pa BJ

II064645

THE IRWIN SERIES IN ECONOMICS

CONSULTING EDITOR

LLOYD G. REYNOLDS
YALE UNIVERSITY

BOOKS IN THE IRWIN SERIES IN ECONOMICS

THE ECONOMIC SYSTEM

THE ECONOMIC SYSTEM

by JOHN M. KUHLMAN
Associate Professor of Economics
University of Missouri

and GORDON S. SKINNER
Professor of Economics
University of Cincinnati

REVISED EDITION

1964

RICHARD D. IRWIN, INC.

HOMEWOOD, ILLINOIS

TO THE MEMORY OF PROFESSOR EDWIN E. WITTE
Teacher, Advisor, and Friend

Economists, like all others who merit the high distinction of being known as scholars and scientists, may never compromise with truth and must have the courage of their convictions. Falsifying, coloring, or twisting the truth is contemptible, whether it be done for compensation, to gain notoriety, or to curry favor.
—Presidential address of Professor Witte, "Economics and Public Policy," *American Economic Review*, March, 1957, p. 13.

PREFACE

Economics represents a curious dichotomy in the lives of most university students. On one hand, affairs of an economic nature constitute a major subject of conversation in the many discussion groups of both a formal and informal nature which are associated with institutions of higher learning. Students, like other people, have opinions regarding the level of prices, the policies of unions, the oppressiveness of taxes, and a host of other similar problems. But in addition to these, the student has economic problems which are peculiar to his status as a student. There is, first, the problem of maintaining himself in the style to which he has become accustomed. Tape recorders, motor boats, hi-fi sets, automobiles, and all of the other accessories which are so much a part of present-day college life pose an economic problem for the student. At a somewhat different level, the student is also faced with the problem of high tuition fees, expensive books, large dining hall bills, costly transportation, and burdensome activity fees. These, too, represent economic problems. To the discussion of such problems the student is willing to devote a good deal of his time and energy. In fact, if all discussion topics were ranked in accordance with the time devoted to each, matters of an economic nature would probably be consistently ranked as second.

At the academic level, however, economics does not seem to arouse the same interest. At this level students are quite often unwilling to devote a great deal of their time and effort to its pursuit. More often than instructors in the subject would like to think, students would, if given a choice, eliminate economics from the curriculum. The study of economics is, to many students, "uninteresting, theoretical, and impractical." In short, it is everything that economics of the campus discussion group is not. But this is not too surprising. Students generally come from a family of practicing economists. The student's present position has been achieved without the aid of a formal education in economics. And, even without such a course, he usually has previously acquired the "right" answers to the pressing economic questions of the day. Under such circumstances, it is no wonder that students see little need for taking a course in economics.

So there is the dichotomy. On one hand, the student finds economics to be lively, interesting, timely, and very practical. On the other, it is deadly, dull, and dismal. This is, indeed, an unfortunate situation, for it is an attitude which makes learning difficult if not impossible.

The authors of this book have attempted to write a book which beginning students in economics will find interesting. A text can probably never be as interesting as an informal discussion group in a college dormitory, but it is felt by the authors that an effort should be made toward an interesting and readable presentation insofar as the text is concerned. Therefore, readability has been kept in mind throughout.

We have attempted to explain the basic principles which underlie the American economic system. Furthermore, we have attempted to clothe these principles with sufficient empirical data to make them meaningful for the students by applying them to situations with which the students are acquainted. In addition, the exercises at the end of each chapter, and this applies particularly to those in Groups II and III, are designed to stimulate the student to do additional work in particular areas with which he may become acquainted or in which he may become interested. But above all, this book is specifically designed and written to make the student think, and to make him think in a logical and rational fashion rather than in a purely emotional form, as is so often the case. If we can get the student to think logically about the economic principles underlying the American economic system, we are on the way to making a better citizen out of that student.

The major change in the revised edition of this book is the introduction of indifference curve analysis. Economists have found the use of this particular tool to be of great value in many areas of economics—demand analysis, production theory, and risk and uncertainty, to name only three. It is our belief that the tool can be profitably used at the elementary level as an aid to understanding. But it is also our conviction that the student should be exposed to the tool for its own sake. The student should have a better appreciation of economics as well as economists. This was a major factor in the decision to revise and expand our introduction to both demand and production analysis.

For some, the introductory course in economics is the first in a series of courses in the field. Others take only a single course in the subject-matter area. For the former group, it is our intention to provide a framework for further study and analysis. For the latter, it is our intention to provide a broad yet selective picture of the economic system and the principles which underlie its operation. Thus prepared, students will be better able to understand its functioning.

The bibliography at the end of each chapter can be used to supplement and amplify the material presented in the text. The paperback reading list which accompanies each chapter will give the student some idea of the vast amount of material which is readily accessible. The use of the book in such a fashion would permit the instructor to introduce a great deal of flexibility insofar as the treatment of the subject is concerned.

The bibliographies and exercises, are designed for the student who finds the subject matter interesting and wants to undertake some work on his own. Such a student will find suggestions for reading which range from works written for the general public, which are of an economic nature, to economic treatises written by and for the professional economist. This arrangement, it is hoped, will not only permit but will actually encourage the able student to do additional work in economics.

A special word should be inserted regarding the exercises at the end of each chapter. They are in three groups. Those in Group I consist of questions that all students should be able to answer or discuss after the material has been covered. They may be used by the instructor for oral discussion or for written quizzes. The exercises in Group II are somewhat more advanced and are intended to be interesting problems which will challenge the student. The exercises in Group III are generally in the nature of topics for term papers, research projects, or subjects for individual study. In some instances they will indicate areas of investigation not taken up by the text. It is hoped that all students will find some problem which will be sufficiently interesting to cause them to put forth some extra effort.

The authors owe a very great debt to former teachers and scholars. To them must go a general acknowledgment for nearly everything in the book, for there is little that is new. A principles text can, at best, be little more than an accumulation of past learning. A debt is likewise owed to our students. It was upon these individuals that the various means of presenting the material were tested. They suffered patiently albeit unknowingly.

A debt of appreciation is owed to Professors David G. Davies of Duke University and Lloyd M. Valentine of the University of Cincinnati, who gave so liberally of their time and intellect. The generous and helpful editorial assistance of Professors Lloyd Reynolds and Robert Clower did much to improve the quality of the work. And, of course, we are appreciative of the permission to quote from the several cited works.

Above all others, however, a debt is owed to the late Professor Edwin E. Witte of the University of Wisconsin. Professor Witte served as faculty advisor to both authors during their years of graduate work at that institution. Only those who knew Professor Witte can appreciate his contribution, but they will be able to discern his influence on nearly every page of the book.

We, of course, assume the burden for the errors.

JOHN M. KUHLMAN
GORDON S. SKINNER

University of Missouri
University of Cincinnati

January, 1964

TABLE OF CONTENTS

Chapter 1

ECONOMICS: A STUDY IN CONTROVERSY

Detection is, or ought to be, an exact science, and should be treated in the same cold and unemotional manner. You have attempted to tinge it with romanticism, which produces much the same effect as if you worked a love story or an elopment into the fifth proposition of Euclid.—Sir Arthur Conan Doyle, *The Return of Sherlock Holmes. The Sign of Four.*

'I should have more faith,' he said; 'I ought to know by this time that when a fact appears opposed to a long train of deductions it invariably proves to be capable of bearing some other interpretation.—Sir Arthur Conan Doyle, *The Return of Sherlock Holmes. A Study in Scarlet.*

In the year 399 B.C., Socrates drank of the hemlock. He had paid the supreme penalty for his crime against society. That crime was the promotion of freedom of thought and inquiry. The list of those who have been persecuted or ridiculed because of their promulgation of new and different ideas is lengthy. Differences of opinion have persisted throughout the ages, and these differences promise to continue in the years ahead.

As any field of intellectual endeavor matures, the area of agreement becomes larger and larger while the area of disagreement diminishes in size. The development of the natural sciences illustrates this fact. Today it is agreed that the earth is round and that the sun is stationary while the earth moves around it, but these facts have not always been accepted as immutable truths. Through centuries-long application of the scientific method, the natural sciences have developed a large body of knowledge which is generally accepted by those in the various fields. This knowledge is expressed in the form of scientific laws or principles. The social sciences, on the other hand, have not received the intensive study accorded the natural sciences. Early philosophers, as well as laymen, were concerned about man and his social institutions, but it has only been in the past few centuries that an intensive study of these subjects has been made by men who might be called specialists in the field. Because of the comparative youthfulness of the subject matter, the social studies are not characterized by a large body of generally accepted knowledge as evidenced by a number of principles or laws.

Although such men as Plato (427–347 B.C.), Aristotle (384–322 B.C.), and St. Thomas Aquinas (1225–1247) were concerned with problems which would now be classed as economic in nature, economics as a separate body of knowledge is among the younger of the social sciences. It is impossible to state that economics began in a particular year with a particular individual, but many would say that the subject had its beginning as an independent study with Adam Smith (1723–1790), who wrote *An Inquiry Into the Nature and Causes of the Wealth of Nations* at the time of the American Revolution. Although Smith was trained as a philosopher and his magnum opus was a philosophical work, the intellectual genealogy of most present-day economic thinking can be traced to his writings.

In the United States, economics has had an even shorter history. At the time of the American Revolution only a few individuals, notably Alexander Hamilton (1757–1804), and Benjamin Franklin (1706–90), were acquainted with Smith's writings. Prior to the Civil War a number of laymen had thought and written about economic subjects, but the professional economist did not appear on the American scene until the latter part of the nineteenth century. Prior to this period, economics, when it was found in the university curriculum, was offered as a part of philosophy. It was toward the end of that century that the first departments of economics were established in American universities, and it was at that time that American economists began making contributions to the advancement of the subject.

Since economics is a young member of the academic community, it should come as no surprise that it has been and continues to be characterized by controversy. As the subject has developed, however, larger areas of the subject matter have come to be generally accepted by all or nearly all economists. Nevertheless, there continue to be areas of disagreement. It is not too far amiss to characterize economics as a study in controversy—a study often characterized by differences of opinion.

A second area of disagreement exists in what might be called applied economics. Nearly everyone works, makes money, and spends that money. Most vote and pay taxes. These issues are basically economic in nature, and it is only natural that all should feel qualified to pass judgment upon such problems of everyday life. While most individuals are quite willing to admit that they are not qualified to pass judgment on questions in atomic physics or medical research, there is no such compunction regarding questions of an economic nature. The mere fact that one is working and earning, spending and saving, and voting and paying taxes seems automatically to qualify the individual to pass judgment upon economic questions. Since so many are passing judgment on these issues, it follows that there will be wide differences of opinion in this area of applied economics, with the controversy centering largely around the role of the government in the economic system.

THE CONTROVERSY AMONG PROFESSIONAL ECONOMISTS

What Is Economics?

Lionel Robbins of the London School of Economics put the matter very succinctly when he said, "We all talk about the same things, but we have not yet agreed what it is that we are talking about."[1] One would exaggerate very little in saying that there are nearly as many definitions of economics as there are economists, but oddly enough, in spite of the heterogeneity of definitions, there is a remarkable degree of homogeneity in the subject matter.

The definition of economics which has probably found more general acceptance among economists than any other is that of Alfred Marshall (1842–1924). He defined economics as "a study of mankind in the ordinary business of life; it examines that part of individual and social action which is most closely connected with the attainment and the use of the material requisites of well-being."[2] A second popular definition is that of Robbins, who has defined economics as being concerned "with that aspect of behaviour which arises from the scarcity of

---

[1] Lionel Robbins, *An Essay on the Nature and Significance of Economic Science* (2d ed.; London: Macmillan & Co., Ltd., 1949), p. 1.

[2] Alfred Marshall, *Principles of Economics* (8th ed.; London: Macmillan & Co., Ltd., 1947), p. 1.

means to achieve given ends."[3] A third is that of H. J. Davenport, who defined economics as "the science which treats phenomena from the standpoint of price."[4] The above are only three of many, but they will suffice to illustrate some of the differences in the definitions of the subject matter.

Davenport's definition imposes severe limitations on the subject matter, for it would treat only that part of human activity which can be studied from the standpoint of price. A study of economics based upon such a narrow interpretation would eliminate such aspects of economics as economic history and economic institutions. However, it must be admitted that the consignment of such areas of the subject to an intellectual limbo would make it possible to formulate a much more exact study, since price is one item which can be measured with preciseness. In other words, a study of price can be quantitative while a study of economic history, for example, has been, to a large extent, qualitative in nature.

Marshall's definition of economics has been criticized by Robbins and others because of its emphasis on the material aspects of well-being. This is a legitimate criticism, for economics is concerned with the non-material as well as the material aspects of well-being. Furthermore, Robbins contends that economics should be concerned not with certain types of human behavior but with a certain aspect of all human behavior. That is, economics is concerned with that part of human activity arising out of the fact that human wants are unlimited and insatiable while the means of satisfying those wants are definitely limited. This is the meaning of his definition of economics—scarce means and alternative ends.

Regardless of which definition is deemed acceptable, all have a single element in common—scarcity. If all the things needed by man were as plentiful as air, there would be no need for economics or economists. Everyone realizes that when any item is scarce, measures must be taken which will result in the greatest amount of satisfaction from the limited resources. The college student, for example, has neither the time nor the money to do all of the things which he might possibly enjoy. He can study, or engage in a variety of extracurricular activities. He can take a course in economics or a course in philosophy, but he certainly cannot take all of the courses listed in the university catalogue. He can buy a new suit or take a weekend at the beach. Individuals, families, business enterprises, and other economic units in our society are under the same neces-

---

[3] Robbins, *op. cit.*, p. 24.

[4] H. J. Davenport, *Economics of Enterprise* (New York: Macmillan Co., 1932), p. 25.

sity to choose certain activities and forego others. None have sufficient resources to meet all of their wants. When one finds one's self in the position of having inadequate resources for his existing wants, provisions must be made for the judicious use of the resources. If any item is scarce, it must be used wisely; in other words, a person must economize. Economics, then, is the study of this act of economizing. It is the study of the means by which human wants are satisfied through the use of scarce resources.

Some limitations must be imposed upon the above definition of economics, for there are some goods which do satisfy human wants but with which economics has no concern. A good may be defined as anything which has utility; that is, it possesses usefulness or the ability to satisfy human desires. There are some goods which are very useful to man but exist in such quantities that no effort or cost is involved in their acquisition. These are free goods and are of no concern to the economist. Fresh outdoor air exists in superabundant amounts and is readily available to all; however, fresh cool air in an office building on a hot summer day is scarce and it therefore becomes an economic good. Water is a free good to a man in a flood, but fresh water is an economic good of great value to a farmer in the Imperial Valley of California.

Economics, then, is concerned with only those goods which possess both usefulness and scarcity—economic goods. It is not concerned with those goods which have usefulness but lack scarcity—free goods. All economists address themselves to the question of how economic goods satisfy human wants.

The Science of Economics

John Neville Keynes (1852–1949) in his book *The Scope and Method of Political Economy* spoke of positive economics as being a systematized body of knowledge concerning what is; of normative economics as being a systematized body of knowledge concerning what ought to be; and the art of economics as being a system of rules for the attainment of a given end. This classification will stand us in good stead.

The area known as normative economics is concerned with value judgments. What ought the policy of the government to be in the field of labor, taxes, foreign trade, and so forth? There is no way of scientifically establishing the validity of value judgments. It is not possible to rank different value judgments so that we might all agree as to which is superior.

The science of economics refers to positive economics. What is? What will be? These are questions to which the science of economics is directed. These are the types of questions that positive economics is intended to answer. The discussion of the science of economics is, then, a discussion of positive economics—of what is rather than what ought to be.

Most definitions of a science will include four parts: (1) objective knowledge (2) methodically arrived at and systematically related containing (3) a body of general principles or truths which can be used as the basis for (4) prediction. One who would be classed as a scientist must enter upon his quest for knowledge with a completely objective frame of mind. There can be no such thing as going into a scientific study with preconceived conclusions. Conclusions can be drawn only after the study has been made. The research should never be designed solely to prove or disprove a particular conclusion, but it should aim to explore all sides of the problem in an effort to discover the truth. This is extremely difficult in the social studies, or, at least, it is much more difficult than in the natural sciences. The chemist, for example, can conduct an experiment in a test tube, and it is not a difficult matter for him to disassociate himself from the experiment. In the social sciences, however, the investigator is in the middle of the experiment, so to speak, and he may well have personal feelings about the matter being investigated.

To the extent that such feelings exist, or to the extent that the research is influenced by such personal attitudes, one cannot be classed as a scientist in any sense of the word. Those doing research for such organizations as the AFL-CIO or the NAM are, in many instances, technicians searching for a particular set of facts to support the policies and programs of the organization for which they work. This is not meant to imply that their approach is wrong, but it is meant to indicate that the views of special-interest groups should be regarded with some degree of skepticism if one is seeking the truth. The "truth" is seldom found in extreme or one-side opinions. For this reason, it is always important to note who writes what one is reading as well as the associations of the author. From the scholar and scientist, one should expect the truth as the investigator finds that truth. From the technician, one can expect a point of view. The two are not the same.

Probably the most important test for determining what is scientific knowledge is the method used. There must be a plan of study. Many people believe that this plan of study is *the* scientific method which is applicable to all fields of intellectual endeavor. Actually this is not the that all should be objective in the search for knowledge. It must be solved. A technique used in the mathematical sciences may not be suitable for the philosophical sciences or the social sciences. The proper methodology to be employed in economics is of such importance that it will be discussed in some detail later in this chapter.

The purpose of economics, like that of the natural sciences, is to formulate general truths. These can be referred to as economic laws or principles. In the natural sciences a law is a statement of a general truth: for example, falling bodies accelerate at a constant rate. In economics and the social sciences, it is somewhat more difficult to arrive at such unqualified truths. So an economic law is less a statement of a general economic truth than a statement of an economic tendency.

All are acquainted with the laws passed by state legislatures or Congress. Such laws are enacted by mortal men, and other men can violate them although the penalty for such violation may be rather severe. We are all likewise acquainted with the moral principles passed on to us by our parents and our religion. These, too, may be violated by man, but here, unlike the case above, there may be no immediate punishment—except that of a guilty conscience.

Economic laws, like those in the natural sciences, are neither jural nor moral in nature, for once the conditions are granted, such laws cannot be violated. The only difference between the laws in the natural sciences and the laws in the social sciences (including economics) is that the latter group has a larger "if." It is a comparatively simple matter to maintain atmospheric pressure at a constant level or to take into account the effect of friction of the air on falling bodies. However, it is extremely difficult to take into consideration the irrational behavior of human beings. Economists have to eliminate certain aspects of human behavior through the use of assumptions. Such assumptions will allow us to arrive at certain general truths, but, as will be pointed out, in making these assumptions one moves away from the actual situation, and thus economics tends to become somewhat abstract.

Moral and jural laws are needed to guide human behavior in the everyday business of living in human society. The general truths or principles which the scholars are seeking are desired for the purpose of explaining the behavior of human beings and nature. In other words, the need is to discover the basic laws that underlie the natural world and human society in order that future states of affairs can be predicted with accuracy. This is the major function of the science of economics.

That part of the totality of economics known as positive economics certainly meets the criteria of a science. The study of scarce means and unlimited wants relates to objective knowledge. There are instances where this criteria has not been met, but intellectual honesty demands that all should be objective in the search for knowledge. It must be recognized, however, that value judgments can creep into the analysis unbeknown to the investigator. Simply living in a particular type of social environment may impair objectivity. This is certainly the case in the USSR where even the most technical of economic articles may be larded with Communist dogma and propaganda.

Economic knowledge is methodically arrived at, although the method may not be, in every respect, comparable to those techniques used in other areas of intellectual endeavor. It should be noted, however, that the increased use of mathematics has resulted in emphasizing the similarities between economics and other fields. Economics does have a body of general truths or laws, but there are not as many as might be found in the natural sciences. And lastly, these principles can be and are used for purposes of prediction. When they are used to predict in the real world, they may predict incorrectly or they may fail to predict with great precision. But neither error nor inaccuracy is enough to deny the scientific status of the subject matter.

The Derivation of Economic Principles

Much of the controversy in the history of economic thought has centered around the proper methodology to be used in establishing economic principles. It would be impossible to list the disputants in any reasonable amount of space. Neither is it possible to discuss all of the different issues. The discussion herein will be limited to what has been loosely known as the analytical and empirical approaches to the study of economics.

The Analytical Method. The analytical or deductive method is what the layman often has in mind when he speaks of the theoretical approach to a problem. This technique places great emphasis on the construction of models and deductive reasoning. Its most vocal proponents would assert that there is no other legitimate approach to the subject. It is so important in the science of economics that it merits our careful and rather detailed attention. Thus we turn to the question of model building in economics.

First, it should be recalled what the objective is. Remember the economist is seeking a *general* principle which can be used to predict. Note the word general. It means that the economist is looking for an economic law which will be widely applicable rather than one which will simply predict the price of a particular commodity at, say, noon tomorrow. To do this, the economist has his choice of two techniques. First, he can collect all the facts possible and see if he can discern some general principle. This is the empirical or inductive method which will be discussed shortly. The second method is that of abstracting from the facts—that is, of moving away from the factual situation. The latter is the deductive method. This approximation of reality is the model. If the economist has done his work well, the model can be used to make predictions which will be useful in understanding the real world.

Of what does a model consist? Basically, it is made up of a number of assumptions and the conclusions that can be drawn from these assumptions. The assumptions may be a very close approximation of the real world, or, on the other hand, the relation between the assumptions and reality may be so remote as to be undiscernable. These assumptions may be behavioral, relating to the way human beings act and the motives or rules they live by, or tautological, specifying certain relationships that exist by definition.

During the initial phases of the construction of the model, facts have a role. The observations of the researcher may suggest certain relationships either to be built into the model or to be avoided. In other words, facts may suggest certain assumptions, but, at this point, that is all that should be expected. Specifically, it is not a requirement that the model correspond to the factual situation.

Once the assumptions are established, what next? The next step is that of deduction. On the basis of the assumptions, what conclusions can be drawn? What implications are there in the assumptions? What predictions might be made on the basis of these assumptions? Here there can be no appeal to reality to prove or disprove the validity of the predictions or the truth of the hypothesis or theory. The experimenter may test his theory against the facts, and he may conclude that the facts and the implications of his theory are consistent or not, as the case may be. But it must be emphasized that such a test is not to be taken as proof of the validity of the theory. The model is not to be judged useless simply because it does not conform in all respects to the factual situation of interest.

There are two questions that might well be asked of any theory. First, is it true? This question can only be answered by checking the logical consistency of the entire model. Does the conclusion logically follow from the premises or assumptions? Secondly, does it work? That is, does it predict with sufficient precision so as to enable us to understand the phenomena in which we are interested? A theory may be satisfactory in that it will predict with a reasonable degree of success. It may also be that there is a second (or third, or fourth, or . . .) theory that will also predict successfully. One is "better" than the other, then, insofar as one is a better predictor than the other. Both may be true in the sense that they are logically consistent. The implications of both may be consistent with the factual situation. But the only means of comparison is to be found in their relative ability to predict.

The economist, when constructing an economic model, is always on the horns of a dilemma. On the one hand it is desirable to have a model of general applicability that can be used for prediction in the greatest number of different circumstances. For example, a model which would predict the price of wheat at noon tomorrow would be of little use, while a model which would predict the price of wheat at any time under a variety of circumstances would be of great use. And even better would be a model which would successfully predict prices for a wide variety of goods and services in a host of different circumstances. Any model can be made more general in its applicability by further abstracting from reality. That is, the more general the model, the more abstract or unrealistic it will be. So the economist has to reach some compromise in his quest for the best economic model. One approach to this problem follows.

Suppose that an abstract model of wide applicability has been constructed. It is logically consistent in that the conclusions follow from the assumptions. The problem is one of making it more realistic in nature. This can be done, in some instances, by relaxing some of the assumptions in the original model. It may have been that some particularly troublesome aspects of the real problem have been assumed out of the model. Then the economist asks what would happen in the absence of this particular variable. Once that question has been answered, he then asks what the effect would be if this variable were brought back into the model.

An extremely convenient assumption for the economist which is widely used in economic analysis is the assumption of *ceteris paribus*. This is the assumption that variables other than the one(s) in which the economist is particularly interested remain constant. It is quite often this assumption that is relaxed in order to make the model somewhat more realistic and to study the effect of those factors which were held constant in the original model.

As an example of model construction, let us assume for the moment that the problem is that of determining the reaction to a change in the price of a commodity. It doesn't matter what the commodity is. What assumptions might be made? First, it might be assumed that there is an inverse relationship between the quantity purchased and the price. Second, it would seem reasonable to assume that there is a direct relationship between the amount offered for sale and the price. Third, it will be necessary to make some assumption regarding the behavior of businessmen, so let it be assumed that they will act in a manner designed to maximize their profit. Fourth, it will be assumed that consumers seek to maximize their satisfaction. Fifth, for this particular problem it might be well to assume that there are so many buyers and sellers that no one of them can have any influence on the price by their individual actions. And last, since the two variables of interest are price and quantity, it might be assumed that all other variables will remain unchanged; that is, changes in population, technology, consumer taxes, income, and the like will be ruled out for the time being.

On the basis of the above assumptions, then, it is possible to generalize about price and quantity sold. A meaningful statement can be made about the price which will prevail as well as the amount which will be exchanged. If we make an additional assumption about the cost structure of the firm, then we can go on and make meaningful statements about the level of output of the firm. But the student should note that all of this was done without any reference to any particular commodity, market, firm, or individual.

Now it may be desirable to test the model against the real world or a particular part of that world. One might want, for example, to see whether the model constructed would permit one to achieve a better understanding of the wheat market. The following questions, among others, might be asked. Does the action of the producer agree with what the model implies? Does the general statement which was made about price and quantity appear to be consistent with that situation which exists in the wheat market? Can the model be used to predict in this market? If not, can the model be successfully used if a few of the assumptions are relaxed or altered? The student will note that we have carefully refrained from stating that we were going into this particular market to see if the theory is true. The only reason for applying this particular model or theory to this specific market was that of seeing whether or not it worked—predicted successfully. If that is so, it is a workable theory which economists will find useful.[5]

The Empirical Approach. The empirical or inductive method is also used to derive economic principles. Rather than emphasizing analysis and deductive reasoning, the empirical approach relies more heavily upon the collection of facts or descriptive material. After selecting the

---

[5] The student with any mathematical training can readily perceive that many of the above assumptions can easily be expressed in a mathematical form. Although a mathematical presentation is not going to be utilized in this book, the student who does have a mathematical background should keep this idea in mind as the different models are presented and discussed.

problem, the scholar using the empirical approach, would accumulate all of the facts he thinks necessary for the particular problem. But the selection and gathering of facts cannot be a hit-or-miss affair such as a child gathering daisies in a pasture. Obviously, there has to be a preliminary hypothesis that can be used as a guide in the selection of facts. This preliminary hypothesis may be derived from the scholar's intuition, or it may be some conclusion which has been reached through analytical reasoning. When a sufficient number of facts have been accumulated, the scholar attempts to derive some general proposition. An economic principle established in such a fashion would differ from one established through the use of the analytical method only in the method use. There would be no difference in the use of the principle itself.

The works of Wesley Mitchell (1874–1948) in the field of economic fluctuations and Selig Perlman (1888–1959) in the field of labor illustrate the use of the empirical technique in economics, although it cannot be said that either of these distinguished scholars relied solely upon the empirical method. Mitchell gathered a mass of data relating to the level of economic activity, and from these data he sought an explanation of the business cycle. He did not, however, seek facts blindly, for his search was directed by the theories that others working in the field, as well as Mitchell himself, had postulated. Professor Perlman, following in the steps of Professor John R. Commons (1862–1944), traced the development of the labor movement both in this country and abroad. From the facts collected, and with the aid of a good bit of analytical thinking, he was able to formulate a general theory of the labor movement.

Two tools which are widely used in, and peculiarly associated with, the empirical method are statistics and economic history. The use of statistics permits the quantification of data. Prior to the development of statistical concepts and the collection of statistical data, it was impossible to do anything but simply record certain descriptive material. The analysis, of necessity, had to be qualitative rather than quantitative. For example, before the development of statistical techniques for measuring price changes, one would merely record that there had been general increases in prices and cite a few examples. Nowadays, however, it is possible to point out that most of a given price increase of a given magnitude results from increases in rents, food, or whatever the case may be.

History is essentially descriptive in nature; that is, history relates how a society has arrived at its present position. The economist using empirical techniques is especially interested in history, for through the collection of historical facts one may arrive at some generalizations regarding human behavior. Economic history, however, if it is to be anything other than "just interesting" must go beyond mere description. It must assist in the derivation of economic principles, and in the hands of capable scholars it does contribute to this end. In the hands of the intellectually naive, history will "prove" anything and everything.

It should not be inferred that statistics and history are not used by the economist employing the deductive or analytical method. An individual using this method might rely upon economic history to indicate a reasonable assumption, or he might use it to test the conclusion. The analytical economist, moreover, is making more and more use of statistics and the statistical tools which have been developed in recent years. The development of new concepts in statistics has enabled the analytical economist to clothe what at one time were pure deductive models with a great deal of factual data.

The controversy between the two schools of methodology has been long and vocal, and it has been characterized by differing degrees of intensity. In Europe during the nineteenth century it took the form of opposition between the English classical economists and the German historical economists. Toward the end of that century, American scholars were studying in Germany, and as a result many American economists supported the empirical approach against the analytical approach associated with English economists. However, since 1890 or so, the number of economists in the United States placing primary emphasis on the analytical method has increased. Today, the members of the profession in this country are divided between those who would emphasize the analytical approach and those who would emphasize the empirical approach. No economist of repute, however, will contend that one or the other is the sole productive technique. Nearly all will agree that there is a vital and significant role for both methods, for it is generally recognized that both have made valuable contributions to the development of economics. With only one of the two, economics would be sterile insofar as the production of economic principles is concerned.

Economics and Ethics

Economics is the study of human wants and the means by which those wants are satisfied. Ethics, on the other hand, is the study of the ends themselves with the purpose of determining whether the ends are proper or improper, moral or immoral. Economics as an analytical science is not concerned with ethics. It is only interested in deriving fundamental truths. There exists a human want for opium, and the supply of opium is scarce in relation to the desire. Thus there is an economic problem—the investigation of this relationship. *As a scientist,* the economist studying this problem has no right to, indeed he is obliged not to, pass an ethical judgment upon the use of opium.

Economics, insofar as it is a science in the strictest sense of the word, seeks to formulate broad general truths. The "truth" itself is the desirable quantum. The physicist does not pass an ethical judgment upon the law of gravity. Of itself, it is neither good nor bad; however, it is desirable that its operations be understood. So it is with economics. Gresham's law, which states that cheap money will drive dear money out of circulation, describes what will happen if two monies circulate. It does not say that cheap money *ought* to drive dear money out of circulation. Neither does it say that it is undesirable that cheap money drive dear money out of circulation. Gresham's law is a statement of fact—a general truth. In other words, economic principles are positive in nature in that they describe what *is* rather than being normative in nature and describing what *ought* to be.

In the area of applied economics, the issue is no longer so clearly defined. The application of economics to the normal activities of the individual, the business firm, and the government is concerned with what ought to be. This is particularly true in the field of governmental policy. What ought to be our policy in regard to labor unions, big business, the farm problem, or the distribution of income? These are not simple questions and have no simple answers. Unfortunately, economics and the social sciences do not, as yet, provide us with answers to question of "what ought to be" such as are provided for the question "what is or what tends to be." This is probably the major cause for a large part of the controversy in the area of applied economics.

Microeconomics and Macroeconomics

J. B. Say (1767–1832) formulated Say's law of markets in 1803, and from that date down to the period following World War I, economists worried little about the level of economic activity. This law simply stated that the act of production creates the demand whereby the output is purchased. Thus the individuals producing automobiles have the wherewithal to buy those cars, but, of course, instead of using all of their income to purchase cars, they would spend an equivalent amount on clothing, food, and other commodities. This theory has an obvious inadequacy in that not all persons will spend their incomes but may save a part of it. Then if there are no others who desire to invest the savings, there will be idle resources. But in spite of this, for over a century the majority of the world's economists felt that the economic system would inevitably move toward a level of full employment. They observed, from time to time, that factors of production were unemployed and that goods which had been produced had not been sold, but such a condition was thought to be transitory in nature. If men were unemployed, the solution was to lower wages, since the cause of unemployment was the fact that labor was asking too high a wage. If goods remained unsold on the shelf, the cause was the fact that the merchant was asking too high a price for his merchandise. For nearly 125 years the study of economics was largely confined to the pricing and output of goods and services and the pricing of the factors of production—that is, the pricing of land, labor, capital, and entrepreneurial activity. This was the age of microeconomics.

To some degree during the 1920's and certainly during the 1930's, economists began to have some doubts about the validity of the classical belief that the economy was always tending toward a level of full employment. During the Great Depression of the 1930's that belief was abandoned for a new faith. The economic system was thought by some to be inevitably moving toward a level of stagnation because of a declining rate in population growth and a lack of investment opportunities. John Maynard Keynes (1883–1946) provided the theoretical underpinning for what has been referred to as the "New Economics." Keynes pointed out that the economy could well be in an equilibrium situation at less than full employment. That is, the economy could move along for an indefinite period with unemployed labor and resources.

Economists, like everyone else, were depression conscious during World War II. The major concern of all was the level of employment which would follow the war. After all, there had been depressions following every war in which this country had participated. Our governmental policies, as well as the policies of some business firms, were directed toward overcoming what was felt to be an inevitable depression. So, largely as a result of the depression of the 1930's and the fear of a postwar depression, the American people, including the economists, became acutely conscious of the level of economic activity.

The period, then, from 1929 to the present has seen a shift in emphasis from the economics of the firm (microeconomics) to the economics of aggregates and national income (macroeconomics). National income statistics were developed which enable one to study the performance of the economy with a high degree of accuracy. As macroeconomics advanced in importance, there was less tendency to investigate the economics of the firm. If one were to generalize regarding the economy and its operation, it was deemed necessary to generalize from aggregates rather than from the circumstances prevailing in a single firm or industry.

The dispute between those who would approach the subject from the viewpoint of the individual firm and industry and those who would approach it from the aggregative viewpoint has varied in intensity. At one time or another, each viewpoint has been considered to be the sole productive method of studying economics. Textbooks, and especially those in principles of economics, have been written from both viewpoints. There have been those who have ignored aggregative economics, while others have ignored nearly everything else. This book, like many others, will attempt a "balanced" approach.

THE CONTROVERSY IN APPLIED ECONOMICS

The controversy in the application of economics takes on a much broader aspect than that associated with the controversy among the professional economists. In this instance the controversy is found in lay circles in addition to the professional brotherhood. There are few individuals who have no opinion on taxes, the farm problem, labor unions, big business, little business, tariffs, or a multitude of other economic problems. The discussion in this field is almost entirely normative in nature in that the concern is with what ought to be rather than with what is. What should be our farm policy? What should be our labor policy? Our tax policy? As citizens all must be prepared to arrive at some form of answer which can be translated into public policy. A collective answer can be no more than the summation of a large number of individual answers under the system of government which exists in this country. Therefore, as citizens, each must have some idea as to the nature of the problem and the alternative solutions. In a free society there is no guarantee that the course selected will be the best alternative; nevertheless, the chances of selecting the course which will have the best chance of solving the various problems can be increased if all have some acquaintance with the problem at hand. The student must keep in mind, however, that there is no such thing as a ready-made answer which can be considered to be *the* single correct answer.

The economist has a very significant role in the field of applied economics. He cannot say what society as a whole ought or ought not to do insofar as questions of public policy are concerned. All that the economist can do is to spell out the alternatives and the economic consequences of each. Thus he would explain what would happen if society followed one policy as against another. The decision as to what ought to be done will be made by parties other than the professional economist in his professional capacity.

With those comments in mind, let us briefly examine some of the controversies in the field of applied economics. The remarks here will merely serve to introduce the problems, and, in most instances, more will be said regarding each in later sections of the text. It should not be inferred that the following is an all-inclusive listing of the economic problems of the nation; life would be simple if that were so.

A quick glance at any reputable daily newspaper will indicate the ubiquitousness of economic problems as well as their characteristically controversial nature. As an exercise, the student might examine the front page of any newspaper to see how many news stories are of an economic nature.

In the summer of 1963, when this was being written, the United States was concerned with many economic problems. First, there is the question of tax policy. Many are contending that a lowered tax rate and a changed tax structure will encourage a more rapid rate of economic growth. Others are arguing that a reduction in taxes will result in a budget deficit of such proportions that the country will suffer serious inflation. There is no unanimity of opinion here, either among the professional economists or the public.

A second problem that continues to face the United States is the role of this country in the community of nations. To what extent should we lower tariffs and encourage world trade? If tariffs are lowered and some domestic industries are subject to additional competition from foreign producers, what kind of relief, if any, should the government provide? The problem of the Common Market in Western Europe and the relationship between the Common Market and the United States promises to be a vexing one. It is an economic problem as well as a political and military problem.

Another facet of the same problem is our relation with the underdeveloped nations of the world. Economic development is, in large part, dependent upon the stock of capital—buildings, machinery, electric generating capacity, etc. With an extremely low level of income, it is almost impossible for some countries to free resources from the production of consumer goods to produce such capital items. Thus the underdeveloped countries turn to the more advanced countries and seek loans or gifts. That raises the question as to this nation's interests. Should we support economic development abroad? If so, what is the best technique for doing so?

Other current economic problems would include the problem of labor and collective bargaining, big business and the antitrust laws, unemployment, automation and the effects of a rapidly changing technology, and agriculture surpluses. The one feature that they all have in common is the fact there is no concensus as to the correct solution. This simply makes the subject matter more challenging and exciting.

CONCLUSION

This discussion does not exhaust the controversy in either applied economics or what might be called the economics of the scholars. Only the surface has been touched, but that must suffice. The student must realize that for each of the problems which have been raised, there are a host of problems which have not been mentioned. The problems in the area of applied economics have a variety of solutions offered by one group or another. Some would solve the labor problem by breaking up all labor unions. Some would solve the problems of big business by socializing private enterprise. Still others insist that the proper farm policy is to let the farmer shift for himself without any assistance from the governments. These represent extreme solutions and are not generally acceptable, or at least they are not acceptable to the parties in question—labor, business, or agriculture. The people of this country have never made a practice of adopting extreme solutions to problems except in times of dire emergency. Lasting solutions to the nation's problems must be moderate in nature.

To the student of today there is a vast variety of ready-made answers. But just as one should be suspicious of persons offering to give away valuable merchandise, so should one be suspicious of ready-made solutions which are offered for the taking. Any item of value has a price. No idea of value can be obtained without effort. No one should be so lazy intellectually that he is forced to rely upon secondhand ideas. It is only through the activities of free-thinking individuals that a free society can hope to survive.

The basis of this country is a profound belief in freedom. And freedom is freedom. There is no hierarchy of freedoms; that is, the freedom of any single individual is no more or less important than the freedom of all other individuals. Thus free enterprise, free speech, free inquiry, and freedom of religion are part and parcel of the same thing.

Here the concern is with one particular aspect of freedom—free inquiry. It is only through free inquiry that we can hope to seek out the answers to our problems. In the process of seeking the "right" answer, the wrong answer may be accepted, but if free inquiry is operating properly, the mistake will be pointed out and the search for truth will continue. In a totalitarian society without freedom of inquiry, mistakes will be accepted and will continue to be accepted as the truth. The answer which is decided upon by those in power automatically becomes the "correct" answer. In a democratic society, answers to problems must be subject to the assault of free intellectual inquiry, and such answers will continue to be accepted as the truth only as long as they are able to meet successfully the challenge of freely inquiring minds.

It takes faith to believe in freedom, for there are numerous temptations to abandon it. There are many who are very vocal in their defense of freedom, but who are, in reality, very doubtful of the value of freedom. If doubts are raised about the propriety of free inquiry in a particular field, this is indicative that the objector either lacks faith or understanding. Free inquiry will serve to strengthen true beliefs, just as it will cause the abandonment of those beliefs which are found to be false or inadequate. One need not be afraid of free inquiry in economics or in any other field.

The purpose of this text is to stimulate intellectual endeavor in the field of economics. Those ideas which are correct will be strengthened. Those which are found wanting will be revised. Those which are found false will be discarded. But let it be emphasized that it is the student who is to do the strengthening, the revising, and the discarding. One must ultimately depend upon one's self for the answers to the pressing questions of the day, for there is no Bureau of Standards to which one can apply for correct answers. This book, then, is not an answer book to be used as a "pocket guide to pressing questions of the day." The sole purpose of this book is to encourage the student to think about the American economic system and its operation as well as about some of the problems associated with that system. Once the student has mastered certain basic tools of analysis, then he should be able to draw his own conclusions regarding the important problems of the day.

EXERCISES[6]

Group I

Explain why the following statements might possibly be false:
1. Economics has no relation to ethics.

[6] The exercises are divided into three groups. Those in Group I represent questions which all students should be able to answer after studying the chapter. Those in Group II may require additional reading and research, and those in the last group would be suitable topics for research papers or independent study.

2. An economic law is a statement of general principle which has been recognized as such by a legislative body.
3. Economics is not a science since it does not use the scientific method which is used in the natural sciences.
4. In economics, a model is an exact duplicate of reality.
5. The only reason that there is controversy in the field of applied economics is that we have not yet found *the* single correct answer for these problems.

Group II

1. What is the process by which our individual decisions in economic affairs are translated into collective decisions as manifested in the economic policy of our government?
2. Is there any guarantee that the answer of the majority of the people will be the "correct" answer?
3. What are the rights of the minority once the policy has been decided upon by the majority?

Group III

1. What is meant by a "value judgment"? How does the scientist handle value judgments? What is the difference between a fact and an opinion? Is the distinction clear-cut or does one shade into the other?

BIBLIOGRAPHY

FRIEDMAN, MILTON. *Essays in Positive Economics.* Chicago: University of Chicago Press, 1953.

KEYNES, JOHN NEVILLE. *The Scope and Method of Political Economy.* 4th ed. New York: Macmillan Co., 1930.

KOOPMANS, T. C., *Three Essays on the State of Economic Science.* New York: McGraw-Hill Book Company, Inc., 1957.

ROBBINS, LIONEL. *An Essay on the Nature and Significance of Economic Science.* 2d ed. London: Macmillan & Co., Ltd., 1949.

PAPERBACK READING LIST

GALBRAITH, JOHN K. *Economics and the Art of Controversy.* New York: Vintage Books, 1959.

HEILBRONER, ROBERT L. *The Worldly Philosophers.* New York: Simon and Schuster, 1959.

<table>
<tr><td>Chapter
2</td><td>SOME BASIC CONCEPTS
NEEDED FOR ECONOMIC
UNDERSTANDING</td></tr>
</table>

Chapter 2

SOME BASIC CONCEPTS NEEDED FOR ECONOMIC UNDERSTANDING

"There's glory for you!" "I don't know what you mean by 'glory'," Alice said. "I meant, 'there's a nice knock-down argument for you!'" "But 'glory' doesn't mean a nice knock-down argument'," Alice objected. "When I use a word," Humpty Dumpty said in a rather scornful tone, "it means just what I choose it to mean—neither more nor less."—Lewis Carroll, *Through the Looking Glass.*

Certain basic concepts must be mastered in any field of endeavor. In some instances this will refer to the tools and basic operations of the trade, and in others it may include a professional language or jargon. In the case of economics, the newcomer must master both basic tools and professional jargon. This chapter will serve as an introduction to some of the basic concepts in economics.

CONSUMPTION AND SAVING

The fields of economics and psychology abut in the area of human wants. The psychologist is interested in the nature and the source of the wants, while the economist is concerned with the means of satisfying those wants. Since this is an economic treatise, primary attention will be devoted to the latter and only incidental attention will be given to the nature and sources of such wants.

Human Wants

The manner in which wants are satisfied will be dependent upon several factors. The amount of income will, in part, determine the manner in which one's hunger pangs are satisfied, just as the geographical location of the consumer will be extremely important in determining the type of clothing and housing as well as food. The society in which one lives will have a major influence upon the manner of gratifying these primary wants. Society does more than merely influence the manner of satisfying the primary wants; it also gives rise to an entirely new set of wants. The desires of a person living in industrial society will be much different from the wants of a person living in a primitive agricultural society. The goals of a person living in a middle-class neighborhood will be different from the goals of a person living in either the slums or in an upper-class neighborhood.

The use of scarce goods to satisfy these wants may be defined as consumption. It includes the use of food to satisfy hunger, water to satisfy thirst, or attendance at a performance of the opera *Carmen* to satisfy one's desire for leisure or culture. Consumption includes the satisfaction of those desires which are approved by society as well as those which may not be so approved.

Two observations can be made. The first is the fact that such wants are unlimited and insatiable—that is, they are incapable in the aggregate of ever being satisfied. A person actually has a hierarchy of wants, and as the wants at the top of the hierarchy are satisfied, the consumer in turn attempts to gratify those wants of lesser urgency. Once the basic wants of food, clothing, and shelter are satisfied, then one may seek better food, more expensive housing, more leisure, travel, security, and so on. There is no possibility that there will ever be a time when the wants of all people are fully satisfied, for one of the astounding factors associated with economic and social change is the change in consumer wants. Those who are living in the middle of the twentieth century cannot imagine what the people living 50 or 100 years from now will want, just as those who lived 100 years ago could not imagine many of the present consumption items which are taken for granted.

Whereas the desires are unlimited and insatiable, the means of satisfying those wants are not unlimited but, on the contrary, are extremely limited or scarce. There are few items which can, in their natural form, satisfy human wants. For the most part, man must combine his efforts with the material provided by nature in order to produce those goods which have the capacity to gratify the wants of man. A time cannot be anticipated when the wants of man will be gratified without human effort. This is essentially the problem of economics.

Decisions of the Individual Consumer

Most individuals are faced with the problem described above. They have, on one hand, a large number of wants, and, on the other, a limited number of resources capable of satisfying those wants. The problem is one of using the limited resources in such a fashion as to obtain the maximum amount of satisfaction. The analysis of consumer behavior may well be the most difficult problem area facing the economist, and it is one in which economists have, until recently, done little. The reason for this is that much consumer behavior is difficult to explain on purely rational grounds. To the extent that a person acts irrationally, there is no means of generalizing or predicting future behavior. But in spite of the difficulties involved, a few comments are in order.

There is (1) a direct relationship between income and consumption, and (2) a definite relationship between changes in income and changes in consumption. No one has failed to observe that the manner in which wants are satisfied is, in large part, dependent upon one's income. It is likewise readily apparent that as income increases, the method of gratifying a given want may change. What may not be so obvious is the fact that as incomes go up, there will be an increase in consumption, but the increase in consumption will not be as great as the increase in income. If, for example, income were to double, consumption would increase, but it would not double. If an individual were spending 90 per cent of his $5,000 income, he might spend only 80 per cent of a $7,000 income. In this case income increased by 40 per cent but consumption increased by only 24 per cent. This is an important consideration in determining the results of government taxing and spending policies. The effect of a tax depends, to a large extent, on which part of the population is taxed, just as a change in spending policies may have a different effect depending upon which income groups receives the expenditures. A person in the lower-income group, for example, might spend a larger part of his increased income than would a person in a higher-income group.

A third observation which can be made regarding expenditures is the fact that the rational consumer will diversify his expenditures in order to achieve the maximum possible satisfaction. The major decision which a consumer must make is how his income is used to satisfy his myriad wants. It is necessary for him to rank his wants and then satisfy those of the most urgent nature first. After those with the highest priority are adequately provided for, then others of lower priority are met. Now if we can assume that units of expenditures of equal size are made in several lines of consumption, any given type of consumption will be followed until the satisfaction received from the last unit of expenditure is equal to the satisfaction received from the last unit of expenditure in all other lines. In other words, a college student will buy milkshakes until the satisfaction derived from the last unit of expenditure is equal to the satisfaction obtained from the last unit of expenditure spent on other consumption goods. If this were true for all types of consumption expenditures, the consumer would gain nothing by increasing one type of consumption expenditure and decreasing another. In fact, under such circumstances the consumer would be achieving the maximum amount of satisfaction from the expenditure of his income. It must be pointed out, however, that the ranking of wants and the satisfying of those wants is a highly subjective process. Because of this fact, it is difficult for the economist to generalize on the behavior of consumers. But it can be said that the consumers, in their efforts to satisfy their wants, guide the process of production which creates the goods and services necessary to the consumer. And their decisions are reached by the process described by the above to the extent that they rationally attempt to maximize their satisfaction.

Nature and Significance of Savings

In addition to dividing his income between different wants, the consumer must also decide to what extent present wants shall be sacrificed for the sake of future wants. The consumer will not ordinarily consume his entire income. That part of income which is not consumed represents an abstention from consumption on the part of the consumer. In fact, savings may be defined as abstention from consumption.

One ordinarily thinks of savings in terms of money, and many would conclude that an economy having no money would have no savings. It cannot be emphasized too strongly that monetary "savings" are in the nature of a façade. The act of saving is the failure to consume, and the student should think of saving in just such terms. Possibly the act of saving can be best demonstrated by referring to Communist China. In 1958 the government of that country organized a large part of the population into communes, which were to take care of all of the wants of the individual members including food, clothing, and burial. The individual, then, worked nearly twelve hours a day, and in return he received food, clothing, and a few other necessities. The total value of what he produced exceeded the total of his consumption. The government thus forced the peasant to abstain from consumption, or, to put it in other words, the peasant was forced to save.

In the United States, the act of saving is usually a voluntary act. In addition, the individual has a choice as to the form of savings. We may hold money, or we may purchase bonds, stocks, or other assets. Whereas we have something which represents our savings, the Chinese peasant had nothing. But, nevertheless, the basic act of saving is the same for the individual in the two economies. Both abstain from consumption. Both save.

The significance of saving is to be found in the fact that it serves as the source of man-made goods to be used in further production—capital goods. Only by abstaining from consumption can an economy increase its stock of investment goods. By not consuming all that it produces, or by saving, the economy can use some of its resources to produce capital goods rather than consumer goods. If the society consumed all that was produced, or, in other words, if there were no saving, it would be impossible for the society to increase its stock of capital. Under such circumstances production would be of the most primitive type. Consumption would suffer, for in the long run there would be less to consume. Economic progress would be negligible.

But savings do not automatically become investment expenditures. An investor must use the funds to acquire capital goods. The conversion of savings into investment is the role of the several financial institutions. To the saver, financial institutions represent alternative methods of savings. To the investor, they are alternative sources of funds which can be used for investment expenditures. Even if the act of saving and the act of utilization of savings are done by the same person, that individual will be acting in two different capacities. The first, that is, saving, will be done in his role as a consumer while the second will be done in his role as an investor or producer. In most instances, however, the act of saving and the act of investing are done by different persons.

Once a society advances to a point where it no longer consumes everything that it produces, the nature of the productive process undergoes a fantastic change. No longer does man work the contributions of nature with his hands. The use of capital provides him with a powerful lever. Abstention from consumption and the creation of capital goods serve as the bases for the world's modern industrial economies, and it makes no difference whether the economy is the capitalist economy of the United States or the communist economy of the USSR.

FORMS OF ECONOMIC ORGANIZATION

If those goods which consumers prefer are to be produced, there has to be some type of organization devoted to the production of the desired goods and services. It may be a very simple organization, such as a single person. Or, on the other hand, it may be an extremely complex institution, such as a modern corporation or some form of government organization. In some economies, as, for example, the United States, such organizations are, for the most part, private in nature; while in others, such as the USSR, the organizations controlling production are a part of the government. This discussion, then, will concern itself with the various types of economic organization in the United States which have to do with the production of goods and services.

The Sole Proprietorship

The sole proprietorship is, basically, an individual in a managing rather than a consuming or laboring capacity. The firm is the individual. The individual is the firm. The individual puts up the money or borrows it from creditors. He decides what to produce as well as how much to produce. He determines whether the product should be changed or abandoned. There is no board of directors to which he has to report, nor does he suffer special attention from the government merely because he is doing business as a sole proprietorship.

The above should at least indicate the major advantages of the sole proprietorship. It is simple to organize and operate. One need not request permission from the government to organize, although the enterpriser may be required to obtain a license to engage in a particular type of activity. Furthermore, within limits the firm will be flexible in its operations since there is no need to consult others before decisions are made. The owner makes the decisions, and the firm can change its policy as quick as the owner can change his mind.

The limitations are likewise evident. The managerial resources are fairly well limited to the founder, although in some instances it is possible to hire competent managerial talent. Quite often, however, the need for new talent has necessitated the reorganization of the firm and the use of a different type of organization. Credit resources, moreover, are limited to the credit resources of the individual. If money is to be borrowed, it must be borrowed on the basis of the owner's credit rating, and his credit rating is a combination of his personal and business activity. Another disadvantage of the sole proprietorship is the fact that the life of the firm is identical with the life of the individual. When the latter dies, so does the firm. This makes it difficult for such a firm to enter into long-term contracts, and it makes the negotiation of long-term loans especially difficult. The last and probably the major disadvantage of the individual enterprise is the unlimited liability which the proprietor assumes. If the firm should fail for any reason, the nonbusiness assets of the owner may be required to satisfy the creditors. In total, the disadvantages of the sole proprietorship are such as to preclude its use in those areas in which large units are requisite.

The Partnership

Unlike the proprietorship, which is confined to small business, the partnership is generally associated with particular types of business such as law and medicine, and it may be of any size. There are many small partnerships with only two partners, but there are some large partnerships with hundreds of partners. On the whole, however, partnerships are not frequently found in the ranks of big business.

The partnership represents a combination of the resources and talents of two or more individuals. These persons quite often complement one another in the sense that each has a particular resource or talent, or it may be that one will represent the firm in one community while other partners represent the firm in other localities. It is quite common in a legal partnership, for example, to find one of the partners specializing in tax law, while a second partner specializes in labor law or some other field of jurisprudence. In an accounting partnership, there may be a partner in each office, and if the firm is an extremely large one, partners may be found in nearly every major city in the United States.

The partnership, like the sole proprietorship, is not a creation of the government and does not require governmental approval. It is, in essence, merely an agreement between two or more individuals to conduct business operations on a joint basis. In an unlimited type of partnership agreement, any of the partners can obligate the partnership. If one of the partners commits the partnership, the other partners share in the liability.

From the brief description of the partnership, its advantages and disadvantages are apparent. It does overcome some of the shortcomings of the sole proprietorship. Greater financial resources are available. The partnership enables the firm to command specialized talent for management. An advantage shared with the proprietorship is the fact that it does not suffer special governmental regulation and taxation.

The disadvantages of the partnership are several. First is the unlimited liability of the partners. In a sole proprietorship, the proprietor bears the responsibility for his own actions, but in an unlimited partnership, each partner is liable for the actions of the others. If one partner acting in the name of the partnership incurs a debt which cannot be satisfied, the personal property of all may be called upon to satisfy the creditor. It is true, of course, that the partnership may be of a limited nature, in which case one or more of the partners has only limited liability; however, the activities of such special types of partnerships must suffer close supervision by the state. A second disadvantage of the partnerships is the fact that the organization lives no longer than any partner. If one should die or drop out of the business, the partnership is automatically dissolved. The partnership of Jones and Smith is not the same partnership as Jones and Smith, Jr. As in the case of the proprietorship, this makes it somewhat difficult to enter into long-term contracts. A third disadvantage is the fact that the partners must agree on the actions of the partnership, and if it should develop that the partners do not have a close working relationship, the life of the partnership may be stormy and troublesome. This might well result in inflexibility in the operation of the firm.

In professional services such as law, medicine, accounting, and architecture, the partnership is well suited, but its disadvantages preclude its widespread use in industry. Although it is as old as the sole proprietorship, it has never been used as extensively.

The Corporation

Chief Justice John Marshall defined the corporation as follows:

A corporation is an artificial being, invisible, intangible, and existing only in contemplation of law. Being the mere creature of law, it possesses only those properties which the character of its creation confers upon it, either expressly, or as incidental to its very existence. These are such as are supposed best calculated to effect the object for which it was created. Among the most important are immortality, and if the expression may be allowed, individuality; properties by which a perpetual succession of many persons are considered as the same, and may act as the single individual.[1]

As the definition indicates, the corporation has a life which is independent of the individuals who organize the firm. It is as though a child were born. The corporation, like the newborn child, has certain rights in its own name. The law of the land regards the corporation as a person and, like a person, the corporation can hold property and sue or be sued, and it is entitled to the protection of the law.

[1] *Trustees of Dartmouth College* vs. *Woodward*, 4 Wheat. 515 (1819).

The requirements for organizing a corporation will vary from state to state, but as a rule they will follow this general pattern. In most instances, a minimum of three adults may organize a corporation by submitting the articles of incorporation to the appropriate agency of the state government and raising the required minimum amount of capital. The articles of incorporation must include such information as the name of the firm, the object for which it is organized, and its place of business, officers, and capital structure. Once these requirements have been satisfied, the state will recognize the existence of a new entity with a personality distinct from that of the incorporators.

TABLE 2–1 (A)

NUMBER OF SOLE PROPRIETORSHIPS, PARTNERSHIPS, AND CORPORATIONS IN
THE UNITED STATES, 1960, BY INDUSTRY
(In Thousands)

Industry	Sole Propri-etorships	Active Partner-ships	Active Corpora-tions
All industries	9,090	941	1,141
Agriculture, forestry, and fisheries	3,480	136	17
Mining	33	16	13
Construction	655	62	72
Manufacturing	193	47	166
Transportation, communication, electric, gas, and sanitary services	288	18	44
Wholesale and retail trade	1,945	291	356
Wholesale	306	41	117
Retail	1,548	238	217
Finance, insurance, and real estate	483	203	334
Services	1,966	159	121

SOURCE: U.S. Bureau of the Census, *Statistical Abstract of the United States*, 1963 (Washington, D.C.: U.S. Government Printing Office, 1963).

The corporation as a form of organizing human activity has had a long and varied history. Dating from the time of Christ, it has been widely used as a form of organization by civic groups, eleemosynary institutions, and business firms. Although the Romans used it in the latter capacity at an early date, it has only been in the last century that it has come to be the single most important form of organization in the field of business [see 2–1(A), (B)]. The reason for its current importance is to be found in the advantages associated with this type of organization.

Life in Perpetuity. A partnership or sole proprietorship exists only as long as the individual or the partners survive. The corporation, on the other hand, receives a charter from the state which grants the corporation a life of indefinite length. The incorporators may bequeath their stock to their heirs or sell it to strangers, but the firm continues regardless of changes in ownership. This is evidenced by the fact that each day several million shares of stock are traded on the stock exchange, and each sale represents a change in ownership.

Life in perpetuity constitutes an advantage for the corporate form of organization, for it permits the company to grow and expand without any thought being given to the necessity for future reorganization. It can undertake projects which will not be completed for a number of years, since the corporation will continue to exist and operate beyond the

TABLE 2–1 (B)

BUSINESS RECEIPTS OF SOLE PROPRIETORSHIPS, PARTNERSHIPS AND CORPORATIONS IN
THE UNITED STATES, 1960, BY INDUSTRY
(In Millions of Dollars)

Industry	Sole Proprietorships	Active Partnerships	Active Corporations
All industries	171,257	72,771	802,791
Agriculture, forestry, and fisheries	27,370	4,352	4,215
Mining	1,501	1,007	10,408
Construction	14,942	6,584	32,362
Manufacturing	6,935	7,372	364,612
Transportation, communication, electric, gas, and sanitary services	4,363	1,000	64,132
Wholesale and retail trade	87,062	39,003	265,363
Wholesale	17,061	12,712	130,637
Retail	65,439	24,787	125,787
Finance, insurance, and real estate	5,294	4,031	39,477
Services	23,256	9,281	22,106

SOURCE: U.S. Bureau of the Census, *Statistical Abstract of the United States*, 1963 (Washington, D.C.: U.S. Government Printing Office, 1963).

death or retirement of the present management and ownership. Long-term loans are facilitated, for it is the corporate entity which will bear the liability through the future years. All of the original incorporators may pass out of the picture; the present management may be retired; but when that obligation comes due, the corporation will satisfy those to whom it is obligated.

Limited Liability.   The corporate form of organization in business enterprise is especially attractive whenever the risk is very great or large amounts of money are required. The feature which lends it this attractiveness is that of limited liability for the stockholders. As has been pointed out, the person or persons doing business as sole proprietorships or partnerships have unlimited responsibility for the obligations of the firm. The corporation, on the other hand, is an entity in its own right, and it can enter into contracts and incur obligations. If it fails to fulfill its obligations, the creditors have recourse against the corporation alone. They have no claim upon the personal assets of the stockholders. Once the stockholder has paid for his stock, his liability for the obligations of the corporation has been fulfilled. If the corporation accumulates debts beyond its means of payment, the creditors must look to the corporation itself for satisfaction. If the corporation is unable to satisfy the creditors, the firm may be reorganized with the creditors assuming control in an effort to salvage their interests.

Limited stockholder liability is an advantage to the corporation, as it enables the firm to use the funds of many people including those with very small amounts to invest. This makes it possible for a single firm to command a tremendous amount of capital, for a janitor or a schoolteacher, to name two, may become part owners in Reynolds Metals, Lockheed Aircraft, Cincinnati Milling Machine, or any of thousands of other firms. Under such a system a large number of individuals are able to finance an operation which would be beyond the capacity of a small number of individuals. It should be pointed out here, however, that when a firm is first organized, limited liability may serve as deterrent to the raising of capital. For a new firm, would-be creditors might prefer that the liability of the owners be unlimited since the corporation has few assets. Once the firm is established, however, the possibilities for growth are much greater with the corporate form of organization.

Flexibility. The fact that the corporation is an extremely flexible form of organization is evidenced by the fact that it has been used for such a multitude of purposes. As has been pointed out, its dominant role in the field of business organization is a comparatively recent development. It was not until the period following the Civil War that the corporation achieved its position of dominance in this country, although it had been used as a method of organizing business activity earlier in the history of the United States.

The wide variety of uses is indicative of its flexibility, but if one considers it in just its role as a form of business organization, it likewise is very flexible in that single capacity. It must be admitted at the outset, however, that it does not have the flexibility of the sole proprietorship or partnership, since the latter are usually smaller, there is no government control, and the decision-making power is vested in fewer individuals. In the main, however, the corporation can move in any direction with ease and efficiency. During World War II, companies changed from the production of automobiles to airplanes, from refrigerators to airplane propellers, from radios to GI helmets, and from a variety of peacetime products to an equal number of different products needed for fighting a war. Such changes were made with a minimum of interruption. The return to peacetime production at the conclusion of hostilities was made with equal facility. The technical change of one tool for another was not a difficult chore, since the going concern with its working rules was well established. This type of organization, with its flexibility, must be given much of the credit for the country's success in the war program.

Life in perpetuity, limited liability, and flexibility constitute the major advantages of the corporate form of organizing economic activity. There are, on the other hand, some disadvantages associated with the corporation, and in some cases the disadvantages are so serious as to preclude its use in certain fields.

Separation of Ownership and Management. Sole proprietorships and partnerships are ordinarily managed by the owners, or the owners are very close to the management of the company. Likewise, there are thousands of small corporations in which the owners are the managers. On the other hand, there are many large corporations which have hundreds of thousands of stockholders who have little if anything to say about the management of the company. In such companies the functions of management are delegated to a few "hired men." The board of directors and the officers of the company make all of the daily operating decisions and practically all of the policy decisions. With the exception of a few questions, such as a bonus plan for executives, it is the hired managers who control the property of the owner. And it might be added that once such a delegation of power is made, it becomes nearly impossible for the stockholders to reassert their control over the corporation and its activities.

Special Regulation. Since the corporation exists at the pleasure of the state, it is subject to special types of regulation which other types of business organization need not endure. In the first place, certain regulations must be respected in the organization of the firm. Information regarding the firm must be filed with the appropriate state agency in the chartering state, and similar information must often be filed in all states in which the firm operates. In addition, the national government will require that firms doing business in interstate commerce and listing their securities on a stock exchange file certain information with the Securities and Exchange Commission.

A second area of special regulation is that of taxation. The individual operating as a sole proprietorship or partnership reports the income from the firm as personal income and pays taxes on that income as an individual. There is no tax on the income of the firm as such.

However, in the case of the corporation, the national, state and some local governments tax the income of the firm. Such taxes are levied prior to the payment of dividends to the stockholders who must, in turn, pay taxes on the dividends. In addition, the state in which the corporation is chartered will levy a tax or fee on the firm at the time of organization. In some states it is a very small amount for all corporations, but in most it is graduated according to the capital structure of the firm. Most states also levy an annual franchise tax on the corporation based on the capital structure of the firm. Finally, to avoid the possibility of a person incorporating to avoid the personal income tax by retaining all profits in the corporation, the national government limits the accumulated surpluses which can be held in the firm without incurring the penalty of additional tax payments. Such a tax is not intended to prohibit the accumulation of surpluses for legitimate business purposes, but it is intended to prevent tax avoidance through the use of the corporate device.

Since the corporation is regarded as a person existing at the will of the state, all levels of government have seen fit to tax it as a separate institution. This causes many people to complain of double taxation, since the income of the corporation is taxed as is the same income when it becomes personal income through the payment of dividends. The effect, it is argued, will be a tendency to dry up the flow of investment funds into corporate enterprise.

Diseconomies of Large-Scale Management. The diseconomies of large-scale management may be considered as more than just a disadvantage of corporations. It is a problem which is associated with all large organizations, and since corporations are generally identified with large-scale enterprise, it does not seem too illogical to class this as a disadvantage of the corporate form of organization. Bureaucracy, the term generally used to describe such a situation, is generally associated with the national government, but it is a product of bigness—large labor unions, businesses, universities, or other organizations.

In summary, it should be obvious by now that the corporate form of organization is peculiarly well suited to industrial and financial enterprise. Its advantages are so overwhelming in the field of industry and finance that it has now become the most important form of business enterprise in this country in terms of output, employment, or any other measure one might want to use with the exception of sheer numbers.

The Government

Some of the wants of society cannot be provided through the forms of economic organization discussed heretofore. National defense, the postal service, inland waterways, and others are provided through governmental activity. There are some activities which can be performed by either private enterprise or public enterprise—electric power, certain credit facilities, transportation facilities such as railroads and canals, and others. When the government at any level attempts to provide some good or service, it may do so through one of the established departments of the government or it may organize a special government corporation. The Army's Corps of Engineers may build a dam, or Congress may charter a corporation such as the Tennessee Valley Authority to build dams. The Commodity Credit Corporation supports the prices of farm commodities. There are a number of other corporations at all levels of government that perform services and provide goods demanded by the people. The major difference between a public corporation and private corporation is the fact that we are all "stockholders" in the public corporation, and the board of directors and the officers are appointed by the individuals who presently make up the government.

The Cooperative

There are several other types of business organization which will not be discussed in any detail. One of the most important is the cooperative, which has had a long but relatively minor history in this country. While there have been numerous attempts to organize producer co-ops in this country, most of them have failed. In such an enterprise the workers are the owners, and they receive not only wages but any profits which are made. It is managed by the elected representatives of the worker-owners. It is not unfair to say that the producer co-op never has been, and is not, an important form of organizing productive activity.

A second type of co-op which has had somewhat more success is the consumer co-op, in which a number of consumers organize in an effort to reduce the costs of buying goods. Each member subscribes to a certain number of shares. He has a vote in the administration of the co-op, and he shares in the "profits" of the co-op in proportion to the amount of purchases made rather than in proportion to the number of shares held. The consumer co-op has attained a somewhat more lasting degree of success than the producer co-op. Its disadvantages are such, however, as to preclude its ever attaining a high degree of importance in the economic system of the United States.

The one segment of the economy in which cooperatives are significant is that of agriculture. Farmers often market their product through a cooperative. On the other hand, there are also a number of farmers' co-ops through which farmers purchase goods. The two largest farm organizations, the Farm Bureau and the Grange, operate such outlets in many agricultural communities. Agricultural co-ops are organized and operate in the same general pattern as other co-ops.

Other organizations which are sometimes classed as cooperatives include rural telephone and electric companies, mutual saving associations, mutual insurance companies, and a few others. As a rule, such firms play a relatively minor role in the economy.

CONCLUSION

Man is endowed with the capacity to consume far beyond his means, for the goods and services available to satisfy his wants are severely limited. The individual must decide (1) how much of his income is to be spent for consumption expenditures and (2) how that expenditure is to be divided among the different outlets. Since the goods and services which man desires do not "grow on bushes," it is necessary that the four factors of production, land, labor, capital, and the entrepreneur, be combined in such a fashion as to provide that which the consumer desires. At one time production was carried on in a very direct manner with man applying his efforts directly to the resources provided by nature. Today, however, production is indirect in the sense that large amounts of capital are used, and production has become highly specialized. In the United States, the most important method of organizing the productive process is the corporation, but the sole proprietorship and the partnership are also used.

The government also produces goods and services, but most of the output of governmental enterprises is of such a nature as to prohibit its being produced by any of the various forms of private business organization. This, it might be pointed out, is in sharp contrast to the economy of the USSR, where nearly all of the goods and services are produced by government enterprise.

The economic system is a set or collection of institutional devices which perform certain functions or fulfill certain goals. The functions and goals are economic in nature rather than political or biological.

Obviously there are many ways in which man may order his economic life. A free economy with decentralized decision making or a controlled economy with centralized planning are only two. Regardless of the specific form which the economic system takes, there are certain principles which can be used to analyze and interpret economic activity and the functioning of an economic system. It is the derivation and application of these principles which is our concern.

EXERCISES

Group I

1. Explain why each of the following would or would not be considered as an act of saving.
   a. Buying a TV set at a sale at $20 below its regular price.
   b. Buying life insurance.
   c. Repaying a promisory note.
   d. Payment of the mortgage on a house.
   e. Buying a share of common stock.
   f. Buying a refrigerator for one's house.
   g. A farmer building a fence.
   h. A Chinese peasant turning over to the government all of the rice he produced except the minimum amount necessary for subsistence.
   i. A gambler playing a slot machine in Las Vegas.
   j. A housewife canning peaches.

2. Why is the corporation the dominant form of business in the United States in terms of employment and production but yet is not the most important form if only numbers are considered?

3. Trace the course of your own personal savings into the production stream. For example, if you have funds in the bank, what did the bank do with them? How has your insurance company invested its funds?

4. Suppose that you are an adviser to one of the countries classed as being underdeveloped. What measures might you suggest in order that savings would be increased?

5. Explain how savings might be achieved in a country without a currency or money in any form.

Group II

1. An important concept in economics is that of "opportunity costs" which may be defined as the best alternative foregone. That is, the real cost of an item is what one has to give up to acquire that particular good. Using the concept of opportunity cost, estimate the cost of your college education. How does it compare with the "out-of-pocket cost?" Compare the cost of a college education for the good student and the poor student. If you eliminate all factors except cost and expected payoff, how would you determine whether or not your decision to attend college was correct?

2. What is the role of the stock market in the saving-investment mechanism?

Is such an institution required in all types of economic systems? If not, why not?

3. Select several shares of common stock from those listed on the New York Stock Exchange. What principles would you use in building up your portfolio? After selecting the shares, graph the price for each trading day for the remainder of the term. If the price fluctuates, what causes it to do so? If you had invested in these stocks, would your investment achieve those goals you used in guiding your original selections?

Group III

1. Large corporations are becoming much more dependent upon internal sources of funds for capital expansion. By using these funds generated within the company, they do not have to go into the capital market and meet the test of the market place. Develop an argument for the proposition: "A confiscatory tax should be placed on retained earnings. This tax should be heavy enough to force corporations to do all of their capital financing through the capital market."

2. What is the role of corporate management in today's very large corporation? To whom do they owe first responsibility—the stockholders, the customers, the wage earners, or to some other entity?

BIBLIOGRAPHY

BERLE, A. A. *The 20th Century Capitalist Revolution.* New York: Harcourt, Brace & Co., 1954. (Also available in paperback.)

BERLE, A. A., AND MEANS, GARDNER. *The Modern Corporation and Private Property.* New York: Macmillan Co., 1931.

DRUCKER, PETER F. *The Concept of the Corporation.* New York: Harper & Brothers, 1941. (Also available in paperback.)

SMITH, ADAM. *An Inquiry into the Nature and Causes of the Wealth of Nations.* New York: Modern Library, 1937.

VEBLEN, THORSTEIN. *The Theory of the Leisure Class.* New York: Modern Library, 1934. (Also available in paperback.)

PAPERBACK READING LIST

MASON, E. S. (Ed). *The Corporation in Modern Society.* Cambridge: Harvard University Press, 1960.

TAWNEY, R. H. *The Acquisitive Society.* New York: Harvest Books, Harcourt, Brace, and World, Inc.

Chapter 3

THE PRODUCTIVE PROCESS

Mr. Podsnap's world was not a very large world, morally; no, nor even geographically; seeing that although his business was sustained upon commerce with other countries, he considered other countries, with that important reservation, a mistake, and of their manners and customs would conclusively observe, "Not English!" when, PRESTO! with a flourish of the arm, and a flush of the face, they were swept away. Elsewise, the world got up at eight, shaved close at a quarter-past, breakfasted at nine, went to the City at ten, came home at half-past five, and dined at seven. Mr. Podsnap's notions of the Arts in their integrity might have been stated thus. Literature; large print, respectively descriptive of getting up at eight, shaving close at a quarter-past, breakfasting at nine, going to the City at ten, coming home at half-past five, and dining at seven. Painting and Sculpture; models and portraits representing Professors of getting up at eight, shaving close at a quarter-past, breakfasting at nine, going to the City at ten, coming home at half-past five, and dining at seven. Music; a respectable performance (without variations) on stringed and wind instruments, sedately expressive of getting up at eight, shaving close at a quarter-past, breakfasting at nine, going to the City at ten, coming home at half-past five, and dining at seven. Nothing else to be permitted to those same vagrants the Arts, on pain of excommunication. Nothing else To Be—anywhere!—Charles Dickens, *Our Mutual Friend.*

One cannot imagine a society, no matter how primitive or advanced, in which no effort of any kind would be needed to fulfill human wants and desires. The most primitive man had to climb trees, hunt and fish, pick berries, or engage in some other form of activity to satisfy his few but basic wants. Modern man living in a highly mechanized and interdependent society must likewise put forth effort, although it is of a much different nature than that of his primitive cousin, so that his wants, which have also changed from those of his primitive ancestors, will be satisfied. In every society—primitive or advanced, capitalistic or socialistic, agricultural or industrial—effort must be put forth before man can have those goods and services necessary to fulfill his wants. The process by which this is done is the productive process.

WHAT IS PRODUCTION?

Everyone is acquainted with the idea of a process. We come in contact with and observe many different kinds of processes each day. The Mississippi River, for example, is a process. There are a number of inputs including water from various sources, soil washed from the hillsides, wastes from industrial plants and municipalities, etc. And then there are a number of outputs including the water that flows into the Gulf of Mexico, the new land area that is constantly being formed at the outlet, and the fish that inhabit the river. Another process frequently observed is that of the housewife baking a cake. She combines flour, milk, eggs, and other ingredients with her labor as well as certain capital items including a mixer, spoon(s), a bowl, etc. The result is a tasty delicacy. Now if the aim of the housewife is simply that of producing a chocolate cake for dinner, it is obvious that she has several choices among different methods which will produce the desired end.

Now that these two examples have been pointed out, the student should be able to observe many examples of processes of one sort or another. It should be obvious, at this point, that production is also a process. It doesn't matter whether the item to be produced is a performance of Mozart's *Don Giovanni,* a book to be used by a university student, or a chocolate cake to be eaten by the family at dinner. In each case there are a number of items which will be needed in the process to achieve the goal.

Those items which go into the process resulting in the production of some good or service are called inputs. The final products are out-puts. Thus, in the case of the housewife, the ingredients, her labor, and the cooking utensils are inputs while the finished cake is the output. Any productive process, then, is some combination of inputs which are brought together in such a fashion so as to produce an output which is, in some way, different from the inputs.

It is important to note the above requirement that the outputs of the process must be, in some respect, different from the inputs, but it should not be inferred that this difference is necessarily physical in nature. The physical difference may, as a matter of fact, be slight (such as a shoe shine on an already highly polished pair of shoes) or it may be very great (as in the case of the conversion of iron ore into automobiles). The important difference between the inputs and the outputs is to be found in their relative ability to satisfy human wants. Production must result in an output which has a greater capacity to satisfy human wants than the inputs. If this statement is not true, production will not take place over any very long period of time in a free market economy.

It has become fairly standard in economics to refer to that ability of a good or service to satisfy a human want as the utility of the good in question. If one good has a greater capacity to satisfy a human want than another, then the first has greater utility. And an output of the productive process will have greater utility than the input.

Production includes five types of utility creation. The first, and probably the easiest to understand, is that of *form* utility. When iron is made into steel, wheat milled into flour, or cotton cloth made into clothing, there is a change in the form of the input which results in a more useful output. *Place* utility is created when a good is moved from one location to another. The mere act of shipping coffee from Brazil to the United States increases the capacity of that commodity to satisfy human desires. Here, one should note, one of the inputs is the necessary transportation facilities and services. *Time* utility is created when the utility of goods is enhanced simply by holding them over a period of time. The warehousing process is a good example. Although Adam Smith in 1776 did not recognize *service* utility, it is now generally recognized that those in the service industries such as medicine, teaching, law, etc. are producing goods (services) even though they are intangible. *Possession* utility is the result of exchange. A real estate agent, by bringing a buyer and seller together and effecting the transfer of property, increases the usefulness of that property. If the property were not more valuable to the prospective buyer and the money of more value to the prospective seller, there would be no transaction. By effecting the transfer, both parties anticipate being better off than they were before the transfer, and by contributing to this end, the real estate salesman must be considered to have made a contribution to the productive process.

All five have one thing in common. All increase the usefulness of the commodity; or, to put it in other words, the ability of the good to satisfy a human want has been enhanced. Because this is so, we can say that its value is increased through production. Production, then, can be regarded as the creation of utility or the creation or enhancement of value.

Out of the productive process come both wealth and income. The factors which create utility receive a payment for their services, which is income. The wealth of an economy is reflected in the products created by those engaged in the productive process. To be classed as part of the nation's wealth, however, a product must be both tangible and transferable. Thus the nation's wealth is increased as the output of steel, automobiles, phonograph records, and other tangible products increases. However, those who render only a personal service have not directly increased the national wealth, although they may have contributed a great deal in an indirect fashion.

One should not read into the above paragraph any moral connotation. It cannot be said that those who do not create a tangible good and thus do not increase the nation's wealth are not productive. Wealth and income are simply two technical terms used to appraise the productive process and the national well-being.

The Factors of Production

In order that human wants may be satisfied, it is necessary for man to combine his efforts with the products of nature in order to produce the desired goods and services. The production of all goods is essentially a result of combining the efforts of man with the resources provided by nature; however, the efforts of man can take different forms and the combination of the two may be of different types. The generally accepted classification discusses four factors of production—land or natural resources, labor, capital, and the entrepreneur or enterpriser.

Land. It has long been the custom among economists to refer to those resources provided by nature as land, but it must be understood that the term as it is used herein refers to anything provided by nature. It includes not only land in the ordinary sense of the word but also air, water, and minerals. It is seldom that the product of nature can be used directly, for in nearly every instance it must be combined with the efforts of man in one form or another.

Labor. Labor consists of the human effort which is contributed to the productive process. The term, as used by economists, is somewhat more inclusive than that which is generally thought of as labor by the layman. Men who dig ditches, teach school, or perform any of a myriad of activities are included in the general classification of labor. If their actions meet the criteria of productiveness established earlier in the chapter, they are considered to be productive. If, however, such human effort does not result in the creation of some form of utility, there is no production and such exertion is not productive activity.

Capital. The third factor of production consists of the man-made goods used in the productive process. When man combines his efforts with resources provided by nature, it is possible to produce either of two types of goods. The first are those which have the ability to directly satisfy the wants of man—consumer goods. The second includes those goods which cannot directly satisfy man's wants but can be used to produce other goods which have this ability. Milling machines, factories, heavy electrical equipment, and the like do not directly satisfy man's wants, but the products which these investment goods produce do meet the needs of man. And there are some goods which may be considered as being either consumer goods or investment goods. An automobile is a consumer good when used for pleasure, but the same automobile is capital when used by a salesman.

One must not, under any circumstances, consider money as capital in the sense meant here. Using our concept of productivity, money is not capable of producing any good which has the ability to satisfy consumer wants.

The Entrepreneur. The productive process is not analogous to a chemical reaction in the sense that you can merely bring land, labor, and capital together and the result will be the production of consumer goods and services. In the productive process someone must assume the risks involved. Someone must create new ideas and new products. Someone must organize and supervise the productive process. Although the latter tasks may be delegated, there is, nevertheless, a necessity that some individual perform the role of risk taker and innovator—tasks which are not classed as labor. The individual who performs this vital role is the entrepreneur.

His identity presents no problem in the case of the small business firm. In the case of the large corporation, it is not so easy to identify the entrepreneur. Common stockholders are the primary risk takers in the modern corporation. To the extent that they purchase stock, they are voluntary risk takers. To the extent that corporate management retains earnings in the company and uses the earnings for capital expansion, the common stockholders might be classed as "involuntary" risk takers. Retaining earnings in the company reduces the dividends of the stockholders, but it opens up for them the possibility of increased earnings in the future. Thus they assume the risk. If no one assumes the risk, there will be no production. This is even true for an economy such as the USSR's, in which the people collectively assume risk.

Methods of Production

Direct and Indirect Methods of Production. The simplest type of production is that which may be described as direct production. Under such a method labor is applied directly to the resources of nature and the result is a good which can satisfy a human want. The cave man picking berries, chasing rabbits, or going to a spring to get a drink was engaged in direct production. Obviously such an economy was very primitive. Very early in history man conceived the idea of building a trap to catch rabbits, a net to catch fish, and a flume to pipe water. In order to construct such items, it was necessary for this primitive individual to abstain from consumption, or save, as has already been described. Through this abstention from consumption, capital was created which could, in turn, be used to produce consumer goods. Capital enables one to engage in indirect or roundabout production. The classic description is that of Böhm-Bawerk:

A peasant required drinking water. The spring is some distance from his house. There are various ways in which he may supply his daily wants. First, he may go to the spring each time he is thirsty and drink out of his hollowed hand. This is the most direct way; satisfaction followed immediately on exertion. But it is an inconvenient way, for our peasant has to make his way to the well as often as he is thirsty. And it is an insufficient way, for he can never collect and store any great quantity such as he requires for various other purposes. Second, he may take a log of wood, hollow it out into a kind of pail and carry his day's supply from the spring to his cottage. The advantage is obvious but it necessitates a roundabout way of considerable length. The man must spend, perhaps, a day in cutting out the pail; before doing so he must have felled a tree in the forest; to do this, again, he must have made an ax, and so on. But there is still a third way; instead of felling one tree he fells a number of trees, splits and hollows them, lays them end for end; and so constructs a runnel or rhone which brings a full head of water to his cottage. Here obviously between the expenditure of the labour and the obtaining of the water we have a very roundabout way, but, the result is ever so much greater. Our peasant needs no longer take his weary way from house to well with the heavy pail on his shoulder, and yet he has a constant and full supply of the freshest water at his very door.[1]

Modern methods of production are indirect or roundabout. Rare is the instance in which a consumer good is produced through only the contribution of land and labor. The first step in the production of nearly any commodity is the creation of large amounts of capital. To build automobiles, large factories with expensive machines are required. To make dish towels, textile mills are built and farm machinery is manufactured. To grow wheat, fertilizer plants are built.

TABLE 3–1

INVESTED CAPITAL PER PRODUCTION WORKER IN SELECTED
INDUSTRIES IN THE UNITED STATES, 1956

Industry	Invested Capital per Production Worker
Food, beverages, and tobacco	$17,416
Textiles and textile products	6,051
Leather and leather products	4,420
Rubber products	15,526
Lumber and wood products	7,529
Paper and paper products	15,841
Printing and publishing	10,959
Chemicals and allied products	28,570
Petroleum	110,096
Stone, clay, and glass products	12,496
Metal products	13,834
Total manufacturing	15,006

SOURCE: National Industrial Conference Board, *Economic Almanac, 1960* (New York, 1960).

In 1956, for every production worker employed by manufacturing firms in the United States, an average investment of $15,006 was required. (See Table 3–1.) In the case of the petroleum industry, the investment was $110,096 for each production worker. The total new investment in plant and equipment for the manufacturing industries of the United States in 1956 was estimated to be $11,409,000,000.[2] If the nonmanufacturing industries as well as agriculture were included, the investment would be considerably larger. Where do such vast sums come from?

The answer has already been given. The source of such funds is the absention from consumption—that is, savings. If everything that was

[1] E. von Böhm-Bawerk, *Positive Theory of Capital,* trans. William Smart (London: Macmillan & Co., Ltd., 1891), p. 18.

[2] National Industrial Conference Board, *Economic Almanac, 1960* (New York, 1960).

produced was consumed, there would be no accumulation of capital. Just as the cave man postponed consumption to make a bucket or build a flume, so must modern man postpone consumption in order to accumulate capital. The end result is beneficial, of course, since at some time in the future far greater amounts will be produced through the use of capital. Thus the net effect of using savings to engage in indirect production is a tremendous increase in production and hence consumption. Capital is analogous to a lever, for it enables man to apply a far greater force on the resources of nature and to accomplish goals which would be impossible were it not for the use of capital. It is impossible to imagine the production of seven million automobiles without the use of capital; in fact, it is impossible to imagine a modern economy devoid of capital.

Accompanying the more extensive use of indirect methods of production has been a movement toward specialization in production. Today, the Jack-of-all-trades is a phenomena of the past, for most people are master of one trade. A single individual may do nothing more in the making of an automobile than attach the wheels or the steering column. Today's farmer often raises only wheat, cotton, or some other single crop. Even the schoolteacher of today teaches only one of the three R's and leaves the remaining two for colleagues. Specialization is characteristic of the modern economic system. It has tremendous advantages, but, as shall be pointed out, there are also some problems.

Advantages in Indirect Methods of Production. Adam Smith first pointed out the nature of specialization in the *Wealth of Nations* in a delightful passage describing the production of pins.

To take example, therefore, from a very trifling manufacture; but one in which the division of labor has been very often taken notice of, the trade of the pin-maker; a workman not educated to this business (which the division of labor has rendered a distinct trade), nor acquainted with the use of the machinery employed in it (to the invention of which the same division of labor has probably given occasion), could scarce, perhaps, with his utmost industry make one pin a day, and certainly could not make twenty. But in the way in which this business is now carried on, not only the whole work is peculiar trade, but it is divided into a number of branches, of which the greater part are likewise peculiar trades. One man draws out the wire, another straights it, a third cuts it, a fourth points it, a fifth grinds it at the top for receiving the head; to make the head requires two or three distinct operations; to put it on, is a peculiar business, to whiten the pins is another; it is even a trade by itself to put them into the paper; and the important business of making a pin is, in this manner, divided into about eighteen distinct operations, which, in some manufactories, are all performed by distinct hands, though in others the same man will sometimes perform two or three of them. . . . Each person, therefore, . . . might be considered as making four thousand eight hundred pins a day. But if they had all wrought separately and independently, and without any of them having been educated to this peculiar business, they certainly could not, each of them, have made twenty, perhaps not one pin a day.[3]

Certainly specialization increases the productivity of the factors taking part in the productive process. Adam Smith pointed out three factors: (1) The worker becomes more skillful at his particular job whereas he could not acquire the same degree of skill over all aspects of a much larger job. (2) There is a saving in time, since each employee works at one job in one place rather than moving from one job to another. This is amply illustrated by the worker on the assembly line who always has the needed materials deposited in front of him. (3) It stimulates technical progress, for the worker who is concentrating on a single task is more apt to think of ways to improve the process than the worker who is scattering his efforts over a number of jobs. Adam Smith includes a picturesque description of a boy working on a steam engine:

In the first fire engines, a boy was constantly employed to open and shut alternately the communication between the boiler and the cylinder, according as the piston either ascended or descended. One of those boys, who loved to play with his companions, observed that, by tying a string from the handle of the valve which opened this communication to another part of the machine, the valve would open and shut without his assistance, and leave him at liberty to divert himself with his playfellows. One of the greatest improvements that has been made upon this machine, since it was first invented, was in this manner the discovery of a boy who wanted to save his own labour.[4]

Since Smith's time, other advantages have been perceived. (4) The time required to learn the task is much shorter. In the machine tool industry, for example, an untrained individual can learn a fairly complicated operation and perform quite competently within a short time. It would take much longer, if it were even possible, for that individual to master the whole process involved in the making of machine tools. (5) The total job is subdivided so that the various abilities of the individual concerned are put to the maximum usage. That part of the job which is extremely complicated can be performed by those persons who are more able, and those jobs which do not require a high degree of ability can be performed by those who are less able. Probably the best example of this is the fact that there is a very important place in modern industry for the physically handicapped. (6) Capital is put to a better use. A single individual producing the entire product would be able to use a given

[3] Adam Smith, *An Inquiry into the Nature and Causes of the Wealth of Nations* (New York: Modern Library, 1937), p. 4.

[4] *Ibid.*, p. 9.

piece of equipment for only a small part of the time, and it would be idle while other pieces of equipment were being used. With specialization in the productive process, each piece of equipment is in constant use.

Costs of Indirect Methods of Production. The result of indirect production and extensive specialization has been a vast increase in productivity, but this has not been without cost. Space does not permit a detailed discussion, but some consideration must be given to problems which have arisen. These problems are not wholly economic in nature, for, in part, they are problems in sociology and psychology. Probably most important is the worker himself. Many claim that increasing specialization results in a narrowing of the personality of the worker, thus producing an individual who is unable to enjoy life. It is further contended that working on a single small part of the total job destroys this worker's creativity. The criticism, then, is that one becomes a slave to the machine in that the individual lives for the machine rather than the machine existing for the person. Certainly, this problem is not as serious as the extreme critics of industrialization would have us believe, for tremendous strides have been made in the fields of education and leisure activities which offset the narrowness of one's job.

A second problem area is the concern of the economist. As productivity increases, the necessities of life can be produced with an ever smaller amount of human labor. At the present time not all of our agricultural resources are required to produce the necessary foodstuffs. The same thing is true of coal and other resources. There is, then, the problem of adjusting resources to the demand for the particular commodity. Such resources must shift from areas where there is an ability to overproduce into areas in which an insufficient amount is being produced. As time passes, a smaller amount of our total resources will be found in such primary industries as agriculture, and a larger and larger percentage will be found in such service industries as entertainment and recreation.

PRODUCTION FUNCTIONS

The fact that there are fundamental laws which underly the behavior of such physical phenomena as falling bodies, ocean tides, light, and the like is generally accepted by all and understood, to some extent, by many. But the fact that there are comparable laws relating to the production of economic goods seems to elicit some surprise, and scepticism, among non-economists. Once one accepts the fact that the productive process is a technological phenomena, the existence and meaning of laws of production should be somewhat easier to understand and appreciate. Moreover, since the principles which are going to be discussed are of a technological nature, it follows that they are independent of the political or economic system which prevails in any given country. In other words, the techniques of analysis and the principles discussed in this section will apply with equal validity to the United States, the Soviet Union, or the underdeveloped nations of the world.

The Concept of the Production Function

The production function may be defined as that physical relationship which exists between the inputs of the several factors and the output of product. For example, there is some relationship between the quantity of wheat produced by a farmer and the inputs of labor, capital, and natural resources. The relationship between inputs and outputs lends itself rather readily to the mathematical formulation in much the same way that a housewife's recipe (production function) for a cake is expressed in terms of quantitative inputs. Most of the advanced work in this field is of a quantitative nature, but here primary attention shall be confined to the more elementary concepts which can be presented in words and diagrams.

There are some instances where there is only a single recipe for the production of a given output. For example, there is only one combination of hydrogen and oxygen which will produce water. Such a relationship is not characteristic of production functions. As a matter-of-fact, a producer generally has considerable freedom insofar as combining the factors of production are concerned and achieving a specified goal.

Once the producer has decided what he wants to produce, he is faced with the engineering-economic task of deciding what different methods of production are available and which of the possible techniques will be used.

Suppose, for example, that a young boy is considering mowing lawns in order to earn spending money. Let's assume that he needs to mow four lawns a week (at $1.50 each) in order to earn the necessary income. In this simple problem, the two inputs will be (1) labor in the form of the number of hours worked per week and (2) capital in the form of a lawnmower or cutting instrument of some type. The contribution of nature in the form of growing grass can be ignored if it is assumed that the grass grows at a steady rate which is just enough, no more and no less, to require one cutting a week.

What are some of the alternatives? One would be that of using a lawn mower powered by an engine and ridden by the operator. Another would be that of using a machine where the operator is the source of power. And one could imagine an extreme case in which the cutting instrument was a pair of shears. These are only three of the many possible combinations of inputs. The young entrepreneur could then list all of the possible combinations of labor and capital which would yield the desired output of four lawns per week.[5]

One of the restrictions on this problem up to this point, was the fact that the individual only wanted to mow four lawns a week—that is, earn $6.00. But he might want to mow more lawns or possibly fewer. So in addition to listing all of the combinations of inputs which would result in the mowing of four lawns, he might also include those combinations would yield a larger output (5, 6, 7, 8, 9, or 10) or fewer (0, 1, 2, 3). The entire table, that is, all the combinations of inputs which would mow 0, 1, 2, ... , 9, or 10 lawns per week is the production function. It would show all of the possible combinations of inputs which would yield each of the several levels of output.

A production function using only two inputs and yielding only a single output, such as the example above, can be presented in graphical form in such a fashion that it is quite easy to understand. What is needed is some sort of a curve (mathematical function) which will represent all of the possible combinations of input which will yield a specified output. Such a production function is shown in Figure 3–1. The horizontal axis indicates the amount of labor input and the vertical axis represents the capital input. The curved lines are constant output curves. Each represents various combinations of the two inputs which yields a given output. The lowest curve, I_1, represents all the combinations of labor and capital which will produce 200 units of output; I_2 represents those combinations which will yield 300 units of output, and so on. The higher the constant output curve, that is, the further to the northeast it is, the higher will be the level of output. These curves are called "constant product curves" or "isoquants."

In its economically significant portion, any curve representing a production function must have the general shape of those in Figure 3–1. That is, it must have a negative slope (downward to the right), and in nearly all cases, it must be concave upward. Why? The negative slope of the function indicates that as more of one factor is used, less of the second is needed. In the example, the larger the labor input, the

[5] He should not forget to list Tom Sawyer's peculiar production function. For it might be possible for this boy to get his friends to work for nothing or even better to pay him for contributing their inputs to the productive process. If he could thus get this "free" help, it would pay him to use more and more labor and less and less capital as well as his own labor.

smaller the amount of capital required in order to produce a given output. Certainly this is consistent with one's observations, for it is hard to imagine a situation in which output would remain constant when all factors are increased which is what would be indicated by a constant output curve with a positive slope (upward to the right).

FIGURE 3–1

THE PRODUCTION FUNCTION

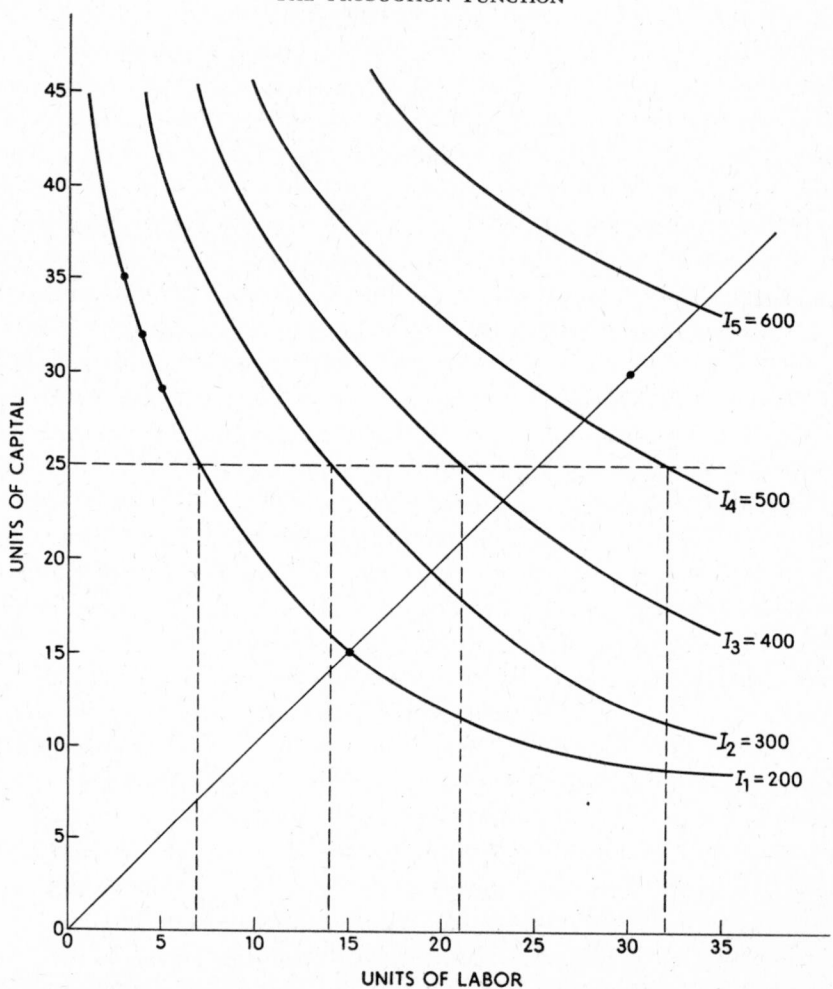

How is the concavity of the function explained? First, contemplate the case where the constant output curve is a straight line sloping downward to the right. Such a function would indicate that a given level of output could be reached by using all labor or all capital. Furthermore, one factor could always be substituted for the other in a given proportion and total output would remain unchanged. In other words, if the constant output curve is a straight line with a negative slope, the two inputs are perfect substitutes for one another—they are the same input. Thus the fact that the two inputs are not perfect substitutes explains why the function must be concave upward. What would the constant output function look like for two inputs which could not be substituted for one another but which had to be combined in a fixed proportion, say one-to-one?

What other information can be gleaned from the nature of the production function in Figure 3–1? In the case of I_1, for example, 200 units of output can be produced with 35 units of capital and three units of labor. The same level of output can be produced with 32 units of capital and four units of labor. One unit of labor is needed to replace three units of capital. However, if the capital input is further reduced by three units (to 29 units of capital input), the labor input would have to be increased by slightly more than one unit. And at that point where 15 units of both inputs are used, it would take five units of labor to replace three units of capital. The more labor that is used, the less valuable one more unit becomes, and thus more labor is required to replace a given amount of capital. And, saying the same thing in a different fashion, the smaller the quantity of capital being used, the more reluctant one will be to substitute additional units of labor for the remaining units of capital. As the producer moves downward to the right on this constant product curve, he becomes less and less willing to substitute labor for capital. Eventually the producer may come to a point where further substitution of one input for the other will no longer produce the desired output.

The Law of Diminishing Returns

The law of diminishing returns is a technological or engineering concept; however, it does play an extremely important role in economics. Suppose that in a particular production process there are two inputs, one of which is held constant and the second is allowed to vary (increase or decrease). The law of diminishing returns states that as additional units of the variable input are combined with a given amount of the fixed input, eventually a point will be reached where the output will not increase proportionately. For example, if land were the fixed factor and labor the variable factor, the producer could double and redouble his labor input while holding the land input at some constant level, but beyond some point the output would not be doubled.

Imagine, for the moment, a person confronted with the problem of applying fertilizer to his lawn without the benefit of any instructions from the manufacturer. He decides to conduct an experiment to determine the effect of varying quantities of fertilizer on the lawn. Using a mechanical fertilizer spreader, he adopts the following procedure. On the first strip, the spreader was closed so that no fertilizer was applied. On the second strip, the spreader was opened one notch; on the third strip it was opened to the second notch; and so on until on the last strip the spreader was opened to the last notch. After the fertilizer was applied, the lawn was carefully mowed a strip at a time and the output for each strip was weighed during the course of the growing season. Our suburban gardener noticed that for the first few strips the percentage increase in grass was greater than the percentage increase in fertilizer. Then a point was reached where the percentage increase in the output (grass) was less than the corresponding increase in the variable input (fertilizer), and eventually the total production of grass actually started to decline. On the last strip no grass at all was produced, because the application of fertilizer was so large that it killed the grass. The point of diminishing returns is that point where the proportionate increase in output is less than the proportionate increase in input. And the law of diminishing returns states that such a point will exist whenever a fixed input is combined in varying proportions with a variable input.

Here we have our first economic model, and since it is a model, there will be assumptions. What are the assumptions underlying the law of diminishing returns? There are two. First, it is assumed that the units of the variable factor are homogeneous—that is, each unit is a perfect substitute for every other unit of that input. This means that diminishing returns is not explained by the fact that the additional inputs of the variable factor are of a poorer grade or quality.

The second assumption is that known as "a given state of the arts," which in this case refers to the state of technology. For example, if capital is the variable input, it is assumed that the additional units of capital represent the same technology as the previous units. If capital is the fixed input, then the additional units of labor all work with the same type of capital; that is, there is no substitution of more productive units of capital for less productive units of that factor.

It should be carefully noted (and remembered) that the law of diminishing returns applies only to those situations where one factor is varied and everything else, including the state of the arts as well as the quantity and quality of the fixed factor, is held constant.

What is the explanation of this phenomena known as the law of diminishing returns? Many students, when asked this question will assert that the explanation is to be found in the fact that the additional units of the variable input are of poorer quality, but this explanation has been assumed out of the problem. So there must be some other explanation.

It is not too difficult to accept the proposition that there is some combination of factor inputs (fixed and variable) which is better than any other combination for producing a given amount of output. For example, if there is a ditch to be dug, the combination of one man and one shovel is probably a better combination than one man and no shovels, one man and two shovels, or one man and a dozen shovels. If the man (the fixed input) is combined with no shovels (the variable input), it will take a considerable length of time to dig the ditch. The reason is the fact that there is too much of the fixed factor for the variable factor being used. Obviously this is not a very good combination unless the cost of shovels is extremely high and the cost of labor extremely low. If a single unit of labor were combined with two or more units of capital, there is too much of the variable factor—in this case, shovels, for the one man can only operate one shovel at a time, and there would be idle units of capital. So whenever two factors can be combined in varying proportions to produce a given output, there has to be some combination which is better than any other.

As a matter of fact, the law of diminishing returns is sometimes referred to as "the law of variable proportions." The latter term has some advantage because it does call attention to the critical fact that, in most cases, factor inputs do not have to be combined in some given proportion, but, on the contrary, can be combined in varying proportions. It follows that there is some proportion which is better than others.

Returns to Scale

Holding one input constant and varying another is only one way of altering the production process. Another possibility is that of altering all inputs; that is, having no fixed input. In such a case, the appropriate principle of production is that of "returns to scale." "Returns to scale" refer to the relationship between changes in output and changes in inputs when all of the latter are allowed to vary.

If all inputs are increased proportionately and there is a proportionate increase in output, this is a case of constant returns to scale.[6]

---

[6] The case of constant returns to scale is of considerable interest at the present time. A production function with constant returns to scale is said to be a homogeneous production function, or some times it is referred to as being linearly homogeneous. Linear programming, then, is a technique of working with production functions which are linearly homogeneous (constant returns to scale). It is a mathematical technique for determining the best combination of inputs under certain conditions, one of which is that of constant returns to scale.

Thus if all inputs are doubled and output is likewise doubled, this is an example of constant returns to scale. If there is a less than proportionate increase in output, it is a case of decreasing returns to scale; and if there is a larger than proportionate increase in output, it is an example of increasing returns to scale.

What is the explanation of this phenomena known as returns to scale? First, take the case of increasing returns to scale which asserts that if all factor inputs are increased in some constant proportion, output will increase more than proportionately. One explanatory fact stems from the indivisibility of certain of the inputs. A large milling machine may be necessary if an enterprise is to produce even a few units of output, even though the machine has the capacity to turn out many thousands of units. Thus a firm which expands its capital input by installing the new machine may find it profitable to, at the same time, increase its input of all other factors in the same proportion. Under such circumstances, a doubling of all inputs may well result in a more than doubling of the output of the enterprise.

A second explanatory factor is that of specialization. In a larger undertaking, resulting from increasing all inputs, each of the inputs can be used to its best advantage. A unit of capital may, for example, be used to produce one particular part of the final product rather than being used to produce several different parts (with the resultant increase in downtime). A laborer may perform only a single task on the assembly line rather than scattering his efforts over a variety of tasks. If increasing the quantity of all inputs will permit greater specialization, the result may well be a more than proportional increase in output and increasing returns to scale.

Rather than seek the explanation of constant returns to scale, let us turn immediately to the question of decreasing returns to scale. If an enterprise is experiencing decreasing returns to scale, then increasing all inputs does not result in proportionate increases in output, though this does not mean, of course, that there will be no increase in output.

What might explain this curious state of affairs? The explanation that seems to be most widely accepted is to be found in the input of managerial talent. As firms get larger and larger, a point is reached where instead of increasing management personnel in the same ratio at the other inputs, it is necessary to increase this particular input by a larger percentage than the others. The fact is well demonstrated by the organization of the armed forces or the educational system. If the number of professors, for example, were to be doubled, the number of deans, assistant deans, directors and assistant directors, and other "management" personnel would be more than doubled. If the school population explosion of the 1960's results in increasing the teaching population by 100 per cent, the administrative population in the school system will increase by a larger proportion. Whenever the armed services of any country reduces the number of enlisted men by a specified percentage, the number of officers (particularly of the upper ranks) must be reduced by a larger percentage. The common denominator in all of the above three instances is what is commonly known as red tape or bureaucracy. It is associated with large enterprises regardless of whether they are public or private, in a capitalistic society or some alternative, profit motivated or philanthropic, etc. Thus there is some point, in terms of size, beyond which further expansion will result in decreasing returns to scale. The particular point where this occurs will vary from one instance to the next and will depend upon the characteristics of the particular production function.

Geometrical Demonstration of the Principles of Production

Figure 3–1 can be used to demonstrate the principle of diminishing returns as well as that of returns to scale.

First, take the case of returns to scale. A line drawn from the origin at an angle of $45°$ will connect those points indicating equal amounts of the two inputs. Thus by moving from one point to another on this line, the two inputs will increase by the same absolute and proportionate amounts. When 15 units of both inputs are used, the total output will be 200 units as indicated by the intersection of I_3 and the $45°$ line. If both factor inputs are doubled, that is, if the productive process is altered so that 30 units of both inputs are used, total output will increase to something greater than 500 units. The $45°$ line would intersect some constant output curve which lies between I_4 and I_5. In such a case, the inputs were doubled and the output was more than doubled. This is a case of increasing returns to scale.

If the constant product curves were renumbered so that I_5 represented 400 units of output and I_4 represented 300 units of output, then doubling the inputs from 15 to 30 units would increase output to approximately 350 units. Since the output was increased by less than 100 per cent, this would represent a case of decreasing returns to scale.

In the case of constant returns to scale, a doubling of the inputs would result in the $45°$ line intersecting a constant product curve representing an output twice that of the original.

The law of diminishing returns can also be graphically demonstrated by using Figure 3–1. Since this principle requires that one of the inputs be held constant while the other is varied, it is necessary that those combinations consisting of a given amount of one input and varying amounts of the second be indicated. On the map of the constant output curves, this can be done by drawing a horizontal (or vertical) line which would indicate a fixed amount of one input and varying quantities of the second input. For example, a horizontal line drawn at the level indicating 25 units of capital would represent all possible combinations of labor inputs with that quantity of capital. Then at the points where this line intersects I_1, I_2, I_3, I_4, and I_5, the quantity of labor can be read off which, combined with 25 units of capital, would produce the quantity indicated. The following table results.

TABLE 3–2

LEVEL OF OUTPUT FOR VARIOUS AMOUNTS OF LABOR
WHEN COMBINED WITH 25 UNITS OF CAPITAL

Number of Units of Labor	Number of Units of Output	Increase in Output per Additional Unit of Input
7	200	--
14	300	$14\frac{2}{7}$
21	400	$14\frac{2}{7}$
32	500	$9\frac{1}{11}$

When the labor input was increased from 7 to 14 units, the average increase in output per unit of input was $14\frac{2}{7}$ units, as it was when the labor input was increased from 14 to 21 units. But when the labor input is increased from 21 to 32 units, the average increase in output per additional unit of input falls off to $9\frac{1}{11}$ units. Thus the point of diminishing marginal returns has been reached. The point of diminishing returns is that point where the increase in output per additional unit of input begins to decline.

The principle of diminishing returns can be graphically demonstrated in a second fashion (see Figure 3–2.). Although this approach appears to be rather dissimilar to the first, this is not so. The two approaches demonstrate the same thing.

One notices in Figure 3–2 that there are only two variables—a variable input and a variable output. Like the first demonstration, everything else is held constant including all other inputs. So this is a diagrammatic representation of the relationship between changes in the quantity of one input and resulting changes in output.

The total product function (TP) simply represents the total output which would be produced using different amounts of the variable input with a given amount of a fixed input. The average product function (AP) is the total product divided by the number of units of variable input. And the marginal product function (MP) is the change in the total output which results from increasing (or decreasing) the amount of variable input. It is the relationship between changes in the two variables. As a rule, the marginal product is defined in terms of the addition (or subtraction) of one unit of input. (This limitation can be dropped through the use of calculus.)

The average product function will increase, meaning that the output per unit of input will increase, for a while, indicating that there is too much of the fixed factor for the variable factor being used. Then as

FIGURE 3–2

THE LAW OF DIMINISHING RETURNS

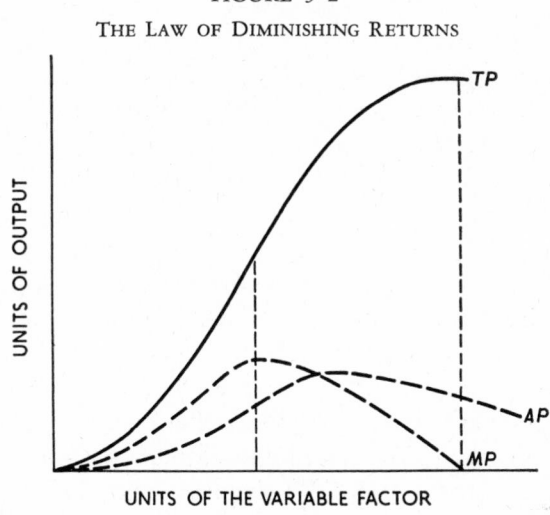

more and more of the variable factor is used with the given amount of the fixed input, eventually a point is reached beyond which the output per unit will fall off. In this range, there is too much of the variable factor relative to the fixed. Note, now, that nothing was said about where the firm should produce or how much of the variable input should be used. More information regarding the cost of the inputs and the demand for the output is necessary before that particular problem can be tackled.

As long as the marginal product function is increasing, additional units of variable input are resulting in a more than proportional increase in output. After the marginal product function begins to decrease, further increases in the quantity of the variable input will result in less than proportional increases in output. And if the marginal product finally becomes negative, this indicates that the additional inputs of the variable factor are actually causing the total product to decline. This is, of course, the case where too much fertilizer is applied to the suburbanite's lawn. That point where the marginal product curve reaches a maximum is the point of diminishing returns, or, as it is sometimes called, the point of diminishing marginal returns.

The relationship between the average product and the marginal product is an arithmetic relationship known to every student, although at first blush it may appear to be somewhat strange. Whenever the additional amount (marginal product) is less than the average amount (average product), the average will be falling. Whenever the additional amount is larger than the average of the series, the average will be increasing. College students know this for a fact, for whenever the last quiz grade is below the average, the average is falling. And whenever the last quiz grade is above the average, the average is rising. The same is true for the golfer who is, in fact, dealing with an average and an additional score. A nine on the last hole would not help the golfer who is averaging five; however, a four on the last hole would bring the same golfer's average down. This is the same principle that is demonstrated in Figures 3–1 and 3–2.

It has already been explained why it might be assumed that the average product is ∩-shaped because of the proportion of the fixed and variable inputs in the productive process. So when the average product is increasing, the marginal product must be greater than the average product; and when the latter is falling, the marginal product must be less than the average product. It follows, then, that a marginal product function must pass through a ∩-shaped average product function at the highest point of the latter. By the same reasoning, one will be able to show, at a later point in the course, a similar relationship between cost functions, only in this case the two functions will be equal at the lowest point of the average function.

CONCLUSION

The production of goods and services is, in part, a technical question. The different methods of producing a given good or service is a question for an engineer. It is an economic problem when prices are attached to the inputs and the interest is in the "best" method of producing the item in question.

To the extent that production is a technical matter, the principles of production are independent of the political system. One would expect to find the same principles of production in a centrally-planned economy as in a decentralized system. Thus the same analytical principles can be used to analyze the productive process, regardless of the existent political system. In other words, differences between economic systems is not to be found in different principles of production.

But even a casual observer is aware that production techniques vary from one country to another. The Soviet Union may use more labor than the United States but less than Communist China or India. Such differences are explained by factors other than the political system. The political system can influence the method of production only insofar as it is able to influence the prices of the inputs or the demands of the consumers.

EXERCISES

Group I

Explain why the following are either true or false:

1. Although there are a number of ways in which a product can be produced, there is one single method which is better than all others, and this one can be determined without any reference to the price of the inputs.
2. The production function shows how many different products can be produced from a given amount of inputs.
3. The concept of the production function would be of no use in a completely planned economy such as that in the Soviet Union, for in such an instance the government decides how each product is to be produced.
4. The law of diminishing returns is "true" because it has no assumptions which might qualify it.
5. Decreasing returns to scale and increasing returns to scale result from changing the proportion of the inputs.
6. Both the law of diminishing returns and the concept of returns to scale are a result of the fact that inferior units of the factor inputs must be used as output is increased.

Group II

1. The absence or presence of economies of scale are an important factor in determining public policy regarding the regulation of business. Write a paper on the "Optimal Sized Production Unit in the Automobile Industry." See the *Study of Administered Prices in the Automobile Industry,* a report by the Subcommittee on Antitrust and Monopoly, United States Senate, 1958.
2. General Motors is generally thought to have been extremely successful in avoiding the diseconomies of large-scale management. How have they done this? Have other companies followed their example?

Group III

1. In a market economy with a freely operating price system, it is the price system which guides production in the sense that one input is substituted

for another as the price of the first falls relative to the second. Now suppose that you are in a completely controlled economy in which all prices are set by the government. How would a government planner determine which factor was to be substituted for others?

BIBLIOGRAPHY

CARLSON, SUNE. *A Study on the Pure Theory of Production.* Reprinted by Augustus M. Kelley, New York, 1956.

HENDERSON, J. M. AND QUANDT, R. E. *Microeconomic Theory.* New York: McGraw-Hill Book Co., 1958.

MANNE, ALAN S. *Economic Analysis for Business Decisions.* New York: McGraw-Hill Book Co., 1961.

Get off the estate.
What for?
Because it's mine.
Where did you get it?
From my father.
Where did he get it?
From his father.
And where did he get it?
He fought for it.
Well, I'll fight you for it.—Carl Sandburg, *The People Yes*. Copyright 1936 by Harcourt, Brace & Co.

Attempts to describe the American economy with short phrases are generally inadequate, for the system is of such complexity that it defies description by slogans. Slogans such as "The American Individual Enterprise System," "The Free Enterprise System," and "The Private Enterprise System," have little, if any, meaningful content. Most academic writers now refer to the economy as a mixed economy, but this tells one little. The only recourse is to devote some time to a discussion of the major characteristics of the system, but it should be

61

pointed out that the following is not all-inclusive. Neither should it be interpreted as being generally accepted, for other writers would describe the system somewhat differently. With those limitations in mind, then, the characteristics of the American economy which distinguish it from other types of economic organization will be discussed. This is a discussion of the economic environment in which the various types of decision-making units function.

CHARACTERISTICS OF THE AMERICAN ECONOMIC SYSTEM

Private Enterprise

Private enterprise is here interpreted to mean a system in which the largest part of the economic decisions are made by private organizations and individuals rather than governmental bodies and public officials. It is not meant to imply that all decisions are so made, for there are a large number of very important decisions which can be made only by the people acting in their collective capacity. But for the most part, in the United States economic decisions are made by private enterprise, for decision making is the essence of such organizations.

In 1962, there were nearly five million business firms and almost that many farms. In addition there were 53.3 million households. In 1963, the population of the country was over 190 million persons. All are constantly and continually making decisions of an economic nature. Business firms are deciding what to produce, how much to produce, and what price to charge. Farmers are deciding whether they should sell all or part of their crops. Householders are buying new cars and new houses or deciding which of the two to buy. All are making decisions as to how time and money should be spent. Should the employer be asked for a raise or should a new position be sought? Should one go to Florida or California for a vacation? In addition to the untold number of decisions being made by the above, there are other private organizations, such as chambers of commerce, labor unions, investment clubs, and women's clubs, which are also making economic decisions.

In contrast to this multitude of private decision makers, we have in the United States slightly more than 100,000 governmental units that make decisions as to whether taxes should be higher or lower, whether new roads should be constructed or new schools provided, whether defense expenditures are sufficient, and many other matters which are beyond the capacity of individuals. But the area of decision making by governmental bodies is comparatively small in this economy dominated by private decision-making units—private enterprise.

The significance of the institution of private enterprise for economics is the fact that it is a decentralized process of decision making in contrast to a more centralized decision-making process in some other systems. Under a system of communism, for example, all except the most minor decisions are made by officials of the government.

There are some who would challenge a system based on private decision making on the basis that an individual in making decisions in light of his own self-interest will make decisions and take actions which are contrary to the general well-being of society. Such a critic would contend that the only technique which would insure that all decisions are compatible with the general welfare would be that in which the government assumed complete responsibility for the decision-making process. Then, it is contended, all decisions would be measured against the "yardstick" of the public welfare. The criticism is brought out most clearly by the socialist criticism of capitalism.

Pursuing one's self-interest does promote the welfare of the society. General Motors' desire to increase profits results in more cars, refrigerators, airplane motors, and other goods for the consuming public. The individual's desire to work, consume, and save promotes the general welfare at the same time that the position of the individual is enhanced. Each in trying to increase personal income is acting in harmony with the interest of others. It should not be thought, however, that there are no exceptions to this rule. A major exception is that of the monopolist, who is in a position to advance his own interest without regard to the interests of others. Because this is so, those who are granted monopoly powers are closely regulated. Other activities which promote individual well-being at the expense of the public are outlawed—robbing banks, for example.

If one group of decision-making units can be singled out as being the most significant, it would have to be the business organizations. Regardless of the form of organization, the business unit is constantly making decisions which affect the lives of all. A dominant factor, and more than likely the most important factor, for business firms in the decision-making process is the profit motive. Decisions regarding the quantity of output and the price, the amounts to be paid to the factors of production, advertising expenditures, expansion of physical facilities, and other matters are all made in light of their effect on the profit position of the firm. The possibility of profit (or loss) encourages the entrepreneur to seek greater efficiency in the operation of the firm as well as to assume risks and take the role of the innovator.

There are some who criticize the profit motive. It has been contended that business, instead of seeking to maximize its profit, should produce with the intention of seeing that the maximum amount of human wants are satisfied. Instead of producing that number of cars which will result in the largest possible profit, the automobile companies should produce as many cars as are compatible with the wants of the people and the resources of the economy. This has always been the complaint of those who criticize the business enterprise for restricting output in order to charge a higher price—the classical indictment of monopoly or those who exercise any monopoly power.

Private Property

The institution of private property may denote no more than the fact that the ownership of tangible goods rests in the hands of private individuals and firms as contrasted to public property, which may be interpreted to mean ownership by the people. If the only concern at this point were a comparison of economic systems, such a limited interpretation might be of some value, but, since the immediate concern is an understanding of the economy of the United States, it will not suffice. A full appreciation of "property" as well as "private property" is essential.

What Is Property? It was not until the advent of the Industrial Revolution that the term property meant anything more than tangible goods; in fact, the common-law interpretation of property denoted a tangible good. In those economic systems which preceded capitalism, the concern was with the use of property—for example, land to provide food and buildings to provide shelter. With the advent of capitalism and specialization, however, property took on a new aspect of great significance. No longer was the concern with the use of property, for the worker did not intend to use what he produced, just as the farmer no longer intended to eat and wear what he produced. As civilization advanced from subsistence to specialization and exchange, the ability of a good to command other goods in exchange assumed a position of primacy. It was still true that tangible property could command other units of property in exchange, but in addition, there was now a vast variety of intangible items which could command other units of property in exchange.

Two examples will suffice to demonstrate the importance of an intangible property right. A barber, when he sells his plant, divests himself of (1) the physical plant and (2) his goodwill. In parting with his goodwill, the barber is selling his liberty to engage in the trade of barbering, for he will agree not to engage in the trade within a certain area for a given period of time. If it were sold without the goodwill, the plant would be worth very little, as the original owner could continue his trade in an adjacent shop and retain all of the old clientele. The original owner in disposing of his goodwill is selling to the purchaser a protected opportunity to do business with the old customers; however, there is no guarantee that this group of people will continue to patronize the shop. The new man may be a poor barber. Nevertheless, it is this intangible piece of property which is known as goodwill which gives the tangible assets their value. Both are property.

A second example of an intangible form of property is involved in the hiring of labor. A workingman will contract to deliver his services rather than the product of his labor. In agreeing to deliver those services, the employee is parting with a segment of his liberty, for he is agreeing that for a certain part of each day his services will be delivered to his employer. Obviously, since his services are not separable from his body, the services must be delivered in person. Thus the employee cannot be at the race track, the beach, or any of a number of places where he might be had he not disposed of a part of his liberty. The intangible concept of liberty is an integral part of the institution of private property.

Property can be defined as a bundle of rights and liberties. Liberty includes one's general freedom of action, and since it can be exchanged for other goods, it must be included in any definition of property. There are limitations on its inclusion, however. An individual cannot be permitted to sell all of his liberty, since that would leave him in a state of involuntary servitude. A minor is likewise restricted in his freedom to dispose of his liberties, as are the mentally incompetent and others. Rights, on the other hand, constitute claims against others. A right must involve two parties—the person who has the claim and the person against whom the claim is levied. For every person who has a right, another must have a duty, and if that duty is not fulfilled, a legal remedy must be available to the injured party.

The most important aspect of property is freedom of contract. Within limits, of course, one is free to contract away part of one's liberties or contract for the liberties of others. A professor may contract away his liberties by agreeing to teach at a university. Once he has agreed to accept the position, he is no longer free to do as he pleases, for he must now appear in the classroom and perform his professorial functions. Thus is established a property relationship, for the professor has assumed a duty and the university has a right to expect fulfillment of the obligation. On the reverse side, the university has the obligation to pay the professor's salary, while the professor has a legal remedy in case that payment is not forthcoming. This freedom of contract to buy or sell, to perform or to abstain from performance, represents an extremely important property right in our economic system.

The largest part of the contractual relationships in this country are between private parties—between individuals, individuals and business firms, business firms and business firms, or private groups. There are certain contractual relationships in which the government is a major party, such as government borrowing, but such contracts are a minor part of the whole. The government is, however, a third party to all contracts, or at least all legal contracts. Without the government's consent, there can be no legal contract, for a society, acting through its government, permits certain types of contracts and prohibits those which it deems undesirable. After deciding what contracts may be considered legal contracts, the government has the additional role of enforcing those contracts not voluntarily fulfilled. It must be pointed out that such situations are rare, for a person or firm cannot afford to have a reputation of reneging on contracts.

The institution of private property may be regarded as that feature of the economy of the United States which distinguishes it most clearly from the economies of the communist countries of the world. Strange as it may seem, the Constitution of the USSR guarantees the right of private property, but the idea contemplated in that legal document is somewhat different from the one entertained in this country. The right of private property which is granted to the citizens of the USSR consists of tangible personal property, such as food, clothing, household furniture, and income from work. In addition the Constitution of the USSR lists certain rights which accrue to the Soviet citizenry as well as the duties which the people must assume. In the former are included the right to work, rest, leisure, and education, and freedom of conscience, speech, press, and demonstration, and others. As for the duties, the citizen of the USSR has, for example, the duty to abide by the Constitution, maintain labor discipline, and defend the fatherland. The duties are supported by legislation to provide for their enforcement, but the rights exist largely on paper. The property relationship in the USSR as contrasted to that in the United States, is a two-party relationship involving the government and the individual. In large part the citizen's rights depend upon the indulgence of the rulers of the country.

The Advantages of Private Property. Private property is a social institution—an institution of man. There are certain advantages which accrue to a system based on private ownership as contrasted to a system based on communal ownership. Probably the most important is that of incentive. A person will, as a rule, take better care of that which belongs to him. Furthermore, the mere fact that that which one earns becomes one's property will cause the individual to put forth a greater productive effort. A farmer will work harder if he is able to keep that which he can produce, just as will the wage earner or the business-man. Certainly if the product of everyone had to be turned over to the government, with each then being dependent upon the government for the means of subsistence, there would probably be a serious impairment of incentive. It should not be inferred, however, that property is the sole form of incentive, for there are others of considerable significance. The desire to do the job well, medals, uniforms, paid vacations and threats of death and exile may serve as an incentive to produce. The first, that is the desire to do the job well, may be the most important of all for many people, but it is generally conceded that the rest do not measure up to the private ownership of property as incentives to produce. It is pertinent to point out that a major problem of both socialism and communism is the provision of incentive.

A second advantage of private property is somewhat abstract and may be difficult to comprehend. Since property represents the exchange value of one's rights and liberties, it constitutes power—that is, the power to command other goods in exchange. A system of private property serves to distribute this power throughout the economy. It is desirable that the totality of power represented by property be divided into a large number of small units rather than being concentrated in a very few or even a single social institution. Insofar as economics is concerned, the reason for this desideratum is the fact that as the amount of property held by a single ownership or managed by a single management increases in size, a point must be reached where further increases will result in inefficiencies in operation. There is an optimum size for a social institution regardless of whether that institution is public or private in nature. In other words, the chances are that a system of private property will be much more efficient than a system based on the public ownership of property.

Because of these advantages, the institution of private property has been deliberately promoted in this country. Private property is not only allowed but is encouraged as a means of organizing economic activity. Its justification is economic and social. It should be kept in mind, however, that since it is an institution of man, it is possible that it can be altered if the people in their collective capacity decide that alterations are desirable. It should also be remembered that power will not be allowed to go unchecked.

The Government and the Institution of Private Property. Those who regard private property as a natural right find it a simple matter to look upon property rights as being beyond the power of government. Whatever the interpretation of the word "natural," property is regarded as having its source outside society and is supposed to have existed prior to government. The social-utility theorists, on the other hand, regard the institution of private property as existing at the pleasure of the people and their government. Under the latter doctrine it is logical for the government to curb property interests in the interest of the general welfare. Certainly this is the doctrine which has prevailed in the United States. A few examples of governmental control must suffice.

The general rule has been that one is allowed to use private property only insofar as that use does not infringe upon the rights of others and is consistent with the general welfare. Ownership of an automobile does not give the owner the right to drive on his neighbor's lawn. Neither does it give him a right to drive as he pleases on the highway. Ownership of land in a fashionable residential district does not carry the right to raise pigs or even run a boardinghouse. In some parts of the country the ownership of rural land does not permit the owner to use it as he pleases. Ownership of copper tubing and other requisites does not permit one to engage in the distillation of alcoholic beverages. The possession of an ability to work does not permit one to dispose of all of his liberties. A minor is not free to dispose of his productive services. These are a few of the countless examples in which the rights associated with private ownership of property are severely limited. What powers does the government have which may be used to curtail one's use of property?

The Constitution of the United States delegates certain powers to the national government. Those powers not delegated to that government are the residual powers which are reserved to the state governments or the people. The police power, which is the general power of a government to protect the welfare of its people, is such a power. Using the police power a state government may seize property without compensation, providing it is done in accordance with the law of the land—due process of law. State governments regulate such diverse activities as conditions of employment, fortunetelling, discrimination against minority groups, gambling, use of land, and many others. All represent the use of the police power to limit the property rights of individuals and business firms. The only limitation on this power is the requirement that it must be in accordance with due process of law. Beyond this, it would appear that there is nothing which cannot be regulated if the state government decides that regulation is in the public interest.

State governments have a second power which may be used to restrict the institution of private property. This is the power of eminent domain. It differs from the police power in that the owner of property which is seized under the power of eminent domain must be remunerated. The state in seizing land for construction of a highway must compensate the owners of that land. This governmental power may be delegated to private organizations such as public utilities. The citizen can appeal to the courts if it is felt that the remuneration is insufficient, but in no case is it possible to challenge the basic fact that the government has the power to seize private property.

The Constitution does not grant the national government the police power, but all governments must have the power to protect and promote the welfare of the citizens. Since the national government is not delegated a police power, it must use others powers to accomplish the same purposes. Whereas a state government can pass minimum-wage laws under its police power, the national government can pass such legislation as part of its power to regulate interstate commerce. A state government can outlaw gambling, but the national government, in order to eliminate gambling, can use the taxing power to levy a tax on gambling and the commerce clause (to prohibit the shipment of gambling equipment in interstate commerce). The same indirect methods are used to regulate the production and sale of sawed-off shotguns, drugs, and other articles which might adversely affect the welfare of the people.

Since property, then, is a social institution, as is government, it follows that the people will insist on regulation of the institution whenever it appears that the private use of property may be inimical to the public welfare, but in all cases private property is protected from arbitrary action by the government. It also follows that since it is a social institution, its nature will change as man's ideas concerning its role in the economy vary from one period to the next.

The Changing Nature of Private Property. Throughout the history of this country the institution of private property has been adjusting to the changing social climate. Probably the most dramatic change in the concept of property was that brought about by the Emancipation Proclamation and the Civil War. Prior to that time slaves had been one of the most important forms of property, and with their liberation a very large amount of property was destroyed.

Another example of the changing nature of property must suffice. In 1918, Congress passed a minimum-wage law which was to apply to women and children in the District of Columbia. Such legislation was termed by the Supreme Court as being a "naked, arbitrary exercise of power" since it deprived women of their freedom to contract to work at a wage below the minimum set by the statute. This, according to the court, was an unjust deprivation of the property of the women. In 1937, the same issue was once again before that court. The Court in this instance held that the minimum-wage law of the state of Washington was a just exercise of the police power in accordance with due process of law. Thus between 1918 and 1937 there was a complete reversal in the position of the Court.

There are many other examples of property as a changing social institution. It would seem safe to predict that it will continue to change, for it is, essentially, a changing social institution rather than an unchanging "natural" institution. But most importantly, it continues to be a system of private rights and duties rather than a system of private duties and public rights.

The Free Price System

A price system is a necessary adjunct to the institutions of private property and private enterprise. There would be little need for a free price system in an economy in which there was neither private property nor private enterprise, although the communist countries presently use a price system to achieve certain goals. The USSR, for example, depends upon the price system to curtail consumption of certain items. This is achieved by simply pricing some items at a point beyond the reach of most of the people. The price system in a controlled economy is not a free price system but, on the contrary, simply represents another facet of governmental control. The price system in the United States is, for the most part, a freely operating price system.

In the American economy, a vast number of private firms and individuals enter into agreements to buy and sell, to work and pay wages, to part with one's liberty or buy the liberty of someone else, and to perform or abstain from performance. This multitude of relations most often is expressed in terms of "price." The laborer sells his services for which he receives a price, just as does the dentist or lawyer. The farmer receives a price for his wheat or corn, just as the capitalist receives a price for the money he lends. And on and on. Each commodity, each service, each participant in the productive process—all have a price. For the most part such prices are determined by the interaction of all the forces of supply and demand. It is a free price system. There are times, as will be pointed out, when such a system breaks down and fails to fulfill its functions, but for the most part the free price system in cooperation with private enterprise and private property works remarkably well.

In a subsistence economy in which everyone has to work on a full-time basis in order to satisfy the basic wants of the individual, there is no problem as to what to produce, how much to produce, or the price to charge. The producer consumes all that he produces. Under such a system there is no overproduction, since it takes all of man's efforts to maintain a minimum level of subsistence. Interestingly enough, there is no advertising in such an economy, for there are not sufficient resources to permit part of the populace to engage in activities which do not produce food, clothing, or shelter. But once man moves beyond the subsistence economy, problems arise. No longer does every man produce for only himself and his family. No longer is his income synonymous with the physical product of his labor. The individual as a consumer is no longer identical with the individual as a producer. Instead of producing the basic commodities for his personal wants, he now produces food, clothing, automobiles, radios, and a myriad of products for other individuals. The producer now produces only a small part of the final product, and by itself, the contribution of the individual is of negligible value. It is now an economy of roundabout or indirect production, of specialization, and of separation of producer and consumer. Means have to be found to determine what and how much to produce, the method of production, and a pattern for distributing the receipts from the sale of the product among those who participated in its production.

There are two methods of approaching these problems. The first is that of a completely planned economy. In such an economy every decision is made by a governmental planning office. Production is controlled by governmental fiat, and since production is so controlled, consumption is likewise controlled. All prices are governmentally determined prices. The government establishes the system of values and decrees the productive methods to be used in the production of the want-satisfying goods and services. Needless to say, this is the system of communism.

The second approach is that of a free price system. The summation of all prices in the entire economic system constitutes the price system, and it is this price system which translates the individual decisions into a collective decision.

Functions of the Price System. The price system establishes a scale of exchange values, assists in the selection of alternative production methods, determines the distribution of receipts to the various factors of production, and provides for change and growth in the economic system.

Establishment of Exchange Values. The price system determines what is to be produced as well as the quantity. The consumers in purchasing various goods and services are, in effect, voters who make their wants known by their purchases. By acquiring one commodity rather than another or one service rather than another, a whole system of priorities or values is established. Many will pay a very high price to watch a boxing match or the world series, while a much smaller number will pay the same amount for classical literature, music, or a learned lecture. More than a few students are willing to spend their lunch money for comic books or candy. Throughout the whole economy, then, the price system establishes a scale of exchange values ranging from that which is considered to be the most valuable down to that which is of least value. The former will have a high price; the latter will have a lower price. Those commodities for which there is a demand will be produced, while those commodities which are not wanted will not be produced. The fact that a few baseball players or lawyers have very large incomes suffices to attract young men into those professions, even though the chance of any particular individual making a similar income is very slight. Just as the price system serves to attract the factors of production to some lines, it also serves to repel the factors from those lines in which the return is very low or is going lower. Thus the price system causes the factors of production to move out of such lines as harness making and blacksmithing. The freely operating price system moves resources from such industries as gas lamps to the electrical industry, from the raising of horses to the making of tractors, from the production of harness to the production of steel, from the production of those goods which are no longer desired to those which are currently wanted by the consumers.

The price system, however, must do more than translate individual desires into collective decisions as to what should be produced. It must also provide the answer as to how much of any product should be produced. Should the automobile companies make five, six, or seven million cars? Should more hi-fi sets be made? More or fewer radios? Television sets? Horseshoes? The price system, representing the interaction between buyers and sellers, automatically provides the answers to such questions. Millions of low-priced cars are produced, while only a few thousand $10,000 cars are required. The consumers, in the act of expressing their desire for one commodity or another, in co-operation with the producers, determine the prices of the products and the quantity of each to be produced.

Determination of the Method of Production. In the production of any commodity, regardless of whether it is a library building, a textbook, or a bushel of wheat, there are alternative methods of production. A large variety of combinations of labor, capital, and raw materials will all suffice to accomplish the desired goal. The combination which is eventually selected depends upon (1) technological considerations and (2) economic considerations. The combination of the two is represented in the cost per unit of output. If a given factor has such a low price that it more than offsets the lower productivity, then larger amounts of the cheap factor will be used in place of the dearer factor. If the greater productivity more than offsets the higher price, then the dear factor will be used instead of the cheap factor. Thus one finds that in areas in which wages are very low, ditches will be dug by hand and hod carriers may carry bricks on their heads. On the other hand, in areas in which wages are very high, ditches will be dug with machines, and bricks moved by mechanical means. Where bricks are cheap, bricks will be substituted for wood in the construction of homes and buildings. The quantity of any particular factor to be used in the productive process, then, depends upon both its productivity and its price. Insofar as the latter is concerned, the price system plays a major role in the organization of production. The method of production to be used is a question to be answered through the operation of the price system.

Distribution of Receipts. Distribution to the economist is different from distribution in the marketing sense. In economic terminology, distribution refers to the distribution of the receipts from the sale of the product among those who participated in its production. Distribution, then, refers to wages, interest, rent, and profit—the returns to the factors of production. It is through the price system that the prices of the factors are determined and thus the returns to the various agents of production. The pricing of the agents of production is similar to the pricing of the finished goods with the exception that the demand for the agents of production is based upon the demand for the finished good. But just as the price system evaluates consumer goods, it likewise evaluates those inputs which are used in the productive process.

The distributive function of the price system is also a co-ordinating function, for it is this aspect of the price system which creates the harmony between the self-seeking individual and the general welfare. The reasoning is as follows. There is a close relationship between the productivity of the individual unit of the factors and the income of that factor unit. The more that is produced, the greater will be the income of the producer, and any reduction in output will generally result in a lessened income to the producer. The wage earner can increase his income by producing more, just as the entrepreneur can generally receive more profits by increasing the amount of risk which he assumes or the amount of innovation which he undertakes. As each member of the economy seeks to increase his well-being through increased production and increased income, the economy as a whole benefits through the increased production, increased income, and the larger amount of goods and services. There are, of course, exceptions to this generalization, but it is generally agreed that such exceptions are rare enough so the general rule is not invalidated.

The income of the individual is a result of the manner in which he disposes of his productive resource or resources. The quantity of income accruing to any given person depends upon the quantity and quality of the productive resource and the method of its employment. A common laborer will have a smaller income than the bricklayer, just as the small property owner will have less income than the larger property owner. The amount of income which one receives, then, determines how large a part of the total product can be purchased by the recipient of that income. The person owning a large quantity of a productive agent and employing it at a high rate of return may live in a $250,000 house and drive a $10,000 automobile, while the person who has only his labor power to dispose of will not be able to live in such an expensive house nor drive such a luxurious automobile. In other words, the price system in evaluating the productive agents also serves to ration consumer goods among the consumers.

Provision for Change and Growth. The price system, in conclusion, brings about an automatic adjustment through time to changes in consumer tastes and changes in technology. In other words, the price system provides for change and growth in the economic system. It has already been pointed out how the price system brought about shifts in resources. Through the price system, the people decide what constitutes progress, and the resources are allocated accordingly. The alternative would be that in which an official of the government decides how progress is to be achieved, and he would move the resources around much as a chess player moves chessmen.

Probably the most important aspect of this particular function of the price system relates to savings and capital investment. The question of consuming and saving in the economy is resolved by the price system. An increase in the interest rate—that is, in the price of savings—will result in a larger amount of savings. Such savings may find their way into increased investment expenditures, and this is a major factor in economic growth.

Limitations of the Price System. There are times when a free price system cannot be permitted to perform its functions because it would impose severe penalties upon society. Furthermore, there are some instances in which the free price system would result in suffering by certain groups in the economic system. In the first instance, the government will set aside the price system and exercise a large measure of direct control. In the second, the people who feel that they are being adversely affected will demand that the government take steps to alleviate their suffering, and if the demand is sufficient, the government will set aside the price system for that particular group. Examples of each follow.

Everyone agrees that the price system cannot be permitted to function without check during time of war. A war economy is a fully employed economy, and all of those participating in the productive process have large amounts of disposable income. At the same time, however, the commodities available for consumption are limited. Normal consumer expenditures would attract resources into the production of such items as electric trains, new clothes, housing, and vacations in Florida. None of these make a contribution to the winning of the war. Missles, airplanes, super-aircraft carriers, GI brogans, and other such items are required to fight a war, and none of these would normally be produced in response to the demands of the consumers. Furthermore, not enough resources exist to produce the large amounts of war equipment in addition to the normal quota of consumer goods. Therefore, means must be found to attract productive resources away from the production of civilian goods and into the production of war material. Since the free operation of the price system will not accomplish this end at an acceptable cost, the government interferes with the operation of the price system for the duration of the war and proceeds to arbitrarily guide production and allocate resources by government fiat.

During a war the price system also fails to function as a rationing device. Since the goods available to consumers are limited and the means of purchasing such goods are much less limited, the government must not only ration the available commodities among the consumers, but it must also control the prices. If there were no such controls, the person with the most money or the first person appearing at the store would receive the largest part of the available supply. The latecomers or those with low incomes would have to do without, but, of course, this is unthinkable when the commodity in question is something as basic as food or clothing.

Therefore, in wartime the price system is supplanted by governmental planning. Consumer goods in short supply are rationed, and the prices are determined by governmental authority. Priorities are established and productive resources are rationed in accordance with this governmentally established system of values. Steel, for example, would go into the production of tanks rather than the construction of race tracks. Nylon, instead of being used to make hosiery for women, would be used to make parachutes for the armed services. This must be the case, for it is inconceivable that a freely operating price system would ever result in the production of atomic submarines, jet bombers, or hydrogen bombs.

Even with extensive governmental controls over the economic system, it is difficult to keep the price system from operating. A major problem associated with such an extensive program of controls is that of the "black market." The black market is nothing but the free price system operating during a period when such free operation is prohibited. In this illegal market all of the forces of supply and demand are operating, and the price is a free-market price. Since the supply of commodities is short and the wherewithal to purchase the same is excessive, the price in the black market will be much higher than that which prevails in the controlled market. Such a market cannot be permitted to operate, for its very operation is inimical to the war effort and the general welfare, since it attracts resources away from the production of commodities needed to fight the war. As soon as the emergency is over, however, the black market once again becomes the free market in which business is done.

In addition to a national emergency such as a war, there are other times when the price system, although not breaking down, may impose a rather severe burden on a particular group. This burden is often not as severe as is commonly supposed, but those who suffer generally demand that something be done to alleviate their distressed conditions. Only a few cases need be mentioned.

During World War II and the immediate postwar years, rental property was at a premium while the demand for such housing was very great. As a result of an increasing population, larger families, and a reduction in the amount of residential construction during the war, there was pressure for increased rental charges. Under a freely operating price system, rents would have risen and resources would have been attracted to the construction of rental housing units. Tenants, however, were not anxious to see such results, and the rent controls established during the war were retained at their insistence for several years after the war was over. In addition to controlling rents, the government also encouraged the construction of nonrental housing units. There can be little question that there would have been more rental housing and less nonrental housing if the government had followed a hands-off policy and let the price system solve the problem. This is not meant to imply that the results were either good or bad, but it is only intended to point out that the governmental action did bring about an allocation of resources different from that which would have otherwise prevailed.

Farmers have long felt that they have been victims of the free price system. Those things which the farmers buy, including machinery, automobiles, trucks, and clothing, have generally been purchased in a market where downward price adjustments are a rarity if not nonexistent. The farmer sells his product in an extremely competitive market where prices are constantly shifting up and down. The price trend of the former, or so it seems to the farmer at least, has always been upward, while the prices of the things he sold seemed to be going in the opposite direction. Most damaging of all was the fact that when farm income decreases, the prices of those goods which the farmers purchase remain constant or drop only slightly. During the 1920's, part of the 1930's, and a part of the period since World War II, farmers' real income dropped compared to the rest of the economy. The farmers prevailed upon the government to protect them from the operations of the price system as early as the 1920's. As with the case of rental housing, this interference has resulted in an alteration in the distribution of resources. It may well be that too large a part of our resources are presently engaged in agriculture. If the price system were free to operate, there can be no doubt that part of those resources presently engaged in agriculture would be driven to other pursuits. This would represent a net gain for the economy if the resources driven out of agriculture were the marginal factors which could be employed in the present line of endeavor only because of the government action supporting agricultural prices at an abnormally high level. It must be admitted, however, that such action would impose a severe burden on those who were forced to leave farming.

A fourth instance in which the price system is set aside is the case of monopolies. The business firm which is the sole seller of a commodity occupies a powerful place—especially if the product is a necessity. In many instances, it is much more economical to have a single seller provide a needed service. Such industries are natural monopolies; they include telephones, electric power, and gas and water companies. In such instances the government limits the price system and imposes a system of governmental controls to protect the consumer. Industries which are of this nature have always been regulated in this country. There is probably only one alternative to regulation and that is public ownership, but there is some question about the efficacy of such an alternative. Most people, however, would admit that this case, like the first example cited, is one in which the price system cannot be permitted to operate.

There are many other instances in which the price system is not permitted to function. In each instance the allocation of resources is affected. Resale price maintenance laws eliminate the operation of the price system for a large part of retail trade. Milk commissions do likewise in the production and marketing of milk in many states. Minimum-wage laws prohibit its operation in most labor markets. Tariffs and quotas in international trade perform the same function on an international basis. There can be no hard and fast rule as to the desirability of permitting the price system to function, for there are some instances when it must be set aside. But, a great deal of caution should be exercised before it is blithely abandoned. It should also be noted that once the free price system is discarded, those who have promoted the abandonment will be forever reluctant to leave their sheltered spot for the rough seas of a freely operating price system.

Criticism of the Price System. The price system and its operation have long been subject to widespread criticism. Some are opposed to the system in its entirety while others are opposed to only a part of the institution. Its critics include those who would replace capitalism with some form of socialism or communism as well as those who are, at other times, capitalism's most vigorous supporters. The following are some of those criticisms.

Instability. The price system, like the tides, is seldom in equilibrium but is generally rising or falling. At one time there may be sharp increases followed by equally severe declines, while at other times the increases and decreases may be very moderate. Regardless of the severity of the change, some people will be adversely affected while others stand to benefit. Because the suffering is somewhat unpleasant and the sufferers somewhat vocal, one cannot be unaware of which groups are being currently pinched by the present fluctuation of the price system.

Historically, farmers have always suffered during a depression because they have generally been debtors. They would borrow money with less purchasing power in times of prosperity which had to be repaid during periods of depression with money of greater purchasing power. Creditors, on the other hand, suffered on the reverse side of the business cycle. They may lend during a period of falling prices and then have to accept repayment during a period of rising prices when money is worth less. One may generalize and say that those with "sticky" incomes suffer on the upswing of the business cycle, for their money incomes either remain constant or fail to increase as rapidly as do prices. As a result, their real income falls. On the downward phase of the business cycle, those with "sticky" incomes stand to gain insofar as they do not lose their source of income. It is here that the farmers, the small merchants, and others subject to intense competition suffer most heavily, for their incomes have no tendency to stick at the high levels. Instead, they fall more rapidly than any other prices in the economy.

Everyone agrees that the price system causes a good bit of suffering because of its instability, but there is no general agreement as to what constitutes proper remedial policy. There are some who would defend instability on the basis that it eliminates the inefficient. A second group would promote a slow but constant increase in the level of prices. A final position would be that of those who would argue that a moderate amount of fluctuation is desirable. Nearly all, however, would agree that the evil of price-level instability would not necessarily be remedied by installing a completely planned economy in which the price system would be replaced by governmental decrees.

The Process of Valuation. As has been pointed out, one of the functions of the price system is to evaluate the goods and services which are produced. The value of an item is its price. Many individuals criticize the price system because they feel it puts too high a value on commodities and services which do not merit the high price. Some offer this criticism because they feel that their own particular service is undervalued. Teachers, for example, may be justified in feeling that something is wrong when they compare their pay with that of a professional baseball player or a Hollywood star. Likewise, some criticize the price system for putting a higher value on comic books than on great works of literature, on technical education rather than a liberal arts education, on what is practical rather than what is interesting. It often seems that the Americans are too materialistic and are interested in a higher price or a larger income rather than the intangible requisites of well-being. And the center of all of this criticism is the price system.

It must be pointed out, however, that the price system only reflects the desires of the people and the distribution of income. Recognizing this fact, the above criticism then becomes a criticism of the wants of the people. One may deplore the fact that children prefer television to intellectual activities, but the fault does not rest with the price system. The establishment of a governmental office to decide what the people should want and have would not be an acceptable solution.

Inequality of Wealth. The price system permits those with larger quantities of scarce factors to receive larger incomes than those with smaller amounts of the more abundant factors. The former make up the upper-income groups while the latter are at the lower end of the income ladder. Some would like to see complete equality based on "from each according to his ability and to each according to his needs"; however, most reject this Marxian doctrine and admit that a reasonable degree of inequality is essential. The only question is whether the price system results in a higher degree of inequality than is necessary for the well-being of the economy. Again, the substitution of governmental decrees is not guaranteed to produce the desired result.

Neglect of Social Costs. For many businesses there are certain nonexpenditure costs which are incurred in the creation of economic goods. These would include such costs as air and stream pollution, defilement of countryside, and other similar activities. To the extent that such costs exist and are not met out of company receipts, the entrepreneur passes them on to society as a whole rather than to the consumers of that particular commodity. These costs, rather than being passed on in the form of higher prices or absorbed in the form of lower profits, are borne by society in the form of higher taxes, poor health, inadequate public facilities, or foul air. Of recent years, such costs have come to be recognized as a part of the cost of doing business, and they are being borne to an ever increasing extent by the producer and the consumer of the product in question. In many instances, however, this assumption of such costs has been as a result of governmental activity. The price system by itself did not result in this assumption of these costs, for as far as the business was concerned, the river flowing by the plant or the fresh air outside the plant was a free good to be had without paying a price.

In summary, then, it must be admitted that the price system is not beyond reproach; however, it must also be granted that it does a reasonably good job. Most important, it performs its functions with a maximum degree of freedom for the individual and with a minimum amount of bureaucratic interference. Although there are strong movements to interfere with that operation, such steps should be regarded with some degree of skepticism, for the results of aiding a few may be deleterious for the rest of society.

CONCLUSION

A society's culture consists of all of its institutions. These institutions or social arrangements shape individual behavior in the interest or welfare of the group to which that individual belongs. Thus competition, labor unions, churches, education, the corporation, and private property are all social institutions, for each represents a technique for influencing individual behavior. Just as the sum of all institutions makes up a society's culture, the sum of society's economic institutions makes up its economic system.

The economic system of the United States is based upon three economic institutions—private enterprise, private property, and the free price system. It is these three institutions which serve to distinguish our economic system from alternative systems such as those found in England, Sweden, or the USSR.

A social institution is continually changing. The determinants of change include forces external to the society as well as internal. An important force for change is found in education and research. To the extent that education and research produce a changing technology, this will be reflected in a changing social structure and changing economic institutions. Thus any nation involved in rapid technological change must also expect to undergo institutional changes. It would seem to be impossible to have the former without the latter.

It is interesting to speculate, for a moment, on the relative quantities of resources devoted to planned technological change, on the one hand, and planned institutional change, on the other. Certainly our present institutional structure is not the best arrangement, for we know that tomorrow it will be changed and, supposedly, improved. We are unwilling to leave technological change to chance. How much planning is done in the case of institutional change?

EXERCISES

Group I

Explain why the following are either true or false:

1. Private enterprise is a characteristic of the American economic system as well as all other economic systems.

2. Private property includes only tangible items which can be exchanged.

3. Private property is a natural right.

4. Private property results in benefits of an economic nature to society.

5. The price system performs no functions which could not be accomplished by other techniques with less trouble and suffering.

6. The instability of the price system does not really affect anyone since, in the long run, those who gain on the upswing lose on the downswing and vice versa.

Group II

1. Private property is an important form of incentive in the United States. What techniques are used in the USSR to provide incentive? Has the USSR adopted some of the means used in this country? (See President Eisenhower's news conference following Premier Khrushchev's visit to the United States in October, 1959).

2. In the United States the price system automatically attracted resources to the production of television sets. How was the television industry established in the USSR? What determined the quantity of sets produced in each country? In the USSR a bureaucratic decision sufficed to guide resources into the production of earth satellites. How was this accomplished in the United States? Is the United States becoming more like the USSR in some respects? Is the reverse true?

Group III

1. Two of the best books on the changing nature of private property are *The Modern Corporation and Private Property* by A. A. Berle and Gardner Means and *Legal Foundations of Capitalism* by John R. Commons. Read one or both of these books and write a report on the changing nature of private property.

2. The role of the corporation in society is a matter of some dispute. Should the corporation use profit maximization as its sole guide to action, or should it consider itself to be a person with social responsibility? Should it be required by law to pay out all of its earnings to its stockholders, or should it be allowed to retain earnings for purposes of capital expansion, aid to education, contributions to charity, and the like? Do corporations have any responsibility in the field of foreign affairs when they are operating abroad? Write a paper on the role of the corporation in modern society.

3. This chapter did not exhaust the subject of economic institutions, for books have been written on the subject. To further develop the ideas in the conclusion, the student might trace the development of Workmens Compensation laws. At one time the workman generally had to bear the burden of industrial accidents, but now this hazard is borne by the consumers of the product. What forces resulted in this change? How did the institutional mechanism evolve? Do you see evidence that a similar evolutionary process is taking place with respect to technological unemployment?

BIBLIOGRAPHY

CLARK, J. M. *Social Control of Business.* New York: McGraw-Hill Book Co., Inc., 1939.

COMMONS, JOHN R. *Legal Foundations of Capitalism.* New York: Macmillan Co., 1924. (Also available in paperback.)

KNIGHT, FRANK H. *The Economic Organization.* Chicago: University of Chicago Press, 1933.

VEBLEN, THORSTEIN. *The Instinct of Workmanship and the State of the Industrial Arts.* New York: Macmillan Co., 1917.

PAPERBACK READING LIST

GALBRAITH, JOHN KENNETH. *American Capitalism.* Boston: Houghton Mifflin Co., Sentry Edition, 1962.

DEMAND AND SUPPLY:
THE BASIS OF VALUE

"I should like to buy an egg, please," she said timidly. "How do you sell them?"
"Fivepence farthing for one—twopence for two," the Sheep replied.
"Then two are cheaper than one?" Alice said in a surprised tone taking out her purse.
"Only you *must* eat them both, if you buy two," said the Sheep.
"Then I'll have *one*, please," said Alice.—Lewis Carroll, *Through the Looking Glass.*

Prices constitute the language of an economic system. Just as individuals communicate their thoughts to one another through a spoken and written language, so they communicate on matters of value through a language of prices. Through prices the value of one's productive services are translated into terms which are understandable by others in the system. Likewise the value of different goods can be compared through a comparison of their prices. So just as one has to learn English to get along in a community speaking that language, so one must learn the language of the price system.

Those commodities which man finds useful, yet which do not exist in such quantities that his wants can be satisfied without effort, are economic goods. Such goods have exchange value, for they command other goods in exchange. Price is an expression of that exchange value, since the price represents the amount of another commodity (money) which the commodity in question can command in exchange. The $20,000 price for a house is its exchange value, just as is the penny which a small boy charges for a glass of lemonade at his sidewalk stand. Such value could be expressed in terms of other commodities, such as cigarettes or chocolate bars, but such a means of expressing value would be extremely awkward. Because of the ease of measurement and expression resulting from the use of money, it has become a nearly universal practice to express exchange value as a monetary unit. The discussion of price, then, becomes a discussion of valuation. Why do goods have value?

AN INTRODUCTION TO DEMAND

One way to introduce the subject is to make a general observation regarding the relationship between price and quantity. As a rule, if only price and quantity are considered, it can be said that a consumer will buy more only if the price is lower, or, on the other hand, he will buy less if the price is raised. (Note that there is a broad assumption of *ceteris paribus* here.) That is, there is an inverse relationship between the price of a good or service and the quantity of that item which will be purchased. This broad generalization is quite valid. It certainly accords with our daily experience, for it is hard to imagine a situation where larger amounts of consumption goods would be purchased at higher prices or even at the same price, if we remember that nothing else changes.

So an analysis of demand must start by presenting a more rigorous explanation of this inverse relationship between the two variables— price and quantity. Simply stating the relationship in broad terms does not enable one to do much in the way of analytical reasoning, which is, after all, our major goal.

Classical economics explained the inverse relationship on the basis of diminishing marginal utility. Each additional unit of a consumer good or service would be of less usefulness to the consumer than the previous unit. A fourth milkshake would yield less satisfaction than a third or a second. A second automobile would provide less utility than the first, and so on. Since additional units will increase one's total satisfaction by steadily diminishing quantities, it follows that the consumer would only consume the larger quantities if the price were lower; thus the inverse relationship mentioned above.

Many, if not most, students express some degree of disbelief when first exposed to the above approach. The question is often asked how a consumer can say that he gets a certain utility from consuming one steak and how this omniscient consumer can compare the satisfaction from a steak with the satisfaction derived from an economics textbook. Classical demand theory based on the utility approach, briefly outlined above, does indeed empower the consumer to make just such measurements and comparisons of utility.

Many, if not most, economists readily admit that this is a rather unrealistic assumption to make regarding human behavior. It is agreed that a consumer is probably not able to measure and compare utility in any really meaningful sense.

To overcome this defect in the logical structure of demand analysis, economists developed a second approach—the indifference technique. This approach to demand requires only that the consumer be able to rank his preferences. Now using only this assumption regarding consumer behavior, one can proceed to offer a logical construction of a demand function—the relationship between price and quantity.

Indifference Curves

The argument can be initiated by assuming that the consumer is faced with the possibility of consuming various amounts of two goods, which will be referred to as Good A and Good B. It doesn't really matter what the two goods are; in fact, one might want to make Good A represent all goods other than Good B. The consumer, then, can choose to consume all A, all B, or some combination of A and B. And the problem is to determine just how the consumption of Good A will change with changes in the price of the good.

The indifference map (Figure 5–1) shows the satisfaction that the consumer will derive from various combinations of Goods A and B. The points on Indifference Curve I_1, for example, represent various combinations of the two goods—A and B. Each point on the curve represents different amounts of the two commodities, but, and this is an extremely important point, the consumer will get the same satisfaction from any of the consumption bundles represented by this particular indifference curve. The consumer is indifferent between the many possibilities represented by this particular curve. The bundle made up of a_1 units of A and b_1 units of B will yield the same satisfaction as the bundle made up of a_2 units of A and b_2 units of B.

As one moves upward and to the right, the successive indifference curves represent a greater total amount of satisfaction. That is, all of the points on I_2 represent greater satisfaction than the points on I_1. Any point on the former would be preferred to any point on the latter. But insofar as any particular indifference curve is concerned, the same basic relationship of indifference holds.

FIGURE 5–1

AN INDIFFERENCE MAP

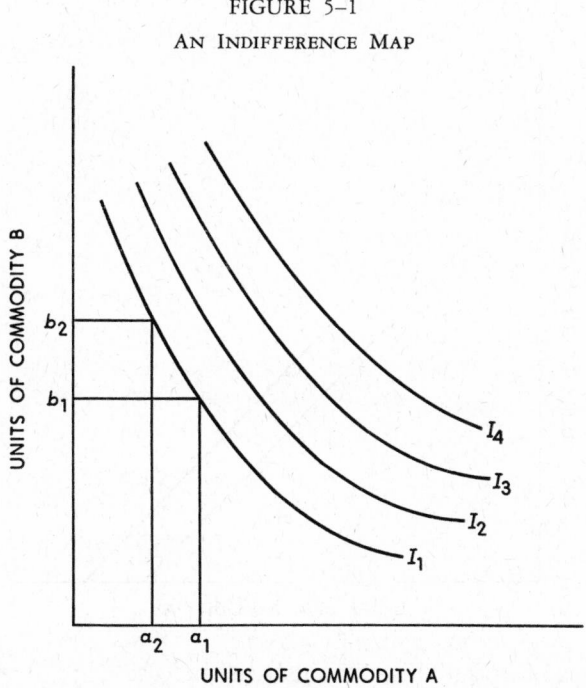

A consumer's indifference map will generally look like that in Figure 5–1. That is, the curves will slope downward and to the right and will be concave upward. Why? Imagine for a moment that the consumer is "moving" downward along I_1—that is, he is substituting Commodity A for Commodity B. He is increasing his consumption of A and decreasing his consumption of B in such a way that his total satisfaction remains constant. As he consumes more and more of A, each additional unit will afford him less satisfaction than previous units, while the more of B he gives up, the greater will be the satisfaction he will contemplate from the remaining units. In short, the more of A he has and the less of B, the less willing he will be to substitute still more of

A for B. The fact that the indifference curves get flatter as one moves to the right along the x axis is a simple geometric demonstration of this fact.

Consider, for a moment, other possible shapes for a consumer's indifference map. One possibility is a straight line from some point on the y axis to some point on the x axis. (See Figure 5–2). The slope of such a line is a constant. This would indicate that the consumer would always be willing to substitute A for B at the same rate, regardless of

FIGURE 5–2

INDIFFERENCE CURVES FOR PERFECT SUBSTITUTES

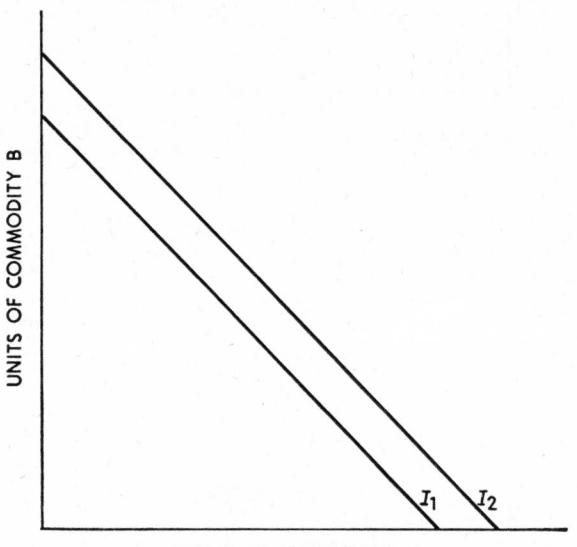

UNITS OF COMMODITY A

the quantities of both. This, obviously, is the case of perfect substitutes —A and B are the same good. The student need only ask himself under what conditions would he always be willing to substitute one good for another at the same rate, regardless of the quantity of either, to see validity of the statement.

Another possibility is that the indifference curve be "L"-shaped. (See Figure 5–3). This would indicate that a_1 units of Good A and b_1 units of Good B would yield the same satisfaction as a_1 units of A and any amount of B (greater than b_1), or b_1 units of B and any amount of A (greater than a_1). Thus Goods A and B must be combined in some fixed or constant ratio, for if such is not the case, the extra amount of the one good does nothing to increase the consumer's total satisfaction. Such goods are clearly complements. Shoes are a good example. Left shoes and right shoes must be consumed in the ratio of one-to-one for nearly everyone. Thus a person with one left shoe would get the same total satisfaction regardless of whether he had one right shoe or a million.

Indifference curves cannot slope upward to the right, for such a function would indicate that the total satisfaction of the consumer would not increase even though he consumed more of both commodities. This would not seem to be very realistic. Such an assumption would probably not yield very useful predictions.

FIGURE 5–3

INDIFFERENCE CURVES FOR COMPLEMENTARY GOODS

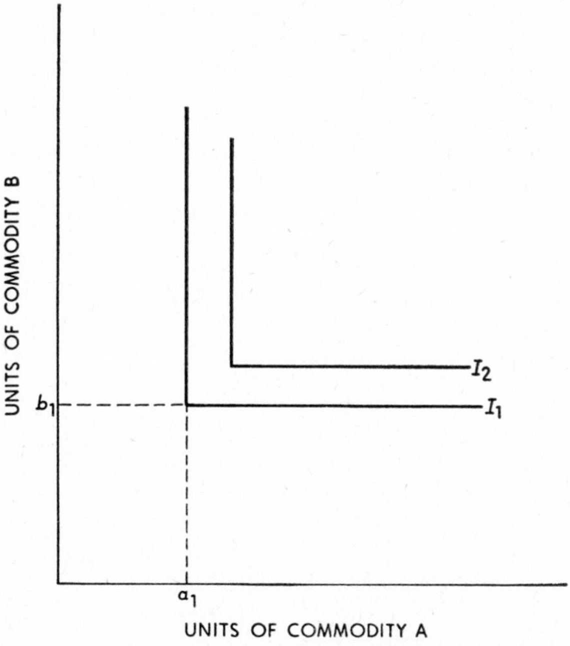

UNITS OF COMMODITY A

Another property of the indifference curves will be indicated, but it will be left to the student as an exercise to establish the reasoning behind this particular point. Indifference curves cannot intersect. That is, it would be impossible for I_1 and I_2 to cross.

The Price Line.[1]

The indifference curves explained the preference pattern of the consumer. Now some function is needed to indicate just what it is pos-

---

[1] All economists agree on the term "indifference curve," but there is no such agreement for the next concept to be introduced. In addition to "price line," it has been referred to as the "consumption possibility curve," "constant outlay line," "the possibility fence," "the budget constraint line," and others.

sible for the consumer to do, in the way of consumption, with a given amount of income. This function, which serves as a restraint, shall be referred to as the "price line." (See Figure 5–4). If the consumer spends all of his income on Commodity A, he can purchase a_1 units, or he can purchase b_1 units of Commodity B with the same income. If these two points are connected by a straight line (b_1a_1), then each of the points on the line represents a possible combination of the two goods which could be purchased with a given income. Thus if a_2 units of A and b_2 units of B were purchased, the total outlay would be the same

FIGURE 5–4

A PRICE LINE

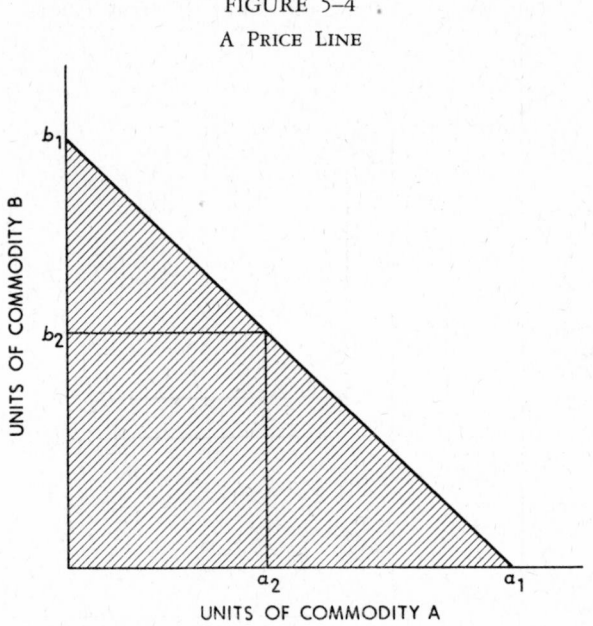

UNITS OF COMMODITY A

as it would had all A or B been purchased. This function, then, is a limit in the sense that it is a constraint on the consumer's expenditures for A and B, for the amounts purchased must be within the shaded area or on the line itself.

This price line can be used to indicate changes in the price of one commodity relative to the other. If for example, the price of A were to fall, more of that good could be purchased with the same total expenditure, and the new price line would be b_1a_2 in Figure 5–5(A). An increase in the price of A would mean that a smaller quantity of A could be purchased and the new price line would be b_1a_2 in Figure 5–5(B). In each case, a_2 represents the amount of the commodity which could be purchased after the price change if A were the only good purchased. The quantity of A purchased is equal to the total expenditure divided by the price of A.

The price line can also be used to show changes in the level of the consumer's income. If the income of the consumer increases, this means that he will be able to purchase more of both commodities. This can be represented by a shift in the entire function to the right and upward (to the northeast). (See Figure 5–6). A shift in the function to the left and downward would indicate a reduction in income.

FIGURE 5–5

CHANGES IN PRICE LINE AS RESULT OF PRICE CHANGES

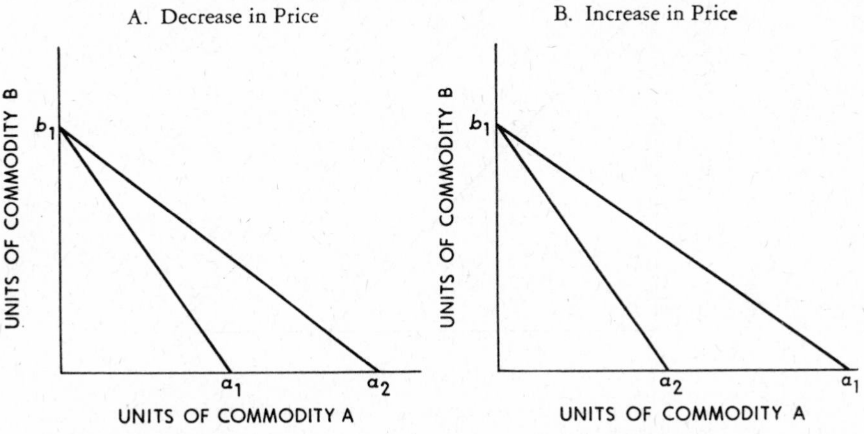

A. Decrease in Price   B. Increase in Price

NOTE: In each case, the quantity of the good is equal to the total expenditures divided by the price. Thus $a_1 = I/Pa_1$ and $a_2 = I/Pa_2$.

Since the price line has been used to demonstrate both price and income changes alone, there is no reason why the two changes cannot be shown together. If the curve shifted upward and to the right at the same time there was a change in the slope of the function, this would indicate that there was both a price change and a change in income.

Particular attention should be given to the slope of the price function. The slope is the ratio of the price of the two commodities.[2]

$$\text{The slope of the price line} = \frac{\text{Price of Commodity A}}{\text{Price of Commodity B.}} = \frac{P_A}{P_B}$$

This ratio of prices is also a substitution ratio, for it indicates the extent to which one commodity can be substituted for the other. If the price

[2] We can ignore the negative sign.

of A is three times the price of B, the consumption of B could be increased by three units for every reduction of one unit in the consumption of A.

FIGURE 5–6

SHIFT IN PRICE LINE AS A RESULT OF CHANGES IN
EXPENDITURES (INCOME)

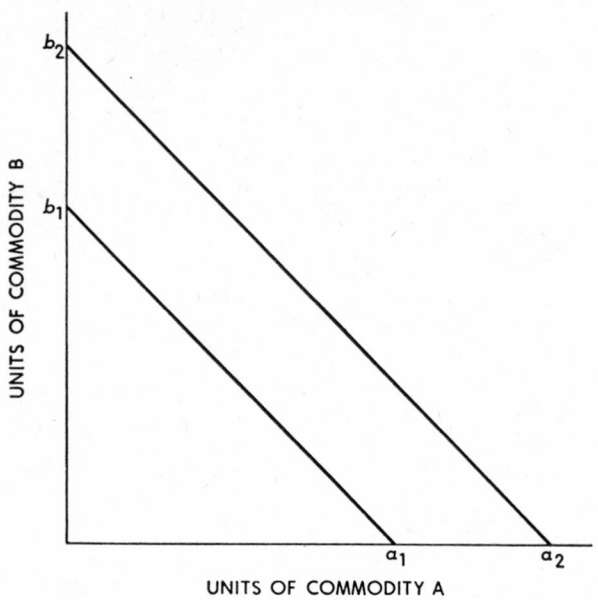

UNITS OF COMMODITY A

NOTE: Given prices of the two commodities, line b_2a_2 represents higher total expenditure than b_1a_1.

The Consumption Decision

The indifference curves and the price line are the tools required for analyzing the consumption decision of the consumer. The first, the indifference curves, indicate his preference pattern. The second indicates what is possible. Now how can these two be used to analyze the consumption decision?

One way to start is by asserting that the equilibrium position will be that represented by Figure 5–7, where a price line, say P_2, is just tangent to an indifference curve—in this case, I_2. The tangency requirement indicates that the consumer is on the highest possible indifference curve, given product prices and level of income. If he moved in either direction along the price line (what is possible), he would be on a lower indifference curve, and thus his total satisfaction would be lessened. He cannot get to a higher indifference curve as long as his level of income and/or prices remain(s) unchanged.

The fact that the slopes of the two functions are equal at this point of tangency indicates that the total income has been divided between the two commodities in such a way that total satisfaction is maximized. If the consumer were to substitute more of A for Commodity B, that is, if he were to move along the price line (for this represents what is possible), he would move to a lower indifference curve. If he moved to a lower indifference curve, his satisfaction would obviously fall. It is clearly impossible for him to move to a higher indifference curve. This point of tangency is an optimal point.

Derivation of the Demand Function

The only task that remains is that of utilizing the tools developed up to this point in the derivation of a consumer demand function.

FIGURE 5–7

THE CONSUMPTION DECISION

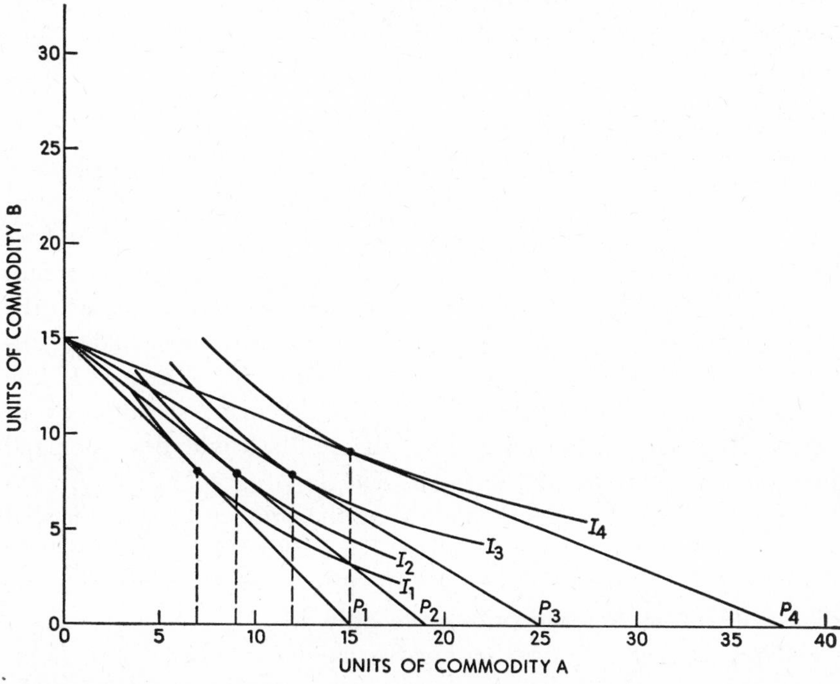

This can be done in the following manner. Start with the indifference map indicated by I_1, I_2, I_3, and I_4 in Figure 5–7. Since the interest at this point is in the relationship between price and quantity, more than one price line must be used to indicate different prices for the good in question. So P_1 indicates a price (for Good A) of \$5; P_2 a price of \$4;

P_3 a price of $3; and P_4 a price of $2. If the price line is P_1, the consumer will consume 7 units of A; if the price line is P_2, 9 units will be consumed; and so on. The entire schedule would look as follows:

Price of Commodity A (Derived from the Price Line)	*Quantity of Good* A *Demanded* (Derived from the points of tangency between indifference curves and price lines.)
$5	7
4	9
3	12
2	15

What has been accomplished? Simply by requiring that the consumer be able to rank his preferences but without requiring that he be able to measure or compare satisfaction, we have established the existence of an inverse relationship between price and the quantity purchased. The table above is known as a demand schedule which might be defined as a schedule of amounts which will be taken during a given time period at various prices providing that everything else remains constant.

The Demand Schedule

Since there are two variables in the demand schedule, price and quantity, it is possible to plot them using the X axis to represent quantity and the Y axis to represent price. A curve connecting the four points derived above is a graphic representation of the demand schedule for the individual consumer. (See Figure 5–8A). It represents the various amounts which would be purchased by this individual at different prices. (Note the *ceteris paribus* assumption here.) If the demand of this individual were added to the demand schedule of all other consumers of this commodity, the result would be a demand curve such as that in Figure 5–8B. The latter graphically portrays the idea that more will be demanded as the price is lowered or that less will be demanded at higher prices. For example, 2,000 units could be sold during a given time period if the price were $4, whereas 5,000 units could be sold if the price were only $1.

The manager of a firm selling Commodity A, then, must decide just what the relationship is between the amount he can sell and the price. He knows, in general, that if he raises the price, less will be sold. He likewise knows that more can be sold if the price is lowered. But he is also aware of the fact that the amount that can be sold will also vary because of changes in factors other than price. The income of the consumer might increase. Unless the commodity in question is a rather

peculiar commodity, increases in income represented by a shift of the
price line to the northeast will increase the quantity of Good A which
is consumed. This would result in a new demand schedule such as D′
in Figure 5–9. This shift in the entire demand function is known as an
increase in demand in contrast to the increase in the quantity sold,
which would result from a lowering of the price with a given demand
curve. The reverse might also happen. If the consumers' incomes were
reduced, consumption of the commodity would be less at all prices. In
this case there is a reduction in the quantity which could be sold at all
prices, and it would appear as D″ in Figure 5–9. Similar shifts might
result from changes in tastes, changes in the prices of other goods, and
changes in other economic and social forces.

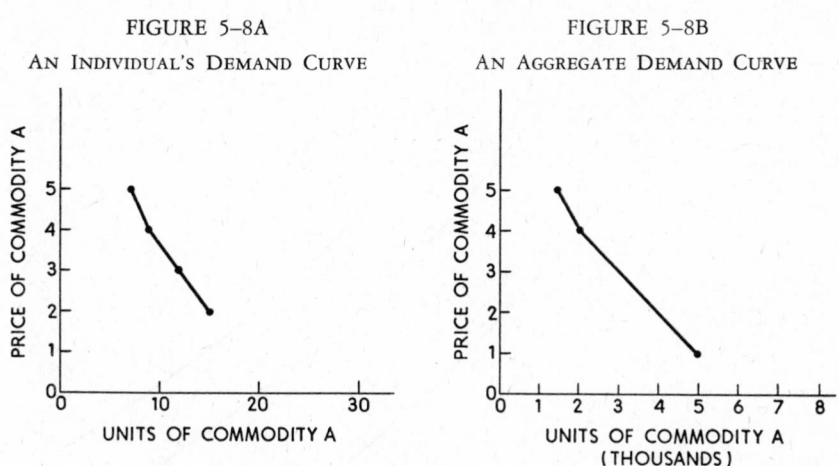

FIGURE 5–8A

AN INDIVIDUAL'S DEMAND CURVE

FIGURE 5–8B

AN AGGREGATE DEMAND CURVE

It is necessary, however, that the person(s) making price decisions
know more about the relation between price and quantity. There must
be some awareness of the relative changes in the two quantities; that is,
what the relationship is between a percentage change in price and the
resultant percentage change in the quantity which can be sold. Will a
10 per cent reduction in price result in an increase in the quantity
which can be sold of 5 per cent, 10 per cent, or 20 per cent? Economists
refer to this relationship between the relative changes in price and
quantity as elasticity of demand.

The specific reaction of quantity changes to price changes can be
described in terms of the elasticity of demand. If the percentage change
in quantity is greater than the percentage change in price, the demand
is said to be elastic. In this case, a reduction in price will be more than
offset by the increase in the amount demanded, and the total revenue

(price times quantity) will increase. If the price is increased, total revenue will decline. Those commodities which have close substitutes will have an elastic demand, for a reduction in the price of such a good will cause consumers to shift from the near substitutes. Likewise, an increase in price will cause them to shift to the substitutes. The demand for a particular brand of television sets, breakfast foods, or cigarettes will be elastic since there are close substitutes.

FIGURE 5–9

CHANGE IN DEMAND

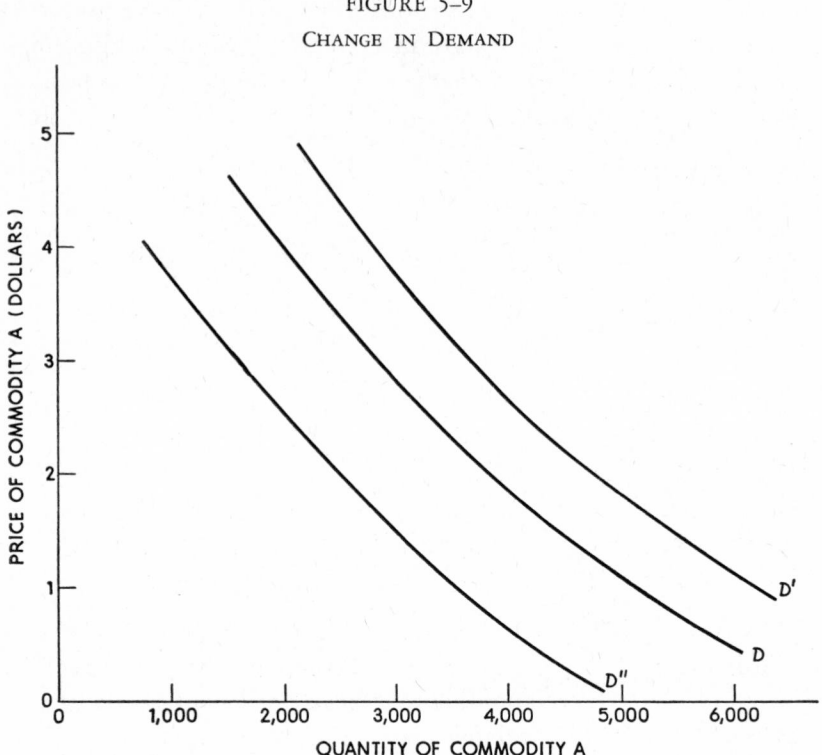

If the percentage change in quantity is less than the percentage change in price, the demand is said to be inelastic. Any reduction in price will result in a less than proportionate increase in the amount purchased, and an increase in price will not result in a proportionate reduction in the amount purchased. If the demand is inelastic and the price is lowered, total revenue will fall, and if the price is increased, total revenue will increase. Commodities which have no close substitutes, which are necessary, or which generally make up a very small part of one's total expenditures will usually have an inelastic demand schedule. Salt, matches, and automobile tires and tubes are examples.

Unitary elasticity is simply a definitional dividing line. In this instance the price changes result in proportional changes in sales, and total revenue remains constant.

Arithmetic examples of the several types of elasticity are presented in Table 5–1. The last part of that table demonstrates a demand curve

TABLE 5–1

ELASTICITY OF DEMAND

Price	Quantity Demanded	Total Revenue	Nature of Elasticity of the Demand Schedule
$10	200	$2,000	
9	300	2,700	(a) An elastic demand between
8	400	3,200	the prices of $6 and $10
7	500	3,500	
6	600	3,600	
$10	252	$2,520	
9	280	2,520	(b) Unitary elasticity between
8	315	2,520	the prices of $6 and $10
7	360	2,520	
6	420	2,520	
$10	200	$2,000	
9	210	1,890	(c) An inelastic demand sched-
8	220	1,760	ule between the prices of $6
7	230	1,610	and $10
6	250	1,500	
$10	100	$1,000	
9	200	1,800	(d) A demand schedule which
8	300	2,400	is elastic between the prices
7	400	2,800	of $6 and $10, has unitary
6	500	3,000	elasticity between $5 and $6,
5	600	3,000	and is inelastic at any price
4	700	2,800	below $5
3	800	2,400	
2	900	1,800	

in which all three types of elasticity are found in the same demand schedule. This is characteristic of most demand schedules, since the demand for most products is inelastic through some price ranges and elastic through others, with a middle area of unitary elasticity. In no instance would it be possible to say that the demand schedule was inelastic or of unitary elasticity at all possible prices. The concept of elasticity has meaning only when it refers to the present price plus and minus a very small change in the price.

One can speak about elasticity of demand in regard to a product of an industry such as breakfast foods, or one can speak of the elasticity of demand for the product of a particular firm in the industry. Insofar as the individual business firm is concerned, it is the latter which is of particular significance. The demand schedule facing the firm is of more importance than the demand schedule for the industry, since it is the firm's demand schedule which the entrepreneur or manager uses as a basis for making price and output decisions.

The demand schedule facing the individual firm will fall somewhere between two limiting extremes. There is (1) the situation in which the individual firm has no control over the price and (2) that in which the individual firm can sell its output at any price it desires. In the first, the demand schedule is perfectly elastic; in the second it is perfectly inelastic. In the first, the seller can have no price policy since he can sell all that he produces at the prevailing market price, and he can sell nothing at a higher price. The second limiting case, that is, a perfectly inelastic demand, means that the seller could sell his stock at any price he wished. There would be no close substitutes for a product which was absolutely necessary. A corner on the stock market approximates such a situation, but other than this, actual examples of this limiting extreme are rare.

The demand for most commodities will be somewhere between these two limiting cases. With the exception of agriculture, most producers will have a price policy in that they can set the price which they think will result in the greatest profit. A more or less characteristic situation would be that of (d) in Table 5–1. Here the seller would have to decide which was the relevant part of his demand schedule, and on the basis of this appraisal (as well as his appraisal of his costs), a price would be established.

Although businessmen may never have heard of the word elasticity in the sense in which it is used here, it is a very practical and often-used concept in the business world. Whenever a price decision is to be made, the person making that decision must have some idea as to the relationship between the two variables. The price would not be increased if it were known that the result would be a reduction in total revenue, nor would the price be lowered if it were known that such a policy would reduce total revenue. Time and events may prove that a wrong decision was made in that it did not correctly anticipate the response to the price change, but, nevertheless, the concept described here was employed in order that the decision could be made in the first place.

AN INTRODUCTION TO SUPPLY

Demand is only half of the economic duo which determines price. The other is supply. If there were no demand, there would be no price, and if the supply were unlimited, there would likewise be no price. The analysis now turns to the matter of supply.

In the case of demand, there is an inverse relationship between the price and the quantity demanded, and the demand curve slopes downward to the right when plotted. In the case of supply, however, there is a direct relationship between price and the amount offered for sale. If the same axes are employed which are used to plot demand, the supply schedule will appear as a curve sloping upward to the right. It demonstrates that as the price increases, a larger amount will be offered for sale by the producers. The reasoning is as follows. First take the case of the individual producer. The proprietor of a student eating establishment would probably not be willing to supply any milkshakes at 5¢ because such a low price would not cover his costs of production. If the price were 10¢, he might be willing to devote a part of his facilities to the production and sale of milkshakes. Then if the price were still higher, he would undoubtedly utilize more of his plant for the production and sale of milkshakes, and if the price went high enough, he would enlarge his facilities in order to sell more milkshakes. His supply schedule might appear as follows:

Price	Number of Milkshakes Offered for Sale per Day at Various Prices
5¢	0
10¢	100
15¢	250
20¢	350
25¢	400

This schedule is represented graphically in Figure 5–10A. But now another factor enters the picture. At the higher prices additional producers will enter the industry. The proprietor in the above example would not supply any at 5¢, and there are others who would not supply milkshakes until the price became 15¢ or even more. At the lower prices some producers cannot make a profit, but at the higher prices even the high-cost producers are able to make a profit. Thus all producers will supply more at the higher prices and there will also be more producers. The supply schedule for the industry is obtained, then, by adding the supply curves of the individual producers. For the example used here, the industry schedule might appear as *S* in Figure 5–10B.

Now supply can increase or decrease just as demand. If more were to be offered at every price, this would represent an increase in supply. If all the farmers planted more potatoes, this would represent an increase in the supply of potatoes. A drought, on the other hand, would cause a reduction in the supply. Such changes in the supply of the commodity are represented by shifts in the supply curve. S' in Figure 5–10B represents an increase in supply, and S'' represents a reduction in supply.

Supply schedules may also be described in terms of their elasticity. If a change in the price will result in a less than proportionate change

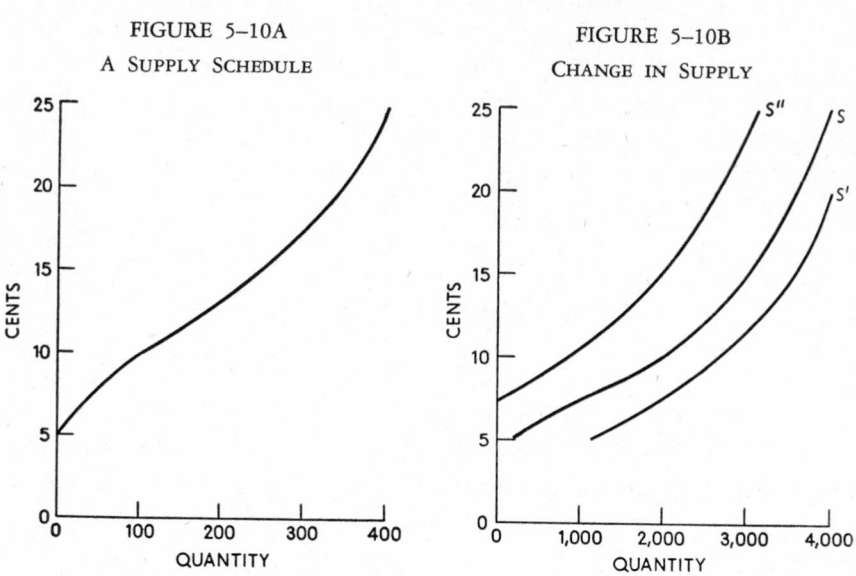

FIGURE 5–10A

A SUPPLY SCHEDULE

FIGURE 5–10B

CHANGE IN SUPPLY

in the amount supplied, the supply is said to be inelastic. On the other hand, an elastic supply is one in which a change in price is accompanied by a larger than proportional change in quantity supplied.

Costs of Production

Since the amount of any commodity which is offered for sale is dependent upon the costs of production, an analysis of costs is necessary. However, before one can discuss costs, certain basic cost concepts must be introduced and understood.

Costs of production are those payments which must be made to the factors of production in order to assure that those factors continue to participate in the productive process. The capitalist must receive interest. The entrepreneur must receive some profit. Labor must receive wages. And the owner of the raw materials must likewise receive a return. If any of these are not forthcoming, the particular factor will be withdrawn and the productive process will be halted. Costs, then, are a special form of prices—prices for the factors of production. But costs as they concern those making price decisions are more than the price of the factor. They are the price of the factor in relation to the productivity of the factor. In other words, insofar as pricing is concerned, the important costs are the cost per unit of output. Thus a high-priced factor of superior productivity might produce a large output with a lower unit cost than a lower-priced factor of low productivity.

For purposes of analysis, costs can be viewed from several aspects. The first is the total cost of production, which is merely the number of units of the factors multiplied by the price of those factors. Included in total costs will be all payments necessary to insure that production continues. This will include the nonexpenditure costs, which are payments made to the entrepreneur for his labor, his capital, and his raw material in addition to the profit which he receives as the risk taker and innovator.

Fixed and Variable Costs. There are some costs which remain constant regardless of the level of output. The cost of the night

TABLE 5–2

COST FUNCTIONS FOR A FIRM

Output	Total Costs	Total Fixed Costs	Average Fixed Costs	Total Variable Costs	Average Variable Costs	Average Total Costs	Marginal Costs
0.......	$ 45	$45	$. . . .	$ 0	$. .	$. . . .	$. .
1........	46	45	45.00	1	1	46.00	1
2........	51	45	22.50	6	3	25.50	5
3........	66	45	15.00	21	7	22.00	15
4........	97	45	11.25	52	13	24.25	31
5........	150	45	9.00	105	21	30.00	53

watchman, for example, is the same whether the firm is producing at capacity or shut down completely. The same is true of the interest on the firm's debt, most executive salaries, some depreciation and obsolescence, certain taxes, and other costs of this nature. These are referred to as fixed costs. There are, on the other hand, costs which vary with the level of output. If the plant closes down, such costs are eliminated, and when the firm increases its level of operation, these costs increase. Labor and raw-material costs are, for the most part, of this nature. These are variable costs.

Rather than being concerned with total fixed costs and total variable costs, those making price decisions are concerned with the average fixed costs and the average variable costs (see Table 5–2). These are, of course, only the total fixed and total variable costs divided by the number of units produced. A few observations must be made about these two kinds of average costs.

Average Fixed Cost. When output is very small the average fixed costs will be high; when total output is at a maximum they will be the least. A firm with a very large percentage of its total costs in

FIGURE 5–11

COST FUNCTIONS

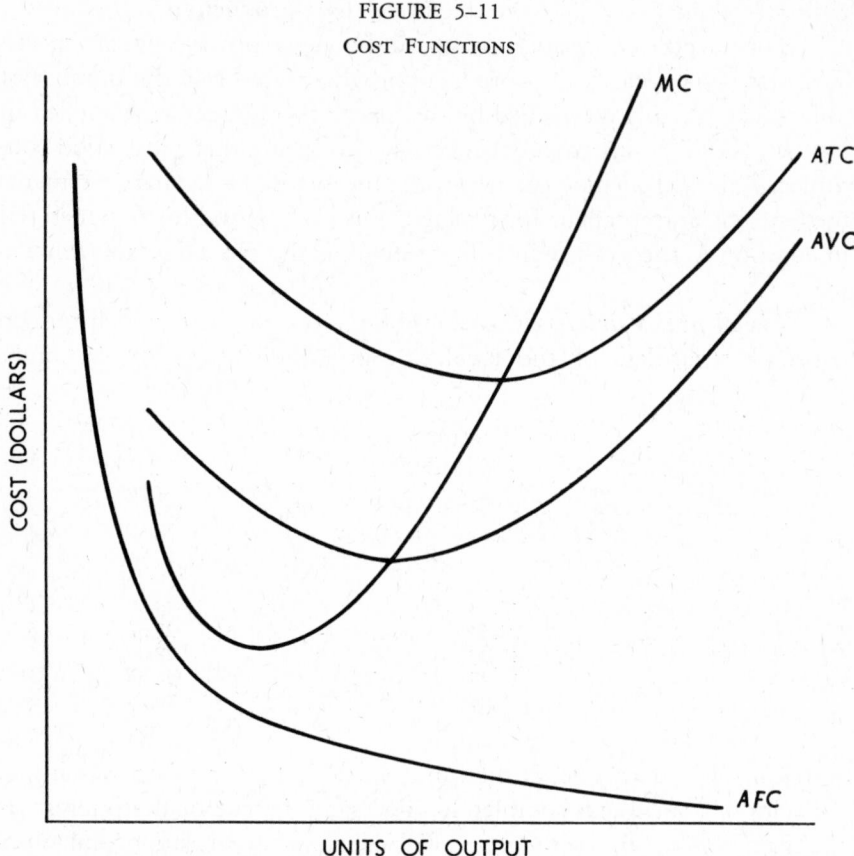

SOURCE: See Table 5–2.

this category will attempt to expand its production, for by doing so it can achieve lower costs of production. Railroads are a good example of an industry in which a high percentage of costs are fixed. If an average fixed cost curve were to be graphed, it would appear as *AFC* in Figure 5–11.

Average Variable Cost. The average variable cost schedule will be of a different nature. Perhaps it can best be explained as follows. As additional units of the variable factor are used in conjunction with a given amount of a fixed factor, the cost per unit of output will decline until some optimum combination of the factors is reached. Beyond this point, the average variable costs will increase. Up to this point there has been too much of the fixed factor for the units of the variable factor being used. Beyond this point there will be too many units of the variable factor. Take, for example, a factory making machine tools. With only a single worker and a large investment in plant and equipment, not much will be produced because of the shortage of the variable factor—in this case, labor. As more and more workers are added, a point will be reached where the number of workers can operate the capital equipment most efficiently. If still more workers are added, eventually too many will be employed for the capital equipment used, and if enough workers are added, one can imagine a situation in which noth-thing will be produced. On purely technological grounds, then, there has to be a combination of the fixed and variable factors which is more efficient than any other combination of the factors. This is the law of diminishing returns.

So far the analysis of the variable factors has been in terms of technological efficiency, but this can easily be translated into terms of costs. As long as there is not enough of the variable factor, average variable costs will decline when additional units are used. When the quantity of the variable factor becomes too great for the fixed factor being used and efficiency declines, the average variable cost will increase. Thus the average variable cost curve will have the general shape of a U; however, the student should be warned against taking the shape of the curve too literally. All that can be said with complete certainty is that as a firm expands production with a fixed factor, there will be a stage when average variable costs are decreasing. This will be followed by a stage of operations in which average variable costs are constant, and this in turn will be followed by a period of increasing average variable costs. The average variable cost curve is usually graphed as *AVC* in Figure 5–11.

Average Total Cost. If the average variable costs and the average fixed costs are totaled, the result will be average total costs. The same result, by the way, could be obtained by dividing the total costs by the units of output. The average total costs will have the same general nature as the average variable costs; that is, they will decline during the initial phases of expansion but will eventually reach a point after which they increase. The point at which the average total costs begin to increase will be beyond the point of increase for the average variable costs, since the average fixed costs continue to decline, which tends to offset the initial increases in average variable costs. The exact influence of the fixed costs depends upon the percentage of total costs which fixed costs represent. In an industry of high fixed costs the average total costs will continue to decline far beyond the point where the average variable costs start to increase. The average total costs appears as *ATC* in Figure 5–11.

Marginal Cost. If the firm is contemplating increasing output, a primary concern will be that of additional costs. How much more will it cost to produce another unit or how much will our costs be reduced if we produce one less unit? This additional cost always represents a change in the variable costs since by definition these are the only costs which change. The change in costs resulting from the production of one more or one less unit of output is known as the marginal cost and appears as *MC* in Figure 5–11.

It has already been explained why it might be believed that the average variable cost schedule is ∪ shaped. When the average variable cost is declining, marginal cost must be less than average cost. When average cost is increasing, marginal cost must exceed average cost. It follows from this that a marginal curve must pass through a ∪ shaped average cost curve at the lowest point of the latter.

These are the costs which serve as the basis for entrepreneurial decisions regarding price and output. The exact nature of the cost schedules will vary from one firm to another, but the principles illustrated here will enable one to make certain generalizations about the pricing and output policies of business organizations.

Time and Price and Output Decisions

Decisions such as those being discussed here are not made in a timeless society, even though certain conditions must be assumed as remaining constant in any individual case. We can, for purposes of analysis, establish three types of decisions on the basis of the time period involved. These are respectively the market period, the short-run period, and the long-run period. The three are defined in terms of cost or supply.

The shortest of the three, the market period, is that time during which the supply of the commodity is fixed. It may be a matter of hours, as in the produce market, or of months, as in the wheat market after the year's crop is harvested. In this period the supply is a stock of goods which cannot be increased regardless of price. The entire stock may or may not be offered for sale.

The second, or short-run, period is that in which the supply can be increased or decreased through a variation in the level of operation of the existing plant and equipment. The entrepreneur must select a particular level of operation. A higher price may induce him to expand his operations beyond the point of minimum average total costs or a lower price may cause him to halt operations at some point below that of minimum average total costs. The student will recognize this situation as that discussed above in the section on costs.

The longest of the three periods, the long run, is that in which the supply may be increased or decreased by building new plant and acquiring new equipment or not replacing the old plant and equipment. In this period, all costs become variable since there is no fixed factor. The entrepreneur thus has to decide on the size of plant he wishes to operate, the number of men to employ, and the amounts of the other factors to use.

Actually a firm is operating in all three periods at once and the entrepreneur or decision maker is simultaneously making decisions relating to all three. For example, policy makers may be faced with the three following questions which are, in order, decisions of the market period, the short-run period, and the long-run period. First, a price must be set which will clear the market of the existing stock, or, if the supply is nonperishable, it must be decided how much of the stock is to be sold today and how much on subsequent days. A second question is that of the proper level of operations for the existing plant and equipment. The third type of decision would be that of determining whether the plant and equipment should be enlarged, whether obsolete equipment should be replaced, or possibly whether the business should be discontinued. These three problems might well confront the management at the same moment, yet they represent the three different time periods with which we shall be concerned.

Now there are certain cost situations which are apropos to each of the several periods. In the shortest of the three periods, the entrepreneur will probably consider that nearly all costs are fixed or sunk. The goods have been produced. There can be no further costs unless there is some cost in selling the goods to the consumer, and even here such costs might well be fixed if the sales costs would be incurred in any event. Any return that the entrepreneur receives will help to defray these costs even though it does not cover all of the costs of production. Since all cost would be lost if the firm closed down, selling at a smaller loss represents a more desirable alternative. Prices in this very short period, then, will be influenced more by the forces of demand than by the forces of supply and cost.

In the short-run period, part of the cost is fixed and part is variable.

The plant has been built and the machinery installed. The cost of such factors is sunk. The firm is better off recovering part of such fixed costs than it is losing all costs. Thus a firm may operate at a price which does not recover the fixed costs; however, it must recover the variable costs, for failure to do so would mean the demise of the firm.

Since there are no fixed costs in the long run and the general proposition is that the price must always cover variable costs, it follows that in this longest time period the price must be sufficient to recover all the costs of operation. In the longest of the three time periods, the firm must recover enough to provide for depreciation and obsolescence, executive salaries, and all other costs.

COST AND SUPPLY

Supply is the amount which will be offered for sale at various prices in a given time period. The amount which any single firm will offer for sale at any price will depend upon the costs of production. The individual firm will not offer additional units for sale if the cost incurred in producing the additional output is greater than the additional revenue which it will receive. Neither will it offer the additional units for sale when the price fails to recover the variable cost. Since there is such a close relationship between cost and supply, let us posit some general principles.

What can be said about the relationship between cost and supply in the market period? In this, the shortest of the three time periods, there is almost no relationship between the two. In the market period all costs are fixed, and this may even include the sales costs. In such an instance, the supply schedule will be perfectly inelastic if the goods are perishable, indicating that a certain stock is to be offered for sale regardless of the price. If the goods are nonperishable, the supply schedule will be less than perfectly inelastic. Its exact nature will depend upon the entrepreneur's anticipations regarding future prices. If he expects future prices to fall, he will sell a larger part of the stock. On the other hand, if he expects an increase in future prices, he will withhold a larger part of the stock for future sales. The higher the present price, the smaller will be the chances for further price increases and the more willing he will be to offer larger quantities for sale. But in no case do the costs of production play an important role in determining the amount to be offered for sale in the market period.

In the short-run period the firm will have both fixed and variable costs. It is possible for the individual firm to increase or decrease its output with its existing plant and equipment. In this time period the firm must cover its average variable costs. And it will continue to expand output as long as the additional revenue which it receives from the sale of the last unit of output exceeds the additional cost incurred in producing that unit.

In the long run, the supply can be either increased or decreased through new firms entering the industry or old firms leaving the industry. The supply curve for the product in such a situation depends upon the cost situation of each of the individual firms insofar as those costs are affected by the industry adjustments; that is, by the change in the amount of plant and equipment and the subsequent change in the level of production for the entire industry. For example, as an industry expands when new producers enter the field, it might be that the costs of all firms in the industry would increase. The larger number of firms producing a larger total output could conceivably bid up the prices of the factors of production, thus increasing costs for all firms. Another possibility would be that the entire industry would be forced to use resources of lesser productivity, again causing costs for the industry to increase. Such instances as these are referred to as industries of increasing costs. The long-run supply curve, under such circumstances will slope upward to the right, indicating that in the long run larger outputs will be forthcoming only at higher prices. The reason is to be found in diseconomies which are external to the firm.

It is also possible that the industry will be one of either decreasing or constant costs. In the first instance the entire industry would experience external economies as production increased. In such an industry (they are rather rare) the long-run supply curve would slope downward to the right, indicating that larger amounts would be offered for sale by the industry at lower prices. In an industry of constant costs there will be no change in the cost situation resulting from a change in the total number of firms in the industry or from an increase in the total capacity of the industry. In this instance the long-run supply curve would simply be a horizontal line, indicating that more could be produced by the industry and offered for sale without any change in the costs of production.

CONCLUSION

Several of the economists' tools, which have been found to be of use in explaining the actions of decision makers, have been introduced in this chapter. The exposure to the tools of the economist has considerable value to the student of elementary economics. A student in elementary chemistry, for example, should acquire some knowledge of chemistry, but probably more important, the student should have some awareness and appreciation of the methodology of the professional chemist. The same is true for the student of elementary economics.

We shall proceed in the next two chapters to complete the construction of several economic models. We shall also indicate just how the economist uses these tools to analyze problems of an economic nature. The student should remember, however, that the goal is twofold. The models have value in and of themselves. At the same time, they enable one to better understand the functioning of the economic system.

EXERCISES

Group I

Explain why each of the following is either true or false.

1. Indifference curves which sloped upward to the right would not indicate any sort of abnormal behavior on the part of the consumer.
2. Unless two goods are perfect substitutes, it would be impossible to draw an indifference curve, because an indifference curve implies substitutability.
3. Changes in the price of either commodity must be shown by changes in the indifference curve.
4. Changes in income can be shown by changes in the position of the price line.
5. The demand function indicates that a consumer will buy more at a higher price than he will at a lower price.
6. If two goods have any degree of substitution, they must have the same elasticity of demand.

Group II

1. The price system serves a very limited role in the USSR as compared to the United States. Investigate and explain the role of the price system in the USSR.
2. The demand for a particular good will change as the level of income changes. What can one say about the changes in the following goods with respect to changes in income: steel, TV sets, houses, bread, beer, and whiskey?

Group III

1. There has been considerable controversy in economics over the measurement of utility. Read George Stigler's article, "The Development of Utility Theory" in the *Journal of Political Economy* (August and October, 1950) and write a report.

BIBLIOGRAPHY

BOULDING, KENNETH E. *Economic Analysis*. 3rd ed. New York: Harper & Brothers, 1955.

DUE, JOHN F., AND CLOWER, R. W. *Intermediate Economic Analysis.* Homewood, Ill.: Richard D. Irwin, Inc., 1961.

LEFTWICH, RICHARD. *The Price System and Resource Allocation.* New York: Holt, Rinehart and Winston, 1960.

SPENCER, N. H. AND SIEGELMAN, L. *Managerial Economics.* Homewood, Ill.: Richard D. Irwin, Inc., 1959.

STIGLER, GEORGE. *The Theory of Price.* Revised ed. New York: Macmillan Co., 1952.

PAPERBACK READING LIST

ALLEN, CLARK L. *Elementary Mathematics of Price Theory.* San Francisco: Wadsworth, 1962.

HENDERSON, H. *Supply and Demand.* Chicago: University of Chicago, 1958.

MARKET STRUCTURE AND FIRM BEHAVIOR

If you think we're wax-works, you ought to pay, you know. Wax-works weren't made to be looked at for nothing. Nohow!—Lewis Carroll, *Through the Looking Glass.*

INTRODUCTION

It is the purpose of economic theory, insofar as pricing is concerned, to predict the future behavior of those making price and output decisions. We are not concerned with what this group ought to do. Our only concern is with describing what they do.

If the entrepreneur is moved by a variety of forces such as a preference for the color blue, a dislike of loud noises, a fondness for children, or a propensity to indulge in gracious living, it would be impossible to predict business behavior. Undoubtedly the motives mentioned above, in addition to many others, have a role in the determination of business policy, but as far as the economist is concerned, it would be impossible to predict any behavior based upon such a multiplicity of motives. The problem would be indeterminate. To overcome this difficulty, economists have assumed that the most important motive underlying business behavior is the desire of the entrepreneur to maximize his profits. This assumption of profit maximization underlies pricing theory, and other possible motives are ignored. It is probable that this is a reasonable treatment of the problem.

It is here that the concept of additional costs and additional revenue, or, to use the economists' term, marginal costs and marginal revenue, are of importance. As a general principle, it can be stated that those who attempt to maximize their profit will continue to expand production as long as the additional cost incurred is less than the additional revenue received from the sale of the larger output. In the short run, the additional cost of the variable factors must be less than the additional revenue. In the long run, the additional cost of all factors, including those which were fixed in the short run, must be less than the additional revenue. Once the additional costs exceed the additional revenue, profits could be increased by reducing total production. Any time a firm increases its cost more than it increases its revenue, total profits are reduced. It follows, then, that if profits are to be maximized, the producer would operate at that point at which marginal costs would just equal marginal revenue. To produce any more or any less would lessen profits.

TYPES OF MARKET STRUCTURE

For the sake of exposition economists have classified business activity into several market types. Then the analysis is conducted in terms of a particular type of market. The final stage of analysis has been to classify an industry or firm according to the type of market in which it operates and then apply the general principles applicable to that particular type of market. This, then, is a description of the market types and the general principles of pricing and output determination found in the several markets.

Pure Competition

The Purely Competitive Market. The purely competitive market is the simplest type of market structure to understand, and thus it makes a convenient point of departure for one first exposed to the subject. Although few industries correspond exactly to the competitive model, there are many instances in which this particular model approximates reality, and in these instances it can be used with profit for purposes of analysis.

The competitive model has the following characteristics. First, there must be a large number of buyers and sellers; so many, in fact, that no single buyer or seller can exercise any influence over the price of the product. The decision to buy or not to buy or the decision to sell or not to sell cannot cause the price to go up or down. Second, all producers must sell a homogeneous product. The product of A is a perfect substitute for the product of B, so the consumer has no preference for the product of one producer or the other. Third, there must be complete freedom of entry into the field and no arbitrary restrictions prohibiting present producers from leaving the industry. This likewise means that the scale of operations is not so large as to prevent producers from entering the market because of a lack of capital. Fourth, there can be no collusion or governmental interference in the industry.

Agriculture, at one time, satisfied the conditions of the competitive model. There were a large number of producers producing a homogeneous product, and there was no collusion among the sellers and no governmental interference. But even allowing for government price supports for agricultural products, the competitive model is still a close approximation of the agricultural industry and thus can make a valuable contribution to our understanding of that industry. The competitive model is likewise a close approximation of the securities and commodities markets as well as of such markets as the used car market. In all of these, an understanding of the competitive model can contribute to one's understanding of the actual world.

Price Determination under Conditions of Pure Competition. The price of the product sold in a purely competitive market is determined by the demand for and the supply of that product. Since the demand schedule represents the amount which would be purchased at the several prices, just as the supply schedule represents the amounts which firms can sell at the several prices, it follows that there can be only one price at which the amount people want to buy just equals the amount others wish to sell. Such an equilibrium situation is represented by Figure 6–1. In this situation the consumers are willing to purchase approximately 3,000 units at 15¢ and the producers are willing to sell the same amount at that price. If the price were higher, the producers would offer more for sale than the consumers would be willing to buy. If the price were lower, consumers would wish to buy more than the producers would be willing to offer for sale. If the price were above 15¢

competition among the sellers would force the price down. If the price were below 15¢ the buyers would attempt to purchase more than was available, and thus the price would be forced upward. Only at 15¢ would there be no forces tending to cause a change in the price.

There are innumerable influences which determine the quantity which consumers will seek to buy or the quantity which producers will

FIGURE 6–1

DEMAND AND SUPPLY

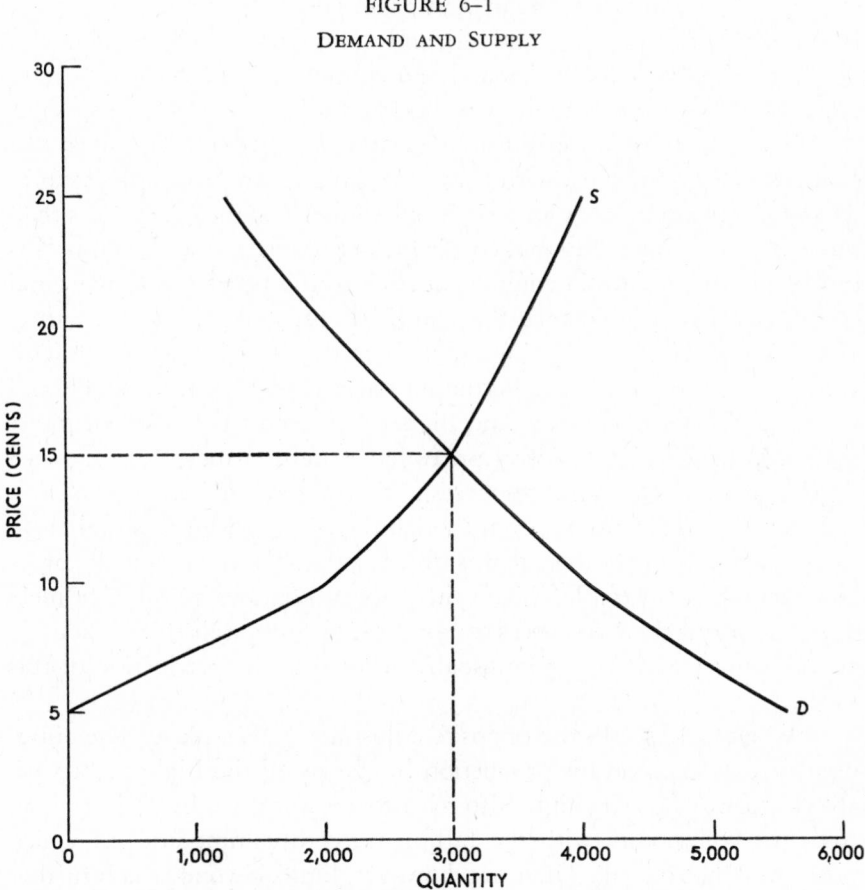

offer for sale. Because a large number of forces determine demand and supply and because no individual producer or buyer is in a position to influence the price, it follows that a competitively determined price will be an unstable price. Anything which increases demand or decreases supply will raise the price. Decreases in demand or increases in supply will lower the price. These forces may be of the most subjective nature and might include such factors as the weather forecast, rumored changes in government policy, favorable or unfavorable crop forecasts, changes in foreign policy of other countries, technological changes, and even a trader's ulcers. A study of wheat prices or any other competitively determined price will reveal this characteristic of marked instability.

Output Determination under Conditions of Pure Competition. The producer operating under conditions of pure competition can make no decision regarding the price of his product other than deciding that he will sell at the market price. He can and must decide just how much he is to produce and sell, and when the price changes because of the total conditions of demand and supply in the market, the individual producer must decide how he is to adjust to the price change.

The entrepreneur operating under these conditions will always be comparing marginal cost with price. He can increase his profits by producing larger amounts as long as the additional cost incurred is less than the price. Once the additional cost is greater than the price, then profits can be increased if production is cut back to the point where marginal cost is equal to price. Since the marginal cost curve is of the nature shown in Figure 5–11 it follows that when the price increases, the individual producer will expand his output to the point where the additional cost is just equal to the new and higher price. This is borne out in actuality. Whenever agricultural prices have risen, farmers have devoted a larger share of their total resources to this particular line of production and increased their output, even though the cost per unit was higher on the larger production than it was on the original production. Potatoes may serve as an example. When the price of potatoes goes up, farmers devote more of their resources to potatoes, even though these resources are not as productive as those usually devoted to the production of this tuber.

When prices fall, the opposite adjustment takes place. The entrepreneur cuts back on his production by not using the higher-cost variable factors. A farmer might also react to a lower price by shifting land from the commodity with the falling price to commodities in which prices were not falling. There are, however, limits beyond which further price reductions will cause the firm to cease producing. In the short-run period, the price can fall no lower than the average variable cost. One may go some time without recovering the fixed or sunk costs, but once the average variable cost is not recovered, the firm must discontinue production. This would be the situation for the firm which did not take in enough revenue to pay the wages of the employees. If the firm's costs are largely of a fixed nature, such as a farm, then costs can fall to extremely low levels before production will be discontinued.

In the long run, however, the price must cover all of the costs of production (see Figure 6–2). If the price fails to provide for the replacement of capital, executive salaries, and other costs which are fixed in the short run, these factors will move to other lines of employment and production will fall. This takes us to industry adjustments to changes in price.

FIGURE 6–2

ADJUSTMENTS IN A COMPETITIVE INDUSTRY

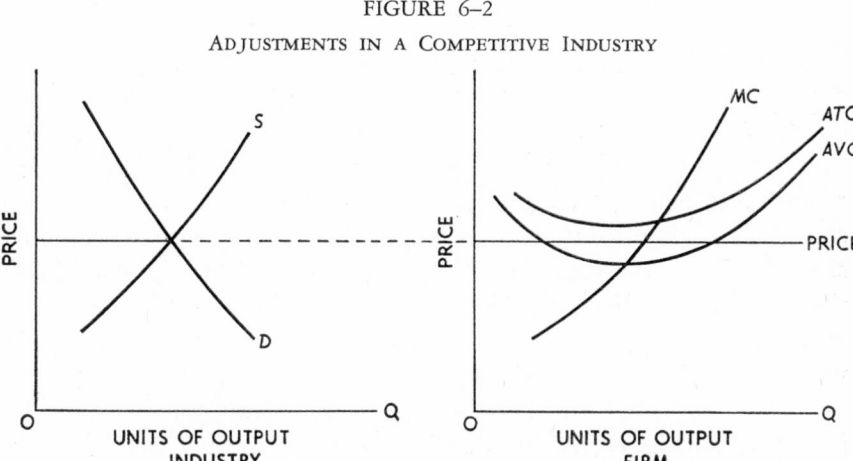

Industry Adjustments to Changes in Price. The industry of which we now speak is merely the summation of all the firms producing products which are perfect substitutes for one another: in other words, a single product. Those adjustments which are something more than the reaction of a single firm to changes in price are referred to as industry adjustments. These take the form of new firms entering the industry or old firms leaving the industry. Such changes are reflected in the industry supply curve.

There is a tendency in a competitive industry for the price of the product to just equal the cost of producing that product. Furthermore, the cost is that cost of production incurred by the most efficient size of company operating at its point of greatest efficiency. In other words, it is the most efficient size of firm operating with the best combination of the variable and fixed factors. If the price were either above or below this point, forces would be present which would result in an industry adjustment.

In the long run in the competitive industry there will be no firms other than those of the most efficient size. Smaller firms of less efficiency would be eliminated. Larger firms of less efficiency would have likewise been eliminated.

Assume for a moment that the price of the product increased because of an increase in demand. The new price is above the cost of production for our representative firm. The firms presently in the industry will thus make a profit in excess of the rate of return required to keep these firms in the industry. In fact, the existence of such profits will suffice to attract new firms into this industry. The addition of new firms to the industry will increase the supply, and the price of the product will fall. And the price will continue to fall as long as the return is greater than that necessary to keep these firms in the industry. This means that the price of the product will fall until it is just equal to the cost of production.

If the price should fall below the cost of production because of a reduction in demand, some firms will leave the industry. The industry supply schedule would thus shift to the left, indicating a reduction in supply. This would result in a higher price. In fact, firms would continue to leave the industry, the supply would continue shifting to the left, and the price would continue to increase until once again the price was just equal to the cost of production for the representative firm.

Any individual firm, then, will be in an equilibrium position if it is maximizing its profits by equating marginal revenue and marginal cost, providing that the price equals or exceeds the costs of production. The industry as a whole will be in an equilibrium position only if there is no reason for new firms to enter the industry or present firms to leave the industry. This latter condition can only exist when the price of the product is just equal to the cost of production for the optimum size of firm (see Figure 6–2).

Industry adjustments as described have frequently taken place in agriculture, which has been a close approximation of the purely competitive model. In both World War I and World War II, new producers entered agriculture because of the large earnings of farmers. New land was broken and used to produce agricultural products. Once, however, that the price returned to what might be termed a more normal level, the marginal land was allowed to revert to its earlier use or even to remain idle. Land in the "Dust Bowl," which could profitably produce wheat during the wars could not do so in the postwar periods.

The same type of adjustment takes place in other industries. Ballpoint pens, for example, were first introduced in the United States in 1945. There was a very great increase in the industry supply because of new firms entering the industry, and the price came down very sharply.

An Appraisal of the Competitive Market. Although the competitive model is a beautiful affair, practice has demonstrated that not all of the expected fruits of that model materialize. In the first place, there are some industries which could be made competitive only at the expense of much higher costs. In such industries as automobiles, aluminum, airplanes, and others of similar nature, the most efficient size of firm may be so large that only a few such firms can produce all that the economy might need. In such industries as these, pure competition would be a very unnatural condition in the sense that it would be inefficient and costly.

Now, once it is granted that some areas of the economy do not readily lend themselves to a competitive type of market, it follows that any industries which do compete will find themselves at a disadvantage. This is essentially the position of the farmers who find themselves in a competitive market insofar as selling their product is concerned, but find that they must buy from industries in noncompetitive markets. Farmers, like others, find competition distinctly distasteful, and, like others, make every effort to eliminate it.

Pure competition has served admirably, then, as a goal, but those who have found themselves competing in what is essentially a non-competitive economy cannot be expected to be extremely enthusiastic about it as a way of life.

Monopoly

In the case of competition it was possible to distinguish between the firm and the industry and conduct a separate analysis for each. In the case of monopoly, it is not so simple to make the same dichotomy. In some instances the firm is the industry and the industry is the firm so that no division at all is possible. In other industries, a single firm may be regarded as the industry in the sense that it produces a branded item, but there may be substitutes for the product which dilute the monopoly power any producer possesses.

The competitive firm, as we saw, could only decide to sell or not sell at the prevailing price. A firm possessing any degree of monopoly power must decide upon a level of output and a price for that output. It may decide upon a price and output simultaneously, or it may adjust both price and output in an attempt to pick that combination which will yield a maximum profit. The monopolist producing a product without any substitutes has more freedom in determining price and output than does the monopolist producing a product with a number of close substitutes, but the principles followed in each case are similar.

The Price and Output Decision of the Monopolist.   As was the case for the competitive industry, the demand schedule facing the monopolist represents an indirect relationship between the quantity which consumers wish to purchase and the price that they are willing to pay. The monopolist will not lose all of his customers if he raises price, and he can increase his sales by lowering his price. This demand schedule is generally referred to as the average revenue schedule, since it is the total revenue divided by the number of units sold. It is represented by *AR* in Figure 6–3.

FIGURE 6–3

REVENUE SCHEDULES IN A MONOPOLISTIC MARKET

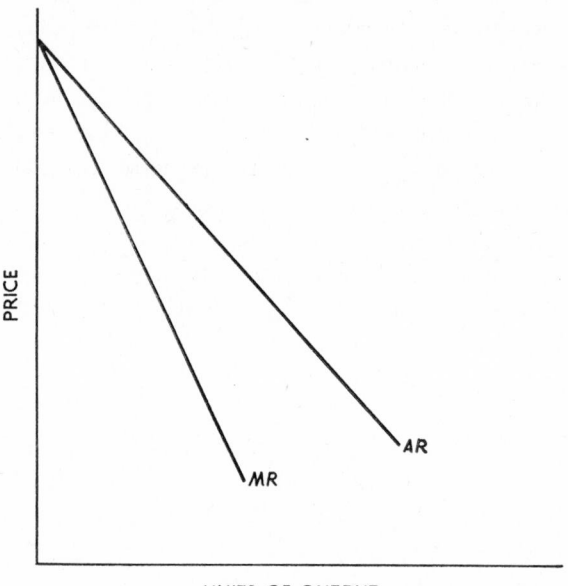

UNITS OF OUTPUT

Under conditions of competition every additional unit sold by the firm increased total revenue by an amount equal to the price of the product. In technical parlance marginal revenue and price were identical. Under conditions of monopoly this is not so. Increased amounts can be sold only if the seller is willing to accept a lower price on the entire output. If the monopolist decides to sell more by lowering his price, his total revenue will not increase by the amount of the price but will increase by the price less that which is lost by selling all of the units at this lower price. The decision to produce and sell an additional unit will force the monopolist to lower the price on all units sold. Thus the increase in total revenue will always be less than the price. This marginal revenue schedule appears as *MR* in Figure 6–3. The table from which Figure 6–3 is derived is as follows:

Units Which Can Be Sold	At These Prices (Average Revenue)	Will Produce Total Revenue of	But Will Increase Total Revenue by (Marginal Revenue)
0	$10	$ 0	$ 0
1	9	9	9
2	8	16	7
3	7	21	5
4	6	24	3
5	5	25	1
6	4	24	−1
7	3	21	−3
8	2	16	−5
9	1	9	−7

This table has one point of significance. The monopolist will not extend production to the point where the increase in cost is just equal to the price, as was the case under conditions of competition. The monopolist will only increase production as long as the additional revenue is greater than the additional cost. This means that the monopolist will produce a smaller output and charge a higher price than a competitive firm with the same cost structure. In fact, the classic characteristics of monopoly are restriction of output and the existence of a price which is somewhat higher than that prevailing in more competitive markets.

The monopolist, however, is not a free agent in the establishment of the price, and this is true regardless of degree of monopoly. A monopolistic position in any single market does not of itself permit the establishment of a high price, nor does it guarantee the existence of profits. In the first place, there has to be a demand for the product. Secondly, it must be possible to produce the product at a cost which will permit a profit. The monopolist is in the same position as any other firm regarding the recovering of the costs of operation. In all instances he must be able to recover his variable costs, and this means, of course, that in the long run he must recover all costs.

If the revenue schedule in Figure 6–3 is accepted and to that is added a cost schedule represented by *ATC* and *MC* (Figure 6–4), it is possible to generalize about the output and price decision of the monopolist. Like any other firm wishing to maximize its profits, the monopolistic firm will expand output with the given plant and equipment as long as *MR* exceeds *MC,* and whenever *MC* exceeds *MR,* output will be reduced. The level of output in this example then is *OQ.* If quantity *OQ* is produced, it can be sold at price *P,* which is what the *AR* schedule represents. Thus to maximize his profits *OQ* will be sold at price *OP.* In this instance the price *OP* exceeds the costs of production which at this level of output are *OC.* Thus on each unit produced the monopolist is making a monopoly profit of *CP.*

Under conditions of competition such excess profit would be eliminated by the entry of new firms into the industry. Under conditions of monopoly such profits may last for extended periods of time if there is no freedom of entry. If the monopoly is based on patents, control of

FIGURE 6–4

COST AND REVENUE SCHEDULES IN A MONOPOLISTIC MARKET

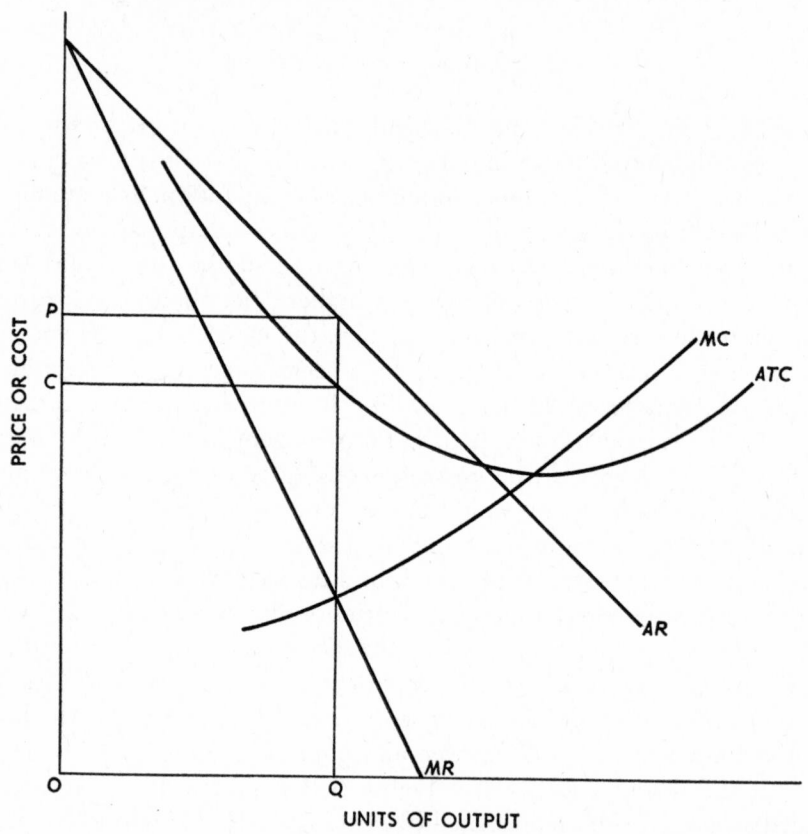

raw materials, control of power sites, or any other such factor, it may be impossible for new firms to enter the industry and thus increase supply, drive prices down, and eliminate the surplus profits. Probably the biggest threat to such surplus profits of a monopolistic firm is the possibility of vigorous enforcement of the antitrust laws.

The Perfect Monopoly. Many producers possess some degree of monopoly power, but few have had or do have a "perfect" monopoly with a completely inelastic demand schedule. A firm having a completely inelastic demand schedule could raise his price without suffering any reduction whatsoever in the quantity which it could sell. Such a monopoly is a rarity. A corner in the stock market would be one example, where the only upper limit on the price of the cornered stock is the ability of the person to pay.

In most instances, however, the demand schedule is less than perfectly inelastic, for there are substitutes for nearly all products. The largest part of the economy's total production is carried on by firms which possess some degree of monopoly power. We might refer to these as imperfect monopolists.

Imperfect Competition

Thus far, the limiting types of market have been considered: namely, pure competition and monopoly. In the case of pure competition, the individual producer has no perceptible influence on the market. The market establishes the price and the individual producer adjusts to that price. On the other hand, the monopolist has considerable control over the market. He is limited to operating within the limits set by his demand curve, but even this might be altered by appropriate advertising and marketing policies. Within these limits, he can establish price and output policies.

It would be somewhat difficult to find examples in the United States of business which could be classified as either purely competitive or purely monopolistic in nature. Most markets in this country are between the two extremes. Within this spectrum, the firms are subject to some of the forces of the competitive market, yet, at the same time, they are able to exercise some of the power of the monopolist.

Within this broad "in-between" market area, there are two general market classifications of primary significance: oligopoly and monopolistic competition. In fact, it is these two market types which are most typical of American business.

Oligopoly. There are a large number of industries in the United States in which a very few firms produce a large part if not all of the total product of the industry. (See Table 6–1.) An industry with so few firms that some or all of them can influence the market is said to be an oligopoly. The oligopoly is "pure" if the products of the several firms are perfect substitutes. Cement is an example. In industries such as automobiles, cigarettes, typewriters, and cereals, the products are close substitutes but cannot be considered perfect substitutes.

The firm in a competitive industry need not worry about the price and output decisions of other firms in the industry. Since there are no competitors in a monopolized industry, the monopolist need not consider competitors. The oligopolist, on the other hand, must consider the actions and reactions of competitors in making his price and output decisions. Since there are so few firms in the industry, the course of action pursued by any individual firm will influence the policies of all other firms in the industry. And it is also true that the decisions of the other firms were, in part, a function of the decision of our oligopolist. This

TABLE 6–1

PERCENTAGE OF TOTAL VALUE OF OUTPUT PRODUCED BY THE FOUR
AND EIGHT LARGEST FIRMS IN SELECTED INDUSTRIES
IN THE UNITED STATES, 1958

Industry	First Four Companies	First Eight Companies
Beet sugar	64	94
Chewing gum	84	93
Distilled liquors, except brandy	60	77
Cigarettes	80	99
Alkalies and chlorine	61	88
Cyclic (coal tar) crudes	89	96
Synthetic rubber	54	75
Biological products	46	66
Softwood distillation	80	92
Salt	81	91
Rubber footwear	66	83
Primary aluminum	82	90
Aluminum rolling and drawing	75	82
Typewriters	79	99
Electric lamps	90	96

SOURCE: *Concentration Ratios in Manufacturing Industry* (Washington, D.C., 1962).

mutual interdependence creates an element of uncertainty which is not to be found in either pure competition or monopoly. Handling this uncertainty remains a vexing problem for the oligopolist.

Decision making in an oligopolistic market takes on many of the features of a poker game. Each time a competitor makes a decision, all the remaining members of the industry (or game) must reassess their position and consider making a new decision on the basis of this new information of changed circumstances. So any individual member in either a poker game or an oligopolistic industry must try to imagine in advance what other members will do in reaction to his decision. Each must be prepared to alter any given decision in light of new decisions made by other members of the industry.

Consider the demand curve of an oligopolist. The general law of demand states that as the price is lowered, the quantity of the product which can be sold is increased. However, in the case of the oligopolist, there is no certainty that this relationship will hold in every situation. If the firm lowering the price has a few competitors producing a close substitute, and if the competing firms do not lower price, then the original firm will experience an increase in the amount demanded. But if the competing firms also lower the price, then the increase in the quantity of the good demanded will be much smaller. In this case, the increase will reflect a general increase in the quantity demanded in the market at the lower price, and the increase for any particular firm will simply be that firm's share of the total market increase. If, however, the competing firms in the industry should actually lower their prices by a larger amount, then the original firm could actually find that sales were reduced at the lower price!

If price increases are considered, a similar uncertainty is found. Most producers in an oligopolistic industry would be inclined to believe that other producers might not follow any price increase. If the producers produced close substitutes, then any firm increasing its price would probably find that its customers had all shifted to the competing firms. Thus, if the oligopolist raised his price, total revenue would fall.

The situation might be summarized as follows. To the oligopolist, the demand schedule appears to be elastic at all prices above the existing price, indicating an increase in price will result in a reduction in total revenue. Below the existing price (or below some lower price), the demand schedule appears to be less elastic, indicating that a reduction in price will add a much smaller amount to total revenue. This can be diagramatically represented by the "kinky" demand curve. (See Figure 6–5). This demand curve indicates that the oligopolist expects his competitors to follow him for any price reductions, but he does not expect them to do so in the case of price increases. The word "expects" takes on particular importance here, for it represents the uncertainty present in the situation. If the firms agree on price and output policy, then the uncertainty regarding the actions of competitors is eliminated.

The "kink" in the demand curve occurs at the current price-output point. The demand schedule is elastic above this point and less elastic below, so there is a discontinuity in the marginal revenue schedule at this point. This is indicated by the gap in the marginal revenue curve at the level of output represented by Q.

If cost curves are superimposed on Figure 6–5, it is possible that they can be shifted upward or downward to a considerable extent without affecting either output or price. This is explained by the peculiar nature of the "intersection" of *MR* and *MC*. If the firm is presently maximizing profit, this means that marginal revenue and marginal cost are "equal" at this level of output—say *Q*. This means that *MR* and *MC* must "intersect" in the gap in the *MR* curve. Since they do "intersect"

FIGURE 6–5

THE AVERAGE REVENUE AND MARGINAL REVENUE
FUNCTIONS FOR THE OLIGOPOLIST

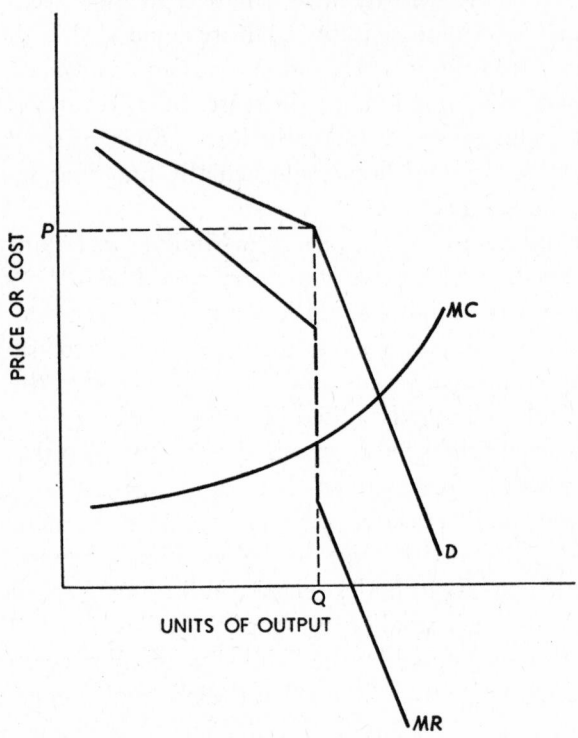

in this vertical gap, it is possible for the whole cost structure, including the marginal cost curve, to shift up and down without changing the level of production at which the two functions are equal. This explains one of the observable characteristics of an oligopolistic industry— namely rigid prices. There can be considerable changes in the costs of production without any change in the price of the product or the level of output of the firm. Where there is any uncertainty as to how competitors might react, it is probably better to stick to a price which is suspected of being the wrong price (in the sense that it is not the price which would maximize profits) rather than incurring the risk of changing the price and possibly opening Pandora's box of troubles.

When the entire industry is faced with the same situation, however, the uncertainty in the situation is reduced. If all of the firms in the industry suffer the same cost increase, then it is more likely that a price change will take place on an industry-wide basis. This is one reason, by the way, that an oligopolist might favor industry-wide bargaining or pattern bargaining over wages and labor costs.

The price-output equilibrium of an oligopolist is largely indeterminate; however, certain ranges may be established. It the firms behave, either accidentally or through collusion, as though they were a single firm, then the price-output results will be that of pure monopoly. In some sense, the firms might try to maximize the profits of the industry. Like firms in other forms of markets, the price to the oligopolist must cover the average variable costs in the short run and the average total costs in the long run. The reasoning here is the same as in the competitive industry.

Because of the uncertainties associated with oligopoly, firms in such an industry commonly seek some avenue of escape. One possibility is collusion. The surest way of reducing the uncertainty surrounding a competitor's actions is to ask him just what he plans to do and then make some mutually satisfactory agreement. But such actions will generally involve infringements of the nation's anti-trust statutes. As far as economic analysis is concerned, the result would simply be a case of monopoly.

A second means of reducing the uncertainty is that of price leadership which will be discussed in the following chapter. A third is that of product differentiation. Here the attempt is to induce customers into believing that the products of the various members of the industry are not acceptable substitutes. If successful, the firm has a greater degree of freedom in setting price and output. Product differentiation is not confined to industries with a few firms, but is also found in those industries with a large number of firms. This is the second type of market structure to be found between the two extremes of pure competition and pure monopoly.

Monopolistic Competition. A market characterized as monopolistic competition has a large number of sellers dealing in products which are substitutes but not perfect substitutes. Each seller attempts to convince the buying public that his product or his particular brand is somewhat different—in fact, somewhat more desirable—than those of competitors. It is basically an attempt to move from what would be the impersonal adjustment of a purely competitive market toward the more enviable position of the monopolist. In fact, the more successful the campaign of differentiation, the greater will be the monopoly power of the seller. In terms of economic analysis, then, the purpose of product differentiation is to (1) make the demand schedule less elastic and (2) shift the demand schedule to the right representing an increase in demand. The first represents a greater degree of control over price, while the second represents a larger level of output and possibly a bigger share of the market.

Product differentiation may take many forms. In some cases there may be an important physical difference in the products. In others the physical difference may be minimal, with most of the difference existing only in the mind of the buyer. Differentiation may take the form of differences in services. Credit, daily deliveries, air conditioning, clean rest rooms, and the like are examples. In still other cases, the difference may be largely illusory, such as the "magic ingredients" in certain products or the fact that a baseball player smokes a particular brand of cigarettes. The important fact is that there need not be any real difference in the product. It is only necessary that the consumer think that there is a difference.

The firm in a monopolistically competitive market will equate marginal cost and marginal revenue if it wishes to maximize profit. It will be profitable to continue operations as long as the price covers average variable cost in the short run and average total costs in the long run. In this particular case, however, the firm must also decide how much to spend in further differentiation of its product. The usual rule applies. As long as the added revenue to be derived from further differentiation is greater than the added cost, the firm would find it profitable to engage in such activities as advertising, expanded services, and similar activities designed to create an image of product superiority in the mind of the consumer. It should be noted, in contrast, that the producer in a competitive industry would feel that the marginal revenue to be gained from such undertakings would be zero, and thus he would not find it profitable to engage in differentiation if there were any cost involved at all.

In the case of monopoly and oligopoly, entry into the field may be severely restricted if not impossible. In the case of monopolistic competition, restrictions on entry are less likely to exist. As a rule, there are too many firms for them to concern themselves about the problem of newcomers to the industry. There are exceptions, however. For example, the dry cleaning industry has been quite successful in restricting entry by getting favorable legislation through city councils.

As long as there is freedom of entry into the industry, those profits which are not necessary to keep the firms in operation will tend to be eliminated. In other words, there is a tendency for price to equal cost. (See Figure 6–6). However, because of product differentiation, firms may have different costs and demands which temper the tendency to move toward that point where price is equal to average total cost. It

FIGURE 6–6

PRICE AND OUTPUT UNDER LONG-RUN CONDITIONS
OF MONOPOLISTIC COMPETITION

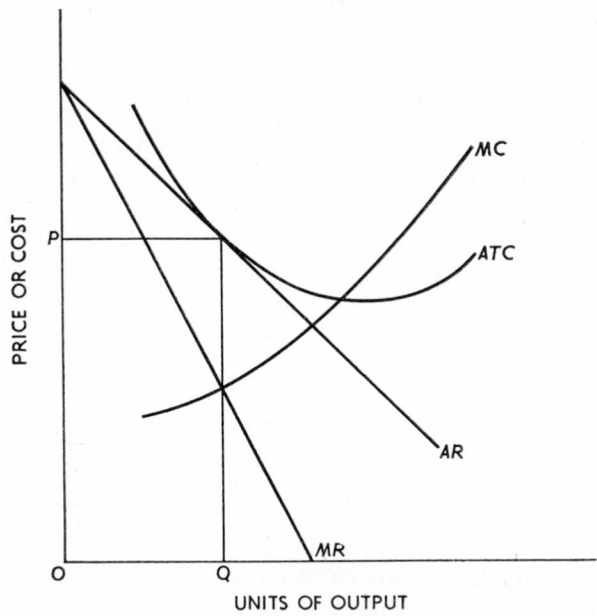

may be that the real differences are generally recognized to be inconsequential by the consumer, and if such is the case, there will be a long run tendency toward equality among the different firms.

Differentiated Oligopoly. A firm in an oligopolistic industry faces additional uncertainty in the fact that it must take into consideration what the competitors might do. One technique commonly used to reduce this uncertainty is that of product differentiation. The differentiated oligopoly—an industry with few firms producing very similar products—is characteristic of much of modern American industry. Insofar as a producer in such a circumstance is successful in convincing the consumer that his product is superior to that of the competitor, it is possible to reduce the impact of the competitor's reaction to one's market policies and thus reduce the uncertainty of the oligopolistic market.

Cigarettes, automobiles, and soap are among the outstanding examples of this type of industry. These industries are characterized by non-price rather than price competition. Firms will spend millions of dollars on advertising of various kinds, but their willingness to engage in such activities is more than matched by their unwillingness to engage in price competition. This raises the following interesting question. Would the gains to society as a whole be increased if some way were to be found which would force the oligopolistic firms to compete with regard to price rather than the nonprice forms of competition which presently characterize so much of the industry?

DECISION MAKING UNDER UNCERTAINTY[1]

In the perfectly competitive model it was assumed that the producer acted as though he knew for certain just what the price would be when the product was sold. Given this price, then, the entrepreneur

TABLE 6–2

OPTIMAL LEVELS OF OUTPUT FOR VARIOUS PRICES

Price	Optimal Output
$ 9	2
22	3
41	4
66	5

chose that level of output which would just equate marginal cost and price, and profits would be at a maximum. This amounted to assuming away any element of uncertainty. But it is obvious that the price which a producer uses as a basis for determining the level of output may not be the actual price in the market at the time the product is sold. And thus realized profits will diverge from anticipated profits to the extent that actual prices diverge from anticipated prices.

The perfectly competitive model which assumed certain knowledge can be made more realistic if an element of uncertainty is introduced. Suppose that our producer feels confident that, on the basis of past experience, the price tomorrow is going to be either $9, $22, $41, or $66. In all of his experience it has never been anything else. If he knew that price were to be $9, for example, he would produce two units, for this would maximize profits at this price. The optimal levels of out-

[1] This section can be omitted if desired. None of the material in the remainder of the book is directly dependent upon this material. It is a presentation of some of the newer work presently being done by economists.

put for each of the possible prices are presented in Table 6–2. Under conditions of certainty, the economist would simply have the decision maker equate price and marginal cost and thus maximize profits. The problem would be solved. So now some way must be found to find a solution to the question of how much should be produced when it is not known which of the prices will prevail.

The first step in the construction of this model is that of constructing a payoff table. (See Table 6–3). A payoff table consists of (a) the possible states of nature, (b) the alternative actions open to the decision maker, and (c) the reward which will accrue to the decision maker for each possible combination of the states of nature and the alternative actions. The state of nature represents the uncertainty in the problem, for this is what the decision maker does not know. If the state of nature were known, then the correct decision could be made without any pos-

TABLE 6–3

PAYOFF TABLE

	Level of Output			
Price	2	3	4	5
$ 9	$-33*	$- 39	$- 61	$-105
22	- 7	0*	- 9	- 40
41	31	57	67*	55
66	81	132	167	180*

* Best level of output for that price.

sibility of error. In this particular model, the unknown state of nature is the price which will prevail tomorrow. The alternative actions are the possible courses of action which are available to the decision maker. In this case the alternative actions are the different levels of production— 2, 3, 4, or 5. And the payoffs or rewards are the profits (or losses) which will accrue to the decision maker for each of the possible combinations of the state of nature and the alternative action. In this case, the rewards are computed by subtracting total costs from total revenue for each level of output and each price.[2]

If the decision maker were certain that the price was to be $9, then two units would be produced and the resulting loss of $33 would be a minimum as compared to the losses which would be suffered at other levels of output and the same price. If, on the other hand, it were known

[2] The figures in Table 6–3 were computed from the formula:

$$\text{Total profit} = px - x^3 + x^2 - x - 45$$

where x is the level of output and p is the price.

that the price was to be $66, profits would be maximized if five units were produced. Thus, one can see that for each possible state of nature (price), there is a best course of action to be taken (level of production to be chosen) which will maximize profits or minimize losses. The best alternative action for each state of nature is indicated by the starred entries in the payoff table.

The significance of the information in the payoff table can, perhaps, be more easily discerned if a loss table is constructed. (See Table 6–4.) Such a table is constructed by subtracting each entry in a given row from the starred entry in that row. The starred entry minus itself will always be zero, and all other entries will be positive.

What does the loss table show? In a very brief form it indicates the loss that the decision maker suffers if the wrong decision is made for a

TABLE 6–4

LOSS TABLE

Price	Level of Output			
	2	3	4	5
$ 9	$ 0	$ 6	$28	$72
22	7	0	9	40
41	36	10	0	12
66	99	48	13	0

given state of nature. Thus if the price turns out to be $66 and four units have been produced, a loss of $13 will be suffered. The difference (in terms of profits) between the best decision and the decision actually made was $13. If five units were produced on the basis of an anticipated price of $66, a loss of $12 would be incurred if the price turned out to be only $41. The figures in the body of the loss table are, then, opportunity losses which result only from making the wrong decision for the realized state of nature. The zeros in the main diagonal indicate that no loss is suffered if the correct decision is made.

Since the price which will prevail is unknown at the time the decision is made, what can be said about the best decision? Under conditions of certainty, the entrepreneur would produce where marginal cost equals price and the conditional loss would always be zero—that is, the best decision or best course of action would be chosen. Now suppose that the decision maker has just a little less knowledge. Instead of knowing what the price is to be, suppose that he knows for certain that the price is going to be either $41 or $66. Then all he has to do is to choose between producing four units (the optimal amount if the price is $41) and five units (the optimal amount if the price is $66). The remaining alternatives can be ignored because they will only be optimal if the price is less than $41. If four units are produced on the assumption that the price is to be $41 and it actually turns out to be $66, the opportunity loss will be $13. The loss will be $12 if five units are produced on the basis of an anticipated price of $66 and the realized price turns out to be $41. In either case, the cost of making the wrong decision will be either $13 or $12. If the decision maker feels that the two prices are equally likely, then he ought to produce five units rather than four. Why?

Now assume that the decision maker—rather than feeling that the two are equally likely—feels that there are three chances in four that the price is going to be $66 and only one chance in four that it will be $41. What will he do? The best decision would be to produce five units for he would suffer an opportunity loss of zero (that is, make the right decision) three times out of four whereas if he were to produce four units, an opportunity loss of $13 would occur 75 per cent of the time.

The problem can be changed still more. Suppose that the decision maker has made 80 observations under identical circumstances, and he has observed that each of the four different prices occured on 20 days. On the basis of past experience, then, he concludes that any of the four is equally likely. If four units are produced, this would be the optimal output for $1/4$ of the time and the wrong output for the remaining $3/4$ of the time. The expected loss would be:

$$(\tfrac{1}{4})(28) + (\tfrac{1}{4})(9) + (\tfrac{1}{4})(0) + (\tfrac{1}{4})(13) = \$12.50.$$

If five units were produced, the expected loss would be $31. The expected loss for both two and three units is larger than $31. So the optimal decision is to produce four units for it will minimize the opportunity loss.

The decision maker need not assume that each of the prices is equally likely. By assigning some other set of values to represent the likelihood of each price, some other output would be selected as the optimum level of production. In general, the action selected will be some function of the probability assigned to each of the possible states of nature. The more likely the higher prices, the more apt the decision maker is to choose a higher level of output. The more likely the lower prices, the more apt he will be to select a lower level of output.

The above example is an extremely elementary application of decision theory applied to a classical economic problem. Instead of assuming that the decision maker knows the price for certain, uncertainty has been introduced in the form of an unknown state of nature. Probabilities are assigned by the decision maker to the several states of nature, and then the "best" output is selected.

CONCLUSION

The use of economic models to explore market structures and pricing policies of business firms gives one some insight into the economic system. The decision-making process of the firm is important for its own sake. But it is also important in that it enables one to better understand the relationship between the self-interest of the firm and the general interest of public.

Moving from the firm to the market or industry, the student of economics can analyze and compare different types of market structures. Such a comparison and evaluation is a necessary condition for a successful social policy. The policy maker must have some idea of the gains to be derived from competition. He must likewise be able to make some estimate of the economies associated with large-scale enterprise. Thus, in a sense, price theory is normative in nature for it helps us to decide just what type of public policy is most apt to achieve the goals of society.

The fact that the economic system consists of a number of industries with a variety of market structures implies further policy problems. That policy which is appropriate for one may not be so for another. One industry, because of its peculiar structure, may benefit at the expense of others. Public policy, then, must take cognizance of such differences in order that the economic system will function successfully and efficiently. To this end, the study of price theory and market structure has an important contribution to make.

EXERCISES

Group I

Explain why the following statements are true or false.

1. The assumption of maximization is basic to a discussion of prices and pricing policy because it makes the model more realistic.
2. A business firm can always increase its total profits by expanding output with its given plant and equipment if, at the higher level of output, marginal revenue still exceeds marginal cost.
3. As the price of a product goes up, existing firms will offer more for sale and additional firms will enter the market if possible.
4. The possession of monopoly power will permit a firm to charge any price it desires.

5. Any firm in a noncompetitive market can increase its profits by raising its price.
6. The poorer the substitutes for the product of an oligopolistic producer, the more control a producer will have over his price.
7. A small firm producing a product which has close substitutes cannot have any monopolistic power.

Group II

1. Make a study of advertising expenditures in the United States. Is there any relation between the type of industry and the total amount spent for advertising?
2. Compare the prices and output of the farm implement industry and some agricultural product—say wheat.

Group III

1. The steel industry poses a peculiar problem in our economy. Explain why this is so. Evaluate the following courses of action: regulate as a public utility; nationalize; or let it alone.
2. Trading stamps are introduced by one firm to attract customers away from other sellers; eventually, however, the industry may not have any more customers, but all of the firms may have higher costs. Write a short paper on the "Economics of Trading Stamps" and explain this peculiar phenomenon.

BIBLIOGRAPHY

BAIN, J. S. *Industrial Organization.* New York: John Wiley & Sons, Inc., 1959.

CLARK, J. M. *Competition as a Dynamic Process.* Washington, D.C.: The Brookings Institution, 1961.

HEFLEBOWER, R. B. AND STOCKING, G. W. (Eds.) *Readings in Industrial Organization and Public Policy.* Homewood, Ill.: Richard D. Irwin, Inc., 1958.

PAPERBACK READING LIST

ADAMS, W. (Ed.) *The Structure of American Industry.* 3rd ed. New York: The Macmillan Company, 1961.

Chapter 7 | PRICING AND BUSINESS POLICY

People of the same trade seldom meet together, even for merriment and diversion, but the conversation ends in a conspiracy against the public, or in some contrivance to raise prices.—Adam Smith, *The Wealth of Nations*.

Of the many decisions made by managers of a business enterprise, those regarding price and output may well be the most sig-

134

nificant. The success or failure of the enterprise depends upon the proper combination of price and output. In addition, the questions of price and output are of social significance. These decisions determine, in part, how much buyers will consume as well as the amount of income the factors of production receive. To all, then, the tools which were developed in the previous chapters become significant as a means whereby problems of the firm and society can be analyzed.

DEMAND AND SUPPLY ANALYSIS

The general proposition established in Chapter 6 was that prices and output are determined by the demand for the product in interaction with the supply. An equilibrium price will be established where the amount supplied is just equal to the amount demanded. There is, in such a situation, no force making for a change. But such an equilibrium can exist only at a moment in time. New forces disturb this equilibrium and cause a readjustment between demand and supply. Through the use of the demand and supply analysis such situations can be analyzed with precision.

The Black Market

Let us start our analysis of the black market by assuming an equilibrium situation as represented in Figure 7–1A. The equilibrium price will be $1.00. At this price the suppliers will supply what the buyers are willing to buy—that is, 10,000 units.

Suppose the country is plunged into war. Employment increases. Wages and prices increase. The government finances part of the costs of the war by borrowing from the banking system. The demand for the product in question increases. The new demand is represented by D' in Figure 7–1B. At the same time, the government imposes restrictions upon the production of civilian goods and thus the supply of this commodity shifts to S'. The price under these conditions would be $1.50 instead of $1.00, and a smaller amount would be sold.

Since the same thing is happening to most of the goods and services produced in the economy, the government imposes a program of direct price controls to prevent inflation. In this case the prewar price of $1.00 is set as the legal price. But under the new conditions of demand and supply consumers are willing to buy far more at a price of $1.00 than the producers are willing to supply. At a price of $1.00, 5,000 units would be supplied and 11,000 units would be demanded. Obviously this is an unstable situation unless the government resorts to some means to reduce the demand to a level at which the quantity demanded at $1.00 is just equal to the quantity supplied at that price.

The price is not now permitted to serve in its historic role as a rationing device. Rather than letting this limited supply of goods and services be distributed on a "first come, first served" basis, the government will, of necessity, have to supplement its price control orders with some sort of rationing device. In the case illustrated in Figure 7–1B, the government would have to allocate the 5,000 available units among consumers willing to consume a larger amount. The shortage of 6,000 units will be distributed among all of the consumers rather than being

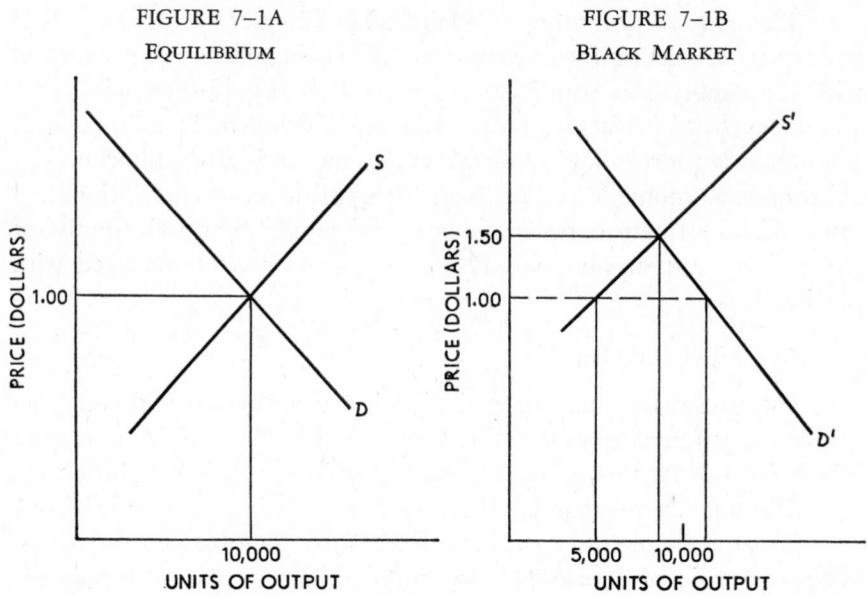

FIGURE 7–1A
EQUILIBRIUM

FIGURE 7–1B
BLACK MARKET

concentrated among those who entered the market after the supply was exhausted, as would be the case if the price system were permitted to operate.

If the program of price control and rationing is supplemented or reinforced by a general atmosphere of patriotism, consumers and producers might live with such a situation. However, those who are not impressed with the motive of patriotism might be quite willing to divert resources to the production of the product in question with the intent of selling their output at a price above the legal price. Consumers of similar low principles might likewise be willing to patronize the black market. In fact, the very term "black market" has an opprobrious connotation.

Producers are willing to supply various quantities at different black-market prices just as consumers are willing to buy various quantities at the different prices. Where the two are equal, that is, where the amount supplied just equals the amount demanded, the black-market price will be established. This price may be higher or lower than the free market price ($1.50), but it will definitely be higher than the governmentally regulated price of $1.00. If the black-market price were to fall to the level of the legal price, the black market would cease to exist. The controlled price and the free price would be the same.

A case in point would be that of governmental attempts to peg the price of currency in various European countries during and after World War II. Those governments would establish an exchange rate between the European currency and the American dollar. Let us take as an example a ratio of 10 to 1. Ten units of the European money would exchange for a dollar. If this rate were too low, that is if a dollar were worth more than the 10 units of the foreign currency, a black market would develop. In this market the dollar could be exchanged for 15, 20, or more units of the currency in question. If, as was often the case, the European country's economy became more stable and economically sound, its currency appreciated in value. Then the free market rate of exchange would move back toward the legal exchange rate of 10 to 1. Once it reached that rate, dollars could be officially and legally exchanged for 10 units of the currency. The black marketeer would thus be the victim of technological unemployment, and the black market would be no more.

The free market price as determined by supply and demand is a powerful force. It can only be offset under the most trying of circumstances, such as war. But even then a free market price will make its appearance unless the government exercises the highest degree of vigilance. Putting a lid on the law of supply and demand is comparable to holding the lid down on a kettle of boiling water.

Agricultural Price Supports

The problem of agricultural price supports lends itself to analysis with the tools of demand and supply. Let us start by assuming the conditions of demand and supply in Figure 7–2A. In this situation 200 million bushels of wheat will be sold at a price of $1.75. The supply is rather inelastic because farmers will not usually vary production a great deal with changes in price.

Now assume that the farmers and politicians feel that a price of $1.75 is too low to enable them to receive a fair return, and a law is passed to raise the price of wheat by restricting output. Each farmer is given an acreage allocation which he can plant and harvest. Let us assume, for the moment, that this restriction of acreage actually reduces the supply of wheat. The new conditions of supply are represented by S' in Figure 7–2B. Now under the new conditions of supply and the unchanged conditions of demand, the price will be $2.00 but a smaller amount will be consumed. If the reduced acreage is farmed more intensively by fertilizing, spraying, and increasing the use of capital equipment, the third period, then, will see an increase in the supply of wheat. Under the new situation, the market price would be $1.50, but the gov-

FIGURE 7–2A

EQUILIBRIUM BEFORE
ACREAGE RESTRICTIONS

FIGURE 7–2B

EQUILIBRIUM AFTER
ACREAGE RESTRICTIONS

FIGURE 7–2C

EQUILIBRIUM (WITHOUT
PRICE SUPPORTS) AFTER
MORE INTENSIVE
CULTIVATION

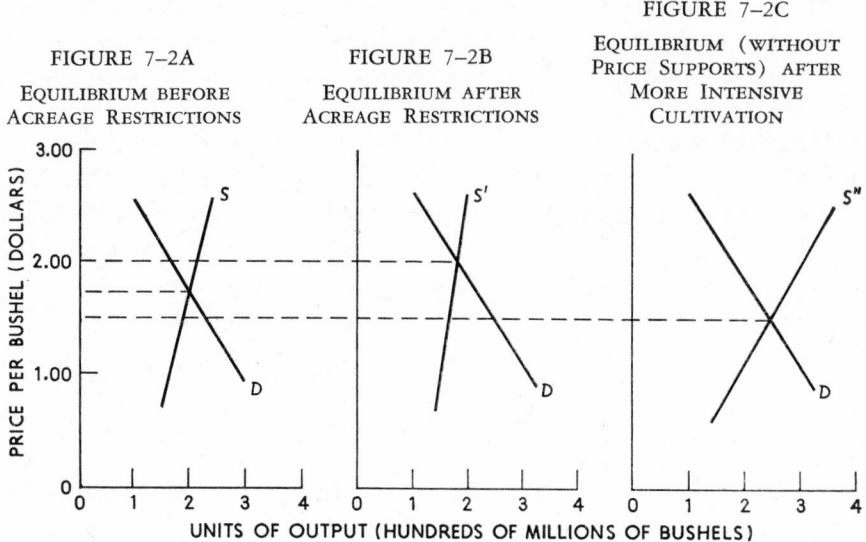

UNITS OF OUTPUT (HUNDREDS OF MILLIONS OF BUSHELS)

ernment is committed to maintain the price at $2.00. In Figure 7–2C, the farmers will offer 300 million bushels for sale at a price of $2.00, but the consumers will buy only 180 million bushels at that price. The government must purchase the difference of 120 million bushels at a price of $2.00 if this price is to be maintained. The moment that the government ceases to buy up this surplus, the price will fall to its market level of $1.50. The government in this example would acquire the ownership of 120 million bushels of wheat at a cost of $240 million dollars. This is what has actually been happening in the instance of governmental support of agricultural prices.

The case of the government supporting a price at a level above the normal market price is just the reverse of the black market in which the price was pegged at a level below the normal market price. The problem of the black market was one of enforcement of the governmentally established price. The problem of the high price support as in agricultural support prices is the handling of the surplus production which consumers will not purchase.

An Excise Tax

A third application of the demand and supply analysis is an excise or sales tax levied upon a particular commodity. Let us start by assuming the conditions of demand and supply as represented by D and S in Figure 7–3A. The consumers are willing to purchase two units at a price

FIGURE 7–3A

EQUILIBRIUM BEFORE EXCISE TAX

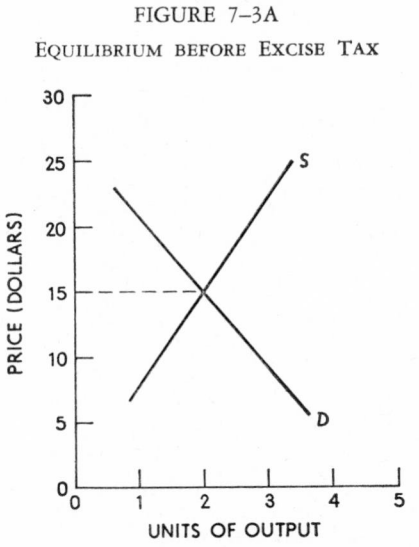

FIGURE 7–3B

EQUILIBRIUM AFTER EXCISE TAX

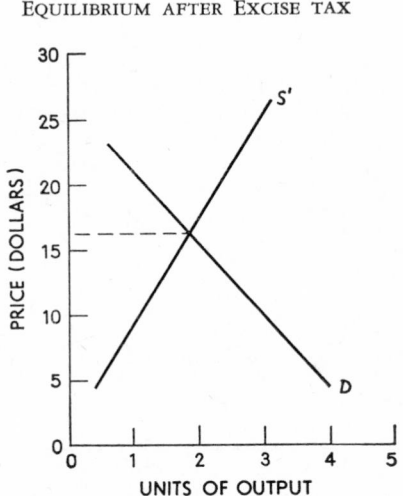

of $15. This is an equilibrium situation as the amount demanded equals the amount supplied at this price.

Now a tax is imposed upon this particular product. The effect of the tax will be that of reducing the supply of the commodity—at every price, less will be offered for sale. So if a tax of $3.00 were imposed on each unit sold, the supply curve would shift upward by the amount of the tax. In other words, the same amounts would be supplied at the original prices plus, in each instance, the tax of $3.00. The consumers originally purchased two units at a price of $15, but after the tax they will reduce their consumption to 1.8 units and will pay a price of $16. This new equilibrium situation is represented by the intersection of D and S' in Figure 7–3B.

The actual effect of a tax on price and consumption, then, will depend upon the elasticities of supply and demand. The following observation can be made. The more elastic the demand, the greater will be the output adjustments. The less elastic the demand, the greater will be the price adjustments. If it were perfectly inelastic, the entire adjustment would be in price. A tax imposed on a commodity with an elastic demand will result in a smaller amount of tax being passed on to the consumer in the form of higher prices. In such an instance, the tax burden would be shared by seller and buyer. For those commodities with less elastic demand, the consumer will bear a proportionately larger portion of the tax in the form of higher prices, and if the demand were perfectly inelastic, the consumer would bear the entire burden of the tax. The case of an excise tax imposed on a commodity with an elastic demand is represented in Figure 7–4A, and that of a tax imposed on one with a less

FIGURE 7–4A

EXCISE TAX—ELASTIC DEMAND

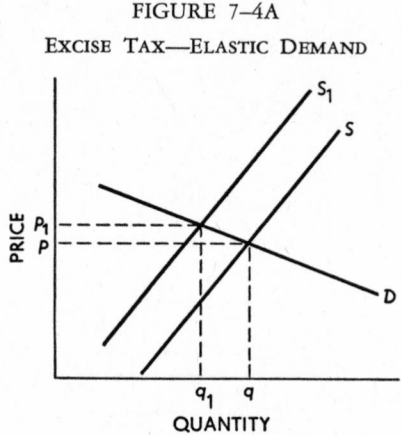

QUANTITY

FIGURE 7–4B

EXCISE TAX—INELASTIC DEMAND

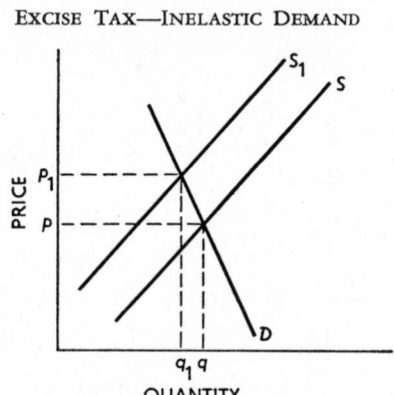

QUANTITY

elastic demand is represented in Figure 7–4B. In the first, the tax burden is divided between the two and in the latter it is borne almost entirely by the consumer. In Figure 7–4A, there is a large reduction in the amount demanded but a relatively small increase in price. In the second illustration the reverse is true.

If a tax is levied upon a commodity with an inelastic demand schedule, there will be little reduction in output and the price will increase by nearly the amount of the tax. Thus there will be an increase in total revenue nearly equal to the tax multiplied by the number of units produced. The tax would be profitable. If, on the other hand, the tax were imposed on a commodity having a very elastic demand, there would be a larger reduction in the level of output and a smaller increase in price. The increase in total revenue would be less than the amount obtained when the tax was multiplied by the units sold. It is for this reason that commodities such as cigarettes, gasoline, and automobile tires are taxed. By the same reasoning, a governmental monopoly on matches will produce more revenue than would a governmental monopoly on jewelry.

Technological Innovation

Whereas a tax causes the supply schedule to shift upward so that less will be offered at every price, technological innovations have the opposite effect. If new and more productive techniques of marketing, production, or organization are introduced, it means that the same amounts can be offered for sale at lower prices. Or, larger amounts could be offered at the same prices. The result would be expressed by shifting the supply curve downward to represent an increase in supply. If it is assumed that the conditions underlying the demand schedule remain unchanged, such a development would cause a reduction in the price of the commodity. Obviously any development which shifted the supply curve to the left and resulted in higher prices could not be classed as technological innovation but would have to be considered as being the reverse or technological retrogradation.

Subsidies

From time to time during the history of this country, subsidies have been used by the various levels of government to encourage production of a particular product. Early colonial and state governments used such a technique to promote the establishment of salt works, canals, iron works, and other industries which those economies needed. The United States government has used the subsidy to promote the construction of railroads, and to encourage agricultural production during times of war.

If the government were to pay the producer a flat amount for each unit produced, the effect would be an increase in the supply, for the same amounts would be offered at the original prices less the amount of the subsidy. In World War II the agricultural subsidy was used in this fashion in an effort to relieve the upward pressure on prices. This was also the essence of the Brannan Plan in the 1940's for agriculture, which was never adopted, as well as the Benson Plan in the 1950's for wool, which was adopted. The net effect is a reduction in the price of the product without a reduction in the amount supplied.

A subsidy for consumers would have the same general effect, but the mechanism would be slightly different. In this case the consumer would receive the payment and it would, in effect, increase his demand for the commodity. Consumers would now be willing to buy more at each price which, it nothing else changed, would cause an upward movement of the price. If the mechanism of the subsidy were such that the consumer were reimbursed for part of his expenditures on a particular commodity, then the effect would be a lowering of that particular price. Consumer subsidies have never been widely used in this country.

Selling Activities

A firm must reach some decision as to the price charged and the output produced. At the same time these decisions are being made, a third decision must also be made, for it is part and parcel of the first two. This third decision is that concerned with the selling activities of the firm. For the price to be charged and the output to be sold are directly dependent, with one exception, upon the effort expended in advertising and other selling activities.

The firm operating under conditions of pure competition can do nothing but sell at the market price. The individual producer gains nothing by advertising, for the product of one firm is a perfect substitute for the product of all others. In addition, the individual producer can sell all that he produces at the market price and nothing at any higher price. So nothing would be gained by advertising on the part of one of the firms in the industry. The whole industry, however, might find it profitable to advertise. The industry demand schedule is not perfectly elastic in the sense that any amount can be sold at any market price. There are substitutes for the product, although they will not be perfectly substitutable. It frequently happens that such an industry finds that the demand for the product is decreasing because of a change in the nature of the buyer's consumption habits. To offset such a development, some competitive industries have levied a small assessment upon the individual producers in order to finance an advertising program designed to increase the sales of the entire industry—milk and dairy products, for example.

A segment of an industry which is essentially competitive might also undertake an advertising campaign if it thought it could possibly remove itself from the confines of the competitive industry. Suppose that the firms in a particular part of the country sell a product which is essentially substitutable for the products of other producers in other parts of the country. There is a single price for all. Now if the consumers can be convinced that the output of this particular part of the industry is superior to that produced by the remainder of the industry, then the group in question can charge a higher price. The consumers, believing that this is a superior product, will continue to purchase the commodity at that higher price. Prime examples of such action include potatoes and cranberries. Housewives no longer merely buy potatoes. They buy Idaho potatoes, Maine potatoes, Wisconsin potatoes, or just potatoes. And the various types of potatoes are not perfect substitutes. In fact, the promotional activities of the Idaho potato producers have been so successful that some consumers are convinced that the Idaho potato is a particular species of potato. Thus through advertising and the various promotional activities the producers of Idaho potatoes have made the demand schedule for their product somewhat less elastic. The result is a higher price for Idaho potatoes than for potatoes produced in other parts of the United States.

It is in the noncompetitive markets, however, that one finds the largest amounts of advertising. Such advertising takes a variety of forms and is intended to accomplish a number of goals. Some is designed to educate the consumer regarding the availability of the product and its quality. Other advertising is for the purpose of persuading the customer to regard the product as being something it is not. Much of the product differentiation exists only in the consumer's mind as a result of the advertising program of the producer. Still another type of advertising may have nothing to do with the product. This is institutional advertising which, at best, has only an indirect effect on sales. And finally, some advertising has as its purpose the recovery of consumers who had substituted the products of other firms for the one now engaged in the advertising program. In such a program consumers are pulled to and fro between the producers, but there is no increase in total production or total consumer satisfaction.

In terms of economic theory, advertising is designed to accomplish either or both of two goals. First, it is hoped that through advertising the demand for the product may be increased. Shifting the demand schedule to the right will enable the firm to sell a larger output at a higher price, although the exact change in price and output will depend upon the elasticity of demand. In general, the more elastic the demand, the greater will be the increase in output, and the less elastic the demand, the greater will be the increase in price. As a practical matter, an increase in demand resulting from increased selling activities will result in readjustments in both price and output.

The second purpose of advertising is to make the demand schedule less elastic. The accomplishment of such an objective permits the producer to increase his price without losing a proportional amount of sales. Thus he could increase his total revenue by selling a smaller amount at a higher price. Furthermore, the less elastic the demand schedule, the less need be his concern regarding the actions of the firm's competitors. If the consumer is convinced that this particular product is superior to all others and that the others are, at best, poor substitutes, then changes in the prices of the products will not cause a material shift in consumption. In other words, through advertising a producer hopes to create a situation which gives him more leeway in his price policy.

Advertising expenditures not only affect the demand, but such expenditures also affect the cost schedules of the advertising firm. As selling activities increase, total costs will increase. The entrepreneur will continue to increase his total outlay for such programs as long as it is anticipated that the additional cost is less than the increase in total revenue. Once the additional costs exceed the additional revenue, no further selling activities will take place.

The net effect of advertising, however, must be discussed in terms of the average cost. Such expenditures are, for the most part, in the nature of a variable cost in that there is a direct relationship between production and sales promotion costs. However, if the increase in costs is less than the increase in output, the average variable cost credited to advertising will be smaller at higher levels of output. Likewise if the increase in costs exceeds the increase in output, the average variable cost resulting from advertising will increase. Just as there is some optimum combination of the factors of production resulting in the lowest average cost, there is also some optimum combination of output and advertising expenditures where the cost per unit for advertising is at a minimum. If because of increased advertising expenditures the firm is permitted to move toward this optimum combination of all factors, including advertising, the average total cost will decline. If this reduction in average total cost exceeds the larger expenditures for advertising, the result will be an enlarged output at a lower unit cost. Where this is the case—which may be rather seldom—advertising benefits society by permitting a greater amount of consumer satisfaction at lower costs.

There is no doubt that many advertising expenditures do not fall in such a cost-reducing category. Some advertising does not result in a more efficient level of operations but merely increases total costs of production without any appreciable increase in output. Such advertising would be hard to justify.

One other point must be made. Advertising does support a great deal of our communication media and provides a large part of our entertainment. Television and radio as well as newspapers and magazines are all supported by the advertising expenditures of the economy's producers. Thus a large part of the ultimate cost of the TV spectacular, as well as of the 25-cent magazine and the daily newspaper, is borne by those who smoke, eat breakfast cereals, use deodorant, or consume other advertised products. This does give rise to an interesting problem, although it is not strictly an economic problem. In effect, the consumers of the TV and radio shows or newspapers and magazines are being subsidized by the consumer of the advertised products. The price for the former is much below that which it would be if the consumer of each product had to pay the full cost. Certainly if each had to receive a price covering its costs, there would undoubtedly be some readjustment of resources.

Summary

The demand and supply analysis is probably the simplest tool employed by economists in the field of pricing. It is of value to the student because it not only explains particular situations but also introduces a more rigorous type of thinking. Through the use of this relatively uncomplicated tool, some rather complicated problems can be resolved. This may be the long-run gain to be derived from these few pages.

PRICE DISCRIMINATION

To this point, the concern has been with demand and supply. Now our attention will turn to the relationship between the demand for the product and the cost of production. It has already been established that the curve representing average cost will go through a decreasing phase followed by an increasing phase. A noncompetitive producer will select that combination of price and output which will yield him a maximum profit; however, as he expands production to take advantage of the lower costs, he will also have to lower the price in order to sell the larger amount of goods. The problem is how to take advantage of lower costs of production at higher levels of output without reducing the price. Price discrimination is one answer to this perplexing question. A policy of price discrimination merely means that the same product will be sold at two or more prices. But before the complexities of price discrimination can be explored, it is necessary to say a few words regarding the fixed costs.

The Importance of Fixed Costs

Steel, aluminum, automobiles, aircraft, appliances, petroleum, transportation, electrical power, and a variety of other industries require a very large capital investment in order to produce any output at all. The fixed costs in such areas constitute a large percentage of the total costs for firms in these industries. In any instance where the fixed costs do constitute a large portion of the total costs, it is possible for a firm to reduce average cost of production by increasing its level of output with existing fixed investment. Expanding the output will lower the average fixed costs, and if this reduction exceeds the increase in the average variable costs, average total costs will fall. And of course, the more significant the fixed costs are, the greater will be the tendency for this to happen. The larger the percentage of total costs which are fixed, the more interest will be shown by management in utilizing the fixed factor in a more efficient manner and the less will be shown regarding the more efficient utilization of the variable factor. More efficient use of the fixed factor will lower average total cost more than the less efficient use of the variable factor will increase average total cost.

Conditions Requisite for Price Discrimination

Any producer operating in a noncompetitive market is aware that there are some buyers who are willing to pay a price in excess of that which they actually pay for the product. He is also aware that there are some who would purchase the product if the established price were lower. In other words, if the price were set at a dollar, there would be some who would be willing to pay more than that while others would buy the product if the price were less. Now if the firm could charge each customer the maximum that the individual was willing to pay, the firm would make a larger profit than that made by charging all customers the same price. Total profits would increase both because sales increased and because the larger output could be produced at a lower cost.

But charging two or more prices for the same product is not a simple feat. It can only be accomplished under certain well-defined conditions. First, the seller must be able to separate his market into its several components based upon the elasticity of demand in each. That part of the market which has the less elastic demand schedule will be charged a higher price. The price will be lower in the market which has the more elastic demand schedule. The several divisions of the market may be separated by distance and prohibitive transportation costs, legal barriers such as a tariff, consumer tastes and preferences, uses of the product, or other similar dividing mechanisms.

The second condition is that it must be impossible for a person to buy in the lower-price market and resell in the higher-price market. If it were possible to move freely from one market to the other, any program of price discrimination would collapse. One reason that a surgeon can charge different prices for the same surgical operation is that a used appendectomy has no resale value.

These two conditions are much more apt to prevail in the case of monopoly than in the other forms of noncompetitive markets. Price discrimination cannot be practiced at all in a competitive market. But even the oligopolist is able to engage in price discrimination since he does have a monopoly on his branded item. And of course if the oligopolists acted in collusion, the industry would be, in effect, one of monopoly, and price discrimination could be practiced.

The Operation of a Policy of Price Discrimination

The first step in implementing a decision to practice price discrimination is that of separating the markets on the basis of the elasticity of demand in each. A sales schedule will be estimated for each of the possible markets to indicate the quantity which could be sold at various prices. Then the increase in total revenue resulting from additional sales in each of the markets would be estimated. Once these separate estimates of average revenue and marginal revenue have been made, the entrepreneur would total these schedules for the several markets. At this stage the entrepreneur has sales schedules and marginal revenue schedules for each of the divisions of his total market, and he also has total sales and total marginal revenue schedules for the firm's entire operation. To maximize the profits of the undertaking, that amount will be produced which will equate total marginal revenue and marginal cost. The only remaining step is to allocate the sales between the different parts of the market and to set a price for each market. The output will be allocated between the markets by equating the marginal revenue in the particular market with total marginal cost. By so doing, the entrepreneur is receiving the maximum possible profit from each market. Nothing can be said in general about the relative amounts sold in the several markets, but the price in the market with the less elastic demand will be higher than the price in the market with the more elastic demand.

Now although the foregoing may sound somewhat technical and unreal, it should be pointed out that price discrimination is a common business practice; in fact, it is probably much more common than most people realize. In addition, the actual practitioners of price discrimination follow the above procedure rather closely. A few examples of price discrimination may serve to illuminate the situation.

Discrimination Based on Time. The elasticity of demand for a particular product will often vary considerably over a period of time. If all other conditions are satisfied, it becomes possible for the entrepreneur to charge different prices during different time periods. The motion picture theater is a prime example. The demand for movies is much more elastic during the day than during the evening hours when there are fewer acceptable substitutes for those who might attend the movies. And the demand is most elastic for the "Saturday morning" crowd who have a countless number of substitutes. So the children who attend the Saturday morning "matinee" may be able to see a picture for 35¢ while the adults may pay 85¢ to see the show in the afternoon and $1.50 to see it that evening. The same thing is true of resort facilities and other commodities where there is a seasonal demand.

The reasoning of the theater manager is as follows. A large part of his costs are fixed. Such costs would include the capital investment, part of the wages and salaries, part of the maintenance and upkeep, a large part of heating and air conditioning, and a part of the firm's taxes. And the shorter the time period, the larger the portion of the total costs which are fixed, until, in the case of a single showing, all costs are fixed in the sense that the total costs will be practically the same regardless of whether the theater is half full or filled to capacity. So the percentage of total costs which vary will always be rather small and will, in some instances, be practically zero. Thus any time that the manager can recover anything above the small variable costs, it will be to his advantage to do so. In fact, in the case of a single showing, as long as an additional viewer contributes anything at all to the total revenue of the firm, it will be profitable to admit him, even if the price has to be lowered to do so. Thus it is profitable to admit children at a fraction of the adult fare just as it is profitable to run a "Saturday morning" matinee or sell the poorer seats at something below the price charged for the better seats. As long as the marginal revenue received by admitting one more customer is positive, it will pay to sell him a ticket.

Discrimination Based on the Use of the Product. A single product may be used in different fashions by the same consumer or it may be used differently by different consumers. If the elasticity of demand varies from one use to the other, then it will be possible to charge different prices providing that it is still impossible to buy in the lower-price market and resell in the dearer market. A good example of this type of discrimination is the sale of electricity. A power company will have a family of rates covering a rather wide range. For the householder, it is often possible to buy power at two rates—one for providing light for the house and a second and lower rate for heating water. Commercial users will pay a lower rate for electric power, and industrial users will pay a still lower rate for the same commodity. The several rates reflect the several elasticities of demand. The demand for power to light a home is very inelastic since there are no acceptable substitutes. The demand for power to heat hot water is more elastic since there are good substitutes—gas and oil. And the industrial user not only has alternative fuels but also the possibility of generating his own electric power.

The generation of electrical power involves a peculiar cost situation which makes price discrimination especially attractive. A power company must have sufficient generating capacity to provide the power required by its customers during peak periods of consumption. If this capacity exists, and consumption is less than this maximum, there will be excess capacity in the sense that turbines will be running idle. If the power company could sell the power which could be generated with existing equipment, it would pay them to do so even if the price had to be lowered. They would be willing to sell it at prices which just covered their variable costs. For this reason many power companies sell electric power for heating hot water at a much lower rate than that sold for lighting if the consumer will agree to use that power during the night when not all of the company's facilities are being used. This is an example of a single consumer paying two different prices for the same product.

Discrimination Based on Geographical Location. It has often been true in foreign trade, for example, that the price in the foreign market has been lower than the price in the domestic market for the same commodity. And this is done, even though the costs in the foreign market are increased by larger transportation costs. This particular practice of price discrimination is known by the technical term "dumping."

The demand for the product in the foreign market will generally be more elastic since the number of substitutes will be larger in that country. In the domestic market the producer may have some monopoly power, meaning the customers feel the substitutes are not quite satisfactory, whereas in the foreign markets the buyers have the products of foreign producers to choose if they so desire. Since there are different elasticities of demand in the domestic and foreign markets and since the costs of transportation preclude its shipment back to the domestic market, it is possible for the entrepreneur to sell at a lower price in the foreign market.

If the producer were to sell the entire output in the domestic market, it would be necessary to establish a price below that which would prevail if only a part of the output were to be sold in this market. However, if a part of the product can be sold in another market, in this case the foreign market, then the producer can still take advantage of the lower average cost at the higher level of production without being forced to lower his price in order to sell the product. Thus the price in the foreign market need be only high enough to recover the variable costs associated with their production, and if such sales do contribute to the firm's fixed costs, that amount can nearly be classified as additional profit. Therefore, the increased profit may not come so much from the foreign sales as from lower average costs of production. Again through price discrimination the producer is able to increase his profits beyond what would have been possible in the absence of such a policy.

Discrimination Based on Differences in Quality (Real or Alleged). Largely through advertising, consumers can be led to believe that one brand is definitely superior to all others, whereas, in fact, the various brands may be so nearly identical as to be indistinguishable. There can be little difference, for example, between aspirin tablets. Different brands of automobile tires selling at different prices are made by the same producer. Practically the only difference between certain brands of appliances is to be found in the name tag. The same product may be sold on different floors of a department store at different prices. Yet in these instances and many others the consumer is so convinced that the products are different that he is willing to continue buying the higher-priced item.

The following hypothetical example may serve to illustrate the reasoning of the producer. Suppose that a producer of washing machines sponsors an extensive advertising program. However, in spite of the advertising, the firm has the physical equipment to produce more washing machines than can be sold at the price selected. This extra capacity can then be utilized if the firm can sell the remaining machines under another brand name at a lower price and through another retail outlet. Of course, the trim and physical appearance will be changed, but apart from the outward appearance the two washing machines are identical or nearly so. Now the demand for the advertised brand will be less elastic, at least if the advertising has been a success, and the demand for the remainder will be more elastic. And since it is impossible to buy one brand of washing machine and resell it as another, the former will have a price above that of the latter. Again the firm will increase its total profit.

Discrimination Based on Differences in Quantity. There are certain economies associated with large-scale production, such as the selling and shipping of large lots, but there have been and continue to be price differences which exceed these economies. When the price differential actually exceeds such economies, price discrimination is being practiced. Such practice is illegal when it serves to lessen competition, and as far as the consumer is concerned, it is probably of little importance.

In summary, it might once again be pointed out that in each of the above cases of price discrimination it was possible to divide the markets on the basis of elasticity of demand. In each case it was impossible to buy in the lower-price market and resell in the higher-price market. Where such conditions prevail, it is possible for the entrepreneur to discriminate between customers in the sense that some customers will pay a higher price for the product than will others. It should be emphasized that this is legal with the one exception noted above. It is a common business practice designed to increase the total profits of the firm. It is especially well adapted to those firms in which fixed costs are a high percentage of total costs. And it can only be practiced where the producing firm has some degree of monopoly power.

PRICING TECHNIQUES

Price competition has undesirable aspects for all business firms, but especially for firms where a large percentage of cost remains constant regardless of the level of output. In those industries the economies of scale are such that a very few producers can supply a quantity sufficient to satisfy the wants of the consumers. Such oligopolistic industries are characterized by a high degree of interdependence. Any time one firm changes its prices, the remaining firms will be forced to do likewise. Under these conditions price competition would be, to say the least, chaotic, for the firms would, in the short run, be willing to sell at any price which would recover only their marginal costs, and this could be a very low price. Such price competition does occur from time to time in the form of price wars, but such a manifestation of competition is regarded as an economic conflagration of the most serious type to be extinguished as expeditiously as possible.

In a competitive market there can be only a single price. The process by which that price is established has already been discussed. Now in an oligopolistic market each firm may have a price policy, and, theoretically at least, there could be as many prices as there are firms. In practice, there is often only a single price. The mechanism by which that price is established, however, is somewhat different than the mechanism which operates in the competitive market.

Price Leadership

Price leadership is that situation in which one producer announces the price for his product and all other producers of that product follow suit. If the products are perfect substitutes, such as steel, all firms will charge the same price. If the products are merely close substitutes, then there may be a difference in the price of the products of the several firms, but even in this instance an announcement of a price change by one would be followed by comparable changes by the others. The differential would be maintained.

Price Leadership by a Single Firm. Price leadership can exist in either of two types of market structures. In industries dominated by a single firm with a very large percentage of the industry's total capacity, the smaller firms have little choice but to follow the actions of the larger firm. If they were to lower their price to such an extent that they began to encroach upon the larger firm's business, the latter might well engage in retaliatory price cutting. And of course nothing would be gained by raising their price above that of the price leader, for it would merely reduce their sales. So in such an industry the smaller producer has little choice but to follow the pricing policies of the industry leader and hope that the latter's decision regarding price is satisfactory for the small producer.

Now such a price policy need not be detrimental to the interests of the smaller firms in the industry. If the large firm desires to be the price leader, it must set a price which will permit the continued operation of the smaller or less efficient firms. If the smaller firms are the more efficient, they will gain, for the price leader will naturally set a price which will cover his costs. And, in addition, the price leader must also take into consideration the potential actions of the government. A predatory policy which resulted in driving smaller firms out of business would result in an antitrust action against the price leader. So a program of price leadership, then, is designed to insure price uniformity rather than to reduce competition by reducing the number of firms in the industry.

Price Leadership by Several Firms. A second situation in which price leadership will prevail or may prevail is that in which a few producers of about the same size follow the same price policy. There may be no single firm which consistently fills the role of the price leader but rather a well-established tradition that whenever one firm changes its prices, the other members of the industry will do likewise. In this instance there is a tenuous line between free and open price determination and collusion. There is nothing wrong when one firm changes its price in response to changes made by another. The theory of oligopolistic pricing would lead one to expect this to happen. But there is some question as to the propriety of the firms getting together and making a collective decision as to the price to be charged and then selecting one of their number to make the decision public. Such a collusive policy would have some of the undesirable features of monopoly.

Instances of price leadership are not hard to find in the history of

American industry. Probably the most famous was that associated with the steel industry during the early years of the present century. The famous Gary dinners sponsored by the president of the United States Steel Corporation served as the media. During the course of these periodic dinners, Judge Gary would state the policy of U.S. Steel in regard to the price of steel, and the steel magnates representing the other firms in the industry would then find their way clear to follow the same pricing policy.

But price leadership has not been confined to steel. At various times it has existed in such diverse industries as crude oil and petroleum, cigarettes, tin cans, farm implements, nonferrous metals, cement, corn products, and many others. The student might find the story of price leadership in cigarettes to be an especially interesting chapter in pricing policy and American history.

The Economic Effect of Price Leadership. A policy of price leadership does not mean that there will be no competition whatsoever in the industry. It means only that there will be no price competition. The firms may and do compete through such means as advertising and product improvements. The latter forms of competition are much more genteel than rough-and-tumble price competition.

If price leadership, then, has a deleterious effect, it must be, in part, because price competition possesses some virtue. This happens to be the case. Price competition is desired because it puts a constant pressure on the producer to lower price in order to increase sales. To lower price, cost must be lowered. To lower costs, the firm must operate more efficiently. Thus the elimination of price competition certainly reduces, if it does not eliminate, an important motive for increasing efficiency of operation. This is probably the great harm stemming from a lack of price competition.

A second disadvantage is the fact that the price leader will generally set a price which protects the more inefficient firm. If it is a lower-cost producer acting as price leader, it must do so in order to preserve its role as the price leader. And a higher-cost producer would naturally do so. In either case the more efficient firms are making profits beyond that which would be necessary to keep them in business. Thus it keeps resources in this industry which might better be in other areas where their contribution to society would be greater.

Basing Point Pricing

A second method of insuring uniform prices is the use of a basing point system of price determination. This technique represents both price discrimination and price leadership. It is a form of price discrimination, since the seller receives differing mill net prices from the several purchasers. It has generally represented price leadership, since it has usually been inaugurated by a single powerful firm or a combination of several firms. Once established, however, it has been followed by all firms in the industry. In fact, a basing point system of pricing could not long exist unless all of the firms in the industry followed the same practice.

What Is Basing Point Pricing? A consumer buying a commodity to be delivered purchases the commodity as well as an additional service—transportation. The consumer making such a purchase usually pays two prices—the price of the commodity and the price of the service. In such an instance all transportation costs are paid by the consumer. Under such a pricing system the individual consumer would pay a price different than that paid by consumers located either nearer to the seller or further from the seller. Now this practice is so common that one might think that there is no other. This is not the case.

The industrial purchaser, like the consumer, purchases two items —the commodity itself and the service necessary to move it from the place of its production to the location of its use. In many instances, however, the purchaser paid a single price for the two, but that price has not always been equal to the cost of the product plus the cost of delivery. The actual price may be either more or less than the actual price plus cost of delivery. In those instances in which the transportation costs constitute a very large percentage of the total costs, there exists a very strong incentive to use the cost of transportation as a means of shaving the price to meet competition or, on the other hand, to increase the firm's profit position by charging the buyer more for transportation services than those services actually cost. The basing point system of pricing permits just this.

A basing point system of pricing may be either a single basing point or a multiple basing point system. First, a few words in explanation of the single basing point system. In determining the price under such an arrangement, all producers will use the price of the product at the basing point. This includes those firms whose plants are not located at the basing point. To this base price is added the transportation costs from the basing point to the location of the customer. All firms use this transportation charge, even though they may not be located at the basing point and their actual transportation costs are different from the producer located at the basing point. The result of such a pricing practice is a single uniform price to the buyer. It matters not whether the supplier is located across the street or across the country. The price in either case is the base price plus the cost of transportation from the basing point to the location of the purchaser.

Under a multiple basing point system a somewhat different arrangement is found. If there are two or more basing points, it is the basing point nearest the buyer which is used in the determination of the price. The combination of the cost of the product at the various basing points and the cost of transportation from these basing points to the location of the buyer is computed. That combination of price and transportation charge which is lower than all other combinations is the one to be used. Thus a producer in City A might use City B as a basing point in computing the price to be charged a buyer in City C. The buyer would then pay the price of the product in B plus the costs of moving the prod-

FIGURE 7–5

BASING POINT PRICING

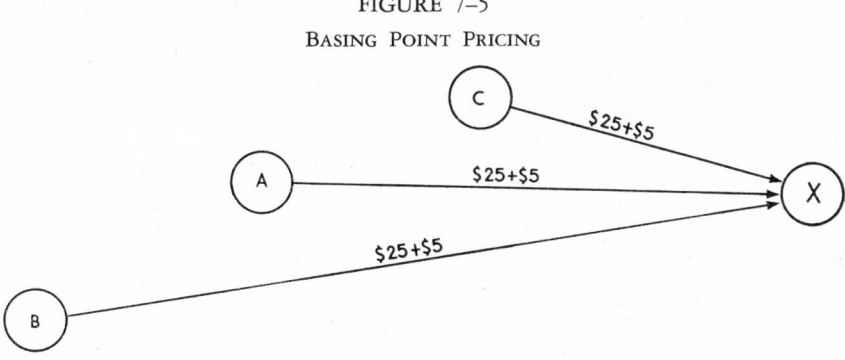

uct from B to C even though the goods were produced in A and were moved from A to C. And the same would be true for producers located in all other cities and selling to a buyer in City C. As was the case under a single basing point system, the result is a uniform price to buyers. There would be no need to shop in anticipation of a lower price, for regardless of producer, the price will be the base price plus the costs of transportation from the basing point.

Under either form of the basing point system there are sales which result in the seller absorbing freight costs and other sales which result in the seller charging more for freight than the services actually cost. The first is known as freight absorption and the latter is known as phantom freight. Let us assume for the purposes of demonstration that there are three producers in an industry, whose locations are represented in Figure 7–5 by A, B, and C. The customer is located at X. A is the basing point. Now let us further assume that the base price is $25 and the cost of moving the good from A to X is $5.00. All three producers, then, will charge the customer at X $30—$25 for the commodity and

$5.00 for transportation. In the case of the producer at *A*, the realized net mill price will be $25. The costs of transportation for the producer at *B*, however, will exceed $5.00 and thus his net mill price will be less than $25. He will be absorbing freight in order to sell to *X*. The cost of transportation for the producer at *C* will be less than $5.00, and his realized net mill price will thus exceed $25. Since he is charging the customer more for freight than that service actually costs, this producer is realizing phantom freight. It would also be possible for the producers at *A* and *B* to realize phantom freight. If the allowances for transportation were based upon the cost of rail freight, then the producers at these two points might be able to ship more cheaply using some other means of transportation. If the producers at *A* or *B* could ship by barge at a cost of $3, they would realize phantom freight. Now of course each seller will be in a position to gain on some sales, but on others he will have to absorb freight. The determining factors are the locations of the seller, the basing point, and the buyer.

The above rather simplified description of the basing point system of pricing represents the basic mechanics of the system as it has been practiced in the United States. This peculiar system of pricing has had a profound effect upon the pattern of development of particular industries within our economic system.

The Economics of Basing Point Pricing. In an economy with a freely operating price system or even in an industry with such a mechanism, each firm or each mill will have what might be termed a "natural" market area based upon its location, costs of transportation, and availability of transportation facilities. The market for the individual producer would extend outward in all directions until the cost of production plus the transportation costs to the buyer were equal to the costs of the firm's competitors. On the border of each such market area there would be a zone of indifference. The buyers in this area would be indifferent as to which firm they purchased from, since the costs of production plus the costs of transportation are equal for the two suppliers. In such a situation the costs of transportation would preclude one seller selling in the market of the other unless that seller were willing to absorb the differences in the cost of transportation.

Such a market situation can be described in terms of elasticity. In the market area in which any producer has a competitive advantage based on location, the demand will be more inelastic within the relevant price range because of the paucity of substitutes. On the other hand, producers will regard the demand for their product as being more elastic in the more distant markets because of the availability of substitutes. Since the costs of transportation preclude the shipment of the product back to the market area of the producing firm, the conditions exist which make it possible for the producer to practice price discrimination. A higher price will be charged in the market adjacent to the plant than will be charged in the more remote market.

Price discrimination will be extremely attractive to many firms with this type of market situation. In industries such as cement and steel, fixed costs constitute a high percentage of total costs. Average variable costs are constant over a wide range of output, for output can be increased from very low to very high levels without any increase in the firm's average variable costs. Since average fixed costs are declining and average variable costs are remaining constant, it follows that the average total costs are declining over an extended range of production. Thus viewed from the cost side, it is to the producer's interest to increase output to take advantage of the lower costs of production at the higher levels of output if this can be done without having to lower the price on the entire output. The market situation makes price discrimination possible; the cost situation makes it highly desirable. The mechanism of price discrimination then is the basing point system of pricing. It permits the producer to realize differing mill nets while at the same time maintaining a single uniform price.

Why is such an elaborate mechanism essential? Why doesn't the producer just openly charge different prices to the individual buyers? The reason again is to be found in the large proportion of total costs which are fixed. A price war or even price competition between firms with heavy fixed costs would be ruinous. A firm could, in the short run, lower its prices until it was only recovering its average variable costs. This would be an extremely low price. Without any form of price control mechanism, there would exist a motive for each firm to invade the market areas of other firms and charge any price which covered marginal costs. Under such a situation there would be a large number of prices and the whole market situation would be extremely chaotic. The basing point pricing system permits the producers to sell in the "natural" market areas of other firms providing they sell at the same price, but it does allow them to realize different amounts of profits on the different sales. To the buyer the prices of all producers are the same. To the seller, different buyers represent different prices.

Such a system of pricing has peculiar economic consequences for the economy. It is what might be termed a monopolistic interference with the free price system and as such it results in an uneconomic allocation of resources. Since each producer is trying to sell in the market areas of competitors, there is some cross-hauling. One firm may be shipping an item into the market area of a second firm while the second is shipping the same item into the market area of the first. Such a practice is an economic waste. For optimum economic efficiency each firm should serve its own market area.

A second result of the basing point system is to be found in its effect on the location of production facilities. The users of steel, for example, would find it to their advantage to locate their plant near the basing point. Since the buyer has to pay the cost of transportation from the basing point, it is to his advantage to locate near that basing point. This is especially true if there is a large weight loss in the productive process. This phenomena took place in the steel industry, for, at least partly as a result of the basing point system of pricing, the steel industry was concentrated in the Pittsburgh area long after it had lost its natural advantage. It was not until there was a large and well-established market for steel in Chicago and Detroit that steel production facilities were built in these areas.

Basing Point Pricing in Action. This type of pricing has been widely used in American industry. Although it has been most often associated with the steel and cement industries, it has also been used in such diverse industries as lumber, petroleum, sugar, and others. Since the first two are the more well known, a few further comments will be made regarding those specific industries.

The basing point system of pricing in steel was first used shortly after the Civil War. Pittsburgh was the sole basing point for most types of steel products. As producers located at other locations, they continued to charge the Pittsburgh price plus the cost of transportation from Pittsburgh to the destination. It was because of this that the pricing system has come to be known as the "Pittsburgh Plus" system of pricing. From time to time other points were used as basing points, but it wasn't until 1924 that the Federal Trade Commission ordered the abandonment of the single basing point system of pricing. It was replaced with a multiple basing point system which prevailed until 1948. In that year the Supreme Court held that even this represented a violation of the country's antitrust laws.[1] As it stands now, the basing point system is largely a thing of the past. It does, however, represent an interesting and important attempt on the part of industrial firms to cope with the problem of large fixed costs while at the same time avoiding chaotic price competition.

[1] *Federal Trade Commission* v. *Cement Institute,* 333 U.S. 683 (1948).

CONCLUSION

A freely operating price system is an integral part of the economic system of the United States. It is the institution which ties the parts of the system together by translating individual decisions into collective decisions. Something like it will be found in all industrialized nations other than those with a highly centralized decision-making apparatus. In the latter, there will be a substitute for the price system for there is no substitute for the functions performed by the price system.

It has been shown in the last three chapter how the price system operates to allocate resources to those ends for which consumers have a high preference. Resources are moved from those goods and services which are not wanted and toward those which are preferred. Any economic system must perform this function. A free price system does it without the services of a government bureaucracy.

But there are other ways of allocating the system's scarce means to the many and varied ends. A system of government planning will do the job. And it is possible, as in Western Europe, to use a combination of planning and prices.

But let us move on and exercise our imagination for a moment. Would it be possible to devise a political system which would perform the functions now performed by the price system with the same results? We might call such a political system the "pure political" model and compare it to the economic model of pure competition.

The first requisite of such a model would be as follows. The political parties would have to be infinitely responsive to changes in public wants. As consumer wants change, the political decision maker would have to be aware of the change and respond appropriately.

A second assumption would be needed to deal with the question of voting weights. Under the price system the weight of any individual in the market place is a function of his wealth. A person with a large stock of wealth exercises more influence than a pauper. In the "pure political" model, each person might be given one vote. This would correspond to a completely equal distribution of wealth. Such arrangement would continue to permit the unsuccessful individual to exercise as much influence as the successful. So if the "pure political" model is to achieve the same results as the economic model, voting rights would have to be assigned on some other basis—perhaps some measure of ability, productive capacity, or wealth.

At this point we will leave it to the student to formulate a rule for the political decision maker to use in the determination of price and output. The student should also consider the relative efficiency of the two methods of making the price-output decisions.

EXERCISES

Group I

Explain why the following statements are true and in what sense they are true:

1. If fixed costs represent a very large part of total costs, pressure is very great to engage in price discrimination.
2. The basing point system of pricing will result in a different industry locational pattern than would exist if the product were priced on the basis of the mill price plus transportation costs.
3. The black market is merely the free market operating during times when the public interest cannot permit its operation.
4. Selling activities are productive activities which benefit the economy as a whole.
5. The monopolist must consider the elasticity of demand for his product in making the price decision.

Group II

1. Is price discrimination an ethical business activity? Explain your answer.
2. Explain how a policy of price discrimination enables a producer to make larger profits than if such a policy were not followed.
3. What would be the results if the price system were to be the sole determining force in selecting what students attended college?
4. Compile a list of the commodities upon which the government has imposed excise taxes. In what cases are the demand schedules relatively inelastic? Why would a government impose excise taxes upon commodities which have relatively elastic demand schedules?

Group III

1. Investigate more fully the agricultural problem. What programs have been used or have been proposed? In what respects did the Republican programs of the 1950's differ from the Democratic program of the 1930's and the 1940's? Can any price support program be devised which will make it unnecessary for the government to accumulate large surpluses? How have the agricultural programs interfered with the allocation of resources?
2. Write a report on "The Economic Effects of Advertising." What evidence do you find that indicates advertising either increases or decreases the cost of the advertised commodity? Does advertising give the large firm an advantage over the small firm in the same industry? How would you analyze the effect of a tax on advertising expenditures?

BIBLIOGRAPHY

BURNS, ARTHUR H. *The Decline of Competition.* New York: McGraw-Hill Book Co., Inc., 1936.

EDWARDS, C. D. *Maintaining Competition: Requisites of a Governmental Policy.* New York: McGraw-Hill Book Co., Inc., 1949.

HOOVER, E. M. AND DEAN, J. (Eds.) *Readings in the Social Control of Industry.* Philadelphia: The Blakiston Co., 1949.

KAPLAN, A. D. H.; DIRLAM, J. B.; AND LANZILLOTI, R. F. *Pricing in Big Business.* Washington, D.C.: Brookings Institution, 1958.

STOCKING, G. W., AND WATKINS, M. W. *Cartels in Action.* New York: Twentieth Century Fund, 1948.

———*Cartels or Competition.* New York: Twentieth Century Fund, 1951.

———*Monopoly and Free Enterprise.* New York: Twentieth Century Fund, 1951.

PAPERBACK READING LIST

LILIENTHAL, DAVID E. *Big Business: A New Era.* New York: Pocket Books, Inc., 1962.

LABOR AND COLLECTIVE BARGAINING

Now let me ask you this question: what can you expect of man seeing that he is a being endowed with such strange qualities? Why, shower all the earthly blessings upon him, drown him in happiness, head over ears, so that only bubbles should be visible on its surface, as on the surface of water; bestow such economic prosperity upon him as would leave him with nothing else to do but sleep, eat cakes, and only worry about keeping world history going—and even then he will, man will, out of sheer ingratitude, out of sheer desire to injure you personally, play a dirty trick on you. He would even risk his cakes and ale and deliberately set his heart on the most deadly trash, the most uneconomic absurdity, and do it, if you please, for the sole purpose of infusing into this positive good sense his deadly fantastic element. It is just his fantastic dreams, his most patent absurdities, that he will desire above all else for the sole purpose of proving to himself (as though that were so necessary) that men are still men and not the keys of a piano on which the laws of nature are indeed playing any tune they like, but are in danger of going on playing until no one is able to desire anything except a mathematical table.—Fyodor Dostoevsky, *Notes from the Underground.*

One of the most important groups of decisions made in any economy are those involved in labor-management relations. Management must decide how many men to hire, what skills are needed, what shall be the hours of work, what wages shall be paid, what other benefits the workers shall receive, how to handle a union, and many other important questions. The worker is concerned with where he will find a job, what kind of a job, what pay he will receive, and what promotions or advancement he might receive. Labor unions are concerned with matters similar to those important to workers, and in addition they have their own worries. What shall they ask for in bargaining? Shall they strike, and if so for how long? Certainly the student can think of hundreds of questions and issues inevitably involved in the pursuit of income through working for someone else.

INTRODUCTION

In 1963 more than 67 million people were working in the United States. Out of a total national income in the United States in 1962 of $458 billion, wages and salaries accounted for $322 billion or approximately 65 per cent of national income.

How and where are the decisions affecting this large segment of the economy made? By whom are they made? The very nature of the employment relationship puts control of labor matters in the hands of the owner of the business. Proprietors and partners have legal control of labor matters in their own businesses. In the corporation, control is usually delegated by the stockholders, the owners of the business, to the board of directors and perhaps in turn to the corporate officers. Historically, the determination of labor matters was very simple. The employer stated his terms of employment, and the worker could either take it or leave it. Of course, the employer's terms had to be competitive with those of other employers, but within the company the employer was the sole determinant of labor questions. The helplessness of the workers in such a situation led to the formation of labor unions through which the workers tried to influence the employer's decisions. Thus, employers surrender part of their prerogatives to their employees when they willingly or unwillingly agree to some or all of the demands of the union. The union's hand was strengthened with the passage of the Railway Labor Act (1926) and the Wagner Act (1935), which force employers to bargain with a properly chosen union of their workers on questions concerning "wages, hours and other terms and conditions of employment." While the employer need not agree to any union demand, he must bargain with the union where a majority of his employees have indicated a desire to be represented by the union.

Since there are only about 18 million union members out of a total labor force of more than 70 million, it might appear that the total union influence upon employment conditions was relatively small. But the figures are misleading. Many people in the labor force are self-employed. Their income is primarily determined by the prices of their product or service. Other members of the labor force are nonunion supervisors and white-collar workers employed by concerns whose production workers are unionized. In such cases, the white-collar wages and other employment benefits are usually strongly influenced by the gains won by the production workers.

In some plants, the union may have only a slight majority of the workers on their membership rolls, yet their contract applies to all of the workers in the bargaining unit. In this case, nonunion workers work under union-bargained terms.

Most nonunion companies are influenced in their determination of terms of employment by union terms in competing and neighboring plants. In order to obtain qualified workers, a nonunion plant may have to meet or better the conditions in the neighboring union plants. And, many companies which have long resisted union organization have done so only by giving their workers wages and other benefits in excess of those won by the union involved. Here again, although the union is not directly involved in setting employment terms, it exercises a strong indirect influence.

Thus, unions in the United States play a significant role in establishing the conditions of employment. In this chapter, we shall discuss unions and management and how they participate in collective bargaining to establish terms of employment. We shall also discuss the role of the government in the field of labor-management relations. In the following chapter, we shall discuss the issues involved in terms and conditions of employment, such as wages, hours of work, security, and other similar matters.

DEVELOPMENT OF AMERICAN UNIONISM

In many ways, labor organizations in the United States differ from similar groups in other countries of the world. Some foreign labor leaders have criticized the American movement as being "immature" in that it does not include an independent political party, espouse socialism, or submit to the leadership of intellectuals with left-wing theories of economics and politics. Yet, in no other country of the world has organized labor achieved such high standards of living as in the United States. American labor focuses its attention on the bargaining arena—either the economic bargain with the employer or the political bargain with the governmental bodies which control and influence labor's economic activities.

Labor unions in the United States differ from other labor organizations not because they are "young" and "immature" but rather because they represent the present stage of a continuing process of evolution—of experiments, of success and failure—through which has been molded a type of organization uniquely suited to the free-enterprise economy. Today's policies are not idle schemes of an intellectual but tested and proven methods of achieving more for the American worker within the framework of the free-enterprise economy. A brief historical review of the development of American unionism will serve to highlight the whys and wherefores of present union policies and methods.

Early Beginnings

There were few labor organizations in the United States prior to the Revolutionary War. There had been scattered instances of typical labor activity, and strikes, but these involved primarily groups resembling medieval guilds more than modern trade unions. That is, the strength of the organization rested upon the employer members, and the bargains frequently were with municipal bodies which regulated prices of certain articles.

Following the Revolutionary War, markets expanded with increasing trade among the several states. Merchant capitalists bought goods from employers and sold them over ever increasing areas of the new country. Competition forced down the price paid to the employer, and he in turn reduced wage rates. Many groups of skilled journeymen and craftsmen such as carpenters, shoemakers, and printers joined together to resist wage reductions. These organizations were local in nature and usually of short duration. The impetus to organization came from the threatened wage reduction, but regardless of whether the journeymen's organization was successful in resisting the cut, the group ordinarily dissolved once the issue was settled. Some of these local craft groups broadened their bargaining demands to include such currently popular issues as shorter hours, apprenticeship regulations, and the closed shop.

Journeymen's organizations were strongly resisted by the employers. The English common-law doctrine of criminal conspiracy was used to suppress concerted worker activities, and an industrial depression in the early nineteenth century brought most of the scattered worker's organizations to their demise. Here is the beginning of a cycle that was to plague American unionism throughout much of its history. In periods of business prosperity, unionism thrives. Prices are rising and real wages are challenged. Business is booming and employers desire to maintain production. Labor is scarce. Rising prices make it easier to pass on wage increases to the public.

However, when the business cycle turns downward, the lot of the union has generally been poor and in many cases disastrous. Unemployed labor is plentiful and ready to undercut union wages. Orders are scarce and strikes do not hurt employers as much as they do in prosperous periods. Constant or even gradually decreasing money wages usually mean rising real incomes for the workingman as prices are falling sharply. Union dues and fees become burdensome to the membership. Traditionally, membership roles have been depleted and many unions have failed to survive economic slumps.

Political and Utopian Programs

When the unions failed to function effectively as bargaining institutions during depressed economic periods, they turned to other methods to attempt to improve the lot of the workingman. Throughout the nineteenth century, many labor organizations undertook political action in an attempt to gain some of their objectives. Some of these political efforts bore fruit. However, their success was fleeting. The initial enthusiasm soon waned, and more skilled politicans adopted the programs of the labor groups and absorbed them into the existing political organizations. And, in the meantime, the expenditures of union funds and leadership effort in politics had marked the end of the union as an effective bargaining institution. This pattern of trade unionism in prosperity and politics in depression characterized the American labor movement until the end of the nineteenth century and was a periodic temptation even later than that.

Another depression diversion was the utopian scheme. Many people felt that workers could never achieve lasting gains under the economic system as it was then organized. They felt that the salvation for the ordinary laborer lay in a new form of society. Many unions turned to producer's co-operatives as an avenue of escape from the fickle wage system. Some of the ventures prospered for a short time, but most failed through a lack of capital or because of inefficient management. And, in those cases where the co-operative was a success, a small group of leaders would gradually seize control of the enterprise and it would take on the characteristics of an ordinary independent capitalistic venture. Other utopian schemes included agrarianism, greenbackism, and experimental communistic societies such as Brook Farm, Massachusetts, and New Harmony, Indiana.

The middle of the nineteenth century was the only time in the history of organized labor in the United States that the labor movement was dominated by the "intellectuals." Most foreign labor movements have always drawn much of their leadership from a group of well-educated intellectuals who are not of working-class origins. American labor has always been suspicious of the intellectual, for its experience during the 1840's and 1850's indicated that, as in the case of political movements, pursuit of utopian objectives saps most of the financial base and leadership effort of the labor organization and deprives it of the essential ingredients for the quest of immediate economic gains.

Development of a National Movement

By the middle of the nineteenth century, the economy had advanced to a point where competition extended beyond the local community, and, in many cases, embraced much of the then existing area of the country. If labor organizations were to improve and maintain standards of employment such standards would have to apply to entire industries. Uniformity of standards was needed throughout each industry, and only national organizations of workers within each industry could insure that uniformity. In the 1850's some local craft unions joined with other locals of their craft to form national unions. The International Typographical Union, the printer's union, dates from this period.

Following the Civil War, there was a movement to form a national labor organization. In 1869, a secret organization was formed in Philadelphia, called the Noble Order of the Knights of Labor. This was a heterogeneous group combining skilled craftsmen, semiskilled and unskilled workers, professional men, and social reformers. The Knights favored the grouping of all members on a geographical basis with the great bargaining power of the skilled workers being used as a lever to improve the status of others. Their membership was never very stable.

The Knights lost several strikes of national prominence during 1886, in part because of lack of effective leadership. Following these defeats the membership fell off rapidly, and The Knights of Labor succumbed to the inevitable lure of politics and ceased to function as an effective labor organization after the 1890's.

The Knights of Labor marked the last significant labor group organized and operated in the pattern which characterized most labor groups up to the latter part of the nineteenth century. Labor seemed unable to profit by its own past mistakes. Rather it continued to pursue the same paths that continued to destroy the movement whenever a period of economic adversity occurred. It seemed that we never would develop a continuing labor movement—an organization that might bend with the winds of economic misfortune but would never bow to them.

The American Federation of Labor

During the period when the Knights of Labor were active there was a small group of labor unions that managed to keep out of the mainstream of labor development in the United States. This small group was organized nationally on a craft basis and dominated philosophically by the cigar makers' union. These trade unionists searched for the weaknesses in the typical American union—weaknesses that resulted in lost strikes and a tendency to fly off on various tangents. They thought the answer lay in the organizational structure. Centralization of power was needed. These unions were organized with most of the governing authority in the hands of the international officers. Dues were raised and benefit programs were established to cement the bonds between the member and the union. Large treasuries were built up to finance the benefit programs, collective bargaining, and strikes. This was a different approach from the "native" emphasis upon co-operatives, utopian dreams, and politics. This was business unionism, concentrating upon the improvement of the economic condition of the trade through collective bargaining with employers. They felt that the average workingman was not particularly interested in some idealistic scheme to change the form of the economy at some remote time in the future. He wanted better pay, shorter hours, and improved working conditions, and he wanted them at the present time. Idealistic schemes gave way to practical, opportunistic objectives.

This was business unionism, pure and simple. Perhaps its philosophy can best be described in Gompers' classic expression of labor's objectives, "More, more, more—now." After almost a century of struggle and frustration, a successful form of unionism was developed, a form peculiarly adapted to the conditions of American society, and a form which has persisted in its basic elements to the present time.

In 1886 the craft unions banded together to form the American Federation of Labor, a federation of national and international trade unions. Each national union was recognized as a sovereign body in its own area. The member unions were almost exclusively organizations of skilled craftsmen. The unskilled men were generally ignored and the only unions embracing many semiskilled or unskilled members at that time were the miners' and the clothing workers' unions.

By the early 1890's, the American Federation of Labor was the unchallenged master of American union organizations. Its member unions continued to grow through that decade and after the turn of the century, even though the early part of the twentieth century was not an easy period for labor unions. They were actively opposed by most employers, and there were few if any rules which limited the employer's ability to strike back. Also the courts generally viewed union activities with considerable hostility. Yet, in spite of this, the movement continued to grow. Union membership reached a high point of approximately five million in 1920—four million in unions affiliated with the AFL. But the momentum generated before and during World War I disappeared and unions suffered a setback. The 1920's marked the only time in our history when union membership failed to grow during a period of economic prosperity. Yet signs pointed to better times. In 1926 the Railway Labor Act was passed. It was the first piece of federal legislation guaranteeing workers the right to organize unions and to bargain collectively with their employers. Only the railroad workers were so protected, but a beginning had been made. Also wages had increased during the decade and the 40-hour week had become general.

The depression beginning in 1929 added to the forces operating against organized labor. Total union membership stood at almost 3.75 million in 1929 but fell to less than 3 million in 1933. But even after a decade of strong opposition, several years of depression, and rather inept leadership in many unions, union membership in 1933 still represented about 60 per cent of its 1920 peak. Labor had come a long way from the nineteenth century.

The 1930's—Labor Finds a New Friend

Almost from the founding of the AFL, that group had remained relatively unconcerned with political events. It is true that the AFL was an active and many times successful lobbyist on behalf of labor, but it did not form any new political organization nor seek to alter the basic structure of the economy through political activities. They operated on a program promulgated by Samuel Gompers—"reward your friends, punish your enemies." But by the 1930's some labor leaders felt that organized labor needed the assistance of the government if it was to advance. Results were almost unbelievably favorable.

In 1932 Franklin D. Roosevelt was elected President of the United States and proceeded with his program to counter the severe depression then in progress. Many of the laws passed in his New Deal program served organized labor well. In 1933 the National Industrial Recovery Act gave labor the right to organize and bargain collectively, although with no effective way to enforce that right. And the National Labor Relations Act (the Wagner Act) in 1935 strengthened labor's position when it gave the worker the legal right to organize unions and bargain collectively with employers. Labor quickly took advantage of the government assistance and union membership again began to grow. But there was one retarding factor. Most of the workers in the country were employed in the mass-production industries. But there were no unions of any consequence in these industries, and the existing craft unions seemed unwilling to give up any jurisdictional rights to the new unions. A few AFL leaders urged the formation of new industrial unions, based on the industry in which the man works as contrasted with the old craft unions whose membership was based upon the type of job performed. John L. Lewis and Sidney Hillman were the leaders of the industrial-union movement; however, they represented a minority in the AFL and their proposals were defeated. Therefore, Lewis and his supporters organized a new group which became the Congress of Industrial Organizations (CIO). By World War II this federation consisted of most of the original unions which had joined with Lewis plus the newly formed industrial unions in the automobile, steel, rubber, and other mass production industries.

The creation of a second labor federation spurred organizational activity, as the unions in both federations attempted to gain new members. The Wagner Act made such organization relatively easy. In 1937 many of the antiunion bastions, including such giants as General Motors and U.S. Steel, fell before the new industrial unions of the CIO. In 1935 there had been less than 4 million union members. By 1940, there were almost 9 million union members, with slightly more in the AFL than in the new CIO.

Labor Comes of Age

Labor union membership continued to grow during World War II, until there were almost 15 million union members in 1945. The immediate postwar period saw the greatest wave of strikes in the history of the country. One hundred sixteen million man-days of labor were lost through strikes in 1946. These strikes only served to add to the distrust of labor which was prevalent among many groups in the country. By the end of World War II, labor was a powerful factor in both collective bargaining and public affairs. Many people thought that it should be subject to more stringent controls. This attitude culminated in the passage of the Labor Management Relations Act of 1947 (the Taft-Hartley Act), which imposed many controls on labor organizations. It retained the controls on management contained in the Wagner Act.

Another problem facing American unions following World War II was the communist issue. Many of the national unions found that some of their leaders were Communists or Communist sympathizers. This was particularly true of the newer CIO unions whose speedy growth in the 1930's had swept all into membership without any real scrutiny of a person's background. Most of the unions faced with Communist infiltration took steps to eradicate the Communist element and generally succeeded in this task within a few years. In 1949 and 1950, the CIO expelled those member unions still found to be Communist-dominated after they had been repeatedly warned to clean up. The CIO immediately established new unions to organize the members of the expelled unions, and many of the Communist-led unions have been driven out of existence.

The split which occurred in the American labor movement in the 1930's served to stimulate the organization of industrial workers, but other than that there was little sense in having two competing labor federations. Each was organized on a similar basis and both pursued fundamentally the same policies. The breach was closed in 1955, when the two federations reunited into the American Federation of Labor-Congress of Industrial Organizations (AFL-CIO) under the leadership of George Meany, president of the AFL, and Walter Reuther, president of the CIO. Meany became the first president of the merged federation.

STRUCTURE AND GOVERNMENT OF UNIONS

While all unions have many basic features in common and all have developed out of the historical context already discussed, their formal organization and their methods of operation differ. Most people are familiar with those unions affiliated with the AFL-CIO, such as the United Steelworkers and the Brotherhood of Carpenters. The national unions affiliated with the AFL-CIO include approximately three fourths of all union membership. Other workers participate in collective bargaining through local unions which are affiliated with national (or international) unions but which have no connection with the AFL-CIO. The United Mine Workers, the Teamsters, and the Railroad Brotherhoods are unaffiliated unions. And, many other workers share in industrial relations decisions through a strictly local organization serving one plant or company. In all of these cases, the workers share in making decisions governing the work relationship through their union.

FIGURE 8–1

STRUCTURE OF AMERICAN UNIONS

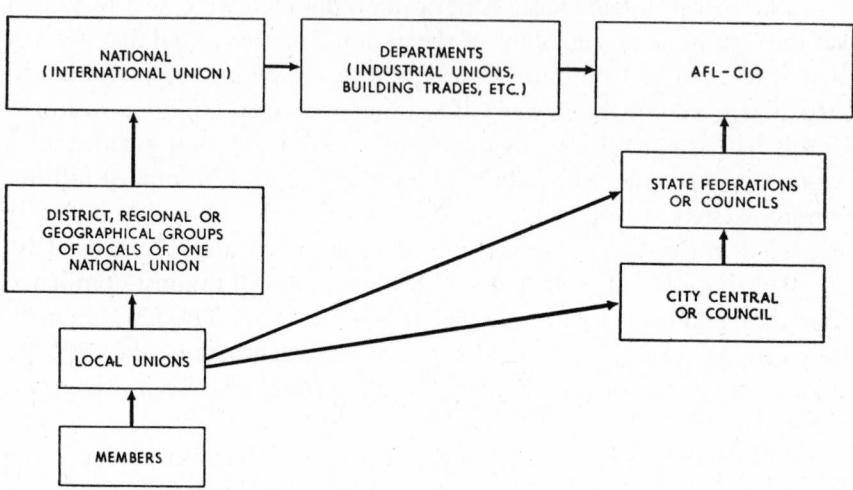

A general structural breakdown showing the interrelationships of the major structural parts of that section of American unionism affiliated with the AFL-CIO is shown in Figure 8–1. The relationships of member, local union, and national union are similar for unaffiliated unions.

Members

The heart of any labor organization is its membership. The purpose of a union is to advance the welfare of its members. Its success or failure will depend largely upon the number of members and their attitude. There were approximately 18 million union members in the United States in 1960. There are 40 to 50 million who are employed who are potential union members. Many industries, such as the trade, service, finance, and government are poorly organized. Many areas of the southern part of the country are predominantly nonunion. And, increasing union membership will not be easy, for those industries already organized are the industries most susceptible to organization. Each additional million members will be harder to enroll than the previous million. But even today, unions are highly organized in such important industries as transportation, communications, mining, and heavy manufacturing.

Local Unions

There are more than 75,000 local unions in the United States. The local represents the member's immediate link with the organization, and it is through the local that he learns of union activities and in turn participates in those activities. Most local unions are openly run, and the member gets every opportunity to participate in union affairs. It is true that in local unions, as in many other organizations, only a small percentage of the membership actively participates.

In locals of large industrial unions, such as the steelworkers and the miners, where contracts are negotiated on a company-wide or industry-wide basis, the functions of the local union are largely administrative. The local collects dues, enlists new members, disseminates union information, and administers the collective bargaining agreement through the grievance procedure.

On the other hand, in cases where contracts are negotiated locally, the local union has more important functions. This is particularly true in industries where the product market is localized, such as newspaper printing and construction. In such cases, the local union may do much of the collective bargaining and call strikes if the bargaining is unsuccessful. However, there is usually considerable power in the hands of the international unions because they control the strike benefit funds. Many internationals must grant their approval before a local may strike.

Officers of local unions are usually part-time and unpaid. In most locals, one of the working members will be elected president, and he may receive a small salary or no pay at all. Many unions retain a full-time secretary, and some of the large locals, such as Local 600 of the United Auto Workers at the Ford River Rouge plant, which at one time had more than 50,000 members, have full-time officers.

Union dues vary from one union to another, but most fall between $2.00 and $8.00 a month. In most unions, approximately half of the dues stays with the local union and half goes to the international. Because the average local union contains only 200 to 300 members, one half of the dues of its members does not represent a large income. Recent financial reports filed with the federal government show that 69.4 per cent of the local unions reporting during 1959 and 1960 had gross receipts of less than $10,000.[1] Out of the rather small income, the local must cover the costs of office space, clerical help, salaries of local officers, and costs of soliciting members.

Most international unions have administrative organizations consisting of groups of local unions. These groups are based upon some common work or job or more commonly upon geographical locations. These organizations are arms of the international union in most cases.

International or National Unions

The centers of power, money, and decision-making in the American trade-union movement are the international unions. In many unions, particularly those dealing with the large mass-production industries, collective bargaining is done by the international union. For example, in the automobile industry, the basic contract is written with the major automobile producers, and the local unions are restricted to bargaining about purely local issues, which may supplement or amplify but not replace the basic agreement.

In the nineteenth century, American unions gradually came to feel that centralization of control of employment conditions in a given trade or industry was essential to union success. This centralization reduced the chances of undercutting of one area by another or of one company by another. In the twentieth century, with the growth of mass marketing, it became even more essential to centralize control of labor matters in a given trade or industry and to standardize the terms of employment insofar as possible. This basic fact has accounted for the degree of power exercised by national and international unions today. And the trend appears to be toward still further centralization of power and control.

Insofar as unions may be said to be "rich," that term would apply only to the national unions, and actually, only a few of the national unions have large treasuries. Of the unions reporting to the Bureau of Labor-Management Reports during 1959–60, 260 were classified as "national unions" and they had total assets at that time of $784.8 million. Twenty-four nationals had assets of $5 million or more. The United Automobile Workers has a strike fund which it is hoped will be maintained at $40 million. But even a fund of this size would not go far if several hundred thousand workers struck a large automobile producer. The United Steelworkers, with more than a million members, receives $2.50 of the $5.00 monthly dues paid by each member. Out of this the union maintains extensive administrative organizations to pro-

[1] *Union Financial Statistics 1959–60,* Bureau of Labor-Management Reports, Department of Labor, 1961.

vide services to members, bargains with the employers, enforces contracts, fights arbitration and legal battles, maintains economic and statistical research agencies, lobbies on the national and state levels, conducts organizing campaigns, and distributes union informational material to members and the general public.

The government of most national unions centers in general conventions. These conventions may meet once a year, once every two years or, in a few cases, once every three or four years. At these conventions, the union membership is represented by delegates from the locals. Regional organizations are also represented. Usually locals vote in proportion to their membership. At the convention officers are elected, rules and bylaws are enacted, and general union policy is established. Between conventions the union is governed by an executive board composed of the top officers of the union and usually so constituted that all major interests in the union are represented. The officers of a national union generally include a president, a secretary-treasurer, one or more vice presidents, a general counsel, an editor, a research director, and organizers.

A frequent criticism of organized labor is that it is internally undemocratic. People point to the long tenure in office of men like John L. Lewis, who was president of the United Mine Workers for more than a generation. On the other hand, a union like the International Typographical Union is noted for the democratic way in which it is run and governed. Most labor unions are basically democratic, and the membership has an opportunity to present grievances against their leaders and have them acted upon. The mere fact that a single man has held the presidency of a union for a number of years does not necessarily mean that the membership has been denied the opportunity of voting for any other man or that their desires have been ignored. Many union officers have spent years working up through the union organization and have proven themselves to be the most capable leaders within the union.

The very structure of unions tends to prolong the tenure of their top officers. The union president and secretary-treasurer are the only union members who are known to all of the membership. There is little opportunity for new men to rise and challenge the incumbent leadership. A topnotch local leader might well make an excellent union president, but his ability will probably be known only to the members in his local and the national officers. The only available media of communications in the union, the national magazine, is probably under the influence of the present leadership. And the national convention will be strongly influenced in its agenda and program by the leaders currently in control. But, in spite of these forces, there is little doubt that most union members are satisfied with the leadership of their national union.

There may even be some question as to whether unions should be overly democratic. An officer who faces a serious challenge to his position every year would probably pursue a program of short-run expediency that might mean more for the member today but ultimately weaken the economic position of the union and industry. An officer who feels secure in his position is better able to pursue an economically sensible course that will maximize the well-being of the union members over the years but perhaps at the expense of a little less in any particular year.

This does not mean that there are no problems in internal union administration. Some national union officials have built up political machines that have been used to perpetuate themselves in office. The use of local "trusteeships" is another device by which national officials have gained control of local unions. In a few national unions, this machine control has been accompanied by the misuse of union funds.

In 1957 an investigating committee of the United States Senate uncovered shocking abuses in several national unions, including the Teamsters, the Bakery Workers, and others. As a result of the investigations, the Labor-Management Reporting and Disclosure Act was passed in 1959. This bill, more popularly known as the Landrum-Griffin Act established rules governing the conduct of and frequency of elections, financial practices of unions, and the form and availability of financial reports. Trusteeships are also regulated. The effectiveness of this law will not be known for some time. Many of its provisions are very general, and their applicability will have to be tested administratively and legally. In the final analysis, however, it is the interest of the union members that will determine the type of organization and leadership to be found in the trade union movement.

Labor Federations

The best-known organization in American labor is the American Federation of Labor–Congress of Industrial Organizations. In 1962 this organization consisted of 132 national and international unions with more than 14 million members. The AFL-CIO is literally a "federation" of national unions and exists at the sufferance of its member national unions. Throughout American labor history, national unions have been jealousy possessive of their sovereignty. They are willing to work with other groups through a federation but will not surrender their sovereignty. Thus the AFL-CIO, representing millions of workers, is a powerful political force and lobbyist, is influential in public affairs, and speaks for labor on general issues, but it is *not* a powerful force in collective bargaining. The federation does not negotiate labor contracts for its constituent unions, and it does not engage in strikes. However, there has been a growing tendency to increase the power and scope of federation actions.

The AFL-CIO is governed similarly to the national unions. It has a biennial convention which formulates federation policy; an executive council composed of the president, secretary-treasurer and twenty-seven vice presidents, which governs between conventions; a general board made up of the executive council members and one officer of each affiliated union, which meets annually and handles policy questions; and an executive committee composed of the president, secretary-treasurer, and six vice presidents chosen by the executive council, which advises the officers on policy questions. George Meany of the Plumbers is president and William Schnitzler of the Bakery Workers is secretary-treasurer. Each held the same office in the AFL before the merger in 1955.

The AFL-CIO is a powerful lobbying force. The organization, representing almost 14 million members, is one of the largest economic interest blocs in the country. Federation leaders face an attentive audience when they present their viewpoints before the federal Congress or a state legislature, and, regardless of the political sentiments of the legislator, careful consideration will be given to the views of organized labor.

The views of labor concern not only cases of direct interest to the worker as a worker. A list of the staff departments of the AFL-CIO includes Civil Rights, Education, International Affairs, and Social Security.

Because it embraces the bulk of organized labor, the AFL-CIO provides the only real avenue through which interunion difficulties can be aired and perhaps solved and through which the various activities of American unions can be co-ordinated. The federation is constantly beset with jurisdictional conflicts between two or more of its members. Procedures have been established in an attempt to provide peaceful settlement of such disputes. Since the only real power the federation has over its member unions is the threat of expulsion from the federation, it must move slowly and carefully in settling disputes between national unions involving matters affecting the latter's jealousy guarded "sovereignty."

In recent years, the federation has become more concerned with the internal administration of its member unions. An ethical practices code provides stringent rules of conduct which must be followed by member organizations. Failure to live up to the standards of these codes can lead to expulsion from the parent federation, a fate already suffered by several unions, including the International Brotherhood of Teamsters.

The AFL-CIO is financed through a 7-cent-per-month per capita tax paid by each national union. This would presently provide the federation with an annual income in excess of $11 million per year. This barely covers the operating expenses of the federation and does not permit it to build up a sizable treasury. However, because the federation does not engage in strikes, the need for a sizeable reserve fund is not as essential as it is for a national union.

There are also state and local federations. Each state has a state federation of labor composed of the local unions within the state which belong to national unions which are affiliated with the AFL-CIO. Likewise, locals affiliated with AFL-CIO member unions make up the membership of city "centrals." The state and local bodies are mainly concerned with lobbying and political activities on matters of state and local interest. Thus, the Wisconsin Federation of Labor would support a bill to increase unemployment insurance benefits in the Wisconsin legislature, while the Cincinnati Central Labor Council would be concerned with a fair employment practices ordinance before the Cincinnati City Council.

MANAGEMENT AND INDUSTRIAL RELATIONS

Since the 1930's, management has become more concerned with industrial relations. Before that time, most companies did not have labor unions to contend with, and their labor problems could be handled with little regard for the workers' interests. It is true that many companies have had long records of sympathetic treatment of their workers. But for most companies, it took the impact of the labor union, either as an accomplished fact or as a potential threat, to force a change in their treatment of labor problems. Collective bargaining forces tremendous changes upon a company. Where once the company had complete control of labor matters, now it must share that control. With unions emphasizing uniform treatment of workers and standardized terms and conditions of employment, and with a multitude of government rules and regulations to be lived up to, companies have been forced to give more time and consideration to labor problems. The responsibility for successful handling of labor problems is now assumed by the highest levels of the management hierarchy. No longer is it possible to delegate authority for handling labor problems to some high-grade clerk in the personnel office. Laws and unions have made labor problems one of the most important phases of business, and mistakes can be very costly.

Ordinarily, the board of directors, representing the owners, will retain ultimate control of the important aspects of labor relations, particularly where the company bargains with a strong union. The board will probably set certain limits within which the officers may bargain with the union, and they will probably keep in close contact with the progress of the bargaining. Certainly, no corporate officer would agree to any clause in a collective bargaining agreement unless he felt relatively sure that the clause was acceptable to the majority of the board. In many cases, the board of directors will have considerable say as to where in bargaining it becomes cheaper to endure a strike than to accept the union's demands.

Once the collective bargaining agreement is in effect, the corporate officers, and in particular the officer in charge of industrial relations, will be in charge of its administration. The job of administering a labor contract is as difficult as writing the contract. Successful labor relations are usually achieved in the shop and not in the smoke-filled bargaining rooms. To have successful relations in the shop, the foremen, supervisors, and other management representatives and the union's shop stewards must be familiar with the agreement and interested in making it work. The lower levels of management must be informed as to what the contract is, what it means, and how it is to be applied. And, in turn, information concerning the working of the agreement must flow upwards through the management hierarchy if successful agreements are to be written.

Professor Reynolds, a leading student of labor-management relations, distinguishes four general approaches of management toward organized labor.[2] They are forcible opposition, peaceful competition, defensive endurance, and positive acceptance. Forcible opposition characterized the attitude of most American management until the 1930's. As the name implies, it involves the use of any and all means to thwart the union and to keep the plant nonunion. In the past, this technique involved the use of labor spies—who worked in the plant and informed management of any union activity—the blacklist, the yellow-dog contract, and many other techniques. Perhaps the most forceful device

[2] Lloyd Reynolds, *Labor Economics and Labor Relations* (3rd ed.; New York: Prentice-Hall, Inc., 1959), chap. 6.

of management in this approach was economic coercion—the threat of loss of job if the worker joined a union or had anything to do with the union. In some cases, this approach involved the use of physical violence as well. Today, this approach has all but disappeared, partly because of government laws outlawing or restricting most of the weapons employed and partly through a more enlightened attitude of American management towards organized labor.

Peaceful competition means fighting the union and competing with it in an attempt to win the worker's allegiance but staying within the limits of law. Paternalism is a good example of this strategy. Management offers the workers higher pay, more employee benefits, recreational programs, and other benefits in an effort to show the men that there is no need for a union. Paternalism—or welfare capitalism—reached its peak in the 1920's but is by no means dead today. Many large companies, such as International Business Machines, National Cash Register, and Procter and Gamble have long resisted outside attempts to unionize their companies through highly organized and extensive employee benefit programs.

Forcible opposition and peaceful competition both are attempts to keep the union out of the company. But, as we all know, most manufacturing, transportation, communications, and mining companies have unions. What are their attitudes toward unions? Defensive endurance probably characterizes the attitude of most unionized companies in the United States. Management accepts the unions as an inevitable part of the enterprise—for better or worse—but it does not give the company away to the union. The company continues to resist union power and actively competes with the union.

In a small and slowly growing number of companies, management has accepted the union as a positive force working for the good of the company as well as for the good of the workers. Union and management trust one another. In some cases, such as in the clothing industry, the union becomes almost a partner in the enterprise, not in the legal sense of that term, but rather as a co-operative force working hand in hand with the management for substantially the same objectives.

Many companies have traveled through all of these strategies, working from forcible opposition to defensive endurance or even positive acceptance. However, one strategy does not necessarily follow another. Many companies have long pursued a single strategy and others have retrogressed from a favorable relation with a union to an unfavorable one. But, the trend does seem to be toward a more mature and co-operative approach on the part of both management and labor.

COLLECTIVE BARGAINING

Industrial Peace

Negotiating the Contract. Collective bargaining exists when workers join together and bargain as a group. Thus, the collective aspect of bargaining rests solely on the worker side of the employment relationship. True, employers may also associate for purposes of bargaining, but the essential feature of collective bargaining that distinguishes it from alternative methods of determining conditions of employment is the fact that the workers bargain as a group rather than as individuals.

Today, when we think of collective bargaining we are apt to think of the annual sessions at which the employer and the union hammer out an agreement to control the work relationship through the following year. But, collective bargaining is more than an annual joust between two forces, each threatening to withhold what it controls and what the other desires. It is more properly a continuing relationship, in which the contract negotiation is but one important part. For the contract does not govern itself. During its life, management and labor must continue to vie with one another over differing interpretations of the agreement.

Collective bargaining is bilateral bargaining—each side has the potential economic power to hurt the other side. Without this bilateral aspect, bargaining would be meaningless. Collective bargaining is essentially an economic tug-of-war with each contestant hoping to gain some advantage over the other. The solution will favor one side or the other depending upon the strength and force each is able to exert. But it is not completely a tug-of-war, as the losing side will usually give in through a compromise before it is pulled into oblivion, and the winning side is usually weary enough to accept.

The bargaining sessions about which we read are not simple arguments that arise on the spur of the moment. Long months of preparation have been spent before the bargaining begins. The union may formulate its general demands years before it presents them to the employer. It should be pointed out that we are accustomed to think that collective bargaining always originates with a union demand for "more." That has been true for two decades and is a function of a favorable economic climate. If economic conditions turned downward, bargaining might well originate in a management demand for a wage reduction, and the union might find itself fighting to retain the status quo. The union demands will perhaps arise from the members of the union, they may be suggested by the actions of other unions or employers, or they may arise from some economic peculiarity of the industry involved. In addition, demands may originate with the union officers who feel a need to present new demands to the membership to retain their interest in the union. Whatever the demands may be, the union will spend much time and money in research to determine the relative merit of the demands and how best to present them. Some demands may first be presented to the members to test their interest in them. The public must be wooed, and newspaper stories, pamphlets, and other materials presenting the union's story will be circulated. The top echelons of the union will review the demands and formulate a formal demand which will be presented to the employer. They will also probably agree upon a minimum amount that they will be willing to accept from the employer without resorting to a strike. Naturally, this later amount is kept secret from the employer. Because of the very nature of bargaining, the initial demands of the union are usually inflated, and the initial counter-offer of the employer is probably well below what he is willing to pay if necessary. In that way, each party is in a position to make concessions by offering more or demanding less, as the case may be, with a minimum amount of sacrifice. Thus it is not unusual to see a union demand a "package" of 50 cents an hour and the employer offer 3 cents an hour. After long days of bargaining they agree on 23 cents an hour. Chances are that if we could have sat in the inner councils of both labor and management, we might have found that labor really hoped to get about 25 cents per hour and that management felt able to pay 20 cents or a little more. Also, the arguments used to support the inflated demands and the deflated offers may be, at least in part, rationalizations that will appeal to the public and be more palatable to the opponent rather than being the real reasons behind the respective stands of the parties. For example, if a union shop is the issue involved, the union will argue that since all workers benefit from the union's activities, all should participate, and the employer will argue that it is undemocratic to force a man to join the union. Never do you hear the union assert that it will have more bargaining power against the employer nor does the employer say that he hopes the union will not have too many members so it will be weaker.

The employer's offer will have been formulated by the top echelons of management. They will also agree upon a certain amount which can be safely given to the union, and the bargainers will be free to bargain up to this point. They will also probably agree on an amount beyond which they would prefer a strike rather than make any further concessions. Again, this latter amount is a well-kept secret.

The actual techniques of bargaining, the number and types of persons on each bargaining team, the site of the bargaining, and the time and length of sessions vary greatly from one bargain to another. At the start of the bargaining each side will feel the other out, trying to determine which issues are the most vital, where a point can be easily won, what the other side dearly wants and will pay much to get, and finally, just how far they can push each other before one side or the other calls a halt. As the threat of a strike is the main factor pushing each side toward a compromise agreement, the approach of the strike deadline results in more serious bargaining and an increasing number of concessions.

The final result of collective bargaining is a labor contract. In most instances the contract is signed without a strike. The contract will spell out the relationship of the parties to one another and will describe the terms and conditions of employment that will prevail for the workers covered for the life of the agreement.

The Grievance Procedure. The employment relationship in a modern industrial plant is so complex and so many issues are involved that it is virtually impossible to write an agreement that will provide a ready answer to all problems which might arise during the life of the contract. Also, it is not always possible to foresee future developments that may effect a basic change in working conditions during the contract term. And, finally, a contract that provided a precise answer for every conceivable problem would probably be too rigid and inflexible to be of any practical use in modern industry. For these reasons, a method must be provided to handle disputes that arise between labor and management while the contract is in force. These disputes most generally concern the application and interpretation of the agreement. A labor contract would be of little use if a dispute over its interpretation destroyed the contract. For that reason, the grievance procedure has been developed as a peaceful means to settle such disputes.

The typical grievance procedure provides a series of consultative steps between increasingly higher levels of officials of both the union and the management. If the grievance is not settled at any one point, it may be appealed to the next step. Commonly, the procedure provides for outside arbitration of the grievance if the parties are not able to settle it within the prescribed steps. This insures that there will be no unsettled issues under the contract. Since arbitration is the final step, the parties themselves, successively through persons having greater discretion and authority, have had ample opportunity to settle the issue without the intervention of an outsider. The settlement becomes part of the total relationship between labor and management.

Industrial Conflict

Inherent in free collective bargaining is a certain amount of disruption of work activity through strikes, boycotts, and lockouts. In collective bargaining, it is unlikely that both sides will agree on what constitutes a fair settlement at the beginning of the bargain. A settlement is finally achieved through the give and take of many days or weeks of bargaining. But each side must give as well as take. Each must be able to exert economic pressure upon the other. The employer has legal control of the jobs—the workers' means of livelihood. The only opposing pressure available to the workers is their ability to withhold their labor. Thus, the strike becomes an integral part of collective bargaining, and in the absence of a right to strike there could be no true bargaining for there would be no reason for the employer ever to concede to worker demands except through his own volition. There can be no question of "liking collective bargaining if it weren't for the strikes." The two are inseparably intertwined.

Because of the nature of the employment relationship, the workers must usually initiate any industrial conflict. The employer need never "start" a dispute as it is usually much more advantageous for him to insist upon his position and let the workers, through their union, call a strike. In that way, the stigma of initiating the breakdown is usually upon the union, regardless of the respective merits of the union and employer demands.

In the United States, strikes have rarely caused a significant reduction in national economic performance. In only one year since accurate statistics have been available (1927) have strikes caused a loss of more than six-tenths of one per cent of the total potential man-days of work in a year. Even in 1946, the worst strike year in our history, when 116 million man-days of labor were lost through strikes, over 200 million man-days were lost through industrial accidents. This is not meant to imply that strikes never cause problems but rather that their impact has most generally been overemphasized and overdramatized. Approximately 43 per cent of the strikes in 1961 lasted less than a week and only 23 per cent lasted a month or more. It is unfortunate that so much publicity is given to the few thousand strikes that occur in any year and so little publicity to the more than 100,000 contracts that are negotiated each year without any loss in production.

What are the different economic "weapons" used by employers and unions when a breakdown in negotiations occurs? The main union pressures are exerted through the strike, boycott, and picketing. On the employers' side, the most popular techniques include the lockout, the use of strikebreakers, and the injunction.

A strike is a concerted refusal to work that is intended to promote the interests of the workers. The strike must be a concerted refusal to work, since individual quitting of work causes little economic pressure upon the employer, whereas the loss of an entire work force usually precludes further production. And, while it may be simply a matter of semantics, it is better to refer to a strike as a "refusal" to work than as a "quitting" of work, since the strikers do not intend to sever permanently the employment relationship. They hope to return to their same jobs at the conclusion of the strike.

When a strike has been called, the employer may try to counter its pressure through the use of strikebreakers. The purpose of the strike is to inflict economic loss upon the employer by stopping his production and subsequently his sales and income. If the employer can recruit and train a sufficient number of replacement workers, he can prevent the economic loss and usually defeat the strike, if not the union itself.

Picketing by the union usually accompanies strikes and boycotts. Picketing consists of publicizing a labor dispute by parading in front of the employer's plant while carrying signs indicating that a dispute is in progress and portraying the grievance involved in such general terms as, "This Company Unfair to Organized Labor." Picketing serves to maintain the strikers participating in the walkout and perhaps to bolster sagging spirits. It also is used as a device to discourage strikebreakers or customers from entering the struck plant. Whereas a strike is an attempt to stop the employer's production, a boycott is designed to cut off his markets. The boycott involves pressure upon parties other than the immediate employer concerned.

The labor injunction has been an important weapon in industrial disputes for almost one hundred years. An injunction is a court order specifying that the named person(s) do something or refrain from doing something. Historically, it was not the injunction itself but the way in which it was used in labor disputes that made it such a *cause célèbre.* Injunctions were written in sweeping terms and applied to any or all persons who might in any way become involved in the dispute. Friendly judges issued sweeping temporary injunctions, and the same judge who had issued the order frequently presided over any contempt proceeding which arose. The injunction meant a speedy end to most disputes, as few unions could withstand contempt orders that depleted their treasuries and imprisoned their leaders. And, all of this might have happened before hearings were held on the propriety of the injunction itself.

Constant pressure from organized labor and a growing support from other groups in the society eventually led to the virtual demise of the labor injunction in federal courts with the passage by Congress of the Norris–La Guardia Anti-Injunction Law in 1932. However, subsequent legislation, particularly the Taft-Hartley Act, has reintroduced the injunction in cases of certain unfair labor practices and in the so-called national emergency disputes.

GOVERNMENT IN LABOR RELATIONS

Throughout history, the public has always seen fit to protect its interest whenever it appears to be threatened by some single force or by some combination of forces within the society. Just as labor problems have been with us since the birth of the United States, so likewise have we always had some form of government intervention and control in the interest of protecting society. Organized labor has grown very powerful in the past two decades, and the consequences of collective bargaining and of breakdowns in collective bargaining have grown proportionately. Today, we find more government intervention in labor problems than ever before. But that fact is mainly attributable to the increasing scope and significance of collective bargaining.

The nature, as well as the intensity, of the government's role in collective bargaining has changed as labor relations have evolved. For the first hundred years of our existence as a nation, government intervention was almost solely through the judicial system, and almost entirely on the side of management. It began with the use of the British common-law doctrine of criminal conspiracy—which virtually outlawed all group labor activity. As Recorder Levy expressed it in the Philadelphia Cordwainers Case in 1806, "A combination of workmen to raise their wages may be considered in a two-fold point of view: One is to benefit themselves . . . the other is to injure those who do not join their society. The Rule of law condemns both." The conspiracy doctrine was tempered in its use by the middle of the nineteenth century and was soon replaced by the labor injunction.

The Sherman Antitrust Act of 1890 was the first Act of Congress to affect labor relations. Although primarily designed to curb business combinations, its general terminology led to its use against organized labor. Efforts to reduce the impact of the Sherman Act upon organized labor by the passage of the Clayton Act in 1914 had little success, as the United States Supreme Court ruled that the amendments gave much less aid to labor than its spokesmen had hoped.

Organized labor was treated favorably by the government for the first time during World War I, which marks a sort of turning point in the relationship between government and labor problems. In 1926 Congress passed the Railway Labor Act. This was an important milestone in several respects. It marked the shift in government intervention from the judiciary to the legislative and executive branches of the government, and, for the first time of any importance, government intervention was at least partially in behalf of organized labor. The Railway Labor Act guarantees railroad workers the right to organize and bargain through unions of the workers' choosing and provides administrative agencies to facilitate the settlement of industrial disputes on the railroads.

Laws favorable to labor unions were prominent in the New Deal. The most important was the National Labor Relations Act of 1935, more commonly referred to as the Wagner Act after its chief sponsor, Senator Wagner of New York. The Wagner Act placed the government in labor relations in a very positive sense. This act was designed to do for workers in general what the Railway Labor Act had done for railroad workers. While the purposes were similar, the methods differed in many respects.

The key part of the Wagner Act was Section 7:

Employees shall have the right to self-organization, to form, join or assist labor organizations, to bargain collectively through representatives of their own choosing, and to engage in other concerted activities for the purpose of collective bargaining or other mutual aid or protection.

These rights were to be protected by limiting employer action in this field. A list of employer unfair labor practices was included, restricting such anti-union actions as firing a worker for joining or assisting a union or interfering with workers' rights to form unions. The Wagner Act required an employer to bargain collectively with the union chosen by a majority of the employees. In order to determine the free choice of the workers, secret elections gave workers the opportunity to indicate which union, if any, they desired to represent them in collective bargaining.

The act was enforced by the National Labor Relations Board, an administrative agency appointed by the President. This agency policed the unfair labor practices and supervised collective bargaining elections.

The Wagner Act was essentially a prolabor law. It was passed during the depression of the 1930's when it was generally felt that the individual worker could not bargain effectively with his employer. And, it was also felt that the individual workers faced a difficult, if not impossible task in trying to work through a labor union in the face of virtually unlimited employer weapons and economic power. The Wagner Act was passed in this setting in an attempt to protect the right of a worker to join and bargain through a labor union so that he might bargain on relatively equal terms with the employer.

The Labor-Management Relations Act of 1947, more commonly known as the Taft-Hartley Act, continued most of the features of the Wagner Act and added many new provisions. Most important of the new provisions was a list of unfair labor practices of unions to counterbalance the unfair labor practices of employers which were continued in almost the same form as in the Wagner Act. The union unfair labor practices restricted secondary strikes and boycotts, jurisdictional strikes and union interference with workers' rights to organize. It required that the union bargain collectively with management.

In addition to the union unfair labor practices, the Taft-Hartley Act made other changes in the Wagner Act. Under the Wagner Act, the role of the government was restricted to an attempt to balance the bargaining power of the contending parties and to force collective bargaining upon the employer. What the parties did in the bargaining was their business. The Taft-Hartley Act not only attempts a new balancing of bargaining power, but also makes the government a party at the bargaining table through restrictions upon what can be made a part of a labor contract and other rules governing permissible use of traditional contract provisions. For example, the Taft-Hartley Act outlaws the closed shop even if both labor and management agree to such a clause. The act also provides detailed rules for pension and welfare programs established through collective bargaining. The Labor-Management Reporting and Disclosure Act of 1959, in addition to the rules concerning union affairs already mentioned, tightened some of the union unfair labor practices, particularly through regulating so-called "hot-cargo" clauses and some types of picketing.

When society is faced with collective bargaining by giant companies and giant unions (or combinations of giant companies and giant unions), laws providing balanced rights and responsibilities on both parties and which protect the worker as well as the public seem to be necessary. We can not expect to reach agreement as to just when a fair balance of power is reached, but when both sides think they are receiving the worst of the bargain, it would appear that we are on the right track.

CONCLUSION

Because of the impact of collective bargaining in the economic system, society has seen fit to regulate the ground rules of bargaining. Certain activities of both labor and management have been outlawed and further abuses or injuries to society may well lead to increased control of collective bargaining. The proper role of government in labor-management relations is one of the major unresolved issues of the day.

It appears to be a generally held view that the exigencies involving the cold war, the battle against inflation, and the conquest of space are such as to warrant the most extreme kind of government interference with free collective bargaining. Steel, shipping, railroads, and newspaper publishing are the most recent examples of government interference in the bargaining process in order to protect the public interest.

Collective bargaining is faced with a problem arising out of the rapid rate of change in technology. Changes in technology are forging a structural shift in the labor force, increasing the need for skilled workers while decreasing the requirement for unskilled and semi-skilled. As a result, some unions are faced with the problem of declining membership. Unions are being forced by their members to take strong stands on the matter of job security. This means that the institution of collective bargaining is having to cope with a problem which it is just not capable of handling. The problem of technological unemployment is a problem of the economic system rather than being a problem of labor and management. It should probably be taken out of the context of collective bargaining, for requiring collective bargaining to wrestle with the problem may fatally impair the institution itself.

EXERCISES

Group I

Explain why the following statements are either true or false:

1. Collective bargaining is an institution which ought to be preserved, but strikes should be outlawed.
2. The AFL–CIO could be eliminated as a labor federation without any appreciable difference in collective bargaining and industrial relations in the United States.
3. Collective bargaining is always characterized by a union demand for increased pay, more fringe benefits, better working conditions, etc.

4. Forcible opposition is the most common management attitude toward unions in the United States today.
5. American unions have enjoyed considerable success in politics.
6. Unionism was illegal until the passage of the Wagner Act in 1935.
7. The Taft-Hartley Act was designed to weaken unions.

Group II

1. What is the significance of "democracy" in union government? How could this be implemented? How democratic should unions be?
2. How does the philosophy of American unionism differ from that of foreign labor movements?

Group III

1. Investigate some of the recent "emergency" disputes. Compare the operations of the Railway Labor Act and the Taft-Hartley Act in handling such disputes. How effective have they been? Consider other proposals such as compulsory arbitration as devices for resolving the conflicting interests involved.
2. In 1963, the steel contract was signed as a result of a labor-management committee known as the Human Relations Committee. This agreement was widely hailed as a "new step forward" in labor-management relations. One provision in the agreement calls for a 13-week vacation every five years for older employees. The "new" approach as well as the specific provisions raise rather interesting questions. Has bargaining been replaced? Has the president of the union become, for all practical purposes, a member of steel management? Is there any question about the long-run viability of the union under such a process? What is the difference between the 13-week vacation in steel (where it was praised) and featherbedding in railroads or payments to farmers for not producing (both of which are roundly condemned)? Is the "long vacation" a reasonable way for the labor force to share a declining number of job opportunities? What will the steel worker do on a 13-week vacation—moonlight?

BIBLIOGRAPHY

CHAMBERLAIN, NEIL W. *Sourcebook on Labor.* New York: McGraw-Hill Book Company, Inc., 1958.

NATIONAL PLANNING ASSOCIATION. *The Causes of Industrial Peace.* Washington, 1948–53.

PERLMAN, SELIG. *A History of Trade Unionism in the United States.* New York: Kelley, 1950.

SLICHTER, SUMNER H.; HEALY, JAMES J.; AND LIVERNASH, E. ROBERT. *The Impact of Collective Bargaining on Management.* Washington: The Brookings Institution, 1960.

TAFT, PHILIP. "Theories of the Labor Movement," *Interpreting the Labor Movement*. Madison, Wisc.: Industrial Relations Research Association, 1952.

PAPERBACK READING LIST

DARROW, CLARENCE. *The Story of My Life*. New York: Universal Library, 1957.

LIPSET, SEYMOUR; TROW, MARTIN; AND COLEMAN, JAMES. *Union Democracy*. New York: Anchor Press, 1962.

ISSUES BETWEEN LABOR AND MANAGEMENT

. . . we are firmly convinced, and can show evidence to prove, that
the blame for past price increases in the automobile industry cannot
legitimately be placed at our door.—Walter P. Reuther, President,
United Automobile Workers in letter of August 16, 1957, to Henry
Ford II.

The rapid increase in wages of automobile workers over the past ten
years—which were negotiated under the duress of your demands—have

unquestionably contributed to inflation.—Henry Ford II, President, Ford
Motor Company in letter of August 24, 1957 to Walter P. Reuther.

All aspects of the employment relationship are of general concern to both labor and management. The terms which are agreed upon in bargaining between employer and employees determine the well-being of the employee and his family. To the employer, the terms of the contract represent a major factor in determining the largest single cost of doing business. Both parties tend to measure the contract in monetary terms—what it will cost or what it will provide. For this reason, then, primary attention is generally given to those parts of the contract which can be readily translated into money terms. Wages, pension plans, health and accident programs, unemployment benefits, vacation rights, seniority rights, and other similar features represent major subjects covered in bargaining sessions. There are, in addition, some phases of the agreement which cannot be easily and immediately translated into money income for the worker or money cost for the employer. These would include such items as the grievance procedure and union security provisions. And lastly, there are some phases of the employment relationship which are only partly subject to collective bargaining but which are extremely important. Particularly important here are the total hours of work. These, then, are the issues between labor and management.

INTRODUCTION

In the absence of a labor union, the employer unilaterally determines the wages to be paid, hours to be worked, and fringe benefits, if any. However, his choice will be limited by the terms of employment offered by competing employers. Most nonunion employers find themselves setting their terms of employment in some relation to those negotiated by union employers.

While it is usual to discuss wages as an issue, hours as another issue, and pensions and other fringe benefits as still other problems, it should be remembered that in actual practice all of these form a single package which comprise the terms of employment. It is not simply a question of first deciding upon a wage rate, then considering hours, and then discussing fringe benefits. They are inseparably intertwined in a total "package." High wages may offset long hours, or a poor pension plan may be overlooked where there are liberal vacations. The total package approach is of particular importance to the employer. Most of the issues in the employment relationship can be reduced to a cost per hour. For example, an extra week of paid vacation may prove to cost the employer 5 cents per working hour when spread over the year's operations. In many cases, the employer will be indifferent as to whether he spends 5 cents an hour on supplementary unemployment benefits or as a direct wage increase. Of course he must be careful to see that his total employment package is so constituted as to attract the type of worker he desires. An employer wishing to hire relatively young workers can pay less attention to a pension plan than one whose work force is composed of older workers.

Workers vary greatly in their desires. Those interested in security may be attracted by liberal supplemental unemployment benefits and strong seniority programs. Others may value social prestige and be willing to sacrifice some pay for a white-collar job in pleasant working conditions. Still others are primarily motivated by pecuniary desires and look for the large wage today with plenty of opportunity for over-time work.

A union will determine its demands in at least partial accordance with desires of the majority of its members. The United Mine Workers, in an industry with high accident and sickness risks, emphasizes health and welfare programs. Unions may also be motivated by considerations of public relations. They may wish to pioneer in the development of some new type of worker benefit or catch up with or exceed the gains of other unions and union leaders.

The interactions of management, union, and worker attitudes toward the job result in a package of terms covering the conditions of employment. This package will determine the success of the employer in obtaining and holding good workers, of the union in winning new members, and of the worker in meeting the basic psychological, social, and economic needs of himself and his family.

WAGES

Wage Concepts

It is easy for one to become confused when discussing wages because of the variety of terms used to express different aspects of the wage picture. Webster defines "wages" as pay given for labor, usually manual or mechanical, at short, stated intervals. The economist usually includes in wages the payments made to the labor factor of production which includes supervisory, professional, and any other labor effort including both mental and manual labor. Whereas wages are considered a payment to manual labor for short intervals, salaries are the payment for work other than manual which is paid on a time basis of more than a day or week. In our discussion we shall use the term wages to encompass all returns to persons furnishing the labor factor of production.

The "wage rate" is an amount to be paid per unit of time, such as $2.00 per hour, $90 per week, $400 per month or $5000 per year. For most workers, the wage rate is per hour or per week. Payments over a longer period of time usually are associated with salaried executive and administrative occupations. Some workers receive "piece-rates" where the wage is determined by the amount the worker produces. The weekly income of a worker depends upon his wage rate and the number of hours worked during the week. In turn, the annual income depends upon the regularity of employment during the calendar year. A worker with a high hourly wage rate may earn less money over the year than a worker with a lower wage rate in a job providing more regular employment. In fact, high wages are often a compensating factor to counteract the existence of irregular work.

Another important wage concept is that of "real wages." Real wages measure what one can buy with the money wage. A worker might have made $3,000 in 1943 and be making $5,500 in 1963. On the surface that looks like a sizable increase. However, when that worker spends the money, he finds that the $5,500 in 1963 buys fewer goods and services than did the $3,000 in 1943. After all, the reason a person works is not to accumulate an abstract sum of money but to enable him to enjoy the goods and services he desires. The real wage measures his standard of living.

The Labor Market

The labor market would include any place where workers (sellers of labor service) and employers (buyers of labor services) can agree upon an employment relationship. It would include state employment service offices, private employment agencies, personnel offices of the employer, college campuses, telephone conversations, application letters —in fact, almost any place or media of communication that enables workers seeking work to communicate with employers with jobs to be filled.

Many economic theorists felt that the labor market would operate in the manner of the competitive price market with a single wage rate established for each type of work. Any unbalance between demand and supply would be corrected through changes in the wage rate. That is, if supply exceeded demand, wages would fall until everyone desiring work was employed.

Instead of a single wage rate for a given type of work, there are almost as many different wages as there are jobs. In the winter of 1958–59, beginning weekly wages for inexperienced women typists in Detroit varied from a range of $37.50 to $40.00 to a high range of $80 and over.[1] How can such differentials, as well as other wage differentials, exist? Why don't workers move to the companies, industries, or areas paying the highest wage for the type of work they do? To answer these questions requires an understanding of the characteristics of the labor market.

The perfectly competitive labor market, where such differentials could not long exist, would have the following characteristics. There would be many workers and employers. No single worker or employer could influence the wage rate by his own activities in the labor market. All of the participants in the labor market would act independently of one another. Both workers and employers would have complete knowledge of the market. That is, they would be generally acquainted with the forces of supply and demand, the wages different workers were willing to accept, and the wages different employers were willing to pay. In a perfectly competitive labor market, there would be sufficient mobility of both labor and capital so that the movement of workers, capital, or both would be such as to eliminate any wage differential.

How does the actual labor market compare with the theoretical model? While there are many workers seeking jobs in most types of employment, the number of employers of different types of labor in a given labor market is usually relatively small. As a result, employers can and do influence the labor market and wage rates by their employment activities. In many communities, a single employer may be the major source of work. In such a case, competition in the labor market is seriously restricted.

Labor unions now number among their members almost one third of the employees in nonagricultural pursuits. To the extent that a labor union bargains about the terms and conditions of employment on behalf of the workers, there is no independent action on the worker side of the market. And if there is also multiemployer bargaining or pattern bargaining in an industry, there is no independent action on either side of the market. Either pattern bargaining or some form of multiemployer bargaining characterizes much of heavy industry today.

---

[1] *Wages and Related Benefits, 20 Labor Markets, 1958–59* (U.S. Department of Labor, Bulletin No. 1240–22).

Perhaps the most important discrepancy between the perfectly competitive labor market and the actual labor market in our economy is the lack of knowledge about the labor market. This is particularly true on the worker side of the market. Few production workers know much more about the labor market than their own employment situation. The average employed worker does not know the wage paid for his particular type of work by more than a handful of other employers if that many. Workers may hear about the wages paid by other firms through friends. Labor unions, themselves inconsistent with the perfectly competitive labor market, also help furnish labor-market information. The laborer seeking a job usually does not have much information about the labor market and ordinarily has little opportunity to learn much about the market. He may gain information and some leads to jobs through newspaper advertisements, and he may find some information through the public employment offices. Unfortunately, except in periods of extreme labor shortages, those firms advertising for employees and more particularly those seeking workers through the public employment offices need to find men for jobs that have been hard to fill through applications at the company. Most of the good jobs have been filled by the laborer who has called at the different plants in the area seeking work.

Even the worker who seeks work from plant to plant does not acquire much information about the labor market in normal economic periods. The worker may have some idea about what wage he hopes or expects to receive. Upon applying at a company personnel office, he is usually offered a take-it-or-leave-it proposition. The worker has little opportunity to solicit offers from different companies, informing them that he will consider their offers and let them know after he has completed the rounds of possible companies. When a job is offered, he may take it if it sounds reasonable. If not, he may look around for alternative job offers, but with the knowledge that the original job is likely to be filled by some other person if he decides that other offers are not as attractive. As a result, many workers will accept the first reasonable offer they receive.

Another discrepancy between the perfectly competitive labor market and the actual market lies in the general immobility of the labor factor. While American labor tends to be more mobile than most other labor forces, there still are many obstacles to mobility in our labor force. Lack of knowledge of alternative opportunities is one important obstacle. The costs of moving are another. When a more attractive opportunity is available in another locality, the relative advantages must be weighed against the costs of moving. Many companies find they must cover transportation expenses to get desired mobility from management personnel. In addition, there are other factors involved in moving. New social relationships must be established—new schools for the children, a different church, and other factors of this type. Even within a given labor market, the worker may be reluctant to shift to a new job. Transportation problems may be involved, including the length of travel time involved, ability to "share the ride," and the costs of transportation. And, any job change involves moving from the known to the unknown. The worker may be happy in his present job, get along well with his fellow employees and his foreman and have settled into a routine where he knows his job and is confident he can do it well. The new job involves new relationships with fellow workers and supervisors and a trial period wherein the worker must prove himself. Some of the current aspects of a job relationship also work against mobility. Many fringe issues, such as pension plans, paid vacations, and seniority, increase in value in accordance with the length of the worker's service with the company. As these rights are accumulated, the worker becomes less willing to move to a new job where he may have to start all over in building up the benefits he now enjoys.

As a result of these labor market imperfections, wage differentials can and do exist. And while there is some long-run tendency toward the reduction of these differentials, it is likely that they will continue to persist for long periods of time.

Demand for Labor[2]

Just what constitutes the demand for a given type of labor? How many workers will an employer be willing to hire at a certain wage? While there are many subjective factors which influence these decisions, the central force is the marginal productivity of the worker. While the marginal productivity theory has been oversold by some partisans and much maligned by overzealous critics, it still stands as a basic explanation of the employer's demand for labor and is a useful analytical tool when properly employed.

Basically, an employer is willing to hire a worker and pay him a wage because the worker will contribute something of value to the concern. It would be very rare to find a worker employed who contributes nothing of value to his employer. Since the worker is hired because of his productive contribution, the important factor in the hiring decision is the relationship between the worker's potential productive contribution

---

[2] An alternative approach to factor demand using tools similar to the indifference analysis of product demand is discussed below. See pp. 203-7.

and the cost involved in employing him. If an employer can hire a man for $10 per day who would contribute daily production worth $20, the employer would be foolish not to hire him. On the other hand, if the worker's daily contribution was only $5, it would be uneconomical to pay him $10. Most employers would readily subscribe to the reasoning above without realizing that they are following the basic principles of marginal productivity.

The results of attempts to increase production by employing more units of any of the productive factors (land, labor or capital) when at least one of the productive factors is fixed in quantity have been described as the law of diminishing productivity. (See Chapter 3.) The change in the total product when one more or one less unit of labor is employed is called the marginal productivity of that unit of labor. The law of diminishing productivity states that, with given conditions of technology, as equal successive units of a variable factor (or factors) are combined with a fixed productive factor (or factors), a point is reached after which additional units of the variable factor yield successively smaller additions to the total product. Notice that this principle applies regardless of which factors are varied or which factors are held constant. In our present discussion, we are concerned with labor as the variable factor. In succeeding chapters, we shall see the significance of this principle when other factors are varied.

In most employment situations, the employer is concerned with a choice of hiring workers or laying off workers without any immediate change in his plant. That is, labor is a variable factor and plant is fixed, thus giving us the conditions necessary for the operation of the principle of diminishing productivity. However, the employer is not simply interested in the number of piston rings the employee would add through his efforts. Rather, the employer is interested in the value of the worker's production.

If we multiply the marginal physical product of the worker by the marginal revenue derived from the sale of that output, we get the value of the worker's effort to the employer. Marginal revenue product has the same characteristics as marginal productivity. In fact, under conditions of pure competition, the marginal revenue product would be identical to the marginal productivity function, as the price and the marginal revenue would be constant regardless of the level of output. Where the employer operated under conditions other than pure competition, the marginal revenue product would be less elastic than if the employer operated in a purely competitive market, because marginal revenue will be less than price and will be declining.

A graphical presentation of marginal revenue product would

approximate the characteristics of diminishing marginal physical product. That is, marginal revenue product would increase for a while as the number of labor units increased, but after a certain number of units were employed, it would begin to decline and would continue to decline as more and more units of labor were employed.

The principle of diminishing productivity assumes the existence of at least one fixed factor of production. For our purposes, we have assumed that labor is the only variable factor. While all other factors are assumed to remain constant, there may be increases in costs associated with the fixed factors as we increase the units of labor employed. Added power may be needed. As machines are run faster and longer, depreciation will increase. As output expands through the use of additional labor units, more materials will be used. As the employer is interested in the added value derived from the employment of an additional unit of labor, he must deduct these incidental expenses associated with the use of additional labor units to determine the net contribution of the labor unit. This is called marginal net revenue product.

TABLE 9–1

DIMINISHING MARGINAL PRODUCTIVITY AND THE DERIVATION OF THE MARGINAL NET REVENUE PRODUCT*

Units of Labor Factor	Total Product	Marginal Physical Product	Price (Marginal Revenue)	Marginal Revenue Product	Increased Costs of Other Factors	Marginal Net Revenue Product
1............10	10	$10	$100	$ 2	$ 98	
2............22	12	10	120	4	116	
3............32	10	10	100	6	94	
4............40	8	10	80	8	72	
5............45	5	10	50	10	40	

* Assuming a fixed quantity of land and capital and the sale of the resulting product in a purely competitive market.

Table 9–1 and Figure 9–1 illustrate the derivation of marginal net revenue product and the characteristics of the *MNRP* curve. The first three columns of the table illustrate the operation of the principle of diminishing marginal productivity. Multiplying the marginal physical product by the marginal revenue derived from its sale (price and marginal revenue are equal in pure competition) yields the marginal revenue product. And, by substracting any incidental expense, we obtain the marginal net revenue product. The curve shows that after the first two units of labor are employed, the net revenue productivity declines as additional units of labor are employed. Assuming that the employer will hire units of labor as long as they contribute more to output than

FIGURE 9–1

A MARGINAL NET REVENUE PRODUCT CURVE

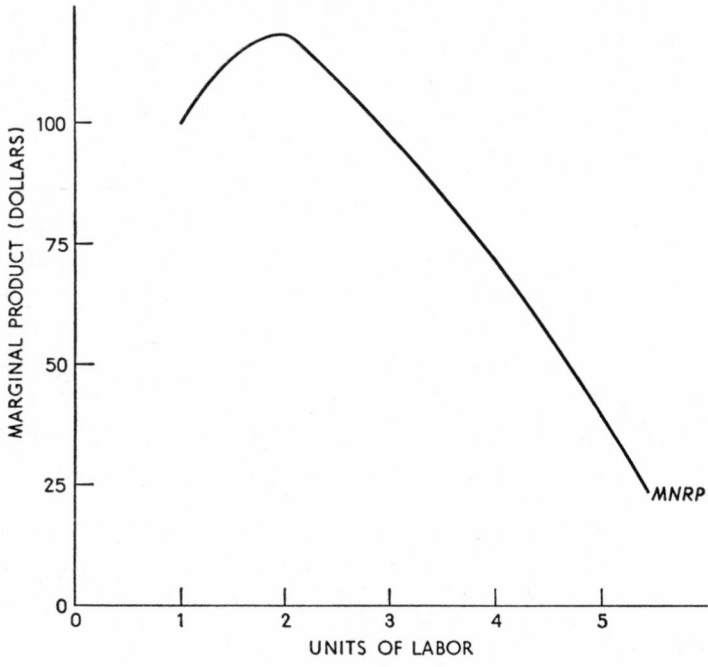

SOURCE: Table 9–1.

the cost of their services, the curve shows more labor would be employed at lower wage rates. That is, the demand for labor will vary inversely with the wage rate.

Supply of Labor

The supply of labor depends upon many different factors. Basically, population is the ultimate source of a labor supply. Increasing population provides an increased labor force and a decreasing population would probably lead to a smaller labor force. While the size of the population is a basic factor in determining the supply of labor, changes in population have only a very long-run effect upon labor supply. Of more immediate importance is the labor-force participation rate. This measures the percentage of the population 14 years of age or older who are in the labor force. Included in the "labor force" are all people at work or looking for work. In the United States, the labor-force participation rate has been remarkably stable, with the labor force ranging from 55 to 60 per cent of the population fourteen years of age or older. However, this stability of the over-all participation rate fails to disclose some significant changes that have occurred. One is the increasing percentage of women workers. Another is the later entering age of workers into the labor force. More and more people are pursuing advanced education, and economic conditions are such that most families do not need the income of the teen-age members of the family. Third, we are experiencing a significant increase in the number as well as the percentage of older people who have retired.

Some economists have used a concept of disutility of labor to explain the behavior of the general supply curve. Here a third variable is introduced. The supply of labor depends not only on the population and the labor force participation rate but also upon the number of hours each worker in the labor force is willing to work. In making his decision, each worker weighs the relative advantage of extra income against the disadvantage (or disutility) of additional hours of work. It is felt that as wages increase, the higher wages more than offset the disutility of added hours of work and workers will increase their hours of work. But sooner or later, a point is reached after which further wage increases decrease the amount of labor supplied. This is because workers feel that with the higher wage rate, they can work fewer hours with the same weekly income but more leisure. There is no doubt that there is some merit to this theory. The payment of overtime and penalty rates on weekends indicate the necessity of paying more to get more hours of work. And, for most workers, there is undoubtedly a level of income beyond which they are unwilling to work any longer in spite of offers of greater income.

Supply of Labor to an Industry. The nature of the supply of labor for any industry depends upon a number of factors and therefore will vary greatly from one industry to another. In the short run, many industries will be faced with an inelastic supply of labor (that is, wage changes will result in only minor changes in the supply offered). This is particularly true with respect to industries which require lengthy and expensive training, such as medicine and college teaching; those which require unique skills, such as opera or big-league baseball; those which may be geographically isolated, such as coal mining; or those industries which have union or industry restrictions governing who can or cannot be employed. On the other hand, industries requiring certain routine skills, or a low level of skill will usually have an elastic supply (indicating that wage changes will bring large quantity responses). This elasticity results from the fact that there are usually large numbers of such workers available who can move from one industry to another. Thus a higher wage will tend to draw large numbers from other industries while a low wage may result in the loss of much of the work force.

In the long run, all industry supply curves will tend to be more elastic. Time permits the training or discovery of new talent and permits the movement of people from one location to another. Even here, however, restrictive hiring practices may still limit the supply.

Supply of Labor to a Company. The supply of labor to any company in the short run will usually be fairly elastic, particularly if the company is located in a large city. The company can attract many workers from other companies by raising its wage offer. If the company is in a small town, it may be the only employer of certain types of labor and its supply will be very inelastic in the short run. Over the long run, workers will be drawn from outside the local labor market or local workers will be retrained, thus making the supply of labor more elastic.

Summary. The demand for labor is based on the productivity of labor, and the supply of labor depends mainly upon the population of working age, the labor-force participation rate, and the mobility and training of labor. The discussion that follows will demonstrate that a simple analysis of supply and demand curves is not an adequate explanation of wages in the economy. However, the demand and supply framework provides a useful tool for understanding the impact of changes in the labor market.

An Alternative Determination of Factor Demand

The demand for a factor of production can also be determined by a method analogous to the indifference curve approach to product demand. Most production can result from varying combinations of the productive factors. If one were to plot on a graph the amount of production resulting from various combinations of labor and capital and then connect points of equal production, the result would be a series of curves such as those labeled "P = 10," "P = 20,". . . in Figure 9–2A. These curves are called iso-quants and show the various combinations of the productive factors which produce a given amount of output.

The iso-quants also illustrate the law of diminishing productivity. For example, with capital fixed at A, as the amount of labor is increased, production rises from 10 to 20 and so on until a maximum product is reached at 40 when B units of labor are employed with A units of capital. As more labor is used with this given amount of capital, output increases but by decreasing amounts. After B units of labor are employed with A units of capital, further increases in the use of labor will actually cause total output to decrease. Since no rational producer will employ a productive factor that decreases his output, he will not use more than B

units of labor with A units of capital. Similar points of maximum output will be reached with differing amounts of capital. The line OX connects such points and would serve as an upper limit to the rational combinations of the two factors.

The same analysis would apply if labor were the fixed factor and capital varied. Output would increase for a while but after a point, it would increase at a decreasing rate. Also, for each fixed quantity of labor, there is some quantity of capital at which output would be a

FIGURE 9–2A

ISO-QUANTS AND RIDGE LINES

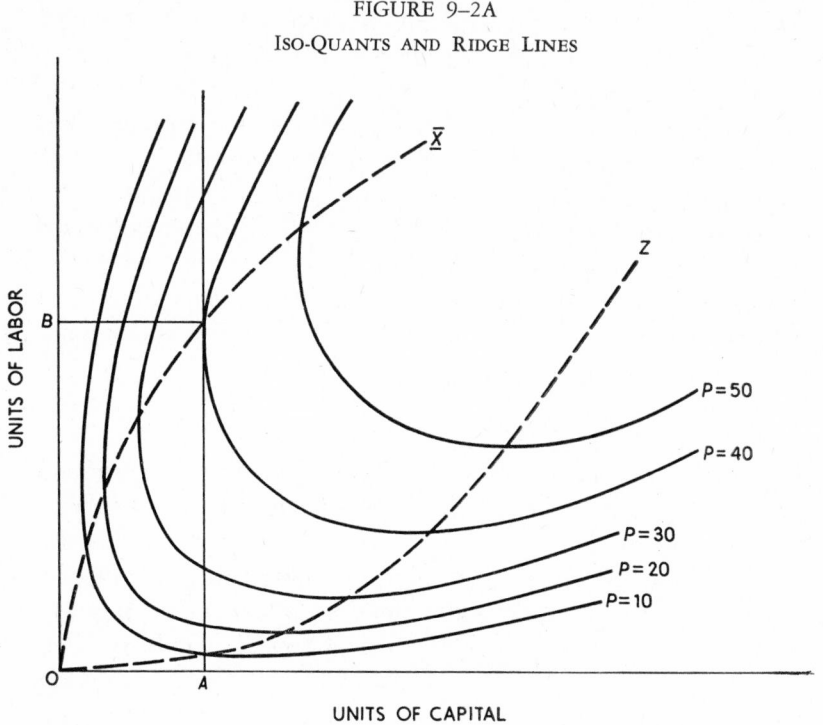

maximum. The enterpriser would lose money if he were to employ more than this number of units of capital. The line OZ connects these points. Thus, the rational area for decision is the area contained between the OX and OZ ridge lines.

The exact combination the producer would employ depends upon the relative costs of the productive factors, the amount of money the producer has to spend for the factors and the amount of production he wishes to achieve. Given the prices of the factors (P_L for labor, P_c for capital) for each level of total costs (C) an iso-cost line can be constructed. Figure 9–2B illustrates a family of such curves (A, B, C, and

FIGURE 9–2B

Iso-Costs

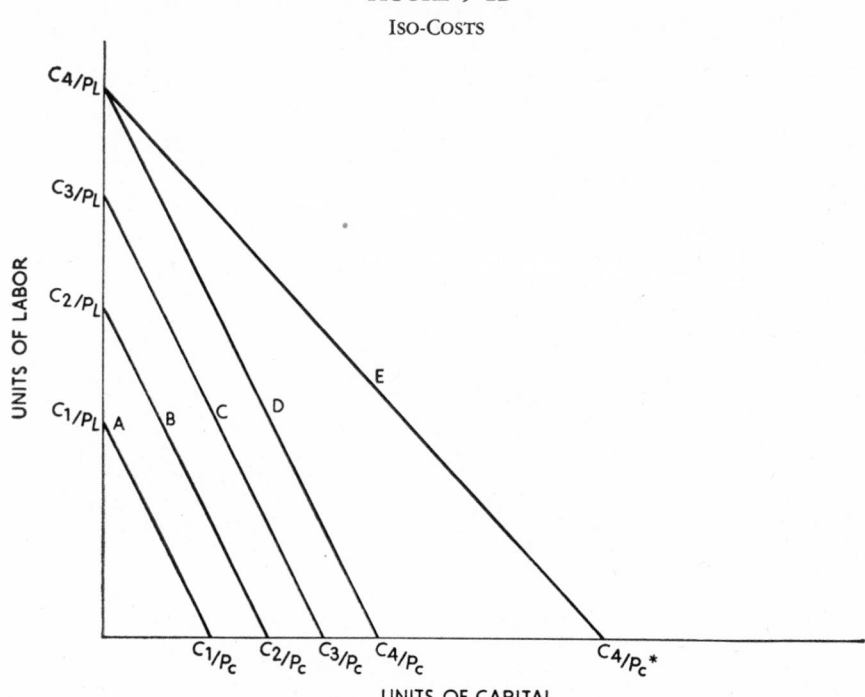

UNITS OF CAPITAL

D). Line E shows the change in the price of one factor when the price of the second factor as well as the total costs are held constant. As the price of the one is decreased, more units can be purchased with a given cost expenditure. The end points of the iso-cost lines can be located by assuming that no units of one factor will be used and dividing total costs by the price of the other factor to determine the number of units of the factor that could be purchased.

Figure 9–3A illustrates the use of the iso-quant and iso-cost curves to determine the demand for a factor of production. For any given cost outlay, the rational producer will try to get the maximum amount of production. This is accomplished by moving back and forth along the iso-cost line until it touches the highest possible iso-quant—the point of tangency. Similarly, to achieve a given level of output, the producer wishes to do so at the lowest possible cost. Again this can be achieved by moving along the given iso-quant until you reach the lowest possible iso-cost—again the point of tangency.

Given a specified total cost outlay (C) and a price of capital (P_c), one can derive a demand curve for labor by varying the price of labor and ascertaining what quantities of labor would be employed. For

FIGURE 9–3A

FACTOR DEMAND ANALYSIS

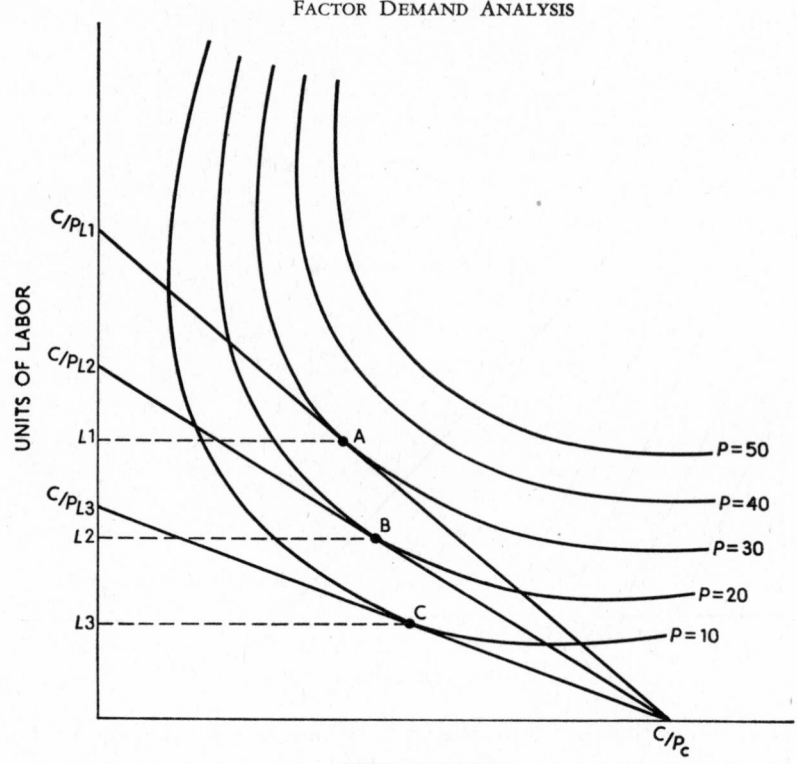

UNITS OF CAPITAL

FIGURE 9–3B

DEMAND FOR LABOR

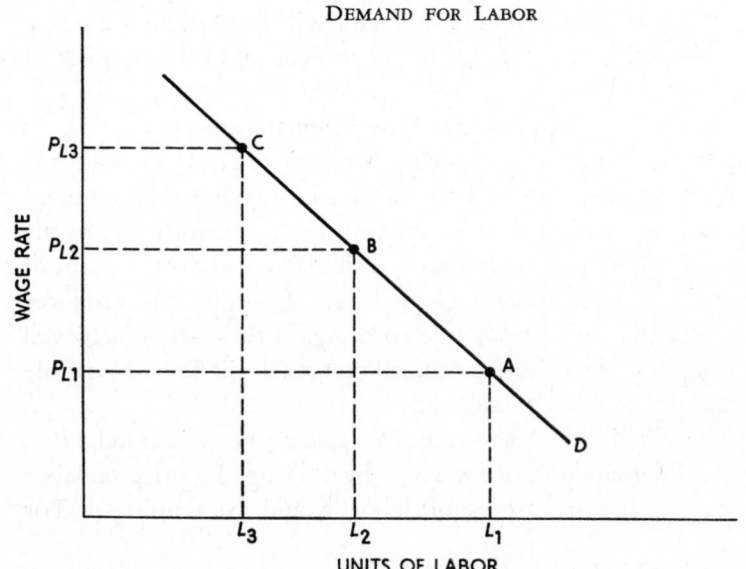

UNITS OF LABOR

example, at P_{L1}, the best adjustment is at A where L_1 units of labor would be demanded. At P_{L2}, L_2 units of labor would be demanded, and so on. By varying the price of labor, it is possible to generate as many price-quantity points as necessary to determine the nature of the demand curve for labor. Three of these points are plotted in Figure 9–3B.

Nonunion Wage Determination

In the absence of collective bargaining, the employer has considerable freedom in setting wages. Sometimes this is referred to as "individual bargaining"; however, in most nonunion situations, there is relatively little "bargaining" between the employee and the employer. The employer has probably established a wage rate for the job in question and the worker's only choice is to take or refuse the job. It is true, however, that some highly skilled workers may be able to bargain individually with their employer, particularly in times of full employment, but this is the exception to the rule.

What factors does the nonunion employer consider in setting his wage rates? Is there any limit to the wages he can pay? Any minimum? Most nonunion employers have a range of possible wages they can pay rather than a single wage rate for each type of work. Certainly the maximum which the employer can afford to pay his workers in the long run is their marginal net revenue productivity. However, this does not mean that the given curve of net revenue product is a fixed upper limit. The curve can be shifted in several ways. Perhaps the most common shift results from increases in the price of the product produced. This increases net revenue productivity by increasing the value of the goods produced. The curve might also shift through the substitution of one factor of production for another. For example, the substitution of capital goods —better machinery—for labor might increase the net revenue productivity of the remaining workers and permit the payment of higher wages to them. Increased effort by the workers will increase the net revenue productivity. And, of course, the opposite of these forces would decrease net revenue productivity.

In the short run, the employer may pay workers in excess of their value productivity. If wages exceed the value productivity of labor, it will be at the expense of the return to other factors of production. As rents and interests are normally fixed through long-term contracts, the most likely victim is profits. But wages cannot continue high at the expense of profits, for sooner or later, the employer will discontinue his business. There may be many cases where the employer pays his workers a wage rate in excess of their productivity because of a mistaken estimate of productivity. Rarely does an employer stop to compute the marginal productivity of a particular job or type of job. Yet the average employer probably does have a reasonably good estimate of the productivity of his work force as a whole.

The minimum point of the range within which the employer is relatively free to set nonunion wage rates is the lowest wage which he can pay and attract the required amounts and types of workers. This minimum will depend upon the supply and demand of labor in the relevant labor market, the wages paid by other employers within the same market, his ability to draw workers from outside the immediate labor market and the relative attractiveness of work in his company as compared to the laborer's alternatives. If there is a large body of unemployed workers in the area, the employer can probably hire workers at a very low wage rate. On the other hand, if there is a shortage of workers of the type needed by the employer, he may have to pay a relatively high wage to ensure an adequate work force.

Alternative forms of employment in the area also affect the "minimum rate." If most of the other employers are unionized, wages in the area are apt to be high. The same situation would prevail if most of the jobs in the area are in heavy industry, construction, or other high-wage industries. On the other hand, if the area is predominately agricultural, or dominated by industries such as furniture and textiles which pay relatively low wages, the minimum wage is likely to be low. Many companies have a reputation as a "good place to work." Such a reputation will make it easier for them to draw the needed workers without paying too high a wage rate. In fact, this firm may even be able to draw workers from outside the normal labor market area. However, this ability is also limited by conditions beyond the control of any one employer, such as available housing, schools and the relative attractiveness of the community as a whole. Some employers must pay a higher minimum wage than other firms in the locality as the price of being considered an unattractive source of employment.

While the range of permissible wage rates open to an employer has been stated in terms of a maximum and a minimum, in reality there may not be much of a range available to a given employer. In fact, it is conceivable that the "minimum" might exceed the "maximum" under certain circumstances. This is possible because the maximum and minimums are established through the operation of different sets of forces. The maximum point of the range depends upon the marginal net revenue productivity which in turn depends upon the physical productivity of the employer's enterprise and the prices of the products which he produces. The prices are established in the product market and the physical productivity is also likely to approximate that of other firms in the industry. Thus, the maximum is dependent primarily upon conditions in the employer's industry.

On the other hand, the minimum point of the wage range is set by conditions in the local labor market. Thus, two different sets of forces operate on opposite ends of the wage range facing the employer. As a result, an employer in an industry characterized by low labor productivity might find it difficult if not impossible to operate in a labor market characterized by high-wage industries. An automobile manufacturer operating in a small town in South Carolina would probably have a much bigger range within which to set his wages than would a textile manufacturer operating in Detroit.

Just where within the wage range the nonunion employer sets his wage depends upon his own subjective decision. Some employers pride themselves upon being wage leaders and will continue to pay somewhere near the maximum point of the range. Others are satisfied to be near the bottom of the range. Some employers will pay a relatively high wage in the hopes that their labor turnover will be reduced, and thus the higher wage will be compensated for by reduced turnover costs. In certain situations, the employer may pay a relatively high wage with the hope that by so doing he may forestall union organization of his workers.

Actually, most nonunion employers do not have too much latitude in deciding upon the wage which they will pay a given type of worker. The community probably has a going range of rates for that job and the employer will set some rate within that range which he feels will best further his own interests. After once deciding upon a certain spot within the range, the nonunion employer will probably change his wage only when local labor market conditions necessitate such a change.

Union Wage Determination

Union wage rates are the result of collective bargaining between the union, representing the workers, and the employer. Except in the rare case of a new plant being started with a union already recognized, collective bargaining is concerned with changes in wage rates rather than the initial setting of a wage rate. In other words, the union and management are not starting from scratch to establish a wage system. Rather they are considering whether the present wage schedule should be continued or in what respect it should be changed.

It is misleading to talk about collective bargaining over wage rates as an independent subject. Collective bargaining embraces all of the terms and conditions of employment, and they are all interrelated in the bargaining. Thus, a wage demand might be lowered if the employer were willing to grant a union shop. However, the different factors considered by labor and management in collective bargaining and the relative merits of some of the principles as a basis for wage setting can be discussed.

Union Position on Wage Bargaining. Union officials will consider many factors before deciding upon their wage position, but it is unlikely that any one factor will be of primary importance. Some of the factors are strictly economic issues. Others are political. Out of all these factors will come the union's demand for wages.

Among the factors considered by the union in formulating wage demands will be the company's ability to pay. The union realizes that the company must make a profit if it is to stay in business. However, the union idea of a "fair profit" will probably be much different from the company's view of the same matter. In most cases, the amount of profit earned by a company in excess of a "fair" amount will usually not provide much of a wage increase if spread among all of the company's employees. And, in addition, a large profit in one year may not necessarily indicate the company's ability to pay over the long run. Of course, ability to pay is evidenced not merely by the current profits of the company but will involve the possibility of offsetting wage increases through price increases.

Closely related to the employer's ability to pay is the productivity of the workers. The union is usually more concerned with benefits accruing from changes in productivity than with the absolute relationship between productivity and wages, and would like to share the resulting gains.

Another factor considered by the union is the cost of living. Whenever prices are rising in the economy, workers find that their money wages are falling. In an effort to maintain their real wages, workers desire wage increases that will at least compensate for price increases. During the inflationary period that followed World War II, it was common to include a provision in the labor contract providing for an automatic adjustment in wages, usually every three months, to compensate for changes in the cost of living. In that way, the money wage rate would always buy the same amount of goods and services. From the worker's point of view, cost-of-living adjustments are fine when prices are increasing, but they are not so popular when prices are decreasing. Most of the cost-of-living agreements are so written that the impact of price decreases is limited.

Some of the factors considered by unions in the determination of their wage demands have political overtones. Wages of other workers in the same industry and of workers in other industries may serve as a base for wage demands. While comparative wages may serve as a good economic criterion of the state of the labor market, their use in wage demands may also indicate a desire of the union in question and its leaders to be at least as successful as other unions and union leaders.

Most unions pursue a program designed to eliminate intercompany wage differentials in their industry. Therefore, wage gains and wage levels in other companies within the industry may serve as an important factor in the union's wage demands.

The internal politics of a union may also be a factor in labor's demands. If a union leader's office is in jeopardy, he may feel that he has to win a large wage increase if he is to retain his office. On the other hand, a leader who is well entrenched in his office can afford to take a long-range view of the economics of the industry and perhaps negotiate a somewhat smaller wage increase than he might have been able to win.

The existence of nonunion competition in the industry will have an effect upon union wage demands. The effect will vary in some proportion to the percentage of the industry which is nonunion. If there is a large percentage of nonunion production in an industry, unionized workers will have to be careful lest they price themselves out of work. Unless there are compensating cost differences, the union wages will have to stay reasonably close to the nonunion wages. Since World War II, the New England textile workers have negotiated wage decreases at a time when most workers in that area were receiving wage increases. However, the textile workers had to accept wage reductions to keep their wages in line with the wages in the southern segment of the industry, which is mostly nonunion. On the other hand, where nonunion competition is nonexistent or makes up only a small part of the industry, the union can usually ignore the nonunion problem in formulating the union wage demands.

Out of the complex of all the factors mentioned, the union leadership will decide upon the wage demands, the supporting arguments to be used (which may be rationalizations), and the minimum amount they are willing to accept without striking. Naturally, only the stated demands are made public along with the arguments and rationalizations used in support of the demands.

Employer Position on Wage Bargaining. Upon receipt of a wage demand by a union, or perhaps in anticipation of such a demand, the management will have to decide what wage increase can be granted.

This decision will be based primarily upon economic considerations with little of the external or internal political forces that influence the union decision. Most of the same economic factors considered by the union will also be weighed by management. However, the relative significance and interpretation of each will differ.

The company's ability to pay is certainly important to management. Ability to pay means ability in the future, not in the past. Therefore, the possibility and the effect of price changes must be considered. There will probably be a significant difference of opinion between union and management as to what level of profit is necessary to maintain the company in business. Thus, while both parties consider this factor it does not mean that each decides upon the same wage increase. Also, the union is likely to use profits as an excuse for wage increases when profits are high and to forget this argument when profits are low. On the other hand, ability to pay will be one of management's big arguments in times of low or nonexistent profits, but this issue will be minimized when profits are high.

The employer will also consider labor productivity. However, he may well feel that rising productivity of labor does not necessarily call for wage increases of a corresponding amount. Management may feel that the increased productivity is a result of investment by the company, and that the fruits of this productivity increase belong to the owners of the company. And productivity by itself may not be a satisfactory basis for wage changes as productivity varies so greatly from one industry to another, from one job to another, and from one company to another. If productivity were the sole basis for wage adjustments, the wage structure would be very chaotic.

The employer will also be concerned with wages paid by other employers in his labor market as they will show how much he may have to offer to continue to attract the labor he desires. The existence of nonunion competition will be of importance to the employer in formulating his wage position. Extensive nonunion competition will seriously limit the employer's ability to grant wage increases, for he cannot permit his wage structure to depart significantly from that of the nonunion producers. The condition of the employer's product market must be considered. The strength and elasticity of the demand for his product will affect the employer's ability to offset wage increases with price increases. Finally, the employer's position with regard to wages will depend upon his subjective attitude toward the labor market and his employees. If he is a "wage leader," he may be willing to grant a sizable wage increase. If he is a wage follower, he will wait until other employers raise their wages before he will make any move.

Out of all of these factors, the employer will agree upon certain wage concessions which can be made. He will decide upon a maximum amount of wage increase which he is willing to grant to avoid a strike. He will formulate a bargaining position that will allow him room for bargaining before he reaches his limit. This bargaining position will be supported by arguments and rationalizations that will help to make the program look fair to the workers and to the public.

The Wage Bargain. We have already mentioned that wages are not bargained in a vacuum. They are an integral part of the total bargain and cannot be considered separately with any meaningful results. But out of collective bargaining will eventually come agreement on all of the issues involved. If the employer's maximum limits exceed the union's minimum demands, a settlement is relatively easy. When the union's minimum exceeds the employer's maximum, a strike is likely. Since the impact of the strike is costly to both parties, it will serve to reduce the union's minimum, and to raise the employer's maximum until a settlement is reached.

Guaranteed Annual Wage

In recent years, the guaranteed annual wage or some other program designed to promote steady work has become a popular union demand. The desire for some form of guaranteed wage or employment stems from the worker's basic interest in security.

The recent interest in guaranteed wages has been led by the United Auto Workers; it was their primary bargaining goal in 1955. The plan which was finally negotiated with the auto industry has come to be called supplemental unemployment benefits (SUB) since such plans usually call for the laid-off worker to receive a benefit from the company in addition to any unemployment insurance benefit to which he might be entitled. The worker receives in unemployment benefits and SUB payments a percentage of his wage. This percentage has been increasing and today is commonly from two-thirds to three-fourths of the weekly wage. The duration of such benefits has also increased from 26 weeks to 39 weeks and, increasingly, to one year. These benefits are financed by a contribution paid by the employer of so many cents per payroll hour (commonly five cents). There are many difficult questions concerned with SUB, including the possible transfer of benefit rights from one company to another; the question of destroying the incentive to work by making benefits too large, and the possibility that SUB reduces employment by making wages more like a fixed cost.

Impact of Unionism on Wages

The effect of unionism on wages is a moot question. Some critics of labor say that labor is simply an inflationary engine, while labor advocates maintain that unions simply bid up wages to compensate for price changes so as to maintain a constant real wage for their members. To date, the evidence is not sufficiently clear to permit a precise evaluation of unionism's effect upon wages. The relative shares of the national income do not offer much assistance. Compensation of employees (70 per cent of the national income of 1961) seems to be increasing slightly as a proportionate share. Most of this increase in the proportionate share share of compensation of employees has come at the expense of income of unincorporated enterprise (11 per cent of the national income in 1961). Income of unincorporated enterprise is a combination of many factor returns but is primarily wages. Since unincorporated enterprise is usually in nonunion fields, this may indicate some shift in the distribution of income from nonunion to union labor.

One fact is evident from the national income figures. If we count income of unincorporated business with wages, the total "labor" income approximates 80 per cent of the national income. Property incomes (corporate profits, rents, and interest) approximate 20 per cent of the national income. These relative shares seem to be reasonably stable. Thus, there is some doubt about labor making significant long-term gains at the expense of the other factors of production.

Although organized labor may win some gains in their income at the expense of the unorganized portion of the labor force, there is a limit here also. If organized labor gains too much, we can expect groups of the unorganized to join unions or similar organizations. This would eliminate the advantage of the organized. The main long-run gain that labor can make in real income is through increases in national income. In a period of relatively full employment, such gains come mainly through productivity improvements. As we produce more goods and services with a given input of productive factors, it is possible for all of the productive factors to experience an increase in real income—that is, to be able to enjoy more goods and services. In light of this fact, it seems rather shortsighted that many labor unions follow practices that discourage rather than encourage productivity gains. However, when technological improvements appear as a threat in its industry, the union has the responsibility to protect its members. The functioning of the economy as a whole is not its major concern. It does little good to tell a worker with a skill acquired over many years of training and work that even though he is going to lose his job, new jobs will appear elsewhere in the economy. He may not be qualified to fill the new job or he may be too old.

Many union activities have had the effect of reducing wage differentials. The reduction in differentials between skilled and unskilled labor has already been mentioned. In addition, unions have generally worked to eliminate wage differences based on race and sex. Geographical differentials have also been reduced when a union covers workers in many areas of the country. This has been particularly true with the large industrial unions such as the automobile and steel workers.

Minimum Wage Laws

In the early years of the United States, there was no general regulation of minimum wages, hours worked, or employment of child labor. The first attempts at regulation of these matters came in the nineteenth century, but these first laws were usually restricted to hours of work and/or child labor in certain occupations or industries. In the early twentieth century, several of the states experimented with the regulation of wages through the imposition of a minimum wage. Again, these laws usually did not have general applicability. The federal government did little in this area until the 1930's. The doubtful constitutional status of a federal law was a big deterrent. However, in 1938, the Congress enacted the Fair Labor Standards Act, which provided for minimum wages, premium pay for hours in excess of 40 in any week, and child-labor regulations.

The Fair Labor Standards Act (more commonly called the Wage and Hours Law) originally provided for a minimum wage of 25 cents per hour with provisions for this amount to increase to 40 cents per hour within a few years. In 1949 the federal minimum wage was raised to 75 cents per hour, in 1956 it became $1.00 per hour, and currently it is $1.25 per hour. The main weakness in the Fair Labor Standards Act is that of its limited coverage. It is ironical that the $1.25 minimum covers mainly workers who make well in excess of that amount, while the workers who currently make less than $1.25 an hour are not covered.

Several states also have laws providing for minimum wages. Most of these laws apply to women and children, with only a few state statutes applying to both men and women. These laws are designed to insure a minimum wage that enables the worker to at least maintain himself at some minimum level of living. Unfortunately, some of the laws do not provide such a standard, and many states do not have any protection at all. State minimum wage laws are of two types. In one, the legislature provides a specific minimum wage (such as 75 cents) in the statute. The other approach is to provide for "boards" or "commissions" which establish minimum wages. These boards hold hearings, investigate conditions in the industry and recommend an appropriate minimum wage to the state labor commissioner, whose orders have the effect of law.

HOURS OF WORK

Along with wages, hours of work are probably the most important aspect of the employment relationship. Some of the most bitter strikes in history have been fought over the hours issue. They would include the eight-hour day strikes in 1886, including the strike which culminated in the Haymarket riot in Chicago, the railroad strike which resulted in the passage of the Adamson Act of 1916 (which prescribed the eight-hour day for railroad crews) and the railroad shop-craft strike in 1922 for the eight-hour day.

In the early nineteenth century, the twelve-hour day was common in the United States. However, there was already agitation for the ten-hour day. The ten-hour day movement continued through most of the nineteenth century. It overlapped the beginnings of the eight-hour day movement. The latter started about the time of the Civil War, but it did not achieve final victory until the 1920's. The building trades and other craft groups were in the forefront of the hours-reduction drive. They were usually successful in achieving the shorter work day well before it was achieved in manufacturing. After the eight-hour day was won, workers turned to the reduction of weekly hours from 48 to 40, in many cases with an intermediate stop at 44 hours. Labor leaders today are talking about the 35-, 32-, and even the 30-hour week.

Why this continual demand for shorter hours of work? In the early days of the movement, worker emphasis was on reducing what was literally a backbreaking day in many cases. Another idea of the workers and unions was undoubtedly to reduce the effective labor supply by reducing the amount of labor any one worker offered. They hoped that this reduction might both relieve unemployment and, more important, raise wages. Most of the hours-reduction movements have been partially rationalized by the argument that it was good for employers as well. This argument stated that long hours of work tired the workers and they produced less than they could have by working at a higher speed for a shorter period. While this argument did prove true in many cases, it was certainly more of a rationalization from the union point of view. As hours were reduced and wages increased, unions and workers paid more attention to the values of leisure time. They could now afford golf clubs, boats and outboard motors, homes in the suburbs with yard work to be done, and the leisure time to devote to these activities.

In recent years, a new bogeyman has arisen. Actually, this is an old menace in a newly phrased disguise—automation. Many unions claim that new machines and techniques are going to put men out of work. Therefore, if hours are shortened, employment will be maintained by spreading the available work among the labor force. Thus far in our history, innovations have increased rather than reduced the over-all demand for labor. However, it is true that many men may see well-developed skills made obsolete, and much retraining and movement of labor may be necessary to reduce the impact of shifting labor needs in a technological economy. This approach has been recognized in present and proposed federal and state legislation.

Reductions in hours of work are one method of distributing the gains of productivity increases. If more can be produced with the same hours of labor effort, the current output can be produced with fewer hours of effort. Historically, productivity adjustments have taken the form of both increased leisure and increased physical production.

The basic practices concerning hours of work are found in state law and the Federal Fair Labor Standards Act. The federal law covers workers engaged in interstate commerce or in the production of goods for interstate commerce. These workers must be paid at least one and one-half times their regular rate of pay for all hours worked in excess of 40 hours in any week. There is no maximum number of hours in the federal law. Some state laws prescribe maximum numbers of hours that can be worked in any period. These apply particularly to women, children, and workers in hazardous industries. With the Fair Labor Standards Act as a base, many employment relationships merely provide for standards which are greater than those required by the law. The most common addition is to provide for overtime payments for hours worked in excess of eight hours in any day. This is not required under the Fair Labor Standards Act.

Some contracts call for overtime premiums in excess of time and one-half. Others call for overtime after periods shorter than 40 hours. For example, overtime is paid after 35 hours in anthracite coal mining. Many union contracts specify starting and quitting times and days of the week to be worked. In general however, management retains the right to make reasonable changes in these factors. It is rather common to provide for "call-in" pay, for those workers who come to work but are not needed. In addition to the overtime pay provided under the law for hours worked in excess of 40 hours in a week, most labor agreements call for premium pay on Saturday and Sunday or on the sixth and seventh days in a week. While individual practices vary, the most common premiums paid are time and one-half for Saturdays and the sixth day of work and double time for Sundays and the seventh day of work.

FRINGE BENEFITS

Since World War II, "fringe issues" have become an increasingly important part of the total employment relationship. There are many different concepts of a fringe issue but in general they would include all supplementary employment benefits that are a cost to the employer but are not part of the regular pay of the worker. They range from pension plans to free meals, and from guaranteed wages to payments for time spent on jury duty. While most of the fringe benefits antedate World War II, it was at that time that they became important in labor relations. During the war, wage rates were controlled by the War Labor Board and few wage increases were permitted. Many companies found it difficult to attract the workers they needed because while their wages might have been the same as other companies, other benefits were not comparable. The War Labor Board allowed companies to have approximately the same fringe benefits. This opened a large area in which companies could give more to their workers without violating the wage ceilings. Thus many companies began providing fringe benefits at that time as a means of attracting labor. And, as most companies were financially able to pay more to their workers, they readily agreed to the fringe benefits. Most of these benefits were continued and expanded after the war.

Fringe benefits are closely related to the basic desire of the worker for security. Pensions offer security against need in old age, accident insurance provides protection against disability, life insurance offers protection for the family, and guaranteed annual wages provide security against unemployment. In addition, fringe benefits open new areas for union activity. Many strong unions find they have increased wages about as far as possible at a given time without completely disrupting the labor market, but they can get further concessions in the area of fringe benefits. Also, the fringe benefits permit the union and the employer to offer a diversified package to the workers. Once the area of fringe benefits was opened during World War II, workers, unions, and employers became interested in them, and they have reached the point that in many package settlements the cost of fringe benefits exceeds the cost of direct wage increases.

TABLE 9–2
FRINGE BENEFITS PAID BY 1120 COMPANIES, 1961

Type of Supplement	Per Cent of Companies
Social security	100
Unemployment compensation	99
Insurance (life, medical, etc.)	98
Paid vacations or bonus in lieu of vacation	97
Payment for holidays not worked	97
Workmen's compensation	95
Pension plans	86
Paid rest periods, wash-up time, etc.	63
Paid sick leave	54
Christmas or other special bonuses	43
Employee meals	21
Separation or termination pay allowances	17
Profit sharing	17
Employee educational expenses	16
Discounts on goods and services purchased	15

SOURCE: Chamber of Commerce of the United States, *Fringe Benefits—1961,* (Washington, D.C., 1962).

The Chamber of Commerce 1961 study of fringe benefits noted that they averaged 24.9 per cent of payroll, 61.6 cents per hour, and $1,254 per year per employee. The estimate includes the cost of compulsory social insurance programs such as workmen's compensation, unemployment insurance, and old age, survivors and disability insurance.

ISSUES OF SECURITY

All of the parties in industrial relations are interested in security. Management, union, and workers are all apprehensive about their future. Therefore, it is usual to find one or more clauses in a collective bargaining agreement offering, with varying degrees of success, some form of protection against future contingencies for each of the three parties.

Management Security

Employers almost universally view the union as a threat to the control of their business. As collective bargaining develops between a union and management, the union gradually exhibits an interest in more and more phases of the enterprise. From a simple contract governing wages and hours, agreements grow to include clauses dealing with shift assignments, introduction of new methods and machinery, time study, safety, sanitary facilities, and many other matters. Management feels that such extensions of the labor agreement pose a challenge to its control.

To protect against future inroads, management usually wishes to have a clause in the contract protecting their "prerogatives." The purpose of such a clause is to spell out management's "rights" and to preclude the possibility of a union challenge of such issues during the course of the contract. Management rights clauses do not have too much effect. Being a part of the contract, they are subject to interpretation under the grievance procedure. In addition, they are effective only for the term of the contract and are not necessarily continued in a subsequent contract. And, being a part of the jointly negotiated contract, they are, for practical purposes, only a guarantee of exclusive management control of those matters that the union has been willing to agree to in bargaining.

Union Security

Unions have never felt very secure in their collective bargaining positions. They see possible threats to their future existence from management, other unions, and membership inertia. To insure their viability as the bargaining agent, they will seek some form of compulsory membership clause in the labor agreement.

Unions want all of the workers in the bargaining unit to belong to the union. The union is legally the representative of all of the workers in the bargaining unit regardless of whether the workers belong to the union. Since all of the workers benefit from the efforts of the union, it is contended all should belong to the union and contribute to its support. Union leaders also feel that having all of the workers belong to the union reduces friction among workers, and the employer benefits through greater output. And, they say that the union will spend less time recruiting and retaining members and more time trying to improve the bargaining relationship.

On the other hand, most managements feel that it is undemocratic to force a man to join a union if he does not want to do so. Management also maintains that if the union is doing a good job, the men will join voluntarily. And, finally, they feel that if all men must belong to the union, there is no check upon the union's operation and efficiency.

Today, more than two thirds of all workers working under a union agreement are covered by some form of union security. Currently, the most common form of union security is the union shop. Under this type of agreement, any worker may be hired, but after a certain period of time, usually thirty days, the worker must join the union and remain in good standing as a condition of employment. The Taft-Hartley Act has restricted the operation of the union shop. Under that act, a worker may be legally discharged by the employer for not belonging to the union only when union membership has been denied or terminated because of the worker's failure to pay the normal dues and initiation fees.

Closely allied to union security is the check-off. The check-off is a system wherein the employer deducts union dues from the worker's pay and forwards the payment to the union. This is an easy and sure system of dues collection for the union, and it may even benefit the employer, despite the increased bookkeeping costs, by reducing the amount of work-time lost by union officers badgering members into paying their dues. Under the Taft-Hartley Act, an employer can only deduct union dues from a worker's pay when the worker has signed a written authorization to that effect.

In addition to the restrictions on the union shop contained in the Taft-Hartley Act, many states have enacted laws regulating or outlawing union security agreements. The laws which outlaw all forms of union security and usually the check-off as well are called "right-to-work laws." The same basic arguments are used for and against the right-to-work laws as are used in the basic union security debate. The Taft-Hartley Act permits the right-to-work laws to take precedence over its own rules permitting the union shop.

Worker's Security

One of the major reasons for workers joining a union is to gain some protection against arbitrary layoffs and other forms of discriminatory treatment at the hands of the employer. This goal is achieved through the incorporation of seniority rules and a grievance procedure in the labor contract. Basically, seniority means the use of the length of a worker's service with the employer as a determining factor in layoff, promotion, rehiring, and other situations affecting a worker's status on the job.

Advocates of seniority maintain that skill and ability tend to increase with length of service so that long-service employees will be better workers than newer workers. Also, that rewarding long-service employees improves the morale of the workers and reduces labor turnover. And, probably most important, it removes the discretionary element from the decisions and eliminates favoritism. The main objection to the use of seniority is that it overlooks ability. Also, it makes it impossible to reward initiative and hard work and tends to remove incentive. To overcome some of these objections, many seniority agreements provide that seniority is considered only where ability is approximately equal or where seniority is considered along with ability.

What decisions will be influenced or controlled by seniority? Seniority is almost universally used in connection with layoffs and rehiring after layoffs. It is less often but still frequently used in cases of promotion, although here it is frequently used in conjunction with ability.

CONCLUSION

Wages probably constitute the most important aspect of the employment relationship for both the worker and the employer. To the worker, they form the major source of his income. To the employer, they are one of the most important items in his costs of production. In the absence of a union, the employer has a relatively free hand to set whatever wages he wishes within the limits set by the labor market in which he is located. Where a union is present, wages represent the joint agreement of the union and the company. Union determination of wages is of primary importance in most of the nonagricultural employment in the United States today. But in union-management negotiations, wages are only part of a total package. Other issues of great importance are hours of work, vacation, pension and welfare plans, and security. The agreement reached by the union and management will constitute a total package describing the employment relationship in detail. No one aspect of this relationship can realistically be separated from the others. Wages, hours and fringe benefits are interrelated, both as to the merits of the job as viewed by the worker and as to their impact on the employer's costs of production.

Some persons feel that unions, in pursuing their goals, have a harmful effect insofar as the economy as a whole is concerned. The effect of negotiated wage increases is most often cited in this respect. Do the unions simply drive up prices so that their wage increases are self-defeating? Do union programs retard technological improvements? Is the power possessed by some unions a transitory thing, or is it a permanent part of the landscape which threatens the very existence of the system? These are only some of the questions which must be answered in determining the future status of labor unions.

Public policy has and will continue to change. The question of what the proper public policy ought to be is a normative question for which there is no single "correct" answer. Whatever policy is adopted will have a better chance of succeeding if it is based on clear and nonemotional thinking. Public policy based on sheer emotion has little chance of succeeding. It matters not whether one considers himself as being "prolabor" or "promanagement" if that position is a result of thought rather than passion, but one who is "prolabor" or "promanagement" as a result of emotion only can make little contribution to successful public policy.

EXERCISES

Group I

Explain why the following statements are either true or false:

1. Nonunion employers do not have to concern themselves with union wages in setting their wages.
2. The employment package rather than just the wage rate is becoming increasingly important.
3. Real annual income is the most important wage concept in determining one's standard of living.
4. The labor market closely approximates the economist's concept of a perfect market.
5. The marginal net revenue product of labor is the basis of the employer's demand for that factor.
6. The supply of labor for an entire industry will be more elastic than will the supply of labor for a particular firm within the industry.
7. If both unions and management are fair and objective, there would be no need for collective bargaining over wage rates.
8. Union security is represented by those demands of the union seeking greater security for the individual workers who are represented by the union.
9. Unions are usually enthusiastic supporters of piecework wage arrangements.

Group II

1. Compare wages in union and nonunion companies in your community. Explain the difference.
2. Make a study of a current bargaining experience. Compare the original demands and offers of the parties with the final settlement. Explain the strategy of the respective parties.

Group III

1. Have unions raised real wages in the economy? Have unions raised real wages for their own members? How have they affected wages of nonmembers?
2. Analyze the proposition that "Labor unions are monopolies." In what respects do they differ from business monopolies and in what respects are they similar? Base your conclusion on reason and facts rather than emotion.
3. It is argued by many that increasing the minimum wage will increase the level of unemployment. Others argue that it will increase the demand for

goods and services and thus increase employment. Investigate and evaluate the two arguments. Can you use the same arguments in the case of union negotiated wage increases—that is, do unions cause unemployment?

BIBLIOGRAPHY

BUREAU OF NATIONAL AFFAIRS. *Collective Bargaining Negotiations and Contracts, Contract Clause Finder.* Washington, D.C. (current).

REYNOLDS, LLOYD G. *Structure of Labor Markets.* New York: Harper & Brothers, 1951.

ROSS, ARTHUR M. *Trade Union Wage Policies.* Berkeley: University of California Press, 1948.

TAYLOR, GEORGE W., and PIERSON, FRANK C. *New Concepts in Wage Determination.* New York: McGraw-Hill Book Co., Inc., 1957.

WOYTINSKY, W. S., and Others. *Employment and Wages in the United States.* New York: Twentieth Century Fund, 1953.

WRIGHT, DAVID MCCORD (Ed.). *The Impact of the Union.* New York: Harcourt, Brace & Co., 1951.

Chapter 10   CAPITAL AND INTEREST

Whereas it has long been known and declared that the poor have no right to the property of the rich, I wish it also to be known and declared that the rich have no right to the property of the poor.—John Ruskin, *Unto This Last.*

The American economic system is distinguished from other economies by the fact that most of the productive plant is privately owned. Private parties furnish the productive capacity required to maintain and advance our high standards of living. Some of the funds to provide this productive capacity come from business firms. In addition, individuals have surplus funds which they make available to business enterprise. Borrowing and lending are commonplace, and a host of institutions service this economic activity.

This chapter, then, deals with capital (the man-made good in the productive process), the return to capital (interest), and the institutions which facilitate the conversion of savings into capital.

INTRODUCTION

Gross and Net (Pure) Interest

Interest is the price paid by a borrower to a lender for the privilege of using funds belonging to the lender. It is expressed as a percentage of the principal—the amount of money being borrowed—and unless expressed in different terms, interest is an annual premium.

Interest is generally associated with capital—one of the productive factors. More properly, interest is the price paid to obtain the funds with which capital may be obtained. But loanable funds may also be used by consumers to finance the immediate purchase of goods for current consumption. Such funds are mobile, so the law of one price might be expected to prevail in the loanable-funds market. However, in actual practice there is a wide variation in interest rates, ranging from less than 1 per cent at some times for certain U.S. government securities to 30 and 40 per cent or more for small loans to consumers. In addition, there are wide variations in interest rates paid for a particular type of loan by different borrowers and for loans of different maturities.

How can such variations prevail in a market characterized by a relatively high degree of mobility and in which most of the participants are well informed about alternative interest rates? The answer lies in the difference between the gross interest rate and the net (or pure) interest rate. Gross interest is the contract interest rate—the actual payment agreed upon between the lender and the borrower. The net interest rate is the premium paid solely for the use of loanable funds. The gross interest rate is more than a payment for the immediate use of funds by borrowers and the abstinence from the use of funds by the lenders.

The gross interest rate will include the net interest payment and a risk premium that will vary with the risk associated with the loan. One of the major problems connected with lending funds is the risk that the borrower will be unable or unwilling to repay the amount he has borrowed. Thus, General Motors will find that it can borrow money at a lower gross rate than can an unknown individual who wishes to borrow several million dollars to finance a projected rocket trip to Venus. The greater the likelihood that the borrower will repay the loan and meet the interest charges, the closer the gross interest will be to the net interest rate.

In addition to the differing degrees of risk associated with different loans, there are also differences in the cost of making loans. These include the costs of investigating the credit risk associated with the loan—an investigation of the borrower's financial status and ability to repay, the location of suitable lenders, etc. In addition the management of a loan and the collection of the principal and interest involve additional costs. Installment loans which require monthly payments and which might involve legal actions to collect are expensive relative to the average size of loan. On the other hand, a loan to a well-known industrial firm calling for semiannual interest payments and repayment of the principal in twenty years involve little or no collection expense. Institutions handling loanable funds include in the gross interest rate a sufficient premium to compensate them for the costs associated with the loan.

Another factor influencing the gross interest rate is the duration of the loan. For a given degree of risk and cost of management, a short-term loan will ordinarily carry a lower gross interest rate than a long-term loan. This is because short-term loans are more liquid—they are more easily converted into cash. Such loans are a more attractive investment for temporary surplus funds of business. In addition, the short-term loan is popular because it eliminates much of the risk of future uncertainty. Suppliers of loanable funds may be reluctant to lend money under long-term commitments because of a feeling that interest rates may be higher in the future. However, by lending for a short term, the loan is continually being liquidated, and the opportunity is always present to take advantage of changes in the interest rate.

Effective Rate of Interest

In the realm of consumer credit, there is considerable confusion as to the actual interest paid by a consumer. This is particularly true in installment loans. In general, the consumer has the impression that he is paying a relatively low interest rate when, in fact, he may be paying an effective rate of interest of two or three times the amount stated in the installment contract. This discrepancy arises out of two characteristics of many installment loans. First, the interest rate is usually applied to the entire amount of the loan for the *entire installment period.* For example, a person borrowing $1,000 to buy a new car is quoted an interest rate of 6 per cent. The bank or other financing institution then charges him $120 interest to cover the two years of the installment contract. They have charged him for the use of $1,000 for two years, but the customer does not have the use of the money for that long. At the end of the first month, he repays part of the loan and by the time of the twenty-fourth monthly payment he has only about one twenty-fourth of the institution's money, not the whole $1,000. The customer has not borrowed $1,000 for two years but has borrowed an amount that is $1,000 for the first month only and then is declining throughout the installment period. Averaging out these declining amounts, the customer has the use of $1,000 for approximately twelve and a half months, or the use of a little more than $500 for twenty-four months.

A second device which clouds the interest rate on installment loans is the "finance charge" which in some cases is in addition to a regular interest charge. The customer is charged 6 per cent interest plus a 2 or 3 per cent "finance charge" to cover the cost of the installment loan. The finance charge is included in gross interest in addition to that amount explicitly stated as interest.

A formula to compute the effective rate of interest is:

$$i = \frac{2mf}{P(n + 1)}$$

Where:

> i is the effective interest rate per year,
> m is the number of payment periods per year (*i.e.,* 12 months, 52 weeks, etc.),
> f is the finance charge plus interest expressed as dollars and cents,
> P is the net amount actually loaned to the borrower,
> n the number of payments to be made.

In our example of a person borrowing $1,000 to be repaid over twenty-four months at a nominal interest charge of 6 per cent, the effective rate would be 11.52 per cent. As a rough approximation, the effective rate will be almost twice the nominal rate of interest on an installment loan. And if an additional finance charge is included, the difference between the nominal and effective interest rates will be larger.

A further confusion exists in the case of some retail establishments which sell on credit. Credit is made available to almost everyone, and thus customers are attracted who cannot afford to pay cash and who do not really understand the cost of credit. In such establishments, the price of the article may be set above the normal price for the article. In that way, the effective financing charges are partially hidden, and the consumer is misled as to the cost of credit. By adjusting the price of the product, almost any effective interest rate can be obtained.

NET INTEREST RATE

The basic payment for the use of funds for a period of time is the net (or pure) rate of interest. It does not include any risk premium or compensation for the cost of making the loan. The net interest rate is determined through the interaction of the demand for and the supply of loanable funds. Thus, a study of the demand and supply of loanable funds is basic to a discussion of the net interest rate.

Demand for Loanable Funds

Consumer Demand. Part of the demand for loanable funds comes from consumers in the economy. Consumers desire loanable funds to purchase goods—furniture, houses, etc. Why are consumers willing to pay a premium in the form of interest to obtain funds to make such purchases? The reasons vary with the nature of the purchase in mind.

In the case of home buying, the demand for loanable funds may arise from simple economic expediency. The alternative to owning one's own home is renting or leasing property. Thus, most individuals will be accustomed to making periodic payments to secure living accommodations. Normally they will pay a certain sum every month to the owner of the property they are using. The payment of rent is a pure consumption transaction. The utility purchased with the monthly rental is dissipated within the month. Nothing permanent accrues to the renter. He may compare this pure consumption payment with the cost of borrowing a sufficient amount of money to enable him to purchase his own home. When the purchase of a home is undertaken, a monthly payment is also called for. However, in this case the payment actually consists of two payments: one, a payment for the use of the borrowed money—interest; and, second, a partial repayment of the principal borrowed. In this way, at the end of a specified number of years, the borrowed sum will be repaid and the borrower will own the asset.

If a family has a budgeted amount it can spend upon living accommodations, the higher the interest rate, the less money they will be able to borrow to purchase a home. A high interest rate means that a larger share of the monthly payment will be in the form of interest, leaving a smaller amount to be applied to the principal. Assuming a fixed period of repayment, that means that the principal must be smaller. On the other hand, when the interest rate is low, a larger sum of money can be borrowed, as the interest part of the monthly payment will be smaller and a larger amount can be applied to the repayment of the principal. Even the family willing to pay a certain amount per month in the form of interest will find that the lower the interest rate, the larger the amount of money they can borrow, and the higher the interest rate, the smaller the sum of money which they can borrow. Thus, the demand for funds to be used in the purchase of homes tends to have the familiar characteristics of the law of demand; namely, the higher the price, the smaller the quantity demanded and the lower the price, the larger the quantity demanded.

Certain other consumer purchases have many of the features of home buying; that is, that the expense of borrowing to buy replaces an alternative consumption expense. A person considering the purchase of a new car might well weigh the alternative costs of public transportation.

Time Preference. It is easy to state that people are foolish to borrow money to purchase an item which is not considered to be a necessity. One might say that it is far cheaper to save the money first and pay cash to avoid the interest and other financing charges. Yet, millions of persons contract debts to enable them to purchase the goods they desire. Partially, this reflects the difficulty most people have in saving for a future purchase. More important, however, is what is called "time preference."

Time preference refers to the relative valuation placed upon a good today as compared to its future value. When a person prefers a good today rather than in the future, he has positive time preference. When a person values a future good higher than a present good, he has negative time preference. It should be obvious that most people have positive time preference; that is, they enjoy present goods more than future goods. For example, a typical family is considering the purchase of a television set priced at $200. This family can budget ten dollars a month for a television set. By saving this amount they could buy the set for cash in little more than a year and one-half. But they want the set now. It is more valuable to them now than in a year and one-half. And as evidence of this greater value, they will buy the set now and arrange to pay ten dollars a month for two full years or a total payment of $240. In other words, the set today is worth forty dollars more to this family than the same set twenty months in the future.

Why do people have a positive time preference? Obviously a person has the use of the good immediately. Another reason is uncertainty. We don't know what conditions will be in a year or two. The present is much more important and certain than the future. It is difficult for some people to project their wants and desires far into the future.

Another factor affecting time preference is the prospect for future incomes. A person with reasonable expectations of an increasing income will have positive time preference. On the other hand, a person expecting a declining income in the future, perhaps because of an impending retirement, might well have negative time preference. But in any case, the more a person discounts his future income through current borrowing, the greater must be his time preference. This is true because as we increase our consumption in the present, we resort to less and less important expenditures yielding less and less utility, and as we give up more and more future purchases, the more important those foregone purchases become. Thus time preference will also give us a demand schedule where the quantity of loanable funds demanded varies inversely with the price of those funds.

Business Demand. An important segment of the demand for loanable funds comes from business organizations. The uses to which these funds are put increase the productivity of the business. As a result, business loans have a marked difference from consumer loans. Business loans will be used in such a way that income is created out of which both principal and interest can be paid. If the businessman has invested wisely, the investment will return not only enough to repay the loan but enough to pay the price of the loan as well. Certainly, if it did not appear that the investment would earn enough, above and beyond other costs, to repay the loan and required interest, it would not be an economically sound investment. On the other hand, it would be wise to invest as long as it appeared likely that the return would be sufficient to repay the loan plus interest. Therefore, the amount of funds businessmen will borrow at various interest rates depends upon the productivity of the investments.

In Chapter 9 the principle of diminishing productivity and its impact upon the demand for labor were discussed. In that instance, it was noted that as additional units of labor were added to a fixed amount of land and capital, a point was reached beyond which further additions of labor yielded successively smaller returns. The same principle operates when capital is the variable factor and land and labor are fixed. As additional units of capital are added to a fixed amount of land and labor, a point is reached beyond which further units of capital yield smaller and smaller additional returns. Until we reach the point of diminishing productivity, the fixed factors are being used less efficiently. Thus, the significant part of the productivity curve is that beyond the point of diminishing productivity. In the case of capital, the marginal revenue product must be expressed as a rate of return so that it can be compared with the cost of capital.

The curve representing the marginal revenue productivity of capital will have a negative slope—that is, as more units of capital are employed, the return derived from its product will decrease. With equal units of capital costing the same amount of money and a declining yield, the difference between the cost of the capital and the return will decline and eventually disappear. It is this difference which permits the payment of interest. So we can say that the lower the interest rate, the more units of capital it will be profitable to use and the greater the demand for loanable funds by businessmen. This will be true even when all of the productive factors are varied. Given the prices of the productive factors and their productivities, there will always be one optimum combination that will enable the businessman to produce at the lowest unit cost of production. At that combination, the marginal costs of the different factors will be in balance. That is, we could not improve our position by replacing a worker with a machine, or a tractor with another acre of land. But if the cost of any one factor increases while the costs of the other factors remain the same, it will then pay to use less of the costlier factor and more of the other factors. Thus if interest rates rose, it would pay to use less capital and more land and labor and if interest rates fell, it would pay to use more capital and less labor and land.

Marginal Efficiency of Capital. A somewhat different approach to the problem of the value productivity of capital was presented by J. M. Keynes (1883–1946) in the marginal efficiency of capital.[1] Keynes based his concept upon a comparison of two values. One, the prospective yield of an investment during its life and the other, the supply price of the capital goods. The prospective yield would be the net money return expected from the use of the capital asset for each year of its life. The supply price of the asset would be the price which would be large enough to induce the manufacturer of the capital asset to produce an additional unit of such asset. We could find a present value for the prospective yields of the capital assets by discounting their future yields by some rate of interest. Keynes defines the marginal efficiency of capital as being that discount rate which would make the present value of the future yields of the capital asset just equal to its current supply price. Or, as he expressed it, ". . . I define the marginal

---

[1] John M. Keynes, *The General Theory of Employment, Interest, and Money* (New York: Harcourt, Brace & Co., 1935), chap. 11.

efficiency of capital as being equal to that rate of discount which would make the present value of the series of annuities given by the returns expected from the capital asset during its life just equal to its supply price."[2]

In ordinary business terminology, the marginal efficiency of capital is the discounted rate of return that could be made from an additional unit of investment in capital equipment. Keynes felt that as the supply of any given type of investment increased, the marginal efficiency of capital would decrease. And as it would pay the businessman to invest in any capital asset whose marginal efficiency of capital exceeded the interest rate, the business demand for investment funds would follow the characteristic demand pattern; namely, the lower the price (interest), the larger the quantity demanded.

Government Demand. Government also borrows. All levels of government participate in this demand; local governments, school districts, county and state governments, the federal government, and various governmental agencies such as turnpike commissions, universities, and public-power authorities. Many of these demands are to be used for purposes that can be considered self-liquidating. A turnpike is supposed to raise enough money through the collection of tolls to cover its operating costs, pay the interest on its bonds, and to provide for the retirement of the bonds themselves. Rental at a state university dormitory is to do likewise. If interest rates are rather high, the authorities concerned may decide not to issue the bonds until a later date or to revise their needs downward to a point where prospective income will cover the costs of the bonds. Thus, this demand bears the usual characteristics of a demand curve.

Many other government projects are financed through borrowed funds. A city may find itself in immediate need of new school buildings. Such facilities will be used for many years and it is common to finance their construction with borrowed funds. The interest on such loans and repayment must come from tax revenues. This demand may be affected slightly by the interest rate. As the expense of the loan is to be borne by tax revenues, there is an effective limit to the total interest charges that can be carried. If interest rates are high this will mean that smaller amounts can be borrowed. If interest rates are low, larger sums can be borrowed without increasing the interest cost to the taxpayer (of course, repayment also must be considered).

Where the government must borrow funds to cover the costs of its general operation, a different problem arises. Ordinarily, such bor-

[2] *Ibid.*, p. 135.

rowing is done only in times of public crisis, such as an economic collapse or a war. At those times the need is so great and the problem so immediate that little regard is paid the interest rate. Funds are needed immediately. However, in many cases of this type, particularly those in which the federal government bears the brunt of the expenditures, the borrowed funds tend to become a permanent part of the government debt. As such they must continually be refinanced, and each time the government is a participant on the demand side of the market. The impact of government on the capital market is discussed more fully later in this chapter.

Supply of Loanable Funds

The supply of loanable funds depends upon the willingness of people and institutions to lend purchasing power to other individuals in return for the latter's promise to repay a larger amount in the future. Individuals, businesses, and the government supply loanable funds. The ability to loan funds depends upon their having surplus funds which are not needed in current consumption. Surpluses arise because income exceeds consumption expenditures, in other words, savings. In addition, commercial banks provide a source of loanable funds through the creation of deposit credit.

Personal Savings. One source of savings in the economy is personal savings. As people receive income, they spend a part of it for consumption goods. For some people, consumption expenditures will exhaust their total income. But for others, some of their income may not be needed in immediate consumption and this amount can be saved. Personal saving is an abstention from consumption by individuals.

Why do people save? There are many reasons. Some save simply because it is difficult to spend all of their current income. People with very large incomes may satisfy all of their consumptions needs without exhausting their income. Unfortunately, not many people are in this predicament. The large majority of people in the United States would have little difficulty in finding uses for their current income. In such cases, saving means a sacrifice of current consumption, and the saver must be compensated for this sacrifice.

Life is such that people face many uncertainties. A blowout of an automobile tire, an illness of a child, the unexpected replacement of a refrigerator—all are uncertainties which cannot be predicted. Their impact may well jeopardize the current financial status of the victims. To avoid this, many people save to meet the vicissitudes of life and to cushion the impact of financial catastrophes.

Another important motive for savings is that of saving for a specific goal. A vacation, particularly an expensive one such as a trip to Europe, a Caribbean cruise, or a month at Miami Beach may be possible through systematic saving of small amounts of money. Saving is not an easy thing for most people to accomplish, for time preference is very strong. And saving for a future goal must appear more valuable than the things one might consume currently. However, a specific goal may offer sufficient attraction to overcome this positive time preference. Dreams of a night on the town in Paris or a swim at Waikiki may induce a person to forego current expenditures.

Another popular goal of savings is education. More and more parents realize the value and importance of a college education for their children. By saving from the time the child is very young, such an education may well be possible. Christmas Clubs and similar programs are another form of savings for a specific goal.

It is interesting to note that the income-producing motive for saving is not very important as a force inducing people to abstain from current consumption. Many early economists felt that people saved to earn money from the investment of their savings. Thus, a greater return was supposed to induce people to save a larger portion of their incomes. The strength of this argument has steadily declined among economists, and today it is generally recognized that the size of a person's income is by far the most important force in determining the amount of an individual's saving. Table 10–1 provides strong evidence for this point.

TABLE 10–1

LIQUID ASSET HOLDINGS* BY SPENDING UNIT, EARLY 1959

Income of Spending Unit	*Per Cent of Spending Units with Liquid Asset Holdings of:*				
	0	*$1–499*	*$500–1,999*	*$2,000–4,999*	*$5,000 & over*
Less than $1,000	61	17	12	5	4
$1,000–1,999	50	24	16	5	5
$2,000–2,999	44	24	16	8	8
$3,000–3,999	28	36	18	11	7
$4,000–4,999	21	45	19	8	8
$5,000–5,999	14	44	24	13	6
$6,000–7,499	7	43	29	15	7
$7,500–9,999	4	28	34	20	14
$10,000 & over	2	12	26	26	34

* Liquid Assets include: U.S. Savings Bonds, checking accounts, savings accounts, shares in savings and loan associations and credit unions.

SOURCE: *Economic Almanac 1962*, National Industrial Conference Board, New York, 1962.

A very important segment of personal savings is the repayment of debts. A person with a $5,000-a-year income may buy a $12,000 house. In that year, his expenditures exceed his current income. But at the same time, he incurs a debt which will involve future repayment. In future years, this individual must consume less than his income and use the difference to repay his debt. When the individual forwards his monthly mortgage payment to the building and loan company, that amount of money is again available for lending. In a sense this is also saving for a specific purpose, except that the purpose has been or is currently being enjoyed rather than being anticipated future satisfaction. Savings of this type also depend upon income levels but here in the sense of making possible the repayment of debt. In a period of low incomes, many people may have to default because of their inability to pay.

The particular form which one's savings may take is influenced by several factors. The first is that of liquidity. Liquidity refers to the ease with which savings may be converted into cash; therefore, the most liquid form of savings is cash itself. Certainly, every saver wants part of his savings in the form of cash and a part in some form which can be readily converted into cash. Secondly, a saver will want security for his savings. There is always a chance that the savings will be lost in their entirety, and one must take cognizance of this possibility. Against this he must balance a third factor, namely, yield. The greater the chance of loss, the higher the rate of return; and the greater the security, the lower the rate of return. The fourth factor which must be considered is the possibility of depreciation or appreciation of savings. Regardless of the form of savings, the purchasing power will vary as the general level of prices changes. Obviously, the person who has saved would prefer to see the value of the savings increase. With these thoughts in mind, then, a few comments may be made about the various forms of savings which are available to the individual.

(*a*) Money savings offer the highest degree of liquidity as well as the maximum amount of security; however, there is no yield. In times of rising prices, the value of such savings will depreciate, but they will appreciate during times of falling prices.

(*b*) Savings in banks and other financial institutions are nearly as liquid as money, and the security of such savings is nearly that of cash. The yield will be small if any, and the value will vary inversely with the price level.

(*c*) Government bonds have a high degree of liquidity, and they offer the same security as money. The yield, however, is less than that paid by some other outlets, although it compares favorably with that provided by some private financial institutions. Bonds, like money, depreciate in value during periods of inflation and appreciate in periods of falling prices.

(*d*) Bonds of private enterprise offer a fourth outlet. Such bonds are fairly liquid, but they offer a lesser degree of security than government bonds. The yield will be somewhat higher than that offered by the other forms of savings mentioned so far. Their value will vary inversely with the price level.

(*e*) Corporate stocks representing an equity investment in corporations have a high degree of liquidity, but one may suffer a capital loss or enjoy a capital gain when such securities are liquidated. Stocks offer less security than bonds, but the potential return is much greater. The price of corporate securities varies directly with the general level of prices. As prices increase, the price of securities increases, and vice versa. This is the great advantage of this type of savings in periods of rising prices, but it is, of course, a disadvantage during periods of falling prices.

(*f*) Insurance is both a means of saving and a means of protection. As a means of saving, it lacks the liquidity and does not have the yield offered by common stock. It suffers the same disadvantages as cash during periods of rising prices, but it enjoys the advantages of cash during periods of falling prices. In most instances savings of this nature have a very high degree of security.

(*g*) Commodities and direct investment offer another outlet for personal savings. There is less liquidity, although this will vary depending upon the particular type of outlet selected. There is less security than most other forms, but there is also the chance of a much higher yield. In some instances the value will continue to increase through depression and prosperity, but for the most part, the value of savings will be endangered during a depression, just as it will be enhanced during periods of price increases.

These are the major outlets for personal savings. The wise saver must pick that outlet for his savings which will provide the desired liquidity, sufficient security, and a satisfactory yield. Furthermore, the saver must institute changes in his savings portfolio as general economic conditions change, for a savings program which is satisfactory for one moment in time may be unsuitable for another.

Business Savings. Business firms also save. Businesses, like consumers, save by not spending all of their income. They may set aside depreciation and obsolescence allowances that allocate the cost of past investments over their useful lives. This provides an important source of funds for business spending on plant and equipment. It is currently estimated that approximately one-half of business capital outlays originate from this source. In 1961, businesses in the United States set aside capital consumption allowances of $45.2 billion. This form of saving simply permits the maintenance of the present level of capital accumulation in the country. And even this is not accomplished in periods of rising prices when the depreciation allowances based on the costs of past investments do not provide sufficient funds to replace these investments at current prices.

Businesses may also save by reinvesting part of their earnings. In 1961, corporate business in the United States made profits of $46.1 billion. Corporate income taxes took $22.8 billion, leaving $23.3 billion of after-tax corporate income. Of this amount, the corporations distributed $14.4 billion in dividends to the stockholders of the businesses. The remaining $8.8 billion was retained by the corporations for reinvestment. Retained earnings are an increasingly important component of capital growth.

Is there any relationship between business savings and the interest rate? Basically, business savings appear to be made independent of the interest rate. Capital consumption allowances, the major portion of business savings, depend upon past investments, current replacement costs, and expected life of investments. None of these factors is directly dependent upon the interest rate. Reinvested earnings depend in the first instance upon the availability of earnings. Having earnings, a business may decide to reinvest its own earnings rather than borrow from others if interest rates are very high. However, this effect is probably not very significant in the total supply of savings. It does mean though, that business firms don't have to enter the market as borrowers, and thus such savings do influence the rate of interest.

Government Savings. The different levels of government may also save. Whenever a government runs a budgetary surplus—that is, when it takes more from the economy in taxes than it returns through expenditures—it saves. On the other hand, when the government spends more money than it takes in—when it runs a deficit—it dissaves. It then appears on the demand side of the loanable-funds market, seeking to borrow funds to make up the difference between its income and expenditures. Permanent government investments—such as the Grand Coulee Dam in the state of Washington or improvements in navigation facilities on the Ohio River—are a form of savings. Such projects involve the use of portions of current income to finance improvements that will yield benefits to production and consumption in future years, which is the essence of savings.

Supply of Bank Credit. Another factor influencing the supply of loanable funds is the quantity of money in the economy. In this sense, we count demand deposits in banks as well as currency and coin as money. Some authorities would also include savings (time) deposits in this definition of money. If there is an increase in the supply of money, more funds will be available to investors than is furnished by savers out of the current income. On the other hand, a decrease in the supply of money would tend to reduce the supply of loanable funds below that amount that would have been supplied if the money influence were neutral.

In our economy, the largest part of the money supply consists of bank deposit credit. Is there any relationship between the supply of this type of money and the interest rate? In other words, does the rate of interest influence the supply of money? The monetary authorities in the government exercise control over the supply of money and regulate the supply in such a way as to influence the over-all performance of the economy. That is, they consider levels of employment, the volume of investment, interest rates, price levels, the economy's need for liquidity, and many other factors. Since the interest rate is only one of many factors influencing the monetary authorities, it would not be too inaccurate to assume that at any period of time, the total money supply is more or less independent of the interest rate insofar as the monetary authorities are concerned.

The banking system is, however, influenced by the rate of interest. Given the lending capacity, a bank would be willing to make more loans and thus increase the supply of money at higher rates of interest. Banks would be less willing to make loans at lower rates of interest, and thus for the banking system there is a direct relationship between the rate of interest and the supply of money.

It is also true that, given the lending capacity, an individual bank will be influenced by its expectations of future changes in the rate of interest. That is, if the bank thought that interest rates would increase in the future, they might be reluctant to make a large volume of loans at the present time, particularly long-term loans, and would prefer to withhold some of their lending capacity until the future higher interest rates were actually available. But this effect involves mainly a shifting of bank loans from short- to long-term loans rather than affecting the total amount of loans made.

Determination of the Net (Pure) Interest Rate

The net (pure) interest rate depends upon the interrelationship between the demand for loanable funds and the supply of loanable funds. The demand for loanable funds bears an inverse relationship to the interest rate: that is, the higher the interest rate, the smaller the quantity of loanable funds demanded; and the lower the interest rate, the larger the amount demanded. The supply of loanable funds bears a direct relationship to the interest rate: the higher the interest rate, the larger the amount of loanable funds supplied and the lower the interest rate, the smaller the amount supplied. The supply will be less responsive to changes in the rate of interest. With these conditions of demand and supply, there will be an equilibrium rate of interest that will clear the loanable funds market. At this rate of interest the amount demanded and the amount supplied will be equal. Figure 10–1 illustrates

FIGURE 10–1

DETERMINATION OF THE NET INTEREST RATE

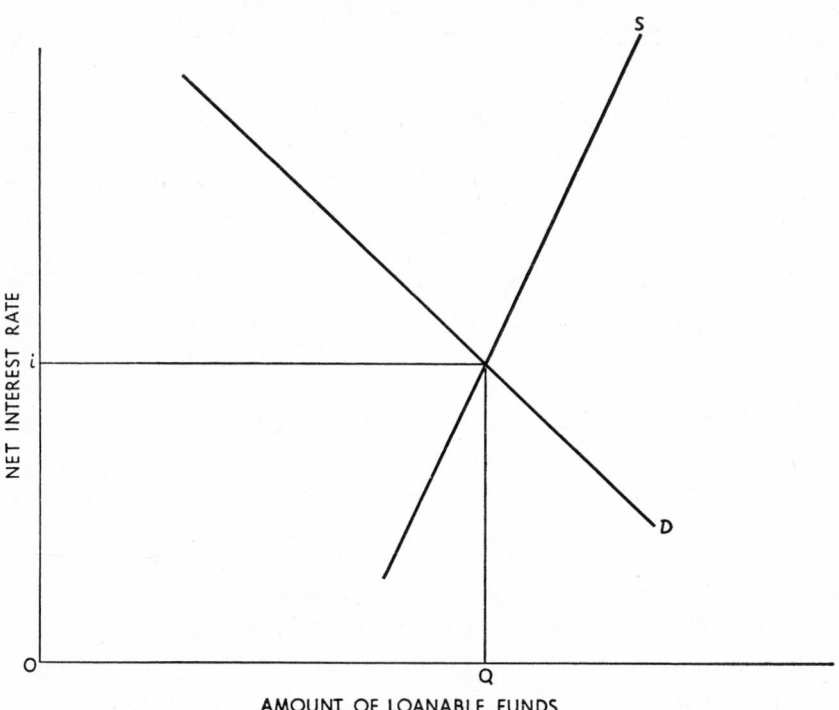

the determination of the net interest rate. The interest rate i is the equilibrium rate. At any higher interest rate, the supply of loanable funds exceeds the demand, and as the suppliers attempt to dispose of their part of the supply, the rate of interest will fall. At any interest rate lower than i, the demand for loanable funds would exceed the supply, and as the investors attempt to borrow, the rate of interest will increase. Only at i is there no inherent force in the market tending to change the interest rate.[3]

Any forces which increase the demand for loanable funds (an increase in the productivity of capital goods, increasing time preference, government deficits, etc.), tend to raise the interest rate. Forces which increase the supply of loanable funds (increased savings by persons or by businesses), tend to lower the interest rate. And, of course, the reverse is true.

The loanable-funds market is essentially competitive. As a result, most borrowers of loanable funds, particularly consumer-borrowers, are faced with a certain interest rate for a given type of loan. Such borrowers can decide upon the quantity to borrow but there is no decision as to the price to be paid. The same situation faces the small saver who finds certain interest rates in effect for different types of savings and adjusts his behavior to those rates. On the other hand, large participants in the capital market may be able to influence the applicable interest rates by their actions in the market.

Capitalization

The rate of interest serves an important function in determining the value of capital assets. The layman ordinarily thinks of the value of a building or a business as being the composite of the costs of the physical parts of the business with perhaps some adjustment to account for any depreciation or an adjustment to account for a difference in the cost of reproducing the asset. Yet business investments are made not to accumulate an abstract mass of physical articles but rather to acquire a source of future income. In that sense, the proper value of any asset is not the cost of its physical components. Its value must reflect its earning capacity. To calculate the value of a capital asset, one needs to know the going rate of return (or interest) on an investment of the particular type. For example, consider the purchase of a piece of city land expected to yield income in perpetuity or at least for a very long period of time. Assume that it is expected to yield an annual

---

[3] An alternative approach to interest rate determination is that of liquidity preference. In this formulation, the rate of interest is the result of the interaction between the demand to hold money and the supply of money. The demand to hold money is a function of the rate of interest. At the higher rates of interest people will be less willing to hold money because of the higher return on securities, and they will be more willing to hold money at lower rates since the possible return on securities is less. The supply of money is, for the most part, independent of the rate of interest; see Chapter 13, "Determination of National Income." This formulation of interest theory is presented in a very readable and understandable fashion in Dudley Dillard, *The Economics of John Maynard Keynes* (New York: Prentice-Hall, Inc., 1948).

income of $5,000, and that the current rate of interest for investments of this type is 5 per cent. What amount might properly be invested in this land and yield the going interest return? Capitalizing the income will give the answer. A capitalized asset value can be computed as follows:

$$C = \frac{I}{r}$$

where:

C is the capitalized asset value,
I the annual return in perpetuity,
r the going rate of interest for such an investment.

In the problem noted above, $100,000 would be the capitalized asset value. If the going rate of return had been 10 per cent, the capitalized value would have been $50,000. On the other hand, if the going rate of interest had been 4 per cent, the capitalized value would have been $125,000. Similarly, increases in the annual income will result in an increase in capital value.

For a capital asset that would be expected to yield a return for only a certain number of years, such as an oil well, the capital value is determined by discounting the income to be received in the future years by an appropriate interest rate. For example, suppose one is considering the purchase of an oil well that geologists estimate will yield $10,000 a year for the next five years and then be worthless. If you think that 10 per cent is a necessary return to induce you to take this risk, you must determine what amount you should currently pay for the well such that if it does yield $10,000 net income for five years, you will get a return of 10 per cent or more on your capital investment.

Year	Return at end of year	Present value of year-end income*
1	$10,000	$ 9,090.91
2	10,000	8,264.46
3	10,000	7,513.15
4	10,000	6,830.13
5	10,000	6,170.89
		$37,869.54

* Determined by dividing return by $(1 + r)^t$ where r is expected rate of return and t is the number of years the return is discounted.

You can pay up to $37,869.54 and receive your desired rate of return. If you had to pay more than that amount, you would be better off by investing in some other area where you could hope to realize your desired rate of return.

THE CAPITAL MARKET

In an industrial economy, savings are a necessary condition for the roundabout process of production. Savings make possible the production of producers' goods such as factories, machines, trucks, and harvesting machines. Savings are converted into investment in the capital market and the institutions associated with it. Some of the institutions in the capital market provide a direct linkage of savings and investments. Investment bankers act as middlemen between large savers and corporations seeking investment funds. But most of the capital institutions serve as links between savers and investors. They serve as a place for people to place their savings, and the collective savings are then available for investment purposes.

The channeling of savings into investments for consumption purposes is primarily through institutions such as savings and loan associations, savings banks, credit unions and finance companies. Typically in these cases the savings are small in amount and the loans vary in size from small consumer needs to home loans. Larger investment needs are met through such institutions as insurance companies, investment banks, commercial banks and other similar agencies which again take small savings but pool them and make them available to meet the large-scale needs of American business. In all types of savings-investment channels, a significant role is played by the United States government through such agencies as the Rural Electrification Administration, the intermediate credit banks and the Commodity Credit Corporation in the agriculture industry; and the Federal Housing Administration and the Veterans Administration in the home mortgage field. Such federal agencies sometimes provide funds themselves directly to borrowers; in other cases they provide funds indirectly through financial institutions and in some cases they provide guarantees which enable private borrowers to get better terms from private lenders.

The Federal Government and the Capital Market

The total amount of credit, the nature of its use and the spectrum of interest rates are of major concern to the federal government. In its role as overseer of the economy, the federal government is concerned with such aggregative aspects of the economy as the level of business investment, amount of consumer credit and its relation to total consumer spending, the amount of savings in the economy, and the level of borrowing and spending by various levels of government. Chapters 14 and 15 will indicate more clearly the key role that these factors play in total economic behavior. At this point we can recognize that all are important phases of the capital market.

The federal government is also concerned with the levels of interest rates. Some of this concern is related to the factors noted above. For example, the government may work toward lower interest rates to stimulate additional business investment. Much of the control over interest rates is exercised through the medium of the Federal Reserve System, as will be explained in Chapter 12. In 1962, the federal government was trying to reduce long-term interest rates at the same time it was trying to increase short-term interest rates. The former objective was in an attempt to increase investment to stimulate a business recovery. The latter effort was directed at stopping the flow of short-term money deposits from American banks to foreign banks which were paying higher interest rates. This was contributing to the adverse balance of payments which the United States has been experiencing.

Furthermore, since the federal government is the largest debtor in the economy it is interested in (1) maintaining its credit rating so that it can continue to borrow funds, and (2) borrowing at as low a rate of interest as is compatible with other policies of the government.

CONCLUSION

Billions of dollars are borrowed every year in the United States by consumers, businesses, and government. In each case, the borrower desires to use the money at the present time and the lender is willing to forego the use of the money until some future date. In return for the current use of the money, the borrower pays interest. The gross interest rate is made up of a risk premium, a premium to cover the cost of the loan, and a net interest charge to pay for the use of the money. The net interest rate is determined by the interaction of the demand for, and the supply of, loanable funds. The demand for loanable funds arises from the desires of businesses, consumers, and governments to borrow. The supply of loanable funds comes from parties willing to postpone their own consumption.

There are a number of financial institutions to facilitate the movement of savings from those who are willing to supply loanable funds to those who seek to borrow. Important private institutions include savings banks, commercial banks, insurance companies, savings and loan associations, and credit unions. Government agencies are significant in the areas of home mortgage financing, agricultural credit, and consumer credit.

There are still some who will argue the question as to whether credit is "good" or "bad." This is a nonsense argument. Credit is a necessity in a higher industrialized economy. Even the USSR makes use of credit. There are likewise individuals who are willing to argue the question of whether a person ought to be permitted to receive interest. This can be dismissed rather summarily by observing that as long as money is scarce, there will be those who are willing to pay interest. Few would presently accept the early church doctrine that interest is morally "wrong."

One problem that many are worried about at the present time is the tremendous concentrations of savings and the power that accompanies such huge accumulations. Life insurance, the government debt, pension and welfare funds negotiated in labor contracts, and the increased use of retained earnings by corporations mean that an ever larger part of society's savings are coming under the control of a relatively small segment of the population. There are, of course, certain economic advantages accruing from such a situation, but there is also the question as to just how much concentration is economically defensible and/or socially desirable.

EXERCISES

Group I

Explain why the following statements are either true or false:

1. The capital market is not a competitive market in any sense because of the wide variations in the interest rates which exist at any given moment in time.
2. Most savers abstain from consumption because of the possibility of earning interest on their savings.
3. Life insurance premiums, purchases of government bonds, and payments on home mortgages all constitute different forms of savings.
4. Business demand for loanable funds is primarily dependent upon the productivity of the capital equipment to be acquired with the borrowed funds. Therefore, business demand for loanable funds has little relationship to the rate of interest.
5. Rising interest rates tend to lower the capital value of assets.
6. No consumer will have negative time preference.
7. The federal government plays a role in the capital market only insofar as the Federal Reserve System is a major lender.

Group II

1. Investigate the rate of interest on various types of loans including government securities, business securities, home mortgages, consumer credit, and others. What is the highest and smallest rate of interest charged to borrowers? Explain the different rates.
2. Why do some businesses prefer to finance capital expansion through borrowing rather than through the issuance of equity securities?

Group III

1. Investigate the methods of reconciling the loanable-funds approach to the determination of the interest rate and the Keynesian analysis of the interest rate.
2. Investigate the amount of government assistance given in the case of (a) agricultural financing, and (b) business financing.

BIBLIOGRAPHY

AMERICAN ECONOMICS ASSOCIATION. "Interest," *Readings in the Theory of Income Distribution.* Philadelphia: Blakiston Co., 1946.

BÖHM-BAWERK, E. VON. *Capital and Interest.* New York: Macmillan Co., 1890.

DILLARD, DUDLEY. *The Economics of John Maynard Keynes.* New York: Prentice-Hall, Inc., 1948.

FISHER, IRVING. *The Theory of Interest.* New York: Macmillan Co., 1930.

KEYNES, JOHN M. *The General Theory of Employment, Interest, and Money.* New York: Harcourt, Brace & Co., 1935.

RENT AND PROFITS

The price of pig,
Is something big;
Because its corn, you'll understand,
Is high-priced, too;
Because it grew
Upon the high-priced farming land.

If you'd know why
That land is high,
Consider this; its price is big
Because it pays
Thereon to raise
The costly corn, the high-priced pig.

—H. J. Davenport

Interest and wages, the returns to capital and labor, are generally contractual expenses incurred by the producer. They may be noncontractual if the enterpriser provides the factors himself, but the determination of the value placed upon such services provided by the enterpriser is based on the principles discussed in the preceding chapters. Those principles involved nothing more than an extension of the principles of pricing to the two factors of production. It was simply a matter of the demand for, and the supply of, the two factors interacting to determine a price and the enterpriser adjusting his employment of the two factors. The productivity of the factors was of primary significance in that decision.

In some cases, the factors of production will have an inelastic supply, meaning that increased amounts of the factor will not be forthcoming at higher prices. Under such circumstances, those units of the factor already employed will receive a return which is greater than that necessary to keep them employed, as well as being greater than what they might be able to earn in alternative employments. Since it is impossible for newcomers to enter this particular type of employment, this surplus can continue over an extended period of time. Better land, talented labor such as baseball and movie stars, more efficient managerial talent, and superior iron ore deposits will receive such a surplus return, which is generally classed as rent.

The price of one factor is not determined by the pricing mechanism and the supply and demand analysis. The last factor to receive its remuneration will simply get what is left after all other costs have been met. The enterpriser gets this residual income, which is called profit.

Rent and profit, then, are the subjects of this chapter. The very neat theory which has been of so much use to date in discussing pricing is of much less use in the case of these two returns. Formulating and presenting a theory of "surplus" returns is somewhat more difficult than presenting the theory of wage and interest determination.

RENT

Contract Rent

Rent is a term with many different interpretations. Popularly it refers to the payment made for the temporary use of any good as distinct from the purchase of the good. A vacationer may rent a car, a college student may rent a tuxedo, or a farmer may rent 100 acres of corn land. In all such instances, it is anticipated that the rented object will be returned to its owner at the end of the specified period. A contractual rental payment will be agreed upon by the owner and the user.

If the desired object is intended for consumption purposes, the determining factor in the borrower's demand is the marginal utility to be derived from the use of the good. The greater the amount possessed, the less useful an additional unit would be and the less one would be willing to pay in contract rent. The rental price would be determined by the interaction of the demand for and the supply of the item being rented just as would the price of the same good if the purchase price were being determined.

The rental price of objects to be employed in the productive process can be handled through the use of the marginal productivity analysis. The demand for such items as land, tractors, machine tools, electronic equipment, shoemaking machinery, and similar items is based on their productivity. The renter will seek to rent additional units as long as the additional revenue from each unit exceeds the additional cost. The aggregate demand for the factors of production and the aggregate supply of the same factors will interact to determine a price which is, in this case, the rental price instead of a purchase price.

Contract rent thus is simply a price for the use of an item rather than being a price for the ownership of the same item. In this sense it is similar to interest in its everyday meaning, which is the price paid for the temporary use of loanable funds. Contract rent, like interest and wages, is a cost of production to the enterpriser who elects to rent rather than purchase factor inputs.

Economic Rent

A Return to Factors with an Inelastic Supply. Historically, economists associated rent with land, and they developed a very rigid analysis of rent determination which failed to explain many significant aspects of this factor income. Early rent theory was associated with David Ricardo (1772–1823) who acquired his interest in rent theory while pondering the politically important problem of grain prices in England in the early nineteenth century. Much of Ricardo's work is still very useful, but the concept of economic rent has been broadened until it is now used to analyze a certain type of return to all factors rather than being confined to the return of a single factor.

If the elasticity of supply for a factor is such that there will be no change in quantity supplied as a result of price changes, the units of the factor presently employed may receive economic rent.

Since the supply of land is extremely inelastic, it may be easier to understand the concept of economic rent if, at the beginning, the discussion is carried on in terms of economic rent accruing to land. Then the concept can be expanded to include other factors of production.

Whenever land is readily available to all who want it without cost, land is a free good. There would be no price on the land and no rent. This was the case in the United States when there was free land on the frontier. But as the demand for the land increases, and since there can be no increase in the supply, a point is reached where

FIGURE 11–1

RENT WITH PERFECTLY INELASTIC SUPPLY

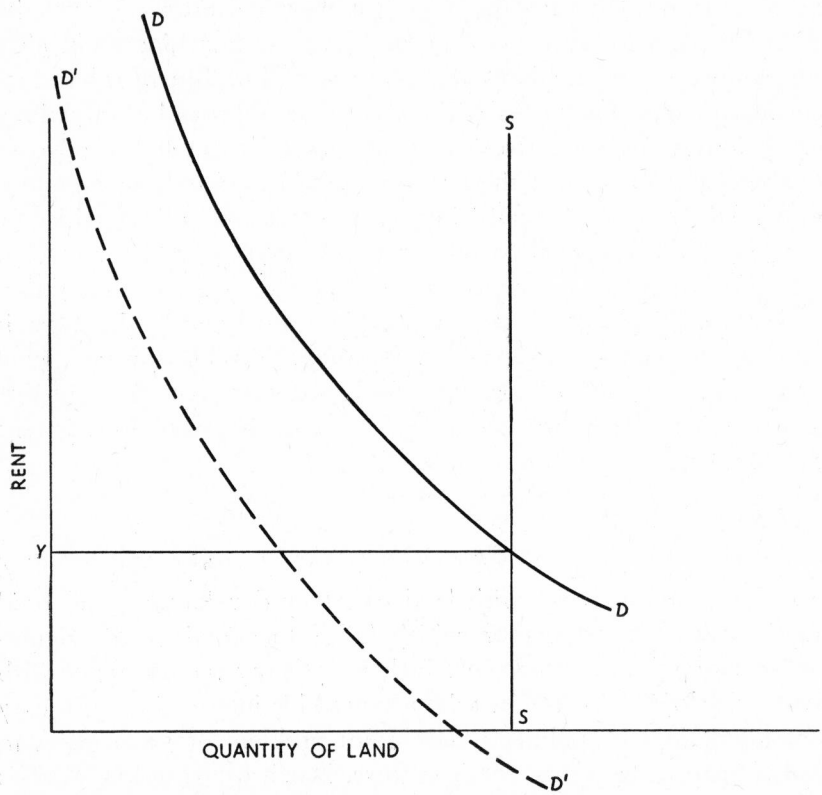

the demand exceeds the supply. When such is the case, rents result because there is no alternative to doing without the land. Figure 11–1 illustrates the problem. The supply of land is represented as being perfectly inelastic. If the demand for the land were $D'D'$, no rent would arise because the supply of land is more than sufficient to meet the demand for land. But when the demand for land is DD, a rent will result because the demand for land exceeds its supply at a price of zero. Persons needing land will compete with one another for the fixed supply, and a rent of r will be established.

The costs of production played no role in the determination of this price. The supply of land was fixed, and the rent return to land depended entirely upon the demand for that factor. Although this is true for the total supply of land and the total demand for land, it is not necessarily true for any particular type of land or the land used by any particular industry. In such a case, land can be shifted from one use to another, and the supply would be more elastic for any particular industry or firm.

Since the total supply of land is fixed, the supply in Figure 11–1 was drawn to indicate that the same amount would be supplied at price zero as would be offered at any higher price. The same situation will characterize factors other than land, if the supply of that factor is perfectly inelastic. For example, consider Babe Ruth, the star baseball player for the New York Yankees. His skill and crowd appeal made him a valuable asset. Moreover, there was only one such player. Certainly there was a minimum figure below which he would not have played baseball; that is, his minimum supply price was not zero. He had alternative sources of employment, but his income in the alternatives would have probably been less than that earned in baseball. Thus that part of his salary above his minimum supply price necessary to keep him in baseball could be considered as being a rent. The New York Yankees, who under baseball law had a monopoly on his services, probably also received a rent from his services by paying less than the value of his product, which he could have gotten had he owned the Yankees.

It is not necessary that all of the factor in question be used before a rental return can accrue. Land is a case in point. All that is necessary is that different grades of land be employed. Land in a frontier settlement might yield a rental return while great quantities of free land existed within a very short distance. The rent-producing land might enjoy the protection of the settlement while the nonrent-producing land suffers the attention of hostile natives. Or the rent-producing land could be more fertile, have a superior location on a river, or enjoy a number of advantages over other pieces of land. Now the same can be said of the other factors. As long as it is necessary that different grades of the nonreproducible factor be employed, the more efficient units of the factor will enjoy a return which is above that necessary to keep them employed in the industry.

To illustrate this principle, consider Figure 11–2. These firms are engaged in the production of corn. The land which Company A has is superior to the land available to the other companies. In this case, the superiority is attributable to natural factors which make Company A land grow a larger crop of corn for a given input of labor and capital. This figure shows the familiar cost curves discussed previously. The average cost of production is lower on Company A land because of its natural superiority. With a small demand for corn, P_1 might be the price of corn and only Company A land would be in production. The price would equal the minimum average cost of production on that land (including noncontractual costs) and no surplus would arise. But

FIGURE 11–2

RENTAL RETURN TO FACTOR WITH AN INELASTIC SUPPLY

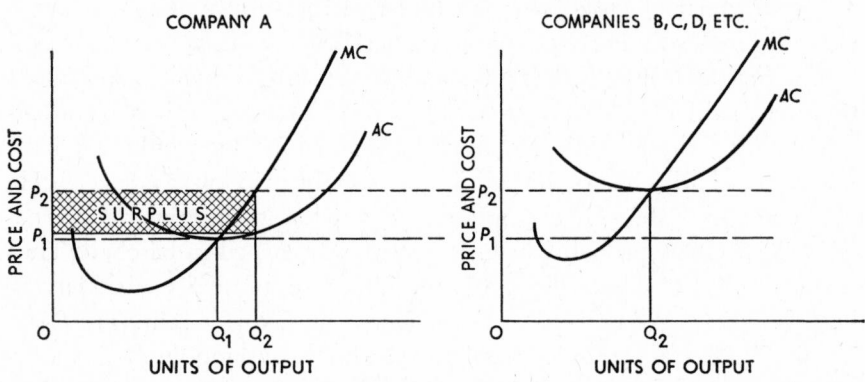

as the demand for corn increases, the price of corn rises and Firm A increases its output, always producing where its marginal cost and price are equal. Since the marginal cost is increasing, the price will have to increase to induce Company A to produce more corn. The marginal cost is increasing because the Company A land is being used more intensively and diminishing productivity is resulting. As the price rises, Company A land earns a surplus. The price may increase to a point (P_2 or higher) where it becomes profitable to use Company B land.

This same illustration can be used to explain rental returns to factors other than land. For example, the companies might be making ashtrays. Company A's superiority is due to a machine it developed and patented which permitted this firm to produce ashtrays at a cost below that of competing companies. The supply of this capital item is inelastic. The competing firms cannot use the new machine, and as long as they remain in operation and the price of ashtrays covers their costs of production, Firm A will receive a return in excess of that necessary to keep it in business. This excess is a rental return to capital in this case.

Another case in which the rental return is obvious and easy to understand is the case of the regulated industries. The regulating body may set a rate high enough to cover the costs of the least efficient unit of capital in operation. Thus the more efficient units will receive a return in excess of that necessary to keep them in operation.

The superiority of one unit of a factor over another results from a number of causes. In agriculture, it is primarily the result of differing natural productivity, including both fertility and location. In the case of urban land, the differential is primarily one of location. For capital, the superiority may be based upon age or technological changes. Differentials in labor may stem from the innate differences in humans. But in any case, where units of the same factor having differing productivity are employed, a rental return will accrue to the more efficient units of the factors.

The Intensive and Extensive Margins. As the demand for the product increases in an industry using a nonreproducible factor, the price (rent) of the factor will rise, and the rent-producing factor will be used more intensively. Additional units of the other factors will be employed in order to utilize the factor with the inelastic supply in a more efficient manner. In fact, additional units of the other factors will be added as long as the additional revenue exceeds the additional cost of their employment. When the last unit of the variable factor yields an increase in revenue equal to the increase in cost, the producer will then use the less productive units of the rent-yielding factor.

There are many examples of this principle. Farmers use superior land more intensively before working the poorer grades of land, since they find that a given amount of labor applied to the superior land yields a greater return than the same amount of labor applied to poorer grades of land. He will only work the poorer grades of land on his farm when the labor applied to this land will yield a larger return than if the same amount of labor has been applied to the better land. Thus farmers combine large amounts of capital and labor with the better grades of land and produce such products as vegetables, corn, dairy products, and the like. On the poorer grades of land they apply much smaller amounts of capital and labor and raise such products as sheep and cattle.

The same principle applies to urban land. The very productive land in Manhattan in New York and the Loop in Chicago will be used more intensively than the land in the suburbs. The height of the buildings is a rough index of the intensity of urban land use. Superior business management will receive a rental return, and the business will attempt to utilize such superiority by increasing the quantities of the other factors employed.

But let us develop somewhat more fully the case of Babe Ruth. In 1931 and 1932 he reportedly received a salary of $80,000—a sizable income for the depth of the depression. He was able to command such a salary because there were no other players of his quality. Thus part of his salary was rent in the sense that the term is being used here.

The New York Yankees, then, were confronted with the economic question as to how to best use this great baseball player. According to our analysis, one would expect them to increase the quantity of other factors in order to utilize Ruth more efficiently. They did this by building a $2 million stadium known as "The House that Ruth Built." The optimum combination, in the management's opinion, was one Babe Ruth, one $2 million stadium, and other sundry items, some of which also received a rental income.

Contract Rent and Economic Rent. Economic rent serves at least as a starting point in determining contract rent or the rental price. If contract rent is the price to be paid for the temporary use of land, then both owner and renter will base their offer on their estimate of the economic rent. They will demand and offer a higher contract rent for the more productive land. Land which produced no economic rent would not generally command contract rent unless the renter was ignorant of its true productivity. The relationship between economic rent and contract rent will depend upon the bargaining relationship between the renter and the owner. In a competitive market with perfect knowledge, the contract rent would just equal the economic rent.

The same principle applies where economic rent accrues to factors other than land. Let us return to Babe Ruth. The economic rent accruing to him was the difference between what they would have had to pay him to just keep him in baseball and the reduction in total revenue to the club which would have resulted had he quit baseball. Let's assume that he would have continued to play for a salary as low as $5,000 and that the New York baseball club would have lost $500,-000 in revenue had he quit the game. The economic rent, then, would be $495,000. The division of this rent between employer and employee will depend again upon the relative bargaining power of each. If Ruth had been free to move from club to club, he could have demanded and received a much larger portion of this rent than was actually the case. On the other hand, if he had no alternatives at all, the wage actually paid would move toward his minimum supply price. Considering the nature of the market in which baseball players are bought and sold, it is probable that his salary came close to being equal to his minimum supply price. The only way that ballplayers can get a larger part of the rent is to convince the management that their minimum supply price is very high. The holdouts each spring are, in effect doing just this by saying that they refuse to play at all for a salary which is less than that being sought. In practice, they usually are willing to play for less.

Rent as a Cost of Production

However determined, contract rent will be a cost to the renter. Even if the owner of an asset employs it himself, he should properly consider the implicit rent as one of his costs. This may sound very simple, but there has been some controversy concerning whether or not rent is a cost of production. Most of the argument results from differences in use of terms rather than from any irreconcilable differences in basic principles.

When economists maintain that rent is not a cost of production they are referring to economic rent. We noticed in Figure 11–2, that the price is high enough to induce the operators of the marginal unit to produce. There is no economic rent on the marginal units, so that this rent does not enter into the price. But this does not mean that there will be no rent at all. This overlooks our first principle, that as we demand more of a factor with an inelastic supply, a rent will arise. This explains the existence of rent in a society as a whole. In addition, land (or other assets) will be distributed among different types of production in accordance with the relative productivity in the different uses. Thus, even marginal corn land will have to pay a rent sufficient to draw the needed amount of land away from its next best alternative use, a golf course or a subdivision, for example. This rent will be a cost of production to the corn industry (and to all of its constituent firms), and it will have to be covered by the price of corn if we are to get the marginal land into cultivation.

Some observers have maintained that rent cannot be a cost to society as a whole. In this reasoning they are concerned with rent of land exclusively. They reason that there is no minimum supply price of land

—it is furnished gratuitously by nature. Therefore, no one "earns" rent. Rents arise through social pressures. Out of this type of reasoning evolved a very interesting economic and political movement, the single-tax movement. This proposal is associated with Henry George (1839–1897), whose ideas are presented in his book, *Progress and Poverty*. The single taxers felt that all economic rent was an unearned income and could in no way be attributed to any efforts of the landlord. Since the landlord had done nothing to earn the rent, they reasoned, it could be taken from him without any harm being done. However, the administrative problems of determining rent and administering such a tax would be insurmountable. Such a tax would discriminate against certain taxpayers, and it would certainly result in a rather drastic reallocation of resources. And lastly, it would not produce enough revenue to finance the operations of today's government. The single tax does not have a promising future in this country's tax picture.[1]

Land Values—the Capitalization of Rent

Rent is the basis of land values. The owner of a piece of land can receive a contractual rental payment approximating the surplus earning ability of the land by leasing the land to a tenant. Or he can receive this return as an implicit rent if he uses the land himself. If he were to sell the land, his loss in income would be the rent which he no longer received. On the other hand, the person buying the land will receive an increase in his income equal to the rent of the land. Economic rent is a major determinant of the sale price of land just as it was in the case of contract rent.

All of the prospective buyers will have a price at which they are willing to purchase land just as the owners will have a price at which they are willing to sell. The buyers' prices will depend upon the anticipated return they expect to get from the property as well as the interest return which they expect. Each prospective buyer will capitalize the rent which he anticipates will accrue to the property. This is done by dividing the rent by the rate of interest. Thus if one purchaser anticipated an annual income of $10,000 and he used a 5 per cent rate of interest, he would offer to pay $200,000 for the property. Other buyers

---

[1] The principle of the single tax is apparently enjoying a resurrection in the USSR Two Soviet economists proposed that Soviet agriculture be reorganized along the lines indicated by the single tax. It was contended that two groups of collective farmers putting in equal amounts of work received different returns because of the difference in the fertility of the land. The two economists proposed that the differential between the good farms and the poor farms be shared by all of the collective farmers. It was not proposed that the differential go to the government or to the consumers. This development was reported in the *New York Times,* August 17, 1958.

anticipating different returns and using other rates of interest would offer to pay larger or smaller prices.

PROFITS

Profits are a second form of surplus or residual income. They are a true residual in that they are the amount remaining to the owners of the firm after all other costs, including contract rent, have been met. Profits are the return to the entrepreneur who undertakes the employment of the other productive factors. He hopes that income will exceed costs, but there is always the possibility that the costs will be larger than the revenue. He thus stands a chance to lose his initial investment in addition to not making a profit.

The entrepreneur performs a vital and necessary function in the productive process. Land, labor, and capital can all be available, but their mere presence does not result in the production of goods and services. Someone must hire and pay for these productive factors, determine what to produce, and how to do it. Even then there is no certainty that the product will sell when completed or that the price will recover the expenses incurred. The entrepreneur assumes these risks.

The function of the business enterpriser is essential in any economic system. It cannot be eliminated. Alternative economic systems may claim that they have done so, but what they have usually done is eliminate the *private* enterpriser. In communist economies, the government assumes the role of the enterpriser, and the entire society takes the risks associated with production. In the United States, we rely primarily upon individuals and private associations to perform the function of risk taking.

Profits are of great significance in the United States economy since they are generally considered to be the single most important force in determining business policy. Most decisions of the firm are made with the intent of maximizing the amount which remains after all expenses have been met.

Gross and Net (Pure) Profits

Gross profits are the total return to the business after the payment of all contractual expenses to the other factors of production. Except for minor differences, gross profits coincide with the accountant's concept of net income. The economist, however, insists that there is a difference between net income and net profits. Some of the items included in the accountant's concept of net income are not included in the economist's concept of net (pure) profits.

If the enterpriser provides other factors of production in addition to his entrepreneurial services, he must be compensated for those additional factors as well as for his entrepreneurial services. And the compensation for each must be considered as being the type of remuneration associated with the particular productive factor. For example, if the enterpriser furnishes labor, a part of his return must be considered as being a wage payment for his labor service. And he would receive interest on any capital which he provided as well as a return on any raw materials which he brought to the enterprise. The return to the factors provided by the enterpriser are implicit returns. There is no provision for a contractual payment.

The problem of distinguishing between these different types of income can be demonstrated by using the example of a small grocery store making gross profits of $7,500. The proprietor's investment is $5,000, he works from 60 to 80 hours a week, and he owns the land on which the building stands. If he could invest the $5,000 at 5 per cent; if he could earn $5,000 by working for someone else; and if he could rent his plant for $1,250; his pure profits would be his gross income minus these implicit returns. In this case pure profits would be $1,000 in contrast to the gross profits of $7,500.

It is this profit figure which is of significance for the economist, and it should be the significant figure for the enterpriser. It is his pure return for operating his business and taking the risks associated with that business. There are many small business firms and many farms which do not earn pure profits. Such individuals would be better off financially if they took advantage of their alternative opportunities.

Necessary Profits and Surplus Profits. Since profits are a residual accruing to the enterpriser, it follows that in some years the profit will be greater than that required to retain the enterpriser in business, and in other years, the profit figure will actually be negative, indicating a loss. A part of profits are like fixed costs in that in the short run they need not be forthcoming. But also like fixed costs, in the long run a certain profit return must be earned or the firm will cease operations. Those profits which are necessary to keep the firm in business are called necessary profits and are as much a cost of doing business as are wages, interest, and contract rent.

However, the enterpriser may earn more than the amount necessary to keep him from quitting. That is, he may get a return which is above his minimum supply price. These are surplus profits. The student will recognize that such profits have all the characteristics of rent; in fact, we can look upon surplus profits as being a rent return to the business enterpriser.

But one must be cautious, for the entrepreneur may be earning a rental income to labor, capital, or land which take the form of implicit income. Thus he might receive a rent element in his wages of management because of his superior ability as a manager. For profits to include an element of rent, it would be necessary that the enterpriser be a superior risk taker. He would have to be a better appraiser of the risks involved and make fewer decisions resulting in losses. As a result, his profits would include an element of rent in comparison to the firms run by less able enterprisers.

In the case of rent, only that part of economic rent which was included as contract rent was included in the firm's cost of doing business. Surplus profits are determined by the price of the product. If the price goes down, the firm will continue to operate, although at a smaller rate of profit. So, surplus profits cannot be considered as being a cost of doing business in the sense that necessary profits represented a cost item.

Sources of Surplus Profits

Surplus Profits and Market Structures. There would be no profits in the long run in a purely competitive industry. Profits or losses can exist in any market structure, including pure competition, in the short run, for the time period does not permit adjustment to be made in respect to changes in demand and technology. Pure profits in the long run under pure competition will be eliminated through the adjustments in the industry. If firms were making profits, new firms would enter the industry, increasing the supply of the product and lowering the price. Profits arise because of risk and uncertainty. To say there would be no profits would require that there be no risk or uncertainty. This would require perfect knowledge of alternative forces present in the market and the mobility to take advantage of such knowledge.

One area in the economy where surplus profits may be made for prolonged periods of time is in monopolistic markets. The monopolist need not worry about what competitors will do, for he has none. He is free to adjust output and to set his price anywhere within the limits of his demand schedule. As a general rule, it is assumed that the monopolist will determine his output policy in such a way that he makes the largest possible profit. As long as there is some price in the monopolist's demand schedule which exceeds his average total costs (including implicit costs), he can make a profit.

To some extent, the ability of a monopolist to maintain his position in his market depends upon the means whereby he has attained his monopoly position. If competitors can enter his industry, his monopoly position will be destroyed. The threat of competitors may be enough to make the monopolist temper his output and price policies so that he doesn't make too large a profit. Very large profits might serve as an inducement for new firms to attempt to break his monopoly power. Large profits may also attract the attention of the Antitrust Division of the federal government. Actually, tempering profit margins—to avoid competition or to avoid government interference—may maximize profits over the long run. A high profit for a few years, followed by intense competition or government interference, is less attractive than moderate profits lasting for many years.

Even a firm in a monopoly situation will usually find that there are other firms which offer relatively close substitutes. A monopoly of public transportation in a city does not insure profits, particularly if the rates are such that people find it preferable to drive their own automobiles. Gas companies are usually monopolies but compete with electricity in many uses. These factors tend to limit the ability of a monopoly to make surplus profits over the long run even if rates are regulated, as they would be in the cases cited.

If there is some restriction on the entry of new firms, a condition likely to exist, the firms in an oligopolistic industry may make profits approximating those that would be earned by a monopoly in that industry. If there is freedom of entry, the prices in the oligopoly may approximate the costs of production and little if any surplus profits would be made.

Some firms under conditions of monopolistic competition may earn surplus profits for a period of time because of an unusually successful advertising campaign or some "gimmick" differentiating their product. This will rarely last for long, as other firms will soon offer a close substitute.

Many industries are actually combinations of the characteristics of oligopolies and monopolistic competition. In this situation, it may be possible for a large firm with a successfully differentiated product to make surplus profits for a long period of time. This is particularly true when there is some restriction of entry into the industry. The big firms in the automobile industry have been very successful profit-wise for many years, and new firms have been unable to break into the industry to share in the profits. Where a differentiated oligopoly also has some degree of collusion, the firms may make pure profits for long periods of time.

Windfall Profits. Windfall profits arise out of some occurrence over which the enterpriser has no control. They are not necessarily associated with any one type of market structure.

One common source of such profits is general changes in the price level. When general prices are increasing, the business enterpriser can profit in two ways. First, buying goods and materials at one time and selling them later may enable him to reap a return greater than his normal markup. Secondly, the enterpriser can gain because cost changes normally lag behind price changes. When prices are increasing, costs will also start increasing but at a slower rate. This increased spread between price and cost increases gives an added profit to the enterpriser.

Sudden changes in the price of a product will usually result in temporary profits or losses for the firms in that industry. Such price changes ordinarily result from changes on the demand side of the market. Changing tastes of the consumer, development of new competitive products, changing patterns of living, and changing income levels can affect the demand for any product.

Wars frequently result in some producers making windfall profits. The necessities of war require the immediate government purchase of items for which it is prepared to pay a premium. Companies in a position to furnish needed goods and services stand a good chance of making profits. Shortages arise during a war period, and producers in industries with facilities that are in short supply may also make surplus profits because of that condition.

There are several other sources of surplus profits. Taxes, tariffs, and subsidies may all permit certain producers to make a profit larger than that necessary to keep the firms in business. Other types of windfall profits are a result of "Acts of God." A severe drought in one part of the country may cause a shortage of certain agricultural products. As a result, prices rise, and farmers in the areas which escaped the drought can make large profits. Technological changes can result in extra profits in any type of market. Innovators benefit from a temporary monopoly in the new methods or products until other concerns have time enough to copy the innovation. Innovation permits the firm to produce at a lower cost than other firms and to profit from this difference.

The Role of Profits in the Economy

Since profits are the residual income, it follows that as business income and expenses fluctuate, profits will likewise fluctuate. Moreover, the other factors have a contractual claim against the income of the firm. Except in the cases in which the firm goes bankrupt and cannot meet the claims of its employees, creditors, and other claimants, there is a bottom limit of zero income for all factors except the entrepreneur. For the latter the minimum is actually an indeterminate negative figure. On the other hand, there is no upper limit as to the total profits a firm can make, while there is such a limit for those factors with prior claim on the earnings of the firm. The result is that there will be greater fluctuations in the profit income of the enterprisers than there will be in the factor income of any other productive service. The actual profits for various industries as well as the disposition of the profits for corporations in the United States can be found in Figures 11–3 and 11–4. The fluctuations in corporate profits from year to year are obvious.

Profits and the Independent Businessman. In the case of the small business enterpriser, it is easy to identify the entrepreneurial function. The single proprietor not only organizes and directs his business, but he is usually the major if not the sole investor of funds in the business. His decisions will be based upon present and prospective profits. The same general conclusions apply to the partnership. Most partners are active in the business and are aware of its success or failure. In both the proprietorship and the partnership, profits and losses of the business are profits or losses of the owner(s). Profits have an immediate effect upon decisions of the independent businessman.

Profits and Corporate Decision Making. Profits also play an important role in the operation of the business corporation. In the small personal corporation, the common stockholders may also manage the company or be directly concerned in making basic management decisions. In this case, they function directly as enterprisers and, as such, are intimately concerned with the profits earned by the corporation. The presence or absence of profits will be the basis for decisions as whether to expand the business, change its nature, continue its present operations, or dissolve the business entirely. An acceptable level of profits will be necessary to continue the venture in the long run.

The situation is somewhat different in the case of a large corporation. The American Telephone and Telegraph Company (AT&T) has 1.5 million stockholders, the overwhelming majority of whom have never attended an annual meeting of the corporation. These people rarely exercise their ownership role in decision making beyond returning voting proxies. Are these common stockholders entrepreneurs? Not everyone would agree on an answer to this question. There are certainly risks connected with the ownership of stock. Dividends may diminish or even disappear. Stock values fluctuate significantly. But the

FIGURE 11-3

CORPORATE PROFITS, TAXES, AND DIVIDENDS
(National Bureau of Economic Research, 1919–29; Department of Commerce, 1929–)

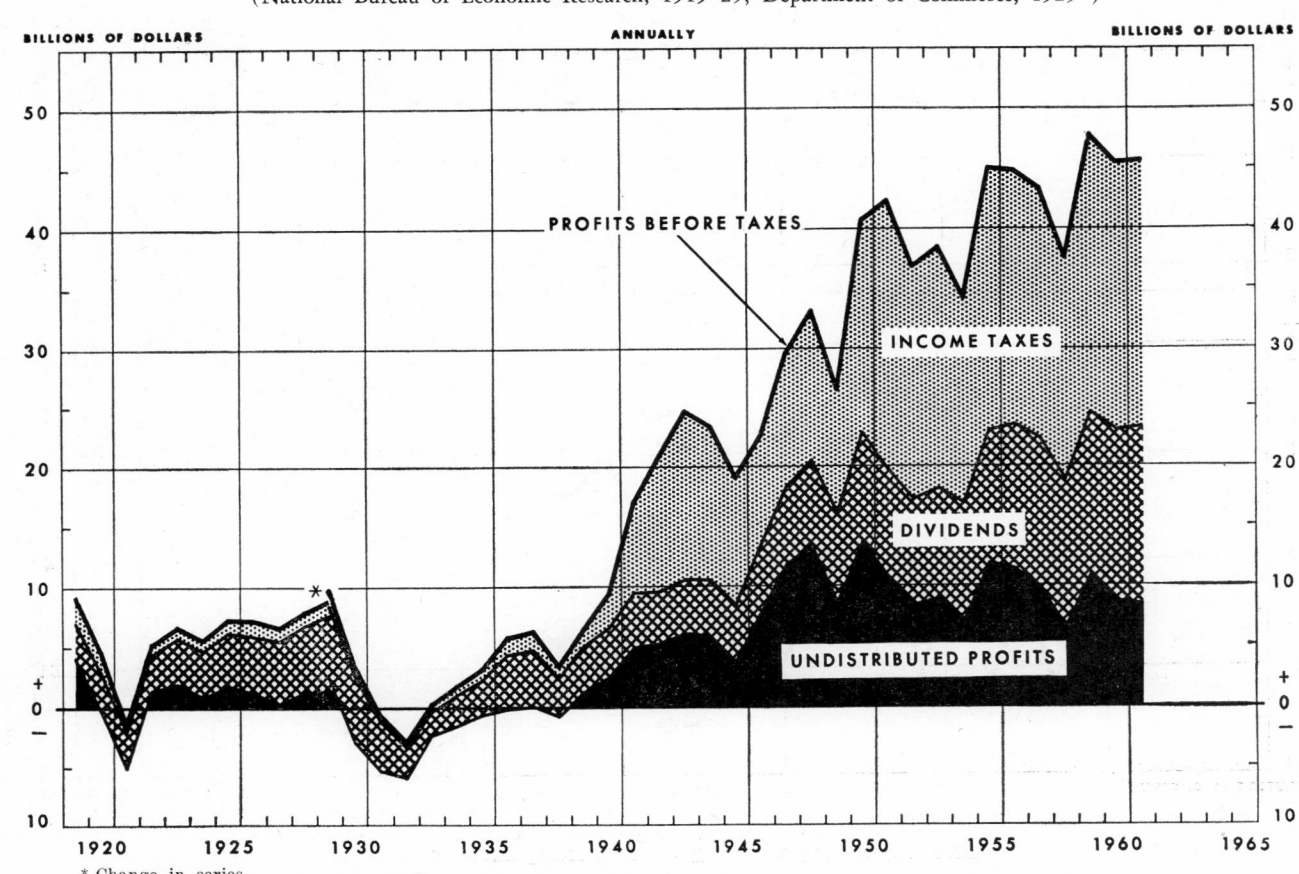

BILLIONS OF DOLLARS

ANNUALLY

BILLIONS OF DOLLARS

PROFITS BEFORE TAXES

INCOME TAXES

DIVIDENDS

UNDISTRIBUTED PROFITS

* Change in series.
SOURCE: Board of Governors of the Federal Reserve System

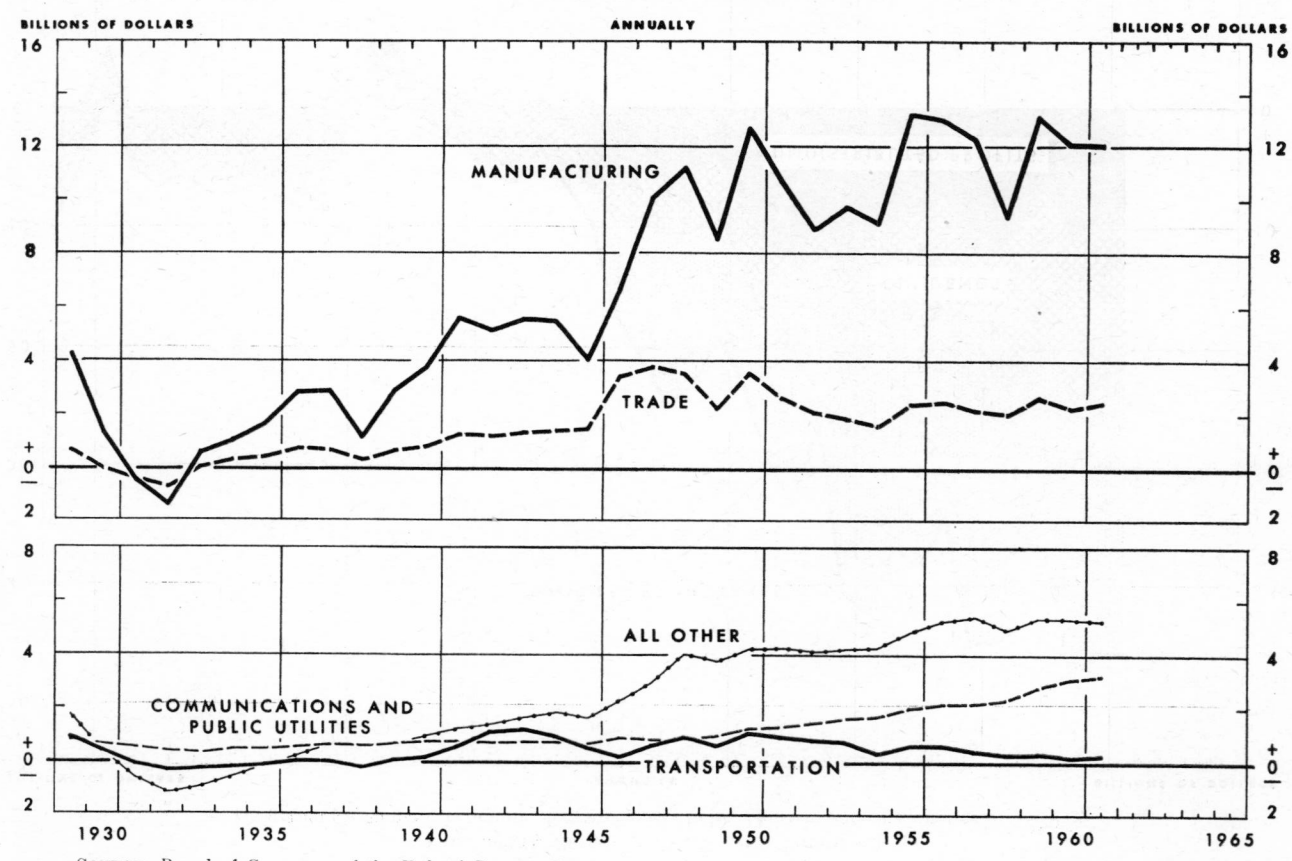

FIGURE 11–4

CORPORATE PROFITS AFTER TAXES BY MAJOR INDUSTRY
(Department of Commerce)

BILLIONS OF DOLLARS   ANNUALLY   BILLIONS OF DOLLARS

MANUFACTURING

TRADE

ALL OTHER

COMMUNICATIONS AND
PUBLIC UTILITIES

TRANSPORTATION

1930   1935   1940   1945   1950   1955   1960   1965

SOURCE: Board of Governors of the Federal Reserve System

import of this risk is different in the case of the large corporation. If profits do not appear sufficiently large to satisfy any particular stockholder, he does not initiate a movement to dissolve the corporation. He cannot recover his investment from the corporation. Rather, he simply sells his stock to some other individual who is willing to make such an investment. And the selling price will vary so that it appears attractive to enough buyers to purchase the shares offered for sale by dissatisfied owners. For most stockholders, it is the size of the dividend payment rather than the total profits that is significant, and their only recourse in most cases of dissatisfaction with dividends is to sell their stock. Regardless of whether or not the common stockholder is called a business enterpriser, he does undertake risks and is influenced by profits in his decision making.

Does this mean that profits have no significance to the modern large corporation? Not at all. But to the large corporation the significance of profits is different from their significance to the sole proprietor. If the returns from salaries, bonuses, and dividends on stock are sufficient to satisfy the controlling interests, they will continue the operation of the venture and can usually forestall any complaints of the "outside" stockholder. This does not mean that the controlling interests do not wish to make large incomes. They are motivated by the same forces as any other individual in the society. But they may receive their satisfaction through large salaries and bonuses rather than through dividends on their stock. And they may be more concerned with the long-run profit position of the company than are the typical small stockholders.

Most corporate enterprises are not satisfied with their present economic status. They want to grow and expand their interests. But this takes money. In some corporations, profits may be the major source of funds for expansion. Many corporations in the United States typically reinvest well over half of their profits and distribute the rest as dividends. Such dividends may not satisfy the outside stockholder, but the general growth of the corporation is important to the controlling interest (and to most stockholders as well). Corporations which rely on such internal financing are understandingly concerned with profits, for profits govern their success in enlarging the concern.

Other corporations finance expansion through borrowing. In order to obtain favorable terms for their loans, the corporation must be financially successful. But the lending agency is not concerned with the size of the dividends paid to the stockholders but rather with the amount of net return that the corporation will have available to pay the interest and principal of the loan.

Still other corporations rely upon equity financing. In this case, it is essential that the corporation maintain a healthy market for its stock so that future stock issues will yield sufficient amounts of new capital. These corporations typically pay a larger share of their earnings in dividends so that the value of their stock stays relatively high. Many public utilities have followed this practice for years in the United States.

It is difficult to overemphasize the significance of profits in the American economic system. Profits are an impersonal economic commissar. When the buying public decides that it would like to attend more drive-in movies, outdoor theaters are constructed. This is not because a governmental official decreed such action, but because there is an increased possibility of making profits by such action. In a like fashion, a decrease in the demand for a product will reduce the prospective profit to be made, and fewer facilities will be devoted to the particular outlet. Changes in the anticipated and realized profits result in a reallocation of our resources.

CONCLUSION

Wages, interest, rent, and profit are prices of peculiar significance, for they are the prices of the inputs in the productive process. And we saw in Chapter 3 that it was a combination of the factor prices and the technology of production which determined the combination of inputs. So the factor prices are important determinants in the allocation of resources among the many different productive processes going on in the economic system at any moment in time.

Profits, moreover, have different characteristics than the other factor prices. Wages, interest, and contract rent are prices which are determined in the market for each of the factors. Profits are a residual return going to the one who organized the particular productive process. There are instances in which the return to entrepreneurial input is larger than necessary to draw forth the factor. Nevertheless, the factor is essential to the operation of the system. Even if the economic system were reorganized on an entirely different basis, the role of the entrepreneur would have to be undertaken by someone. One possibility would be that of having the entire society assume the role of risk taker. But regardless of the system, the entrepreneurial factor must be forthcoming if the economy is to function.

EXERCISES

Group I

Explain why the following statements are either true or false:

1. Rent is of no significance in explaining the values of residential land.
2. An increase in the price of the product will increase rents.
3. Rent arises solely in the case of land and in no other productive factor.
4. Rent comes into being because of the law of diminishing returns.
5. Gross profits and pure profits are always identical.
6. Profits can be made a contractual return which can be guaranteed to the owners of the businesses.
7. In the long run, there will be no pure profits in the economic system.
8. Being a residual return, profits could be taxed at a rate of 100 per cent without affecting the operations of the economy.

Group II

1. Profits, in the United States, represent the key factor in the making of business decisions regarding employment, output, and pricing. What role does this return play in decision making in the USSR and England? If profits do not play an important role in these two economies, what takes the place of this factor return?
2. What are the respective factors which motivate the stockholders and the management of the nation's large corporations? Are their objectives consistent? What influence can the stockholders exert over the activities of the hired manager?

Group III

1. Explain the popularity of shopping centers located outside large cities. Does this development contradict rent theory?

BIBLIOGRAPHY

AMERICAN ECONOMIC ASSOCIATION. *Readings in the Theory of Income Distribution,* pp. 533–95 and 599–659. Philadelphia: Blakiston Co., 1946.

GEORGE, HENRY. *Progress and Poverty.* New York: Appleton-Century, 1879.

GORDON, ROBERT A. *Business Leadership in the Large Corporation.* Washington: The Brookings Institution, 1945.

KNIGHT, FRANK H. *Risk, Uncertainty and Profit.* Boston: Houghton Mifflin Co., 1921.

Chapter

12

AN INTRODUCTION TO
MONEY AND BANKING

Civilization is possible only through confidence, so that we can bank our money and go unarmed about the streets. The bank reserves or a policeman keeping order in a jostling multitude of people, are only slightly less impudent bluffs than my uncle's prospectuses. They couldn't for a moment "make good" if a quarter of what they guarantee was demanded of them.—H. G. Wells, *Tono Bungay*.

Money and the monetary system are creations of man. They are social institutions which guide the conduct of members of society. Decisions regarding money and the monetary system are a mixture of public and private decisions. Some represent unilateral action of an individual or firm. Some are bilateral decisions involving two or more individuals or firms. And some represent collective decisions of society. Individuals, business firms—especially banks—and the government make decisions in this area of economic activity. This chapter,

268

then, is a study of the monetary system and its role in the economic system.

AN INTRODUCTION TO MONEY

What Is Money?

It is possible to imagine a primitive economy in which no money is required. If perchance a member of such a society should produce more than was needed to fulfill his personal wants, the surplus could be traded to a neighbor. Such a situation would be extremely awkward and inconvenient. In bartering it would be necessary to find a second party that possessed what you desired and wanted what you in turn owned. Or lacking that, it would be necessary to find a third party who could successfully complete the transaction. It would be quite possible that the trading process would be more circuitous than that just mentioned. Today some nations trade on a barter basis, and in this country there are "swap shops" in many communities, but most bartering is confined to small boys trading marbles.

Specialization makes bartering impossible. There is no way by which a man who works on an automobile assembly line can trade the product of his labor for needed food and clothing. The individual worker cannot be paid a car or even a part of a car. If he were paid "two cars a year," the problem of converting his "wages" into milk, bread, eggs, and other goods and services would be insurmountable. In an economy of specialization, therefore, each producer is paid a monetary equivalent of his physical production. This monetary equivalent is converted into goods and services which the individual wants. Just as a producer can be rewarded for making a very small contribution to the total productive process, a consumer can divide his income into small units of expenditure.

Primitive people soon learned that something was needed to serve as a medium to express the value of commodities and facilitate the process of exchange. Salt, rice, pigs, carabaos, fish, and tobacco have been used as money at various times and places. During World War II, cigarettes and candy served as money. Such commodity monies, however, have never been satisfactory, and they have been replaced by metallic and paper monies. At the present time, the most important type of money is bank credit or "checkbook money." Money, then, must not be regarded in a narrow sense as a particular type of metallic or paper money but must be considered as anything which is generally used as a medium of exchange. The fact that marbles may be accepted as a settlement of a debt between schoolboys does not mean that marbles are money. Cigarettes, however, would have had to be classed as money during World War II in many parts of the world. But most important for us at this point is the fact that demand deposits must be classed as money, for this is the medium most often used in the settlement of debts.

Characteristics of Good Money

While many different items have served as money at one time or another or one place or another, some have been better monies than others. What, then constitutes a good money? What features have resulted in the widespread use of certain types of monies and the limited use of others? William S. Jevons (1835–1882) listed seven qualities which were deemed to be desirable.[1] Those listed by Jevons over sixty years ago are still the generally accepted criteria of a good money.

Money must have value. If money commands other goods in exchange, as it obviously must, then it has exchange value. Unlike other goods, however, money need not have intrinsic value. Gold and silver coins have nonmonetary value, but the nonmonetary value of paper money and demand deposits is negligible. Both serve satisfactorily as money.

A good money not only has value, but that value must be rather stable. Money serves as a link between the present and the future, and since it serves in this temporal capacity, it follows that fluctuations in value are undesirable. If money loses or gains value, the possessor of money becomes poorer or richer, even though his holding of money is constant. A good money should purchase about the same amount at some indefinite time in the future as in the present.

Next, a good money must have both portability and durability. Many items which have great value could not be used as money because they are too large and unwieldy to serve the purposes for which money is employed. Automobiles, steel beams, and cows all have value, but none would fit into the shopper's purse. Silver dollars in the United States have limited circulation because they lack the quality of portability. The disadvantage of such commodity monies as cigarettes and chocolate bars, even though readily portable, is that they lack the durability that a good money should possess. Even paper money wears out sooner than is desirable.

Lastly, a good money must be recognizable, and it must have

[1] W. S. Jevons, *Money and the Mechanism of Exchange* (New York: Appleton & Co., 1898).

homogeneity and divisibility. A money which is readily confused with a nonmonetary item or with some other money would indeed be a poor money. Furthermore, equal weights of a money should have equal value. If a money were divided into equal parts, the sum of the value of the parts should equal the value of the whole. Gold and silver monies both have a high degree of homogeneity and divisibility; however, commodity monies such as fur or cigarettes lack these two essential qualities. The fur of an animal would lose most of its value if it were cut into equal parts. A fourth of a cigarette is not worth 25 per cent of the value of the whole cigarette—especially if the quarter happens to consist of the filter tip.

The perfect money, like the perfect mate, does not exist. One must be content with that money which comes closest to satisfying the requirements of the ideal money. Various types of money have been used in this country during the past century and a half. For many years, the most important forms of money were metallic—gold and silver—and paper monies. But for nearly a century now there has been an ever increasing use of demand deposits as money. Although such money has some shortcomings, the inadequacies are relatively minor.

The Functions of Money

Most people if queried as to whether they have all the money needed would indicate that they do not. College students are convinced that their need for money is unlimited, whereas the supply is extremely limited. The latter is undoubtedly true, but as regards the first part of the statement, the only person who has an actual demand for money is that individual who desires to hold his assets in a liquid form. For most, however, money is desired because it will perform certain functions. The ultimate or basic want is for the goods and services which money can command. Money, itself, cannot satisfy human wants, except insofar as it may satisfy a psychological desire for security. It cannot be worn or eaten, nor does it provide shelter or entertainment. Money cannot produce physical goods, but it can be converted into factor inputs which can produce economic goods. What, then does money do? What are the functions of money?

First, it serves as a standard of value—a common denominator for the measurement of value. The various units of weight serve as a common device for the measurement of weight, just as units of distance serve to measure distance. A mile in Florida is the same as a mile in the state of Washington, and a pound in California is the same as a pound in Maine. It is just as necessary to have a device for measuring value. In an economy dominated by specialization, money performs this function.

Secondly, money serves as a medium of exchange. With it, one can convert productive power into want-satisfying goods and services. Anything which has value may be converted into money, and the money in turn may be converted into commodities and services. A laborer in a machine tool plant converts his labor power into money, which is then exchanged for bread, books, and other economic goods. Through the use of money as a medium of exchange, the producer of Maine potatoes can purchase Florida grapefruit, and the peanut planter of Virginia may take a winter vacation in Sun Valley.

There are two other functions of money which are generally accorded a position of secondary importance. Money serves as a store of value and standard of deferred payment. A few words of explanation will suffice. Just as it is possible to store electrical power in a storage battery, it is likewise possible to store value. One may store value by purchasing coal with the intention of reselling it at some future date. One may also store value in land, rare books, securities, or any other commodity, however, money is commonly used as a store of value.

Money's function as a standard of deferred payment is closely allied to its function as a store of value. In both cases it is a matter of relating present and future value. Contracts commit one to a future performance. The obligations incurred are often monetary obligations. It is necessary to know at the time of the incurrence of the obligation what the burden of repayment or fulfillment will be. Money performs this function and does so in a manner more satisfactory than other commodities.

Why Does Money Have Value?

For purposes of this discussion money can be divided into two types—standard or full-bodied money and fiduciary money. Standard money has a commodity value equal to its monetary value. Such is the case with gold coins. If a country were on a full gold standard, the owner of a gold coin could, if he desired, melt it and sell the bullion for the original amount of currency. Whether it is in the form of bullion or money, the value is the same. The value of such a money is determined by the forces of demand and supply, and the demand consists of both a monetary and nonmonetary demand. If there were an increase in the demand for gold for nonmonetary uses, its value as money would increase. If there were an increase in the supply of gold, both its monetary and nonmonetary value would decrease, other things remaining equal.

One of the major arguments for a gold standard stems from this very fact. Most of the gold which has been produced is still in existence. Furthermore, the amount produced in any given year is a very small percentage of the total supply. There will not be great fluctuations in the supply of gold, and its value will tend to be relatively stable. For this reason many people consider it to be the best basis for a monetary system.

The second type of money, fiduciary money, has a monetary value in excess of its commodity value. There is not a dollar's worth of silver in a silver dollar, nor is there a penny's worth of copper in a copper cent. There is the same amount of paper in a dollar bill and a ten thousand dollar bill, but in neither case is the value of the paper equal to the monetary value of the bill. If it were not for the fact that these particular pieces of paper were money, they would be of no more value than any other piece of paper of equal size. Various countries have, from time to time, suffered such extreme increases in the price level that the monetary value of the money fell to such a low level that it was worth little more than its commodity value—in fact, little more than nothing. In such instances it may require a wheelbarrow full of money to buy a loaf of bread.

Why does fiduciary money have monetary value, or, more properly, why does it have a monetary value which far exceeds its commodity value? There are two factors. The first is its reserve. Nearly all of the present-day money used in the United States has a reserve of some sort. Federal Reserve notes, which are the most important form of currency, are backed by gold equalling 25 per cent of the value of the notes with the remaining 75 per cent consisting of government bonds. The 25 per cent reserve is actually in the form of gold certificates held by the Federal Reserve bank which issued the currency, but these gold certificates are claims on gold held by the United States Treasury. Demand deposits, which are a prime example of fiduciary money, likewise are backed by a reserve consisting of gold certificates and instruments of debt.

The mere existence of a reserve is not enough to give money value. Neither the student receiving his allowance nor the merchant accepting payment for merchandise is concerned about the amount of gold at Fort Knox. Nevertheless, the reserves play an important role, since the reserve requirement limits the supply of money. If the supply of money were unlimited, the value of money would decline as more were put into circulation until finally it lost all value and would cease to be money.

Probably a more important factor contributing to the value of money is the fact that it is generally acceptable. A student accepts money for working in the bookstore because he knows that the dining hall will take the money in payment for board. The dining hall accepts the money because it is confident that the produce house will take it in payment for fruits and vegetables. And the operator of the produce house takes it because he knows his son can spend the money at the bookstore to buy books. There could be no better example of circular reasoning, but it is a fact that people take money because they have confidence that others will take it. When they are unwilling to do so, then the money can no longer be used to settle debts, and it is no longer money. This faith combined with the fact that the supply is limited gives money its value.

The Development and Use of Money in the United States

The development of money in the United States is a lengthy but interesting story. Until 1900 the country was on a bimetallic standard, which meant that gold and silver dollars served as a standard of value. Although both served as a standard of value, in practice only one or the other served as a medium of exchange. There was a time during the Civil War when large amounts of irredeemable paper currency were issued. These "greenbacks" had no metallic reserve and could not be exchanged for metallic monies. At the turn of the century, the United States went on a full gold standard in which the gold dollar was the standard of value and gold coins and certificates served as the medium of exchange. Since 1933, the country has been on a limited gold bullion standard. Gold coins and certificates do not circulate, since it is now against the law for gold to be held for purposes other than industrial uses or as collector's items.

At the present time, there are three major forms of money. Metallic money (coins) constitutes a very small part of the money supply; nevertheless, it is extremely important since it gives the monetary system the essential quality of divisibility. All coins are fiduciary monies, since in no case is the bullion or commodity value equal to the monetary value.

A larger part of our monetary supply consists of paper money. At one time, paper money was issued by nearly all banks. At the time of the Civil War, the right of issue was restricted to the national banks; that is, banks chartered by the national government. A special tax was levied on the notes issued by the state banks, which drove the state bank notes out of circulation. In 1914, the Federal Reserve System was established and today the Federal Reserve banks are the sole banks of issue. Approximately seven eighths of the paper money in circulation consists of Federal Reserve notes issued by the twelve Federal Reserve banks. The remainder is made up of minor issues. For all practical purposes, the Federal Reserve notes and the silver certificates make up our paper money supply.

The last type of money, and by far the most important in terms of amount, consists of demand deposits. When one establishes a checking account in a bank by depositing currency or checks, or by borrowing from the bank, the depositor can write checks on the account. These checks are the most widely used form of money in the United States (see Table 12–1).

TABLE 12–1

THE UNITED STATES' MONEY SUPPLY, APRIL, 1963
(In Millions of Dollars)

Type of Money	*Amount*
Federal Reserve notes	$ 31,429
Treasury currency—total	5,381
Standard silver dollars	486
Silver bullion	2,102
Silver certificates* (duplication)	(2,125)
Subsidiary silver coin	1,802
Minor coin	676
United States notes	347
In process of retirement	170
Demand deposits	118,600

* Silver certificates are to be retired and replaced by Federal Reserve Notes. The silver reserve will be used for industrial purposes and to coin silver coins.
SOURCE: *Federal Reserve Bulletin.*

Demand Deposits as Money

Some form of money is essential in an economy of specialization such as that found in the United States, and it is probably necessary that it be credit. Modern industrial economies are speculative in nature, since the consumer has not generally committed himself to the purchase of the good at the time of its production. The producer is combining the factors of production to produce a good which will be consumed at some unknown time in the future by some unknown person at an unknown location who will purchase the commodity at an unknown price. It may be a matter of days, months, or even years before the end product is finally consumed. The extreme case is the industry which requires large amounts of capital investment, in which case it may be several years from the time plans are first advanced until the finished product is available to the consumer. In other cases the time lag may be much shorter, but in any event, this time lag between production and consumption necessitates extensive use of credit.

Credit is used at all levels of economic activity. The consumer makes extensive use of credit. Rather than saving money and paying cash for a car, he often borrows from banks or other financial institutions. The consumer does not borrow paper or metallic money, he just borrows. The debt may be repaid with paper or metallic money, but more often it is repaid with checkbook money—credit.

The merchant likewise makes extensive use of credit. He may buy a consignment of goods with the intention of selling the various items over a three-month period. He may not have the cash to make immediate payment or he may not wish to tie up his available cash. So he gives the supplier a 90-day note which he will pay off at the end of the three months with the receipts from the sale of the merchandise. The manufacturer, on the other hand, may want cash, since he is in the business of producing this commodity rather than lending money. So he may take the note to the bank and sell it to the bank and receive deposit credit. The buyer then has purchased his goods and has 90 days in which to get the funds necessary for repayment; the manufacturer has made what is, in effect, a cash sale; and the bank has made a loan which earns interest. At the end of 90 days, the note will be retired by the merchant making payment to the bank rather than to the manufacturing concern to which the note was originally given.

Large industrial firms, particularly those in the utility field, make extensive use of credit. The American Telephone and Telegraph Company may finance the expansion of its communication facilities through a bond issue rather than sell additional stock in the company or plow back earnings. This indebtedness is retired over a period of years or even over decades.

Much of the government's borrowing is of this nature. Governments borrow to build roads, schools, sewage disposal plants, etc. Repayment is over an extended period of time.

The above examples may be taken as being representative of the three major types of credit transactions: (1) consumer credit, (2) commercial credit, and (3) investment credit. The three have important differences. Consumer credit is used to finance consumer goods which are not self-liquidating. The purchase of a refrigerator does not increase the housewife's income to provide funds for repayment, although it may make life much pleasanter. Both commercial credit and investment credit, on the other hand, are self-liquidating since both provide for increased funds in the future which can be used to retire the debt. In the case of commercial credit, the funds for repayment come from the sale of the goods, and in the case of investment credit, the funds for repayment come from increased earning power. There is a distinguishing feature regarding the latter two types of credit. Commercial credit is usually short-term credit while investment credit is long-term credit. The credit instruments also differ. In the instance of commercial credit, the credit instrument is either a promissory note or an order to pay, while the bond is usually the credit instrument used in the case of long-term investment. The net effect of all types of credit is the same, for it permits one to use the good while paying for it.

Although there are a few other credit institutions such as savings and loan companies, insurance companies, and other specialized lending agencies, banks are the ultimate custodians of credit and the guardians of the credit system. The decisions as to the expansion or contraction of credit and the granting or refusing of requested loans are banking decisions. An understanding of credit and the credit system is essential for an appreciation of economic enterprise, and for all of this an understanding of banks and the banking system is a prerequisite.

AN INTRODUCTION TO BANKING

The banking system in the United States consists of two parts. The first, the private banking system, consists of the commercial banks handling the financial and credit transactions of individuals, firms, associations, etc. The second is the Federal Reserve System which consists of twelve Federal Reserve banks and their branches. They perform the same general functions for the commercial banks as the latter perform for their customers. These banks are aptly referred to as bankers' banks. In addition the Federal Reserve banks provide banking facilities for the government of the United States.

The Private Banking System

The private banking system consists of approximately 15,000 privately owned banks. State banks are chartered by state governments, while others received their charters from the national government and are known as national banks. The latter must belong to the Federal Reserve System, and the state banks may belong if they wish. Those which belong to the Federal Reserve System are known as member banks while those which do not are referred to as nonmember banks. All banks may be members of the Federal Deposit Insurance Corporation (FDIC) which was established in the 1930's to insure deposits. All banks are regulated by the state and/or national government. It is these private banks which represent that part of the credit system with which most individuals and businesses come into contact.

Operation of a Commercial Bank. The operations of a commercial bank may best be understood by following the actions of a hypothetical bank. Assume, first, that a group of individuals start a bank with a charter from the national government. Each of the incorporators subscribe to a certain amount of the stock of the bank. The bank must have a paid-in surplus before it begins operations. This paid-in surplus can be acquired by issuing the stock at a premium. One other requirement of a national bank is that it belong to the Federal Reserve System. This means that the bank will have to buy stock in the Federal Reserve bank of its district equal to 3 per cent of its capital stock plus surplus. When all of the above have been done, the balance sheet would look as follows:

Assets		*Liabilities and Net Worth*	
Cash...............	$1,164,000	Capital stock........	$1,000,000
Stock of Federal Reserve		Surplus (paid in)......	200,000
bank............	36,000		
Total.............	$1,200,000	Total............	$1,200,000

The owners of the bank then purchase bank furniture, buy a building and some accounting machines. These purchases total $214,000. Then $900,000 of the remainder is deposited in the Federal Reserve bank to serve as a reserve against deposits. When these transactions have been completed, the balance sheet will look as follows:

Assets		*Liabilities and Net Worth*	
Cash...............	$ 50,000	Capital stock........	$1,000,000
Stock of Federal Reserve		Surplus..............	200,000
bank............	36,000		
Furniture and			
equipment.......	214,000		
Reserves............	900,000		
Total.............	$1,200,000	Total............	$1,200,000

The bank has no earning assets except its stock in the Federal Reserve bank, which yields 6 per cent. Since the bank was organized to make a profit, it behooves the management to put some of their assets in an income-producing position. This is done by receiving deposits and making loans. During the first day's operation of this bank, customers brought $35,000 cash and deposited it in their checking accounts. The balance sheet then appeared as:

Assets			*Liabilities and Net Worth*		
Cash	$	85,000	Demand deposits	$	35,000
Furniture and equipment		214,000	Capital stock		1,000,000
Reserves		900,000	Surplus		200,000
Stock of Federal Reserve bank		36,000			
Total		$1,235,000	Total		$1,235,000

The bank still has no additional assets which will produce income. A bank can earn income only by making loans. Individuals and businesses borrow money from the bank in order to purchase automobiles, new capital equipment, or inventory. The customers will pay interest on the money they borrow, and this interest is income for the bank. When a bank makes a loan, the bank acquires an asset in the form of the borrower's note, and it incurs a liability in the form of a demand deposit. The loan is an income-producing asset.

There is a limit to the amount of demand deposits which any bank can create. The bank in our problem will be required by law to maintain a reserve behind all of its deposits. The $900,000 of the incorporators will serve as the reserve against any deposits which the bank might create in the process of lending money to customers.

Credit Expansion. Let us initiate our discussion of lending and credit expansion (creation of demand deposits) by assuming that the above balance sheet represents the only bank in the system. All checks written on demand deposits will be redeposited in this bank. There would be no need to settle accounts with other banks as a result of checks being deposited in banks other than the one upon which they were drawn. In this situation, then, the bank is able to loan out more than it has in its reserve account. If we assume for the sake of argument that the reserve required by law is 20 per cent, the banking system can increase loans until demand deposits are five times the reserve. If this were done, the balance sheet would appear as:

Assets			*Liabilities and Net Worth*	
Cash	$	85,000	Demand deposits	$4,500,000
Furniture and equipment		214,000	Capital stock	1,000,000
Reserves		900,000	Surplus	200,000
Loans and discounts		4,465,000		
Stock of Federal Reserve bank		36,000		
Total		$5,700,000	Total	$5,700,000

There need be no concern here because the bank has loaned out five times as much as it has in reserves, since there is no chance that all of the depositors would want cash at the same time. The original depositors will write checks on their accounts and give those checks to others. The recipients of the checks, rather than demand cash from the bank, will deposit the checks in the same bank and receive deposit credit. The new depositors will then write checks on their deposits to pay their obligations. In any event, the demand for cash is small and frequently offset by cash deposits. Most business is transacted through the medium of demand deposits.

The situation becomes somewhat more complicated when instead of a single bank in the banking system there are 15,000 banks. Instead of having the balance sheet represent the entire banking system, we will now assume that it represents the financial position of only a single bank. In such a situation many of the checks drawn on the demand deposits of any one bank will be deposited in other banks. The bank which created the demand deposit must be prepared to have the entire amount of the loan deposited in other banks, although as a practical matter some of it will be redeposited in the bank of origin. Under these circumstances, then, it would be unwise for a bank to lend out more than it has in reserves. If it did so, other banks would present the checks drawn on these deposits for payment, and the original bank would be unable to meet these obligations.

So now let us examine the balance sheet of our bank. Remember that we had $35,000 in demand deposits. Since we have $900,000 in reserves, we can expand demand deposits to a total of $900,000. The balance sheet would look as follows:

Assets		Liabilities and Net Worth	
Cash and due from		Demand deposits..... $ 900,000	
other banks......$	85,000	Capital stock........ 1,000,000	
Furniture and		Surplus............. 200,000	
equipment.......	214,000		
Reserves............	900,000		
Stock of Federal			
Reserve bank....	36,000		
Loans and discounts..	865,000		
Total...........$2,100,000		Total...........$2,100,000	

The checks written on the new accounts will be deposited in all banks in the system. The checks deposited in other banks will result in a reduction of this bank's reserves and an increase in the reserves of the other banks. They, in turn, can increase their loans on the basis of their increased reserves. If we assume a reserve requirement of 20 per cent, then for each dollar in increased deposits, banks can loan out 80 cents and keep 20 cents as reserve. But still additional checks will be written on these deposits, and they will, in turn, be deposited in still other banks which will cause another shifting of reserves and another increase in demand deposits. The net effect will be the same as in the example above where we assume that the one bank represented the entire banking system. If a 20 per cent reserve is required of all the banks in the system, then any increase in the reserves of the banking system will permit a fivefold expansion in demand deposits.[2] Thus the entire banking system is in a position to expand credit to some multiple of its reserves. This is something an individual bank cannot do, for if it did so, there would be a continual drain upon its reserves until it could no longer meet the demands of those who held checks drawn upon that bank.

Since this principle is crucial for an understanding of the problem of economic stability and its control, let us examine what would happen if a bank received a demand deposit of $100 against which a 20 per cent reserve was required. It would have to hold $20 as a reserve, but it could loan out $80. The borrower of the $80 would then write checks on the demand deposit, and these checks might be deposited in a second bank. The second bank would have to keep $16 in reserves and could loan $64. This process would be repeated and repeated until finally there was a total increase in demand deposits of $500, an increase in loans and discounts of $400, and an increase in reserves of $100. This is represented in Table 12–2.

TABLE 12–2

THE MULTIPLYING CAPACITY OF RESERVE MONEY IN BANK TRANSACTIONS

Transaction	Amount Deposited in Checking Accounts	Loans and Discounts (Amount Lent)	Amount Set Aside as Reserves on Deposit at Reserve Banks
Bank 1	$100.00	$ 80.00	$ 20.00
Bank 2	80.00	64.00	16.00
Bank 3	64.00	51.20	12.80
Bank 4	51.20	40.96	10.24
Bank 5	40.96	32.77	8.19
Bank 6	32.77	26.22	6.55
Bank 7	26.22	20.98	5.24
Bank 8	20.98	16.78	4.20
Bank 9	16.78	13.42	3.36
Bank 10	13.42	10.74	2.68
Additional banks	53.67	42.93	10.74
Total, All Banks	$500.00	$400.00	$100.00

SOURCE: Board of Governors of the Federal Reserve System, *The Federal Reserve System, Purposes and Functions* (Washington, D.C., 1954).

[2] In practice there will be some leakages which will not permit this much of an expansion in deposit credit. For example, bankers will need to hold more currency as demand deposits increase.

The above example represents an increase in reserves and an expansion in deposit credit. The opposite effect will be noted where there is a reduction in bank reserves. For example, if there were a reduction of $100 in the member bank reserves, there would have to be a $500 reduction in demand deposits if we again assume a reserve requirement of 20 per cent. It is important to note that in both cases there is a multiple expansion or a multiple contraction of bank credit—that is, demand deposits.

Clearing of Checks. The demand deposits created by the depositing of cash or checks or by borrowing are drawn upon by the borrower as he writes checks. If the checks are deposited in the same bank, there is no change in the total amount of that bank's demand deposits. There is merely a transfer in deposit credit from one depositor to another. If they are deposited in other banks, as most checks are, then the bank upon which the check is drawn must be prepared to make payment to the bank which received the check. At the same time, however, that checks drawn on this bank are being deposited in other banks, depositors with accounts in those banks are writing checks which are in turn being deposited in the bank of this example. All banks in a banking system owe money to other banks. Since this is true, it becomes possible to settle interbank debts arising out of changing demand deposits by a rather simple procedure. This is referred to as the clearance of checks.

Check clearance operates as follows. The banks present the checks they have received drawn upon other banks. These checks represent money owed to the bank presenting the checks. The representatives of the other banks are also presenting checks, which means that each bank will also owe money to all other banks. All banks are owed money; all banks owe money. This may be presented as follows:

DUE FROM OTHER BANKS
(*Thousands of Dollars*)

Bank A	Bank B	Bank C
B 25	A 13	A 11
C 20	C 28	B 31
45	41	42

DUE TO OTHER BANKS
(*Thousands of Dollars*)

Bank A	Bank B	Bank C
B 13	A 25	A 20
C 11	C 31	B 28
24	56	48

In the above example, Bank A presents checks drawn upon Banks B and C which total $45,000. Bank B has checks drawn on Banks A and C to the extent of $41,000, and Bank C possesses checks drawn on A and B amounting to $42,000. At the same time, Banks B and C have presented checks drawn on Bank A which they have cashed which total $24,000. The comparable figures for Banks B and C are $56,000 and $48,000 respectively. It will be noted that the total amount due to other banks is equal to the total amount due from other banks. Both equal $128,000. A second check is that the net amount due the banks must equal the net amount due from the individual banks. In this instance, Bank A is owed $21,000 more than it owes. Bank B owes $15,-000 more than it is owed and Bank C owes $6,000 more than it is owed. Note that $21,000—$15,000—$6,000 equals zero.

The only step that remains is that of settling the balances. It would be possible to settle the net balance through the movement of cash, but such a means of settlement would be awkward. A more satisfactory method is through the maintenance of clearinghouse accounts by all banks. If the above banks have such accounts, then Bank A's account would be increased by $21,000 and Banks B and C would have their accounts reduced by $15,000 and $6,000 respectively. The method most commonly used is that of settling balances through a Federal Reserve bank.

If the balances are settled by adjusting the balances of the banks at the Federal Reserve bank, then Bank A's reserve account will be increased by $21,000. The bank is now in a position to use this additional $21,000 as a reserve against new demand deposits. Of course, there is always the possibility that tomorrow Bank A will owe rather than being owed. If this should be the case, it would mean that the lending capacity of the bank would be reduced. It should be obvious from the above that it would be impossible for a single bank to expand credit. If a single bank were to do so, there would be more checks drawn on it and presented by other banks for payment. The net result would be a continued adverse balance and a continuing reduction in reserves and lending ability. This would not happen if all banks expanded credit together, for those checks drawn on one bank and deposited in other banks would be counterbalanced by an approximately equal number of checks moving in the opposite direction. So even though there were no regulation of reserves, it would be impossible for one bank to expand credit while the remainder of the banking system did not.

The Federal Reserve System

The Structure of the Federal Reserve System. With the exception of the First and Second Banks of the United States (1791–1811 and 1816–1836), the United States did not have a central bank until the passage of the Federal Reserve Act in 1914. That act, rather

FIGURE 12–1

BOUNDARIES OF FEDERAL RESERVE DISTRICTS AND THEIR BRANCH TERRITORIES

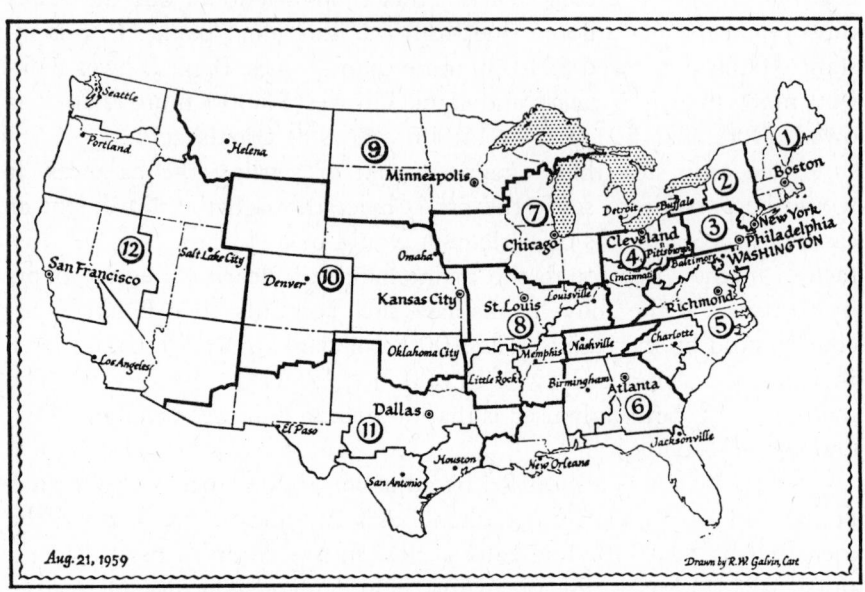

Legend

— Boundaries of Federal Reserve Districts —Boundaries of Federal Reserve Branch Territories

✪ Board of Governors of the Federal Reserve System

◉ Federal Reserve Bank Cities   • Federal Reserve Branch Cities

than providing for a single central bank bowed to the general belief in decentralization and provided for twelve regional banks (see Figure 12–1). Each of the Federal Reserve banks is owned by the commercial banks of the district which are members of the Federal Reserve System. Each member bank subscribes to the capital stock of the Federal Reserve bank in accordance with its own capital stock and surplus. The member banks receive a dividend amounting to 6 per cent on their investment. The individual Federal Reserve banks are managed by a board of directors consisting of nine individuals. The Class A and Class B directors are elected by the member banks. The first may be bankers, but the Class B directors must represent some business (including agriculture) other than banking. The Class C directors are the public members of the board, and they are appointed by the Board of Governors. One of the public members is designated to serve as chairman of the board, and he will also serve as the agent of the Board of Governors of the Federal Reserve System.

The Board of Governors in Washington, D.C., exercises general supervision over the entire system. There are seven members appointed by the President of the United States with the advice and consent of the Senate. These individuals serve for terms of fourteen years which are staggered so that there is a single term expiring every two years. One of the members is designated to act as chairman of the Board of Governors. In addition to supervising the various Federal Reserve banks, the Board of Governors represents the Federal Reserve System in its numerous contacts with the United States government. It is an independent agency, but it works closely with the Treasury Department, although at times their interests are not identical. The seven members of the Board of Governors plus five other persons representing the Federal Reserve banks comprise the Open Market Committee. This committee has general supervision of the securities held by the Federal Reserve System, and it will buy and sell those securities as the situation may require.

In summary, it should be emphasized that the Federal Reserve System is a private banking system, even though it is under the general supervision of a governmentally appointed board. It provides services for the commercial banking system of the country. The Federal Reserve System also fulfills the role of a central bank in performing certain functions for the government and promoting certain governmental policies.

Functions of the Federal Reserve System. *Issuing Federal Reserve Notes.* The Federal Reserve banks issue Federal Reserve notes, the largest single component of our currency. The process by which Federal Reserve notes are put into circulation is interesting. Assume for a moment that because of increased spending at Christmas more currency is needed in a particular Federal Reserve District to serve as a medium of exchange. Once the Federal Reserve bank of that district has decided to issue the currency, it deposits collateral with the Federal Reserve Agent to serve as a backing for this new issue. The collateral consists of gold certificates equal to at least 25 per cent of the value of the currency, with the remainder being made up of either government bonds or certain commercial paper which the Federal Reserve bank holds. Nowadays, with the tremendous stock of government bonds, there is little use of commercial paper. Upon receipt of the collateral, the Federal Reserve Agent releases the currency which has been printed by the Bureau of Printing and Engraving. This currency is paid out to the commercial banks as they request additional cash during the Christmas shopping season. This money circulates through the economy, but once Christmas has passed, there no longer exists such a need for currency. Currency will be deposited in the commercial banks by business firms and individuals. The banks, rather than hold idle cash in their vaults, will deposit the money in their Federal Reserve banks where it will serve as reserve for new loans. Once the currency is deposited in the Federal Reserve bank it will be sorted, and that which is in fit condition will be returned to circulation as needed while that which is worn out will be destroyed. As the currency is retired from circulation, the Federal Reserve Agent will be notified, and he will release the collateral put up by the Federal Reserve bank. This, in brief, is the story of our currency.

Clearing Checks. The Federal Reserve Banks clear checks. Of the many checks written in the daily course of events, a large number are written in favor of firms or individuals that are hundreds or even thousands of miles removed from the bank on which the check was drawn. A check drawn on a New York bank will be sent to California, or a check drawn on a Texas bank will be sent to the state of Washington.

In such instances as these, the facilities of the Federal Reserve System will be used to clear the checks. An example of such a clearing involving two Federal Reserve banks follows.

Assume for the moment that a college student in Palo Alto, California, purchases a book from a publishing company in New York City and pays for that book with a check on his checking account in the Bank of America. The publishing company will deposit the check in its bank—say, the Chase Manhattan, and the Chase Manhattan will credit the publisher's account, thus increasing the firm's demand deposit. The Chase Manhattan will send the check to the Federal Reserve Bank of New York, and the reserve account of the Chase Manhattan will be credited by the amount of the check. Now the publisher has his money. The bank has its money. The New York Federal Reserve Bank will then forward this check along with the others drawn on banks in the twelfth Federal Reserve District to the Federal Reserve Bank of San Francisco. Now a new agency, the Interdistrict Settlement Fund, enters the picture. Each of the Federal Reserve banks maintains a balance with the Interdistrict Settlement Fund in Washington, D.C. When a Federal Reserve bank is owed more money by other Federal Reserve banks than it owes, its account in the fund is credited, while those Federal Reserve banks which owe more than they are owed will have their accounts charged by the net amount which they owe to the system.

In the instance being discussed, the account of the Federal Reserve Bank of New York would be credited and the account of the Federal Reserve Bank of San Francisco would be charged the amount of the check. The check in the meantime has been sent to the Federal Reserve Bank of San Francisco, and it is now charged against the account of the Bank of America, thus decreasing its reserves in the Federal Reserve Bank of San Francisco. The check itself is sent to the Bank of America, where it is finally charged against the maker's account and the transaction is finally completed when the canceled check is returned to the maker with his statement. A book has been paid for with a series of bookkeeping transactions although several thousand miles separated buyer and seller. The purchaser's check was sent from California to New York, and in returning, it passed through the two commercial banks and two Federal Reserve banks. Each bank made the proper accounting entries to charge the account of one party and credit the account of another. The net effect was an increase in the publisher's bank account and a reduction in the bank account of the college student a continent away.[3]

Essentially the same process is followed in the intradistrict clearance of checks, but in this case only one Federal Reserve bank will be involved in the clearing process. Suppose that a check drawn on a bank in Richmond, Virginia, is presented for payment to a bank in Clarksburg, West Virginia. The receiving bank would return that check along with other checks drawn on banks in the Fifth Federal Reserve District

[3] In practice there will be a time lag, for a bank will not credit an account until the check has cleared; that is, the Federal Reserve bank will wait two days before crediting the account of the New York member bank.

to the Federal Reserve Bank of Richmond. There the account of the bank which received the check would be credited, while the bank upon which the check was drawn would be charged the amount of the check. The check would then be returned to the originating bank, which would send it to the depositor.

Holding Reserves of Member Banks. The Federal Reserve banks hold the reserves of the member banks. Under the National Banking System (1863–1914), the reserves of the commercial banks were pyramided. Commercial banks deposited their reserves against customer's deposits in other banks and thus earned interest. A bank in rural Pennsylvania might deposit part of its reserve in a bank in Harrisburg, and that bank in turn might deposit a part of its reserve in a bank in New York where it could earn interest. The same thing happened all over the country. The result was a concentration of the reserves in New York banks. In a situation such as this, any call for cash at the local level would involve much of the commercial banking system. This is what happened in the Panic of 1907, which resulted in a great deal of pressure for a revision in the method of handling bank reserves.

In the Federal Reserve Act of 1914, Congress established the reserve requirements for member banks. Country banks were required to have a 7 per cent reserve, reserve city banks a 10 per cent reserve, and central reserve city banks were required to hold 13 per cent in reserves.[4] Furthermore, these reserves had to be kept in the Federal Reserve bank for the district in which the bank was located, and no interest could be paid on such reserves. The Federal Reserve Bank Act was amended in 1935 to enable the Board of Governors to increase the reserve requirements. Under that amendment, the reserve requirements against demand deposits could be raised to 26 per cent for central reserve city banks, 20 per cent for reserve city banks, and 14 per cent for country banks. For time deposits in all banks the reserve requirements could be set between 3 per cent and 6 per cent. The law was changed again in 1959. The minimum and maximum legal reserve requirements for central reserve city banks and reserve city banks are 10 and 22 per cent. At the same time, the law was changed to permit banks to include vault cash in their legal reserves.

The 1935 amendment enabled the Board of Governors to control the total amount of bank credit, and thus influence the level of eco-

---

[4] The central reserve city banks are large banks in the financial districts of New York and Chicago. The reserve city banks are those found in 62 of the larger cities of the country. The remainder are termed country banks.

nomic activity. As long as a bank has reserves in excess of that required for deposits, it can continue to make loans and create new deposits. Once, however, a bank has no excess reserves, it must either borrow from the Federal Reserve bank or cease making loans. If a bank needs additional reserves, they can be obtained by any of several techniques. A method which is often used by commercial banks is that of borrowing on the promissory notes of the commercial bank backed by collateral consisting of commercial paper or government bonds. It can also sell commercial paper or government bonds to the Federal Reserve bank.

The reserves maintained with the Federal Reserve bank do not consist of currency or gold. The reserves of the commercial banks in the Federal Reserve bank are similar to the checking account which an individual might maintain in a commercial bank. The depositor's account is a bookkeeping entry appearing as a liability on the commercial bank's balance sheet. The reserve of the commercial bank appears as a liability on the balance sheet of the Federal Reserve bank. The Federal Reserve bank, like a commercial bank, will not maintain a 100 per cent reserve against deposits. It maintains a 25 per cent reserve against deposits of commercial banks in the form of gold certificates. Since the gold certificates actually represent an equivalent amount of gold, credit, like currency, is based on gold, but the amount of gold backing either is small.

Providing a Market for Commercial Paper. The Federal Reserve banks provide a market for commercial paper or to put it in technical terms, the Federal Reserve banks rediscount commercial paper. Commercial paper includes such credit instruments as orders to pay or promises to pay which arise out of commercial transactions. For example, a merchant in Cincinnati might purchase $10,000 worth of merchandise from a Chicago manufacturer. The transaction may be financed by the seller drawing an order to pay upon the purchaser, which the latter accepts. The seller of the merchandise can sell or discount the note at his bank and receive deposit credit equaling the amount of the note less the discount. The bank in turn might desire additional cash or reserves, and it could sell this note to the Federal Reserve bank. Since this would be the second time that the note is sold, it is referred to as rediscounting.

The Federal Reserve bank, like any other bank, does not lend money without charging interest, and when a member bank borrows from the "Fed," it must pay for that service. The rate which is charged borrowing banks is the rediscount rate, and it is set by the Federal Reserve banks. There will be an inverse relationship between the rediscount rate and the eagerness (or lack thereof) of the member banks to borrow from the "Fed." The higher the rediscount rate, the more reluctant the commercial banks will be to borrow, and the lower the rediscount rate, the more willing they will be to do so. As the rediscount rate increases, the rate charged by the commercial banks will increase, and there will be a reduction in the number of loans made. To the extent, then, that member banks need to borrow funds from the Federal Reserve banks, changing the rediscount rate will make money cheaper or dearer.

A major purpose of providing rediscounting facilities for the commercial banking system is to provide the latter with liquidity. If, for any reason, there should be a large number of depositors wanting their funds from a given bank, that bank could sell the commercial paper that it holds, or it could borrow on its promissory note, using the commercial paper as a collateral. In this fashion it could weather the crisis. A second purpose of control over rediscounting is the promotion of economic stability, which will be discussed in some detail.

Promoting Economic Stability. Since 1935, the Federal Reserve System has been charged with the promotion of economic stability— a problem plaguing the United States for the past century and a half. Periods of widespread prosperity have been followed by periods of general unemployment. Prices, instead of remaining stable over the decades, have fluctuated; or to put it in other words, the value of money has been unstable. The Federal Reserve System is charged with maintaining a stable monetary system. To accomplish this purpose, the Board of Governors and the Federal Reserve banks have certain tools which can be used to influence the decisions of bankers as well as the individual citizen and business firm.

Attempts to promote economic stability through the use of monetary controls are based on the premise that there is a direct relationship between the quantity of money and the level of economic activity. Although it is possible to control the amount of currency in circulation, primary reliance must be placed on the control of credit if the level of economic activity is to be influenced. If the amount of lending is restricted or made more costly, it will tend to reduce expenditures by individuals and businesses. On the other hand, if it is made possible for banks to expand demand deposits, individuals and businesses will be encouraged to borrow and thus increase expenditures. The Federal Reserve System may (1) influence the amount of credit or (2) the cost of credit. These monetary controls are indeed powerful weapons, but, as will be pointed out, they are more effective in combating inflation than depression. Following are ways in which the Federal Reserve System promotes economic stability.

(*a*) Changing the rediscount rate. As has been previously explained, the member banks may sell commercial paper to the Federal Reserve banks if increased reserves are needed, or they may borrow on their promissory note. In either case the member banks are borrowing and paying interest. As the rediscount rate increases, the cost of borrowing increases, and as it goes down, the cost decreases. Possibly as important as the cost effect is the psychological effect. If the rediscount rate is raised, the public is informed that the banking officials feel that there is an overextension of credit and steps are being taken to remedy the situation. A change in the rediscount rate may portend other more drastic measures in the near future.

(*b*) Open market operations are the most powerful and most frequently employed tool used to promote economic stability by the Federal Reserve System. The Federal Open Market Committee makes all sales and purchases in the name of the Open Market Account. The Federal Open Market Committee meets frequently to survey credit conditions and the national economic outlook in order to plan future actions. The actual operations are supervised by the manager of the account who is associated with the New York Federal Reserve Bank. All of the operations are conducted in the New York financial market.

The Open Market Committee buys and sells government securities for the most part, although it has dealt in bankers' acceptances. In open market operations, the Federal Reserve System is taking an active and forcing role as contrasted to the passive and permissive role associated with the changing of the rediscount rate. By buying or selling government bonds, the reserves of the member banks will actually be increased or decreased. When government bonds are sold, the member banks may be forced to reduce loans or to borrow from the Federal Reserve banks. It is for this reason that the open market operations are a favored tool in the promotion of economic stability.

For the sake of illustration, assume that the Open Market Committee decides that money is too tight or scarce and wise public policy decrees a loosening of credit conditions. The committee would purchase government securities from private bond brokers. This would increase the reserves of the commercial banks and would enable them to expand loans. The following entries in a commercial bank balance sheet may help to explain this point.

Assets	*Liabilities and Net Worth*
Reserves with Federal	Demand deposits.... +\$10,000,000
Reserve bank... +\$10,000,000	

If the above entries are taken to represent the aggregate balance sheet of the banking system, the \$10 million which the member banks received as deposit credit can be used as a basis for expanding credit. If the reserve requirement is assumed to be 20 per cent, the banks could increase demand deposits by \$50 million. In the meantime, changes have been taking place in the balance sheet of the Federal Reserve banks. Their holdings of government securities and deposits of member banks have increased by \$10 million. In terms of the Reserve banks' balance sheet, the changes would appear as follows:

Assets	*Liabilities and Net Worth*
Government	Deposits of member
securities......... +\$10,000,000	banks............ +\$10,000,000

In the sale of securities the procedure is merely reversed. The Open Market Committee sells government securities to private bond dealers and receives payment in the form of checks drawn upon commercial banks. These checks are collected by charging the member banks' reserve accounts in the Federal Reserve banks. This reduces their reserves and lending capacity. If the reduction takes the banks below the required level of reserves, the commercial banks will have to reduce loans or borrow from the Federal Reserve banks. The effect will be a general tightening of the money markets, especially if the rediscount rate is increased at the time when the member banks wish to borrow from the "Fed."

Dealing in the open market is the most powerful tool which the Federal Reserve authorities have at their command. Nevertheless, selling in the opening market is a much more powerful tool than is buying. In selling operations, the reserves of the member banks are being reduced, and this may force the banks to reduce loans or raise the rates charged on loans. Buying, on the other hand, increases reserves and enables the member banks to expand loans if they desire, but making such action possible is not the same as consummating new loans. In other words, buying in the open market is permissive in nature while selling is compulsive.

(c) The Board of Governors can change the reserve requirement for member banks to promote economic stability. The policy has been one of raising the reserve requirements during times of threatened inflation and lowering the reserve requirements during times of threatened depression or falling prices. These actions are based on the same principle which underlies open market operations and changes in the rediscount rate. If prices are increasing and it is felt that a major cause is too much credit, the Board of Governors would increase the reserve requirements to restrict the lending power of the member banks. If there were an insufficient amount of credit which might result in a decline in business activity, reserve requirements would be lowered in an effort to increase lending by the private banking system. For example, $100 of excess reserves would serve as the basis for $500 in demand deposits if the reserve requirement were 20 per cent. If the reserve requirement were reduced to 10 per cent, the same reserve would serve as the basis for $1,000 in demand deposits. Or, if the reserve requirement were increased to 33⅓ per cent, the $100 would serve as the reserve for only $300 in demand deposits.

There are several limitations on the use of reserve requirements. First, there is the general handicap that all monetary controls have in promoting higher prices or prosperity. It is permissive only. Secondly, in the past reserve requirements have been raised, but for several reasons the commercial banks have had such large amounts of excess reserves that the higher reserve requirement did not affect their operations. There is the added difficulty that changing reserve requirements is, at best, a cumbersome method of regulation. A very small change in reserve requirements will (or could) result in a much larger change in the amount of credit. Furthermore, if the reserve requirements were changed frequently, the banking system would become characterized by uncertainty and confusion. Thus, for the day-to-day control of the credit supply, chief reliance is placed on open market operations and changes in the rediscount rate, both of which can be used with a great deal of finesse. The reserve requirements are changed only when action of great magnitude is desired.

(*d*) The Federal Reserve System has been given certain regulatory controls which are not strictly a part of the banking and credit system, but, nevertheless, are instruments to be used in the promotion of economic stability. One of these is the power to control margin requirements in the stock market. If one purchases stock on the margin, a certain percentage of the purchase price is paid in cash and the rest is borrowed from the broker. If the margin requirement is 10 per cent, a buyer can buy $1,000 worth of stock with $100; but if the margin requirement is 50 per cent, he could buy only $200 in securities. Raising the margin requirement has a dampening effect upon those who could purchase stock by reducing the number of shares which can be purchased with a given amount of money. This is, in effect, control over a special type of credit.

There cannot be much questioning of the fact that there is a direct relationship between the availability of credit for stock-market activities and the level of prices in that market. Certainly the fact that the margin requirement was only 10 per cent in 1929 contributed to the tremendous increase in stock prices which preceded the crash of that autumn, but this is not meant to imply that there were not other contributing causes.

(*e*) The Board of Governors has from time to time been empowered to exercise certain direct controls over credit and its use. During World War II, Regulation "W" was imposed to regulate the size of down payment and limit the period of repayment for goods purchased on installment credit. Regulation "X" imposed the same type of controls on housing credit. These controls were also used during the Korean War and to some extent during the interwar period. It is felt that direct controls are a necessary tool in the program of promoting economic stability during war, although the cost of administration is extremely high. Such controls are based on the same general philosophy as that underlying the controls previously discussed. A limitation on the quantity and use of credit will have an anti-inflationary effect, while a relaxation of such controls will at least permit an expansionary movement. The method of operation is, however, in sharp contrast, for rather than regulate the amount of credit at the source, direct controls attempt to regulate the use to which credit is put.

It should be emphasized in conclusion that all of the monetary and credit controls which have been discussed operate much more effectively when used to curb inflation than when used to promote spending and prosperity. One may stop a horse by pulling upon the reins, but that horse cannot be made to move forward by pushing on the reins. The same is true in the case of monetary controls. The formation and use of credit may be restricted and thus exercise an anti-inflationary influence, but it proves much more difficult to give the credit system more freedom and thus promote an expansion of credit and economic activity.

Acting as Fiscal Agents. The Federal Reserve banks act as fiscal agents for the national government. In many countries a governmentally owned central bank serves the government in carrying out its financial operations. There is no such governmental bank in this country, and the United States government must rely upon private banks for the necessary banking services. These private banks are the Federal Reserve banks.

Millions of individuals and firms are continually paying taxes to the government with checks drawn on their accounts in commercial banks. If the check is very large, the government deposits that check in the bank on which it was drawn so that there will not be any great difficulty caused by its being cashed in some other bank. From time to time, the Treasury will announce that a certain percentage of its accounts in the commercial banks are to be transferred to the various Federal Reserve banks, so that eventually all the funds paid in taxes find their way into government deposits in the twelve Federal Reserve banks. When the government makes a disbursement, a check is written on an account in one of the Federal Reserve banks and the payment is made to the veteran, the farmer, the soldier, or whomever might be the recipient of the governmental payment.

The Federal Reserve Banking System also performs other functions for the government. During World War II, the system purchased a large number of war bonds to help finance the war. It assists the Treasury Department in selling bonds to commercial banks and other financial institutions which may desire to make such investments. The Federal Reserve Bank of New York represents the government in dealing in foreign exchange. There are, in addition to the above, other services which the Federal Reserve System performs for the national government.

CONCLUSION

The price system is the institution which "ties" the various parts of the economic system together and consolidates them into a unified entity. Money, on the other hand, is a unit of expression. A single monetary system means that all of those in the economic system speak the same language—use the same expression. An economic system with two or more monetary systems would be extremely awkward. And an economic system without a monetary system is inconceivable in today's industrialized society. It also seems inevitable that, as the barriers between nations are broken down, present national monetary systems will take on an international flavor.

What this really means is this. The economic system is made up of two distinct parts. One is the goods and service sector in which real goods and services are produced, exchanged, and consumed. Alongside it is the money sector—a market in which savings are accumulated and funds acquired for investment expenditures and other ends. The two sectors of the economic system are not independent. Actions in one affect the other. And, most important, money and the money market can be manipulated in order to bring about desired results in the other sector of the economy. This will occupy much of our attention in the remainder of the book.

EXERCISES

Group I

Explain why the following statements are either true or false:

1. All monies will always fulfill all of the functions of money.
2. It is possible for something to serve as money without having value.
3. Since the banking system can lend out some multiple of its reserves, it follows that each individual bank must also be able to do so.
4. If the Federal Open Market Committee buys government bonds in the open market, the result will be a reduction in the reserves of the member banks.
5. The government should raise the reserve requirement and lower the rediscount rate if the policy is one of combating inflation.
6. Some type of credit money is essential in an economy characterized by specialization.
7. Monetary controls exercised by the Federal Reserve System are permissive rather than coercive in promoting recovery, although they are coercive in curbing inflation.

Group II

1. Evaluate the silver purchase policy of the United States over the past 75 years.
2. What is the relationship between changes in the rediscount rate and changes in the rate for prime commercial paper (Treasury bills)? Do changes in the prime rate follow or precede changes in the rediscount rate? Empirical evidence can be obtained from the *Wall Street Journal* for 1957–58.

Group III

1. One of the proposed banking reforms which has received a great deal of attention but little sympathy is popularly known among economists as the "Chicago Plan of Banking Reform." An article describing this plan by Albert G. Hart appeared in the *Review of Economic Studies,* Vol. II (1935) and was reprinted in *Readings in Monetary Theory.* What is the Chicago plan? What shortcomings was it devised to meet?
2. Technically, the United States is still on the gold standard. From time to time, however, there are proposals that the country return to the full gold standard which prevailed between 1900 and 1933. What are the arguments for and against the gold specie standard? Is the country ever apt to return to this standard?
3. During the entire nineteenth century the United States was on a bimetallic standard. What are the arguments for such a monetary standard? Why was this standard abandoned? Did this standard work in practice?

BIBLIOGRAPHY

AMERICAN ECONOMICS ASSOCIATION. *Readings in Monetary Theory.* Philadelphia: Blakiston Co., 1951.

RITTER, L. S. (Ed.). *Money and Economic Activity—Readings in Money and Banking.* 2nd ed. New York: Houghton Mifflin Co., 1961.

ROBERTSON, D. H. *Money.* New York: Pitman Publishing Co., 1948. (Also available in paperback edition.)

WOOD, ELMER. *Monetary Control.* Columbia, Missouri: University of Missouri Press, 1963.

PAPERBACK READING LIST

BAGEHOT, WALTER. *Lombard Street: A Description of the Money Market.* Originally published in 1873 but reissued by Richard D. Irwin, Inc. in 1962.

REPORT OF THE COMMISSION ON MONEY AND CREDIT. *Money and Credit: Their Influence on Jobs, Prices, and Growth.* New York: Prentice-Hall, Inc., 1961.

<table>
<tr><td>*Chapter*

13</td><td>THE DETERMINATION OF

THE LEVEL OF INCOME</td></tr>
</table>

LOVE IN THE BOOM

He: Darling, the gross national product is still climbing and we are nearing the cyclical peak of the family-formation curve.

She: So what?

He: Well, I thought possibly we too, ought to constitute a household unit.

She: And what'll we use for personal disposable income?

He: Well, I have been thinking of entering the labor force, because automation will probably create more jobs than it destroys.

She: That may be, but I must warn you that I have an awful marginal propensity to consume.

He: Angel! Another thing we hold in common! But my annual increases in productivity are bound to keep the rate of growth of our consumption sustainable . . .

She: . . . and reduce inflationary pressures, other conditions remaining the same.

He: Yes, you do see. There really are no significant disincentives.

She: But are you sure I'm the one?

He: Well, I've tried a random sample and you were modal.

She: . . . Sweet.

He: You're all the future I ever extrapolated for. Say you will!

She: But I never made a long run projection.

He: We could have the dearest little dwelling unit.

She: I don't know . . . Do you think we should form a farm or a nonfarm household?

He: Nonfarm, definitely. At the same time I believe in outmigration from the high-density urban area.

She: So do I. I have my heart set on a single-family dwelling in a one class neighborhood.

He: What sort of a fertility pattern do you think we should have?

She: Well, as you know, I've always thought of myself as an average sort of girl. I'd like 1.87 children—if I said yes, of course.

He: Then say it!

She: The Federal Reserve Index of production has topped 140, at that.

He: And it would make the Census Bureau so happy.

She: Well, I probably will.

(They embrace, as the curtain descends at a rate of ten feet per second.)—Bennett Cerf, "Trade Winds," *Saturday Review,* December 3, 1955.

Determining the level of income and the forces influencing the level of income for an economic system resolves itself into two problems. First, there is the problem of measuring the level of income. How much does the economy produce in any given year? Measuring the output of goods and services for an economy as productive as that of the United States is not an inconsequential task. The first few pages of this chapter, then, will be devoted to a discussion of the tools used to measure the level of income.

After the first problem, which is largely mechanical in nature, is solved we can turn to the second and more important question. The second area of intellectual exploration is that of determining the forces which cause the level of income to change from one period to the next. Why is income high in one period only to be followed by a period of low income? What are the forces within the economic system which might cause changes in the level of income? Does the economic system move toward an equilibrium from which there would be no disposition for it to move to some other level of income? After we have analyzed such questions as these, we will be in a position to go on to the following chapters and discuss the business cycle and the attempts of the government to influence the level of economic activity.

NATIONAL INCOME ACCOUNTING

Introduction

The American economic system is a fantastically productive economy. The task of measuring that productivity for any given year is a task of Herculean magnitude. An individual worker, businessman, or farmer can state with exactitude his production in physical terms. A business firm or individual may produce houses, cars, or bushels of wheat, but since it is impossible to add cars, wheat, and houses, a physical inventory of the total production of the economy is likewise impossible. To make such an inventory, a common denominator is needed which can be used to measure output regardless of the physical unit—tons, ounces, barrels, performances, etc. All of the above, however, have one thing in common—value which can be expressed as prices. By converting physical units into monetary equivalents, it is possible to arrive at a monetary figure which represents the productivity of the economic system, but it must be kept in mind that it is the monetary value of the economy's productivity.

Expressing the value of the total output of the nation in monetary rather than physical terms can be misleading during periods of changing prices. Most measuring devices for distance, pressure, weight, etc., remain constant. That is, an inch represents the same distance at all times. In the case of value, however, the measuring device varies when prices change. Assume for a moment that 1,000 units of a good were sold at a price of $1.00 per unit in 1960. In 1961, the same quantity sold for $1,250. In this example production did not increase, but the monetary value of the production increased by a total of $250. In a period of declining prices, the reverse would be true. Thus changes in the value of the economy's output may represent changes in physical output and/or changes in the prices of the goods and services.

The changes in the value of total output which result from changes in prices can be eliminated statistically. If the figures for total production are adjusted for changes in prices, the resultant series will represent productivity in terms of dollars with constant purchasing power. This can be done by selecting an appropriate price index and dividing each of the total value figures by the corresponding figure for the price index. Thus, the total value of goods and services produced in 1964 would be divided by the price index for the same year. If the price index were based on 1959, the resultant figure would represent the total value of goods and services produced in 1964 in terms of a dollar having the purchasing power of the 1959 dollar. Such figures would be comparable with others in the series, for they would represent the changes in total output and would not reflect changes in the price level.

Those working in the field of national income accounting have need for various kinds of data depending upon their particular field or problem. Whereas one may be interested in the total market value of the product, another may be interested in consumption or saving. To meet these diverse requirements, the Department of Commerce computes a number of accounts which are available in the *Survey of Current Business,* the *Federal Reserve Bulletin,* the *Economic Report of the President,* and a number of other publications which publish statistical data on the nation's economy. The student would do well to examine at least one of the above publications to get some idea of the available information.

Gross National Product

The market value of the final goods and services produced in the economic system during a given period, usually a year, is the gross national product (GNP). It is a summation of all the prices paid (plus some which don't have a price such as farm produce consumed by the farmer) by the final users of the goods and services produced in the current accounting period. It includes the amount the housewife pays for a loaf of bread, the price of a ticket to the opera, the price of a new car, as well as the price of an appendectomy, and a host of other goods and services. Since the goods and services are valued at their market price, the GNP is the most inclusive of all the national income accounts and is the largest of the several concepts. In 1962 the gross national product was $553.9 billion (see Table 13–1). This means that the American economic system produced $553.9 billion worth of goods and services—an amount so large as to be incomprehensible. No other country comes close to this level of production.

In the computation of the GNP, care must be exercised to eliminate double counting. If, for example, the value of the farmer's wheat, the miller's flour, and the baker's bread are all included, the resultant figure would be too high, since the retail value of the bread includes the value of the wheat and flour. To eliminate this difficulty, only the value of the final product is included in the GNP. It would be possible to arrive at the same result by computing the value added at each level of the productive process, but the method explained above is somewhat easier to understand and compute.

"GNP" is a measurement of the productivity of the economy in a given year, and because it is so defined, only the production of that year is included. Thus the value of the new car is included, whereas the price of the used car is not. The latter constitutes a consumer expenditure, but as the car was actually made in a previous accounting period, it was included in the GNP of that earlier period. If it were included in more than one accounting period, the resultant figures would have an upward bias of considerable magnitude. The same reasoning applies to the sale of securities, used housing, etc.

TABLE 13–1

GROSS NATIONAL PRODUCT OR EXPENDITURE
(Department of Commerce Estimates, in Billions of Dollars)

Item	1962
Gross National Product	$553.9
Personal Consumption Expenditures	356.7
Durable goods	47.5
Nondurable goods	162.0
Services	147.1
Gross Private Domestic Investment	76.6
New construction	44.5
Residential, nonfarm	23.3
Other	21.2
Producers' durable equipment	28.9
Changes in business inventories	3.2
Net Exports of Goods and Services	3.3
Exports	28.4
Imports	25.2
Government Purchases of Goods and Services	117.3
Federal	62.4
National defense	53.4
Other	9.7
Less: Government sales	.8
State and local	55.0

SOURCE: *Federal Reserve Bulletin.*

The GNP is the summation of personal consumption expenditures, domestic investment expenditures, government purchases of goods and services, and net foreign investment (see Table 13–1). Personal consumption expenditures, the largest single account, consists of all expenditures made by consumers for goods and services produced in the particular period. It includes expenditures for consumer durable goods, nondurable goods, and personal services.

Government purchases of goods and services represents the second largest segment of GNP. The $117.3 billion spent by all levels of government in 1962 includes expenditures for such diverse goods and services as rockets, highways, sewage disposal plants, and school crossing guards. In 1962 government purchases represented approximately 20 per cent of the total GNP, but during World War II, government purchases accounted for as much as 45 per cent of the total GNP. National defense is the largest component of government expenditures.

The third segment of GNP is domestic investment, which includes new construction, new producers' durable goods, and changes in inventory. Investment expenditures include both those expenditures to replace present equipment and those expenditures to increase the economy's stock of capital goods. Investment expenditures are very volatile in the sense that there is a great deal of variation from one year to the next. This is particularly true in the case of inventories and producers' durable equipment.

The fourth and final division of the GNP is net exports. This figure represents the difference between exports and imports of goods and services. If more is exported from the United States than is imported, there will be a net flow of money into this country. If more is imported, there will be a net balance of payments in favor of those who sold goods in the United States. If exports exceed imports, the net figure is positive. If, however, more was imported than was exported, the net figure to be used in the computation of GNP would be negative, and it would be deducted from the sum of the other components of gross national product. In 1962, net export of goods and services was a positive figure indicating that exports exceeded imports.

Net National Product

In producing $553.9 billion worth of goods and services in 1962, some of the nation's productive resources were worn out or became obsolete. Other resources were destroyed by accident or lost. The GNP does not make an allowance for such depreciation or loss. Net national product (NNP) does, however, for it is computed by subtracting an allowance for capital consumption from the GNP. It is thus a measure of net current production. In a very short period of time, depreciation is negligible, and in such an instance it is not inaccurate to use the GNP; however, over a longer period of time, the NNP would be a better representation of the economy's productivity, if accurate data could be obtained for depreciation and obsolesence allowances.

National Income

National income (NI) is the total output of the economic system valued at factor prices as contrasted to GNP, which is the output valued at market prices. In any given year, the four factors of production— land, labor, capital, and the entrepreneur, will receive a return for their participation in the productive process. National income is the summation of wages, interest, rent, and profit. National income is the summation of wages, interest, rent, and profit.

National income can be computed by deducting from NNP those items which do not become factor income, although they are included in the market price of good or service in question. Indirect business taxes (sales taxes) are included in the market value of the goods and services, yet the revenue obtained from such taxes goes directly to the government rather than to the factors of production. Business transfer payments represent payments made by business firms for which no productive service is rendered. Business transfer payments will be included in GNP and NNP, but they must be deducted from the latter in order to compute national income, since they do not become factor income. So NNP minus business transfer payments and indirect business taxes equals national income.

There is, however, a second method of computing national income (see Table 13–2). Since it is the total factor income, it is possible to

TABLE 13–2

NATIONAL INCOME, BY DISTRIBUTIVE SHARES
(Department of Commerce Estimates, in Billions of Dollars)

Item	1962
National Income	$458.0
Compensation of Employees	321.6
Wages and salaries	295.8
Private	239.7
Military	11.0
Government civilian	45.2
Supplements to wages and salaries	25.8
Proprietors' Income	49.8
Business and professional	36.8
Farm	13.0
Rental Income of Persons	12.8
Corporate Profits and Inventory Adjustments	51.5
Profits before tax	51.3
Profits tax liability	25.0
Profits after tax	26.3
Dividends	15.9
Undistributed profits	10.3
Inventory valuation adjustment	.2
Net Interest	22.2

SOURCE: *Federal Reserve Bulletin.*

compute NI by totaling wages, interest, rent, and profit. As it is impossible to separate total factor income into the four categories used by the economist, the following are used: compensation of employees, income of unincorporated businesses, rental income of persons, corporate profits, and net interest. Although some, such as the income of unincorporated businesses, will include wages, interest, profit, and rent, a summation of the five will equal a summation of the four forms of factor income. This second method of computing national income thus serves as a check upon the accuracy of the statistician's computations in computing national income from gross national product.

Personal Income and Personal Savings

Personal income is that part of national income actually received by individuals, for not all national income gets into the hands of individuals. For example, contributions to social security, corporate profits taxes, and undistributed profits represent factor income, but none become personal income. The first two are paid to the government by the corporation, and the latter is retained by the company, which eventually uses it for capital expansion. But there are also some items which do not represent returns to the factors in the current accounting period but do constitute personal income. Government transfer payments and business transfer payments are of this character. The first include such benefits as those received under Social Security and the various veterans' programs. The second would include business contributions to charity. To the extent that such payments become personal income, they must be added to national income in order to compute personal income.

In 1962 personal income was $440.5 billion. After paying $57.6 billion in personal taxes, consumers retained $382.9 billion in disposable income. Of this they spent $356.7 billion and saved $26.2 billion.

Summary

Table 13–3 represents a tabular explanation of the various concepts and the relationship between each. By starting at the top of the table and working toward the bottom, one can grasp the relationship between each of the several measures of aggregate economic activity. Tables 13–1 and 13–2 simply broke down two segments of this table in order to explain the component parts of GNP and national income.

Figure 13–1, shown on page 307, on the other hand is a graphic explanation of the national income concepts. In this instance all figures are omitted as well as some of the minor accounts. This diagram portrays the circular nature of the flow of income which is not so easily observed in the tables. The student should pay particular attention to the savings and investment relationship, for it is of crucial importance.

TABLE 13–3

RELATION OF GROSS NATIONAL PRODUCT, NATIONAL INCOME,
PERSONAL INCOME, AND SAVING
(Department of Commerce Estimates, in Billions of Dollars)

Item	1962
Gross National Product	$553.9
Less: Capital consumption allowances	47.6
Indirect business tax and nontax liability	51.6
Business transfer payments	2.1
Statistical discrepancy	−3.6
Plus: Subsidies less current surplus of government enterprises	1.7
Equals: National Income	458.0
Less: Corporate profits and inventory valuation adjustment	51.5
Contributions for social insurance	23.9
Plus: Government transfer payments	32.4
Net interest paid by government	7.4
Dividends	15.9
Business transfer payments	2.1
Equals: Personal Income	440.5
Less: Personal tax and nontax payments	57.6
Federal	49.1
State and local	8.5
Equals: Disposable Personal Income	382.9
Less: Personal Consumption Expenditures	356.7
Equals: Personal Saving	26.2

SOURCE: *Federal Reserve Bulletin.*

THE CLASSICAL THEORY OF INCOME DETERMINATION

Knowledge of a single fact contributes little or nothing to our understanding of the society in which we live. Simply knowing the magnitude of the various national income accounts for a single year or even for all the years since the country began would be of little use to the person possessing such knowledge. In fact, that is the position of the student who has reached this point, for the basic accounting concepts have been presented and, it is hoped, mastered by the student. But as it stands, this newly acquired knowledge is of no usefulness except possibly to test the student's ability to memorize.

We must go on and explore the complex relationships between the different sectors of the economy. It will be possible to establish certain general propositions which enable one to predict future behavior. It is the purpose of the theory of income determination to establish these generalizations.

Classical Economics and the Business Cycle

The classical economists are generally considered to include that group of economists who lived, thought, and wrote between the Amer-

FIGURE 13–1

FLOW OF INCOME AND EXPENDITURES

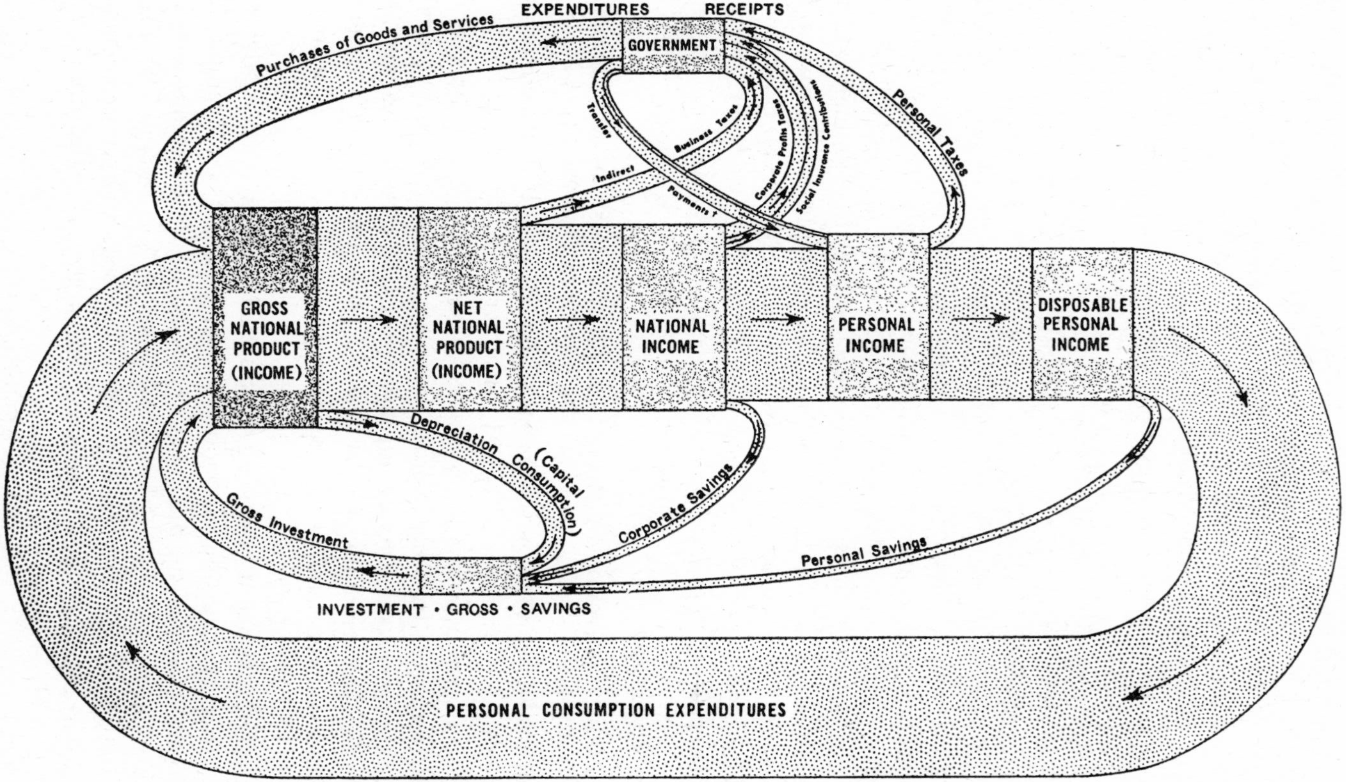

SOURCE: J. F. Dewhurst and Associates, *America's Needs and Resources: A New Survey* (New York: Twentieth Century Fund, 1955).

ican Revolution and World War I. For the most part they were English-men, although there were some individuals who must be included in the group who lived on the continent of Europe and in the United States. The first classical economist, without much question, was Adam Smith who has been mentioned from time to time. Alfred Marshall (1842–1924) might be considered as being the last of the school, although he is sometimes referred to as a neoclassicist since he did much to reconcile the writings of the classicists with other schools of economic thought.

The term "classical" is not used in the sense of traditional, although out of this particular group of individuals a body of economic doctrine developed which has, for the most part, withstood the challenge of time as well as intellectual attack. The main contribution of this group is that body of economic doctrine known as microeconomics or the economics of the firm and industry. Although some individual economists were concerned about the level of employment, the classical school as a whole demonstrated little concern with this economic problem which is of such importance today. Their lack of concern, however, was a result of their failure to perceive that such a problem might exist. How can this failure to see a problem, which is so apparent to everyone today, be explained?

Say's Law

The problem of unemployment for the classicists was eliminated by the French economist J. B. Say (1767–1832) in his proposition which is known to the world as Say's Law. He divided the economy into two groups—producer units and consumer units. The first, that is, the factors of production, work as laborers, save, take risks, and provide natural resources. In other words, they provide the productive services necessary to produce goods and services desired by the consumer units. For their contribution, the factors of production receive a monetary payment in the form of wages, interest, rent, and profit. The total of these four factor returns must be just equal to the price of the product.

Thus the act of producing creates the income to purchase the product. In producing an automobile costing $2,500, for example, that amount is earned by those who participated in its production. This group has the purchasing power necessary to buy the product created. In the aggregate, then, the total value of goods and services produced must just equal the total purchasing power created by the production of goods and services.

But there are going to be some factor owners who do not desire to spend all of their income for consumption goods and services. In other words, some are going to save. At the same time, some producer units will spend more than that currently received as income in order to expand their supply of capital equipment. As long as the amount which society wants to invest equals the amount society wishes to save, the circular flow of income remains undisturbed. All of the income received by the factor units is spent for either consumption goods or capital goods. If savings and investment should not be equal, the total amount spent by the factor units would be more or less than their total income, and some adjustment would be necessary.

Say, and the classicists who followed him, held that such adjustments would be made automatically. If the amount saved exceeded the amount invested, the rate of interest would fall. This would cause savings to be reduced and investment to be increased to a point where they would once again be equal. If investment exceeded savings, then the rate of interest would increase to that point where equality would be established. The interest rate, then, was of primary importance in the classical structure for it was the equilibrator of savings and investment.

The classicists, using this proposition of Say's, said that there was an inexorable tendency for the economy to move toward a full-employment equilibrium. If unemployment did exist, it was a temporary phenomena which would be eliminated by automatic adjustments. If any factor was unemployed, it was because its price was too high. If it was labor, the wage rate was too high, and as soon as it was reduced, labor would be fully employed. If it was capital, the interest rate was too high, and as soon as it was lowered, savings would once again be fully utilized. And if consumption goods were not being purchased, the price again was too high, and the situation would be remedied with a reduction in the price.

This, then, was the reason why the classical economists never concerned themselves about the level of employment. To them there was no such problem, for the economy contained forces which would always push it toward a full-employment level.

THE NEW ECONOMICS[1]

In 1935 John Maynard Keynes (1883–1946) published *The General Theory of Employment, Interest, and Money,* which has been regarded as either (1) a complete revolution or (2) a major evolutionary change in economic thinking. To some, Keynesian economics, as it has come to be known, is the sum and substance of all economics, while to

[1] Taken from the title of the book edited by Seymour Harris entitled *The New Economics* (New York: Alfred A. Knopf, Inc., 1947).

others the mere name is an anathema. But all of the thinking in the field of economics during the past 30 years has been profoundly affected by the writing and thinking of this English economist. And today, practically all economists accept his work as a major contribution to economic thought.

Keynes turned the attention of the profession to the question of the level of employment and away from the question of price and output determination for the individual firm. It was probably propitious that the book was published in the middle of the Great Depression, for had it come out a decade earlier, it might have passed unnoticed. It was not difficult for Keynes to call attention to the problem of unemployment when there was 15 million unemployed in the United States.

Following in the path of Keynes have been a host of economists concerned with the problems of aggregative economics. They took the work of Keynes and used it as the basis for still further advances. Errors were corrected. New fields and new problems were explored. The "New Economics," then, is more than Keynesianism. It is concerned with that entire school of economic thought which places primary emphasis upon the economics of income and employment rather than upon the economics of the firm and the industry. We can now turn our attention to this more modern version of the theory of income determination.

The Basic Structure

Expenditures and Income. Total expenditures (Y) in the economy consist of (1) consumption expenditures, (2) investment expenditures, (3) government expenditures, and (4) exports or expenditures by foreigners for goods and services produced within the economy. These four categories correspond to the major component parts of the GNP. This relationship can be expressed in a very elementary mathematical form as:

$$Y = C + I + G_e + F_e$$

where G_e refers to government spending and F_e refers to exports.

It is a simple truism to state that the expenditures of one individual constitute the next person's income. The same is true for the economic system. The total expenditures for a given economy give some indication of the state of aggregate well-being of the individuals of that economy.

Since the total expenditures constitute the income for those receiving the expenditures, we might inquire as to how that income is used. Just as there are four different kinds of expenditures above, there are four ways in which the income can be used: spending for consumption goods, saving, paying taxes, and purchasing goods and services from producers in other economies (imports). Since expenditures and income are really the same thing from two different points of view, we can denote total income as (Y), and the formula for its disposition becomes:

$$Y = C + S + G_t + F_i$$

where G_t represents government income (taxes) and F_i represents imports.

The economic system will be in equilibrium when total expenditures and total income are equal. In this model, the equilibrium situation can be expressed by the following equality:

$$C + I + G_e + F_e = C + S + G_t + F_i$$

The components of total expenditures when summed for the economy just equal the sum involved in the disposition of the total income. An equilibrium flow has been established. The left side of the equation indicating the way incomes are generated is equal to the right side indicating how the income is used. For this equilibrium flow to be maintained, any leakages would have to be replaced by new injections of income from some other source.

This model can be simplified by reducing the number of terms in the equation above. In the formula for total expenditures, government spending could be reclassified as either consumption expenditures (spending for currently-used goods and services) or investment expenditures (spending for capital projects such as a hydroelectric facility). Similarly, foreign purchases of goods and services could be classified as consumption or investment expenditures. In the formula for the disposition of income, payments to the government and purchases of foreign goods could likewise be reclassified as either consumption expenditures or saving (where capital investments are made). Our formula for the aggregate economy becomes:

$$C + I = C + S,$$

or

$$\text{The creation of income} = \text{The disposal of income.}$$

This, in turn, can be reduced to:

$$S = I,$$

but the discussion of this relationship will have to be postponed for a few pages.

Elimination of government and foreign transactions does not imply that they are of no significance in the economy, for, in fact, the contrary is the case. If, for example, government expenditures exceed payments to the government, it would mean that the government was putting more into the income stream than was being withdrawn, and this would have an expansionary effect. On the other hand, if payments to the government were larger than government expenditures, the government would be taking more out of the income stream than it would be adding to that stream, and the effect would be of a contractionary nature. The relationship between foreign spending in the United States (exports) and spending abroad (imports) is similar.

The component parts of the expenditure-income relationship must be examined in some detail. Our interest will be in questions of the following nature: What are the factors which determine the level of consumption and investment expenditures? What is the relationship between changes in one and changes in the others? What are the conditions necessary for the establishment of some equilibrium level of income? And in the following chapters the question will be raised as to what the government can do to influence the level of income.

The entire discussion will be based on the value judgment that the desired level of income is one which will provide a high level of employment. Once this value judgment is accepted, the question then becomes one of determining what can be done to influence any one of the component parts of total expenditures in order to achieve this end.

Consumption Expenditures. Aggregate consumption expenditures in any economic system are, rather obviously, merely a summation of the consumption expenditures of all the individuals living in that economy. An explanation of total consumption expenditures must, perforce, start with an explanation of the consumption expenditures of individuals.

Any individual's consumption expenditures in a given time period will depend upon (1) the size of his income and (2) the amount of saving he might wish to do at a particular level of income. Generally those in the lower income groups will spend a larger part of their total income on consumption goods than will those in the higher income groups. It follows, then, that the aggregate consumption function for the economy is also dependent upon (3) the distribution of income among consumer units.

The general nature of the relationship between consumption and income is what one might suspect. Consumption and saving increase as income increases, but the increase in consumption is less than the increase in income.

The aggregate consumption function (C) is presented graphically in Figure 13–2. To aid in interpreting the national income graph, it is customary to draw in a guideline such as Z. This line indicates an equilibrium relationship between the two variables of the graph (income = expenditures). The guideline (Z) is the set or collection of all points where total expenditures and total income are equal. Its significance will become apparent as the analysis is developed.

If all the income received for producing the total supply of goods and services were spent, the consumption function (C) would be the same as Z. The actual consumption function indicates that at lower levels of income, the consumers actually spend more than they receive as income. At higher levels of income, consumption expenditures are less than total income. To the left of the intersection of C and Z, people are consuming out of assets—dissaving, and to the right of that intersection the consumers are saving—abstaining from consumption. In this simplified structure of the economy, people either spend or save. These are the only alternatives. Therefore, if C is subtracted from Z, the result will be the aggregate savings function for the economy. The savings function (S) indicates that aggregate savings are negative for lower income levels and positive for higher income levels.

At the higher levels of income, consumption expenditures make up a smaller part of the total income, whereas at the lower levels of income, the consumption expenditures actually exceed income. This relationship between total consumption and total income is known as the average propensity to consume (APC) and may be expressed as:

$$APC = C/Y.$$

It has already been pointed out that consumption will increase by less than income even when both are increasing. So the relative changes in the two is of significance. The relationship between the change in income and the change in consumption is known as the marginal propensity to consume (MPC). For example in Figure 13–2, as income increases from a to b ($=x$), consumption increased by an amount equal to y. Thus we could write:

$$MPC = dC/dY$$

where dC represents the difference in consumption and dY represents the difference in income. In Figure 13–2 the MPC could equal y/x.

The marginal propensity to consume is the slope of the consumption function. The consumption function (C) in Figure 13–2 was drawn as a straight line indicating that the *MPC* is a constant.

The slope of the savings function is likewise known as the marginal propensity to save (MPS). It is the relation between changes

FIGURE 13–2

CONSUMPTION AND SAVING

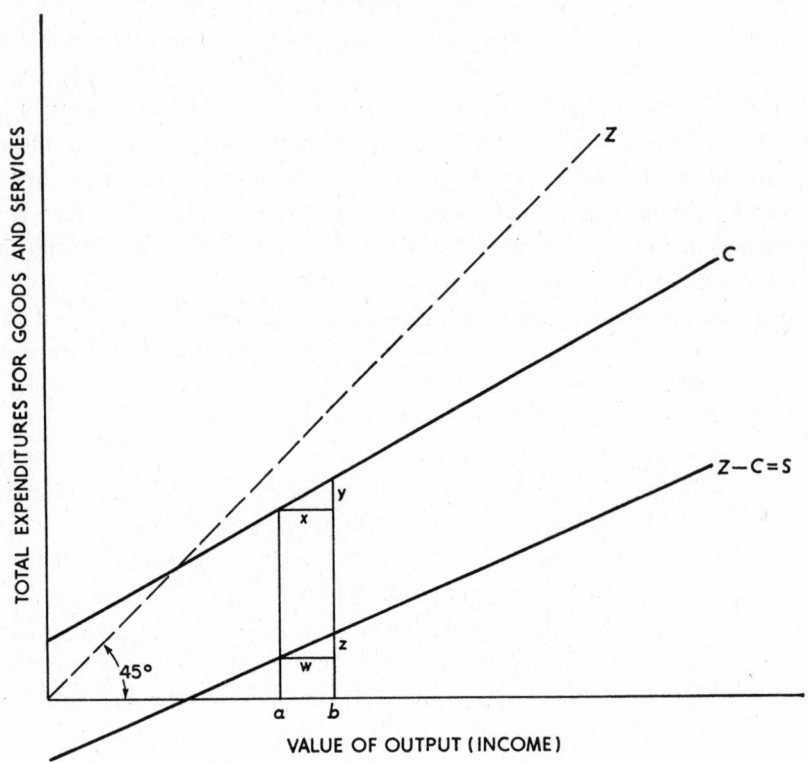

in saving and changes in income. In Figure 13–2, as income increases from a to b $(=w)$, savings increase by an amount equal to z.

$$MPS = dS/dY = z/w.$$

Since, by definition, an individual and the economy must dispose of any increment of income by either spending it or saving it, the marginal propensity to consume plus the marginal propensity to save must equal one.

The relationship between changes in income and changes in consumption and saving are of vital significance in explaining changes in the level of income, as will be pointed out shortly.

Investment Expenditures. In the Keynesian structure the level of investment is determined by (1) the rate of interest and (2) the anticipated rate of return.

The interest rate in this model is a function of (1) the supply of money and (2) the demand for money to hold in preference to securities. The supply of money is determined by (1) the government and the central bank and (2) the commerical banking system. As far as the government and the central bank are concerned, the interest rate is only one of many considerations influencing the supply of money. The commercial banking system gives more weight to the rate of interest insofar as the supply of money is concerned. In Figure 13–3B the supply function has been drawn in such a way as to indicate that a part of that supply is independent of the rate of interest.

The demand for money, on the other hand, is a function of three different motives. The *transaction* motive represents the demand for money to purchase goods and services. This is, primarily, a function of income. The *precautionary* motive represents the demand of people to hold money to meet unforeseen contingencies—"something for a rainy day." These two motives are not significantly affected by the rate of interest. The *speculative* motive is the desire to hold money in anticipation of a higher return at some time in the future. If the interest rate is low, the holder of funds is sacrificing less in the form of foregone interest income than he is if the interest rate is higher. Moreover, by holding assets in cash, he will be able to take advantage of any future increase in the interest rate. On the other hand, if interest rates are very high, income is foregone by holding money, and the holder of assets would prefer to have them in the form of earning assets.

The intersection of the supply of money and the demand for money (liquidity preference-*LP*) determines the rate of interest in the Keynesian system. (See Figure 13–3B.) At any rate higher than *r*, the supply of money exceeds the demand. Someone has to be holding the money so that some people are holding more money than they want. In an effort to get out of money and into securities, the price of securities will be driven up and the interest rate will be driven downward. On the other hand, if the rate of interest is lower than *r*, the demand for money will exceed the supply and some people will be unable to hold money as they wish. In their efforts to get out of securities and into money, the price of securities will be lowered, which is the same thing as saying the rate of interest will be increased. Only at an interest rate of *r* is there an equilibrium in the money market.

The interest rate is the cost of investing, regardless of whether one borrows or not, and it must be compared to the anticipated rate of return to make an investment decision.

The anticipated rate of return, which is known as the marginal efficiency of capital, is the second determinant of investment. The demand for any factor of production is based upon its productivity. The marginal efficiency of capital is a productivity concept. It is the relationship between the quantity of investment per period and the anticipated rate of return. The latter is, in turn, a function of the physical productivity of the investment good, and the quantity of final good sold.

FIGURE 13–3

KEYNESIAN INTEREST RATE DETERMINATION AND THE LEVEL OF INVESTMENT
A. Level of Investment   B. Rate of Interest

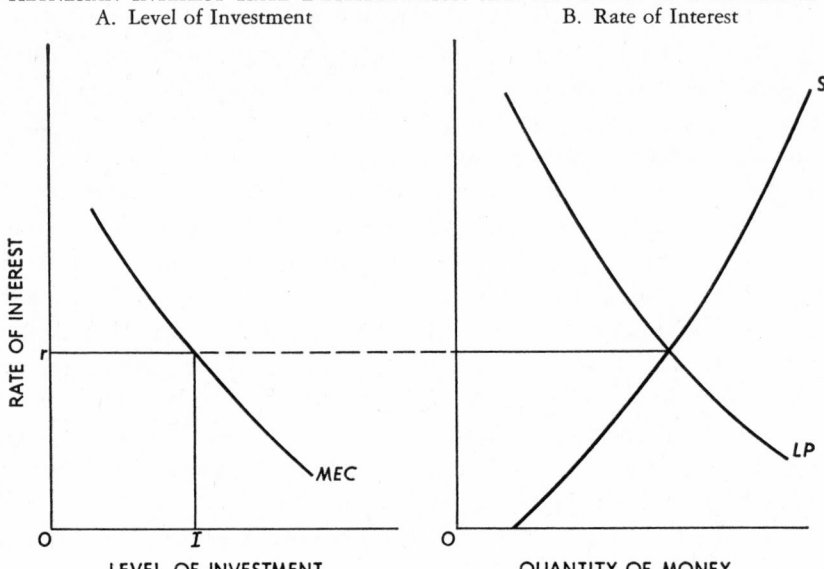

Measuring the productivity of capital, or the anticipated rate of return, is somewhat more difficult than measuring the productivity of other factors of production. In the case of labor, for example, marginal productivity is a manageable concept since the productivity of labor is usually realized within a relatively short period of time. In the case of capital investments, however, the planning horizon may be in terms of years or even decades. Thus in estimating the marginal efficiency of capital, the entrepreneur must have some idea of the income-producing power of the particular capital item over this extended time period.

In addition to this, future income must be translated into terms of present value, for an anticipated $1,000 income ten years from now is not equal to the same income at the present time. The $1,000 that a machine will produce for each of the next ten years must be discounted back to the present in order to obtain the present value of that future income. In other words, the pertinent sum is the present value of a future income stream.

Basically, then, the marginal efficiency of capital is the relationship between the discounted dollar return anticipated as a result of the investment and the total amount of investment. It is expressed as a percentage rate of return.

The marginal efficiency of capital (*MEC*) schedule represents the demand for capital. As larger and larger amounts of capital become available, the increase in the anticipated return for the last unit becomes less. This is the principle of diminishing marginal productivity as applied to capital.

As the entrepreneur observes the situation, he makes the same observation. The larger the stock of capital at any given moment, or the more investment which is currently underway, the smaller will be the anticipated rate of return on any additional investment. Graphically, this is represented by the *MEC* schedule in Figure 13–3A. With an interest rate of '*r*' and the marginal efficiency of capital schedule as depicted, the level of investment will be *OI*. If the marginal efficiency of capital remains unchanged, any reduction in the rate of interest will cause an increase in the level of investment, and any increase in the rate of interest will cause a reduction in the level of investment.

The *MEC* is extremely volatile. There are any number of factors which might cause the investor to anticipate either a higher or lower rate of return. The possibility of war or peace, a presidential illness, labor union activity, unrest in the Congo, population growth, technological changes, and a host of other things will cause the *MEC* to change one way or the other. Technological advances, for example, would cause the function to shift to the right. This would indicate an increased amount of investment at the same rate of interest. Anything which caused the *MEC* schedule to shift to the left would mean a reduction in the level of investment if there were no corresponding change in the rate of interest. The student should observe that the ever present assumption of *ceteris paribus* is implied.

The level of income was not listed as a determinant of the level of investment. Certainly, anticipated changes in the level of income would affect the marginal efficiency of capital; however, at any given level of income, investment is dependent upon the interest rate, and the anticipated rate of return and is independent of the level of income.

This can be graphically portrayed by a straight line parallel to the x axis (see Figure 13–4).

Consumption plus Investment. At the beginning of this section it was pointed out that

$$Y = C + I$$

where G_e and F_e have been reduced to consumption and investment type expenditures, and included in C and I respectively. (C and I have been graphically portrayed in Figures 13–2 and 13–4). If I is added to C, the result will be the diagrammatic presentation of Y in Figure 13–4.

FIGURE 13–4

CONSUMPTION AND INVESTMENT

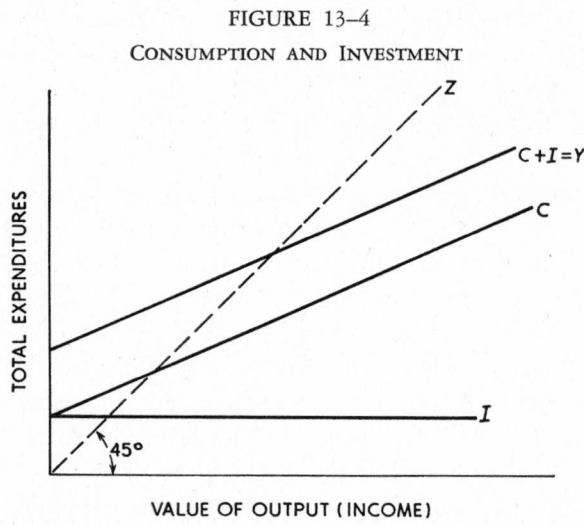

VALUE OF OUTPUT (INCOME)

The curve labeled $C + I = Y$ represents total spending in the economy for consumption and investment goods. It should be emphasized that this includes government, nongovernment, foreign, and domestic expenditures.

The Level of Income

Savings and Investment. The relationship between savings and investment has been accorded primary significance in any discussion of the level of income. The classical economists, as was pointed out earlier, contended that changes in the rate of interest would always establish such an equality. Furthermore, this school of thought contended the equality would always be such as to provide for the full utilization of the savings of society.

Developments in the theory of income determination in the past few decades have put even greater emphasis upon the relationship between savings and investment. The two basic equations for the creation of and the disposal of income become:

$$Y = C + I$$

and

$$Y = C + S$$

At any time period, the two C's must be equal as they are simply two sides of the same transaction. Thus, the two equations imply that savings must equal investment.

An individual saves by abstaining from consuming his entire income. But the savings of one individual may be just offset by the dissaving of some other person. In the aggregate, then, a society can only save when the total consumption of all consumer units in the economy is less than the amount produced. But the economic structure has already been defined in such a way as to make savings and investment definitionally equal. This equality, then, can only be true if the savings and investment referred to are the realized or actual savings and investment, that is, *ex post* savings and investment. Anticipated or planned savings and investment, which are sometimes referred to as *ex ante* savings and investment, need not be equal.

One might wonder how a difference could arise between anticipated and realized savings and between anticipated and realized investment. A few brief examples might help to explain this dichotomy. Suppose that consumers plan to save more than the investors plan to invest. This means that total expenditures (consumption and investment) will be less than the value of output. This means that some production must go unsold and inventories will increase. And larger business inventories are a form of business investment even though it may be involuntary investment. So the system will force an equality between savings and investment by increasing realized investment.

Another type of adjustment might take place in the same circumstances; namely, where planned savings exceed planned investment. The deficiency in planned investment could result in a decrease in income as expenditures fall. People who had planned to save may revise their plans in light of their falling income and either reduce or eliminate their savings. Thus again the system has forced an equilibrium between actual savings and investment by forcing consumers to reduce their savings.

In summary, then, it is the *ex ante* or planned savings and investment which are the important factors in the determination of national income. These are the two concepts with which we will be concerned. And it is the anticipated or planned savings and investment which have been presented in Figures 13–3 and 13–4.

The student should have noticed that in the preceding discussion the rate of interest no longer served as the equilibrating device. The equality of savings and investment is established by changes in the level of income rather than changes in the rate of interest.

The Equilibrium Level of Income. The level of income must either increase or decrease as long as planned savings and planned investment are unequal. When there is equality between the two, there will be no force promoting a change in the level of income.

In Figure 13–5 planned savings are equal to planned investment at Point Q. At that same level of income the total planned expenditures by consumers and investors (represented by $C + I$) intersects the Z line. This will always be true because savings (S) are the difference between consumption (C) and the Z line. At the point Q,

$$C + I = Z$$

or

$$Z - C = I.$$

Therefore, S and I must be equal at this level of income because both are the difference between consumption and the guide line Z. Thus at income level Q, the total expenditures just equal the total value of the output of the economic system. At any point to the right of Q, the total expenditures will be less than the total value of the economy's output. This is sometimes called a deflationary gap since there will be a downward pressure on prices, output, and income. Whenever expenditures are less than income, income will fall. In terms of Figure 13–1, more is taken out of the income flow than is being put back in.

At any point to the left of Q, the total planned expenditures of consumers and investors will be greater than the total value of the product. This difference is sometimes referred to as the inflationary gap since pressure will exist to increase both the level of output and the level of prices. In this case, more is being put into the income flow than is being taken out. If output cannot be increased, the result can only be increased prices—inflation. So if total expenditures are not equal to the total value of the output (or total planned savings are not equal to total planned investment), the economy is in a state of disequilibrium. Whenever such conditions exist, there will be forces present to cause a change in the level of income.

Unlike classical theory, there is no guarantee that the equilibrium level of income will be such as to provide for the full employment of the factors of production. In Figure 13–5, an equilibrium level of income was established, but it is possible that there might well be large

FIGURE 13–5

EQUILIBRIUM LEVEL OF INCOME

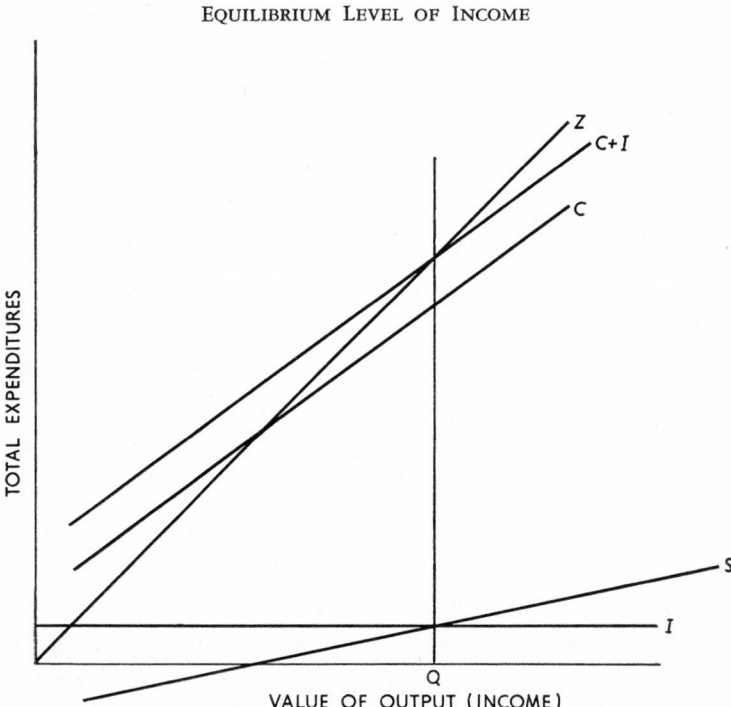

quantities of unemployed labor, for example. If a new equilibrium level of income is to be established which would provide for full employment of the factors of production, there must be an increase in total expenditures. This would be represented by an upward shift in the $C + I$ function.

The nature of the original total expenditures function provides some clue as to the forces which might cause this function to shift upward. An increase in consumption spending, an increase in investment expenditures, or increasing government spending or exports would all result in a higher level of total expenditures in the economic system.

Changes in Investment and Changes in Income. Any new investment expenditure will increase income. But by how much? Obviously it will increase income by the amount of the new investment expenditure, but, and this point may not be quite so obvious, it will increase income by something more. The magnitude of the total increase in income is explained by the "multiplier."

As each income recipient receives income resulting from the original investment expenditure, he will spend part of the increased income and save the remainder. The division of the increased income will depend upon the marginal propensity to consume.

If we assume an *MPC* of $\frac{4}{5}$, we know that out of every additional increment of income, the income recipient will consume $\frac{4}{5}$ and save $\frac{1}{5}$. Out of $1,000 in new investment, the first income recipient would spend $800 and save $200. Upon recieiving the $800 in new income, the second would spend $640 and save $160, and so on. Ultimately there would be a fivefold increase in income. The multiplier is simply the reciprocal of the marginal propensity to save, and it enables one quickly and simply to compute the total increase in income resulting from an increase in new investment.

This multiplicative effect will result from a number of different factors. Certainly, an increase in investment financed by an expansion in the supply of private bank credit would start it. But so also would an export-import balance which results in a net inflow of funds into the economy. Government investment expenditures financed through the borrowing of funds from the central bank would also serve as a starter for the operation of the multiplier.

One must note that the multiplier works in both directions. Anything which reduces the level of planned investment will result in a larger reduction in the level of income. If investment expenditures in one sector of the economy are increased at the expense of investment expenditures in some other sector of the economy, there will be no net multiplier effect or at least a much reduced effect.

The operation of the multiplier can also be demonstrated graphically. The original conditions in Figure 13–6 are represented by the investment function I_1 and the savings function S. The marginal propensity to save (1 minus the marginal propensity to consume) is $\frac{1}{4}$, and the multiplier is thus 4. The original and equilibrium level of income was Q_1. The economy then experienced a net increase in new investment represented by I_2. The new equilibrium level of income would be that where $S = I_2$ or Q_2. The increase in income measured along X axis is just four times as great as the increase in investment expenditures measured along the Y axis. If the $C + I$ function were drawn in for both I_1 and I_2, one would find that the new total expenditures function would cross the Z line at a point directly above Q_2, the new equilibrium level of income.

FIGURE 13–6

THE MULTIPLIER

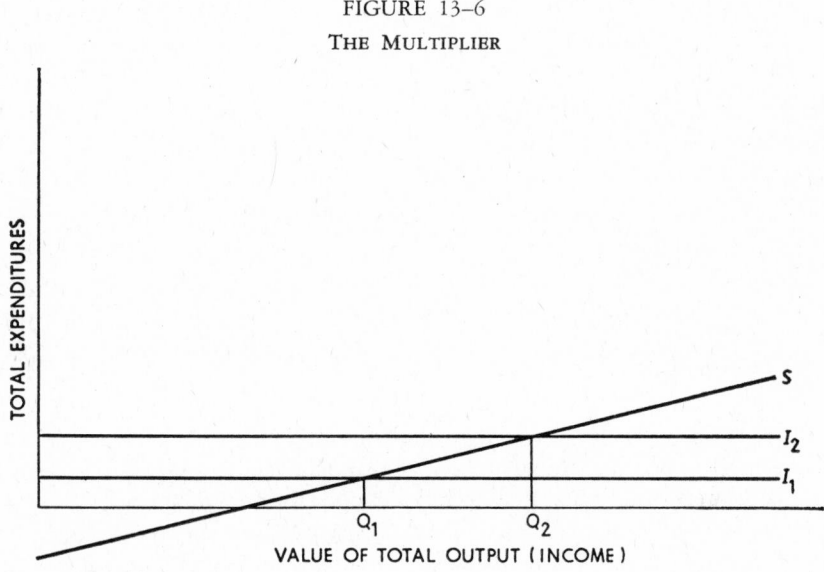

CONCLUSION

The economic system, like a household or business firm, generates a flow of goods and services, and like these two smaller units, the economy requires a measure of that activity. That measure is the set of national income statistics. These statistics impart, with some precision, knowledge of the level of activity within the economic system at any particular point in time.

But the data must do more than simply provide a measure of past and present performance. If this was the sole purpose of such statistics, it is doubtful whether it would be worth the effort to construct the model and collect the data. National income statistics (1) enable us to better understand the forces which determine the level of activity and (2) permit us to do a better job of predicting changes in the level of economic performance. In other words, national income analysis is important for its aid in analysis rather than its aid in description.

Although much of the discussion will be, as it has in the preceding pages, in terms of money, the interest is in the real sector of the economic system. That is, the significant problem is the level of consumption (how well are the people living?), the level of employment (what percentage of the factors are employed?) and the rate of growth (what is the rate of growth of employment opportunities?).

EXERCISES

Group I

In each of the following questions two economic concepts are presented. The student is to compare or contrast each pair. How are they alike or how do they differ? Is there a relationship between the two? How does their use in economics compare or differ?

1. Planned savings and investment and realized savings and investment.
2. Gross national product and national income.
3. The marginal propensity to consume and the multiplier.
4. Savings and investment as determinants of the equilibrium level of income.

Group II

1. Compare the economic philosophies of President Herbert Hoover and President Franklin D. Roosevelt regarding the questions of unemployment and the level of income. Could it be said that Hoover represented the classical school of economists and Roosevelt represented the newer approach?
2. Compare the behavior of both money savings and real savings in the United States since World War II. How have they fluctuated in both actual amounts and as a percentage of national income? Do such fluctuations contribute to an understanding of the fluctuations in income and employment? Explain.

Group III

1. Inventories represent a very sensitive indicator for the student of economic fluctuations. Inventories may increase (or decrease) for either of two reasons: (1) businessmen may decide to increase their stocks or (2) they may be forced to increase inventories because of a drop in buying by their customers. Select several industries and investigate the behavior of the inventories. Is it possible to discern the reason for changes in inventory holdings at a particular time? What is the relationship between the particular fluctuation and the corresponding change in inventory?
2. The marginal efficiency of capital will fluctuate sharply. The rate of interest appears to be much more stable. Investigate the importance of each insofar as the investment decision is concerned. Does it appear that one or the other is more important in the long-run situation in contrast to a shorter period?
3. Malthus and Ricardo engaged in a friendly debate regarding various aspects of economics. An important segment of that debate concerned the level of economic activity. Investigate the two approaches. How might the history of economic thought have been altered had Malthus and his approach been given more consideration? Is there an intellectual kinship between Malthus and Keynes?

BIBLIOGRAPHY

DILLARD, DUDLEY. *The Economics of John Maynard Keynes.* New York: Prentice-Hall, Inc., 1948.

HABERLER, G. (Ed.) *Readings in Business Cycle Theory.* Philadelphia: The Blakiston Co., 1944.

HARRIS, SEYMOUR (Ed.). *The New Economics,* Part IX. New York: Alfred A. Knopf, Inc., 1947.

KEYNES, JOHN M. *The General Theory of Employment, Interest, and Money.* New York: Harcourt, Brace & Co., 1935.

PAPERBACK READING LIST

HANSEN, A. H. *A Guide to Keynes.* New York: McGraw-Hill Book Co., Inc., 1953.

KLEIN, LAWRENCE R. *The Keynesian Revolution.* New York: The Macmillan Co., 1947.

Chapter 14 · TAXATION AND PUBLIC FINANCE

His horse went dead, and his mule went lame,
And he lost six cows in a poker game;
Then a hurricane came on a Summer day,
And blew the house where he lived away;
An earthquake came when that was gone,
And swallowed the land the house stood on.
And then the tax collector came around,
And charged him up with the hole in the ground.
> —Author unknown. Reproduced in H. L. Mencken (Ed.), *A New Dictionary of Quotations* (New York: Alfred A. Knopf, Inc., 1942), p. 1179.

A government, in some respects, is like a household or a business firm. To provide the goods and services the people demand, it must have a source of revenue. The breadwinner of the household and the business firm earn income by selling goods and services. The government produces some goods and services for sale, but for the most part, the services provided by government cannot be sold nor can their costs be allocated among the citizenry. National defense, the judicial and educational systems, business services, law-enforcing agencies, welfare programs, and many others cannot be organized to produce the income needed to finance them. To finance the largest part of governmental activities, financial dependence is placed upon the productivity of the members of society. The government takes a portion of the income produced by that productivity through taxation.

Although there are similarities between government and households and business firms, there are also important differences. The government, for example, may raise funds through taxation without any intention of spending such funds. The purpose of such action may be that of depriving the people of the power to spend. Or the reverse may happen. The government as a deliberate policy may spend more than it taxes. That is, the government may go into debt simply because doing so will increase the power of the people to spend. The government may use its powers to tax, spend, and borrow to promote economic stability. This is in contrast to the individual who uses his powers to produce income, borrow, and spend in order to satisfy his wants for goods and services.

The government is the ultimate authority in society. It is the only institution which may use force to insure compliance with its decrees. It is the only entity which, rather than being forced to rely upon its own resources, is permitted to fall back upon the income-producing power of every citizen and every business firm in the society which it governs.

The study of the government and public finance can be divided into three parts: taxation and tax policy; governmental borrowing and debt management; and government spending. These are the subject matter of this and the following chapters.

PRINCIPLES OF TAXATION AND TAX POLICY

Characteristics of a Good Tax

Writing in 1776 Adam Smith listed four characteristics of a good tax. They are almost universally used at the present time in any attempt to evaluate a particular tax. We shall not be an exception to the rule.

In the first place, Smith said that a person should be taxed in proportion to his means. Thus the poor man should pay less than the rich man, even though both receive equal benefits or possibly the poor man might even receive greater benefits. Today most tax authorities agree that an equitable tax is one which imposes nearly equal sacrifices on different individuals, although the actual tax payment may vary over a wide range. The second criteria of a good tax is that of certainty. The tax ought to be certain in the sense that the time, the method, the place, and the amount ought to be clear to every taxpayer. Third, a tax ought to be convenient. Undue inconvenience for the taxpayer imposes an unnecessary burden upon the individual. It may lead to disrespect for the law and eventually evasion. The fourth characteristic of a good tax to be pointed out by Adam Smith was that it should be profitable in the sense that a tax should produce more in revenue than it costs to administer. Those taxes which cost a good deal to collect yet bring in very little revenue are poor taxes if their purpose is to produce revenue for the government. It is now commonly recognized, however, that there are some regulatory taxes which are not intended to produce revenue. If such a tax produces revenue, it is not accomplishing the purpose for which it was enacted. Such a tax cannot be judged by Adam Smith's fourth canon.

Taxes are similar to money in that economists can list the desirable features of both but can never find a tax or a money which fulfills the qualities desired. In a moment the individual taxes will be briefly examined, but before that is undertaken, certain basic principles of taxation must be understood.

Benefits Received vs. Ability to Pay

Taxes may be apportioned among the taxpayers in accordance with either of two principles. "Ability to pay" means that taxes are levied in accordance with one's ability to bear the tax burden. "Benefits received" means that taxes are levied in accordance with the benefits the taxpayer receives when the government spends the money. Of the two, the first has been and continues to be of major import in the United States.

Most tax authorities agree that the principle of ability to pay is essentially an extension of Adam Smith's canon of taxation—equity. Using "ability to pay" as the guide for tax policy, there is no concern with benefits derived by the citizen when the tax funds are spent. The rich pay more than the poor merely because they are able to do so, rather than because they receive greater benefits. One may be taxed to support the school system, although the taxpayer may have no children. One may likewise pay taxes to maintain public parks, even though the taxpayer has a passionate dislike for parks. And so on. All taxpayers are required to support activities from which no direct benefits are to be received, although most would contend that such tax support promotes the general welfare. Needless to say, such a system of taxation has not been free from criticism.

In the first place, measuring ability to pay presents some difficulty. Income is the most generally used criteria, but there is general recognition of the fact that one may not have a large income yet have considerable ability to pay taxes. For example, the holding of property may indicate ability to pay. A second criticism is that of injustice, for some contend that those who are taxed to support government activities from which they receive no benefits are being discriminated against. A third criticism is that such taxation has a deleterious effect upon incentive. The contention is that the taxpayer who works hard and accumulates great wealth is penalized by such taxes. A fourth criticism is an adjunct of the third, for it is further contended that such a tax will reduce savings and thus impede economic progress because of the subsequent reduction in investment.

Most tax authorities as well as politicians have rejected the above arguments either in whole or in part. The problem of measuring ability to pay does have workable solutions. Most concede that it is possible that such a tax will have an effect on incentive. The deleterious effect on savings and investment is a popular criticism, but the fact remains that both have increased steadily for the past 25 years, during which time greater and greater reliance has been placed upon taxes based on ability to pay. Among the politicians there is perhaps even greater acceptance of such taxes for the simple reason that there are more poor folks than there are rich folks. This is in addition to sound economic and sociological reasons for such taxes. The matter can be summed up by noting that taxes based on ability to pay are so well entrenched in our tax system that it would appear very unlikely that this particular tax philosophy will ever be abandoned.

The principle of benefits received is little used. It must be established that the taxpayer does receive a peculiar benefit from the expenditure of tax funds. If such a direct relationship can be established, the taxpayer should support such services through a special tax. If he is the sole beneficiary, he should bear the entire burden. If he is only a partial beneficiary, he should bear only a part of the financial burden. If the society as a whole benefits in any way, then the community must share the burden, although this individual taxpayer may pay more than other taxpayers.

There are few examples of taxes based on benefits received. Taxes on motor fuels, truck tires, and other motor vehicle products are such an example, since the receipts are generally ear-marked for the construction and maintenance of highways. Some states levy a tax on the fuel sold for use in airplanes and use the funds for the construction and maintenance of airports. Another example, although not generally considered to be a tax, is that of fees and special assessments. The first includes those charges for public services which provide a special service to the individual. This includes court fees, educational fees and title registration fees. Special assessments are charges against property owners to finance public improvements from which special benefits will accrue to the property owners. Assessments for street improvements are of this nature.

Levying taxes based on the principle of benefits received is subject to major difficulties. In the first place, it is often difficult if not impossible to measure the benefits which the individual taxpayer receives from a given public expenditure. How are the benefits of expenditures made for national defense, courts, education and welfare, to be allocated? A second difficulty is the fact that those who receive the benefits may be financially unable to bear the burden, and if they were required to pay for such services, it is likely that such services would never be rendered. The very poor would probably have to forego the education of their children. There would be no public assistance program for the needy. If such programs are socially desirable, and most would agree that they are, it is necessary that they be financed in large part by those who will not receive a direct benefit, although the indirect benefits may be considerable.

A major argument in support of the benefits-received principle is what might be termed tax consciousness. This contention holds that those who receive governmental benefits and are not required to contribute to the support of such programs may be promiscuous in their consumption of governmental services. It is thought by many that if each person were financially liable for a part of the governmental services consumed, all would exercise greater forbearance in demands for increased governmental spending. There is probably more than a modicum of truth in this idea. Nevertheless, the difficulties of putting the principle of benefits received into practice are of such magnitude that it is unlikely that primary reliance will ever be placed upon such taxes.

Shifting and Incidence

The person who sends the tax payment to the government may or may not bear the burden of that tax. Those taxpayers who are in a position to shift the burden to someone else will do so. This shifting of the tax burden is the essence of shifting and incidence.

The point where the tax is originally imposed may be referred to as the point of impact. The incidence refers to the taxpayer who bears the ultimate burden of the tax. The movement of the tax burden from the point of impact is known as shifting—the transfer of the tax burden.

Not all taxes can be shifted, and where the tax burden can be shifted, the shifting may be in different directions. The tax burden is shifted forward when it is passed on to the final consumer in the form of price increases. A tax burden is shifted backward if it is transferred to the suppliers of the inputs in the form of lower prices for their goods and services. In some instances it may be shifted to other industries in the form of lower prices for their products. And in still others the process of shifting and the bearing of the ultimate burden is so complex and obscure that it is difficult, if not impossible, to trace the full effects of a particular tax. But in a discussion of any tax, it is necessary to analyze the incidence of the tax if the economic effects are to be understood.

Rate Structure

Before we can go on to a discussion of the individual taxes, one last observation must be made regarding the basic principles of taxation. This refers to the rate structure. Certain terms used to describe rates will be introduced at this point.

A progressive tax is characterized by increases in both the tax rate and the tax base—the amount upon which the tax is levied. Thus as taxable income increases, the rate of taxation also increases. For example, a person with $2,000 of taxable income would be taxed at a rate of 20 per cent while a person making $4,000 would be taxed at a rate of 21 per cent. A proportional tax is one in which the tax rate remains the same regardless of the base. Thus a 3 per cent sales tax is a proportional tax, for the rate is 3 per cent regardless of the tax base. A third type is a regressive tax. In this case the tax rate declines as the tax base increases. In common terminology, however, another definition of a regressive tax is used. Most people refer to a regressive tax as a tax which takes a larger proportion of the low-income taxpayer's income than it does of the upper-income taxpayer's. The retail sales tax without any exemption is proportional as far as rates are concerned, but it is regressive in effect since the low-income groups pay a larger percentage of their income to the government as taxes than do the upper-income groups.

THE AMERICAN TAX SYSTEM

The government of the United States is a federal government and thus consists of two sovereign levels—the national and the state. The latter, in turn, has subdivisions including counties, cities, irrigation districts, school districts, and others. Over 100,000 governmental units impose a variety of taxes, for it is through taxes that all receive their revenue. There are times when all governments find it propitious to borrow rather than tax. So, before the subject of taxing and borrowing by governments is pursued further, it is necessary to take a brief look at the spending activities of government.

The breakdown of governmental expenditures is presented in Table 14–1. The major fields of activity for the several governments are clearly indicated. The national government's major expenditures are for national defense and foreign affairs—or, to put it in other words, war—past, present, and future. Highways, education, public welfare, and hospitals are the major items of expenditure for the states, and at the local government level the largest expenditures are for education, public roads, public welfare, sanitation, and police protection.

In 1961 the several governments of the United States raised a total of $116.3 billion from the various tax levies. The difference between this figure and that for total governmental expenditures is explained in part by other types of governmental revenue, such as the receipts from the operation of utilities and liquor stores, fees and special assessments, license fees, payments into retirement funds, etc., and government borrowing.

TABLE 14–1

GOVERNMENTAL GENERAL EXPENDITURE (DIRECT AND INTER-GOVERNMENTAL), BY FUNCTION AND LEVEL OF GOVERNMENT

1961

(In Millions of Dollars)

| | Amount ($1,000,000) | | | |
Item	All Govern-ments	Federal	State	Local
Total..........................	$139,161	$89,971	$29,118	$37,393
National defense and international relations	49,387	49,387	....	....
Postal service.........................	4,025	4,025	....	....
Education............................	21,214	1,669	9,775	16,782
Highways............................	9,995	2,738	7,496	3,645
Natural resources.....................	11,409	10,214	924	421
Health and hospitals..................	5,682	1,750	2,243	2,092
Public welfare........................	4,779	2,238	3,913	2,442
Housing and urban renewal............	1,320	655	37	936
Air transportation....................	1,800	1,442	55	386
Social insurance administration...........	636	655	351	....
Interest on general debt................	9,309	7,485	584	1,240
Other and combined...................	19,604	7,714	3,760	9,448

SOURCE: U.S. Bureau of the Census, *Statistical Abstract of the United States, 1963*, (Washington, D.C., 1963).

The income tax, including both the personal and corporate income taxes is the most productive tax in the entire tax system. It is followed by the sales tax or gross receipts tax (general sales tax). The property tax ranks third but well below the other two. (See Table 14–2.)

The Personal Income Tax

Probably the best known tax in the United States is the income tax. The United States government, as well as a number of states and

TABLE 14–2

GOVERNMENTAL TAX REVENUE BY SOURCE, 1942–61
(In Millions of Dollars)

Year	Individual Income	Corporation Income	Sales, Gross Receipts, & Customs	Property	Other Taxes (incl. Licenses)
1942	$ 3,481	$ 4,999	$ 5,776	$ 4,537	$2,000
1950	16,533	11,081	12,997	7,349	3,140
1952	28,919	22,072	15,689	8,652	3,735
1955	29,984	18,604	17,221	10,735	4,527
1957	37,384	22,151	20,594	12,864	5,649
1959	38,713	18,310	21,769	14,983	5,862
1960	43,178	22,674	24,452	16,405	6,411
1961	43,951	22,220	25,112	18,002	7,047

SOURCE: U.S. Bureau of Census, *Statistical Abstract of the United State, 1963* (Washington D.C., 1963).

local governmental units, use the income tax as a major source of revenue. There are two income taxes. First is the personal income tax which individuals pay on income. The second is the corporation income tax levied upon corporate income. In 1962 the national government received 53 per cent of its total revenue from the former and 27 per cent from the latter. State governments received 18 per cent of their revenue from income taxes, while local governments received one per cent from the same general type of tax (Table 14–3).

TABLE 14–3

GOVERNMENTAL TAX REVENUE BY SOURCE AND BY LEVEL OF GOVERNMENT
IN THE UNITED STATES, 1961
(In Millions of Dollars)

Tax	Federal	State	Local
Personal income	$41,338	$ 2,355	$ 258
Corporation income	20,954	1,266	. . .
Sales, gross receipts and customs	12,649	11,031	1,432
Property	. . .	631	17,370
Other taxes, including licenses	2,529	3,774	744

SOURCE: U.S. Bureau of the Census, *Statistical Abstract of the United States, 1963* (Washington, D.C., 1963).

Several states used the income tax prior to the Civil War, and it was first used by the national government at the time of that conflict. The rates of this early national income tax were very low, but, nevertheless, it was very unpopular and was allowed to expire in 1872. In 1894 Congress again levied an income tax but it was declared unconstitutional within a year of its passage. The income tax became a permanent feature of the economic and constitutional landscape in 1913 when the Constitution was amended to permit an income tax without obliging the government to apportion the receipts among the several states according to population. Prior to 1913 only a few states had used the income tax, but more and more states have adopted this form of taxation until approximately two thirds of the states now rely upon it as a source of tax revenue.

The Mechanics of the Personal Income Tax. The personal income tax is a progressive tax. The rate ranges from 20 per cent on the first $2,000 of taxable income to 91 per cent on all taxable income over $200,000. But it must be kept in mind that the person making $200,000 is taxed at a rate of 20 per cent on the first $2,000 of income like everyone else. The tax rates vary, then, from 20 per cent to 91 per cent, but taxes as a percentage of income will not vary between the two extremes. A person having only $2,000 of taxable income will have a $400 tax bill, which is 20 per cent of his income. The individual earning $200,000 of taxable income will have a tax bill of $156,820 which is 78 per cent of his taxable income. And the person making $1,000,000 in taxable income would have to pay 88.5 per cent of it in taxes. Taxes as a percentage of income, then, will get closer and closer to 91 per cent, but no one will actually pay this rate on his total income.

Taxable income is not, however, the same thing as gross income or total income. In the first place, certain types of monetary gains are excluded. Interest on state and local bonds, benefits received from life insurance policies, damages received as a result of injury, inheritances, benefits paid by the Old Age and Survivors Insurance fund, and receipts from the sale of property are not included. Once income is determined, there are still further adjustments to be made to compute taxable income. First, expenses incurred in the production of income are deducted. Second, the taxpayer is allowed to take personal deductions, including charitable contributions, certain medical expenses, interest on money borrowed to purchase a home, and others. And finally, the taxpayer is allowed a $600 deduction for each dependent, except that in some instances a larger allowance is permitted. What remains, then, is taxable income, and it is to this amount that the tax rate is applied. Taxable income may be a rather small part of total income.

The income tax of the national government is administered by the Director of Internal Revenue. All of those who receive their income in the form of wages or salary have their taxes withheld by the employer. Others must make tax payments at stated times during the year. For those taxpayers who feel that they have been wronged by a decision of the Office of Internal Revenue, there is a Tax Court to which the taxpayer may appeal, and the decisions of the Tax Court may be reviewed by the United States Courts of Appeals.

Administration of the state income taxes is essentially similar. The definition of taxable income will vary from state to state. The rates will likewise vary but are much lower than the rate of the national income tax. They are usually graduated. And there will be a state tax commission which is charged with the responsibility of administering the tax.

An Appraisal of the Personal Income Tax. The income tax imposes a burden which roughly approximates the ability to pay of the taxpayers. So, if ability to pay is accepted as the criteria of equity, then the tax is equitable. The tax is certain. Rates, definition of income, exemptions and deductions, and other major aspects of the law are established by Congress. Major revisions affecting all taxpayers are rare. Unfortunately in the administration and interpretation of the law there are some uncertainties. The income tax is probably as convenient as it possibly could be for the millions who have their taxes withheld by employers. In fact, some would criticize it as being too convenient. And lastly, the tax produces a prodigious amount of revenue.

There are, however, problems in administering the income tax. In the first place, the tax revenue will vary over a wide range without any change in the tax rates. Since the tax bill is a percentage of income, any time incomes change, the tax take likewise changes in the same direction. Thus the same tax rate will produce more revenue during prosperity than during depression. Although this may be desirable as a part of a general governmental program to promote economic stability, it does create problems for those governments which depend upon it for their revenue. This instability of tax revenue is an especially serious problem for state and local governments using the income tax.

There is, secondly, a questionable effect on incentive. The income tax is a tax on productivity. Thus the more one produces and earns, the larger the tax payment, for there is an increase in taxable income as well as the tax rate. Some contend that the effect of such a two-way increase must inevitably be a reduction in man's willingness to produce and earn. The income tax may cause a shift of funds from an investment where the receipts are taxed to an investment where they are not. It may, in some instances, cause a person to put some sort of upper limit on the quantity of work done. But it is questionable, however, that the income tax does cause a serious reduction in incentive. In fact, there is some evidence that it may actually result in the reverse.

There is, thirdly, a purely administrative problem associated with the income tax. Some groups are able to avoid payment of the tax. Those who have their taxes withheld by their employer have little chance to evade their tax payment, but others can avoid payment of their share of the nation's tax burden. It is not an accident that one seldom hears of an employee charged with tax evasion. An income tax, probably more so than most other taxes, is dependent upon a friendly environment for success, for if a large number of people deliberately set out to evade the law, its enforcement would be extremely difficult. In addition to the administrative problem of evasion, there is also a legislative problem of tax avoidance. There are some groups strong enough to have provisions written into the law itself which provide favorable tax treatment for that particular group. The depletion allowance for natural resources is considered by many to be of this nature. There are others.

The income tax is not perfect. It does not administer itself but is administered by a particular group of human beings that have all the faults generally associated with the human species. As long as governmental spending remains at its present high level, any modification of the income tax which resulted in reduced revenue would have to be offset by tax increases in other areas. When this possibility is advanced, the income tax looks even better.

The Incidence of the Personal Income Tax. A personal income tax is difficult to shift. Any attempt by the taxpayer to shift the tax by increasing the price of the product or service he sells will result in increased revenue, if the demand is inelastic, which will be also taxed, and it may well be taxed at an even higher rate. If the demand is perfectly elastic, there is no possibility of raising the price. So if this is described as a short-run effect, it might be summarized by saying that in the short run the possibilities of shifting the tax are limited if not nonexistent.

Over a longer period of time, however, the income tax may affect the supply of the factor involved, although there is a difference of opinion as to the exact effect. Insofar as it may affect the supply of labor, there are two possible alternatives. One is that of reducing the supply of labor forthcoming. This follows the classical approach which asserts that more of the factor will be forthcoming at the higher price and less at the lower price. The second possibility is the reverse. If a given level of living is to be maintained, then an income tax may actually mean that more labor will be forthcoming to maintain present standards. Either may prevail in particular cases.

Insofar as savings are concerned, one can be a little more definite. An income tax will decrease the income which the taxpayer has at his disposal, so it must reduce either consumption or savings. Since it is a progressive tax, most appear to be inclined toward the proposition that an income tax will reduce savings more than it will reduce consumption. One of the common criticisms of this tax is the fact that it will reduce savings and thus investment and will eventually lead to economic stagnation. Of course, those who support this proposition must explain why investment has been so high in the decade following World War II when income taxes have also been extremely high. With those few indecisive words, we now turn to a cursory examination of another income tax, the corporate income tax.

The Corporate Income Tax

Originally the corporate income tax was an adjunct of the personal income tax in that it served as a device for collecting the tax on personal income from corporations. Today, however, it has a place in its own right in the tax structure of the country. It is a tax on a part of the earnings of incorporated business enterprises. There is no such tax on an unincorporated enterprise such as the proprietorship, for the entire net income of the latter is taxed as personal income.

The Mechanics of the Corporate Income Tax. The basic mechanics of the corporate income tax are similar to that of the personal income tax in that certain deductions are subtracted from total income to compute taxable income. Most important of the deductions are those expenses incurred in the production of the income, but also included are contributions to charity, taxes, and other specified items. There are only two rates of corporate income taxation. All taxable corporate income under $25,000 is presently taxed at a rate of 30 per cent, and all taxable corporate income exceeding $25,000 is presently taxed at a rate of 52 per cent.

The Incidence of the Corporate Income Tax. As was pointed out previously, the corporation is considered to be a person by law, and, at least in some respects, it receives the same consideration. However, since it is what might be termed a fictitious person, it can neither eat nor sleep, nor can it vote, go to church, nor bear the real burden of a tax. The burden of any tax must ultimately rest upon some individual or some group of individuals. So although the corporation remits the tax payment to the treasury, the corporation, because of its very character, must shift that tax to some group of real persons.

Since the tax must be shifted, there would appear to be two possibilities. It might be shifted forward to the buyers of the product, or backward to the factors of production, including the stockholders. It seems probable that the lattter group assume the larger part of the burden in the form of lower dividends or smaller capital gains. The remainder would then be borne by the customers in the form of higher prices and the other factors of production in the form of less factor income.

In the case of the corporate income tax, there will be a smaller return to the stockholder for the assumption of risk. Reducing the reward for risk taking may result in a smaller amount of that productive function by the entrepreneurial group. To the extent that this is so, and it may not be very significant, then the burden of the corporate income tax is finally shifted to society as a whole, which must bear the burden of the tax in the form of reduced investment, reduced production, and a lowered level of living.

The reason most commonly advanced as to why this might be so is the principle of double taxation. The corporation first pays the corporate income tax on the profits of the firm. Then a part of the remaining profits are distributed to the stockholders in the form of dividends. Since these dividends constitute personal income to the recipient, the government taxes them. The double taxation of this particular type of income is supposed to cause a diminution in the supply of investment funds and thus lower the level of investment.

The reduction in the assumption of risk is not the only possible effect of corporate income taxation. Corporate income taxation will also affect the pattern of corporate financing, for it may cause corporate managers to prefer debt financing to equity financing. Corporate income taxation is an important factor in the internal operations of the firms, since it means that business expenses are borne in part by the people as a whole. Gifts to charitable organizations and the expense accounts are all deducted from gross income in computing taxable income. Therefore, giving a dollar to charity or to a hat check girl does not cost the firm a dollar but something a good deal less than that amount. In effect, the corporate income tax undoubtedly contributes to managerial laxity.

The corporate income tax raises many perplexing issues. Can such an abstract being as the corporation have an ability to pay, or is this a characteristic confined to real persons? Is the corporate income tax a clumsy device to tax a certain type of income? Is it not possible that there may be a more satisfactory method of taxing this type of income? Is it possible that the corporate income tax can be more easily justified on the basis of (1) its ability to produce revenue, (2) the political attraction of taxing corporations rather than voters, and (3) the general lack of knowledge regarding the tax and its incidence?

The Sales Tax

The sales tax, in its various forms, is the second most productive tax in the American tax system being used by both the national and state governments. It was first used by the national government in a rather minor way during World War I. The states, however, adopted it during the depression of the 1930's. During this period the income tax failed to produce sufficient revenue because of the decline in national income. To make up for this loss, many states enacted sales tax statutes, and today approximately two thirds of the states have such laws in one form or another. The state statutes generally provide for a retail sales tax. There is no general sales tax at the national level. Instead there are a number of sales taxes on specific commodities, which are generally referred to as excise taxes. In addition to the state and national governments, more and more local governments are enacting some type of sales tax ordinances. Most are excise taxes, but some, notably New York City, do have a general retail sales tax.

The Mechanics of the Sales Tax. The sales tax is usually a proportional tax levied upon the sale price of the commodity. The tax may be and is imposed at practically any level in the business structure—manufacturer, wholesaler, or retailer. The Internal Revenue Act of 1954 levies a manufacturers excise tax on motor vehicles, tires and tubes, petroleum products, certain household appliances, and a few other items. These taxes are paid to the government by the manufacturer of the product, but the tax is passed on as higher prices. The national government also levies selective excise taxes at the retail level on such products as jewelry, furs, toilet preparations, luggage, and some personal service industries such as transportation and entertainment. Here the retailer collects the tax and sends the tax revenue to the government. He then collects part or all of the tax from the customer.

The retail sales tax commonly employed by the state governments is a proportional tax. It is a percentage of the retail price. The retailer commonly remits payments to the state government after the tax has been collected from the customer. A tax of this nature is usually complemented with what is known as a use tax which prohibits residents of a sales tax state from purchasing taxable items in a nontax state. People living in Cincinnati, Ohio, might, for example, purchase their automobiles across the river in Kentucky to avoid payment of the sales tax in Ohio. If this is done, however, the buyer will pay a use tax when he applies for an Ohio title.

The details of the general sales tax vary from one state to another. All, however, exempt very small sales. Several states including Ohio exempt purchases of food. Rental payments for housing are not taxed. Few service expenditures are taxed. In some cases no attempt is made to tax intangible items such as bonds and bank accounts. The rates vary from state to state, but most states tax retail sales at a rate of 2 or 3 per cent.

An Appraisal of the Sales Tax. Among economists the sales tax has long been considered as a rather poor tax, but in the past few years it has crept upward on the ladder of respectability.

The most general criticism concerns the equity of the tax. Although the sales tax is a proportional tax, it is regressive in effect. Consider two taxpayers in the circumstances indicated by the accompanying table. In this case Taxpayer A spends his entire income on items which

	Taxpayer A	*Taxpayer B*
Income	$4,000	$100,000
Taxed purchases	4,000	50,000
Rate of sales tax	2%	2%
Amount of tax	$ 80	$ 1,000
Tax payment as percentage of total income	2%	1%

are taxed at the rate of 2 per cent, and thus 2 per cent of his income is his tax burden. Taxpayer B, however, spends only half of his income on taxable items. The $50,000 is taxed at a rate of 2 per cent and tax payment of $1,000 represents only 1 per cent of his income. The tax burden of B is lighter than that of A.

This regressivity can be reduced by building certain exemptions into the statute. Exempting purchases of food grants the low-income taxpayer tax-free income equal in amount to his purchases of food. Since the low-income groups spend a larger proportion of their income on food than do the upper-income groups, it follows that such an exemption will reduce the tax burden of the lower-income groups more than the upper-income groups. This exemption of food is the only significant measure which has been taken to reduce the regressivity of the tax. There have been, however, proposals to make it less regressive if not progressive. These proposals generally call for a refund of tax payments. The amount of the refund would depend upon the income of the taxpayer, dependents, etc. Thus a low-income taxpayer with a larger family might get back all of the sales tax which he paid while the person with a large income might not get any refund. To date, all such programs must still be classed as proposals.

There are some uncertainties surrounding the sales tax and its enforcements, but they are a result of the structure of government rather than the sales tax. The problem of interjurisdictional sales, for example, raises some uncertainty. An item sold in a tax state to be delivered in a nontax state is not taxable, but an item sold in a nontax state to be delivered in a tax state is taxable. This creates problems of enforcement as well as record-keeping for business firms doing business in both tax and nontax states. In addition, there is some uncertainty surrounding the question of what is to be taxed or not taxed. Although it has not been used in this country, some taxing authorities have avoided this element of uncertainty by imposing a universal transactions tax which imposes a tax on any and all transactions. A tax is levied whenever anything is bought and sold.

The sales tax is a major producer of revenue with many states obtaining practically their entire revenue from this single source. And if present rates don't produce sufficient revenue, the rates can be raised with a fair degree of assurance that more revenue will be produced. It is a profitable tax since the costs of administering and collecting the tax are a small percentage of the tax revenue. There are, however, many problems associated with its administration. Although the retailer and other business firms serve as the collectors, the tax agency still needs the services of tax enforcement authorities. There is always the problem of ascertaining whether the proper amount of tax was collected and sent to the tax collection agency of the government. In addition, there are a number of administrative decisions to be made which have to be applied on a state-wide basis, since it is manifestly impossible to permit each of the collectors to make such decisions. The taxing authority must establish policy and then insure compliance by the nongovernmental collection agencies. This contributes to the administrative difficulty of the law and reduces its profitableness, but this is probably a rather minor cost.

In this "Age of Installment Buying" the sales tax must be classed as very convenient. It is, in effect, a buying of government goods and services with nothing down and 365 days to pay. Even on large purchases the sales tax may be financed along with the cost of the car or other item. Thus, taking a $100 out of the taxpayer's pocket a few cents at a time is considerably more convenient for the taxpayer than a tax calling for a payment of $100 in a lump sum. Some would contend that the tax is too convenient because the taxpayers aren't sufficiently tax conscious.

With the exception of the question of equity, the shortcomings of the sales tax are probably no more serious than those of other taxes. But before the sales tax can be fully assessed, the economic effects of that tax must be analyzed.

The Incidence of the Sales Tax. The point of impact for all sales taxes is some level of business—manufacturer, wholesaler, or retailer. It is not expected, however, that the burden of the tax will finally rest on the firms which pay the tax. They are merely tax collectors. They will shift all or part of the tax. In the case of the manufacturer's excise tax, the final price of the product may be raised by more than the amount of the tax since each firm involved in the distribution of the product will base his markup on the cost plus the tax.

The first reaction of a businessman who must start sending a tax payment to the government based on his sales is to pass the tax on to the buyer of the taxed commodity. He knows the price and the tax rate so he may mark up the price of the product by the amount of the tax. But the buyer reacts as though the total of the two were merely a single price representing the price of the product. If the demand schedule for the item is extremely elastic, the amount demanded will be considerably reduced. In such a case, the seller may absorb part of the tax. If, on the other hand, the demand is inelastic, the higher price will not result in a proportionate reduction in the amount demanded.

But now a whole panorama of possible effects has been opened. The exact effect will depend upon a variety of factors, including the availability of substitutes, the level and distribution of income, the level of employment, and other economic factors. Let us explore some of the possible reactions.

If it is assumed that this is an excise tax on a single commodity which has a rather elastic demand schedule, it follows that as the consumers reduce their purchases of this particular commodity, the producers will produce less, and the resources which had previously gone into the production of the commodity will now seek employment in other industries. To the extent that they are able to do so, the supply of such goods will increase and there will be a downward pressure on the price of these commodities. If the alternative lines of employment are not available for the released factors of production, then these resources may remain idle.

If, on the other hand, the tax is levied on a commodity with an inelastic demand schedule, the purchasers will not reduce the level of consumption of this particular good. But unless there is an increase in income, consumers must either reduce the consumption of other commodities or the rate of saving. Under these conditions the tax burden is transferred to the producers of other goods.

Now let us turn from an excise tax to a general sales tax. Here there can be no shifting by the consumer from a taxed commmodity to an untaxed good. There can and will be a shifting from one taxed commodity to another taxed commodity because of differing elasticities of demand. For example, a general sales tax may cause consumers to reduce their purchases of commodities with elastic demand schedules in order to maintain their consumption of commodities with more inelastic demand schedules.

So regardless of whether the sales tax is an excise tax on a particular commodity or a general sales tax, the effects of the tax will spread out from the point of impact to include a large part of the economy. The business firm will pass it on to the consumer. The consumer will make adjustments in consumption, and this will result in a reallocation of the factors of production. The total effect of a sales tax is not easily discernible.

The Property Tax

The property tax has long been the main source of revenue for local governments, although in recent years it has become common to supplement it with either a sales or a local income tax. The use of the property tax in the United States predates the American Revolution, but even though it has had such a long history, time has not eliminated the barrage of criticism levied against this tax on wealth.

The Mechanics of the Property Tax. There are three types of property which have been subject to a property tax. The first and more common type of taxable property is real property, including land and permanent improvements such as buildings. The second type, which is less often subject to the property tax, is intangible property such as securities, bank deposits, and the like. And the third, which is seldom taxed at the present time, is purely personal property such as diamond rings and household furniture. Since the first is more common, the present discussion will be confined to the tax on real property.

A property tax has two variables, and before any tax bill can be computed, some value must be assigned to each. The two are (1) the tax rate and (2) the assessed valuation. The first step in computing a tax bill is the establishment of some value for the property. Even if the taxable value were the full market value, there would have to be some basis for determining that value. But property is seldom if ever taxed at its full market value. Instead, the taxable value is usually some percentage of market value, and this percentage will vary from one taxing jurisdiction to another and even within the same taxing jurisdiction. A house that might sell for $25,000 may be carried on the tax rolls at $12,000. This is the assessed valuation.

The second variable used in the computation of the tax bill is the tax rate. The rate is usually expressed in tenths of a cent (mills) or so many dollars per thousand dollars of assessed valuation. The total rate is obtained by adding tax rates assessed for various purposes. The local governing authority may legislate so many mills to support the general operation of the government. The electorate may vote additional tax levies to finance capital improvements such as schools, sewers, and streets. The total of these taxes imposed for the several purposes is the tax rate.

Once the assessed valuation and the tax rate are established, the computation of the citizen's tax bill involves nothing more than multiplying the assessed valuation by the tax rate. Thus if a house were assessed at $10,000 and the tax rate were $30 per thousand, the tax bill would be $300 per year. The revenue would then be divided among the various activities of the government in acccordance with the taxes imposed for specific purposes.

The property tax is generally administered by the local governing authority under the general supervision of the state government. The degree of control exercised by the state government will vary from one state to another. The state definitely has an interest in the local tax picture since it is the state government which will often be called upon to supply any deficiency in funds for local governments. This interest on the part of the state government has resulted in the establishment of state boards of equalization in some states. Such boards are charged with the responsibility of insuring more or less equal assessment ratios in the different local governments. For example, it might adjust all assessments so that in each county or municipality the assessment ratio was 50 per cent rather than having it set at 75 per cent in some counties and 15 per cent in others. This form of state participation is the most extreme form of intervention in what is essentially a local tax.

In all taxing jurisdictions the taxpayer will have a right to appeal insofar as the assessment is concerned, and such appeal can be carried into the court system if the taxpayer wishes. But once the property is assessed and the assessment upheld, then the taxpayer must pay his tax bill or the government will file a tax lien against the property and will eventually sell the property in order to satisfy the tax claim.

An Appraisal of the Property Tax. The property tax is based on both the principle of ability to pay and the principle of benefits received. The ownership of property is some evidence of ability to pay; however, some property owners possess little or no ability to pay. Widows, the aged, and homeowners in a depression would be in this category. The benefits-received argument rests upon the fact that the property owner receives peculiar services from the government such as police and fire protection and public improvements.

There is, however, considerable evidence that although the rate structure of the property tax is proportional, it is, like the sales tax, regressive in effect. The reason is the assessment procedure. It appears that generally the higher-priced property is assessed at a lower percentage of the market value than the lower-priced property. Thus a $15,000 house might be asssessed at $10,000 while a $100,000 house might be assessed at only $50,000. The tax burden, then, would be relatively heavier on the owner of the smaller house.

The property tax has some rather serious shortcomings insofar as the certainty of the tax is involved. Most of the uncertainties arise from the assessment of the property, although in some instances there are some uncertainties involved in the establishment of the rates. Few taxpayers clearly understand the process by which the assessed valuations are established. Many local governments have, in the past, merely duplicated the tax rolls from one year to another without any serious attempt to assess the property. Reassessment is a task of considerable magnitude and cost. Moreover, reassessment of property will always result in a flock of angry taxpayers frantically demanding an explanation as to why their property was assessed at such a fantastically high figure.

The property tax offers a certain degree of inconvenience for those who pay their tax bill in the form of a single lump-sum payment. But for those who pay their property tax in monthly installments, the matter of inconvenience is largely eliminated.

And lastly, the property tax produces large amounts of revenue without a large cost of collection. However, there is the question of whether it produces all that it should. The administrative problems associated with the property tax are numerous, and if it were to be administered in a fashion designed to produce all the revenue that it should, there would be a very sharp increase in the costs of collecting the tax. In this instance the tax authorities have to strike some compromise between what is possible and what is desirable. Possible tax revenue must be sacrificed because of the desire to keep administrative costs in bounds. And all of this is even more true for the personal property tax, which is nearly impossible to administer.

The Incidence of the Property Tax. A tax levied on the property of a business firm will be treated as a cost of doing business, and it will be passed on to the consumer in the form of higher prices. The amount of the tax to be passed on will depend upon the elasticity of demand for the product. The same is true for a tax on rented property. In this case the landlord will shift part or all of the tax to the tenant.

Insofar as a tax on owner-occcupied residential property is concerned, the property owner must bear the tax. There is no way in which the tax burden can be shifted to others. Furthermore, the present owner may have to assume part of the tax of future owners if the property is sold. This statement can be explained in the following manner. Assume that a new tax is imposed on one's property. Now that property is sold. The prospective owner would have paid $18,000 without the tax, but now that there is the additional tax payment to be made, he is unwilling to pay that amount. He, in effect, capitalizes the tax or part of the tax and deducts that amount from the price which he would have paid in the absence of the tax. If this sale is made, the new owner has shifted at least a part of the tax burden to the original owner.

A major result of the property tax might possibly be more properly described as a consequence of the structure of the nation's government. The property tax rates vary from one county to the next as well as from one community or municipality to the next. Unlike the federal income tax, which has the same rate structure throughout the country, the property tax has a multitude of rates as well as assessment practices. Thus it can happen, and often does happen, that the mere fact that a person lives on one side of the street or the other makes a considerable difference in the tax bill.

As a general proposition rural tax rates will be lower than urban tax rates since rural governments generally provide fewer services for the taxpayers. Tax rates between communities will vary because of different services provided as well as because of differences in the amount of taxable property. So both business firms and individuals will consider these tax differences in determining the site for a plant or home. This explains why many people want to live just beyond the city limits but not so far beyond that they are deprived of many of the benefits of the city, which are financed by those living within the city limits. If there were a single uniform pattern of assessment as well as tax rate, the property tax would not influence economic activity in the fashion that it presently does.

Death Taxes

Property or wealth is always being transferred from one party to another because of deaths. This acquisition of wealth by the recipient cannot be regarded as income and taxed as income since no productive service has been rendered. But, on the other hand, here is a moment in time when a part of the community's total wealth is fully exposed to public examination since the estate will be settled through the courts. The person who accumulated the wealth is dead. His beneficiary is reaping what might be termed a windfall. The former can feel no pain nor can he bear any burden. The latter's burden can only be psychological in nature. This situation has proven to be irresistible for tax-writing legislators.

The Mechanics of Death Taxes. Both the state and national governments impose taxes on the estates of those who die. The national government and a few of the states supplement the death taxes with a gift tax. The tax levied on property transferred at the time of a person's death may take either of two forms. The first is an estate tax levied against the estate of the deceased. This tax is paid from the estate. The second is the inheritance tax levied against the inheritance received by the beneficiary or beneficiaries. The tax rate depends on the size of the legacy as well as the relationship between the parties. The rates increase as the size of the inheritance increases. They are also graduated in that the more remote the relationship the higher will be the tax rate.

At one time several of the states tried to attract elderly people to their state by not taxing property of the deceased or taxing it at very low rates. This competition ended when the federal government started taxing such property, for one of the avowed purposes of the federal statute was that of promoting uniformity among the states. The system operates as follows. The national government imposes a graduated inheritance tax, but up to 80 per cent of the tax liability can be satisfied through tax payments to the state having jurisdiction. If the state has no death tax, the entire tax liability would accrue to the national government. Obviously, with this sort of an arrangement, all states have death taxes.

An Appraisal of Death Taxes. If the ability to pay is adjudged to be synonymous with equity, death taxes are equitable. At no time would the ability to pay be greater than after death and at no time would less sacrifice be demanded, for, after all, the beneficiary is not giving up anything he already possesses. The tax is convenient insofar as any tax is convenient. In those cases where the payment of such a tax would require the dissolution of the estate, the government will allow up to ten years in which the tax may be paid. Insofar as certainty is concerned, the rates, exemptions, and deductions are either known or easily ascertainable. The only element of uncertainty is the establishment of the situs of taxation for certain property which is interstate in nature. It is not, however, a great producer of revenue. This fact alone is sufficient to keep it from ever being considered as a tax of major significance in this country's tax system.

The Incidence of Death Taxes. The incidence of a death tax must be at the point of impact, for neither the deceased nor the beneficiary are in a position to shift the tax. Death taxes are, however, widely criticized for their supposedly adverse effect on incentive and capital accumulation. Let us take a few moments to examine such contentions.

First, many contend that death taxes reduce incentive. It is asked why a man would work if it is known that the government will tax whatever property he accumulates. Many college students, for example, seem to be under the impression that the only reason their fathers are working is in order that the student will be given a start in life. It seems somewhat doubtful whether this is a prime motive for working. There is probably not much reason for believing that people will put forth less effort because of the inheritance or estate taxes.

The second criticism asserts that such taxes reduce property accumulation since death taxes cause going concerns to be broken up. Since such taxes must be paid in some form of money, it is conceivable that a large estate with few liquid assets might have to liquidate at least part of the estate in order to satisfy the tax bill. This probably happens so seldom that it is, at best, a minor criticism.

One last comment. Obviously under our existing economic system, the death tax rates are not going to increase to such a point that private wealth would be confiscated. The institution of inheritance is an integral part of the institution of private property. Confiscatory taxation of such wealth would soon eliminate all privately held property and thus destroy the capitalistic system. We are not so jeopardized at the present time.

Regulatory Taxes

Although many are unaware of the fact, the various levels of government in the United States levy taxes which are not intended to produce revenue. Since the national government was not granted a police power by the Constitution, it has used the taxing power as a tool to promote the general welfare.

As examples of this type of tax, one might cite the present gambling tax as well as taxes on opium, isonipecaine, opiates, coca leaves, and marihuana. In addition to taxes on drugs, the national government also taxes sawed-off shotguns and bank notes issued by state-chartered commercial banks with the intent of eliminating both items. The national government has, until recently, taxed oleomargarine in order to assist the dairy farmers. The government has long taxed many imports in order to protect domestic producers. At the state level one finds a variety of regulatory taxes including taxes on oleomargarine, fortune-tellers, traveling circuses, and many others. In many of these cases the taxes are set so high as to be prohibitive.

Regulatory taxes cannot be judged by the same criteria that were used to judge those taxes designed to raise revenue. The fact that the gambling tax does not produce enough revenue to pay the cost of administration does not make it a poor tax. If it did produce large amounts of revenue, this would be evidence of gambling and the failure of the tax to eliminate this nefarious practice. The question which can be raised, however, is one of governmental structure and operations. Is it proper and fitting that the tax collection agency should be assigned the task of eliminating gambling and the production and sale of narcotics or is this more properly a function of a police agency?

Summary

These pages have served as an introduction to the basic taxes in the American tax system. An attempt has been made to evaluate each in light of the criteria set down by Adam Smith nearly two centuries ago. The economic effects of each tax were briefly examined. Unfortunately, no answer can be given as to which tax is the best tax, for each has its merits as well as certain unattractive features. The particular tax to be used depends upon the circumstances.

THE PUBLIC DEBT

Neither the individual nor the business firm can spend more than is taken in. The government, with limited and rather unimportant exceptions, is in the same position. However, all can spend more than is currently taken in as income in the case of the individual or business firm, or tax revenue in the case of the government. When this happens, the deficiency must be made up by borrowing. The government borrows against its future tax revenue in order that it may provide goods and services in the present and pay for them in the future.

All levels of government borrow in order to finance a portion of the governmental activities. There are, however, usually limits on the amount a government can borrow. The national government is limited by statute, although the limit can easily be raised. Local governments in most instances are limited to some percentage of their taxable valuation. And some state governments have constitutional prohibitions against borrowing.

Historically, governments have borrowed for only a few purposes. In the case of local and state governments, it has been for the construction of such capital projects as schools, highways and sewage facilities. The national government has borrowed for two major purposes—national defense and promotion of economic recovery. The latter explains the increase in the national debt during the 1930's. Since the economic catastrophe of that decade, borrowing as an antidepression device has come to be generally accepted. It is this aspect of the public debt with which we are going to be most concerned.

The Growth of the National Debt

It may appear to be a paradox, but the only method of establishing one's credit rating is to acquire a debt. A family moving into a new community will never acquire a credit rating without first acquiring a debt. The same is true of a new government entering the community of nations. It happened in the case of the United States 150 years ago.

One of the first proposals of Alexander Hamilton, George Washington's Secretary of the Treasury, was that the United States government assume the debts incurred in the Revolution. The debts were those of the previous national government as well as the debts of the states. Hamilton's major argument in support of the debt was the fact that it would establish the credit rating of the nation. But he also argued that a national debt was necessary for the well-being of the country. This view is not accepted by all even today.

Within two years of the inauguration of Washington, the new nation had acquired a debt of $75 million. From that time to this, the debt has increased in size with but few years seeing a reduction in the country's debt (see Table 14–4). The debt per person has fallen since World War II.

The present national debt of more than $300 billion means that the burden on each citizen is slightly more than $1,500. The interest payments alone amount to more than $9 billion per year. How did this happen? Is this an insufferable burden? What are the mechanics of raising the funds and servicing the debt? Does such a debt have some virtues? How big should the debt be? These are some of the questions to be explored in the following pages.

TABLE 14–4

DEBT OF THE UNITED STATES GOVERNMENT FOR SELECTED
YEARS, 1791–1962
(In Millions of Dollars)

Year	Debt
1791	$ 75
1800	83
1825	83
1850	63
1875	2,156
1900	1,263
1925	20,516
1950	257,357
1955	274,374
1960	286,331
1961	288,971
1962	298,201

SOURCE: U.S. Bureau of the Census, *Statistical Abstract of the United States, 1963* (Washington, D.C., 1963).

The Mechanics of the Debt

The debt of the United States government is a domestically held debt. The debt is owed to American citizens, business firms, and banks rather than to foreigners. The problem, then, of increasing or decreasing the debt merely involves the transference of money from one group of people to another within the economy. It does not involve the transference of wealth from one country to another. Neither does it involve problems of foreign exchange or foreign control of American activities.

The government borrows from two sources within the domestic economy. First, it borrows from individual persons and firms. This group may be classed as nonbank investors. Farmers buy bonds in order to establish a reserve for future capital expenditures. Insurance companies purchase bonds to provide low-risk investment paper for their portfolios. Employees save by purchasing bonds through a payroll deduction plan. Industrial corporations buy securities as a long-run investment or as a means of earning some income on assets which would otherwise be held as idle cash for a short period. In all of these cases the person who buys the bond is, in fact, lending the money to the government which, at the same moment, acquires a debt. The bond is the debt instrument.

The second source of borrowed funds for the government is the banking system, including both the commercial banks and the Federal Reserve banks. The banks lend money to the government just as they lend to private borrowers. A bank, when lending money to the government, creates a deposit for the government in the amount of the loan, and the bank receives in return a bond for the same amount. In exchange for the new liability the bank receives this asset, which yields a fairly low return but involves little or no risk.

Table 14–5

PERCENTAGE DISTRIBUTION OF THE DEBT OF THE UNITED STATES
IN SELECTED YEARS SINCE 1940

Group	1940	1945	1950	1955	1960	1962
U.S. Government agencies and trust funds	15.0	9.7	15.3	18.4	19.0	18.3
Bank investors						
Federal Reserve	4.3	8.7	8.1	8.8	9.4	10.1
Commercial	34.0	32.6	24.1	22.1	21.6	21.9
Mutual savings	6.3	3.8	4.2	3.0	2.2	2.0
Private nonbank investors						
Insurance companies	13.5	8.6	7.3	5.2	4.1	3.8
Other corporations	3.9	8.0	7.7	8.4	6.8	6.6
Individuals	20.8	23.0	25.8	23.2	22.8	21.7
Other*	2.4	5.6	7.5	10.9	14.2	15.6

* Includes state and local governments, pension funds, nonprofit institutions and others.

SOURCE: U.S. Bureau of the Census, *Statistical Abstract of the United States, 1963* (Washington, D.C., 1963).

The distribution of the debt among the various groups is shown in Table 14–5. During World War II the banks held nearly half of the total debt, but this percentage has declined steadily until bank holdings are only a third of the total. In general, as interest rates have risen, those business firms which invest primarily for profit rather than security have reduced their holdings of government bonds, and those parties primarily interested in security have increased in importance as holders of government securities.

The reason why such a large percentage of the debt was held by the banking system at the end of the war can be explained in terms of the method of financing the war. As an anti-inflationary measure it was deemed desirable to raise as much of the borrowed funds as possible from nonbank investors. However, the government could not rely upon this group to buy all of the bonds to be sold. And, of course, the war could not be stopped because nonbank investors refused to purchase 100 per cent of a particular bond issue. To overcome this problem the banking system purchased whatever part of a bond issue remained unsold after the public had purchased what it wanted. In this way the government was always assured of having the funds necessary for the conduct of the war. This was not an entirely one-sided bargain, for the government relieved the banks of the necessity of maintaining reserves against these Treasury War Loan Accounts.

Once the debt is incurred, however, there remains the task of servicing it. First, Congress must provide sufficient funds to pay the interest on the debt. Second, there is the considerable task involved in refunding the debt. A large part of the debt matures each month. In addition, there are large numbers of bondholders who desire to sell their holdings of government securities for one reason or another. If, for example, a billion dollars worth of securities are sold or mature within a given period, the government must be able to reimburse these bondholders when they present their bonds. If the funds are not available from current tax revenue, the government must borrow from someone else in order to pay off the present bondholders. This means that the government is borrowing funds, even though it may be receiving more in revenue than it is spending.

In borrowing new funds or borrowing to refund existent debt, the Treasury may issue a number of different kinds of securities. The maturity dates vary from 90 days to over 20 years. The yields ranged from less than $\frac{1}{2}$ per cent to $2\frac{1}{2}$ per cent during World War II, but since then, both lower and upper limits have risen. Some securities are marketable in that they can be bought and sold, while others are nonmarketable, meaning that the holder must hold them until maturity. In short, the Treasury has at its disposal a stable of different types of securities which it can issue. The particular type of security to be issued depends upon the money market, the economic conditions existent at the moment, and government policy.

During World War II it was the policy of the government to keep interest rates low to minimize the cost of borrowing. In order to do this, great reliance was placed upon securities with shorter maturity periods since these carried lower rates of interest. But such financing meant that the government had to be continually conducting refunding operations of considerable proportions. Since 1950 there has been a change in the policy of the government. For the past few years there has been a shift from short-term securities to securities with longer maturity periods. There has been an accompanying increase in the level of interest rates. But the size of the refunding operations has been reduced and the management of the debt has become somewhat less complicated.

The Economic Effect of the Debt

There are two extreme attitudes toward the public debt. One group holds that it imposes a nearly impossible burden on the present and future generations which can only lead to national bankruptcy. The second holds that since the debt is owed by one group—the taxpayers—to another group—the bondholders—there is really no such effect as that seen by the first group. The debt cannot lead to bankruptcy, it is contended, since servicing the debt merely means that we take from one group and give it to another. No wealth has left the economy. The same group argues that the burden is not passed on to future generations since the generation which inherits the liability also inherits the asset. So the debt merely means that future generations must take money away from the taxpayers and give it to the bondholders, just as the present generation is doing.

It appears quite probable that neither of these extreme viewpoints regarding the debt is accurate. First, let us examine the size of the debt. The magnitude of the debt is of considerable importance at any given moment, although there can be no such thing as some absolute amount beyond which the debt should not go. A debt of $5.00 may appear very large to a person without any income, but a debt of $5,000 may not appear so large to a person with a $500,000 income. The same is true for a government. The important relationship is the size of the debt in comparison to the gross national product. The present debt would have presented an impossible burden in the early 1930's, just as some future debt might well be an impossible burden if it existed at the present time. As the gross national product of a country increases, the size of the debt can increase without increasing the burden of the debt. This is not to imply that the debt should always be increasing in size.

An ever increasing debt does have certain implications. In the first place, a debt involves a redistribution of income from taxpayers to bondholders. The larger this debt, the greater will be the redistribution and the problems associated with that redistribution. Secondly, as long as economic activity fluctuates, there is always the possibility that a debt incurred during periods of prosperity will become an insufferable burden in a subsequent period of depression.

There are reasons for having a rather large debt; in fact, a large government debt has probably become an operating necessity in our economic system. It would probably be inadvisable to do away with the debt, even if some practical means were available whereby that could be done. In the first place, the debt is the largest single asset to be found in the balance sheets of the nation's banks. It is a major asset in other financial institutions such as insurance companies. Where there is a need for investment without risk, that investment almost has to be in the government. A second reason why a debt is desirable is to be found in its use in the promotion of economic stability. Government operations of taxing and borrowing, of purchasing goods and services, and retiring the debt are of such magnitude that they can be used in such a fashion as to exert a countercyclical influence. Government decisions in these areas may be taken in light of their effect on economic activity. And it is thus we turn to the question of the relationship between Treasury action, the banking system, and the supply of money.

TREASURY ACTION AND THE MONEY SUPPLY

The Treasury Department collects the tax revenue and writes the checks to pay the bills incurred by the government. The Treasury does have deposits in the nation's commercial banks, but it can only write checks on deposits in the Federal Reserve banks. Thus the Treasury is constantly depositing money in the Federal Reserve banks and writing checks on those accounts. In this fashion, then, the Treasury exercises some control over the banking system just as the Federal Reserve System does.

Taxing and Bank Reserves

A taxpayer will usually satisfy his tax obligation to the government by drawing a check on his demand deposit and sending it to the government. This check will reduce the demand deposits of the commercial bank (a). The check may be returned to the commercial bank, and the Treasury deposit in that bank will be increased (b). Since the Treasury cannot write a check on that account, it must be transferred to the Federal Reserve bank. This is done by reducing member bank reserves (c) and increasing Treasury deposits in the Federal Reserve bank (d).

Commercial Bank		Federal Reserve Bank	
	Demand deposits $-(a)$		Reserves........$-(c)$
Reserves.. $-(c)$	Treasury deposits $+(b)$		Treasury deposits$+(d)$
	Treasury deposits $-(c)$		

Most checks are sent directly to the Federal Reserve bank by the Treasury, and the amount of the check is transferred from the reserves of the member bank to the Treasury deposit. In either case there is a reduction in the reserves of the member banks. In fact, one can generalize and state that whenever taxes are paid to the Treasury, there will be a reduction in the reserves of the member banks.

The student will readily observe that government purchases of goods and services will have just the reverse effect. The check drawn on the Treasury deposit in the Federal Reserve bank will be deposited in a commercial bank. This will increase the member bank's reserves and thus offset the reduction which resulted from the payment of taxes.

Government Borrowing and Bank Reserves

When the Treasury sells bonds to nonbank investors, the effect on bank reserves is the same as that in the above example. The purchaser of the bond gives the Treasury a check, and the check is collected by reducing member bank reserves. So we can now broaden the above generalization and state that whenever the government raises money through taxing or borrowing from nonbank investors, there will be a reduction in the reserves of the banking system.

But when the government borrows from the banking system, the effect is somewhat different. Take first the case of commercial banks. When such a bank buys a bond, payment is made by creating a demand deposit (a). These funds are then transferred to the Treasury account in the Federal Reserve bank (b) through a reduction in reserves (c). In this case there has been no reduction of private demand deposits.

Commercial Banks		Federal Reserve Banks	
Bonds....$+(a)$	Treasury deposits $+ (a)$		Reserves ....$-(c)$
Reserves.. $-(c)$	Treasury deposits $- (b)$		Treasury deposits $+(b)$

The third source of borrowed funds consists of the Federal Reserve banks. In this case there is no effect on private demand deposits or the reserves of the member banks. The bond holdings of the Federal Reserve bank increase and there is a corresponding increase in Treasury deposits.

Debt Retirement and Bank Reserves

Insofar as bank reserves are concerned, the spending of tax revenue just counterbalances the effect of taxes. Insofar as retiring the debt is concerned, the effect will depend upon what portion of the debt is retired.

First, take the instance of debt held by nonbank investors. In this case the Treasury writes a check on its account in a Federal Reserve bank to pay for the bond. This check is then deposited in a commercial bank. When the check is cleared, the commercial bank receives reserve credit. Thus the repaying of nonbank-held debt will increase the reserves of the member banks.

TABLE 14–6

EFFECT OF TREASURY TRANSACTIONS ON MEMBER BANK
RESERVES AND DEPOSITS

Treasury Transaction	*Direct Effect on Member Bank Reserves*	*Direct Effect on Member Bank Deposits*	*Possible Further Expansion or Contraction of Member Bank Deposits*
1 Treasury raises money:			
a) By taxes............	−	−	−
b) By selling securities to nonbank investors....	−	−	−
c) By selling securities to member banks.......	−	0	−
d) By selling securities to Federal Reserve banks	0	0	0
2 Treasury uses money:			
a) To pay bills.........	+	+	+
b) To retire debt held by nonbank investors....	+	+	+
c) To retire debt held by member banks.......	+	0	+
d) To retire debt held by Federal Reserve banks	0	0	0

SOURCE: Federal Reserve Bank of Philadelphia, *Exercises in the Debits and Credits of Bank Reserves.*

The same thing is true if the debt held by commercial banks is retired. In this case the commercial bank receives a check drawn by the Treasury on its account in the Federal Reserve bank. This check is cleared by granting the member bank reserve credit.

But this is not the case when the debt held by the Federal Reserve banks is retired. Such bonds are retired by drawing against the Treasury deposit in the Federal Reserve bank. There is a reduction in Treasury deposits in the Federal Reserve bank and there is a reduction in bonds held by that bank. There is no effect on member bank reserves.

All Treasury transactions and their effect on the banking system are represented in Table 14–6. One can obtain the net effect of any two operations involving (1) raising money and (2) using money by combining the signs for the particular operations. A plus and a minus offset one another. A plus and a zero will increase reserves, just as a zero and a minus will reduce reserves.

The Treasury, in addition to the Federal Reserve System, can influence the activities of the commercial banking system of the country. Through taxing, borrowing, spending, and debt retirement, the Treasury can change the reserve position of the commercial banking system and the deposit position of the nation's bank depositors. The Treasury is in the same position as the Federal Reserve System insofar as the multiple contraction or expansion of deposits is concerned. The United States Treasury and the Federal Reserve System share joint responsibility for the nation's monetary system. They are jointly charged with the responsibility for maintaining economic stability. Any effective program depends upon the co-ordination of the programs and policies of these two agencies.

CONCLUSION

The United States government is the largest single operation in the economic system. The national government is presently operating on an annual budget of nearly $100 billion. The debt is in excess of $300 billion requiring annual interest payments of nearly $10 billion. In addition, there are thousands of lesser government units collecting taxes, selling securities, and spending the receipts. The absolute magnitude of the operations means that it is impossible for a single individual to master the complexities of the nation's fiscal structure. One can, though, get at least some understanding of the principles involved in order that particular aspects of the situation can be analyzed.

The level of government expenditures provides a rough index of the magnitude of the government's role in the economic system. Present conditions probably preclude much of a diminution of the government's role in the near future. It is unlikely that there will be either a drastic reduction in expenditures or taxes in the near future. Instead, the long-term trend of both will probably continue upward.

The role of the government in the economic system is a function of the exigencies of the moment and the desires of the people. "Taxing a little less" or "spending a little less" will not result in a major reversal of the government's role. To reverse the trend will require a major revaluation of society's goals as well as an assessment of the alternative methods of achieving such goals.

EXERCISES

Group I

Explain why the following statements are either true or false:

1. Some taxes cannot be imposed according to the principle of benefits received because (1) in some cases it is impossible to compute and assign benefits and (2) in some cases there are no benefits received by anyone.
2. The principle of ability to pay is an attempt to impose an equal burden on all.
3. The primary basis for judging all taxes is the revenue-producing power of each.
4. There is no limit to the government debt since we owe it to ourselves.
5. What might be an insufferable debt at one time in a nation's history might represent no burden at all at another stage of a country's development.
6. Whenever the government raises money, whether by taxing or borrowing, the result is inflationary.
7. Whenever the government retires debt, the effect is anti-inflationary.

Group II

1. Alexander Hamilton presented a very strong case for a national government having a debt. Read his *First Report on Public Credit.* What were his arguments for a public debt and how valid are they today?
2. A strong argument has been centered around the contention that "the size of the debt is not important as long as it is domestically held." Explore this argument. How much validity does it have?
3. How does the financing of government operations in the USSR compare with that in the United States?

Group III

1. Write a paper on the subject: "Debt Policy of the United States since World War II."
2. Compare the positions of the National Association of Manufacturers, the Committee for Economic Development, and the AFL-CIO regarding tax policy.
3. Is there an economic justification for a progressive income tax?
4. Evaluate the sales tax and the income tax as devices for counteracting inflation.

BIBLIOGRAPHY

DUE, JOHN F. *Government Finance.* Rev. ed. Homewood, Ill.: Richard D. Irwin, Inc., 1959.

GROVES, HAROLD M. *Financing Government.* New York: Henry Holt & Co., 1950.

MUSGRAVE, R. A. *The Theory of Public Finance—A Study in Political Economy.* New York: McGraw-Hill, 1959.

MUSGRAVE, R. A., AND PEACOCK, A. T. (Eds.). *Classics in the Theory of Public Finance.* New York: Macmillan Co., 1958.

SMITH, ADAM. *An Inquiry into the Nature and Causes of the Wealth of Nations.* New York: Modern Library, 1937. (Available in paperback editions.)

PAPERBACK READING LIST

BATOR, F. M. *The Question of Government Spending—Public Needs and Private Wants.* New York: Collier Books, 1962.

HAMILTON, ALEXANDER. *Papers on Public Credit, Commerce and Finance.* Edited by Samuel McKee, Jr. New York: The Liberal Arts Press Division, The Bobbs-Merrill Co., Inc., 1957.

Chapter
15

THE BUSINESS CYCLE AND ITS CONTROL

I saw your friend Keynes. He left a whole rigamarole of figures. He must be a mathematician rather than a political economist.—Franklin D. Roosevelt.

[I] had supposed that the President [Roosevelt] was more literate, economically speaking.—John Maynard Keynes. Both quotations from Frances Perkins, *The Roosevelt I Knew* (New York: Viking Press, 1946).

The economic system, rather than moving on an unchanging course through time, oscillates; that is, the level of economic activity fluctuates from one time period to the next. Periods of intense economic activity are followed by periods of less activity. Such changes in the level of activity are not confined to particular parts of the economy but refer to the aggregate level of activity.

These cyclical fluctuations have their cause in the structure of society and are a phenomenon of a freely operating economic system.

362

This chapter is concerned with the business cycle as it exists in a modern capitalistic economic system. What is its nature? What are its causes? What measures can be undertaken to control the business cycle?

FLUCTUATIONS IN ECONOMIC ACTIVITY

Types of Economic Fluctuations

Although the concern here is with a particular type of fluctuation, that is the business cycle, there are several types of fluctuations in economic activity which have been classified as follows. The secular or long-run trend represents a change covering a period of years, decades, or even longer. It may be in either an upward or downward direction. Many examples of trend may be found. The trend in population in the United States has been upward for over three centuries. The secular trend in infant mortality has been downward. And the production of harness for horses was upward for many years, but for the last two decades or so it has been downward.

Seasonal fluctuations are recurrent and periodic. That is, there is a particular type of change at a particular time of the year. Seasonal fluctuations are less than a year in length. Quite commonly, they are associated with physical phenomena such as weather, but they are also found arising out of the institutions created by man. Examples of the first would include the sale of winter clothing, swimming suits, coal, or air-conditioning equipment. Examples of the latter would be those variations resulting from holidays, such as the sale of fireworks during the period preceding the Fourth of July or the increase in department store sales during the month of December. Since seasonal fluctuations are periodic, it is possible to predict their occurrence with a high degree of accuracy. Business firms, for example, know that there will be a change in their level of operations at a particular time of the year, and steps are taken to prepare for such changes. The practice of introducing the new model automobiles in the fall of the year was intended to offset the seasonal decline in the sale of cars. The ice company combined with the coal company in order to offset the seasonal fluctuations found in both.

Cyclical fluctuations or business cycles are not periodic in the sense that they recur at definite periods. They are, however, recurrent. An average may be computed to represent the length of the business cycle, but like any average, it is only a representative figure, and it is an accident if it fits any individual cycle. It may, for example, be three years from the low point of one cycle to the low point of the next, whereas the subsequent cycle may be either longer or shorter. Since the business cycle is of no definite duration and since it is not periodic, predictions of future levels of economic activity must still be classed as one of the more difficult problems facing economists and statisticians.

There are other types of fluctuations, with which we will not be concerned. There are extremely long wave-like fluctuations covering periods of several decades. There are random or irregular fluctuations resulting from such events as wars or strikes. This chapter, then, will ignore, for the most part, all of the various types of economic fluctuations except the cyclical. This is an examination of the business cycle and of the possibilities of controlling this peculiar economic phenomena.

The Business Cycle

What Is the Business Cycle? Everyone has observed that some years are better than others insofar as economic activity is concerned. The college student, for example, may have no trouble finding a job one year but may experience a great deal of difficulty the next. Business firms may enjoy a profit in one year only to suffer a loss the following. Employees may receive a high wage rate and work a great deal of overtime, or they may have to work for a lower wage rate for only a part of the work week. Everyone, then, has good years and bad years.

If the economic activities of all were cumulated, one would find that the entire economy operates at varying levels of activity. Periods of high production, high incomes, rising prices, and low levels of unemployment are followed by periods of lower incomes, falling prices, and higher levels of unemployment. The returns to the several factors of production, that is, national income, reflect these recurrent changes in the levels of economic activity. This is the business cycle. It is the change in the aggregate level of economic activity rather than the change in a particular industry or a particular part of the economy. These cyclical fluctuations in the level of economic activity in the United States are shown in Figure 15–1.

Cyclical fluctuations can be measured in terms of physical production—employment, freight car loadings, and other physical measurements. They can also be measured in terms of changes in the monetary value of goods and services (GNP) or national income. The business cycle is a combination of both real fluctuations and monetary fluctuations, although at a particular time one or the other may be of more significance. Inflation, for example, is a monetary fluctuation since real production cannot be increased beyond some upper limit, while declines in economic activity may be in either real or monetary terms.

Phases of the Business Cycle. For purposes of analysis, economists have generally divided the business cycle into four parts or phases—prosperity, recession, depression, and recovery. Although the layman may think only in terms of prosperity and depression, it is important for purposes of analysis to think of the business cycle as having four phases.

Prosperity is a period of high-level economic activity. Production of goods and services is high. Nearly everyone is employed. Business firms are making a profit. Prices, including the factor prices, are high. Large sums are invested in capital equipment. Bank credit has expanded and excess reserves are low. These are "good" times.

A period of prosperity is sometimes referred to as a period of full employment, but in this case the term "full employment" is not confined to the labor force. Full employment means that all of the factors of production are nearly fully employed. Employment and unemployment of labor is merely the most observable factor. The concept of full employment does allow, however, for frictional unemployment, which represents those units of factors temporarily out of work because they are in the process of changing jobs. In the case of labor, for example, there will always be several million unemployed during periods of peak employment. Full employment is a real or physical concept as contrasted to a monetary concept, and for most people it represents the goal of our monetary and fiscal controls. That is, social policy should promote full employment.

A period of full employment involves certain hazards. It may be followed by either a period of recession or inflation. An economy enjoying full employment may, in fact, be walking a tight rope between the pits of recession and depression on one side and inflation and hyperinflation on the other.

If an economic system is fully employed, there is no possibility of immediately increasing the output of goods and services. Over a longer period of time the labor force may increase in size and additional capital equipment may be acquired. But in the short run this is impossible. Under such circumstances anything that provides buyers with more purchasing power or anything that causes the people to spend their money faster can have only one consequence. That is, either an increase in the supply of money or an increase in the speed with which money moves from hand to hand can only increase prices. There can be no increase in production. In a depression this need not be the case,

FIGURE 15–1. AMERICAN BUSINESS ACTIVITY SINCE 1790

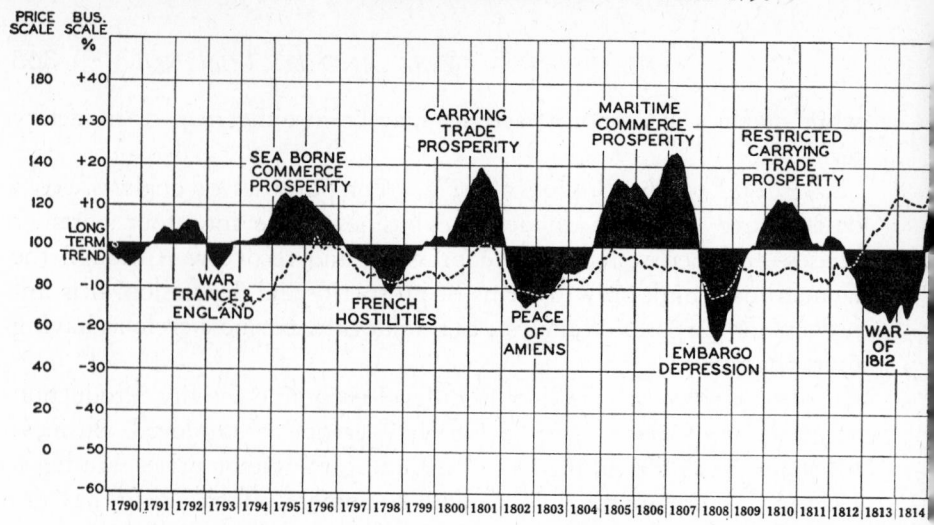

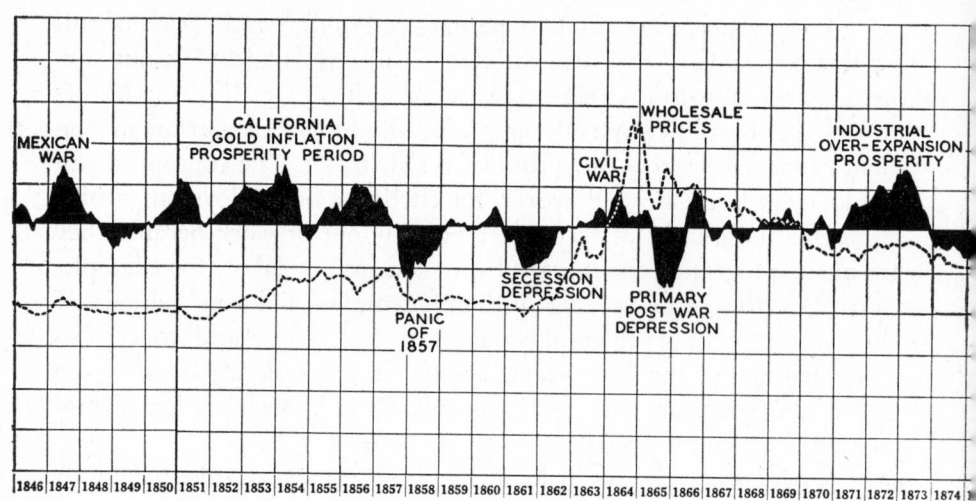

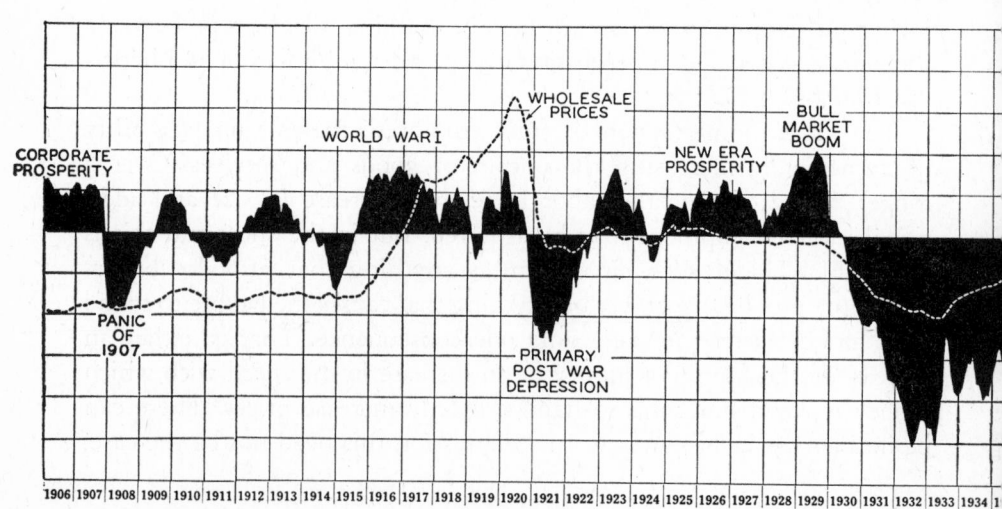

SOURCE: The Cleveland Trust Company

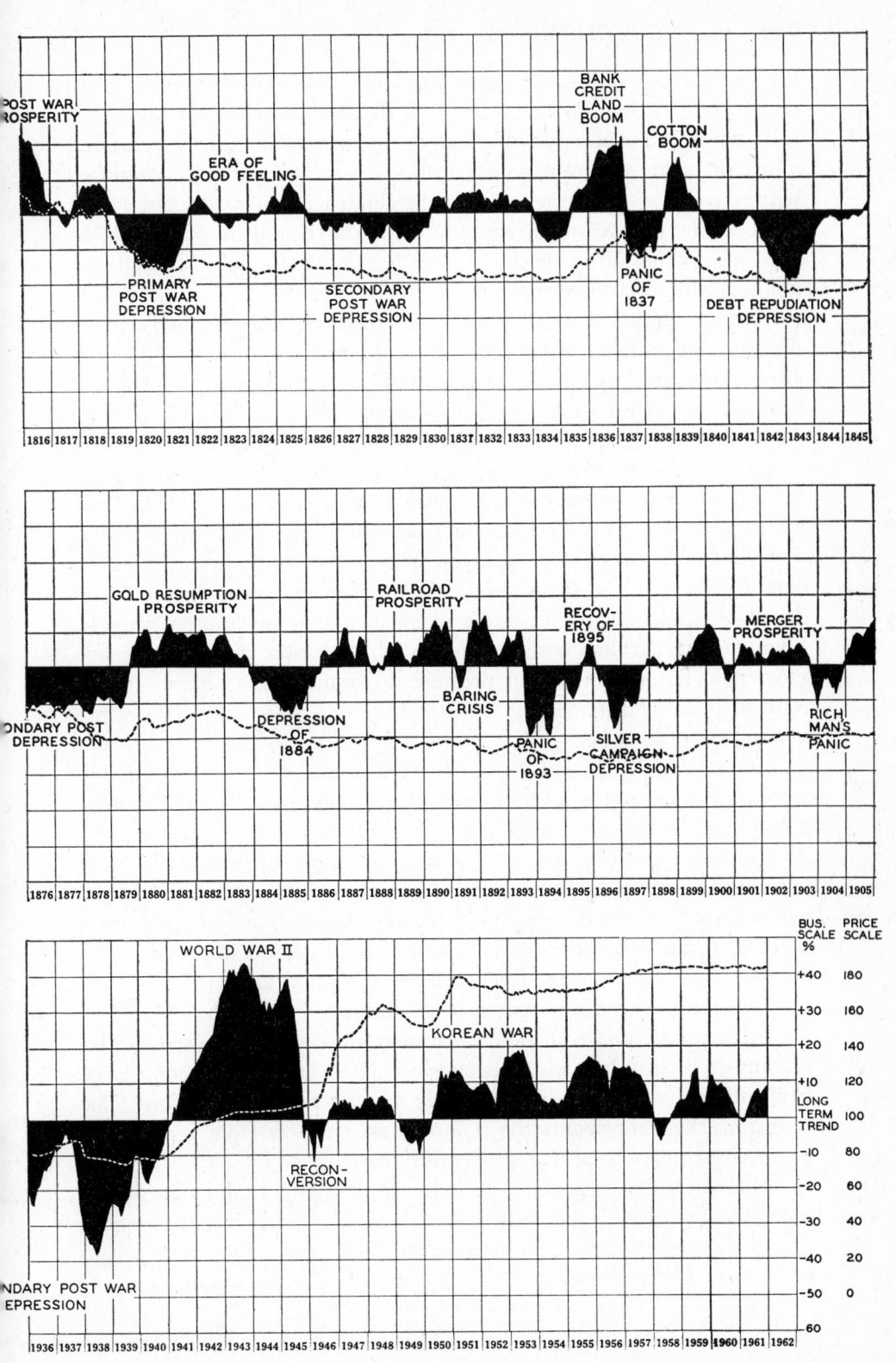

Chart 1 (1816–1845):

POST WAR PROSPERITY

ERA OF GOOD FEELING

BANK CREDIT LAND BOOM

COTTON BOOM

PRIMARY POST WAR DEPRESSION

SECONDARY POST WAR DEPRESSION

PANIC OF 1837

DEBT REPUDIATION DEPRESSION

1816 | 1817 | 1818 | 1819 | 1820 | 1821 | 1822 | 1823 | 1824 | 1825 | 1826 | 1827 | 1828 | 1829 | 1830 | 1831 | 1832 | 1833 | 1834 | 1835 | 1836 | 1837 | 1838 | 1839 | 1840 | 1841 | 1842 | 1843 | 1844 | 1845

Chart 2 (1876–1905):

GOLD RESUMPTION PROSPERITY

RAILROAD PROSPERITY

RECOVERY OF 1895

MERGER PROSPERITY

SECONDARY POST WAR DEPRESSION

DEPRESSION OF 1884

BARING CRISIS

PANIC OF 1893

SILVER CAMPAIGN DEPRESSION

RICH MAN'S PANIC

1876 | 1877 | 1878 | 1879 | 1880 | 1881 | 1882 | 1883 | 1884 | 1885 | 1886 | 1887 | 1888 | 1889 | 1890 | 1891 | 1892 | 1893 | 1894 | 1895 | 1896 | 1897 | 1898 | 1899 | 1900 | 1901 | 1902 | 1903 | 1904 | 1905

Chart 3 (1936–1962):

WORLD WAR II

KOREAN WAR

RECON-VERSION

SECONDARY POST WAR DEPRESSION

BUS. SCALE %	PRICE SCALE
+40	180
+30	160
+20	140
+10	120
LONG TERM TREND	100
−10	80
−20	60
−30	40
−40	20
−50	0
−60	

1936 | 1937 | 1938 | 1939 | 1940 | 1941 | 1942 | 1943 | 1944 | 1945 | 1946 | 1947 | 1948 | 1949 | 1950 | 1951 | 1952 | 1953 | 1954 | 1955 | 1956 | 1957 | 1958 | 1959 | 1960 | 1961 | 1962

for increased spending may draw forth idle resources and result in increased production. As an example, a defense program imposed on a fully employed economy will create tremendous inflationary pressures, while the same program imposed on an economy not fully employed will not create the same inflationary tendencies. The student might compare the immediate effects of World War II and the Korean War.

In a period of prosperity, certain forces develop which may result in a recession or at least make it possible for the economy to move into a recession. Banks may overextend themselves. Certain inefficiencies may develop in the economy, including the utilization of marginal employees and raw materials as well as the establishment of inefficient business firms. Marginal firms may operate successfully as long as demand is strong. However, the slightest decline in business conditions will usually mean losses and perhaps failure. Their failure may jeopardize the solvency of institutions which have advanced credit to these marginal firms. Consumer credit also builds up until the slightest drop in hours, wages or employment causes a significant increase in defaulting on loans. Inventories may increase as consumption is reduced. A slight decline in prices may mean that inventories must be liquidated at less than cost. Residential construction may exceed home purchases. Empty houses put pressure on home prices and apartment rentals, possibly threatening the solvency of construction companies and owners of rental property.

Once these conditions exist, the stage is set for a cumulative downward movement in the level of economic activity. In such circumstances the marginal efficiency of capital will fall, and it may fall rather sharply. As the MEC declines, investors will reduce their level of investment expenditures. As consumers come to anticipate lower prices in the future, they likewise will postpone present consumption expenditures in favor of future consumption outlays. This will cause a still further reduction in the level of investment expenditures and further decreases in income. Planned savings will exceed planned investment.

If the early phase of the downturn is marked by some spectacular economic catastrophe such as the crash of 1929 or the failure of a large bank, then the recession may actually assume panic proportions. The recession, then, represents the economy as it moves from a period of prosperity toward a period of depression.

During such a transitory period, certain changes take place in the economy. Prices will generally fall, although in some instances rigidities in the price system may prevent or delay price adjustments. And even when prices do fall, not all prices will fall at the same time or at the same rate. Some prices are rather sticky, and they will generally start falling rather late in the recession.

During the recession, production and employment will decline. Although inventories originally increased as consumption fell, eventually inventories will be liquidated. And if reduced inventories don't appear to be a sufficient adjustment to the lower level of consumption, producers will cut back on their planned construction of new plant and equipment. When these adjustments in prices, production, and investment have been made, the economy has moved from the recession phase of the cycle into the depression.

Depression! A period of low prices, low production of goods and services, unemployment, business failures, contracted bank loans and excess reserves, foreclosures on all types of property, extremely low level of investment—all of these and others characterize a depression. In the United States there have been a number of depressions, but that of the 1930's is most vivid in the memory of the American people. This depression was the most severe of all of those which the country has suffered. It was, in fact, a major factor in the reshaping of the economy which occurred in that decade. The slumps of 1949, 1954, 1957–1958, and 1960 were rather insignificant phenomena when compared to the Great Depression of the 1930's.

During a depression certain forces build up which eventually put pressure on the economic system to move toward recovery or at least make it possible to move into such a period. Some purchases cannot be postponed indefinitely. As prices continue to fall, cash reserves increase in value. There comes a time when those with liquid assets feel that prices will fall no more. This, to them, is an opportune time to convert liquid assets into nonliquid assets. As costs continue to decline, eventually a point is reached where the entrepreneur feels that he can produce and sell at a profit. The inefficient firms have fallen by the wayside, leaving the more efficient firms with a better chance of making a profit. As far as the banks are concerned, excess reserves have accumulated in the banking system, and it is possible for them to expand credit should the business outlook improve. Once these forces cumulate to such an extent that there is an upward movement in economic activity, the same snowballing effect will be encountered as was found in the case of recession and depression. Once there is a restoration of confidence, the economy will move into the last phase of the cycle—recovery.

The recovery phase of the business cycle is marked initially by an increase in production. Idle resources are employed. As production increases, confidence returns. Investors increase capital equipment expenditures, and banks express a willingness to expand credit based on their excess reserves. Incomes increase, which results in increased consumption expenditures. And finally as the level of income continues to rise, prices will also start to move upward. Again, though, the sticky prices will move upward somewhat later and somewhat slower than other prices. Thus the economy successfully maneuvers through this second transitory phase and moves from the depression to prosperity.

The business cycle is a self-contained force in that each phase creates the conditions necessary for the subsequent phase. It does not depend upon exogenous forces to move from one phase to another. However, such movement may be greatly accelerated by some outside force. For example, the economy may move from prosperity to recession as a result of a bank failure or stock-market crash. On the other side, a war may promote recovery and prosperity for a depressed economy, but this again is an exogenous factor and not an integral part of the business cycle.

In closing this discussion of the cycle, it should be pointed out that it is impossible to state with exactness when the economy passes from one phase to another. In fact, it is impossible to state with certainty just what phase of the business cycle the economy may be in at a particular moment. Politicians, for example, often differ. The party in office may maintain that the economy is enjoying a period of prosperity, while the party which is out may insist that the economy is in a period of recession if not depression. Economists often suffer similar disagreement. And lastly, it must be pointed out that it is impossible to predict just when the economy will pass from the present phase to the next. In fact, it may be impossible to look backward and proclaim just when the economy passed from prosperity into recession or from depression into recovery. The student should not expect too much preciseness.

Why the Concern about the Business Cycle? The problem of the business cycle or level of employment and prices may well be considered as being one of the major problems facing the American people midway through the twentieth century. It is of such importance that Congress has passed a law in favor of full employment. The legislative branch of the government spends a great deal of its time investigating why the economy is not at full employment or what is being done to threaten the continuation of full employment. The Treasury is constantly concerned with the level of employment, as is the Federal Reserve System. So, most people would probably rank the maintenance of economic stability as one of the two major problems facing the country at the present time. Why is economic stability given such an extremely high ranking on our list of problem areas? The reasons are several.

Many of the harmful consequences associated with the business cycle are of a monetary nature. During the later phases of recovery and during prosperity and inflation, the value of money is depreciating. As the prices fall during a recession and depression, the value of money is increasing. In other words, a dollar buys less as prices increase, and it will buy more as prices fall. In this inverse relationship between prices and the value of money is to be found one of the more deleterious effects of the business cycle.

During a period of rising prices, several groups suffer from the depreciation in the value of money. Those who hold their assets in the form of money or near-money actually suffer from a decline in the value of their assets. Those saving in the form of money, life insurance, or bonds are adversely affected. A second group which suffers includes those who live on relatively fixed incomes. Pensioners, for example, may get a specified payment per month, and as prices increase, the pension decreases in value inasmuch as it will purchase less. There is a reduction in their real income. This category would include veterans, those receiving social security benefits, and the increasing number receiving retirement benefits from company retirement plans. A third group, which might actually be considered as part of the second, would include individuals whose incomes are not fixed but are relatively sticky in that their incomes do not increase as fast as the general price level. Public employees, white-collar workers, and teachers are in this category. A final group consists of creditors. If the general price level rises between the time the loan is made and the time of repayment, the creditor suffers a loss in principal, since the amount repaid will purchase less than the amount lent. This has been the position of those who purchased government bonds during World War II and then cashed the bonds a decade later. These persons loaned their savings to the government to fight World War II, but when the government repaid the loans, the principal plus the interest had less purchasing power than did the original principal.

On the downswing, or during the periods of recession and depression, prices are falling and money is becoming dearer. The purchasing power of money is increasing. It follows that those who lost during the period of rising prices now stand to gain. Creditors will be repaid in dearer money. Those living on fixed incomes will experience an increase in real income. Those with sticky incomes will not experience the same rapid decline in real income as will those with incomes which are not sticky. And those saving in the form of money or near-money will find that their savings are appreciating in value. But all of this depends upon one proviso. The source of income must not be destroyed or adjusted downward. The creditor will receive repayment in dearer money if the debtor does not default. Those with fixed or sticky incomes gain only if they keep their source of income. So as long as the fluctuations are minor in nature, any gains are largely offset by losses. But when the fluctuations become excessive, the assets of the creditors are destroyed during the upswing and the assets of the debtors are destroyed during the downswing of the cycle. It should be noted again, for emphasis, that it is the change in the price level which is damaging, for it is the changes in the value of the dollar which upset the relationship between the debtor and creditor. Stable prices would not do so regardless of the price level.

In addition to the above, which is essentially a monetary phenomenon, there are also nonmonetary aspects to the problem of depression. First, there is the problem of unemployment among the factors of production. It is possible for all factors to be unemployed, but it is common to speak only of labor and unemployment in the labor force. Unemployment in a highly industrialized and specialized economy is probably one of the greatest catastrophes which can occur in the life of a wage earner. Lack of adequate food and clothing, inability to provide educational opportunities for the wage earner's children, and marital stress and strain are only three of the more readily observable results of unemployment. The plight of this group is compounded by the fact that most wage earners are debtors, and a depression results in an inability to pay and a loss of property.

A third effect of a depression is to be found in the area of economic growth. The growth of any economy is similar to the growth of a savings account drawing compound interest. For such a saver, the interest for each period is added to the principal, and both accrued interest and principal draw interest in subsequent periods. If the depositor withdraws his savings for one year, the earnings for that period are reduced by the amount of interest he would have received. But more than that, future earnings will always be less, even though he redeposits the same amount which he withdrew.

Economic growth is, in large part, dependent upon the economy's accumulation of capital assets. It is estimated that the rate of capital accumulation for the United States has been approximately 3 per cent per year. In any year in which the rate of capital accumulation is less than 3 per cent, there will be both an immediate effect and a long-run effect. For that year, investment expenditures will be low and thus national income will be reduced. In the following years, when the rate of capital accumulation is normal, the actual amount of growth will be less than it would have been had there been no depression. So in addition to the immediate consequences of lower national income, there is the long-run consequence of a reduced rate of economic growth.

The above three propositions are only the most noticeable and significant aspects of the cyclical declines. There are other undesirable results, and there are facets of depression which are somewhat beneficial. But in totality, there can be little doubt that the consequences of cyclical fluctuations are such that there can be little question that stability, or at least a high degree of stability, is desirable. This value judgment serves as the basis for public policy in this field. The student might pause again at this point to ponder the propriety of this value judgment.

THE GOVERNMENT AND THE PROBLEM OF FULL EMPLOYMENT

No one, or practically no one, of responsibility would presently suggest that the government do nothing about the problem of the business cycle. In fact, the problem of what should be done about the level of employment and depression and inflation has been one of the nation's most important problems of a purely domestic nature for the past 25 years.

To be sure, there is disagreement about what policy the government should be following at a particular moment. But there is a general consensus that the government do something; there is an almost unanimous demand for the government to undertake some positive program to maintain a high level of employment and economic activity. What, then, can the government do to influence the level of employment and output? What can the government do about the problem of the business cycle?

Fiscal and Monetary Controls

After the Panic of 1907 the need for a central banking system empowered to exercise some control over the money supply was obvious. The result was the passage of the Federal Reserve Act of 1914. After the crash of 1929 and the Great Depression of the 1930's, it became evident that additional controls were needed. The result was the passage of the Banking Act of 1935. From World War I down to the present time, the Treasury Department and the Federal Reserve

System have assumed more and more responsibility for maintaining a high level of economic activity.

The powers which these two agencies have which can be used to achieve this end were explained in the preceding chapters, but it is necessary at this point to relate the powers possessed by the two agencies to the general problem of economic stability.

The Quantity Theory of Money: A Basis of Fiscal and Monetary Controls. A Frenchman by the name of Jean Bodin (1520–1596) was the first to clearly state the quantity theory of money. He observed that following the tremendous importation of gold and silver into the various countries of Europe there was a sharp increase in prices. He ascribed primary importance to the inflow of precious metals. From that time to this, economists have accepted the quantity theory of money, albeit with varying degrees of enthusiasm and qualifications. It can be used here with profit to explain the basis of fiscal and monetary controls.

In its simplest form the quantity theory of money is a tautology or truism, for it merely states that, for some time period, the amount of money multiplied by the number of times it is spent is equal to the amount of goods and services purchased multiplied by the price of those goods and services. If M represents the total supply of money, V the number of times the money is spent, P the general price level, and T the total amount of goods and services, then the relationship can be expressed in the following form:

$$MV = PT.$$

The equation can then be written so as to express price as a function of the other three variables. It would appear as:

$$P = MV/T.$$

In this form, the equation states that any increase in M or V or a decrease in T will result in price increases and vice versa. And if the changes in T should be the same as the changes in MV, there would be no changes in the price level. It must also be pointed out that there is a distinct possibility that the reaction will go from P to the other elements of the equation. For example, a change in prices might well induce a change in velocity, but this is probably a relatively unimportant phenomenon. Insofar as the student of the business cycle is concerned, the interesting problem is what will happen to the level of prices if either the supply of money (M) or the velocity of transactions (V) is changed.

The supply of money and the velocity with which it is spent are the more active elements in the equation. M consists of currency plus bank money. The supply of money is a function of the government and the banking system, and it is subject to control. But the same control cannot be exercised over the velocity. Insofar as T is concerned, much will depend upon the level of employment. During times of depression, T can be increased because of the existence of large amounts of unused resources, but during times of full employment, there can be little increase in T. This means that an increase in M or V is much more likely to cause price increases during times of full employment than the same increase in the two variables during a depression.

Any of the three variables, that is, M, V or $T,$ may cause changes in the price level. The sharp inflation following the conclusion of World War II was largely the result of increased velocity. In the case of the Korean War, there was a rather large increase in the quantity of money, which contributed to the inflation. During both wars there was a reduction in the goods and services available, but after World War II, the available goods and services were increasing. In this instance MV was increasing more than T. The result was rising prices.

The quantity theory of money can do much to explain changes in the price level, but for our purposes it is more important as a basis for understanding monetary and fiscal controls. It is, in effect, the theoretical basis for such controls. The Federal Reserve System and the Treasury regulate the money supply on the supposition that increases in the supply of money will tend to push prices upward, while decreases in the supply of money will have a restraining effect on prices.

Monetary Controls as a Determinant of Consumption and Investment Expenditures. In discussing the Federal Reserve System, it was mentioned that that banking system has the responsibility of promoting economic stability. In times of depression it uses its powers to promote recovery. In times of inflation or threatened inflation, it is to use its powers to curtail price increases. These powers include (1) changing the rediscount rate, (2) changing the reserve requirements for member banks and, (3) buying and selling in the open market. Let us first examine how these powers would be used in a period of inflation.

During such a period the quantity of money and the speed with which money changes hands will increase faster than productivity. People want to purchase more goods and services than are available. The result has to be higher prices. As a counterforce, the Federal Reserve authorities will take steps to reduce the supply of money. This will include raising the rediscount rate, raising reserve requirements, and selling securities in the open market.

Selling securities will reduce the reserves of member banks, and impair their lending position. If the banks are fully loaned out, that is, if there are no excess reserves, the banks will be forced to reduce their outstanding loans, liquidate other assets to increase reserves, or borrow from the Federal Reserve bank. If the member banks do have excess reserves, selling in the open market will reduce or eliminate such excess reserves. Under such a situation, the member banks may find it necessary to increase their reserves by borrowing from the Federal Reserve bank or rediscounting commercial paper. If the rediscount rate has been raised, this means that it will cost more for member banks to maintain their reserve position. Raising the rediscount rate in such a situation will reduce the member banks' willingness to make loans to borrowers. The total effect will be an upward pressure on interest rates and a reduction in consumer borrowing and investment. And finally, the Board of Governors may decide to raise the reserve requirements if those requirements are not already at the statutory maximum. This would further impair the lending position of the member banks, for now the same reserve would support a smaller amount of demand deposits.

During a period of recession and depression, monetary policy would be reversed. Reserve requirements would be lowered, the rediscount rate would be lowered, and the Federal Open Market Committee would purchase securities in the open market. All of these actions make money more readily available to the public at lower rates and thus promote spending and recovery.

Monetary controls are, however, less effective during a period of depression than during a period of inflation. The latter is a monetary phenomenon representing a desire to buy more than is available. By reducing the amount of money, the ability to buy is reduced, and thus there is a tendency to establish an equilibrium. But a depression is a real phenomenon in the sense that production is low, unemployment is high, and consumption and investment are low. To bring about recovery, it will be necessary to increase consumption and investment. Insofar as these activities are concerned, relaxation of monetary controls is only permissive, for making the money available does not mean that people will begin to spend. This makes it necessary to augment monetary controls with stronger measures if the government is to be successful in increasing the level of income. These more powerful antidepression tools are to be found in fiscal controls.

Fiscal Controls and Economic Stability. The monetary controls influence the level of consumption and investment expenditures in the equation $Y = C + I + G$. Fiscal controls influence both C and I, but they are also designed to change the value of G in an attempt to promote stability.

The word "fiscal" pertains to the operation of a public treasury. Thus when the fiscal operations of the government are referred to, reference is generally being made to raising and spending funds by the United States Treasury, although one can also refer to the fiscal operations of state and local governments. For purposes of economic stability, the latter can largely be ignored.

The fiscal operations of the government include (1) the raising of funds, and (2) the disposing of those funds by the government. Funds may be raised through (1) taxation or (2) borrowing, and the government may use its funds to (1) buy goods and services, (2) make transfer payments, or (3) retire debt.

All of these activities raise numerous policy questions. What type of taxes are best suited for the different phases of the business cycle? What portion of the revenues should be raised through taxing and what portion through borrowing? As for the borrowed portion, how much should be borrowed from banks and how much from nonbanks? Insofar as expenditures are concerned, there are also questions of policy. If the government has a choice, should it make transfer-type expenditures for which there are no current productive services, such as payments to veterans, or should it purchase goods and services? If debt is to be retired, which part of the debt should be retired, or does it make a difference?

Historically, the general attitude in this country has been that the government should spend only that amount of money necessary to provide the goods and services which the people could not provide in their private capacity. Using such an approach, it was decided how much was to be spent in a given year, and then sources of revenue were sought which would provide the necessary funds. The raising of funds was simply a means to an end. This viewpoint is changing. The government's fund-raising and spending operations have become so large and occupy such an important place in the total operations of the economy that they can and do affect the level of income. Changes in policy which result in more or less spending, more or less taxes, or a change in the debt will affect the total spending in the economy.

The first departure from the historical viewpoint is to be found in the idea of a cyclically balanced budget. Rather than balance the budget each year, proponents of this concept would balance the budget over the business cycle. During periods of depression the government would run a planned deficit, and during periods of prosperity or inflation the government would run a planned surplus. To accomplish this goal, government spending would be reduced and taxes either raised or maintained at a high level during the latter period, and the policies would be reversed during a period of depression. As a counterdepression measure, increased government expenditures would tend to raise income while lowered taxes would permit larger consumption and investment expenditures in the private sector of the economy. In times of higher incomes, high taxes would reduce consumption and investment expenditures and relieve inflationary pressure, as would reduced government expenditures.

With such a program there are a multitude of problems. First, there is the matter of financing the deficit during the depression. If the money is merely borrowed from the people and given back to the people, there will be no change in the total amount of expenditures unless the funds were borrowed from people who would not spend them for either consumption or investment. In other words, borrowing from the people and spending the money will only increase income if the funds are borrowed from those with a high marginal propensity to save and spent on those who have a high marginal propensity to consume. Or we might put it still a third way. Such government action will only increase income if the money is borrowed from groups holding large cash balances and spent on groups holding smaller cash balances.

A much greater expansionary effect will result if funds are borrowed from the Federal Reserve banks. Such an operation is equivalent to printing money. In this case there is no reduction in the private holding of money. There is, moreover, an increase in the private holding of money when the government spends the borrowed funds. And when the government does spend the money, there will eventually be an increase in the reserve position of the private banking system, which will permit a further expansion in private consumption and investment expenditures.

As far as taxes are concerned during a depression, the tax program should be such as to have a minimal depressing effect on private consumption and investment expenditures. An income tax, since it is based on income, will take a smaller percentage of private income during a period when incomes are low. Furthermore, since the income tax is a progressive tax, the tax rate on any individual's income will fall as income falls. Thus both the taxable base and the tax rate fall, and a smaller part of private income goes to the government. A sales tax will probably have a much more repressive effect on consumption expenditures. In contrast to the income tax, a sales tax is a more certain producer of revenue in a depression, and it was for this reason that it was advocated by some as a means of providing revenue for the national government during the depression of the 1930's. A sales tax cannot be classed as an effective antidepression tool.

The government may purchase goods or services, or it may make public assistance payments or other transfer-type payments. It is desirable that the government spend as much as possible for goods and services and as little as possible for transfer payments in times of depression. This is so because government purchases for goods and service have a larger multiplier than do transfer payments. So, a given expenditure for the former would result in a larger increase in income than would the same expenditure on the latter. Building a dam will have a greater expansionary effect than making payments to the poor.

In a period of prosperity, problems of a similar nature are to be found. If the government is taking in more tax revenue than it is spending for current operations, some decision must be made as to the disposition of the excess. If the funds are held in the form of government deposits in the Federal Reserve banks, there would be a reduction in private expenditures, since there is a reduction in both private demand deposits and member bank reserves. As a practical matter the government will not hold large amounts of money in this fashion while the country has a debt in excess of $300 billion. In practice, surpluses will be used to reduce the debt. The simple act of retiring the debt will put money in the hands of those who are holding the debt. In times of prosperity, it is preferable to retire that part of the debt which will do the least to increase spending. It is desirable to retire debt held by the Federal Reserve banks in preference to that held by commercial banks or nonbank investors, because the former will be neutral insofar as the effect on bank reserves and credit expansion is concerned. Such action is neither inflationary nor deflationary and would be preferred to those policies which would be inflationary in nature.

In the case of tax policy, it is desirable that a larger part of private incomes be taken by the government if the policy is one of preventing inflation. The income tax will automatically provide a larger tax take since both income (the tax base) and the tax rates will go up as incomes increase. But there is considerable doubt whether a graduated income tax can be of much use as an anti-inflationary measure. What may be needed in such a period is a tax which puts a penalty on spending (and a premium on saving) rather than a penalty on producing and earning. In addition, the tax will, of necessity, have to impose a heavy burden on the lower- and middle-income groups, which, in the aggregate, do the largest part of the nation's spending. A very good argument can be made for the imposition of a sales tax as an anti-inflationary tool.

In times of full employment, when inflation is a very real possibility, government spending should be reduced. However, it is here that economic theory runs into a formidable foe in the form of practical politics. Some spending, such as national defense, interest charges, and the like, cannot be varied in accordance with the level of income. Spending on such projects as roads, post offices, dams, and the like could be varied as income rose and fell, but the citizenry will not permit delaying the completion of a highway until income falls.

There are some expenditures which rise and fall on a counter-cyclical basis. These would include payments for unemployment insurance and public assistance payments. It would probably be desirable to have a larger part of the government expenditures vary countercyclically.

Direct Controls Employed by the Government

Most of the direct controls used by the government to promote economic stability were discussed as being among the powers of the Federal Reserve System. They will only be mentioned again at this point to indicate that the government has exercised such powers in the past and that there is always the possibility of using such controls again.

The direct controls exercised by the Federal Reserve System have included the establishment of margin requirements for trading in securities and the establishment of minimum down payments and maximum repayment periods for installment purchases. The government has controlled prices and wages through elaborate price control mechanisms. It has also allocated scarce materiel such as iron and steel. It has imposed extensive controls over labor, even going so far as to regulate the movement from one job to another. It has controlled production so as to curtail, or even stop, production of some goods. But all of these measures have been undertaken as an adjunct to the nation's war effort. Some were designed to reduce inflationary pressure, but most were designed solely to channel the nation's resources into the production of war goods.

Direct controls of this nature have been little utilized in the United States in dealing with the problem of the business cycle. From time to time, various individuals have proposed that the government adopt a peacetime program of price and wage controls as a means of combating inflation, but such proposals have received little sympathy. Most people seem to feel that slight fluctuations represent a more desirable alternative than an extensive program of governmental controls.

CONCLUSION

A high degree of short-run stability of employment and prices is generally considered to be desirable by both economists and laymen. Specifically, this means that the economic system should not be permitted to undergo periods of rising unemployment or rapidly increasing price levels. This is not to say that it should avoid long-run changes in the level of prices and employment. This chapter has only been concerned with cyclical fluctuations in the level of economic activity.

Controlling the level of economic activity is a problem that can only be handled on an aggregate basis. If everyone followed their own best interest, the result might well be a worsening of the situation—prices might go up further in the case of inflation, or unemployment might increase faster in a recession. There seems to be no alternative to government action, but there is a considerable degree of choice as to what kind of action should be undertaken by the government.

If nothing is done, all will have the maximum degree of freedom. Any program to achieve economic stability will, of necessity, restrict someone's freedom. If it doesn't, obviously nothing is being achieved.

That leaves us with two problems. What should be the goal? Are some slight fluctuations desirable, or should we strive for complete stability? Once the end is established, what type of controls offer the best chance of success? But the technique selected must be consistent with our social institutions—particularly freedom. Those who argue that freedom is so important that the government should do nothing should review the situation that existed in this country in 1932. Very few were making that argument then.

EXERCISES

Group I

Explain why the following statements are considered as being true.

1. The business cycle is only one of several different types of fluctuations or changes in the level of economic activity.
2. It is possible for an economic system to be at a full-employment level, yet there may still be changes in the level of prices.

3. A fully employed economy is more susceptible to inflation than is an economy which is less than fully employed.
4. It is possible that changes from one level of prices to another are more harmful than the maintenance of any given level by the economy.
5. Monetary controls are of a permissive nature rather than a coercive nature, and are therefore less effective during a depression than during inflation.
6. The attempts of the government to regulate the level of economic activity are based on the premise that there is a direct relationship between the quantity of money and the level of prices and economic activity.

Group II

1. What should the policy of the government be toward the problem of economic instability? That is, should we follow a policy which will promote a gradually rising level of prices, stable prices, fluctuating prices, or some other goal? Would the economist and the sociologist agree on which is the most desirable policy? Can the economist say which policy is the *best?*
2. Evaluate the argument that the progressive nature of certain taxes nips prosperity in the bud. That is, a small increase in the level of income will cause the income tax take to increase more than proportionately and thus curtail private expenditures.

Group III

1. Explain the dispute between the Treasury and the Federal Reserve System during the period immediately following World War II.
2. Write a report on the efficacy of automatic stabilizers.
3. Many people contend that labor unions are the cause of inflation. How do they arrive at this conclusion? Professor Walter Morton's article entitled "Trade Unionism, Full Employment and Inflation" (*American Economic Review,* March, 1950) is probably the best article on the subject and is a good starting place for the student in studying this particular problem.
4. Some have argued that running a governmental deficit will increase aggregate demand regardless of the nature of the expenditures made by the government. Others contend that running a deficit to finance space exploration will not get at the problem of structural unemployment. That is, the second group contends that greater attention needs to be given to the type of expenditures made by the government. And there is also the argument that expenditures for space-related research do not have the stimulating effect on the consumer sector of the economy that would result if the funds were channeled into research on consumer goods. Evaluate these arguments.

BIBLIOGRAPHY

AMERICAN ECONOMIC ASSOCIATION. *Readings in Business Cycle Theory.* Philadelphia: Blakiston, 1944.

DILLARD, DUDLEY. *The Economics of John Maynard Keynes.* New York: Prentice-Hall, Inc., 1948.

HART, ALBERT G. *Money, Debt, and Economic Activity.* New York: Prentice-Hall, Inc., 1948.

KURIHARA, KENNETH. *Monetary Theory and Public Policy.* New York: W. W. Norton & Co., 1950.

LERNER, ABBA P. *The Economics of Control.* New York: Macmillan Co., 1944.

PAPERBACK READING LIST

GALBRAITH, JOHN K. *The Great Crash, 1929.* Boston: Sentry Edition, 1961.

HABERLER, GOTTFRIED. *Prosperity and Depression.* New York: Atheneum, 1963.

SHANNON, D. (Ed). *The Great Depression.* New York: Prentice-Hall, Inc., 1960.

Chapter
16

THE ROLE OF THE GOVERNMENT IN THE ECONOMY

Why, if there is anything in supply and demand, life is the cheapest thing in the world. There is only so much water, so much earth, so much air; but the life that is demanding to be born is limitless. Nature is a spendthrift. Look at the fish and their millions of eggs. For that matter, look at you and me. In our loins are the possibilities of millions of lives. Could we but find time and opportunity and utilize the last bit and every bit of the unborn life that is in us, we could become the fathers of nations and populate continents. Life? Bah! It has no value. Of cheap things it is the cheapest. Everywhere it goes begging. Nature spills it out with a lavish hand. Where there is room for one life, she sows a thousand lives, and it's life eats life till the strongest and most piggish life is left.—Jack London, *The Sea Wolf.*

Few people in the United States might be classed as confirmed anarchists in the sense that they wish a complete absence of government. Likewise, few want the government to assume complete responsibility for every aspect of economic life. Yet the role of the government in the economy has been and continues to be a subject of great and bitter controversy. Unfortunately, economics and the social sciences in general have not been developed to the point where "correct" answers can be derived for questions of a normative nature such as, "What ought to be the role of government?" The most that can be hoped for is logical thinking based on a complete collection of facts and a thorough acquaintance with the historical background. The question of the role of government will then be decided by majority vote. The sounder the thinking underlying that collective decision, the better the chance that it will be the "correct" decision.

THE GOVERNMENT AS A REGULATOR OF ECONOMIC ACTIVITY

It is probably in its role as a regulator of economic activity that the government has been the recipient of the most criticism. No one likes to be told what can or cannot be done, although regulating someone else is not so odious. There has to be, moreover, a minimum amount of regulation, for that is the purpose of government. People cannot live together without each giving up certain rights in the interests of the whole. What, then, is proper regulation and what is improper regulation? Possibly a brief examination of the existing regulatory programs will assist in answering these questions.

Antitrust Legislation and the Regulation of Business

The Genesis of Antitrust Legislation. The period following the Civil War was one of the most fascinating in American history.

It saw the rise of a highly industrialized economy. It gave birth to the modern labor union movement. It was the day of the robber baron, the muckraker, railroad scandals, and the "shame of the cities."[1] The philosophy of *laissez faire* was being proclaimed as *the* economic philosophy at the very time that system of belief was being buried for all time. Andrew Carnegie, espousing a doctrine which has come to be known as Social Darwinism, held that the strong would succeed and the weak would fall by the wayside through the competitive process. President Grover Cleveland, in vetoing a bill which would have provided $25,000 for aiding drought-stricken farmers, proclaimed that "It was the business of the people to support the government and not the business of the government to support the people." It was out of such a period that the antitrust laws were conceived and enacted.

There were individuals who gave lip service to the philosophy of *laissez faire* but were unwilling to accept it in its entirety. According to them, the government's role as a regulator should be held to a minimum, but they were unwilling to rely upon competition. Competition was wasteful. It was to be eliminated as expeditiously as possible. J. P. Morgan successfully eliminated competition within the steel industry when he organized the United States Steel Corporation. He performed the same service for such industries as railroads and ocean shipping. John D. Rockefeller successfully eliminated competition in oil with the organization of the Standard Oil Trust. Andrew Mellon established a monopoly in the field of aluminum which lasted for half a century. The tobacco industry was dominated by the Consolidated Tobacco Company which controlled practically all of the output. The American Sugar Refining Company produced 90 per cent of the total output of sugar. Other industrial giants exercised a similar degree of control in such fields as powder, whiskey, cottonseed oil, lead, and others. It was in this manner that competition, the cornerstone of *laissez faire,* was laid to rest.

The three forms of business organization commonly used to eliminate competition were the pool, the trust, and the holding company. A pool was an organization of independent producers in which each gave up part of its general freedom to operate the business. In the area in which the managerial prerogative was surrendered, the pool made the decisions for the entire industry. This included such activities as pricing, market allocation, production quotas, etc. The pool was an informal association with little power over the members. If it could be

---

[1] Lincoln Steffens, *The Shame of the Cities* (New York: McClure, Phillips & Co., 1904; reprinted by Sagamore Press, 1957).

proven that a pool existed, it was also contrary to the common law. For these reasons the pool was never extremely popular or widely employed.

The trust issued trust certificates for the stock certificates which the owners of the various corporations surrendered to the trustees. The trust certificates, instead of indicating ownership of a single company, would indicate an interest in the companies in the trust. The trustees made the decisions for all companies in the trust, and the holders of the trust certificates received a return based on the profits of all companies. The most famous trust was the Standard Oil Trust of Rockefeller which was dissolved in 1901 under the common law of the state of Ohio.

The holding company became possible when New Jersey amended its corporation laws to permit one corporation to hold stock in another for purposes of control. Through the use of the holding company device, a person with a very small investment could control vast industrial enterprises. Mr. Rockefeller was quick to see the advantages of such an organization, and he reorganized the Standard Oil Company as a holding company several years after the dissolution of the trust. Probably the most elaborate holding company ever organized was that of Samuel Insull, which was reputed to have been so complicated that even Mr. Insull was not completely certain of the organizational structure.

As it became obvious that competition was fast disappearing and could no longer perform its assigned role, the demand for government regulation of business combinations became widespread. The clamor for such regulation was so general that both political parties included planks in their platforms calling for regulation of the "trusts." In 1890 both parties combined to pass the Sherman Act.

The Sherman Act. In its totality, the Sherman Act is an extremely short statute with its substantive provisions being contained in the first two sections of the law.

Section 1. Every contract, combination in the form of trust or otherwise, or conspiracy in restraint of trade or commerce among the several States, or with foreign nations, is hereby declared to be illegal. Every person who shall make such a contract or engage in any such combination or conspiracy shall be deemed guilty of a misdemeanor.

Section 2. Every person who shall monopolize, or attempt to monopolize, or combine or conspire with any other person or persons, to monopolize any part of the trade or commerce among the several States, or with foreign nations, shall be deemed guilty of a misdemeanor.

The punitive provisions of the law provided for fines, imprisonment, injunctions, and triple damages to the injured party. As far as the substantive provisions of the law were concerned, there was nothing new in the statute. It merely adopted the common-law doctrines of restraint of trade, conspiracy, and monopolization. However, instead of such agreements merely being declared void, they were now crimes and punishable at law. The law was thus intended to cope with existing restraints and monopolies by declaring them to be contrary to public policy and illegal. It was remedial rather than preventive.

The next quarter century seemed to indicate the Sherman Act possessed few remedial powers. Business continued to get bigger. The nefarious practices went unhindered. In the first major court test of the statute, the Knight Sugar Company case, the Supreme Court held in 1895 that the American Sugar Refining Company was not a monopoly although it controlled 98 per cent of the country's sugar refining capacity. In 1904 the Supreme Court held that a holding company involving the Northern Pacific and Great Northern railroads was an illegal combination. In 1911 the Court held in the American Tobacco and Standard Oil cases that only those combinations which unreasonably restrained trade contravened the law. The 1911 cases accepted the common-law doctrine that those restraints which were ancillary to the main contract were permissible, but those contracts in which the restraint was the major provision were to come under the ban of the law. It must be pointed out that the companies involved in the 1911 cases were broken up.

By 1912 many people had come to the conclusion that the Sherman Act was a failure in spite of vigorous prosecution under Presidents Roosevelt and Taft. In that year Woodrow Wilson was elected President of the United States with the aid of a split in the Republican party. His program included legislation designed to curb the unfair competitive practices of business which, it was felt, were the cause of the continued growth in the size of business units.

Antitrust Legislation of 1914. The Federal Trade Commission Act created the Federal Trade Commission (FTC) and charged that three-man commission with the enforcement of the 1914 legislation. The FTC Act also stated that "unfair methods in commerce" were illegal, but just what constituted such unfair methods was to be left to the FTC to spell out. The law was amended in 1938 to provide that any unfair or deceptive acts were illegal, for up to that time there was actually no protection for the consumer under the law. In addition it has been supplemented by legislation requiring the proper labeling of wool and fur products, as well as by a statute which makes it illegal to manufacture clothing out of flammable material.

The Federal Trade Commission has been most active and successful in the area of misrepresentation. In various cases it has held that businesses cannot misrepresent the origin of the commodity, the nature or usefulness of the good, the price of the product, or the nature of the producer's business. An important part of the program against misrepresentation is that of curbing false or misleading advertising. The FTC continues to exercise vigilant control over the practices of the country's business firms.

The Clayton Act of 1914 was more specific, for it listed certain practices which were illegal. It made the acquisition of stock for purposes of control illegal where the effect was to lessen competition. This section was amended in 1950 to include the acquisition of assets. The Clayton Act also made it illegal for a single individual to serve as a member of different boards of directors where the effect was to lessen competition. It was likewise illegal for a producer to require a distributor to handle a less desirable line of merchandise in order to get the more desirable. Nor could a producer require the distributor to handle only his line. It was also illegal to charge different prices to distributors except where the differences were based on quantity. In 1936 the Robinson-Patman Act amended this section to require that any differences based on quantity actually represent differences in the cost of handling.

The above activities were thought to be major causes of the continued growth of business. That is, it was thought that business was getting big through undesirable means rather than through economic efficiency. The 1914 statutes were designed to curb future growth by such means. They were, in contrast to the Sherman Act, preventive rather than remedial.

Since the first antitrust statute was passed, a fairly comprehensive list of actions which constitute restraint of trade has been compiled. Professor Corwin Edwards[2] listed the following general categories of restraint which are probably illegal: agreements to exclude competitors from the market, agreements to restrict output, agreements dividing markets or purchases, agreements to fix prices, agreements to eliminate opportunity or incentive to compete, and agreements involving coercion.

Regarding the question of monopoly as a violation of the antitrust statutes, there is no such comprehensive listing. Until recently there has been little success in attempting to enforce the statutory provisions against monopoly. The Knight Sugar Company case has already been

---

[2] Corwin D. Edwards, *Maintaining Competition: Requisites of a Governmental Policy.* (New York: McGraw-Hill Book Co., Inc., 1949), pp. 41–42.

cited. U.S. Steel was found not to be a monopoly in 1921, although it had controlled about two thirds of the nation's steel capacity at the time of its founding. In 1927 International Harvester was found not to possess a monopoly on farm equipment, although it had controlled 85 per cent of the industry at the time of its organization. In both of the above cases a smaller percentage was controlled at the time of the trials, although both were the dominant firms in their fields. Following World War II the courts held that monopolization, per se, was a violation of the antitrust statutes. In the aluminum case the court held that since the Aluminum Company of America produced 90 per cent of the virgin aluminum ingots in this country, it was a monopoly. It was to be broken up, but the court order was not be be enforced until the government had disposed of the aluminum reduction facilities built during World War II. In selling these facilities, Kaiser and Reynolds were given preference over ALCOA. The result was an industry of three firms rather than a single firm. ALCOA did have to sever its ties with its Canadian affiliate—Aluminium Limited. Since the aluminum case, there have been other cases in which monopolization as such has been declared illegal. Nevertheless, there is no clear-cut doctrine here as there is in the case of restraints of trade and unfair trade practices. The most progress has been made in the latter fields.

Exceptions to the Antitrust Laws. If the antitrust laws were religiously enforced, the result would be a fair degree of competition. Competition, however, is a very severe taskmaster, so once such statutes are on the books, many groups seek exemption from their enforcement. The following is not an all-inclusive listing of such exempted areas, but it does represent the major exclusions.

a) Labor was the first to seek exemption, and this group was successful in 1914. The Sherman Act had actually been used more effectively against labor unions than against business combinations. Labor leaders went to jail whereas business leaders never did so. As a result of subsequent court decisions, labor's exemption was short-lived, but in the early 1930's the exemption became permanent.

b) Those businesses engaged in foreign trade were permitted to form associations to conduct foreign trade without violating the antitrust laws after the passage of the Webb-Pomerene Amendment of 1916. These firms were generally competing against international cartels, and they argued that they should be permitted to form domestic associations in order that they might compete more effectively.

c) Agricultural co-operatives were exempted in 1922 and 1926. Those engaged in agriculture are permitted to organize co-operatives and then process and market their product on a collective basis. Since 1933 the Secretary of Agriculture has been permitted to enter into agreements with farmers restricting output without such agreements being in conflict with the antitrust laws.

d) In 1937 the Miller-Tydings Act was passed, which permitted the states to pass resale price maintenance laws. Under such laws the producer of a product can enter into an agreement with a single retailer which stipulates the retail price of that commodity. The price then binds every retail seller of that product, and if some individual sold it at some other price, the law would be violated. Of late several state courts have held that the nonsigner clause is unconstitutional, but the question of resale price maintenance continues to be one of the more controversial aspects of antitrust policy.

e) Patents are granted by the government to promote technological development. A patent grants the inventor a monopoly of the product or process, and he has the sole right to develop and exploit that patent. For many years this was regarded as an unlimited right not to be fettered by the antitrust laws. Of late courts have been willing to restrict the rights of the patent holder if it is evident that the patent is being used for purposes which are not compatible with antitrust policy.

f) Others which are exempt include fisheries co-operatives, transportation agencies, insurance companies until 1944, producers of hog cholera serum, and some of the regulated industries.

Summary. It is impossible to state that the antitrust laws have been a success. In the first place there has been more lip service than there has been financial support, and the laws are not self-enforcing. Secondly, there is no general agreement as to just what should be accomplished. As long as the people don't know just what is desired, there can be no eminently successful policy.

The Regulation of Public Utilities

There have always been certain businesses which have been considered to be peculiarly affected with the public interest. First, they offer a product or service which the public must have and for which there is no adequate substitute. Secondly, the nature of the business is such that a single firm can provide the service more efficiently than could a number of competing firms. Such firms are classed as public utilities and provide such goods and services as gas, electricity, water and transportation. Because of the nature of the product and the disadvantages of competition, society must select one of two alternatives—public ownership or private ownership with public regulation. Private ownership under regulation has generally been the accepted policy in the United States, but other countries have placed greater reliance upon public ownership.

Professor Eli Clemens[3] has stated that a public utility has (1) the duty to serve all comers, (2) the duty to render adequate service, (3) the duty to serve at a reasonable rate, and (4) the duty to serve without discrimination. Since the forces of competition are not present to insure the fulfillment of such duties, government regulation is undertaken with that goal in mind. Public utility commissions regulate the prices charged by the utility. Changes in rates or services rendered by the utility must first receive governmental approval. The regulating agency may require the firm to install additional equipment or provide additional service. If it is felt that the utility does not and will not provide adequate service, the regulating body may revoke the company's charter. Within the limits of public regulation the manager is free to make the decisions regarding the operation of his company. This is one solution to the problem of natural monopolies in public utilities.

Business firms of this nature have always been regulated. Until approximately 1840 such regulation was accomplished by the legislatures of the various states. That legislature would grant the company a charter in which the prices would be listed for the various services the firm was to render. Such regulation was rather awkward, and regulation by legislation was replaced by regulatory commissions. The legislature creates the public utility commission, and that commission is charged with the day-to-day regulation of the public utilities of the state. Although there are variations from one state to another, it can be said that in most of the states public utility commissions regulate those firms providing electricity, manufactured gas, street railways, interurban railways, motor buses, water, telephone, and telegraph.

The national government has also adopted the commission type of regulation in dealing with those public utilities which provide services on an interstate basis. Congress passed the Interstate Commerce Commission Act (1887) which gave the Interstate Commerce Commission control over interstate railroads. At the present time practically all regulation of railroads is vested in this group. In addition it regulates truckers, domestic water carriers, and pipelines. The Federal Aviation Agency which succeeded the Civil Aeronautics Authority in 1959 regulates air transportation, and the Maritime Commission regulates shipping in foreign commerce.

[3] Eli W. Clemens, *Economics and Public Utilities* (New York: Appleton-Century-Crofts, 1950), p. 10.

Since a great deal of electrical power is transported in interstate commerce and since the national government has jurisdiction over the nation's navigable streams, that government also regulates power companies. The Federal Power Commission (1920) licenses construction of hydroelectric projects. Since 1935 the FPC has exercised close control over rates, accounting procedures, issuance of securities, etc. In 1938 its powers were extended to the transportation of natural gas.

The Federal Communications Commission (1934) regulates firms providing interstate service in the fields of wire and radio communication, including television. It controls the rates charged as well as the service, and it exercises rather detailed control over accounting procedures.

The regulation of public utilities, in summary, is generally designed to protect the consumer; however, regulating agencies must also consider the well-being of the producing firm. Rates cannot be allowed to go too high, yet they must be high enough to provide a satisfactory return on invested capital. This means that the ICC and other regulatory commissions must balance the interests of consumers against the interests of the regulated enterprise. The alternative to private ownership and public regulation is public ownership.

Other Regulatory Activities of Government

Antitrust legislation and supervision of public utilities are only two of many regulatory activities of government. Other examples of regulation by all levels of government can only be listed. The Securities and Exchange Commission regulates the sale and issuance of corporate securities. Packers and stockyards are regulated. The Treasury Department supervises the use of gold. The production of alcohol is closely controlled. The exportation of domestically produced goods is supervised by several agencies. The banking system is regulated by both state and national government. The extensive regulation of labor and labor relations has been discussed in an earlier chapter. Then, in addition to all of the above, there are the practically unlimited regulatory powers which the national government acquires during time of war.

At the state and local level, one finds another imposing list of governmental regulatory activities. Various states have commissions which regulate industries other than public utilities—dry cleaners, milk, oil and gas, and beauticians—to name a few. In addition, the state and local governments in their exercise of the police power enact zoning laws; Sunday blue laws; licensing laws; inspection laws; laws regulating special businesses such as places of amusement, slot machines, fortunetelling, and production of drugs; and many others. Government at all levels regulates economic activity.

Summary

Regulation of economic activity is of two types. The first includes those programs designed to maintain competition, and the second is designed to eliminate competition and substitute governmental controls for competition as a protection for the consumer. A perverted type of regulation, which is becoming more common, is that which eliminates competition in fields in which competition would function quite satisfactorily. Competition can only be eliminated if a satisfactory substitute is available. Any successful regulatory policy must carefully differentiate between those economic areas in which competition is desirable and those in which monopoly is desirable. The solution which is applicable to the first will not do for the second, just as the reverse is true.

THE GOVERNMENT AS A SUPPORTER OF SPECIAL GROUPS

No matter what the government does, it will help one group more than another. But all governments have, at various times, purposely set out to help particular groups at the expense of all others. Early colonial governments in this country subsidized salt works. Early state governments subsidized canals and railroads. For the past 100 years, the national government has actively subsidized many groups. The government's role as a subsidizer of special groups is a well-established role and a role that is probably not to be abandoned.

Aid to Agriculture

Among the several economic sectors, aid to agriculture has probably received more attention than any of the subsidizing activities of the national government. Agricultural subsidies have a very long history. The colonies and the English government assisted colonial agriculture. For many years the United States government either gave farmers land or sold it to them very cheaply. Agricultural colleges were established with the aid of federal funds at the time of the Civil War. Extensive credit facilities have been made available to farmers. Electricity was brought to many American farms through governmental action. In short, there has seldom been a time when agriculture was not receiving some form of aid from the government. However, after World War I the situation changed, and by the 1930's a new, and what appears to be a permanent, change in the country's agriculture policy was brought about.

The Economics of Agriculture—Briefly. Agriculture fairly well approximates the economist's concept of the competitive market, or at least it did prior to present governmental interference in the determination of farm prices. There are a large number of farmers selling products which are, in the most part, fairly homogeneous. Agricultural income is quite unequally distributed, so that even in times of prosperity many farmers have comparatively low incomes. Thus the withholding power of farmers is very low, even if the commodity is capable of being withheld from the market. The combination of the two—a large number of farmers and limited withholding power—means that the farmers will have little or no control over the price of the product which they produce. It is produced. It is sold at the market price. The product cannot be withheld to force the price upward.

The demand for agricultural products is rather singular in nature. The consumers of farm products will only change their consumption very slightly in response to changes in incomes or changes in prices. If personal incomes increase, consumers will save more or spend it on items other than food. A reduction in agricultural prices will not materially increase the consumption of those goods. As far as the supply is concerned, however, a reduction in agricultural prices may actually result in an increased supply, as the farmers seek to maintain their income through increased production. This only increases the downward pressure on agricultural prices. The net result is a tremendous fluctuation in farm prices as compared to comparatively small fluctuations in nonagricultural prices. As the prices of the goods which the farmers sell have gone down precipitously, the prices of the items which the farmers buy have declined very slightly if at all. Farm prices have been among the first to start falling and among the first to start up. They go down further and up further than nonagricultural prices. During periods when prices have gone up, the farmer historically has gone into debt to buy more land and equipment. During the ensuing depression, farmers have been hard pressed to repay their indebtedness. The position of the farmer as a debtor plus the realization that farm prices are extremely erratic account for the fact that the farm interests have been in the forefront of most cheap money and antimonopoly movements in this country. America's farmers have never been reluctant to turn to the government in an attempt to alleviate their peculiar economic position.

Prior to World War I the farmer's position in the economy was fairly satisfactory. The United States had been a debtor nation since its founding, and the output of the nation's farms had served as a means of meeting that debt. Agriculture was the major export industry of this country, and as long as the United States owed money to the rest of the world, agriculture could not suffer too much. After World War I, however, the United States became a creditor nation—the rest of the world owed money to the United States. Instead of buying our wheat and cotton, foreign nations now sought to sell goods and services to the United States in order to satisfy their obligations. As they sought markets in this country, Congress raised the tariff rates to keep foreign goods out of this country. This only accentuated the plight of the farmers.

In 1920–1921, the entire country suffered a very sharp depression, but for all except agriculture the recovery which followed was just as sharp. American agriculture was in a depressed condition from World War I until World War II. The Great Depression of the 1930's, which was new to most, was merely an intensification of an existing situation for the nation's farmers.

Political Attempts to Solve an Economic Problem. It was during the normal 1920's that the agricultural interests began pressing for governmental assistance in a drastically revised form. First the Republicans and then the Democrats recognized this demand of the farmers. Today both parties agree that the peculiar position of the farmer in today's economic system, in addition to his peculiar political position, make him eligible for governmental assistance.

The Republican Program of 1929. During the Republican administrations of Presidents Harding, Coolidge, and Hoover, five McNary-Haugen bills were introduced to alleviate agricultural suffering through governmental support of farm prices. None became law. In 1929 Congress passed, and President Hoover signed, the Agricultural Marketing Act. It created the Federal Farm Board which was authorized to spend up to $500 million to purchase farm commodities in an effort to support these prices. By 1931 it had spent nearly all of its appropriation for wheat and cotton, and the prices of both had continued to fall. In that year the board discontinued its operations. It started to sell its accumulated stocks and forced prices down further. In the end most of the board's accumulated stores were given to the Red Cross, which distributed them in China. The cost to the American taxpayer was in the neighborhood of $400 million. The program was a failure since no provisions were made for controlling production. It will always be impossible to support the price of any commodity if that commodity can be produced in unlimited quantities.

The New Deal Program for Agriculture. The several programs of the Democrats and Secretary of Agriculture Henry Wallace all involved restricting output in order to increase prices. The Agricultural Adjustment Act (1933) permitted the Secretary of Agriculture to enter into agreements with farmers in which the latter would agree to restrict their output of seven basic agricultural commodities. For restricting their output, they were to receive payments from the government. As a result of the early New Deal crop restriction policies, there were some increases in agricultural prices, but more credit should probably be given the Great Drought which accompanied the Great Depression. In 1936 this first AAA was declared to be unconstitutional on the grounds that there was an improper delegation of powers as well as an improper use of the taxing power.

The first farm program was quickly replaced with a second, embodied in the Soil Conservation and Domestic Allotment Act of 1936. The Great Drought had brought to light many poor agricultural practices and had made evident the need for improved conservation practices. Under the 1936 legislation the farmer was encouraged to take land out of production and put it in some form of conservation program. For planting trees, fertilizing, terracing, plowing under cover crops, deep plowing, etc., the farmer was to receive payments from the Treasury. Also included in this program was a new concept—that of parity. Parity relates the purchasing power of things which farmers sell to those which farmers buy. It was the intention to maintain agricultural prices in the same position relative to nonagricultural prices as that which prevailed in some base period. By doing so, the farmer could buy the same amount with a bushel of wheat, for example. If the prices of other commodities rose, the price of wheat would be raised to that point where it could once again buy the same amount as during the base period. Now, once parity was determined, the question arose as to whether the price should be supported at 100 per cent of parity or something less—say 90 per cent. Most often, agricultural prices have been supported at 90 per cent of parity, but in some instances the support prices have been permitted to drop much below that figure.

The price support mechanism has generally operated as follows. Once the farmer harvests the wheat, or other nonperishable crop, he can either sell the wheat or borrow from the government at the support price. If the market price should be $1.85 and the government is supporting the price at $1.80, he would obviously sell the wheat in the open market. If, however, the price of wheat in the free market is only $1.75, the farmer could borrow $1.80 (interest free) from the government for each bushel put up as collateral. If during the following months the price of wheat should go above $1.80, the farmer could sell the wheat and repay the government loan. If, on the other hand, the price of wheat should continue below the support price, the farmer would not repay the loan but would permit the government to take possession of the wheat. In this fashion, the government has come into possession of vast quantities of farm products.

A second method of supporting prices is used for the perishable commodities. Under the commodity purchase plan the government enters the market and buys the commodity in question at a price which is supposed to maintain the level of farm prices at some predetermined percentage of parity. Under this program the government has become the owner of large quantities of butter, cheese, eggs, etc. The disposal of these surpluses has proven to be a most vexing question.

When World War II broke out, the farm program combined three elements—soil conservation payments, parity payments, and payments for restriction of output. World War II brought prosperity to agriculture. Now, rather than for restricting output, the demand was for unlimited agricultural production. Rather than depressed prices, the concern was now over skyrocketing agricultural prices which would push up consumer prices. The government imposed price ceilings and the net result was that agriculture had both a minimum and maximum price established by the government. For once, there was no problem of surplus commodities. In those rare instances in which the government did buy farm commodities, there was no problem of disposal. However, there was the problem of encouraging production without permitting prices to go up. This problem was solved by the introduction of the direct farm subsidy. The farmer received a price for his output which was set by the government. Then, the government, in order to encourage him to produce more, gave him a direct payment—a subsidy. Thus the consumer was protected from higher prices, and the producer was assured a greater income.

Like so many wartime measures, this one was not completely discarded when peace was restored.

Republican Postwar Agricultural Programs. In 1948 the Republican-controlled 80th Congress gave that party its first chance in nearly 20 years to write a piece of agricultural legislation. There were no radical reforms; instead the general policy of the preceding twenty years was continued. There were only minor changes in the method of computing the parity price, but even those changes were inserted only to make the law more favorable to agricultural interests.

In 1954 President Eisenhower and Secretary of Agriculture Ezra Taft Benson were ready to make some rather far-reaching changes in the agricultural support program. Until that time the prices of the basic commodities had been supported for the most part at a rigid 90 per cent of parity. The Republicans announced that they were going to abandon the program of rigid price supports for one of flexible supports. The Secretary of Agriculture was to be empowered to raise or lower the support price as conditions dictated. If there were a surplus, the support price would be lowered to discourage further production. If there were a shortage, the support price would be raised to encourage production. The bill as passed was not as revolutionary as its backers had originally proposed since the support price was permitted to vary from 82½ to 90 per cent of parity. And the restrictions that Mr. Benson had originally planned for land taken out of production were considerably revised before the election in 1954. In 1958, supports were lowered for some crops and controls were relaxed.

Whether the legislation of 1954 was a causal factor in the agricultural depression of that year can be debated. Nevertheless, many farm voters and politicians were willing to give it credit. By 1956 politicians of both parties agreed that something must be done to aid agriculture and that it must be done before the elections in November. The first bill was vetoed by the President. The second, which became law, embodied the "Soil Bank Plan" which looked very much like the early New Deal programs. Under this plan the farmer was to take land out of cultivation and plant trees, grass, or other crops which were not to be sold. For this, the farmer received a check from the government. It was intended to reduce production because of the smaller acreage under cultivation and increase the soil resources of the nation. The long-run effect may be just the reverse, for the conservation practices may actually increase production in the future. Unless the use of the land is carefully and extensively controlled, the program may merely change the nature of the surpluses rather than reduce them.

During the quarter century under review, there was a single agricultural program which raised more controversy than any other, although it never became law. It was the famous (or infamous) Brannan Plan.

The Brannan Plan.   President Truman's Secretary of Agriculture, Charles Brannan, advanced an agricultural program which was drastically different from those that had gone before or those that followed. It would have abandoned direct price supports. It was designed to aid the small farmer who supported it. Everyone else opposed it.

The essence of the Brannan plan can be explained in a few words. It would have permitted the prices of agricultural commodities to seek their own level rather than being pegged at an artificially high level. The farmer's income would be maintained by giving him a subsidy payment to make up the difference between what he got in the market for his crop and what was needed to allow him a predetermined level of income. In order to be eligible for payments, the farmer would have to follow sound conservation policies and abide by stringent limitations on output. Payments would have been limited. A small farmer might have had his entire crop supported while the large farmer might have received little aid.

The program was almost universally condemned because it was supposed to be a step toward "socialism" if not the final one toward the state-controlled society. Oddly enough, however, the principle of the Brannan Plan was embodied in the Republican farm legislation of 1954. Wool was to be sold at its market price and then the government would make a subsidy payment to the wool producers. The same type of program was adopted in 1962 for lead and zinc.

The Wheat Plan of 1963. The problem of huge stocks of agricultural surpluses plagued the Kennedy administration as it had the two preceding administrations. In 1963, the administration proposed a new wheat law which would have continued the high price supports but would have required the farmers to submit to tighter controls. The farmers rejected this proposal, and as it stands now, the farmer will be free to plant as much as he likes in 1964 but he will not be guaranteed any minimum price. If he agrees to restrict output, the price will be supported at 50 per cent of parity or just over $1.00 per bushel.

At the time of writing, it appears that a free market may operate in the case of wheat. If such an event should occur, the student might consider the following questions. How much did the price of wheat fall between the summer of 1963 and the summer of 1964? How much did the price of bread fall? Why didn't the price of bread fall by a larger percentage? What happened to the production of wheat? Did the method of production change—that is, did the farmers substitute one factor for another? What was the change in the size distribution of farms; that is, did the small farms tend to disappear while the large farms increased in number? And, finally, how will the problem of rural poverty be handled in the wheat areas if a free market price replaces the governmentally established support price?

Concluding Observations. After nearly 30 years of agricultural programs, what can be said of the government's attempt to support a particular segment of the economy?

On an economic basis there can be little justification of a governmental program which maintains prices at an artificially high level. By arbitrarily repealing the price system, the government promotes an uneconomic allocation of resources. As it applies to agriculture, the governmental programs have undoubtedly kept too large a proportion of the country's resources in that industry. Some people would also contend that such a program in agriculture is necessary for general prosperity. This is not necessarily so. In the 1920's and the 1950's general prosperity was not accompanied by agricultural prosperity.

It is much easier to justify an agricultural subsidization program on a sociological basis. Farming is a way of life. Farm ownership, like private ownership of property in general, is a desideratum. A stable farm class contributes highly desirable middle-class values to any society. Thus the sociologist may be much more able to justify the farm program than can the economist.

On political grounds all politicians agree that something must be done to aid agriculture, and their concern varies directly with the proximity of the next election. In nearly all state legislatures and in the United States Senate the farmers are overrepresented. In many key states the farm vote means the difference between political success and political defeat. Politicians will always want to do something for farmers.

The programs of both Republicans and Democrats since 1929 have demonstrated a single incontrovertible principle. If the government is to support the income position of the farmer, the cost to the farmer is an extensive system of governmental controls. The government cannot tell the farmer that it, the government, is ready to buy all that agriculture can produce.

Since controls are the cost of price supports, what type of controls probably offer the greatest chance of success? To date, controls on production have largely been acreage controls. Limiting the acres planted has never prevented an accumulation of surpluses since the farmers usually set aside their poorer land and worked the remaining land much more intensively. At the same time other divisions of the government have been working to increase agricultural production through experimentation, agricultural education, irrigation projects, production of fertilizer, and other such programs. The chances are very good that the government will eventually be forced to limit the amount which farmers can market.

The farmer is at a disadvantage economically since he operates in a very competitive field as a seller, but as a buyer he operates in a noncompetitive field. If his bargaining power is to be enhanced to match that of other sectors of the economy such as labor and business, it will probably have to be done through governmental action. The farmer today feels that he is only beginning to enjoy what other groups have enjoyed for years. The farmer can hardly be expected to compete unless all other groups are forced to do likewise.

Aid to Business

Nearly all governments have subsidized business with the intention of developing an economy which would support a larger population at a higher level of living. All levels of government have done so in the United States, starting with the colonial governments and ending with the present national government. With the exception of the tariff, which has always been a major aid to business in the United States, and is discussed elsewhere, the major aid programs are listed below.

Aid to Transportation. The development of an adequate transportation system has always constituted a major problem in the economic development of a country with a large land mass. In some the problem was solved by the government building the transportation system. In others, such as the United States, the major part of the transportation system was built by private enterprise with the government subsidizing the private firms.

Railroads. Prior to the Civil War, the state governments either supported private enterprise in building railroads or the state government undertook the project itself. During and following that war, these small intrastate systems were consolidated into the present large interstate systems. In addition, it became politically feasible to build transcontinental systems. In this period railroads were the recipients of tremendous subsidies from the national government in addition to subsidies from state and local governments. Proposals for aid to railroads are again being given serious consideration.

Trucking. The trucking industry has benefited directly from the large expenditures made on the nation's highway system. The industry does pay taxes which contribute to that construction, but there is some question as to whether it pays its full share.

Merchant Marine. A strong merchant marine has always been considered a necessity for national defense. For that reason the government has always subsidized this industry. Congress very early required that coastal shipping be carried in American bottoms. From time to time it has been required that certain goods shipped abroad be carried in American ships. Construction subsidies have been granted as well as operating subsidies. The government has likewise subsidized the industry by maintaining inland waterways and harbor and dock facilities.

Airlines. This newest of the transportation agencies has not been absent when public subsidies are being paid. Until recently all airlines have received operating subsidies, although at the present only the feeder lines do. All receive a subsidy, however, since the government builds and maintains the airport facilities as well as an extensive system of navigational aids. The United States government is committed to subsidize the development of a supersonic commercial aircraft by providing 75 per cent (or more) of the cost of development.

Other Subsidizing Activities of Government. Although other examples are not as spectacular as the subsidizing programs in agriculture and transportation, they are of significance in illustrating the general principle. Newspapers and periodicals mailed in the county of their publication are carried free by the post office. Magazines do not bear all of the cost of their mailing. The same is true of advertising. Patents, copyrights, and trade-marks confer important benefits upon business. Various governmental agencies engage in statistical research and reporting, which is of immense aid to business. Mining industries and the oil industry are allowed depletion allowances, which reduces their tax bill considerably. This is supposed to encourage exploration for new sources of ore and petroleum. Some business firms are allowed to amortize their investment more rapidly, thus reducing their tax payments. The sugar industry has long been the recipient of substantial subsidies as well as other forms of aid. In addition to this, a very large part of all governmental expenditures go directly to business for the construction of schools, highways, sewage disposal plants, tanks, aircraft carriers, shoes, etc., etc.

State and local governments also aid private enterprise. The most common and perhaps the most important are programs found in many states and localities designed to attract industry through tax exemption and the provision of land or building. Business is also aided through the construction of streets and utility facilities as well as by the police and fire protection which is provided by the local government.

Summary. The government cannot spend money without helping one group more than it helps others. This is even true of money spent in the interests of national defense. An army camp near Richmond, Virginia, helps that community more than the community without such a military installation, although both are deriving the benefits of defense. In the final sense, every governmental program must aid someone; it it did not, there could be no justification for the program. Some benefits can be easily justified while others can be justified on no grounds except those of political expediency.

PUBLIC ENTERPRISE IN THE UNITED STATES

Although the economic system of the United States is dominated by private enterprise, there are important areas in which the taxpayers undertake in their collective capacity to provide goods and services. Public enterprise refers to the instances when the government provides goods and services. This area of governmental activity has caused more concern than any other. As a result of the vocal disturbance, many endow it with considerably more significance than it actually possesses.

The Generation and Transmission of Electrical Power

All levels of government—local, state, and national—are in the power business. Of the three, the state is of the least significance since only the state of New York actually produces power. Local governments, however, have been in the business since the earliest days of the industry. Today, most municipally owned electrical systems are found in smaller communities, but this type of enterprise also exists in such well-known cities as Los Angeles; Seattle; Tacoma; Memphis; Nashville; San Antonio; Jacksonville; Kansas City, Kansas; and Columbus, Ohio, in addition to many others. Just above the local level of government a new type of organization has made its appearance in Nebraska and the Pacific Northwest—the public utility district. A public utility district may include several counties and municipalities, which are provided with complete electrical service by this public organization. In part, at least, because of a favorable tax situation, the districts have been actively buying up the assets of private utilities as well as building new facilities. The dispute, however, over public power is not an ideological dispute involving all public power. It is a dispute involving the approximately 15 per cent of the total power generated by the facilities of the national government.

The Tennessee Valley Authority. The problem of navigation on inland waters and flood control have always been in the domain of the national government. The Tennessee River is a good example of the government's attempt to solve those twin problems and its resultant entry into the electrical industry. Prior to the 1930's the Tennessee River ranged from a raging flood of water to a practically dry creek bed. It could not be relied upon for navigation, but it could usually be relied upon to provide a devastating flood. When the TVA was created in 1933, it started the construction of a series of dams to retain the spring flood waters and then slowly discharge them over the dry summer months. Today, there are no floods, and the river is navigable for some 600 miles above its junction with the Mississippi.

Water falling over a concrete barrier represents energy—energy which can be converted into electricity. A flood control project can then generate electrical energy as a by-product. The TVA installed generating facilities and proceeded to dispose of the power. The purchaser of electricity, however, wants a constant supply of power. Generating facilities in a flood control project may not be generating all of the time since the demands of flood control are primary. This means that once electrical generating capacity is installed in a flood control project, steam generating capacity must be constructed to complement the hydro. So TVA built steam plants until today half of its total power is generated by such plants.

Much of the controversy surrounding the TVA stems from the prices charged for the power. That price depends upon the allocation of costs. The critics of TVA contend that electricity should bear more of the cost and flood control and navigation less. Others would contend that flood control and navigation should bear all of the cost of the facilities. Actually about one third of the joint costs have been assigned to the generation of electrical power, with the rest being assigned to flood control and navigation. Largely as a result of this cost allocation, the rates charged for electrical power in the TVA area are among the lowest in the country, and they are often used as a "yardstick" to measure the rates of private power companies.

The Tennessee Valley Authority is a government corporation chartered by the national government. It is administered by three men appointed by the President and approved by the Senate, with the daily administration in the hands of a general manager. The corporation is not dependent upon Congress for operating funds but is for capital expenditures. State and local governments exercise no control over the TVA. It pays no taxes to these governments, although it does make payments in lieu of taxes. In addition to the three activities mentioned, TVA is promoting soil conservation, establishing recreational centers, developing fish and wildlife resources, promoting industrial development, producing fertilizer, and engaging in other activities. What was once one of the most depressed areas of the country has become one of the nation's show places.

The Rural Electrification Administration. A second venture of the national government in electrical power is the REA. It was established in the early days of the New Deal to assist in farm electrification.

At that time only 10 per cent of the farms were electrified. Today, practically 100 per cent of America's farms have electricity.

The approach of the REA was somewhat different than that of TVA. The REA loans money to rural co-operatives. With the borrowed money the REA co-ops construct transmission lines and, in some cases, generating facilities. The power was sold to the co-op members, and the revenue was used to repay the loan. The program has been a success by any measure one might want to use. It has electrified many farms. It has caused the electrification of many others by private utilities. The farmer has turned out to be a tremendous user of electricity. Rare is the farmer who criticizes REA and rare is the politician who is against REA.

Other Power Projects. The national government has constructed a number of dams on various rivers, including Hoover Dam and others on the lower Colorado; Grand Coulee, Bonneville, Chief Joseph, Hungry Horse, and others on the Columbia and its tributaries; and the Shasta Dam on the Sacramento—to name a few of the more important ones. These are all multipurpose in that they generate power, improve navigation, control floods, and provide water for irrigation. Some were started as relief measures. Many, and possibly all, were beyond the capacity of private enterprise at the time they were started. There have been some proposals to establish additional regional authorities such as the Columbia Valley Authority, but such proposals have never passed. At President Eisenhower's behest, Congress provided for the development of the Upper Colorado River Basin, but this was done without the establishment of a semiautonomous authority.

The Post Office and the Government Printing Office

The Constitution delegated to the national government the authority to establish a post office, and today that operation is one of the largest peacetime operations of the government. This multibillion dollar enterprise employs approximately 500,000 persons in conducting its nation-wide business. For the greater part of its existence it has been an inefficient, unwieldly, overcentralized organization run on political rather than economic principles. The head of the organization has usually been the dispenser of patronage plums. Until lately, huge subsidies have been hidden in the annual operating losses.

The Post Office is competitive with private enterprise but in only a very limited sense. Parcel post competes with railway express. The Postal Savings Program offers a means of saving which puts it in competition with private savings institutions. Mailbags are produced by federal prisons for the Post Office, and that service also maintains locks. There is competition with private enterprise, but it is very small.

Another government operation which might be considered as competitive with private enterprise is that of the Government Printing Office, which is probably the largest printing operation of all time. It produces the *Congressional Record* as well as Congressional Hearings and all other official publications. It prints and distributes millions of documents a year. Unlike the Post Office, it is a profitable operation and, also unlike the Post Office, it has come in for little criticism.

Other Business Enterprises of Government

The government is the sole producer of helium. It has been making rope at the Boston rope walk since the Revolutionary War. It operates a tin smelter in Texas and it makes rum in the Virgin Islands. The government operated a barge line on the Mississippi River until 1953, and it still operates a railroad in Panama and another in Alaska. The U.S. government has a monopoly on the production of atomic energy— the biggest single government enterprise. It is raising abaca in Latin America and operating concessions in the national parks, as well as meat-cutting plants. In addition it produces such diverse products as boxes, paint, bread, warships, coffee, ice cream, cement, and a multitude of others.

State and local governments also operate innumerable business undertakings. The state of Virginia operates a system of ferries and owns part of a railroad. The state of California owns a railroad as does the city of Cincinnati. A number of cities operate public transit systems and still more operate their own utilities. Several states have a monopoly on the sale of liquor, while in others the state competes with private enterprise. North Dakota sells hail insurance and has operated a grain elevator and a flour mill. It still operates a bank. The New York Port Authority operates dock facilities, airports, bus terminals, exhibition buildings, tunnels, etc.

The above are only a few of the instances in which the government competes with private interests. It would be difficult to measure the total amount of competition, but it does appear that such competition is slight. In some areas the goods and services could be provided by private enterprise, but in others they could not.

Lending and Insurance

Another area in which government operations are very extensive is that of lending and insurance. The government may actually lend the money or write the insurance, or it may merely assist private firms through the guarantee of loans or partial assumption of insurable risks. A few examples follow.

The Veterans Administration guarantees home loans for veterans and the Federal Housing Authority will do so for nearly anyone. The Public Housing Administration will give or lend money to municipalities for slum clearance, and it will lend money to colleges for construction of housing. The Federal Deposit Insurance Corporation guarantees bank deposits, and the Federal Crop Insurance Corporation will write insurance on agricultural crops. The Commodity Credit Corporation lends money on crops. The Farmers Home Administration lends money to farmers to acquire farms or improve farm property. The Farm Credit Administration lends money to farmers for the improvement of farm land or the purchase of equipment. The Export-Import Bank will lend money to assist in the financing of foreign trade. The Reconstruction Finance Corporation started out lending to banks in 1932 and ended up by lending money to hotels and other businesses following World War II. It was succeeded by the Small Business Corporation which is supposed to lend to small business but has been criticized because of its failure to do so. Insofar as insurance is concerned, the major areas are those of Old Age and Survivors Insurance, Workmen's Compensation, and Unemployment Insurance, to be discussed in the following pages.

Like other fields of government endeavor, there appears to be little chance that the government's role in insurance and lending will be reduced. There may well be a need for some party to assume risks which are too great for private enterprise.

Summary

It can be seen that the American economy is not one consisting solely of private enterprise. All levels of government provide goods and services. Why has this happened? There are several reasons: (1) A failure of private enterprise to provide a necessary service has often caused the people to turn to the government—electric power, for example. (2) The depression caused an expansion of governmental activity as relief measures. (3) National defense is a third argument which cannot be negated. There is, however, a tendency for wartime measures, like depression measures, to become a permanent part of the landscape. (4) Some services are normal by-products of government activities which have never been questioned. The generation and sale of electricity from a flood control dam is one. The deliberate expansion of government activities at the behest of socialist-minded individuals has been very slight, if there has been any such at all.

SOCIAL LEGISLATION

The Constitution charged the government to promote the general welfare. The Congress was given the power to levy taxes and spend that money to promote the general welfare. Yet today the term "welfare state" has become one of approbrium. The welfare state generally refers to the governmental programs which may be classed as social security. In some countries, social security provides benefits from birth to death. The Social Security program found in the United States is not as inclusive as that found in most European countries or in Canada. At best, it is designed to assist the individual in meeting the most serious of the hazards of life. It is not a guarantee of a life in which productive labor is not required.

Social Insurance

Social insurance is the most important of the several institutions generally classed as part of social security. Such hazards as unemployment, old age, industrial accident, and illness or disability are often of such magnitude that the individual does not have the resources to meet such a contingency. On an individual basis, one would have to provide for the maximum hazard. By associating with a large number of individuals, one need only provide for the average hazard of the entire group. This is the principle which underlies all insurance—public and private. These hazards are, furthermore, of such magnitude or so unpredictable that it would be nearly impossible for private insurance companies to provide the protection if the programs were on a voluntary basis. There has to be a very large number of people in each program to reduce the average hazard to a manageable proportion. To do this and to provide protection, governments have instituted several social insurance programs. The term "social" implies that it is a government program. The role of the government will vary from program to program, but some general observations can be made. In the first place, all programs are compulsory. Once the government decides who is covered, that group has no choice but to abide by the law. Secondly, the government decides what benefits are to be paid. It will either establish a formula to compute the benefit or it will specifically state what the benefit is to be. Thirdly, the government will either administer the program itself or it will exercise close supervision over its administration.

In the United States there are only three social insurance programs of significance—Workmen's Compensation, Unemployment Insurance, and Old Age, Survivors and Disability Insurance. At various times a compulsory Health Insurance plan has been proposed, but it has never been adopted. Several states do have a disability insurance plan to complement the Workmen's Compensation program, but its use has not become widespread.

Workmen's Compensation. Until early in the twentieth century the only protection which the employee had in the case of industrial accident was the common law, but that did not offer much solace or relief to the injured workman. First, the workman had to prove that the employer was negligent, and if that point were successfully proven, the workman had the further burden of proving that neither he nor his fellow workmen were negligent, as well as proving that he had not in any way assumed the risk when he was hired. Under such a legal program it was difficult for the employee to collect any sort of remuneration for injuries received on the job. To correct this situation, the various states passed Workmen's Compensation laws during the first half of the twentieth century, with most of the laws being passed early in that period.

The employer is now required to provide protection for his employees in event of injury while working. Some states permit private underwriters of insurance to write the policies, while in others the state itself writes the policies. Some states permit the employer to elect out of the program so that he does not have to take out an insurance policy, but in this case the employer must make the same payments to injured employees. The payments, however, would be made out of the company's general funds. The payments are stipulated in the statute. Regardless of who writes the policy or even if there is no policy, all workers in a state who have the same injury will have their payment computed by the same formula. To be eligible, there need only be an accident. There is no requirement of employer negligence nor can the claim be invalidated because of employee negligence. The cost of the program is borne in every instance by the employer, who in turn probably passes most of the cost on to the consumers of the product. Industrial accidents are inevitable in an industrialized economy and to the consumer of the output of such an economic system, it is an additional cost. Finally, the program is a state program in every instance, with the national government playing no part in the compensation for industrial accidents except for workers under its jurisdiction.

Unemployment Compensation. The economic system has long been subject to cyclical fluctuations about which the individual person or firm can do little or nothing. Men find themselves unemployed as a result of no shortcoming of their own or lack of planning on the part of their employers. Especially with the increasing popularity of consumer credit, a period of unemployment constitutes a very serious hazard for the worker and his family. It is of such proportion that no employee can accumulate sufficient savings to see him through. Likewise, a private insurance company could not provide insurance against a hazard of such monumental proportions.

In 1935 Congress levied a 3 per cent payroll tax on nearly all employers engaged in interstate commerce. The statute provided that if the individual states establish a program of unemployment insurance, 90 per cent of that amount is due to the states with the remaining 10 per cent to be paid to the national government to cover the cost of administering the program. The states, naturally, passed unemployment insurance laws.

This insurance is financed by the employer, but it is probable that a good portion of the cost is finally borne by the consumer. The program is administered by the state governments, but the national government has established certain criteria which must be met. Benefits vary from state to state, but in most instances the benefits are less than half of the worker's usual wage. Furthermore, all states limit the time period during which benefits can be drawn. Workers who voluntarily leave their employment, go out on strike, or refuse to accept suitable employment are generally ineligible for unemployment insurance benefits. The whole program is designed to meet temporary periods of unemployment. The benefits are not such as to permit the unemployed worker to lead a life of luxury.

Old Age, Survivors, and Disability Insurance. A major and lasting contribution of the New Deal to the American economy is the Old Age, Survivors, and Disability Insurance program which is popularly referred to as Social Security. It is designed primarily to meet the hazard of old age in a highly specialized economic system.

This insurance program is financed by a tax on both employer and employee. When the law went into operation in 1936 the rate was one per cent on both. The rate stands at $3\frac{5}{8}$ per cent on each in 1963, and it will gradually be increased until both are paying $4\frac{1}{2}$ per cent. Presently the employee is only taxed on the first $4,800 of income, so he pays at a maximum an annual rate of $174 which is matched by the employer.

To be eligible for benefits a worker must have reached age 65.[4]

[4] It is possible to retire at an earlier age but with reduced benefits.

In addition he must have been in the program for a minimum period of time. If his earnings exceed $1,200 his benefits will be reduced. The size of the benefit payment is based on the worker's earnings during this period of employment, but in no case can benefit payments to a family exceed $254 per month. In addition to benefits to the retired worker, benefits will be paid to wives of retired workers as well as the dependent children of the worker. In the case of death, dependents of insured workers are eligible to receive survivor's benefits. These benefits are likewise based upon the earnings of the insured worker. None of the benefits are large; however, OASDI benefits in combination with other forms of savings, including private insurance, provide considerable security for the retired worker and his dependents.

At the time the statute was enacted, it excluded such groups as the self-employed, agricultural workers, farmers, employees of non-profit institutions, public employees, and others. Since its passage, coverage has been continually expanded until nearly all employed persons plus a large number of the self-employed are presently covered.

The program is administered in its entirety by the national government. The employer deducts the tax from the check of the employee and then sends both his contribution and that of the employer to the United States Treasury. When a person becomes eligible for benefits, payments are made directly to the individual by the Treasury Department. Funds received by the government which are not needed for benefit payments are invested in government securities. The interest earned on this investment then goes to help meet the expenses of Old Age, Survivors, and Disability Insurance including the payment of benefits.

Social Assistance and Social Services

Social Assistance. Since the passage of the Elizabethan Poor Laws in 1601, most civilized nations have assumed the responsibility for those citizens who are not able to provide for themselves. At times the care of the poor has been the responsibility of the church or the family, but as an economic system becomes more specialized and industrialized, the governments of the world have assumed a larger and larger portion of the burden.

Social assistance programs are not insurance programs in which eligibility is established by the payment of premiums. Eligibility for social assistance is determined by need. All programs are administered by state and local governments, but since 1935 the national government has participated in the financing of many of the programs. To be eligible for such financial aid, however, the local programs must meet certain standard criteria established by the national government. This promotes uniformity among the various state programs.

a) General relief or poor relief is the program of the local government to take care of the needy poor. In those instances in which the local government is unable to finance the program, the state government renders financial assistance. The national government has no part in this program.

b) Old age assistance provides small payments to the aged who are incapable of providing their own support. This is a state program, but the national government does render financial assistance through grants-in-aid. That government does stipulate certain conditions which must be met, however, before the state is eligible for such financial aid.

c) Aid to the blind, a state program, likewise receives financial assistance from the national government through grants-in-aid.

d) Aid to dependent children began just before World War I to afford underprivileged children a fair opportunity in life. It is most frequently used in the case of fatherless children, but such benefits are available where the parents are separated, and for other dependent children. This program is also a state program which receives financial aid from the national government providing the state program meets the minimal requirements established by the national government.

e) Aid to the permanently and totally disabled was provided for in the 1950 amendments to the social security law. Under the provisions of this law, the federal government provides financial assistance to the several states for aiding those individuals who are permanently and totally disabled. In general, the arrangement is similar to that found in other assistance programs.

Social Services. Social services, as part of the general institution of social security are a close adjunct of social assistance. Aid to dependent children, aid to the blind, or general relief can take either of two forms—cash payments to the needy, or social assistance and special services to the needy (social services). As far as the cost to society is concerned, and certainly insofar as the individual is concerned, it is wiser to rehabilitate the handicapped than to provide them with assistance payments for an indefinite period. In the case of medical services, for example, it may be much cheaper for the state and municipality to provide medical service for the needy poor rather than make payments to this group and let them obtain their own medical services. Vocational training, to take another example, is much more valuable to the physically handicapped than continued cash payments. The major social service programs include the following.

a) Vocational rehabilitation, which provides for retraining of those who are incapacitated to such an extent that they are unable to carry on their former occupation. It will also provide for the training of those handicapped persons who never had a trade or profession.

b) Services for children and expectant mothers are provided by the several states, with the national government assisting the financing through grants-in-aid. Certain health facilities are provided through the school system. Health clinics are maintained, as well as a public health nursing service. A very important part of this program are those services provided in the crippled children's program. Since the passage of the Social Security Act in 1935, every state has adopted a program to seek out and care for the crippled children in its jurisdiction. Another aspect of the services for children is found in the child-welfare program in the local welfare agency. This agency works with local authorities and local groups in promoting the welfare of the community's younger citizens.

c) The blind are assisted in various manners in order that they will be more nearly able to lead normal lives. The government provides schools for the blind as well as workshops and certain field services. These programs are all administered by the states and partially financed by the national government.

d) Veterans' services, while not generally classified as part of social security, are becoming so important that possibly the services rendered this group should be noted. Two world-wide conflagrations, the Korean War, and a decade and a half of the military draft have all combined to make veterans out of a large part of the country's males. The service rendered this group varies from state to state, but it will generally include educational training, vocational training and re-habilitation, and medical care. The largest part of the program is administered and financed by the national government, but a number of the states do have extensive programs for veterans.

Summary

Social security in the United States is largely a product of the first half of the twentieth century, with most of the developments coming in the decade of the 1930's. At the present time nearly everyone regards it as a legitimate and proper role for the government to assume. The chances are that such programs will be expanded rather than contracted in the future; however, it is probably unlikely that many new programs will be adopted as long as the economy enjoys a high level of prosperity. Should the economic system suffer a severe depression, it might well be that the programs included in social security would be expanded and enlarged.

There are undoubtedly many cases in which the various programs are abused. Cases have been cited in which people drawing unemployment insurance were vacationing in Florida or people on relief were taking vacations in Europe. Poor administration should not be confused with, or interpreted as, an unsound program. None of the programs are, nor should they become, such a lucrative source of income that the recipients would rather draw their social security benefits than work. Social security is to catch those who fall rather than provide a permanent support for all.

CONCLUSION

The American people are pragmatists. They are interested in that which works. Few are socialists in the sense that they believe in socialism as a matter of principle. Even fewer are communists or monarchists or fascists. The belief in free enterprise and private property, however, is rather passive. Most regard private enterprise favorably as long as it works. When it fails, there is no compunction about turning to the government for assistance. If the government provides the necessary goods and services, that is what matters. The belief in private enterprise is not so strong that people would prefer accomplishing certain goals through that media or not at all.

Government operation of economic enterprises as well as government subsidization of private groups has been at the request of private citizens, private firms, and private groups. It has not been as a result of some philosophy or of pressure from a particular group which has been consistently pushing that body of beliefs over the years. Government interference in the economic system, thus, has not shown a consistent pattern. There is extensive governmental interference in one area but none in others. Government may subsidize one group but offer no aid to another.

In trying to evaluate the role of government, one runs into obstacles. There are no final answers. There is no way of ascertaining whether the role of government is correct. There is no way of ascertaining whether a particular government program is accomplishing its intended goal.

The same comments may be made about regulation. Most Americans do not believe in *laissez faire* with the fervor of a religious zealot. Each individual wants only a minimum amount of regulation for himself. However, each one of us is willing to admit that there are others who might well be regulated. In fact, we agree that some people *must* be regulated in the interests of society, but fortunately these people do not belong to one's own group. The net result of such an attitude is a continual expansion of the areas in which government exercises regulative powers.

There are, undoubtedly, times when all would agree that a particular governmental program of either aid or regulation is not only desirable but essential. In times of war, nearly all agree that extensive regulations are needed. There are hazards facing those living in the twentieth century which must be met through government action because suitable private enterprises do not exist. However, before any measure is adopted, the problem should be carefully analyzed. If regulation is needed, it should be decided what goal is to be achieved and whether that goal is compatible with the general welfare. Then there are certain principles of regulation which should be followed in order to insure that the regulatory policy has the best possible chance of success. The same can be said of governmental programs designed to assist certain groups.

In conclusion, it should be pointed out that the economic system will not operate without any attempt on the part of those who make up the system to make sure that it does operate successfully. Private enterprise, for example, must provide for the wants of the people. At any time it fails to do so, the people will turn to the government in an effort to get such goods and services. Every time a particular group turns to the government for a subsidy, the more reason there is for a second and a third to do likewise. Although it is improbable that the clock shall ever be turned back, it does not follow that we need look forward to a continually larger and larger area of governmental operations.

EXERCISES

Group I

Explain why the following are either true or false:

1. The Sherman Act of 1890 was largely remedial in nature while the antitrust legislation of 1914 was largely preventative in nature.
2. A public utility is no different from the corner grocery store, and the government should treat both alike insofar as regulation is concerned.

3. Government regulation is undesirable. It follows, then, that the best government is one which did no regulating whatsoever.

4. A problem such as that which exists in agriculture would never occur in such industries as steel or automobiles.

5. The political solutions for the farm problem have generally emphasized a reduction in supply rather than an increase in demand; however, this is not important since the effect is the same.

6. The cost of industrial accidents and unemployment are borne, at least in part, by the consumer in the form of higher prices.

7. There are some risks of such magnitude that no individual or firm can assume the burden of the risk, nor can a private company even underwrite such risks.

Group II

1. There have been a number of exceptions written into the nation's antitrust laws. Explore the rationale behind each of these exceptions. If these were valid at the time of their enactment, are they still equally valid?

2. Should the antitrust laws be once again extended to labor? Why or why not?

3. From time to time it has been proposed that some sort of health insurance plan be adopted. Outline such proposals and evaluate the arguments for and against them.

4. Is there a need in our economy for a government lending institution which would lend to those individuals and firms which cannot borrow from private lending sources? Why or why not?

Group III

1. A major government activity at the present time is the financial support of research. In some cases the research is directed toward national defense; some research is a form of subsidy to private enterprise; and other research is not easily classifiable—for example, space exploration. What criteria has the government used in determining the areas of government support? Can the doctrine of opportunity cost be useful in analyzing the impact of research expenditures?

2. State supported universities and colleges, as well as private institutions, engage in a number of activities which are ancillary to the educational program. Why do universities operate such activities as placement offices, housing offices, dining and living accommodations, health clinics, printing operations, building and maintenance operations, and many others? Outline a procedure by which one of these functions could be performed by the private sector of the economy and the services purchased in the market.

3. Certain industries in the United States, for one reason or another, present interesting problems for the government. And the reason will vary from one industry to another. Consider the following industries: agriculture, steel, airlines, railroads, urban transportation systems, aluminum, electricity, and shipbuilding. What is the nature of the problem with which the government is or has been concerned? Does the nature of the problem vary from industry

to industry? What has been the objective of government regulation? How successful has the government been in achieving its goal?

BIBLIOGRAPHY

EDWARDS, C. D. *Maintaining Competition; Requisites of a Governmental Policy.* New York: McGraw-Hill Book Co., Inc., 1949.

GLAESER, MARTIN G. *Public Utilities in American Capitalism.* New York: Macmillan Co., 1957.

SIMONS, HENRY C. *Economic Policy for a Free Society.* Chicago: University of Chicago Press, 1948.

PAPERBACK READING LIST

HOOVER, CALVIN. *Economy, Liberty and the State.* New York: Doubleday & Co., Anchor Books, 1961.

Chapter

17

THE UNITED STATES IN
THE WORLD ECONOMY

Says th' Sinitor fr'm Louisyanny: "Louisyanny, th' proudest jool in th' dyadim iv our fair land, remains thrue to th' honoured teachin's iv our leaders. Th' protictive tariff is an abomynation. It is crushin' out th' lives iv our people. An' wan iv th' worst parts iv this divvlish injine iv tyranny is th' tariff on lathes. Fellow-Sinitors, as long," he says, "as I can stand, as long as nature will sustain me in protest, while wan dhrop iv pathriotic blood surges through me heart, I will raise me voice again a tariff on lathes, onless," he says, "this dread implymint iv oppressyon is

419

akelly used," he says, "to protict th' bland an' beautiful molasses iv th' State iv me birth,' he says.

"I am heartily in sympathy with th' Sinitor fr'm Louisyanny," says the Sinitor fr'm Virginya. "I loath th' tariff. Fr'm me arliest days I was brought up to look on it with pizenous hathred. At manny a convintion ye cud hear me whoppin' again it. But if there is such a lot iv this monsthrous iniquity passin' around, don't Virginya get none? How about th' mother iv Prisidints? Ain't she goin' to have a grab at annything? Gintlemen, I do not ask, I demand rights f'r me Commonwealth. I will talk here ontil July Fourth, nineteen hundred an' eighty-two, again th' proposed hellish tax on feather beds onless somethin' is done f'r th' tamarach-bark iv old Virginya."

A Sinitor: "What's it used f'r?"

The Sinitor fr'm Virginya: "I do not quite know. It is ayether a cure fr' th' hives or enthers largely into th' mannyfacture iv carpet slippers. But there's a frind iv mine, a lile Virginyan, who makes it, an' he needs th' money."

"Th' argymints iv th' Sinitor fr'm Virginya are onanswerable," says Sinitor Aldrich. "Wud it be agreeable to me Dimmycratic collague to put both feather beds an' his what's-ye-call-it in th' same item?"

"In such circumstances," says th' Sinitor fr'm Virginya, "I wud be foorced to waive me almost insane prejudice again th' hellish doctrines iv th' distinguished Sinitor fr'm Rhode Island," says he.—Finley Peter Dunne, *Mr. Dooley: Now and Forever.*

The United States is not, never has been, and never will be a self-sufficient economy in the sense that it need not depend upon the rest of the world. Life in the United States is, to a large extent, dependent upon what happens in the rest of the world. And rather than becoming less so, it appears that we will become even more dependent upon other economies and peoples. Although the more readily apparent aspect of this interdependency is political and military in nature, a vitally important facet of the relationship is economic. This economic interest is expressed, for the most part, in the buying and selling transactions between individuals and businesses in the United States and individuals and businesses in the other countries of the world. In addition, however, there is some buying and selling, some trading, and some investing at the government level. And governments may and do regulate the conditions of trading between individuals.

This chapter, then, is more than just an examination of international trade. It is an investigation of the economy of the United States insofar as that economic system is related to the economies of other nations of the world.

INTERNATIONAL TRADE

The Basis of International Trade

Specialization and International Trade. The major advantage of specialization is increased productivity. The old saying, "Jack of all trades and master of none" is certainly true in this respect, for the person who attempts to do the entire job will be more inefficient than the person who specializes in doing a particular part of an operation.

A major type of specialization is geographical specialization. Farmers in northern Minnesota do not grow cotton, but neither does Florida produce iron ore. Texas produces oil while the state of Washington produces wheat. Within the United States or any other national economy, as well as within the world as a whole, there will be specialization based on geography. Each area will produce that commodity in which it has a peculiar advantage, or, if there is no product which it can produce with an advantage, it will produce that commodity in which it has the smallest disadvantage.

In addition to geographical specialization, there is personal specialization. By this it is meant that an individual will produce what he is able to produce most efficiently, or if he cannot produce anything as efficiently as others, he will produce the commodity in which his handicap is the least. The college professor teaches his classes and hires someone to paint his house, even though he might be a better house painter, just as the lawyer practices law and hires a secretary to type, even though he might be a better typist.

If production within an economy is conducted in accordance with this principle, production for the economy will be at an optimum. But the same thing is true for the world as a whole, for what is applicable to a single economic system is equally true for the entire world. Specialization on an international basis will produce an optimum amount of goods and services for the entire world.

The Law of Comparative Advantage and International Trade. The law of comparative advantage simply states that one should produce that product in which the advantage is the greatest or the disadvantage the least. The examples in the preceding paragraphs are demonstrations of that principle.

The law of comparative advantage is true for entire economies just as it is for individuals. Any given country may have an advantage in the production of a particular commodity, or it may have an advantage in the production of all commodities. There could be a country which had no advantage in producing any commodity. But even in the extreme case of a country suffering a disadvantage in producing everything, it would still be to the advantage of all countries to specialize and trade. Total world output would be maximized if each country produced that product in which it had the greatest advantage or the least disadvantage.

David Ricardo (1722–1823), in his classic example of international trade,[1] expressed costs in terms of man-years of labor. In Portugal, 80-man years of labor could produce the same amount of wine as 120 man-years of labor could produce in England. And 90 man-years of labor in Portugal could produce the same quantity of cloth as 100 man-years in England.

TABLE 17–1

Country	Man-Years of Labor Required to Produce:	
	Wine	*Cloth*
Portugal.................	80	90
England.................	120	100

Ricardo went on to demonstrate that both countries would find it to their advantage to trade, even though Portugal was the more efficient producer of both wine and cloth. Portugal's advantage is obvious. For an expenditure of 80 units of labor (to produce wine), Portugal could obtain a quantity of cloth from England which would require 90 man-years of labor to produce in Portugal. Portugal would have found it profitable to trade as long as it was possible to trade the wine produced by 80 units of labor for the quantity of cloth which that country could produce with 90 units of labor.

England, on the other hand, would produce cloth and exchange it for wine as her disadvantage is least in the production of cloth. For an expenditure of 100 units of labor (to produce cloth) England could obtain a quantity of wine which would have necessitated the use of 120 man-years of labor to produce in England. England would continue to trade as long as the cloth produced by 100 units of labor could be exchanged for the quantity of wine produced by 120 units of labor.

In such a simple model as this, both countries will profit by specialization and trade. If the two countries tried to produce both wine and cloth, there would be a reduction in total output.

The comparative advantage or disadvantage which a country en-

[1] David Ricardo, *The Principles of Political Economy and Taxation* (Everyman's Library; New York: E. P. Dutton & Co., Inc.. 1911).

joys may be expressed in physical terms, such as Ricardo's example, but it is more realistic to discuss a country's advantage or disadvantage in terms of costs. It is the differences in the costs of goods between countries which give rise to international trade. A country which enjoys an advantage in the production of all commodities in comparison with other countries would find that it could produce the products at a lower cost. A country suffering a disadvantage, on the other hand, would incur higher costs of production. This cost differential between countries is the basis of international trade.

A particular country may enjoy an advantage in the production of a given commodity because the factors needed in its production are more plentiful or more efficient than are the factors needed to produce the same product in other countries. Although the matter of factor pricing and costs was discussed in earlier chapters, a few comments must be inserted at this point, insofar as the subject matter is peculiar to international trade. Specifically, the student of international trade is interested in knowing what forces exist which result in cost differentials between nations.

First, there is the matter of the relative supplies of the factors of production. Wherever a particular factor is in great supply, the price of that factor will be forced downward. In some parts of the world and at different times in history, land has been very cheap. This was true in the United States for many years. In western Europe, however, land has always been very dear because of the short supply. The labor situation has been the reverse. Labor has quite often been scarce and dear in the United States whereas it was in great supply and somewhat cheaper in Europe. And today, the labor supply in the countries of Asia is such that wage rates are pushed to extremely low levels. But in addition to land and labor, the stock of capital or investment goods also varies from one country to another. Today the United States has a very large stock of such goods while the underdeveloped nations of the world have a small supply. In all of these cases the plentiful factor is less costly compared to the same factor in other countries.

In addition to the supply of a particular factor, the productivity of that factor must also be considered. The cost of production depends upon the price of the factor and its productivity. Low wages do not necessarily mean low labor costs, since the low wages may be accompanied by low productivity. Wage rates in China are much lower than wage rates in the United States, but since the productivity of Chinese labor is much below that of the United States, the labor costs in that Asian country may actually be higher.

The productivity of labor is, in part, dependent upon the amount and quality of capital employed. Thus if two countries employed similar amounts of capital and similar technological processes, then differences in wage rates would result in price differentials between the two countries. An example of this is to be found in the case of some industries in the United States and Japan. Where both use similar production methods, the lower wage rates in Japan give that country an advantage over the United States. But where lower wages are not accompanied by similar productive processes, the high-wage country may actually enjoy an advantage in the form of lower labor costs.

Countries having a plentiful supply of labor will generally find that their greatest advantage or smallest disadvantage is to be found in the production of those goods which do not lend themselves to the large-scale use of capital but do require large amounts of labor. In such

TABLE 17–2

Factor	Price of the Factor in Country		Quantity of the Factor Required to Make Product		Cost of Product X in Country		Cost of Product Y in Country	
	A	B	X	Y	A	B	A	B
Land........$1		$2	2	2	$ 2	$ 4	$ 2	$ 4
Labor......... 4		1	2	4	8	2	16	4
Capital........ 3		5	4	2	12	20	6	10
Total Cost..............................					$22	$26	$24	$18

instances the productivity of labor is very low and the possibilities of increasing productivity and thus lowering costs are slight.

To illustrate cost differentials and international trade, we might imagine two countries producing Products X and Y. In Country A, land and capital are cheaper than in Country B, but the latter has a price advantage in the form of lower wage rates. We will assume that the productive process is the same in the two countries. We will express all costs in terms of dollars (see Table 17–2).

The total cost of Product X in Country A is $22 while the cost of the same good is $26 in Country B. Country B, on the other hand, has a cost advantage in the production of Commodity Y. Under such circumstances, it is obvious that both countries would profit by specializing and trading. Country A would produce Product X and trade it to Country B for product Y. Country A would continue to find it profitable to purchase Y as long as the price of that good was less than $24, and Country B would find it profitable to buy X as long as the price was less than $26. These two upper limits represent the cost of producing the particular good in the country not having an absolute advantage in that commodity.

If the price of labor in Country B were increased to $4.00, the total cost of production in that country would be $32 for Product X and $30 for product Y. Country A would now have an advantage in the production of both commodities, but its relative advantage would be greater for Product X. Even under these circumstances, international specialization and trade would result in a greater total output than would a policy of economic self-sufficiency. The student might satisfy himself on this point by figuring the most efficient method of producing 4 units of both X and Y so that both countries will have 2 units of the two commodities.

The argument can be summed up in this fashion. Costs of production will vary from one economy to another because of differences in prices and productivity of the factors of production. The individual countries will find it to their advantage to produce that commodity in which they have the greatest advantage or the least disadvantage. If production is in accord with this principle, total world output will be maximized.

Free Trade. Free trade means that there are no restrictions on trading between nations other than the natural obstacles of time and distance. Most often it refers to that situation in which the governments of the various nations do not impose a tariff on imports or exports, but it will be used here to exclude all restrictions on trade such as quotas, currency controls, etc.

Free trade between nations has not been widely practiced. Great Britain did not levy tariffs on imports for most of the period between the American Civil War and World War I. The United States has always imposed tariffs on imports although it has never imposed a tariff on exports because of a Constitutional prohibition.

The economic argument for free trade is difficult to refute. It rests upon the law of comparative advantage. Through a system of world-wide free trade, total output and thus total satisfaction could be maximized, but this maximization of output and satisfaction has never served as a guide for the regulation of international trade.

The Regulation of International Trade

An Introduction to Tariffs and Tariff Policy. The tariff has long been used as an instrument of national policy. The various countries of Europe made extensive use of the tariff in the sixteenth, seventeenth, and eighteenth centuries in order to reduce competition from foreign producers and encourage domestic industry. The United States, like the countries of western Europe, has always used the tariff as an instrument of national policy.

A tariff can be and is used for two purposes. The first is that of producing revenue. In such an instance the rates are set to produce a maximum amount of revenue. The United States depended upon the tariff for a major part of its revenue for many years. A second use of the tariff is to protect domestic industry. Such a tariff restricts the sale of the foreign-produced item in the country levying the tariff. A tariff which was completely protective would produce no revenue since there would be no imports. In practice, no country has had a tariff system which prevented the importation of any product, but in the case of individual goods, tariffs have often eliminated competition from foreign producers. On the other hand, if the tariff is to raise revenue, the rates cannot be set so high as to reduce imports to such an extent that governmental revenue is reduced.

Basically, a tariff is a tax on consumption, and it can be analyzed in much the same fashion as such a tax. There are only two parties who can bear the burden of the tariff—the foreign producer and the domestic buyer. The division of the tariff burden between these two parties depends upon the elasticity of demand for the product in question. If the demand for the product is highly elastic, increasing the price by the full amount of the tariff will result in a more than proportionate reduction in the amount demanded and a reduction in total revenue. If the producer is to continue to sell the same quantity of goods in the country imposing the tariff, it will be necessary for him to absorb at least a part, if not all, of the tariff. If part of the tariff is passed on to the consumer, a smaller amount will be sold. In the case of goods for which the demand is relatively inelastic, the producer will be able to pass on a larger part of the tariff burden to the consumers, for the increased price will not result in a more than proportionate reduction in amount demanded and a reduction in total revenue. The domestic consumer, in both cases, assumes a large part of the burden of the tariff in either reduced consumption or higher prices. The two examples are demonstrated in Figure 17–1. In both cases Q_1 and P_1 are the pre-tariff quantity and price, and Q_2 and P_2 represent the quantity and price after the imposition of the tariff. The amount of the tariff is represented by the vertical distance between S and S_T—the original supply function and the supply function following the imposition of the tariff.

A tariff, like a tax, will result in an allocation of resources different from that existing in the absence of such an impost. This is true for both the world economy and the economy of the country imposing the tariff. Behind the protective wall of a tariff, countries will find it to their advantage to produce products where there is no natural advantage or where their natural disadvantage is greater than that for other products which might be produced. World output will be less and it will be produced less efficiently than would otherwise be the case.

Within an individual economic system, resources will be shifted to those industries enjoying protection. In such industries the returns to the factors employed will be higher than that which would prevail were

FIGURE 17–1

EFFECT OF A TARIFF ON GOODS HAVING
ELASTIC AND INELASTIC DEMAND SCHEDULES

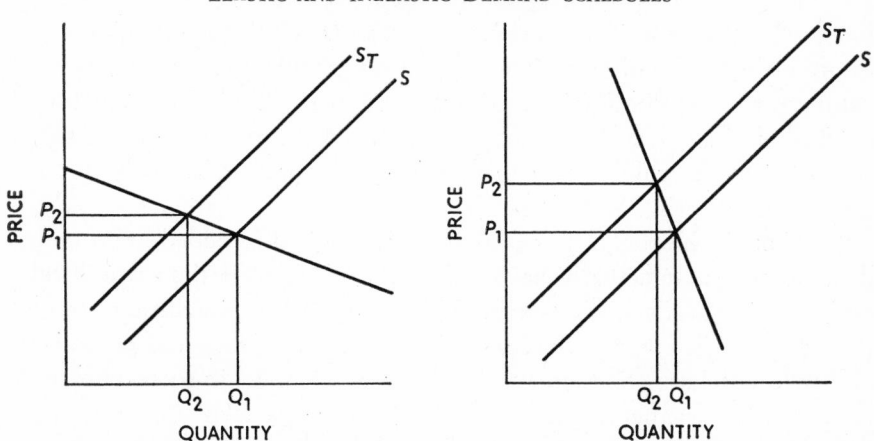

there no tariff. To the extent that this return is above that for nonprotected industries, a shift in the factors of production will result. At the same time, a tariff may reduce exports either because (1) foreign nations cannot acquire the means to pay for such exports or (2) because other nations engage in retaliatory tariff increases. In this event production in the export industries will fall off and factors will shift to industries not so afflicted.

The Argument for a Protective Tariff. Everyone admits that protective tariffs interfere with the free flow of goods between countries, for that is their purpose. Most economists, at least, would agree that a world-wide system of free trade would be superior to a system of national tariffs. Yet all countries have tariffs. Why?

First, underdeveloped countries use the tariff as a means of promoting economic development. Such economies generally face an acute shortage of capital. Methods of production will be somewhat primitive. Productivity of labor will be low. There will be a desire to establish industry as a part of their development program. But competing against the well-established industries in highly developed economies constitutes a fairly bleak prospect. The tariff protects new industries in the underdeveloped economies and enables them to compete with the established industries in the more highly developed areas.

In the early days of the United States, domestic industry suffered a cost disadvantage in competing with the industry of England. In order that industry might be established in the New World, tariffs were imposed on imports into this country to protect the new industries and encourage economic development. The underdeveloped countries of the world are doing the same thing today.

This argument has limitations. What was once an infant industry in a backward country may eventually become a fully matured industry in an advanced economic system. Once a particular industry is able to compete with the industries in other economies, this justification for a tariff is eliminated. Unfortunately, it would appear that once an industry gets used to the pabulum of protection in its infancy, it is difficult to forego the diet in later years.

There is the possibility, moreover, that a tariff intended to promote development may actually have a deleterious effect. If the underdeveloped country needs foreign exchange and can only get it through trade, then tariffs will eventually reduce the country's exports and curtail its ability to purchase goods and service abroad. Planners in such countries, however, have generally felt that the gains for a tariff outweigh the potential losses.

A second argument for a tariff is that of national defense. Just as the war power in the Constitution of the United States can be used as the legal basis for almost any activity of the government in time of war, so can the war itself be used as a justification for programs which could not otherwise be justified on economic grounds. Therefore, this argument would lose all content if the threat of war were permanently removed. In any event, however, as long as the necessity to defend a country prevails, that nation must attempt to insure adequate supplies of defense matériel. There is general agreement that it is proper and fitting to use the tariff to encourage the development of those industries essential to the defense of the nation.

A third justification often advanced for the cause of the tariff is that of protecting the exchange position of a particular country. Suppose, for example, that a country does not have a sufficient amount of the means necessary to pay for imports from the United States. It is necessary that a certain key items be purchased, but in order to do this, the importation of nonessential items must be reduced to conserve that country's supply of dollars. The tariff would reduce foreign purchases, but it should be pointed out that direct controls may be more efficacious.

A final argument sometimes advanced to support a tariff is that of increasing employment. It is argued that a country suffering from unemployment can increase employment by reducing the purchase of goods from foreign sources. Thus the buyers would substitute the goods of domestic producers for those of foreign producers. This would provide increased employment opportunities in the country imposing the tariff and fewer employment opportunities in the foreign country. In this fashion, a tariff is supposed to export a nation's unemployment. But obviously, if all countries followed such a policy, little would be accomplished. The net effect of any such tariff will be the shifting of unemployment from industries producing for domestic consumption to those producing for export.

Other arguments have been advanced for protective tariffs, but few have any degree of validity. It is impossible to refute the economic argument for free trade. However, the noneconomic arguments for a tariff have nearly always carried more weight than the economic arguments for freedom of trade between nations.

The Mechanics of International Trade

Introduction. A person living in New York City and buying an item in San Francisco would experience no difficulty in paying for the commodity since both buyer and seller conduct business in dollars. However, if the same New Yorker tried to buy the same item from a merchant located the same distance to the east, some difficulty would be encountered because the buyer would conduct his business in dollars, but the seller would do business in pounds sterling, marks, francs, or some other currency.

Assume that a person living in Columbus, Ohio, desired to purchase wine from a winery in France. The French producer wants francs, but the American buyer has to make payment in dollars. If the American purchaser knows someone who has francs and is willing to exchange them for dollars, the problem is solved albeit somewhat cumbersomely. It so happens, however, that there are going to be a number of people who want francs, just as there are a number of people who want to exchange francs for dollars. But instead of demanding the actual currency, all are willing to accept bank credit in dollars, francs, pounds, or other currency. Since there is a sufficient demand and since those doing business are willing to do business through the medium of deposit credit, the banks of the world provide facilities for exchanging one currency for another. All major banks in the United States, for example, have departments which deal in foreign exchange. The individual in Columbus can purchase the required number of French francs from his bank in Columbus. He would make payment to his bank by depositing the corresponding number of dollars or by having the bank deduct it from his deposit. The American would have, in effect, deposit credit in a French bank which could be used to pay the producer of the wine. The deposit of the American bank in the French bank will then be reduced by the amount involved. The Frenchman may then decide to travel in the United States. He will go to his bank and convert his francs into a credit instrument which he can cash in the United States for dollars. And again the two banks involved would adjust the balance.

Now if an individual deposits his pay check in a checking account, he is said to receive deposit credit. If he takes the same check and converts it into a foreign currency, he is said to have purchased foreign exchange. He does not actually acquire the currency of the foreign country but gets a draft drawn in terms of that currency which can be converted into currency when the occasion arises. If a buyer wants to purchase a commodity from a foreign producer, he must acquire the exchange of that country unless it should happen that the seller desired currency of the country in which the buyer resided.

International banking operations, then are similar to the operations of a branch banking system. Instead of dealing in a single currency, the depositor may deposit one money in one bank and withdraw a different money from a second bank. This mechanism makes it possible for the seller to receive payment in his money while the buyer is enabled to make payment in his. The only remaining question is that of determining the rate of exchange. How many dollars does the man in Columbus have to give up in order to acquire a specified number of francs which represent the cost of the wine?

The Rate of Exchange. A student might note in a book catalogue that a book can be purchased for 1 pound sterling. But, assuming that he wishes to purchase the book, he does not know how many dollars the book is going to cost. If the pound sterling is worth $4.05, then the book will cost $4.05, but if the pound sterling is exchanging for less than that amount, then the price of the book will likewise be less. In an international transaction, there are two variables—the price of the commodity or service and the price of the foreign exchange in terms of the domestic currency. The latter is the rate of exchange.

The rate of exchange may be defined as the amount of one currency which must be given up to acquire one unit of another country's currency. Thus if a resident of the United States could acquire one pound sterling for $2.85, the rate of exchange is said to be one to $2.85. And then, of course, there will be a rate of exchange for all possible pairs of currency in the world economy, and each pair can be stated in terms of either currency.

In the absence of any restrictions, the rate of exchange will be determined by the demand for and the supply of the particular exchange in question. If, in the United States, there existed a very great demand for French francs while the supply was very small, the rate of exchange would go up and one would have to give up more dollars in order to acquire the same amount of franc exchange. Or, if the situation is reversed, an excessive demand for dollar exchange accompanied by a shortage of the same exchange would force the residents of France to give up a larger number of francs to acquire a given amount of dollar exchange. So anything which influences either the supply of, or the demand for, a particular exchange will affect the exchange rate.

Let us examine this generalization somewhat further in terms of England and the United States. We want to know what factors might cause the price of dollar exchange to rise or fall in terms of the British pound sterling. Any transaction requiring the movement of funds to the United States will increase the demand for dollar exchange. British imports from the United States, British tourists traveling in the states, repayment of debts owed to American creditors or British investment in this country require the movement of funds from England to the United States. These represent demand for dollar exchange and as any of these factors increase, the price of dollar exchange will likewise increase. On the other hand, any transaction which results in a movement of funds from the United States to England will increase the latter country's supply of dollar exchange. British exports, American tourists traveling in England, repayment of debt or the payment of interest by American debtors to English creditors, or American investment in England will serve to increase the supply of dollar exchange available in England. Any force which serves to increase the supply will exert a downward pressure upon the price of the item—in this case, dollar exchange.

Gold and the Exchange Rate. As long as the major trading countries of the world were on the gold standard, gold served as a limiting device insofar as fluctuations in the price of foreign exchange were concerned. Debtors always had the alternative of making international payments through the shipment of gold rather than through the remission of foreign exchange. Any time that the price of foreign exchange went above the cost of gold plus the cost of shipping gold (which was comparatively small), the purchaser would elect to make payment in gold. On the other hand, when the exchange rate fell below the price of gold less the cost of shipping gold, the seller would elect to receive payment in gold rather than in foreign exchange. The price of foreign exchange could only fluctuate between those two limits.

Although gold is no longer used as a medium of exchange in domestic trade, it is still used in international transactions. But rather than being used in individual transactions between residents of differing nations, it is used to effectuate a balance between national economies. When any given country does not have sufficient foreign exchange to cover its purchase from other countries, gold may be used as a means of making payments. But its use is limited since most countries have a very small stock of gold. There is, moreover, a second reason for the decline in the importance of gold. At the present time, conditions of demand and supply are not generally permitted to interact freely and thus determine the various exchange rates. As we shall see in the next section, the various governments have undertaken to establish exchange rates between the several countries. Once this is done, there is no need for gold to serve as a limiting device insofar as the fluctuations in exchange rates are concerned.

Government Regulation of the Exchange Rate. It is possible that exchange rates could be determined by conditions of demand and supply without governmental interference. However, governments have not been reluctant to interfere with the establishment of exchange rates. A variety of controls have been imposed for one purpose or another by one government or another.

The first type of control may be referred to as "pegging" the exchange rate. The operation is similar to that conducted by the government of the United States in supporting the prices of agricultural commodities. The government doing the pegging will always buy and sell exchange at the pegged price. There would be no need for one to pay more than this official rate since he could always buy the needed exchange from the government. And no one would ever have to dispose of exchange at a price below the official rate because he could always sell to the government at that rate. In some instances, the government may set upper and lower limits rather than set a single price. The purpose of this type of control is to limit the fluctuations in the price of a nation's foreign exchange.

A second control may take the form of rationing of foreign exchange. This includes some prohibitions. A government may allocate foreign exchange by permitting a citizen to use limited amounts for certain purposes. Or it may simply prohibit the use of foreign exchange for purposes which the government thinks undesirable. England has done this for much of the period since World War II. Englishmen were permitted such a small amount of dollar exchange for purposes of traveling in the United States that such travel was nearly prohibited. And for other purposes, the English citizen was simply prohibited from using dollar exchange. The purpose of such regulation was to control the use of the limited supply of dollar exchange since the government needed it for national defense. The United States is presently exercising controls over the use of foreign exchange.

A third type of control includes measures undertaken as a part of a comprehensive national policy of trade promotion, defense, or economic alliances. For one reason or another, the rate of exchange is manipulated in an attempt to achieve certain goals. There are a number of examples. Nazi Germany established a number of exchange rates between the German mark and various foreign currencies. One rate was used to encourage the importation of strategic materials. Another was to promote trade with Latin American countries. There were others, but in each case the German government subsidized a particular group within Germany in an effort to promote the policies of the government. Multiple exchange rates have been widely used in the countries of South America. Chile, for example, has had a number of different rates of exchange designed to promote Chilean state policy. The USSR as part of the tactics of the Cold War, appears to have established rates of exchange which apply only to certain groups of Westerners. In all of these cases, the rate of exchange is a governmentally determined rate.

A final form of governmental interference with the exchange rate is the revaluation of a nation's currency. A country may devalue its currency in terms of gold as did the United States in 1933. This was a domestic measure designed to increase prices by permitting the larger dollar value of gold to support a larger supply of money. But revaluing a currency will have international complications even in those instances when it is not done specifically as a foreign-trade measure. In 1949 England devalued the pound sterling from $4.03 to $2.80. Prior to this devaluation an item costing one £ cost the American purchaser $4.03. After devaluation it cost only $2.80. So, although the price in terms of pound sterling remained the same, there was actually a price reduction for an American buyer of 31 per cent on commodities purchased in England. England hoped to increase her exports to the United States and thus increase her supply of dollar exchange. But within any particular economy there can be an increase in the production of export goods only at the expense of other production if that economic system is operating at a level of full employment as was the case in England in 1949. This means that there will be a movement of resources from those industries producing goods and services for domestic consumption to those industries producing goods and services for export. The result almost has to be an inflationary pressure in the country devaluing its currency. As prices start to rise, the advantage which was gained through devaluation may be eliminated. Devaluing a country's currency, then, can increase exports only insofar as the subsequent price increases do not eliminate the international price advantage gained from devaluation.

Following England's lead in 1949, the rest of the major countries of the world, with the exception of the United States, devalued their currencies in terms of the American dollar. During the course of World War II and the subsequent postwar inflation, the currencies of these countries had become worth less and less while the dollar remained relatively sound, although it did depreciate some. An exchange rate which was reasonable and reflected the basic economic conditions before the war became entirely unreasonable and did not reflect the prevailing economic conditions in the postwar period. Prices were so high in the foreign countries and the exchange rate so low that it was nearly impossible for foreign producers to sell in the American market. These countries devalued their currencies in an effort to increase their exports to the United States and thus increase their supply of dollar exchange.

Since 1957, the position of the United States has been reversed. Instead of the rest of the world having a dollar shortage, we are now in the position of having the rest of the world holding large balances of dollar exchange. The most readily apparent aspect of this changed position is the outward flow of gold from the United States. Foreign holders of dollar exchange will get out of dollar exchange any time they can get a higher rate of return in some other part of the world. Therefore, one approach to the gold-outflow problem is to raise the domestic rate of interest and thus encourage the holder of dollar exchange to keep those balances in this country. But such a policy would not necessarily be consistent with a domestic stabilization policy. High interest rates might well contribute to a solution of the exchange problem, but at the same time such a policy would discourage domestic investment expenditures. This is a real dilemma.

In summary, then, controls over foreign exchange will result in the same type of reallocation of resources which were noted to exist in the case of tariffs. If the world economy is to move toward freer trade between nations, the direct controls presently exercised over the exchange rates will have to be relaxed.

THE BALANCE OF PAYMENTS

Concept of the Balance of Payments

An individual or firm may receive money from the sale of goods and services; from gifts, the sale of assets, or repayment of loans; and through borrowing from others. In turn, this money may be used in any of several ways. It may be spent for goods and services. It may be invested. It may be given to others as gifts. Debt may be retired. The money may be saved by depositing it in a bank, by using the services of some other type of financial institution, or by burying it in the back yard. If we can disregard the source and refer to all acquisitions as receipts, and if we can refer to its disposal as payments regardless of the nature of the disposal, then it can be said that money receipts must always equal money payments. Payments in any period can be no more or no less than receipts. If one were to draw up a balance sheet representing the receipts and payments for the individual, it would represent his financial position vis-à-vis the rest of society. It might be called his balance of payments.

Although this concept is not used by individuals, it is widely used in discussing the position of various countries of the world vis-à-vis the rest of the world. This statement is known as the balance of payments. The reasoning is the same as that described above, but instead of individuals, we will now speak of all of the residents of the various countries. People living in the United States purchase goods and services from practically every country on earth just as citizens of other countries buy goods and services from us. Americans travel abroad while others travel in the United States. We invest in foreign enterprises and build plants abroad just as foreigners invest in American enterprises and build plants in this country. And we give money to the rest of the world. In all of the cases funds must be transmitted. For any particular country there will be some transactions which involve payments to residents of other countries, and at the same time there will be transactions which involve receipts. The two combined, that is payments and receipts, represent a nation's balance of payments. And like the individual's "balance of payments," the nation's balance of payments must always balance. Receipts must equal payments.

The balance of international payments for the United States is shown in Table 17–3 and Figures 17–2 and 17–3. In 1962, total ex-

TABLE 17–3

U.S. BALANCE OF PAYMENTS

(In Millions of Dollars)

Item	1959 IV	1960 I	1960 II	1960 III	1960 IV	1961 I	1961 II	1961 III	1961 IV	1962 I	1962 II	1962 III	1962 IV[p]
Exports of goods and services, total[1]	6,448	6,280	6,882	6,581	7,270	6,820	6,952	6,656	7,638	6,995	7,881	7,143	7,795
Merchandise	4,343	4,615	5,008	4,691	5,145	5,012	4,922	4,673	5,308	5,015	5,497	4,895	5,159
Services[2]	2,105	1,665	1,874	1,890	2,125	1,808	2,030	1,983	2,330	1,980	2,384	2,248	2,636
Imports of goods and services, total	5,944	5,740	6,045	6,018	5,385	5,276	5,595	6,078	5,974	5,882	6,318	6,494	6,305
Merchandise	3,974	3,830	3,858	3,551	3,484	3,400	3,458	3,682	3,974	3,946	4,077	3,974	4,196
Services	1,216	1,139	1,429	1,670	1,179	1,106	1,381	1,697	1,278	1,184	1,495	1,790	1,331
Military expenditures	754	771	758	797	722	770	756	699	722	752	746	730	778
Balance on goods and services[1]	504	540	837	563	1,885	1,544	1,357	578	1,664	1,113	1,563	649	1,490
Unilateral transfers (net)	−675	−582	−620	−624	−680	−694	−706	−633	−696	−748	−686	−648	−714
Private remittances and pensions	−206	−201	−202	−207	−232	−216	−218	−213	−231	−228	−221	−223	−252
Government nonmilitary grants	−469	−381	−418	−417	−448	−478	−488	−420	−465	−520	−465	−425	−462
U.S. long- and short-term capital (net)	−595	−883	−1,131	−1,088	−1,885	−1,372	−540	−1,104	−1,863	−1,263	−1,168	−493	−1,251
Private, total	*−838*	*−653*	*−741*	*−943*	*−1,545*	*−989*	*−955*	*−637*	*−1,372*	*−861*	*−722*	*−518*	*−950*
Direct investment	−419	−303	−331	−327	−733	−441	−324	−341	−369	−196	−496	−314	−371
Portfolio and short-term investment	−419	−350	−410	−616	−812	−548	−631	−296	−1,003	−665	−226	−204	−579
Government	243	−230	−390	−145	−340	−383	415	−467	−491	−402	−446	25	−301
Foreign capital and gold (net)	620	851	1,014	1,239	1,156	506	185	916	1,469	763	365	848	1,180
Increase in foreign short-term assets and Government securities	425	586	740	548	254	38	314	626	890	414	487	319	783
Increase in other foreign assets	123	215	180	54	−19	122	201	20	123	160	85	−21	22
Gold sales by United States[3]	72	50	94	637	921	346	−330	270	456	189	−207	550	375
Errors and omissions	146	74	−100	−90	−476	16	−296	243	−574	135	−74	−356	705

[1] Excludes military transfers under grants.
[2] Includes military transactions.
[p] Preliminary

[3] Beginning with the first quarter of 1961, net of change in convertible currencies held by U.S. monetary authorities.

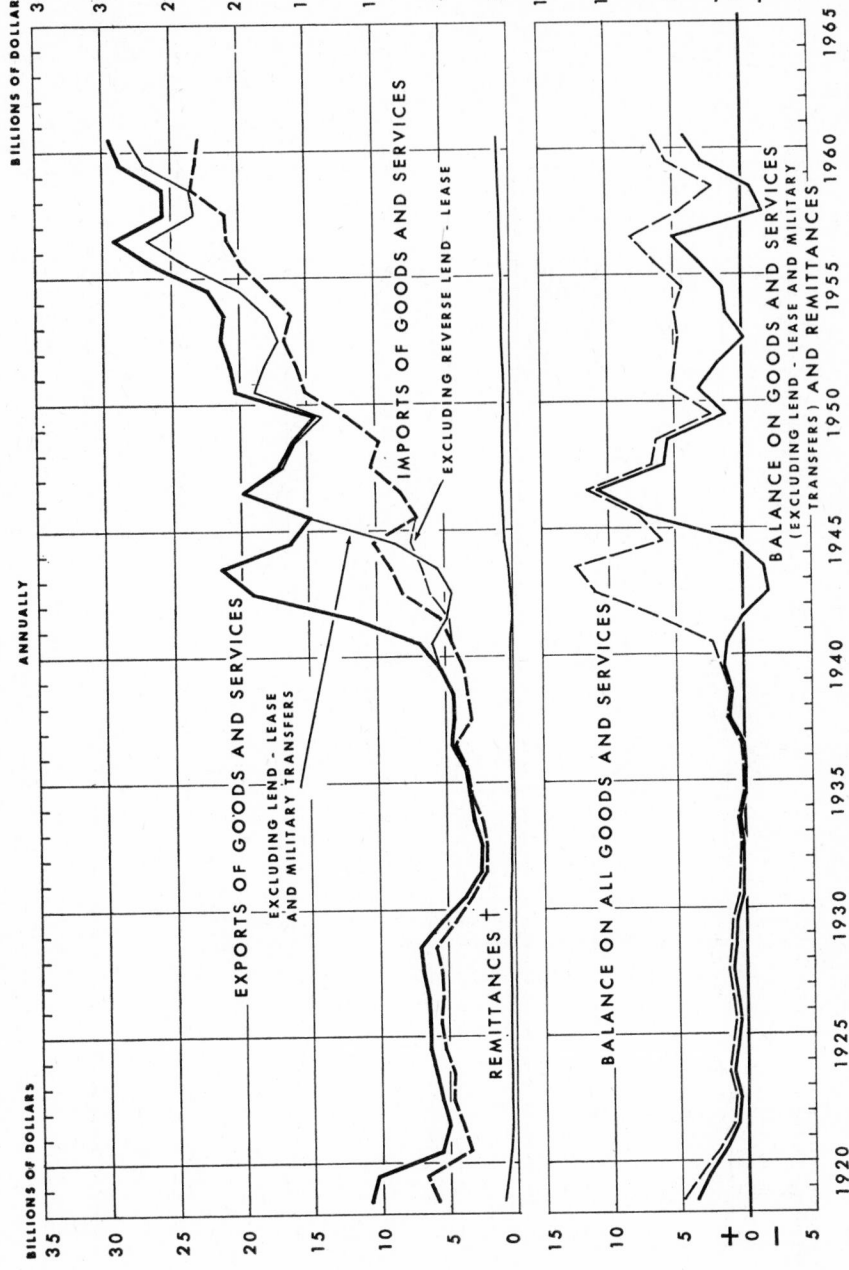

FIGURE 17-2

U.S. BALANCE OF PAYMENTS

Source: Board of Governors of the Federal Reserve System
† Net Payments from the U.S.

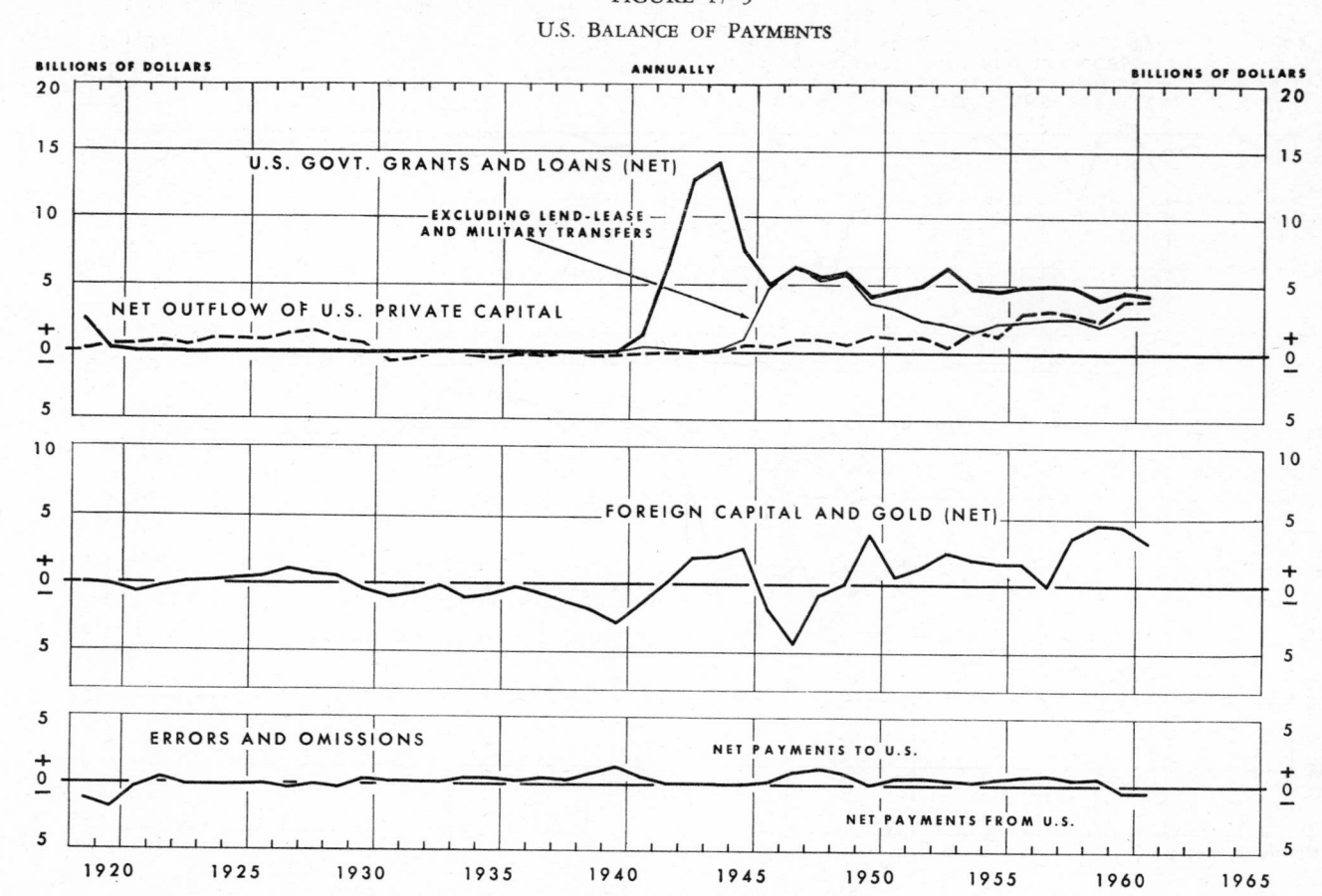

FIGURE 17–3

U.S. BALANCE OF PAYMENTS

SOURCE: Board of Governors of the Federal Reserve System

ports of goods and services were $30 billion, while imports of goods and services were $25 billion. If only goods and services were considered, the United States had an export balance of approximately $5 billion. During the same year, residents of the United States and the government sent $2.8 billion to citizens of other countries and other governments for nonmilitary grants. A total of $3.2 billion was invested abroad by both private and American citizens and this government.

Exports, unilateral transfers, and private and government capital expenditures all cause funds to move away from the United States. Imports result in funds moving to the United States. At this stage in the balance of payments, then, the United States had more funds moving away from this country than moved toward it. The difference in 1962 amounted to $475 million.

But there are other transactions which will cause funds to move toward the United States. If foreign nationals and governments invest in this country, funds will move in our direction. The same is true if we sell some of our assets—say, for example, gold. In 1962, the total flow of funds to the United States from the sale of gold and foreign investment in this country amounted to $3.2 billion.

Since this is a balance sheet, it has to balance. Since all possible transfers have been included, the balance at this point should be zero. Since it is not, the last item, errors and omissions, is included. In 1962, errors and omissions were $1 billion.

Significance of the Balance of Payments

In its totality, the balance of payments tells one little or nothing, but by observing the various components, much can be discerned. It provides a convenient porthole through which the problems arising from the economic relations between nations can be analyzed. A few observations using this new tool might now be made.

Since 1958, the United States has suffered from an acute balance of payments problem. Since that time our economy has run persistent deficits in its international accounts. In 1960, the problem gradually claimed the attention of the American people as it began to result in a large flow of gold to foreigners. Since World War II, the United States has consistently exported more goods and services than it has imported. On the average, the rest of the world owed this country $5 billion more than was owed to them. After World War II, there was a serious problem as to how foreign countries could pay for the excess of goods which they were buying from the U.S. Most often, the balance was established through the use of unilateral grants of funds by the United

FIGURE 17–4

Merchandise Exports and Imports

SOURCE: Board of Governors of the Federal Reserve System
* Change in series

States to foreign governments for economic or military aid. Much of the money would be expended in purchasing goods and services in the United States for use in the country receiving the aid. Under such an arrangement, foreign countries could import from the United States but they did not need to acquire dollar exchange in order to pay for such purchases, since the U.S. had provided the necessary funds.

For many years following World War II, the government appropriations for economic and military aid usually served to balance the international accounts of the United States. What has happened recently to change this picture? First, the economies of Western Europe and Japan have grown and prospered and are increasingly able to compete on favorable terms with the United States in foreign markets. Some of this remarkable recovery is directly attributable to foreign aid from the United States. Secondly, as the Western European economies prospered they re-established external currency convertibility which greatly facilitated international capital flows. Thirdly, the establishment of the "common market" offered a promising market to American companies who rapidly increased their investments in Europe. Fourthly, American overseas commitments, particularly in the military sphere, came to be a permanent part of our international payments picture rather than a stop-gap measure. Finally, the world military picture stabilized to the point where there was no longer great fear of holding large financial resources in Western Europe.

As most of the Western European countries began to show positive balances of payments, their reserves of dollars quickly rose. For some time now, the dollar has served with gold as the major unit of international trade. As dollar reserves built up and as the balance of payments problem of the U.S. seemed to indicate that they would continue to build up, many of the foreign countries elected to convert some of their dollar balances into gold. Thus, the gold flow problem. U.S. gold reserves declined from $24.6 billion in 1949 to $16.2 billion at the end of 1962. During the same period, foreign government and private holdings of dollars and short-term dollar claims increased from $7.5 billion to $25 billion. And, at the present time, approximately two-thirds of our current gold supply is needed as backing for our domestic monetary system.

While liquidation of foreign claims could wipe out our gold supply, this is not likely to happen as long as we can maintain foreign confidence in the dollar. A continued deficit in international payments could lead to increased claims for gold and to doubts about the efficacy of holding dollars as international reserves.

One of the problems which has intensified the gold drain in the last few years was mentioned above—the convertibility of foreign currencies. This has permitted easy transfer of funds from one country to another. In the last few years interest rates in the United States have been lower than rates in Europe. As a result there has been an outflow of short-term funds seeking the higher interest return. This has caused a serious policy problem for the U.S. government. Domestic unemployment in the early 1960's begged for attention. One of the ways in which a domestic recession can be fought is by lowering interest rates to stimulate investment. However, such a move would lead to further outflows of capital funds intensifying the balance of payments problems.

What can the United States do about its balance of payments problems? It can attempt to increase the favorable goods and service balance through increasing exports. This is becoming increasingly difficult in the face of intensified foreign competition and the development of regional economic blocs such as the Common Market. Import restrictions could be imposed. The United States could attempt to reduce its unilateral payments for economic and military assistance. However, the arguments for such payments are pervasive enough to cast doubt on this avenue as a means of alleviating the payment problem. In 1960, the country attempted to reduce the unfavorable balance by bringing home families of servicemen stationed overseas and by limiting purchases made by such families abroad. This offered little long-run hope of solving the problem. At the same time, we tried to get the Western European countries to shoulder a larger share of the common military burden and to participate on a larger scale in aid to the underdeveloped economies. Restrictions could be imposed on capital flows overseas although this would be contrary to our historic principles. And such capital movements eventually result in favorable balances as profits are brought "home" from overseas. The U.S. could also devalue the dollar by increasing the price of gold and thereby decreasing the gold content of the dollar. However, this would greatly disturb established foreign trade practices and might give support to doubts of the long-run stability of the dollar. Attempts to bargain tariff reductions with the Common Market would reduce the incentive for investments in that area as would changes in the tax laws which would affect the status of earnings on overseas investments.

Is the U.S. living "beyond its means" internationally? By no means. At the end of 1960, the U.S. government owned foreign assets totaling $21 billion, in addition to its gold holdings of almost $18 billion; and U.S. citizens owned another $50 billion in assets abroad. The

U.S. is rather in the position of the banker whose long-run solvency is assured but is embarrassed by short-run liquidity problems.

INTERNATIONAL INVESTMENT

Introduction to International Investment

Different economic systems are, at any moment in time, at different stages of economic development. Some countries are capable of producing more than the residents may desire to consume, while others are so primitive in their methods of production that they cannot produce the basic essentials. In the more advanced countries, savings will accumulate which can be translated into investment. In the underdeveloped countries, savings will be an impossibility for most people, and the total amount of savings will be small. However, these countries will have a dire need for investment which would increase productivity. The higher level of production, in turn, would permit the production of still more capital goods. Under such conditions there will be different rates of return to capital investment, and at least a part of this differential is to be explained by the state of economic development. Since the rate of return differs, it follows that there will be a movement of investment funds from one country to another. Viewed in this light, international investment is only a special facet of international trade.

Foreign investment may take any of several forms. It may, first, take the form of debt financing by corporations in other countries—foreign firms. Once such a firm decides to float a bond issue, it may then decide that it would be to the firm's advantage to float that issue in some market other than that located in their own country. Thus a French firm might float a bond issue in the United States. A second form of investment is that of selling equity securities, that is, stocks, in a country other than that in which the issuing corporation is located. A Canadian company, for example, might sell stock in the United States. In such a situation residents of the United States become shareholders in a Canadian firm. A third type of foreign investment is of a direct nature in the sense that an American firm builds a plant in some foreign country. The oil companies of the United States have done a great deal of this particular type of investment, for they have drilled wells, built refineries and pipelines, and provided other facilities for the production of oil in the Middle East and Latin America. General Motors and Ford both have production facilities in western Europe, and many other firms have similar operations. In all such cases the foreign plants are as much a part of the firm as are the domestic plants, but since they are located in another country, they represent a type of foreign investment. The last type of foreign investment includes investments made by governments. Governments lend to one another for such purposes as national defense and economic development. In situations where private investment is impossible because of a high degree of risk, governments sometimes assume the burden of international investment, and thus the risk is distributed among all of the people the lending government represents.

The *raison d' être* of international investment is much the same as that of international trade in goods and services. It is, essentially, a matter of supply, cost, and anticipated return. The individual person or business with funds to invest will seek out the more profitable outlet. If both domestic and foreign investment outlets exist, the investor will select that opportunity which promises to yield the highest return with the least risk. If the country in need of foreign investment is an underdeveloped country with a record of political instability and a propensity to nationalize foreign investments, the risk may be considered by investors to be so high as to preclude investment from abroad.

Debtor and Creditor Nations

Some countries are net creditors in the sense that they lend more to others than they borrow, while other countries borrow more than they lend and are debtors.

The United States was a debtor nation prior to World War I. Residents of other countries had invested more funds in this country than residents of the United States had invested in foreign countries. Much of our economic development was dependent upon these foreign funds. This was particularly true in the railroad industry, which attracted a great deal of English capital. Servicing of this debt and the repayment of the debt required that the United States acquire sterling exchange, since most of the debt was held by English investors. Sterling exchange was rather easily acquired since England was eager to buy goods produced in the United States—particularly wheat and cotton. With the sterling exchange so acquired, those who had lent money in the United States could be repaid.

After World War I there was change in the debtor-creditor status of the nations, and this change was emphasized by World War II. By the time of World War I, Great Britain had investments throughout the world. The return on these investments provided a supply of foreign exchange to pay for the many items she needed to import. In fighting two major wars within 25 years, a severe strain was imposed on her economy. In order to increase the supply of foreign exchange and thus enable her to increase purchases abroad to support her war effort, England liquidated a large part of her foreign investment. In other words, England sold assets in order to acquire foreign exchange. But in disposing of these investments, she was disposing of her major source of foreign exchange, that is, the return on these investments. By the end of World War II, England's supply of foreign exchange was insufficient to support her former role in the international economy. England, as well as other countries in which the wars were fought, faced another difficulty. Capital was destroyed by the war itself. So, through liquidation and combat, both foreign and domestic capital was lost. There was no longer a return from foreign investments. There was a shortage of domestic capital. Instead of being in a position to lend to the rest of the world, England, as well as other countries in western Europe, sought to borrow funds in the international capital market. The former creditor nations now became debtor nations.

The United States, on the other hand, has not suffered in this respect. A small part of this nation's foreign investment was seized in the two wars and some was lost through hostilities, but this loss was negligible. There was no loss of plant and equipment within the continental United States. So, as England's position in world trade declined, that of the United States was in its ascendancy. This country, starting with World War I, loaned money to foreign governments to fight that war as well as World War II. Private investors in the United States began lending money abroad or investing in foreign operations. As a consequence, the United States in the period since World War I has changed from a debtor nation to the world's leading creditor nation.

Even though American investment abroad is a small percentage of domestic investment, the fact still stands that the country as a whole is a creditor rather than a debtor nation. A trade policy which is satisfactory for the latter may not necessarily be so for the former. As a country changes from a net debtor to a net creditor in the family of nations, there must be a change in that country's trade policy. A creditor nation will have to permit the debtor nations to accumulate a supply of exchange in order that interest payments may be made to the holders of that debt in the creditor nation. As a long-run proposition, this probably means that the creditor nation must be willing to accept an increased amount of imports from those economic systems in which the investments have been made. This England was willing to do as long as the country remained a creditor nation. In large part, it explains that country's willingness to abstain from imposing a tariff on imports for the better part of a century. The United States, on the other hand, has made some progress in this direction since World War II, but not a great deal of change has been noted. Certainly, there is a need for a continuing examination of this country's status in the world as a creditor nation as well as a need for revising the trade policy of the nation.

FOREIGN TRADE POLICY

The United States

The Tariff in the United States. Between 1500 and 1776, mercantilism was the dominant economic philosophy in Europe. Mercantilists believed that a strong central government was necessary for the development of the national state; in fact, mercantilism is sometimes referred to as a philosophy of "state building." One factor in the mercantilistic programs of the several states was that of providing protection for domestic industry through the use of a protective tariff in addition to other controls over international trade. Insofar as England was concerned, it was the mercantilistic control measures that finally drove the colonists in the New World to armed revolt.

At the time the Americans were in armed rebellion against mercantilism, the economist Adam Smith had taken up his pen in protest against the same philosophy. He denounced the various regulations as being inimical to the best interests of the people. An important part of his program of *laissez faire* was international free trade. If free trade were to prevail between nations, the welfare of all of the people would be enhanced. One might suppose, now, that since both the colonists and Adam Smith were objecting to the same thing, that the colonists would adopt the doctrines of the economist and philosopher. They did not. Instead, they accepted the doctrines of mercantilism. But instead of England imposing these onerous regulations upon the colonies, the colonists imposed the same regulations upon themselves.

A major problem facing the First Congress of the United States was that of finance. Where was the money to come from to support the operations of the government of the United States? In response to this question, Representative James Madison, from Virginia sponsored a bill enacting a modest tariff for purposes of raising revenue. This bill was passed. The tariff continued to be an extremely important source of revenue for the national government for nearly a century. The Secretary of the Treasury under President Washington, Alexander Hamilton, looked upon the tariff as more than merely a source of revenue. He proposed that the initial rates be raised to such a level as to offer some protection for the industries of the new country. The rates were raised, but it was not until after the War of 1812 that the tariff really offered a significant amount of protection.

From 1789 until 1828, the rates were adjusted upward until they reached a high point in the latter year. At this point, the southern states objected. The South was dependent upon the export of cotton, and to the extent that imports were reduced, they feared that the market for cotton would be lost. The South has remained in favor of low tariffs until the present, but there is some indication that this section also is moving toward a protectionist position. As a result of southern opposition, the tariff rates were adjusted downward for the thirty years preceding the Civil War.

In the 1850's there were three issues dividing the country—slavery, free land, and the tariff. The South wanted slavery. The West and the wage earners of the East wanted free land. And the business and manufacturing interests of the Northeast wanted a protective tariff. The Republican party was formed with free land and a protective tariff as the two planks which tied West and Northeast together. From Lincoln's inauguration in 1861 to Franklin D. Roosevelt's inauguration in 1933, there were only four presidential elections in which the Republican Party was the loser. It was only during the administrations of Cleveland and Wilson that there were reductions in the tariff rates.

Toward the end of the 1920's, Congress was asked to provide relief for farmers. This group was supposed to be suffering from excessive foreign competition, and the relief was to take the form of a protective tariff for agricultural products. By the time the law was passed, Congress had raised rates in more than 800 cases on the premise that if higher rates helped agriculture, such changes would also help other industries. Other countries raised their rates in retaliation, and the result was a rather substantial reduction in international trade at the very time when all countries needed increased production and trade.

The Reciprocal Trade Agreements Act. Just as Congress passed the Smoot-Hawley Tariff in 1930 to promote recovery, so did the following administration pass the Reciprocal Trade Agreements Act in 1933 to promote recovery. The first raised rates to an all time high, and the second provided for lower rates.

The Reciprocal Trade Agreements Act made a basic change in the method of establishing tariff rates. Up to this time, Congress set the rates. This mechanism was unwieldy and promised to become more so. Under the Reciprocal Trade Agreements Act more power was delegated to the executive branch of the government insofar as tariffs were concerned. That branch of the government was empowered to enter into executive agreements with other sovereign governments regarding tariffs. The President could lower tariffs as much as 50 per cent if corresponding concessions could be obtained from the countries with which the agreements were negotiated.

In the quarter of a century since the passage of the first Reciprocal Trade Agreements Act, there has been a progressive lowering of tariff rates on imports into the United States. But even as the rates were being lowered, other barriers to trade were retained and new ones were added. Since the statute is of limited duration, Congress has periodically renewed the legislation. It has been in this fashion that certain restrictive features have been added to what is basically a tariff lowering statute.

A peril-point amendment has been added to the law. This amendment provides that any time proposed reductions in the tariff imperil a domestic industry the Tariff Commission must hold a hearing to determine whether the industry is imperiled and what tariff rate is needed to protect that industry. The President's power to lower tariffs is thus limited. Fig growers, hatters, watch manufacturers, garlic producers, wool producers, and others have sought relief under this amendment, but few have gained the desired relief.

A second restraint imposed by Congress is to be found in the "Buy American" Act which was originally passed as a recovery measure in 1933. This statute provides that the government must purchase from domestic producers in preference to foreign producers unless the price of the latter is more than 25 per cent less than the price of the domestic producer.

Dairy products received a special type of protection during the Korean War. Congress enacted a statute which prohibited the importing of dairy products where it would interfere with the production and marketing of domestic producers. Since the government was then supporting the price of dairy products, the executive branch of the government interpreted this statute to mean that no dairy products were to be imported. Denmark and a few other producers of dairy products did not like this legislation.

A fourth type of restraint is to be found in the restrictions Congress has imposed on shipping. By legislation certain shipping has been reserved for ships of American registry. For example, countries receiving foreign aid from the United States were required to transport goods which they had to buy in the United States in American bottoms. And this was required even in those instances in which cheaper means of transportation were available.

And lastly, a word might be said about the administration of the tariffs. This is so complex that the complexity itself eliminates some imports. The determination of the value of the product, the classification, the applicable rate, and even the determination of the nature of the product must be decided. All take time. International trade is reduced because of the bureaucratic red tape. In addition, much of the bargaining authority of the Reciprocal Trade Agreements Act has been used up and it is increasingly difficult to enter into meaningful negotiations leading toward reductions of tariffs. Nevertheless, the Reciprocal Trade Agreements Act represented a reversal of direction insofar as the level of tariff rates are concerned. However, the protectionist philosophy dies a hard death.

The emergence of the Common Market as a powerful economic bloc with no internal tariff and a common tariff wall against outsiders resulted in increased interest in the United States in providing additional bargaining authority to the executive to bargain down tariff walls and increase the opportunities of American business in world trade and particularly in the lucrative markets of Western Europe.

The United States and the Common Market

If the world is to move toward increased trade between nations, it will probably be done through multilateral agreement involving a number of nations. Such attempts have been and are being made.

Following World War II, there was a general recognition among nations of the desirability of increasing trade between nations. This was particularly true of the countries of western Europe. This area had long been divided into a number of small national states with a tariff wall around each. The United States was envied for her large domestic market with a single external tariff. After the war, western Europe witnessed the establishment of the Soviet satellite system with its possibilities for international specialization and trade. The impetus toward a reduction of the trade barriers was tremendous.

The first step in this direction was the formation of the Benelux Customs Union composed of The Netherlands, Belgium, and Luxembourg. The three countries agreed to impose no tariffs on goods moving from one sovereignty to another. They also agreed to adopt the same tariff schedule on goods being imported into any of the three nations. Some, although not all, of the other restrictions on trade between the three nations were eliminated.

In 1952 the three Benelux countries, France, Italy, and West Germany, established a unified market for coal and steel. And in March

1957, the same six countries signed the Treaty of Rome establishing the European Economic Community—the Common Market. The six countries agreed that within a 12–15 year transition period they would work toward the following objectives:

1. the removal of tariffs, quotas and other barriers to trade within the community;
2. the creation of a uniform external tariff between the six and the rest of the world;
3. the abolition of restrictions on the movement of labor, capital, and business enterprises within the community;
4. the coordination of monetary and fiscal policies in order to promote balance of payments, high employment and price stability in each member country;
5. the establishment of an Investment Bank for Europe and a Development Fund for Associated Overseas Territories.

In 1959 Britain, Norway, Sweden, Denmark, Switzerland, Austria, and Portugal met and agreed to form their own trade area—the European Free Trade Association. This group had a more modest program. By the early 1960's, most of the members of the EFTA were petitioning for membership in the Common Market. And the Common Market accelerated its tariff programs in an effort to eliminate internal tariffs by 1966 and establish common external tariffs by 1969 if not sooner. The external tariff will be the average of the four customs areas—France, West Germany, Italy, and Benelux.

If Britain and other members of the EFTA join the Common Market, the resulting group will more than match the international economic role of the United States. It would have a population (1960 figures) of approximately 250 million and foreign exchange reserves of almost $24 billion. Under existing conditions, this enlarged market would send one-fifth of its exports to the U.S. and obtain one-fourth of its imports from us. In turn, the U.S. would send over 30 per cent of its exports to the enlarged Common Market and would buy 27 per cent of its imports from that group.

The United States faces a real economic challenge from these economic integrations. It must be prepared to negotiate tariff reductions with these groups or find itself priced out of its most lucrative markets. Since the U.S. is so closely integrated with the Common Market in military alliances, it behooves both groups to foster the interdependence with a satisfactory economic alliance. The U.S. and Canada are now equal participating members with the Western European countries in the Organization of Economic Cooperation and Development (OECD), which in 1961 replaced the Organization for European Economic Cooperation (OEEC), set up to help administer the Marshall Plan in 1947. Many problems confront the U.S. and the other free nations in working out better trade relations. Japan must be considered as well as the underdeveloped nations of Africa and South America. It would do little good to reach an agreement which kept the emerging countries from earning their way in world trade.

In 1962 Congress passed the Trade Expansion Act. The impetus for this legislation came largely from developments in Europe. The exciting progress of the Common Market and its development as a large free trade area, the impending entrance of England as well as additional West European countries, and the propensity of the Common Market countries to erect a high common tariff against outsiders made it necessary for the United States to reconsider its trade policy.

The Trade Expansion Act of 1962 permits the President to bargain with other nations on broad categories of goods rather than on specific commodities. Some tariffs can be eliminated, others cut in half; and if the United States and the countries of the Common Market conduct 80 per cent of the total trade in a commodity, the United States can bargain for the total elimination of the tariff. Domestically, the 1962 legislation authorized the government to render various types of financial assistance of a transitional nature to firms and employees adversely affected by increased imports.

As this is written, the Trade Expansion Act is not living up to the high hopes held for the legislation. The failure of Great Britain to join the Common Market means that tariffs can be eliminated on only a few rather minor products. The Common Market itself seems to be much more protectionist-minded than most had imagined. Politically, it is nationalistic rather than internationalistic. And there is the very real fear that the underdeveloped countries will be "left out in the cold" as the developed countries start setting up trading blocs. All of this means that we cannot revert to the trade policies of the pre-World War II period; indeed, we cannot even revert to the policies of the 1950's.

CONCLUSION

Since World War I, the position of the United States in the family of nations has changed. Economically and politically, this country is the most powerful in the world. This has come about because technological changes in production, increasing use of capital goods, increased productivity, abundant supplies of natural resources, faster methods of travel, etc. That is, our position of leadership is largely based on the fact that the economic system is more productive than the economies of other countries. However, powerful blocs of countries in Western Europe have begun to challenge this position.

Changes in the physical environment, such as those mentioned above, will necessitate changes in the social environment. It has often been observed, moreoever, that the social changes will lag behind the changes in the physical environment. That is, it is easier to change the method of production than it is to change the social institutions. This is certainly true in the case of international trade. Because of our changed status in the world, there will be, of necessity, a change or reappraisal of the social institutions associated with international relations and international trade in particular. Some of these changes are already evident. We have changed our method of setting tariffs. The attitudes of particular groups toward the tariff as a protective device has changed. In some cases, those who were, at one time, staunch protectionists have become free traders. There are some examples of the reverse.

The question of what our policy ought to be is another of those normative questions. All that an understanding of economics can do is to explain some of the consequences of alternative policies. The ultimate decision as to what we ought to do has to rest with the people.

EXERCISES

Group I

Explain why the following statements are either true or false:

1. Production in accordance with the principle of comparative advantage would result in a maximum amount of production for the entire world.
2. The economic case for free trade is irrefutable; however, there are strong arguments of a noneconomic nature against such a national policy.
3. The trade policy of a creditor nation should, on economic grounds, be different from the trade policy of a debtor nation.
4. Any individual country can always increase exports by devaluing its currency.
5. The international balance of payments for the United States will always be in favor of this country since we consistently export more than we import.
6. Any individual country can export goods and services to other countries without ever accepting any imports from the countries receiving the exports.
7. Increased investment in backward countries depend upon higher incomes and increased savings, but increased incomes and savings depend upon increased investment.

Group II

1. Since World War II, Japan has been making inroads in the American markets in such industries as textiles, maritime construction, and precision and electronic equipment. What has happened to the costs of production for Japanese industry which has permitted these gains?

2. For nearly a century Great Britain followed a policy of free trade. Why was such a policy adopted in the first place? Why was it abandoned? How did that policy compare with the present policy of the United States? Is the position of the United States at the present time similar to that of Great Britain during the period when such a policy prevailed in Great Britain?

3. Since World War II there has been no shortage of outlets for investment funds in many of the underdeveloped areas of the world. At the same time there have been large amounts of investment funds available in the United States. Why have the investors avoided these foreign outlets for their funds? Has anything been done to make such investment opportunities more attractive?

Group III

1. Historically the Republican party has been the high-tariff party and the Democratic party has been the low-tariff party. However, since World War II, the dichotomy is no longer so clear-cut. Why have major segments within both parties changed their position on this subject?

2. How has the USSR used international trade as a weapon in the struggle between international communism and the free world? How did Hitler use international trade to further his aims prior to World War II?

3. What role can the economist play in deciding what the policy of the United States *ought* to be regarding the tariff and foreign trade?

4. In Silverton, Colorado, there is a large sign advertising gold claims for sale. These claims, it is alleged, will undergo an incalculable increase in value when the government ceases to fix the price of gold at an artificially low level. As a matter of fact, the government imposed price controls over this industry 30 years ago and since that time no increases in the price of this commodity have been permitted despite considerable increases in the cost of production. How can price controls over a single private industry be justified? How can one justify the failure of the government to allow price increases in the light of increases in the cost of production? Why not subsidize the producer of gold?

BIBLIOGRAPHY

AMERICAN ECONOMIC ASSOCIATION. *Readings in the Theory of International Trade.* Philadelphia: Blakiston, 1950.

MYRDAL, GUNNAR. *An International Economy.* New York: Harper & Brothers, 1956.

PIQUET, H. *Aid, Trade and the Tariff*. New York: Thomas Y. Crowell Co., 1953.

SCHELLING, T. C. *International Economics*. Boston: Allyn and Bacon, 1958.

SMITH, ADAM. *The Wealth of Nations*. New York: Modern Library, 1937.

PAPERBACK READING LIST

TRIFFIN, R. *Gold and the Dollar Crisis*. New Haven: Yale University Press, 1960.

Now, *here*, you see, it takes all the running you can do to keep in the same place. If you want to get somewhere else, you must run at least twice as fast.—Lewis Carroll, *Through the Looking Glass.*

455

INTRODUCTION

Economics and Growth

Introduction. Adam Smith's book entitled *An Inquiry into the Nature and Causes of the Wealth of Nations* was an inquiry into the economics of growth. Since that time, economists have shown some tendency to specialize. At any moment in time, certain parts of economics have been emphasized at the expense of others. For roughly 25 years following 1929, the major concern of economists was with cyclical stability. But starting in the early years of the decade of the 1950's, the subject of economic growth became the major preoccupation of economists.

Economic growth is, however, of concern to more than economists. Current national election campaigns find most candidates promising programs which would result in a "high" rate of growth. The Congress of the United States, the United Nations, and the governing bodies of other nations are continually debating the question of growth and the policies best designed to promote a high rate of growth. "Growth" has joined the ranks of those virtues which one can't very well be against.

Economic Growth—What Is It? The concept of economic growth itself is not unambiguous. Although everyone knows, in some general sense, what is meant, the economic analyst needs to define the term with some precision.

It might first be observed that the concept of economic growth refers, in some way, to the output of an economic system, and, by implication, it refers to an increase in that output (although a reduction in output can be regarded as negative growth). Thus it does not refer to the growth in the size of the government, increases in population or employment, or any of the countless things that "grow." Obviously, though, economic growth and growth of specific parts of the economy are interrelated.

Such an increase in output is the result of several factors. For instance, if the output is measured in terms of a monetary unit, the total output can increase in magnitude as a result of an increase in the price level. The relevant economic growth is not a monetary concept but is real economic growth—growth in terms of constant prices.

Increases in real output can result from simply increasing the level of inputs. If one man produces ten units of output and a second person is added who also produces ten units, there has been no increase in the "aggregate well-being." A nation's output will increase as its population increases, but if the increase in output is just proportional to the increase in population, the larger population will be no "better off" than the smaller. A more relevant concept is total real output divided by the population or real per capita output. Economic growth is the increase in real per capita output. The rate of increase in real per capita output is the growth rate.

Here an issue in normative economics must be recognized. If growth is defined as above, then a comparison of the growth rates for different societies may not be too meaningful unless an examination of the types of growth is undertaken. Examine, for a moment, the ratio

$$\frac{\text{Total real output}}{\text{Population.}}$$

There is no ambiguity in the denominator—it is simply the number of people in the country in question. But the numerator is not so clearly defined. The nature of the output in one country may be considerably different from that in another. For example, one nation may be devoting nearly all of its resources to armaments, another may be producing nearly all capital goods, and a third may be concentrating on the production of consumer goods. The real per capita output could, however, be the same for all three. A higher rate of growth does not imply a higher standard of living. Indeed, a high rate of growth and a declining level of living are not incompatible. It is not even possible for the economist to say that a high rate of growth is always superior to a lower rate.

The growth rate is a percentage figure and it behaves as such. Consider, for the moment, a baseball player. During the first game of the season, his batting average may go from .000 to .500 if he gets a hit the second time at bat after going hitless the first. As the season progresses, the additional hit will have less and less effect on his batting average. The point is that large percentage increases are easier to achieve when working from a small base. The same thing is true in the case of economic growth. An increase of ten for a nation with a base of ten would be a one hundred percent increase while it would only be a ten percent increase for a country with a base of one hundred. This does not mean, however, that one can conclude that the first nation's rate of growth will automatically fall off to that of the second as the former experiences further growth, nor does it mean that the first is bound to catch up and surpass the second.

The Problem of Growth—An Analogy. Before turning to an analysis of economic growth, let us first examine the growth process of a hypothetical firm. If we assume that this firm is a sole proprietorship, the owner must choose between using the profits for personal consumption expenditures or reinvestment.

What strategy would result in the largest rate of growth for the business? Obviously this maximum rate could be obtained by plowing all of the profits back into capital equipment. The only difficulty with this strategy is that the family might starve to death in the process. For this entrepreneur, then, the rate of growth for his business is a function of the saving (lack of consumption) by his family. The more that he can induce his family to reduce their consumption, the greater the rate of growth for the firm. The less willing the family is to abstain from consumption, the slower will be the firm's rate of growth.

The rate of growth for our hypothetical firm is a function of more than simply the absolute amount of profits which are put into the firm. For that which is reinvested in the present time period will create greater profits in future time periods. The profits of period t, for example, are a function of the capital which was created through reinvestment in some previous period—say $t - 1$, as well as the amount of capital which was already in existence at the beginning of that time period. In short, there is a compounding effect just as there is when a person deposits his savings in a savings account.

This compounding effect is a double-edged sword. As long as the firm is showing growth, the rate of increase in any given period will be dependent upon the growth of previous periods. But suppose that growth was currently falling off because of a reduction in the willingness of business firms to acquire additional units of capital goods. The immediate effect would be a reduction in the rate of growth resulting from the reduced acquisition of capital goods. There would also be a long-run effect since the capital goods which might have been acquired will not be available in future time periods to serve as a base for the compounding effect. So if our businessman succumbs to family pressure and buys a new house with all of the accoutrements, the immediate cost is a reduction in the growth of the firm in the present time period. There will be a long-run effect of reduced growth in future time periods, even though the entrepreneur once again starts plowing profits back into the firm.

Two Theories of Development

The subject of growth and development transcends economics, for it is a subject of interest to scholars in many of the social sciences. There have been various attempts to formulate general theories of development, of which two will be examined here.

Karl Marx and Historical Development. Karl Marx (1818–1883), although not the first communist, was the first "scientific socialist." Marx constructed what he considered to be a scientific basis for the development and establishment of the socialist state. His theory of socialism has served as the theoretical base to which today's practicing Communists at least pay homage.

Marx was a historical materialist. He saw all social changes resulting from changes in economic forces. Society consisted of (1) an economic base and (2) a social superstructure. The economic base consisted of the forces of production which includes man as a productive force, the productive factors with which he works, and the techniques he employs. The superstructure includes such social institutions as the state, laws, business organizations, property, church, etc.

The relation between the economic base and the social superstructure was one of cause and effect. For each type of economic base, there was a particular form of superstructure. One method of production would result in a feudal type of society while another would result in a capitalistic type of society. The causal relationship went from the economic base to the superstructure, for it was only by changing the base that changes could be effected in the structure of society. This reaction could not be reversed.

Any society, according to Marx, consists of classes based on ownership or nonownership of property as well as the degree of personal freedom. The class structure of society depends upon the method of production. Thus the class structure in a feudal society would be different from that in any other form of society.

To Marx, history involved action and reaction. Thesis, antithesis, and synthesis was the core of Marx's dialectical theory of historical change. The thesis contains contradictory forces which eventually negate the original proposition and establish the antithesis, but the antithesis contains negating forces which eventually result in the establishment of the synthesis.

Marx saw feudal societies containing forces which would eventually negate that society and lead to the establishment of capitalism, but capitalism would be replaced by a socialist society. The class struggle is of the same nature. The class structure of the feudal society would be replaced by the class structure of a capitalist society, and this would eventually be replaced by the class structure of the Marxian socialist society. In the last stages of capitalism, the class structure would consist of two classes—proletariat and capitalist. In the socialist society there would be a single class—the proletariat.

The demise of the capitalist class was explained by Marx as follows. Labor was the source of all value, but the capitalist appropriated part of that value for himself leaving labor only that amount necessary for its continued subsistence. Part of that value appropriated by the capitalist was consumed and part invested. The invested capital was laborsaving in the sense that capital was substituted for labor. Thus the number of workers employed was reduced, and an army of unemployed was created. The net result of the capitalist appropriation of this surplus value was (1) the capitalists got richer, (2) wages remained at a subsistence level, and (3) the number of the unemployed increased. These were the contradictory forces in capitalism which were ultimately to result in the revolution of the proletariat and the demise of the capitalist class.

Following the proletarian revolution, there was to be a period of transition during which time the economy was to be administered by a dictatorship of the proletariat, but this was to be eventually succeeded by a classless society. In the last and highest stage of society envisaged by Marx, the state would simply atrophy, for there would be only minor tasks for it to perform.

In this ultimate society, all prices would be based on labor value. There would be no interest return to the capitalist. There would be no rent return to the owner of natural resources, and of course there would be no need for the private entrepreneur and profit. Labor would get the full value of the product.

Although Marx acknowledged the need for foreign markets in the capitalist stage of development, little attention was given to this particular phase of historical development. Nikolai Lenin (1870–1924) extended Marx's theory of historical development to include an age of capitalist imperialism which was to be the last stage in the development of capitalism.

Domestic capital accumulation would encounter certain limits, for the investment opportunities in the domestic economy are limited. The finance capitalist, who was to become increasingly important according to Lenin, would turn to foreign investment outlets, which would result in his eventual domination of all of the noncapitalistic economies.

The "scientific socialism" of Karl Marx has not fared well. His theory of historical development has not predicted future happenings; in fact, it has proven even too rigid for the Communists in the USSR. Marx did not anticipate the flexibility of social institutions in such capitalistic nations as the United States and Great Britain. The development of trade unions and the improved status of the industrial workers have resulted in a distinct lack of interest in communism and the revolution of the proletariat on the part of the workers.

Among economists and historians of the free world, Karl Marx has little acceptance, yet his beliefs have become the "dogma" of the communist world. Marx's teachings have never found a great deal of acceptance in industrialized economies. On the contrary, communism has found its most fertile fields in the underdeveloped sections of the world. Russia in 1917 was one of the more backward and underdeveloped nations of the world. China following World War II was in the same economic position. The countries of eastern Europe would also have to be classed as underdeveloped with the exception of Czechoslovakia.

Rostow's Stages of Economic Growth.[1] Professor W. W. Rostow has tried to formulate a general theory of economic growth to serve as a substitute for Marxian analysis. Unlike the Marxian approach, Rostow's is independent of the particular type of social organization found in society. Marx thought that the path of development led inexorably toward a system of Communism, while Rostow claims that his theory is equally applicable to a highly controlled economy as well as a decentralized economic system.

Rostow identified five stages in the economic development of any country. The earliest stage of growth is that characterized by the *traditional society* and is associated with many underdeveloped countries. A country in this stage of development would be characterized by low productivity, a disproportionate share of its populace engaged in agriculture as compared to the more advanced countries, a rigid social structure, and a rather primitive technology. In short, there will be an effective limit to the level of per capita output which can be achieved within the existing physical and social restraints.

The second stage is referred to as the *preconditions for the take-off*. This is a period of development—a period of transition during which certain of the prerequisites of growth are established. Most important, the views of the people are changing. The idea of progress itself comes to have value. Social institutions, such as banks and business firms, are established. The center of political power as well as the purpose for which that power is exercised is shifted from those more interested in maintaining the status quo to those more interested in change. Individuals appear who are willing to engage in nonagricultural productive activity. Some social overhead capital (roads, schools, communication

---

[1] W. W. Rostow, *Stages of Economic Growth* (New York; Cambridge University Press, 1960). This book is available in a paperback edition. The student will find it to be interesting and challenging reading.

facilities, etc.) is created. In brief, this is a period when the groundwork is being laid for future development.

The third stage is the *take-off*. In this period the forces making for progress finally outweigh those forces resisting progress. New techniques, institutions, ways of thinking, and industries replace the old. More of the economy's resources are devoted to investment as the consumers save more of their income. Specifically, Rostow says that the following conditions must be met.

(a) Investment must increase from 5 per cent or less to 10 per cent or more of national income.

(b) One or more significant manufacturing sectors must be established which will have a greater rate of growth than other sectors of the economy.

(c) Changes in the social structure must be sufficient to utilize changes brought about by the development of the leading manufacturing sectors. These changes must give the process a continuing basis.

It is important to note that the take-off requires that the economy enter a period of self-sustained growth.

The *drive to maturity,* the fourth of Rostow's five stages, is that period in which the level of investment becomes more or less constant. Output is increasing faster than population so that there is an increase, in some sense, in the general well-being of the populace. Such an economy has a broad range of industrial undertakings centering around technological processes of a more complex type. It was this stage that the United States went through just about 60 years ago, and the USSR entered in the period following World War I.

The final stage—the *age of high mass-consumption*—is that stage in which consumer durable goods become relatively more important. The automobile, for example, is the symbol of this stage in the United States. At this stage in a country's development there is an increased interest in social welfare and security. Resources, which in an earlier stage were used for capital development, can now be devoted to increased welfare—increased aid to the aged and the unemployed, for example. The United States entered this stage following World War I while the countries of Western Europe and Japan did so after the Second World War. It is this stage which the USSR is ready to enter, but for which its leaders appear to be unwilling to accept the consequences. High mass consumption and totalitarian communism may be incompatible.

What follows the age of mass-consumption? Rostow, of course, doesn't know, but he points out that in the United States, at least, the next stage may be marked by a preference for larger families. Another possibility may be that of increasing our stock of social overhead capital —schools, hospitals, recreational facilities, and the like. Space exploration is another possibility.

It must be pointed out that both Marx and Rostow are occupying controversial ground. Are there laws of development which can be used to describe the general process of historical development? If so, can they predict the future? Certainly Karl Marx does not enjoy a high batting average. It remains to be seen whether Rostow will do better. But both present an extremely interesting and challenging approach to the problem of development. Both, however, take a broader approach than we will be interested in here, for our interest is in the economic aspect of development rather than the overall development process which cuts across many fields.

DETERMINANTS OF ECONOMIC GROWTH

Noneconomic Factors

There are many noneconomic factors which are necessary but not sufficient conditions for economic growth. Without them, there can be no sustained economic growth. With them, there may be.

There is the question of changing social institutions. A growing economy beginning to industrialize or planning to industrialize will require a different set of social institutions than a rural, underdeveloped, agricultural economy. Business firms must be organized. Facilities for credit must be established. Legally enforceable contracts must be available to facilitate exchange. There must be provisions for the assumption of risk—either private or public entrepreneurs. Rules governing the use of property will be required. There will often have to be a complete change in the attitude of the people toward work. If work is degraded and left to those of a lower caste or inferior station, economic development will be thwarted if not stopped. Business must have "status" in the community. It cannot be left to the untouchables.

Economic development depends upon education. An uneducated populace may well suffice in a primitive agricultural economy, but only a highly educated and skilled labor force will do in a more advanced society. And as society develops still further, the same society must eventually produce the necessary scientists and professional people.

Eventually a growing economy must spawn a flow of innovations. It is inconceivable that an economy could be forever dependent upon others for new productive techniques, new products, and new processes.

Somehow or other, a society's system of education and its reward for innovators must be such as to make a contribution to economic growth.

This short discussion of noneconomic factors is not intended to minimize the role of such factors. In the total picture, the noneconomic factors may be considerably more significant than the economic factors.

Economic Factors

Introduction. The progress of any economy depends upon two basic economic conditions. The first is the absolute quantity of the factors of production—land, labor, capital, and entrepreneurial ability; but such absolute magnitudes are not sufficient. A second determinant is the productivity of the several factors. A large quantity of any given factor will be of little use if that factor is of very low productivity, and a shortage of a particular factor may be offset by its superior productivity.

The productivity of any factor will be a result of two basic conditions. The first is the quality of the factor itself. Poor land, hungry and undernourished workers, obsolete capital equipment, and incompetent management are examples of factors of low quality. The second determinant is the combination of the existing factors. That is, there must be a proper balance between the inputs if the highest level of output is to be achieved. A very large, healthy, hardworking labor force would produce little without capital, just as fertile land will produce little of use if there is no capital or labor.

There are many examples where the lack of a particular factor results in lowered production and little progress. Many of the underdeveloped countries today have a very large supply of labor, but lack necessary raw materials, capital, and entrepreneurial ability. For many years the United States lacked the labor force needed to permit better utilization of the nation's raw materials. It was not until after the Civil War that there was a more nearly adequate supply of capital goods in this country. The backward countries of the world are presently trying to establish a more balanced relationship between the factors. China is attempting to increase its stock of capital goods through centralized planning and forced saving. India is attempting to do the same thing through centralized planning as well as encouraging foreign and domestic private investment. Russia is increasing the amount of land being utilized for agriculture and has also made tremendous additions to her supply of capital goods. Most underdeveloped countries, however, act as though the shortage of capital is the only barrier to further development.

Suppose, however, that an economy does exist which has sufficient amounts of capital, labor, and raw materials. The mere existence of the three factors does not guarantee that development will take place. Someone must make the necessary decisions as to the combination of the factors. Someone must take the risk associated with innovation. Someone must assume the responsibility of management. In short, economic development cannot proceed without such a decision-making group. In a private enterprise economy, this would be the entrepreneurial input. In a socialized economy, the government would undertake the role of the entrepreneur. But in any case, the functions generally associated with the entrepreneur in a private enterprise economy must be performed. And there are many who would add that this entrepreneurial input is the key to development.

Savings and Capital Accumulation. The stock of natural resources and the supply of the human factor in the productive process, at any given moment in time, have rather inelastic supply functions. Changes over time for these two factors are rather slow if possible at all. The labor supply can be increased by (a) a growth in the population and/or (b) an increase in the percentage of the population which participates in the productive process. Natural resources may be increased as a result of (a) exploration and development and (b) improved technology which makes it profitable to utilize existing resources.

Capital, being the manmade input, is more amenable to man's control. The act of abstaining from consumption releases resources which may be used to increase the economy's stock of capital. Thus it may be possible to increase the stock of capital rather quickly. Bohm-Bawerk's caveman increased the stock of capital when he reduced his consumption of water in order to build a bucket and then a flume. A modern farmer increases the stock of capital when he decides to terrace his fields rather than take a vacation trip to Florida. In some cases, the process of capital creation may cover a period of years (building a steel mill), but in others the process may be extremely short (terracing land).

Capital, including all of the man-made goods which enter the productive process, includes a variety of goods. One of the features which distinguishes one type of capital from another is the payoff period. In some instances, capital will start producing a flow of income immediately, but in others the increased income may not be discernible for years. Investment in education, for example, does not increase income at once—in fact, the increase in income may be negligible for a period of years after the initial investment. Investment in health and recreational facilities are of the same type. On the other hand, a new steel mill will start producing a visible flow of income immediately upon the commencement of operations as would capital investment in agriculture. Choosing between those investment opportunities with a payoff in the near future as opposed to those with a payoff in the more distant future is a difficult decision. The former may yield large benefits in the not-too-distant future while the latter may yield much larger gains in the more distant future. The solution has often been to leave those with the more distant payoff to the government. This has been the practice in the United States, for example.

The Allocation of Capital. Simply increasing the stock of capital does not mean that the problem of economic growth is solved. Some decision has to be made as to just how the increased supply of capital is to be used. This is the by-now familiar allocation problem.

There are, of course, various noneconomic considerations in any economy. Military preparedness and national prestige are important considerations in all economic systems. But in even the most completely planned economy, some consideration must be given to economic factors. It is these economic factors in which we are interested.

First, there is the choice as to present sacrifices, future benefits, and time. For example, a very small sacrifice at the present time may result in a rather modest future benefit at a point not too far removed in the future. Another possibility is that of a large present sacrifice in return for a very great increase in benefits at a more remote point in time. Between these two, if we may consider them to be in the nature of extremes, there is a whole continuum involving the three variables of time, sacrifices, and benefits. Which combination is the more desirable? The economist certainly cannot answer this question for it involves a value judgment that only individuals acting as individuals or in their collective capacity can answer. The economist can, however, indicate the results of choosing among the alternatives.

The method used to get people to abstain from consumption will vary. This is a function of the interest rate in a system relying upon a free price system. Khrushchev has apparently had considerable success in convincing the people of the USSR that they should make a large sacrifice at the present time (in the form of reduced consumption) for the good of the Fatherland and future generations. Communist China has used the force of the government to reduce present consumption. Religious institutions have had considerable success in reducing present consumption in return for promises of great benefits in the hereafter. Using one means or another, the substitution of future for present satisfactions is a problem that any developing economy must solve.

A second aspect of the problem of allocation is that of the

productivity of the capital input. Here the concern is with the relation between changes in the quantity of capital and the resulting change in output. This is often expressed as a ratio:

$$\frac{\text{Change in quantity of capital}}{\text{Change in the total output}}$$

A very large capital-output ratio indicates that a large increase in the stock of capital will increase total output by very little. For example, a four million dollar investment in heavy industry may increase total output in a given year by one million dollars. Investment in the form of improved agricultural practices (insecticides, fertilizing, deeper plowing, etc.) may call for relatively small investment, but the change in total output may be sizeable. Additional investment in educational facilities may increase total output by a negligible amount, at least in the short run.

This "marginal capital-output ratio" will serve as a measure for comparing different investment possibilities. In general, the smaller the ratio (that is, the larger the denominator is with respect to the numerator) the more favorable the investment is to economic growth.

This raises a question of policy. That is, what is the proper strategy for economic growth? Some would argue that growth should proceed on all fronts, in all sectors of the economy. Others contend that growth should proceed on an uneven basis with one industry being emphasized at the expense of others.

There is no agreement, either, as to whether investment in capital goods industries should have priority over investment in consumption goods industries. The former will certainly generate further increases in income. The latter may, however, do likewise if it causes the laborers and other suppliers of factors to work harder and produce more in order that they can buy the output of the consumer goods sector. Thus a bicycle factory may induce additional output simply because people will work harder in order to buy a bicycle.

Balanced vs. Unbalanced Growth.[2] There has been and there remains a considerable difference of opinion among economists as to which of the two possible approaches to economic development should be pursued. Briefly, the arguments for balanced and unbalanced growth are as follows.

The proponents of a program of balanced growth would have the

[2] A. O. Hirschman, *The Strategy of Economic Development* (New Haven, Yale University Press, 1958). Professor Hirschman presents an interesting review of the controversy, although he is committed to the concept of unbalanced growth. This book is available in a paperback edition.

economy advance on all fronts simultaneously. Agriculture and industry must advance together. And as these two basic areas develop, the necessary social overhead capital must be supplied as needed. The argument for the simultaneous advance on all fronts rests on the assertion that such development will make certain economies available to all, whereas piece-meal development will not result in any general economies.

Another argument for balanced growth goes as follows. Before any given sector of the economy can successfully expand, a market for its output must either exist or be anticipated. And the only way that markets will be available for all sectors of the economic system is for the entire economy to expand in step. Markets for agricultural products can only exist if the industrial sector is expanding. If only a single sector developed, there would be no market for the output.

The doctrine of balanced growth is criticized because it, in effect, assumes away the problem. If the economy is capable of pursuing such a policy, that is, if a country has all of the resources for balanced growth, what explains its lack of growth? Certainly a lack of growth implies that one of the necessary ingredients is missing. Hirschman finds that lack in the decision-making capacity of the economy.

The proponent of the unbalanced growth approach would have an economy concentrate on a few sectors for initial development. Leading sectors would be established. These sectors would be given priority and would develop faster than the rest of the economy. This would put pressure on the remainder of the system. Thus a steel mill creates pressures for the development of a consumer goods industry so that the workers in the steel mill will be able to dispose of their income. The construction of the steel mill will likewise require the development of the ancillary industries, both to provide the inputs and to make use of the outputs.

The idea of unbalanced growth is roughly comparable to the policy of the USSR. In that country, leading sectors are designated in each of the five- (or seven-) year plans. These sectors are then singled out for more rapid development than the rest of the economy. Heavy industry has been developed at a faster rate than most other sectors of the economy. Other countries have also used this approach.

UNDERDEVELOPED ECONOMIC SYSTEMS

The Underdeveloped Economies

Just as there are individuals who have and those who have not, there are also nations which have and those which have not. Between geographical regions of the world, and even within an individual nation, there are wide disparities in the level of living. Some people enjoy a high level of income, freedom, good health, plenty of good food, recreational and cultural facilities, and the other prerequisites of good living, while others enjoy none of these. The latter are referred to as the under-developed economies. They generally have a low level of income (per capita) but possess some possibilities of increasing the level of individual income. There are a number of other criteria which might be developed to support the existence of the problem of underdevelopment and its magnitude. These would include such criteria as degree of literacy, quantity and quality of diet, adequacy of housing and clothing, and the extent of individual freedom. With so many variables and so many different viewpoints on the part of those making the decisions, the task of delineating the underdeveloped areas is still a relatively difficult task in spite of the work done by the United Nations as well as individual scholars. We can, however, develop our analysis without specifically identifying the countries and areas which might be classed as underdeveloped.

Problems of Underdeveloped Economies

Underdeveloped economies have both technological and social barriers which hinder economic development. If the rate of development is to be accelerated in such economies, it will be necessary to change the techniques of production. But it will be just as necessary that certain social institutions be altered, for a changing technology will come to naught if it is imposed upon an unchanging social environment. It may well be that the social environment is the more difficult of the two to alter.

Problems in the Social Environment. The social environment will differ from one country to another, but in general, the following conditions exist in most of the underdeveloped areas.

(*a*) The governments are generally antiquated and inefficient. There is no tradition of public service nor is there a Civil Service such as exists in the United States and Great Britain. Very often the governments are of a feudal type long ago disestablished in western Europe. They administer the affairs of the nation to benefit the privileged few rather than the unprivileged masses.

(*b*) The underdeveloped economies have little private enterprise such as we know and take for granted in the United States. As in the case of the governments, the skills necessary for the efficient administration of business units are largely lacking. The sole proprietorship is the most common form of business organization. The corporation is not widely used to organize business activity. The acquisitive spirit, which is so important to capitalism, is often nonexistent. None of the underdeveloped economies has anything which might be called a business system which could efficiently utilize the technology of an industrial economy. Industrialization would require the machinery, techniques, *and* institutions of industrial organization and operation. Such institutions need not be private.

(*c*) Land reform has been accomplished or at least undertaken in some of the underdeveloped economies, but it will be necessary to make still further progress. In some instances land holdings are concentrated in the hands of a very few families. In others small holdings make efficient utilization difficult if not impossible. More efficient use of land and labor devoted to agriculture is a necessary part of economic development.

(*d*) The level of education is abysmally low. An educated labor force is necessary for the efficient administration of both government and business enterprise.

(*e*) Depending upon the circumstances of the individual country, other changes in the social structure will be required. In some, religion is a deterrent force. In others, a rigid caste system precludes development. And in still others the businessman will have to be given a position of social prestige instead of his present position of inferior social standing.

Population Problems. It can happen that an economy will have too large a population—overpopulation. The Reverend Thomas R. Malthus (1776–1834) predicted that population would naturally increase at a faster rate than would the supply of goods and services needed to support the population. He asserted that the population would increase geometrically (1,2,4,8,16 . . .) and that the food supply would increase arithmetically (1,2,3,4,5 . . .). Thus it would only be a matter of time until the population increased to such proportions that the food supply would be grossly inadequate. His dire predictions have not come true for the United States even though the rate of increase in population has often approximated the rate forecast by Malthus. Most of the economically underdeveloped countries have too many people relative to their resources. The specter of Malthusian overpopulation is very real for many countries, for the increases in population either (*a*) exceed the increase in food or (*b*) have the potential for exceeding the increase in the supply of food. In both southeast Asia where the population density is very high and in southwest Asia where the density of population is very low, the population is so large relative to the resources that the majority of the people live only slightly above the subsistence level.

The pressure of the population on resources will become more acute. One of the first phases of development is that of health. As underdeveloped societies experience a falling death rate because of improved diets, better health and sanitation facilities, and more and improved medical facilities, there will be an increase in the natural rate of population growth. The increased pressure of population on resources thus becomes more acute unless (*a*) resource utilization is improved, (*b*) the increase in population is held down through a reduction in the birth rate, or (*c*) some means are found to export the surplus population to areas where the pressure is less severe. The latter means was used by the countries of Europe as long as the United States was willing to accept immigrants. Italy and Japan attempted to use this technique in the 1930's and the 1940's, but their experiments accomplished little. Since World War II, Japan has adopted some measures designed to reduce the birth rate, but controlling the birth rate is relatively difficult for most societies.

Natural Resources and Their Utilization. Many people often make a general statement to the effect that the underdeveloped countries lack natural resources. This is too general to have validity. Underdeveloped countries do not have the variety and quantity of resources found in the United States or the USSR, but even these two countries were underdeveloped fifty or a hundred years ago.

Some of the underdeveloped countries lack a particular resource, but for most the difficulty is a failure to utilize the resources which are available. Egypt has unutilized power resources in the form of the Nile River, and Saudi Arabia and Iran have power facilities in the form of oil and natural gas which are not being presently used to power domestic industry. Some of the underdeveloped countries, such as those in Northern Africa and the Middle East, lack fresh water, but others in southern Asia have much more than can be used. In some instances the soil is practically sterile; in other areas the soil is fertile but requires water; and in still other areas the soil is as productive as any in the world. Some have rich deposits of minerals, and others have extensive stands of forests. Few, if any, have no resources whatsoever.

The lack, then, of quantities of different resources makes economic development more difficult, but insofar as natural resources are concerned, economic development is the development of more efficient means of utilizing the existing resources or the development of new resources. One might compare the economic development of Israel with that of its neighboring countries in order to assess the significance of natural resources in the development process.

Capital Formation. Since there is neither a shortage of labor nor a general paucity of natural resources, the lack of economic development has to be a result of the manner in which the resources are being utilized. The utilization of resources is a function of the quantity of capital goods. All of the underdeveloped countries have a shortage of capital goods. Production is, in large part, direct, primitive, and inefficient. The success of any program of economic development hinges upon the economy's success in accumulating a stock of capital goods in order to change the method of production.

It has already been pointed out that any economy builds up its supply of investment goods by saving—that is, by abstaining from consumption. Saving, and thus capital formation, depends upon (1) the people having a sufficiently high level of income so that not all will be consumed and (2) the existence of a group of individuals who are willing and able to utilize the savings by converting them into investment goods.

The underdeveloped countries are on the horns of a dilemma. Savings are required for progress, but incomes of most are so low that abstention from consumption is impossible. That is, some minimum level of income is necessary before a consumer can save, and this minimum level of income is not being attained by large segments of the population in the backward nations. Once incomes increase so that saving is possible, economic development is facilitated. Nothing contributes to economic progress like progress itself.

In the aggregate, an economy may save, even though there is a large number of people whose incomes are so low as to preclude their saving. This is possible if there is an unequal distribution of income. The United States and other advanced countries as well as the backward nations have an unequal distribution of income; and it is probable, at least, that the degree of inequality is greater in the underdeveloped nations. In such countries many of those with large incomes have little inclination to invest their savings, but would rather use their incomes to support the most blatant forms of conspicuous consumption both at home and abroad.

It is probable, however, that if all those who were in a position to save did so, the problem of capital formation would not be solved. The investment institutions which might utilize the savings of individuals do not exist nor are there firms which are both willing and able to utilize such savings. It is ironic that the savings of some persons in the underdeveloped countries seek investment outlets in such economically advanced countries as the United States, Great Britain, France, and Switzerland, even though the need for such investment expenditures is much more pressing in their own underdeveloped nations.

The situation might be summed up as follows. Most people in the underdeveloped nations can't save. Most of those who can, don't; and of those who do, the institutions as well as the desire to invest in domestic industry are lacking.

The problem of capital formation is not insoluble. The wealthy might be induced to save and invest. Some technological advances that would increase income and thus permit savings are possible without large capital expenditures. Income can also be increased by shifting labor from areas of low productivity into areas of higher productivity. There is a possibility of attracting foreign investment. And lastly, the governments of the various countries may force the people to abstain from consumption.

GROWTH OF A MATURE ECONOMY

Growth and Development in the United States

Population and the Labor Force. In 1610, the estimated colonial population was 210 persons; by 1700 it had increased to 275,-000; by 1800 the population was 5.3 million; and the United States currently has a population in excess of 190 million. Furthermore, the Bureau of the Census estimates that the total population of the United States will be between 231 and 273 million in 1980.

Figure 18–1 is a graphic presentation of the population growth in the United States. The population figures are plotted on a logarithmic scale so the slope of the curve indicates the rate of change. Where the slope is steeper (until 1870 or 1880) the rate of increase was greater than where the curve has less slope (1900 to 1940). Between 1760 and 1860, the rate of increase was almost constant. After that the rate of increase fell off slightly, although the largest absolute increases in population were recorded after 1860. It is interesting to note that the rate of increase has risen since the beginning of World War II.

The population growth of any country is dependent upon two factors. First, there may be a natural increase resulting from a birth rate which exceeds the death rate. At the present time the birth rate in the United States is about 2.5 times as large as the death rate. This has not always been so for there has been a spectacular decline in the death

FIGURE 18-1

POPULATION IN THE UNITED STATES, 1760–1980

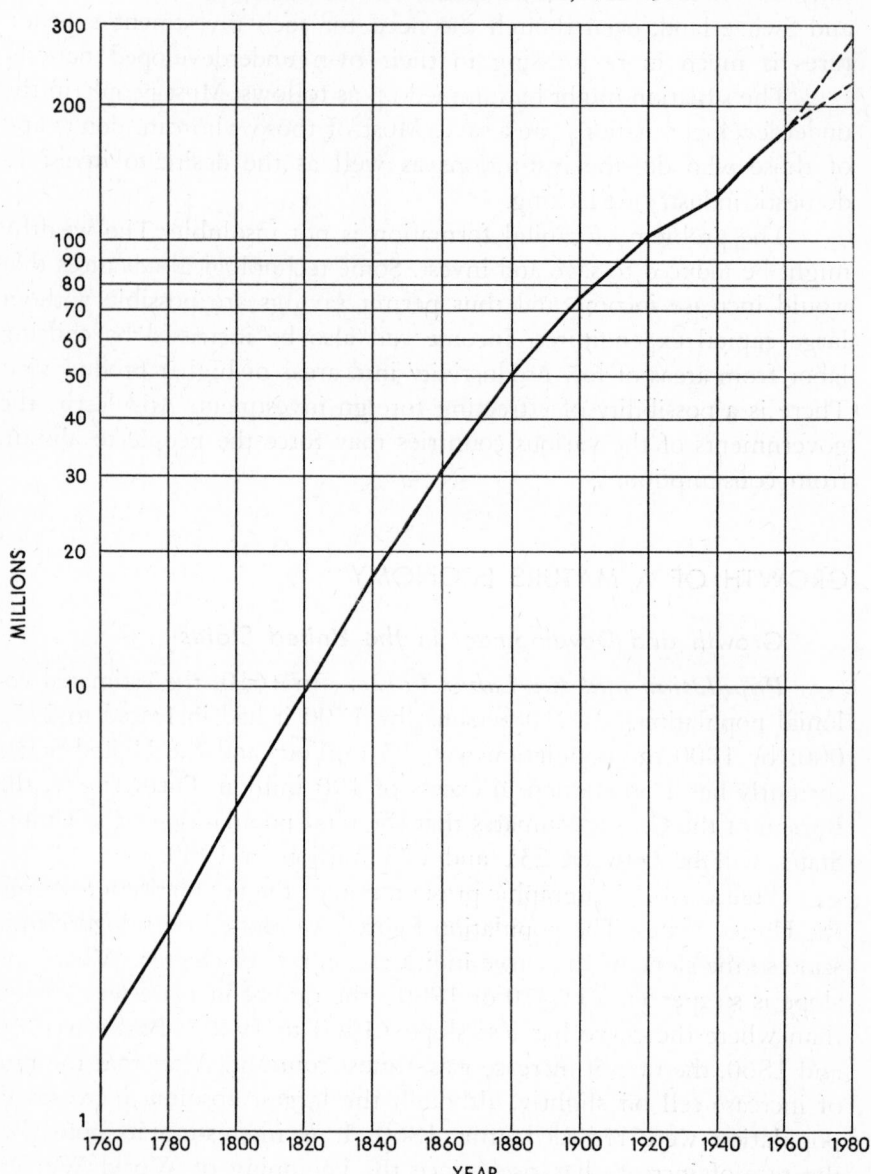

SOURCE: U.S. Bureau of the Census, *Statistical Abstract of the United States, 1961* (Washington, D.C.: U.S. Government Printing Office, 1961).

rate over the past 50 years. In addition, there has been a considerable reduction in the infant mortality rate.

A second factor which is no longer of such great import as it was at the turn of the century is that of immigration. From the Civil War to World War I, great numbers of persons migrated to this country from nearly all parts of the world. The total reached nearly 30 million persons. Since World War I the country has adopted more restrictive policies, and for this as well as other reasons the number of people migrating to the United States has dropped sharply.

Population growth through immigration has one great advantage. As the population increases in size, the number of people who are able to work also increases; whereas if the increase results from an excess of births over deaths a number of years must pass before the newcomers can take their place at the nation's workbench. In the case of the immigrant, then, the United States was able to take advantage of his education and training without having to bear the cost or wait for him to reach an age which enabled the immigrant to take a job.

There may well be a second factor which is a little harder to pin down. It is probable that the process of immigration acted as a separator. That is, the hardier and more ambitious persons immigrated to the United States while the less ambitious tended to remain behind. Thus the United States gained a superior part of the populace.

Not all of the population need be considered as participating in the productive process. That part of the population which either has or is seeking gainful employment is known as the labor force. The labor force in the United States is presently in excess of 74 million, which is less than 40 per cent of the total population. It is the quality of the labor force and the ratio between the labor force and the other factors of production which is important in determining the level of production and economic progress. If labor is the scarce factor, an increase in population will not, per se, overcome the problem, for to the extent that such an increase consists of an increasing number of the aged and the very young, there will be no increase in those able to work. A forced-draft program of economic development would, insofar as labor is concerned, concentrate on improving the quality and quantity of the labor force. This was, of course, the effect of the migration to this country mentioned above.

Productivity. Although we speak of the productivity of each of the factors of production, it is difficult if not impossible to measure the productivity of some, such as the entrepreneur. The computation of a measure of productivity for labor is somewhat easier and more meaningful. If the total output is compared with the amount of labor used, one can gain some idea of the productivity of the factors. But it must be kept in mind that measuring the output per unit of labor will produce a figure which reflects the quantity and quality of all of the factors of production as well as the combination of the several factors.

Basic steel and agriculture represent two industries of fundamental importance in this country. Steel is an industry in which there has been and is a large quantity of capital goods per worker. Agriculture is an industry which has witnessed a greatly increased use of capital in the last twenty years or so. The two may be taken as being more or less representative of the economy, although there are significant types of employment which will differ from either of these two. The increases in productivity in both of these industries has been nothing less than spectacular (see Tables 18–1 and 18–2). There has been a twofold in-

TABLE 18–1

AGRICULTURAL PRODUCTIVITY IN THE
UNITED STATES FOR SELECTED YEARS,
1930–1961*

Year	Output per Man-Hour
1930	53
1940	67
1945	84
1950	112
1955	149
1957	168
1958	188
1959 (prel.)	191
1960 (prel.)	205

* 1947 = 100
SOURCE: U.S. Bureau of the Census, *Statistical Abstract of the United States, 1961* (Washington, D.C.: U.S. Government Printing Office, 1961).

TABLE 18–2

PRODUCTIVITY IN THE BASIC STEEL
INDUSTRY, 1935–1959*

Year	Output per Production Worker Man-Hour
1935	62.9
1939	79.3
1950	111.9
1955	129.4
1959	141.9

* 1947 = 100
SOURCE: U.S. Bureau of the Census, *Statistical Abstract of the United States, 1961* (Washington, D.C.: U.S. Government Printing Office, 1961).

crease in steel productivity since 1935 and a fourfold increase in agricultural productivity since 1930.

The reasons for such spectacular increases in productivity are many. The United States was blessed with a variety of raw materials of high quality. Its location in the temperate zone is conducive to productivity. Water resources exist in sufficient quantities for the most part. But probably more important than the gifts of nature are the contributions of man.

Of paramount importance is the stock of capital goods and the quality of that stock. The more capital that labor has to work with, the more productive labor will be. New capital will generally be more productive than old. Technological changes will result in increased productivity. And the substitution of mechanical energy for human energy will do likewise. Much of the credit for increasing productivity in the United States has resulted from the existence of these favorable factors.

The people of the United States have sacrificed present consumption in order to increase the stock of capital goods. Each year prodigious amounts have been spent to maintain and increase the nation's stock of capital goods (see Tables 18–3 and 18–4). The amounts

TABLE 18–3

GROSS CAPITAL FORMATION—AVERAGES PER YEAR
BY DECADES, 1869–1938
(In Millions of Dollars)

Year	Gross Capital Formation*
1869–1878	$ 2,278
1874–1883	3,192
1879–1888	4,202
1884–1893	5,483
1889–1898	6,499
1894–1903	7,573
1899–1908	8,932
1904–1913	10,733
1909–1918	12,556
1914–1923	13,824
1919–1928	15,760
1924–1933	13,920
1929–1938	10,743

* In 1929 prices.
SOURCE: Simon Kuznets, *National Product Since 1869* (New York: National Bureau of Economic Research, 1946).

TABLE 18–4

GROSS PRIVATE DOMESTIC INVESTMENT EXPENDITURES IN THE UNITED
STATES FOR SELECTED YEARS, 1929–1962
(In Billions of Dollars)

Year	Gross Private Domestic Investment*
1929	35.0
1933	4.0
1940	29.0
1945	17.0
1950	55.9
1955	62.5
1960	72.4
1961	69.3
1962	76.6 (prel.)

* In 1954 prices.
SOURCE: U.S. Bureau of the Census, *Statistical Abstract of the United States, 1963* (Washington, D.C.: U.S. Government Printing Office, 1963) and *Historical Statistics of the United States* (Washington, D.C.: U.S. Government Printing Office, 1960).

spent for capital goods alone in the United States exceed the total value of all goods and services produced by most other countries in the world.

One of the most important aspects of capital investment as far as economic progress is concerned is reflected in the amount of non-human energy produced in the economy. Mechanical power to replace and supplement human power increases the productivity of labor and the other factors. Abundant power means progress, and lack of power is a problem of severe consequences for underdeveloped countries. Between 1920 and 1960, there was nearly a twofold increase in the production of energy from mineral fuels and water power in the United States (see Table 18–5). Power "made" the Pacific Northwest and the

TABLE 18–5

ENERGY FROM MINERAL FUELS AND
WATERPOWER—ANNUAL SUPPLY,
1900–1962
(In Trillions of British Thermal Units)

Year	BTU'S
1900	7,893
1905	11,772
1910	15,375
1915	16,882
1920	21,340
1925	21,571
1930	22,060
1935	19,727
1940	24,969
1945	32,123
1950	34,422
1955	35,365
1960	41,844
1961	42,295
1962	43,979 (Prel.)

SOURCE: U.S. Bureau of the Census, *Statistical Abstract of the United States, 1963* (Washington, D.C.: U.S. Government Printing Office, 1963).

TABLE 18–6

PATENTS GRANTED BY THE UNITED STATES
PATENT OFFICE, 1790–1960

Year	Patents Granted
1790–1850	18,410
1851–1900	702,129
1901–1925	942,930
1926–1950	1,068,285
1951–1955	208,964
1955–1960	251,872

SOURCE: U.S. Bureau of the Census, *Statistical Abstract of the United States, 1963* (Washington, D.C.: U.S. Government Printing Office, 1963).

Tennessee Valley area. The student might speculate on the consequences of cheap power to such countries as Egypt, Arabia, and India.

Another factor contributing to the productivity of the economy is that of innovations and technological advancements. The United States seems to have possessed a rather peculiar capacity to produce men who have been able to develop products and processes which have benefited the whole society in the form of increased productivity (see Table 18-6). Thomas Edison, Eli Whitney, Benjamin Franklin, Robert Fulton, Alexander Bell, the Wright brothers, Henry Ford, and many others have made substantial contributions. Today, the nation's business firms are devoting a larger and larger part of their resources to the development of new products and new processes. It is interesting to speculate on the causes. Undoubtedly the environment was significant, for the inventor has been encouraged through the granting of patent monopolies. The possibilities of financial gain have been great. It is interesting to note, at this point, that the USSR is presently using the motive of financial gain to encourage scientific research.

Education is also a significant contributing factor. An educated labor force is more productive than an uneducated labor force. The task of learning new operations is eased. Individual initiative is stimulated. Consumer demands for goods and services are increased. The fact that public education was initiated early in the history of the country and has existed in most of the country for a century or more has contributed to the increased productivity of the economy.

Lastly, a few words might be added about the social environment. It must suffice at this point to indicate that the whole social environment has always been sympathetic to those forces which contribute to increased productivity. Risk takers and innovators have been encouraged by the possibilities of earning very large returns. Private property and the possibility of private gain have served as a stimulus for more productive efforts on the part of employees. The security of private gains and private property have been guaranteed by the government. The welfare of the productive forces has always been a major concern of the government. Society itself has generally reserved a place of honor for the successful businessman or corporate manager. To be a member of corporate management today indicates personal success. The Puritan ethic has likewise been a significant feature of the social environment. Work and economic gain have been regarded as being morally right, while laziness and inactivity has generally been frowned upon as morally improper. Such social forces as those mentioned above are significant, but it is impossible to quantify them or assess them in any exact manner. The subjective statement of their existence and the assertion of their importance will have to suffice.

Table 18–7 indicates the economic progress of the United States

TABLE 18–7

GROSS NATIONAL PRODUCT FOR THE UNITED STATES IN SELECTED YEARS

Year	(1) GNP (Current Dollars) (Billions)	(2) GNP (1954 Dollars) (Billions)	(3) GNP per Capita in 1954 Dollars
1929	$104.4	$181.8	$1,493
1933	56.0	126.6	1,007
1940	100.6	205.8	1,558
1945	213.6	314.0	2,244
1950	284.6	318.1	2,096
1955	397.5	392.7	2,376
1958	444.2	401.0	2,304
1959	482.1	428.0	2,417
1960	503.2	439.2	2,442
1961	518.7	447.9	2,438

SOURCE: U.S. Bureau of the Census, *Statistical Abstract of the United States, 1963* (Washington, D.C., 1963).

during the period between 1929 and 1961. The figures in Column 1 represent the total market value of all goods and services produced in the country during each of the selected years. The value is expressed in terms of the current dollar, which means that there will be fluctuations from one year to the next because of changes in the value of the dollar. For example, prices fell considerably between 1929 and 1933, so the decline in terms of current dollars was greater than the decline in actual production. Likewise, most of the increase in the value of goods and services produced as measured in current dollars (Column 1) between 1945 and 1950 represent price increases. Price changes alone do not indicate economic growth.

The price fluctuations have been removed in Column 2. This was accomplished by dividing the entire series by a price index. This operation is known as deflating the original values. The result is the value of goods and services produced in terms of dollars with constant purchasing power rather than in terms of current dollars with varying purchasing power. In this case, the constant dollars are 1954 dollars. One will notice that the figures for the years prior to 1954 were increased in the process while those for later years were decreased. This results from the fact that the dollar was worth more in terms of its purchasing power in the years preceding 1954 than it was in the years following.

Once the effects of a changing price level have been removed, the resultant figures can be divided by the population of the United States to get a per capita figure for total output. These figures are in Column 3. It is these figures which are indicative of the economic growth which has occurred in the United States since 1929.

Professor Simon Kuznets (1901–   ) working at the National Bureau of Economic Research has estimated the value of goods and services produced in the United States for the 60 years preceding 1929, the year for which data is first available. His estimates are to be found in Table 18–8. The decade estimates refer to the average value of

TABLE 18–8

VALUE OF GOODS AND SERVICES PRODUCED IN THE UNITED STATES
BY DECADES, 1869–1938

Decade Estimates	*Per Capita Output of Goods and Services* [*]
1869–1878	$237
1874–1883	304
1879–1888	355
1884–1893	378
1889–1898	396
1894–1903	443
1899–1908	505
1904–1913	556
1909–1918	578
1914–1923	615
Averages of Annual Estimates	
1919–1928	689
1924–1933	687
1929–1938	649

* In 1929 dollars.
SOURCE: Simon Kuznets, *National Product Since 1869* (New York: National Bureau of Economic Research, 1946).

goods and services produced in each year of the particular decade. Thus for the decade 1869–1878, the average per capita production was $237. The estimates for the last two decades overlap the material presented in Table 18–7, but this will enable the student to compare the two series. Otherwise the two series are not directly comparable, since Table 18–7 is in 1954 dollars and Table 18–8 is in 1929 dollars.

Table 18–8 does, however, provide a fairly accurate picture of the economic progress in this country between the Civil War and World War II. The per capita value of goods and services produced increased almost threefold. This, it should again be noted, represented a real increase, since all price-level changes have been eliminated.

So year after year and decade after decade per capita production of goods and services has increased. In only a few instances has production for any single decade or year been less than for the preceding period, and these have been periods of depression. The decade 1929–1938 covered two depressions. The economy was recovering from a depression in 1950, and 1954 was marked by a lower level of economic activity. But in spite of these temporary setbacks, which are remarkably few in number, the long-run trend of economic progress has been upward.

Government Policy and Growth in a Mature Economy

The Stagnation Thesis. In the 1930's and again in the 1950's and 60's there was widespread doubt about the possibility of continual increases in the level of investment expenditures in the United States. In the 1930's it was the stagnation thesis. In the 50's and 60's, it was an inadequate rate of growth. Between 1950 and 1959, the rate of growth in the United States was smaller than that in nearly all of the countries of Western Europe as well as that of the Soviet Union. (See Table 18–9).

TABLE 18–9

GROWTH OF GROSS NATIONAL PRODUCT PER MAN-YEAR,
SELECTED COUNTRIES, 1913–59
(Per Cent per Year)

Country	1913–59	1950–59
Japan	2.6	6.1
Italy	1.7	4.7
Germany	1.4	4.5
France	1.5	3.6
Netherlands	1.3	3.4
Norway	1.9	3.1
Sweden	1.7	2.8
United States	1.8	2.2
Canada	1.5	2.0
Denmark	1.2	1.8
United Kingdom	.8	1.7

SOURCE: *Economic Report of the President* (Washington, D.C., U.S. Government Printing Office, 1962).

The stagnation thesis (in large part a product of the Great Depression) asserted that investment expenditures were at such a low level that unemployed resources were a permanent characteristic of the economic system. According to the stagnationists, the United States had undergone changes so there was no longer a tendency for the economy to move toward a full employment level of income. Instead, they foresaw a situation where planned investment would be equal to planned savings at a level of income below the full employment level of income.

The changes which were to result in this situation were the: (1) reduction in the rate of population growth; (2) disappearance of the frontier and the atrophy of the entrepreneurial spirit; (3) unlikelihood of further great innovations, such as the automobile, which would spark huge new investment expenditures; and (4) changing nature of capital itself which would mean that a given level of investment would produce a much larger increment of income. Obviously, the stagnationists were gazing into a rather murky crystal ball, but the issues raised were there and remain with us.

There is a general consensus that a necessary condition for a constant rate of growth is an increasing volume of investment expenditures. If the rate of growth is to increase, there will have to be an even greater increase in the volume of investment expenditures. The lower rate of growth reflects (a) the desire of consumers to consume rather than abstain from consumption—that is, the level of savings is too low and/or (b) an unwillingness on the part of investors to invest.

The shortage of savings may be explained by high time preference; that is, people prefer present consumption goods to future goods. And it may be that as more and more of man's wants are taken care of through social welfare plans, it will become more and more difficult for the private sector of the economy to generate the necessary savings to provide resources for capital replacement and expansion.

Investors may be unwilling to invest because of the high cost of capital—that is, a high rate of interest—or because the marginal efficiency of capital may be too low. Either will reduce the level of investment.

On another level, investment has been criticized on a qualitative basis. In response to consumer desires and the profit motive, business has not been reluctant to invest capital for purposes of product differentiation—particularly in automobiles. Some economists, *qua* social philosopher, have pointed out that society has more to gain from comparable investments in education, health, recreational facilities, and the like. The student might contemplate the contribution to the long-run growth of the economy resulting from increased investment in education vs. further investment in product differentiation or "investment" in space adventures.

Government Policy for More Rapid Growth. The Employment Act of 1946 committed the government of the United States to a policy of economic stability. Though there has been no such formal commitment in the case of economic growth, the government is just as surely committed to a policy of growth. What powers does the government have to encourage a more rapid rate of economic growth?

We already know the relationship between the level of investment and the rate of interest. A lower rate of interest encourages investment while a higher rate will have the reverse effect—other things remaining the same. So any government policy designed to bring the interest rate down to a lower level tends to encourage investment—if everything else remained constant. But here the qualification becomes extremely important. A lower rate of interest is also conducive to increased consumption and increased short term investment. Thus a lower interest rate will encourage spending and higher prices. If the economy is in a period of rising prices, the government's goal of cyclical stability calls for higher interest rates while the goal of long run growth requires a lower rate. The use of monetary policy for both short run stability problems and long run growth problems will often end up in this impossible situation.

Government may encourage growth in the private sector of the economy by adapting its tax structure in such a way as to increase the amount of earnings which private firms may retain in the firm without penalty. Allowing corporations larger depreciation allowances may permit them to retain more funds in the firm to be used for capital expansion. Of course, this assumes that the corporate officers will invest these funds. For there to be a net gain, moreover, there must be some reason for believing that the stockholder (consumer) would not reinvest the funds if they were paid out as dividends.

In addition to its monetary controls and its power to alter the tax structure in order to make investment more favorable, the government has the power to act directly in some areas. Increasing government expenditures for social overhead capital—education, transportation, health facilities, and the like—will contribute to increased growth. In the United States, government construction in production facilities—such as aluminum and steel mills—has largely been confined to the emergencies of war, although prior to the Civil War such direct participation was more common. Even now, though, the government is a major investor in such areas as hydroelectric power, atomic energy, and the construction of defense plants.

The government also makes major expenditures for research and development, and such expenditures are increasing. In the recent past, we note that the government made a major contribution to the development of jet aircraft and its use in the civilian air transportation industry. The government is presently pledged to spend nearly a billion dollars to aid in the development of a commercial supersonic jet transport. And it is estimated that the government will spend as much as $40 billion by 1970 in an attempt to put a man on the moon.

There are other examples which could be cited. But the important point is the fact that the government has powers which it can and does exercise in the interests of a more rapid rate of growth. It is possible that the government will come to rely more and more on this facet of its activities rather than on monetary controls to achieve a higher rate of growth. Another possibility is increased central planning, but this topic will be reserved for the last chapter.

CONCLUSION

Underdeveloped countries develop. Mature economies grow. And regardless of the economic system or the level of development, growth or development are given a high priority in the ranking of society's goals. For the United States, it is a matter of national prestige—this economic system must grow faster than that of the USSR simply to show that ours is the better system. Growth and development are ends in themselves.

Just how much current consumption is to be restricted in order to promote a faster rate of growth is a question for the people in this country to decide and for the government to decide in the centrally directed economies. Under a free market system, the people cast their decision in the market place. It now appears that the market place does not provide a fast enough rate of growth and we are increasingly turning to the government to stimulate growth of the economy. An underdeveloped country may have to depend upon strong government direction and leadership. Do we? Why?

EXERCISES

Group I

Explain why the following statements are true or false.

1. The only way to increase the rate of saving necessary for economic growth is through an increase in the rate of interest.
2. Marx argued that a nation's social institutions determined the method of production.
3. A government cannot force people to save.

4. The "best" program of economic development is always that program which increases the rate of investment in heavy industry prior to increases in the level of investment in other industries such as consumer goods.

5. The problem of development can always be condensed to a lack of one of the factors—land, labor, or capital.

6. Basic to the stagnation thesis was the idea that population would increase at a faster rate than resources.

Group II

1. The question of balanced vs. unbalanced growth is an extremely interesting and timely question. Explore, in more detail than was done in the text, the arguments in support of each. Is one or the other correct?

2. Has Communism enjoyed a high degree of success in the matter of economic development? That is, have the underdeveloped systems been able to use this type of social organization to bring about a rapid rate of development? Think this through carefully and substantiate your assertion with factual evidence.

Group III

1. In the United States it appears that there is considerable conflict between stability and growth. This is true at both the economic and political levels. In the case of the first, economics indicates that the two goals may be, to some extent, mutually inconsistent. At the political level, goals which are intended to foster one may actually impede the other. Explore this topic more fully and write a paper on "The Inconsistencies Between Growth and Stability."

BIBLIOGRAPHY

HIGGINS, B. *Economic Development: Principles, Problems, and Policies.* New York: W. W. Norton & Co., 1959.

HIRSCHMAN, A. O. *The Strategy of Economic Development.* New Haven: Yale University Press, 1958. (Also available in paperback.)

JOINT ECONOMIC COMMITTEE. *Comparisons of the United States and Soviet Economies.* Washington, D.C.: Government Printing Office, 1959. Parts 1, 2, and 3.

PAPERBACK READING LIST

ROSTOW, W. W. *The Stages of Economic Growth: A Non-Communist Manifesto.* Cambridge: Cambridge University Press, 1960.

PLANNING FOR AN
ECONOMIC SYSTEM

To the biologist the problem of socialism appears largely as a problem of size. The extreme socialists desire to run every nation as a single business concern. I do not suppose that Henry Ford would find much difficulty in running Andorra or Luxembourg on a socialistic basis. He has already more men on his payroll than their population. It is conceivable that a syndicate of Fords, if we could find them, would make Belgium Ltd. or Denmark Inc. pay their way. But while nationalization of certain industries is an obvious possibility in the largest of states, I find it no easier

to picture a completely socialized British Empire or United States than
an elephant turning somersaults or a hippopotamus jumping a hedge.
—J. B. S. Haldane, "On Being the Right Size," *Possible Worlds* (New
York: Harper & Brothers, 1928).

INTRODUCTION

To plan or not to plan is *not* the question. The question
is how much and what kind of planning is required to achieve the
accepted goals of society.

Man is distinguished, at least in part, from other animals by the
fact that he can anticipate the future. That is, man can anticipate how
he will feel if certain events come to pass. Some events will be more
desirable than others. As soon as this characteristic of the human being
is recognized, it becomes obvious that he will plan to bring about the
more desirable event and to prevent the happening of the more undesirable events. Families plan the pattern of expenditures. Business
firms plan. Students plan or at least they are advised to plan. Municipalities plan. Social organizations plan. As a matter of fact, it is impossible to think of any social institution which doesn't plan, for it
would appear that this is a major reason for their organization and
viability.

The United States, in the 1960's, is not an unplanned economy;
in fact, it never has been an unplanned economy. One might say that
the very reason for its initial organization was to increase the amount
of planning. In the course of this text, we have seen some of the ways
the government plans and makes decisions. Yet in spite of a long history of planning and extensive planning activities at present, there is a
significant body of public opinion in this country which feels quite
strongly that planning is a form of socialism and therefore undesirable.
And just as obviously, there are very few politicians who, if given the
chance, would materially reduce the quantity of planning operations in
the United States.

In what ways does the United States government plan? First, it
plans in an effort to maintain a high level of employment and a certain
amount of stability in the price level. The tools are monetary and
fiscal controls. Secondly, it plans in the field of economic development.
The TVA, to name only a single example, represents planned economic development. Third, it has engaged in extensive planning in
agriculture in order to insure a higher income to farmers. A fourth

example would be the field of transportation where government planning has aided the development of a national transportation system. Railroad subsidies, maritime subsidies, subsidies to the builders of aircraft as well as airlines, the St. Lawrence Seaway, the highway system, navigational facilities, and other related efforts all stand as evidence of the government's interest in this field. The student can think of other areas where the government has stepped in and planned for the orderly development of a particular part of the economy rather than letting it develop willy-nilly.

On the whole, though, public planning in the United States is restricted to those areas where private enterprise has shown some inability or unwillingness to venture. Planning in other countries refers to the exercise of control by the government over areas where decision making is largely private in nature in the United States. Any extension of planning in this country will undoubtedly mean the imposition of further restrictions on the decision-making capacity of private firms and individual persons.

One may get some ideas as to which way this country might move by making a cursory inspection of planning in other countries of the world.[1]

PLANNING IN FRANCE[2]

The French Economy

The period since 1940 has been one of turbulence for France. This proud nation was conquered, occupied, and liberated in World War II. Since then she has fought two "wars" in Indo-China and Algeria; she has given many of her colonial territories their independence; and she has faced her share of the Communist threat both internally and externally. In addition, the nation has been faced with internal political instability as well as the external problem of European integration. Certainly the situation called for heroic measures. One result was a degree of economic planning by the central government.

Of the major industries in France, the people, through the government, own the railroads, communication facilities, some power and energy facilities, and a part of the automobile producing capacity.

[1] In each of the following cases the authors have relied very heavily on the material in the indicated footnotes. The student who is interested in economic planning should read the literature cited in the footnotes as well as those items in the bibliography.

[2] See "Economic Planning in France" which is a record of a conference organized by the National Institute of Economic and Social Research in London, April 20–22, 1961. It was published as Vol. XXVII, No. 454 of *Planning*, August 14, 1961.

Major industries still privately owned include steel and oil. It can be described as a mixed economy but with a larger proportion of public enterprise than is the case in the United States.

Since planning, to be effective, requires controls, it follows that planning in a mixed economy will present problems. It raises the basic question as to how freedom of private enterprise and the interests of society are to be reconciled.

The public sector of the economy can be controlled directly through government actions. That which is private is not so easily directed, and in this area France's planning takes on extremely interesting features. But the important point is the fact that planning is possible. The French experience indicates that the alternative to complete planning is not a complete lack of planning.

The Planning Mechanism

The Purpose of Planning. In 1945, when France was facing the problem of re-building a war-ravaged economy, the country was leaning toward some form of socialism including state ownership of the major means of production. Economically, the country was behind some of the other countries of Western Europe as well as the United States. And as a condition for receiving Marshall Plan aid from the United States, there had to be some form of central planning for recovery.

Initially, then, planning was the means of promoting economic recovery. However, after recovery was a matter of record, the planning mechanism was not dismantled and set aside. Instead its goal became that of promoting long run growth.

Drawing up the Plan. The uppermost organization in the planning hierarchy (the entire planning organization is almost too small to be referred to as a hierarchy) is the *Commissariat General du Plan.* This governmental organization is a part of the office of the Minister of Finance and Economic Affairs. Its role is that of proposing, advising, estimating, and coordinating. It has no funds of its own which it can spend, nor does it manage any projects. It simply serves as a means by which information is passed between different groups both within and without the government.

At the next level, the Modernization Commissions are made up of representatives of private industry, the workers (through trade union representation), government officials from various departments, and, finally, experts for the particular industry. There is a hierarchy of such commissions. At the top, there is a single commission which devotes its attention to the entire economy. The remainder deal with particular industries and are subordinate to the first. The function of these commissions is to lay out, in general form, a program of national development. But note that it is not a government program, but is, on the contrary, a program put forth by a group representing all segments (public and private, business and labor, rural and urban) of the society. It is a concensus of what ought to be achieved during the planning period.

The *Commissariat General du Plan* initiates the planning mechanism by drawing up a preliminary outline embodying some assumption about the desired rate of growth for the economy. In other words, it formulates a national goal in the form of a desired rate of growth which can be taken as a guide by all segments of the economic system in their planning. In setting up this desired rate of growth, all segments of the economy are consulted and their advice sought.[3] Once the broad outline of the plan has been decided upon, the plan is turned over to the Modernization Commissions which, in turn, spell out the plan in greater detail. Those commissions representing particular industries such as agriculture, housing, chemicals, and the like provide the technical content of the plan. Other commissions, concerned with problems common to the entire economy, deal with labor, saving and investment, regional imbalance, and so forth. And, finally, there is a mechanism provided to reconcile any differences between the Modernization Commissions. The final plan is then presented to Parliament for approval. (See Table 19–1.)

Implementation of the Plan. The French planning authorities feel that much of the force behind the implementation of the plan stems from the method used in drawing up the plan. The fact that all parties concerned have had a part in drawing up the plan means that those same parties have some interest in seeing that it succeeds. But further, the coherence that the plan itself brings about is a gain insofar as the participating interests are concerned. Private firms, for example, find the plan to be of considerable aid in their long-run planning of investment.

In addition to the above congruent interests, the government has other means of influencing the private sector of the economy and thereby inducing the private interests to go along with the plan. Tax

[3] In a democratic society it is probably vital that the public, in some manner or other, has a voice in the formulation of the plan. This does not mean that the public has to participate in the detailed planning, but it does mean that it should have a voice in deciding upon major issues such as the rate of growth, nature of the national wage policy, and the like.

TABLE 19–1

THE FRENCH FOUR-YEAR PLAN*

(Billions of U.S. Dollars; $1 = 5 Fr. Francs, 1961 Prices)

	1961 (Actual)	1965 (Planned)	Per cent Increase
Gross Domestic Production	$ 54.2	$ 67.2	24.0%
+Imports	+ 6.6	+ 8.0	21.2
−Exports	− 7.8	− 9.4	24.2
Total Available Resources	53.0	65.8	24.2
Investment	11.8	15.4	31.0
Consumption	41.2	50.4	22.3
Total Use of Resources	53.0	65.8	24.2
Industry Breakdown			
Agriculture	7.6	9.0	19
Energy	5.2	6.4	24
Metals	2.8	3.6	23
Chemicals	3.8	4.8	29
Manufacturing	32.4	40.0	23
Construction	7.4	9.8	32
Transportation and Communication	4.8	5.8	21
Housing Services	1.8	2.2	23
Other Services	10.2	12.8	27
Total	76.0	94.4	24
−Intermediate Industrial Consumption	−21.8	−27.2	
Gross Domestic Production	54.2	67.2	24

Total Increase in Industrial Labor Force	930,000
Natural Increase	180,000
Immigration	290,000
Release from Military Service	190,000
Switch from Agriculture	270,000

Total New Jobs	930,000
New Jobs in Industry	290,000
New Jobs in Services, Trade and Government	640,000

* Behind these figures are detailed projections of spending by every industry and by government—on new plant and equipment, research and development, education, housing, highways, and other investments.

SOURCE: *Business Week*, April 7, 1962.

adjustments, credit controls, depreciation allowances, subsidies, interest rate adjustments, and similar means can be used by the government to cause the private interests to move toward the planning goals.

A more direct means of implementing the plan is that of direct government investment. As large sectors of the economy are nationalized (as compared to the United States), direct government investment in these areas will have considerable overall effect insofar as meeting the objectives of the plan are concerned. French planning authorities estimate that 50 per cent of total investment expenditures in the country are affected by government investment policies in the nationalized industries. In addition, there is a secondary effect in related private industries.

Summary. The goal of French planning is long-run economic growth. Its success depends upon the government being successful in getting the private interests in the economy to go along with the plan. Through a combination of indirect controls, psychological incentives, and direct investment expenditures, it appears that the government has had considerable success in implementing the plan. And the general consensus appears to be that centralized planning has made a considerable contribution to growth of the French economy.

The French approach to centralized planning is not consistent with present political and economic thought in the United States. Disregarding a rather deep hostility to the concept of planning in this country, the French planning process requires a degree of cooperation among business firms within the same industry which would be unthinkable in the United States. This cooperation is found in the Modernization Commissions for the various industries which make estimates of future demand and supply, of investment expenditures, capacity, technological changes, labor problems, and other problems of the industry. Out of these commissions comes a plan for the industry. Obviously, when put in these terms, the idea of the steel industry in the United States engaging in such activity is unimaginable. To say the least, it would require some change in our attitude toward the antitrust laws.[4]

PLANNING IN YUGOSLAVIA[5]

The economic system of Yugoslavia represents an interesting departure from the Soviet model. In fact, the divergencies between the two systems are intimately bound up in the differences between the two countries at both the political and economic level.

In the USSR it is, by definition, impossible for there to be a divergence of interests between the workers and the state. The state owns all property, and since the state represents the workers, the property is, perforce, operated in the welfare of the working class. In

[4] For an interesting article on planning in the individual countries in Western Europe, planning in the Common Market, and possible developments in the United States, the student is encouraged to read "Europe Charts its Business Future" in *Business Week,* April 7, 1962.

[5] This section relies heavily on "Postwar Changes in the Yugoslav Economic System and Methods of Planning" by T. P. Alton which appeared in the *Papers and Proceedings of the American Economic Association,* 1956 and *The Economy, Liberty, and the State* by Calvin Hoover (New York: Twentieth Century Fund, 1959.)

Yugoslavia, on the other hand, the government is reducing the amount of state ownership and operation of industry and is returning it to the working class. Ownership and control is being vested in the workers of the individual enterprises. In other words, producer cooperatives are replacing state-owned enterprises. To the Yugoslavs, this process represents the "withering away" of the state. There is no evidence that the Communist Party in the USSR envisages any comparable withering process even though Marx predicted such a phenomenon in a Communist society.

The Yugoslav enterprise is operated by a "board of directors" elected by the worker-owners. This board of directors hires a manager as operating head of the firm. Each firm then sells its output in the market for the best price obtainable. Prices are market-determined prices rather than being centrally established prices. The income of the workers is directly dependent upon the profitability of the enterprise. Without any restrictions such a means of determining remuneration would result in wide variations between workers in different enterprises. To prevent such an occurrence, the government "equalizes" returns to workers by charging interest on capital, levying taxes on wages, and imposing a rental fee on natural resources. These worker-owned firms have the same propensity to get together in order to increase total profits as exists in an economy of private enterprise. The government has responded by passing what is, essentially, an antitrust law to preclude such collusion.

Centralized planning, as it is known in the USSR, is absent. The central government uses its monetary and fiscal powers as well as some direct controls over credit to achieve such broad goals as economic stability and growth. The central government does exercise some control over investment by the producer cooperatives. Those enterprises which want to expand their capital plant "bid" for the available resources. The firm which is willing to pay the highest interest rate, above some minimum, gets the funds and the command over the resources. In this way the resources are allocated among the various possible ends.

The government of Yugoslavia has used its powers to force the people to save and encourage investment. The existence of a police state certainly restricts the liberties of the citizenry. Although the Soviet Union regards the Yugoslavian experiment as an experiment in anarchy, there appears to be no possibility that the state will ever be dismantled.

PLANNING IN THE SOVIET UNION

The Structure of the Economic System[6]

Government. The USSR consists of (1) a number of republics and (2) a central government. It is similar in structure to the government of Great Britain in that the republics are divisions of the central government rather than being sovereign governments as is the case with the states in the United States.

The Communist Party is the only political party, and it operates the government. In practice the leadership of the Communist Party also makes up the top echelons of the government of the USSR. The Presidium of the Communist Party is the ruling council of the party and the Council of Ministers is the governing body of the USSR.

Prior to the reorganization in 1957, the Council of Ministers included a number of ministries which are not normally associated with government in noncommunist countries. It was both a political and economic institution. In addition to ministries of foreign affairs and defense, it also had a large number of purely economic ministries who were charged with the administration of such diverse activities as the production and marketing of lumber, automobiles, clothing, etc. In 1957 nearly all of these industrial ministries were abolished and were replaced by regional councils (*sovnarkhozy*) which now administer all the firms found within a particular geographic area. In other words, it was a shift from organization by industry to organization along geographical lines.

The government of the USSR receives most of its revenue from a turnover tax which is essentially a sales tax. It levies an income tax, but the rates are relatively low compared to the United States. Any profit made by any of its industrial enterprises accrues to the government. Some income is received in the form of agricultural products turned over to the government by farmers. The government has also sold bonds to both bank and nonbank investors. Other minor sources of revenue would include tariffs, insurance premiums paid to the government, etc.

Agriculture. Until 1860, most of the agriculture in Russia was carried out under a feudal system of landlords and serfs. By 1917 land

[6] This section relies heavily on *Russia's Soviet Economy* by Harry Schwartz (New York, Prentice-Hall, Inc., 1954). Dr. Schwartz is the specialist on Soviet affairs for the *New York Times.* His articles on current happenings in the USSR and the Soviet bloc appearing in that newspaper are excellent.

reform programs had abolished serfdom and established a landowning peasant class. Immediately following the Communist revolution, peasant ownership of the land was still further increased as the large agricultural units were seized, broken up into smaller farms, and distributed to the peasants. But within a decade of the Communist takeover, however, this policy was reversed and the peasant ownership of land has diminished to insignificant proportions in accordance with the Communist dogma.

At the present time, agriculture is carried on by two types of enterprises. The collective farm or *kolkhoz* is a producer cooperative. The members of the co-op cultivate the land which is owned by the state. Capital equipment, such as tractors, trucks, and combines, are owned by the co-op. Theoretically, at least, the cooperatives are self-governing, but as a matter of fact, they are controlled by the state. The members of the *kolkhoz* receive their remuneration in form of a share of the "profits," but they only share in the "profits" after certain deductions have been made by the government.

The second type of farm organization is the state farm or *sovkhoz*. The *sovkhoz* is a state enterprise in the same sense that a steel plant or a railroad is a state enterprise. The farmers who work on the state farm are employees of the government and they receive their remuneration in the form of wages just as any other employee of the state. In the past few years there has been an increasing emphasis on state farms, and in many cases it has been at the expense of the collective farms. That is, the Soviet government has been encouraging the *sovkhoz* as a form of agricultural organization while at the same time discouraging the *kolkhoz*.

Until 1958, the machine tractor stations were a significant element in Soviet agriculture. The machine tractor stations operated the heavy agricultural equipment such as combines and tractors. This was thought to be a more efficient technique of utilizing scarce capital equipment. Under Stalin the machine tractor stations served as a means of checking on the performance of the cooperative farms as well as providing another source of income for the government. Any person even remotely acquainted with agriculture can easily imagine the difficulties which would ensue if the major farm equipment were under the control of someone other than the farmer or farm manager himself. Increased agricultural efficiency was, presumably, a major reason for the abandonment of the machine tractor stations in 1958.

Soviet agriculture has been and remains of importance for several reasons. In 1917, less than one fifth of the population was classed as urban. At the present time, just about one half of the population lives in the urban areas of the USSR. Like the United States, the rural populace has served as a source of supply for urban labor, although, unlike the United States, it still takes an extremely high percentage of the total population to fulfill the agricultural needs of the country. It is planned that the rural population will be a major source of supply of labor needed to carry out the ambitious plan for further industrialization of the Soviet Union.

A second major point of significance for Soviet agriculture is its role in capital accumulation. Two points must be recognized. First, a major limiting factor in a growth situation is the shortage of capital. Secondly, the underdeveloped economies, including the Soviet Union during the first decade of this century, are predominantly rural and agricultural in nature. Consequently, any drive for industrialization must feed upon the agricultural sector of the economy. So in addition to providing the labor supply, the agricultural sector must also provide the savings necessary for capital accumulation. Since agriculture is the dominant industry, it follows that it is the only sector which has any significant capacity to save—abstain from consumption. In the Soviet Union, agriculture has served as a major source of capital accumulation.

On the other hand, agriculture is important for the problems it presents. The success or failure of the Soviet program depends, to a large extent, on agriculture, and thus on the success or failure that the government has in overcoming the problems associated with agriculture. First, there is the matter of low agricultural productivity.[7] The per capita output for agriculture is considerably lower than comparable figures for the United States. In the latter country the problem is one of surpluses while in the Soviet Union it is one of continuing shortages. Khrushchev has devoted a good deal of his personal efforts toward the goal of increasing agricultural output. To the extent that he is successful, both the means (increased industrial labor and increased savings) and the end (higher standard of living) of the Soviet program will be achieved.

Labor in the Soviet Union. Karl Marx never thought of the labor unions as being a satisfactory device to improve the lot of the working man. Labor unions, to Marx, had as their major function the overthrow of capitalism. To Marx, the exercise of political power was

[7] D. Gale Johnson and A. Kahan present detailed statistics and an extremely interesting discussion of agricultural productivity in "Soviet Agriculture: Structure and Growth" in *Comparisons of the United States and Soviet Economies* (Washington, D.C.: Government Printing Office, 1959.)

the only means that the unions had of improving the lot of the working man. Labor unions have never fulfilled the role that Marx saw for them. Communism has not been established through the efforts of the working class in any industrialized country. It has enjoyed its greatest successes in those countries which are predominantly rural in nature with a small industrial work force.

In the Soviet system there is no place for a free trade-union movement as it operates in the United States. By definition, the interests of the workers and the interests of the Communist party and hence the government are the same, so according to the Marxist dogma it is inconceivable that the government does not represent the interests of labor. In short, the system has defined the labor problem away. There is no need for strikes by unions for there is nothing to strike about. Collective bargaining is unnecessary since the interests of the workers already enjoy the protection of the government.

If labor unions don't bargain with the employer and can't strike, just what do they do? As they are an arm of the government, they have a role in carrying out the various plans of that government. For example, unions are responsible for seeing that the individual workers meet their quotas. The wage structure is administered by the unions. Unions are likewise in charge of the various fringe benefit programs such as maintaining vacation centers, and the like. A comparatively recent development marks the major similarity between the Soviet trade union and the American union. In the Soviet Union a grievance procedure has been developed to protect the workers from the arbitrary and capricious acts of management, and the trade union is responsible for its functioning.

Organization of Industry. All industrial enterprises in the USSR are owned and operated by the government. There are some producer cooperatives in fields other than agriculture, but they are relatively insignificant. And there are a few independent businessmen, but their total output is negligible. It would not be too far amiss to say that everyone works for the government including the common laborer as well as the head of the industrial combine. This industrial operation dwarfs any other economic enterprise in the world.

Prior to 1957, Soviet industry was organized along industry lines. The major industries were classed as all-union industries and each was headed by a cabinet minister. That is, the head of each all-union industry would be a member of the Council of Ministers of the USSR. In such industries the administration was centered in the ministries in

Moscow with control being tightly centralized. Other industries, of lesser importance, were less centralized in their organization. These industries might still be headed by a cabinet minister in Moscow, but there would be, in addition, republican ministries for that particular industry in each of the Soviet Republics.

Immediately below the office of the minister, there was a subministry in charge of a particular part of the industry or a particular region. Below the subministry was the trust or combine which was a group of plants organized as a single administrative unit. And at the bottom of the ladder was the enterprise which was a single plant or a number of plants.

The enterprise or producing unit is comparable to the firm in the United States. It has its own bank account. It can borrow funds (from the government). It keeps accounting records. It can sue and be sued. And it will do business with other producing units. In short, even though all producing units are owned and operated by the state, the individual producing units have many of the attributes associated with individual firms in the United States. It would appear that the difference between the Soviet firm and its American counterpart is not so much to be found in the nature and operation of the firm, though there are significant differences, but is more to be found in the management structure and management control.[8]

Reorganization of Industry in 1957. After the death of Stalin in 1953, it became increasingly obvious that Soviet economy organized along industry lines was not functioning efficiently. The distance, both geographically and bureaucratically, between the minister of the industry at the top and the manager of the enterprise at the bottom of the managerial hierarchy meant that the enterprise could not be effectively controlled. The chain of command was defective in that decisions of the higher units were not effectively and efficiently transmitted to the lower echelons of management. Likewise, the upward flow of information from the lower to higher management units was faulty.

The major change was a shift from vertical organization of industry (which has already been described) to a geographical or territorial organization. Nearly all of the industrial ministries were

---

[8] The student is urged to read *The Red Executive* by David Granick. This book is available in a paperback edition—Anchor A246. It is a well written and extremely interesting comparison of Soviet and American business. The student may well be surprised at the similarities and disappointed at the lack of differences.

abolished. Organization was on a geographical basis so that all of the industries, regardless of the nature of their output, were grouped together in a given area simply because of their physical proximity. The enterprises within the geographical area are supervised by regional economic councils (*sovnarkhozy*). The Council of Ministers for the various Republics rank just above the *sovnarkhozy* in the managerial hierarchy, and then at the top is the USSR Council of Ministers.

There were other changes in 1957. The chairmen of the Council of Ministers for the Union Republics were made members of the Council of Ministers of the USSR. The national planning agency (*gosplan*) was given more representation in the Soviet Council of Ministers. The *gosplan* was also given considerably more power in the operation of the economy.

The reorganization of 1957 was simply another phase in the long and continuing struggle between centralized control and decentralized decision making.[9] Any firm or enterprise, regardless of the system of which it is a part, has to find some solution to this problem. Control must be exercised from the top downward. It will take the form of limits; that is, lesser units will be allowed to make decisions within limits set by the higher administrative units. Within such limits, any unit of the enterprise must be allowed some freedom to make operational decisions. Obviously it would not make sense to require the firm to refer all decisions to the top, although it appears that this has happened from time to time in the USSR. Likewise, it would not make sense to let the lower-level units have complete freedom to operate without controls or guidance. The reorganization of 1957 can probably best be interpreted as only another experiment in the never-ending attempt to find some balanced solution to the problem of decentralized operational decision making and centralized control. It may well be that this reorganization, rather than striving for increased efficiency through more decentralized decision making, was seeking to bring the local decision makers under more effective central control.[10]

The *gosplan* is a committee of the Council of Ministers and is the planning agency for the entire economy. A few key industries such as medium machine building, electric power station construction, and

---

[9] Granick, *op. cit.* has an extremely interesting discussion of this particular aspect of the problem.

[10] See "The Soviet Industrial Reorganization of 1957" by Oleg Hoeffding in the *Papers and Proceedings of the American Economics Review,* May, 1958.

defense production still have representation in the Council of Ministers. State Committees for such areas as atomic energy, shipbuilding, defense technology, and other broad areas exercise a coordinating function for activities which cut across wide sectors of the economy.

In each of the Soviet Republics there is a Council of Ministers, and the chairman of each is a member of the Council of Ministers of the USSR. Various industrial ministries still exist at this level, although the number was sharply reduced in the 1957 reorganization. Ministries of construction, municipal services, local industries, highways, and the like are examples of industries retaining ministerial standing within the republics. Each republic will also have a planning agency. This state planning agency plans for the republic as well as transmits the plans and orders of the national planning commission.

Subordinate to the Republic Council of Ministers is the *sovnarkhoz* or regional economic council. This agency is responsible for the industry within a geographic area. Over 100 regional economic councils were established in 1957. The *sovnarkhoz* appears to serve two masters—the USSR as well as the individual republic. Its role is not yet sharply defined but is in the process of developing and adapting to particular circumstances.

At the local level, one finds provincial, county, and city administrative units. And at the very bottom of the entire industrial structure is the enterprise, but even this more or less basic unit takes on different forms. It may, for example, be a single plant producing a single commodity, or it may be a complex of plants producing a wide variety of products.

The Planning Process

Types of Planning: There are two different types or levels of planning in the Soviet Union. First, there is a long term plan for five or seven years. This plan outlines, in broad detail, the anticipated development of the economy for the specified period. It does not contain any plans for the detailed operation of the economic system. This plan has to be of sufficient length so that such projects as the construction of capital projects can be carried through to a conclusion.

The second type of planning is a short term plan which is, in most cases, a plan for a single year although it may be broken down into semi-annual or even quarterly plans. At this level the planning mechanism specifies output levels for all segments of the economy. It further specifies prices, wages, capital construction, exports, and imports, in fact, nearly everything.

The essence of this short-term planning operation is the control over inputs which is commonly referred to as supply planning. By controlling the supply of goods and services, the government through its planning mechanism effectively controls production and allocates resources. In the United States a producer is free to purchase any good or service that he desires, and the only requisite is that he have the necessary purchasing power. During World War II, the government of the United States, in effect, specified that the producers had to have, in addition to the purchasing power, a government authorization to procure certain scarce goods such as steel. These two, purchasing power and authorization, are both required as part of the normal process of acquisition in the Soviet Union when the enterprise sets out to acquire the necessary inputs.

Supply planning takes as given the goals set forth in the long run plan by the government and the Communist party. Increases in productivity, increased capital capacity in one industry or another, increased agricultural output, emphasis on production of consumer goods rather than investment goods, changes in national defense policies, further encouragement of education or particular types of education, and other goals are the long-run objectives toward which each supply plan is oriented.

The supply plan itself is concerned with the establishment of some sort of equilibrium in the system. That is, the total output of any particular good is supposed to just equal the total demand for that same good. And this equality between demand and supply has to be extended to the economy as a whole so that a general equilibrium is at least approximated (if all goes well).

Supply planning is carried out in terms of materials balances which are balance sheets expressed in units of the physical commodities rather than monetary units. And, since it is a balance sheet, a balance must be established between total output of one industry and the total demand. The total amount of steel produced must equal the total amount of steel used. The student might, as an excercise, draw up a diagram of the steel industry showing the various inputs, the different users of the outputs, as well as the other suppliers of inputs to those industries using steel. Thus the automobile industry draws upon the steel industry in addition to the chemical, textile, glass, aluminum, rubber, and electrical equipment industries. And some of these are, in turn, dependent upon the steel industry. Thus one may get a vague idea of the complexity of the supply planning problem.

The Planning Mechanism. The planning hierarchy is as follows:

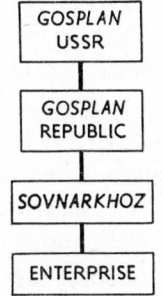

The planning process itself involves a two-way flow of information and orders through this hierarchy. The process is initiated when general orders are passed downward from the central planning agency (*gosplan*) to the republic *gosplan* and on down to the enterprise. This initial information is based upon the long-term plan presently in effect, past performance of the system and industry, and projected performance for the coming year. After these broad directions are received by the enterprise, it works out target outputs specifying what the planned output is to be for the ensuing year. The target outputs are passed on to the *sovnarkhoz* which combines all of the estimates for the enterprises in its area, and this combined estimate is then passed on to republic *gosplan.* Here all of the plans for the *sovnarkhoz* in the republic are combined. Finally, these regional plans are sent to the Soviet *gosplan* where the whole program is coordinated for the entire economy. In working out these target outputs, it is also necessary to make estimates for the needed inputs. So when the process is completed, a materials balance for both projected outputs and projected inputs has been constructed. When this part of the planning process is completed, the Soviet *gosplan* has drawn up a complete materials balance for the entire economy so that the total planned output for each commodity is just equal to the total planned supply of that commodity.

The next phase of the planning process involves a downward flow of orders through the planning structure. Those goods of a critical nature will be under the direct control of the Soviet *gosplan,* and it will allocate these goods among the republics. The republic *gosplan* will in turn distribute its allocation among the *sovnarkhoz,* which in turn allocates it to the various enterprises needing these particular inputs.

The last phase of planning is again an upward flow of orders or requests. Each enterprise places an order for the controlled goods with the regional economic council which in turn passes an order for the controlled goods to the next level. Finally these orders are collected at the Soviet *gosplan* which in turn assigns the orders to specific producers of the controlled outputs.

The process is completed when the suppliers and the buyers sign agreements for the production and delivery of the commodity.

The above description applies just to goods which are controlled by the central government which may mean somewhere between 800 and 1500 different items. Other commodities are controlled by local governing bodies, and there are some which are completely controlled by the individual enterprise. Such a ubiquitous material as sand, for example, is not controlled.

Such complete control over the economy and the magnitude of the planning process itself clearly strains the imagination of one not used to such extensive control by the government. It has ceased to be amazing that the system works. It continues to be amazing that the system works as well as it does. There remain some individuals, however, who continue to act as though some "elf" were coming in at night and spinning the straw into gold.

Problems in Planning

Coordination. In the United States, the price system coordinates the components of the economic system. Interfirm and interperson transactions are carried out in the market place (for the most part). Scarce commodities in great demand will have a higher price and additional resources will be moved in this particular direction. Idle resources in a particular area will exert a downward pressure on the price of the inputs which in turn will cause greater amounts of that particular input to be used. The activities of one firm are coordinated with those of other firms or the factor inputs through the market and the price system. Within the firm, decisions regarding the use of the inputs is an administrative decision.

The price system fails to function in the interest of the country as a whole during time of war, and during such an emergency, the government may actually suppress the price system. This means that the government will undertake to coordinate the various parts of the system in order to insure that productive activity will be directed toward the successful prosecution of the war.

In the Soviet Union the price system serves as a coordinating device for a relatively small part of the total economy. Most of the coordination is done through the administrative mechanism of the government. And since the coordinating task is so large, it comes as no surprise to find that there are certain problems associated with it.

Suppose, for example, that it is decided to increase the production of farm equipment in the next planning period. What ramifications will this have? First of all, of course, all inputs will have to be readjusted. More labor, steel, iron ore, electricity, coal, and many other factor inputs are going to be required to increase this particular output—farm equipment. These additional inputs can only be achieved if (a) other industries use less either by reducing their output or increasing the efficiency of their inputs or (b) the production of all of these required inputs for the production of farm equipment is increased. But this only removes the problem one step. If the production of steel is to be increased, inputs must be drawn away from other areas of production, factors must be used more efficiently, or the production of all inputs used by steel must be increased.

To some extent, increased production can be achieved by increases in supply of labor and the increased exploitation of the nation's natural resources. However, as output increases, it may become increasingly difficult to expand the quantity of these two inputs. One of the most apparent barriers to Soviet development at the present time is the chronic shortage of labor. Thus, an increased use of labor in one industry may be offset by a reduced input of labor in some other industry—usually agriculture. Occasionally in the period since World War II, increased use of labor in industry has been at the expense of the Soviet military machine. Eventually, the impact of increasing inputs in one industry will be absorbed by the rest of the economy. It is a problem of coordination to see that the effect is minimized and consistent with the overall goals of the society.

Suppose, for the moment, that this aspect of coordination can be solved—that is, the necessary additional factor inputs can be found. There remains the purely administrative problem of seeing that everything is in the right place at the right time in order that production can proceed. An increased output of farm equipment will require that new plants be built, additional supplies of steel and labor procured, additional machine tools be acquired, additional electricity supplied, and so forth. There is nothing, however, which guarantees that all of the inputs will arrive at the right place at the right time, just as there is nothing that guarantees that the luggage of an air traveler will always arrive at the same destination and at the same time as the traveler himself. The additional capacity may be installed, the additional labor on the job, and nothing may be produced because the machine tools were not delivered on time. For example, Premier Khrushchev reported in the fall of 1961 that millions of square feet of factory space were idle because the necessary machinery was not available. At the same time, in other parts of the USSR, hundreds of millions of dollars of machinery was standing idle because the necessary installations were not yet ready.[11] This is an interesting as well as significant point, for the critics of capitalism (including the Communists) have long emphasized the tendency of capitalism to result in idle capacity and unemployment. These critics of capitalism have maintained that a system of planning would eliminate the existence of idle resources, and yet here is evidence that planning does not eliminate unemployment but on the contrary seems to create a kind of unemployment of its own.

A device by which the interrelationships between the various parts of the industrial economy are made more evident and the problem of coordination made somewhat more tractable is the input-output table. An input-output table is a mathematical representation of an economic system. First, it will indicate just how the output of a given industry is divided among all the users of that output. Steel, for example, will be used by the steel industry itself as well as many others. Second, the input-output table will show just what inputs are combined in order to produce any particular product. Again using steel as an example, the inputs needed for the production of steel include coal and coke, electric power, machinery, steel, and others. Thus, the input-output table shows (a) the total quantity of steel produced and how it is used and (b) the total quantities of all the inputs required to produce the given amount of steel. And it does this for a number of commodities. Using the input-output table, one can determine how given changes in the quantity of any output will affect the rest of the industries in the economy.[12]

The development and use of such devices as the input-output table and linear programming will at least make the problems of coordination somewhat more manageable. Thus, it is probably safe to predict that there may well be fewer instances of malfunctioning as management techniques improve. Such a tendency may also result if the Soviet Union

[11] *The New York Times,* October 29, 1961.

[12] The student is urged to examine an input-output table for the USSR on pages 88–89 of *Soviet Economic Power* by Robert W. Campbell. This book is published by Houghton Mifflin Company and is available in a paperback edition. The student will find the entire book to be enjoyable and interesting reading.

adopts a policy of restricting central planning to a smaller segment of the economy.

Allocation of Resources. The planners in the Soviet Union have a problem which is just not present in an economy with a freely operating price system. In the latter, the price system will allocate resources. In a planned economy, resources are allocated by government fiat. And when the heavy hand of the bureaucrat replaces the invisible hand of the price system, problems arise.

In the first place, it is necessary to allocate resources because the resources are scarce. If they were not, there would be no limit to the use of any particular resource or the production of any given output. But how does one know where the various resources should be used? Obviously, one criterion should be the urgency of the needs, but, and just as obviously, there are other criteria including the cost of the factors and the "social usefulness" of the output. In our study of production, we saw that cheaper factors will be substituted for dearer factors in the productive process if the goal is to achieve some optimum combination of output and cost.

Since the cost of an input is an essential bit of information in determining which of the many possible production techniques to use, it follows that each input must carry a meaningful price. That is, the price must reflect both the scarcity of the input and its productivity. Any price determined in a freely operating price system does just this. A price determined by a government bureaucrat may or may not. If, for example, a government set a price of zero on a particular input, that is, if the input were taken to be a free good, too much of that particular input would be used while too little of other inputs would be used. On the other hand, if the price were set too high, the result would be a failure to use a good when it really should be used. In either case, the result is an improper proportioning of the factor inputs.

In the Soviet Union, the most interesting problem involves the pricing and use of capital in the productive process. Marxist economists have long regarded interest (the return to capital) as an illegitimate return. To them, labor is the source of value, and wages constitute the single legitimate factor return. The Soviet planners, in accordance with this Marxian dogma, long treated capital as not having a price—as being a free good. The result was an improper proportioning of the factors of production in many instances. By 1962, Soviet policy had begun to change. The interest rate was achieving a degree of respectability. The government was loaning money to Soviet enterprises and charging interest for the stated purpose of increasing efficiency—that is, a better proportioning of the factor inputs.[13]

The movement of labor within any economy presents problems. In the United States, with a free price system, it is difficult to get labor to move from an industry or area with little need for labor to some other industry or area where the need is greater. During World War II, the lure of high earnings (as well as the motive of patriotism) resulted in wholesale shifts of labor in this country. And during much of the history of the United States, there has been a continuing flow of labor from the rural to urban sectors of the nation. In general, reliance has been placed upon the price system to effect these adjustments.

The Soviet Union has much the same problem. If there were no meaningful price system, why would farmers and rural residents migrate to the cities? Why would laborers move from less essential to more essential industries? Why would people move from the settled areas of the country to the frontier in the Eastern part of the USSR? The Soviet Union has, since the death of Stalin in 1953, relied upon the same means that have been used in the United States. In the United States, the price system will put a high price on labor in areas where it is needed. The Soviet planners have, through government decree, put a higher price on labor in undesirable locations or jobs and thus attracted labor. They have also used the patriotic motive as well as forced labor, but it would appear that both of these are of lesser importance now than previously.

Land use in the Soviet Union is rather closely controlled. Productivity in Soviet agriculture is so low that it acts as a deterring force in the country's attempt to maintain a high rate of growth. Low productivity limits the supply of food as well as the migration of labor to urban industry. As a result, Soviet authorities have experimented freely with changing agricultural methods including changing land use in an effort to increase agricultural productivity. It is probably safe to predict that insofar as the agricultural sector continues to lag behind the rest of the economy, this sector will continue to be subject to considerable direct control by the government.

Incentives. Getting people to work, to save, to invest, to spend —that is the problem, and it is a problem that any society must solve regardless of how that society is organized. The nature of the problem in terms of its importance as well as the nature of the solution will vary from one type of economic system to the next, but the problem remains. That is, how do you get the people to do what needs to be done?

[13] *The New York Times,* October 29, 1961.

In the United States, the price system provides much of the answer. That which is needed the worst bears the highest price which in turn induces a greater amount of the particular activity to be forthcoming. In the Soviet Union, the problem is, perforce, different because of the different economic structure. Because of the shortage of consumption goods there is little need to encourage consumption expenditures. The problem is that of curtailing consumption expenditures (increase saving) in order that there will be a greater output of capital goods.

The Soviet Union, like any other economy, has to get people to work and save. Somehow, communism must provide the incentive for the population to produce and then, in turn, abstain from consumption. Let us first look at the incentive used to get people to work.

Obviously, if income is tied to productivity, this fact alone will serve to increase productive effort. If productivity increases, income increases and if productivity decreases, income does likewise. The relationship between productivity and income was discussed in Chapter 9 in the context of a free labor market.

Insofar as labor is concerned, the piece-work system of payment ties income directly to production and the only way that income can be increased is through an increase in production. In the United States, the elimination of the piecework system of pay has long been a major objective of unions, and to a very large extent, they have been successful. At the present time in this country, labor is most commonly paid on an hourly basis and thus their income is not directly tied to the amount that is produced. The piece-work system of pay has been, in the past, one of the most criticized aspects of American capitalism.

In the Soviet Union, the piece-work system of pay is widely used at both the management and worker level. Management of a Soviet enterprise receives a basic stipend, but a large part, and in some cases most, of his pay is in the form of a bonus based on the performance of the unit for which he is responsible. Thus the monthly remuneration of a plant manager depends upon the productive performance of the plant for that month.

Establishing some criterion which can be used to measure performance presents interesting problems. In the United States, management bonus plans are generally based upon profits which are defined with reasonable clarity. Management in this country is moved to reduce costs, increase sales, and achieve some optimum combination of advertising, output, and price.

Soviet planners, on the other hand, don't have the same convenient criterion. Rather than using profit as the basis for management bonuses, the planners may use maximization of physical output, reduction of costs, reduction of waste, exceeding planned output, economizing in the use of certain inputs, and the like. As one would expect, management with its eye on the possible bonus then sets out to operate the system in such a way as to maximize that bonus—to fulfill and over-fulfill the plan. If the quota calls for so many thousand pairs of shoes, the manager may elect to produce that kind of shoes which can be turned out in largest numbers rather than the kind that is more difficult to produce or in greater need. A printer, with a quota of so many pages, may decide to use a larger type and leave more space between the lines. A manager may neglect the upkeep of capital in order to use his facilities for production. The manager may likewise resist change for fear that it would be more difficult to meet the quota if a new product or new technique were introduced. In reporting to higher authorities, figures may be falsified to show that the quota was filled. In short, the system of managerial incentives gives rise to a host of different reactions by Soviet management, and not all of these reactions make a positive contribution to the objectives of the planners.

As interesting as it is, the important point to note is the fact that Soviet management is remunerated in accordance with output, and the relationship between production (meeting the plan) and remuneration is probably closer than is the relationship between production and remuneration for corporate management in the United States. The result of the Soviet system for managerial compensation is a wide difference in income between the Soviet management and the Soviet worker. Soviet management enjoys a status and level of living far above that of the laboring class. And within the managerial class, there is a sufficient difference to afford the incentive for anyone to struggle toward a higher position in the managerial hierarchy.

For the laboring group, the USSR has used a variety of incentives in the past, but more and more it appears that they are relying on the same incentives so commonly used in the capitalistic nations. Under Stalin, there was considerable use of such negative incentives as forced labor and threat of imprisonment. At the present, however, workers, like management, are generally paid on a piece-work basis. Within the laboring group the planning authorities make considerable use of wage differentials. That is, a higher remuneration goes to those who are willing to take the less desirable jobs.

In total, for both management and labor, the incentives are surprisingly capitalistic in their nature. It is at least interesting, if not surprising, to note that Premier Khrushchev, the leading Communist, when visiting the United States in 1959 explained to President Eisenhower, the leader of the major capitalist power, the nature and significance of incentives in the productive process.[14] One might have expected that the direction of the explanation would have been the reverse of what it was.

CONCLUSION

This concluding section, like those that went before, is intended to (1) tie the material in the chapter into the theme of the book—the economic system and (2) raise what we hope are provocative questions in the student's mind. But here we want to do a little more. We would like to think that at this point we are launching the student on a long and fruitful career as a student of economics—not necessarily as an economist but as a thoughtful observer of the contemporary world.

At this point, the student might do two things. First, contemplate for a moment just what has been covered in this book and the course. What concepts have been introduced which help one to understand the operation of an economic system? What are the problems peculiar to an economic system organized on the basis of private property, a free price system, and private enterprise? What are the problems associated with the organization of a centrally directed economy? Do the two types of economic system perform the same basic function? How do they compare or differ? Are the peoples' wants influenced by the type of economic system which prevails? How do we achieve a more rapid rate of growth in a free economy? Is there any conflict between faster growth and personal freedom? There are many other questions which could be raised.

Now the student might turn his thoughts to the future. We don't know what the exact nature of the economic system will be, but we do know that change will be the order of the day. The exact nature of the change cannot be predicted, but we do have the power to bring about the kinds of change that we prefer.

One might speculate as to just what directions the changes will take. Will this country move toward more central planning or will it move toward a more decentralized system? If the private interests of big business and big unions become incompatible with the commonweal, what reforms will be attempted? Is there something short of comprehensive price and wage controls or nationalization? Turning to the place of our economic system in the community of nations, is it possible

[14] See the President's press conference on October 28, 1959 as reported in *The New York Times* on October 29, 1959.

that this nation will move firmly and forcefully toward a position of free trade? How much of our national interests are we willing to sacrifice in order that we can serve as the world's banker? Is the increased nationalism shown by the countries of western Europe going to force this country to take a more nationalistic position with less interest in the concerns of the rest of the world?

These are only a few of the host of questions that could be raised. We are fortunate that speculation about the future, which is so enjoyable, costs so little.

EXERCISES

Group I

Explain why the following statements are true or false.

1. Supply planning in the USSR is a part of the five-year plan.
2. The planning hierarchy in the USSR makes no use of prices in its supply planning.
3. The USSR has a problem of coordination that the United States does not have because the latter relies on the function of a free price system.
4. Eventually the problem of allocation in the USSR will be eliminated.
5. Regardless of the nature of the economic or political organization, there has to be an interest rate.

Group II

1. Compare in some detail the role of trade unions in the United States, France, Yugoslovia, and the USSR. Are unions in the United States and the Soviet Union becoming more or less similar?
2. Explain why the United States has steadily been moving away from a piece-work pay system while the Soviet Union is making extensive use of this "capitalistic" system.
3. Compare the productive processes in the United States and the Soviet Union for particular industries. Does there appear to be a significant difference in the proportioning of the factors? If so, what is the explanation?

Group III

1. The United States and the USSR both purposively set out to reorganize the industrial sectors of their respective economies. The United States does so through the antitrust laws while the USSR does so through government decree. Examine the 1957 reorganization in the Soviet Union and compare that action with the efforts to apply the antitrust laws to American industry. Are the goals the same? What can be said about the success of the two approaches?

BIBLIOGRAPHY

HOFFMAN, G. W. AND NEAL, F. W. *Yugoslavia and the New Communism.* New York: The Twentieth Century Fund, 1962.

JOINT ECONOMIC COMMITTEE. *Comparisons of the United States and Soviet Economies.* Washington, D.C.: Government Printing Office, 1959. Parts 1, 2, and 3.

NOVE, A. *The Soviet Economy: An Introduction.* New York: Frederick A. Praeger, 1961.

SCHWARTZ, HARRY. *Russia's Soviet Economy,* 2nd ed. Englewood Cliffs, N.J.: Prentice-Hall, Inc., 1954.

PAPERBACK READING LIST

GRANICK, DAVID. *The Red Executive: A Study of the Organization Man in Russian Industry.* New York: Doubleday & Co., Anchor Books, 1961.

INDEX

This book has been set on the Linotype in 12 point and 10 point Garamond #3, leaded 1 point. Chapter numbers and titles are in 18 point Spartan Medium. The size of the type page is 27 by 46½ picas.